WILSON:

The Struggle for Neutrality

1914-1915

BY THE SAME AUTHOR:

Wilson: The Road to the White House
Wilson: The New Freedom

WILSON

THE STRUGGLE
FOR NEUTRALITY
1914-1915

By ARTHUR S. LINK

PRINCETON, NEW JERSEY

PRINCETON UNIVERSITY PRESS

1960

General

99919

NOV 1 7 1960

E
767
L75
v.3

FOR

RAYMOND B. FOSDICK

WILSONIAN

THIS, the third, volume in my biography of Woodrow Wilson and the history of his time covers the first fifteen months of the First World War. This period from the outbreak of hostilities in the summer of 1914 to the dispatch of the note to the British government of October 21, 1915, has a natural unity. It was the time when the basic American public attitudes toward the war in Europe took shape. It was the time, also, when President Wilson and his advisers laid the foundations of American neutrality and sought to find accommodation to the ever-encroaching maritime systems of Great Britain and Germany. It was a period characterized on the American side, in short, by a relentless and unending struggle for neutrality and noninvolvement. New policies and bolder efforts and approaches—for example, the President's decision early in 1916 to run the risk of belligerency in the hope of ending the war through mediation—still lay ahead and will be described in the following volume.

This book would have been far easier to write (and less burdensome for the reader!) if I could have stayed always on the main theme of the American response to the war. However, events in Mexico, the Caribbean, and the Far East insisted upon intruding and creating nagging problems for President Wilson and his advisers all during the period when they would have preferred to concentrate upon domestic affairs and developments in Europe. I could not ignore the digressive and peripheral problems any more than Wilson could. But I must confess that there were times when I wished that Mexico, the Far East, and the Caribbean region had been transplanted to another planet!

Readers of this volume might well remark upon what seems to be the absence of any attention to the details of President Wilson's personal life during the months under review. The criticism would not be unfair, and I can only say the following in palliation: In the second volume of this biography I tried to deal with many general aspects of Wilson's personal life during his first term in the presidency—the routine of life in the White House, how Wilson exercised leadership of the people, his relations with Cabinet and Congress and newspapermen, and the like. Wilson underwent two great personal experiences during the period covered by the present volume. The first was the agony that he endured after Ellen Axson Wilson's death in August 1914. I have written about this in the second volume. The second was the joy that he knew in finding Mrs. Edith Bolling Galt a year later. I will describe this in the opening chapter of the fourth volume. During the interim between Mrs. Wilson's death and the discovery of Mrs. Galt the President had, actually, very little "personal" life. He found salvation only by losing himself in the problems that followed hard upon the outbreak of war in Europe. We can see his "personal" life—his thought and character, and his methods of leadership—during these months only by following him day by day as he toiled over drafts of diplomatic notes, wrestled with crises in Mexico or the Dominican Republic, and fought epic battles with Congress.

I have, I think, said enough already in the Prefaces to the first and second volumes about my methods and general objectives in this biography. They have not changed. I can only hope that to some degree I have succeeded in purging my mind of preconceived interpretations, that I have not imposed my own pattern upon the period, and that I have let men and events speak for themselves without passing judgment on them but with all due sympathy.

I have been engaged in the research for and writing of this volume for more years than I like to remember, and all the while I have continued to pile up a burden of debt to institutions and individuals in an almost unconscionable way. Grants from the Guggenheim Foundation, the Princeton University Research Committee, and the College of Liberal Arts of Northwestern University enabled me to begin research on this volume from 1948 to 1951. The Northwestern University Research Committee added timely contributions, particularly in the summer of 1957. Finally, the Rockefeller Foundation made it possible for me to mine the treasures of the Asquith and Bryce Papers at Oxford and of other depositories in England. I might have had all the determination in the world, but I could not have gotten very far without the unstinting support of these institutions.

If there is any merit in this book, the credit should go to generous uncomplaining friends who have sustained and guided me in my work. I think gratefully upon a host of men and women in libraries from Oxford to Evanston, but particularly of Miss Katharine E. Brand, formerly of the Manuscripts Division of the Library of Congress, to whom all Wilson scholars owe a debt that cannot be measured, and of the late Dr. Carl L. Lokke, head of the Foreign Affairs Section of the National Archives, who went far beyond the call of duty in helpfulness.

I remember the help that the late Professor Edward Mead Earle of the Institute for Advanced Study gave at an earlier time. And I acknowledge my gratitude to Professors Gray C. Boyce and Moody E. Prior, chairman of the History Department and Dean of the Graduate School, respectively, at Northwestern University; Mr. Herbert S. Bailey, Jr., Miss Miriam Brokaw, and Mr. P. J. Conkwright of Princeton University Press; Mr. Konrad C. Mueller, Mrs. Maria P. Alter, and Dr. Kenneth Negus, for their help in work among the German sources; Professor Chihiro Hosoya of Hitotsubashi University, Tokyo, for his translation of materials in the Japanese Foreign Office and of secondary works in the Japanese language; and my assistant, Mr. Neil Thorburn, for his help in checking footnotes and bibliography.

My deepest thanks belong to those persons who out of love or friendship were willing to read and criticize various drafts of this manuscript. My wife, Margaret Douglas Link, had perhaps the worst task of all, that of reading the first pencil-scrawled draft. Three English friends, Mr. Herbert Nicholas of New College, Mr. R. A. C. Parker of The Queen's College, and Sir Patrick Devlin of the Royal Courts of Justice, gave such criticism as only profound students of modern European history could offer. Professor Ernest R. May of Harvard University not only read the manuscript but also shared his abundant knowledge of recent German history. The dean of American diplomatic historians, Professor Samuel Flagg Bemis of Yale University, interrupted what would otherwise have been a pleasant summer holiday to read and criticize the semifinal draft. Professor Roger F. Hackett of Northwestern University and Professor Hosoya read and made detailed comments on the ninth chapter. My two colleagues in The Papers of Woodrow Wilson, Dr. John W. Davidson and Mr. David W. Hirst, contributed help and criticism at the end. I owe an old and special debt to Miss Jean MacLachlan of Princeton. She worked as my research assistant in 1948-1949; and she has edited this volume with the same devoted care that she gave to the preceding one. Not finally but throughout there was my loyal colleague and friend, Professor Richard W. Leopold of Northwestern University. Along with my wife he continues to be my most helpful critic and reader. It goes without saying that all these friends did the best they could, and that I alone am responsible for the errors that remain in this book.

I have dedicated this volume to the man to whom all Wilson scholars owe an enormous debt for his labor of love in helping, as chairman of the Publications Committee of the Woodrow Wilson

Foundation, to make possible the publication of *The Papers of Wood-row Wilson. Student and friend of Wilson, he has exemplified the President's own ideals of public service throughout a distinguished career.

A.S.L.

Evanston, Illinois
December 26, 1959

CONTENTS

W|ILLUSTRATIONS|W

Following page 354

CHAPTER I

Initial American Reactions to the War

SPRING was coming to an end in Washington. Young cherry trees had long since blossomed feebly in the tidal basin, and the days were bringing heat that hung like an oppressive pall. Never since his inauguration as twenty-eighth President had the days been so crowded or the nights so restless for Woodrow Wilson as during late May and early June of 1914. The danger of war with Mexico raised by the American occupation of Veracruz in April now seemed safely past, but there were new perplexities in that strife-torn land. On Capitol Hill the two houses were mired in confusion over antitrust bills, and a furious debate raged in the Senate over some of Wilson's nominees to the new Federal Reserve Board. Nor could the President find relief by turning his thoughts away from Washington or inward to his family circle. The country was in shock over the outbreak of civil war in Colorado, the culmination of a bloody conflict between the United Mine Workers and mine owners, and appeals for action were pouring daily in upon the White House. More agonizing still was Ellen Wilson's failure to recover from a long illness and the gnawing fear that she might not get well.[1]

In the background, not yet urgent in the President's thoughts, was the mounting crisis in Europe and the threat of war. His concern was aroused not so much by the events themselves, for he ordinarily gave scant attention to European affairs, as by the reports of his most intimate adviser, Colonel Edward M. House. Impelled by the fear that a general European war would ensue if some way were not found to alleviate the growing tension, House had gone to Berlin and London in May and June of 1914 to explore the possibility of an Anglo-German-American *entente*. By such means the Colonel hoped to draw two of the European rivals into a new orbit and thereby to break the impasse between the Triple Alliance on the one hand and the Triple Entente on the other.[2]

[1] For an account of these events, see the last chapters of A. S. Link, *Wilson: The New Freedom*; hereinafter cited as *Wilson*, II.

[2] Charles Seymour (ed.), *The Intimate Papers of Colonel House*, I, 235-275; A. S. Link, *Wilson*, II, 314-318.

This was, of course, the eve of Armageddon. Crisis had followed crisis since the late 1890's, and by 1914 the European situation was such that any rude incident might lead to general war. House had read the storm signals accurately before he went abroad in 1914. In Europe he saw that catastrophe impended unless something were done quickly to avert it, and he wrote alarmingly, as if to awaken the President to the immediacy of the peril: "The situation is extraordinary. It is jingoism run stark mad. Unless some one acting for you can bring about a different understanding, there is some day to be an awful cataclysm. No one in Europe can do it. There is too much hatred, too many jealousies. Whenever England consents, France and Russia will close in on Germany and Austria. England does not want Germany wholly crushed, for she would then have to reckon alone with her ancient enemy, Russia; but if Germany insists upon an ever-increasing navy, then England will have no choice."[3]

The match was put to the fuse a month later, on June 28, 1914, when a Serbian nationalist murdered the heir to the Austrian and Hungarian thrones, the Archduke Franz Ferdinand, and his young wife, the Duchess of Hohenberg, in Sarajevo, the capital of the province of Bosnia. A short time later the Austrian government, convinced that the Serbian authorities were implicated in the assassination, decided to use the incident as a pretext for action to put an end, once and for all, to Serbian activity and propaganda aimed at the union of the South Slavic portions of the Hapsburg Empire with the Kingdom of Serbia.

Americans read the news of the murder on the front pages of their newspapers with interest and unconcern on June 29. Officials in the State Department, informed of the tragedy by Ambassador Frederick C. Penfield in Vienna, paused from deliberations about more important problems to prepare the necessary ritualistic condolences. A personal telegram from the President to the aged Emperor Franz Joseph, drafted probably at the Department, was dispatched to Vienna on June 29,[4] while Secretary of State William J. Bryan added his regrets in a note to the Austrian Ambassador in Washington on the following day.[5] No one in Washington (or, for that matter, in most of the European For-

---

[3] E. M. House to W.W., May 29, 1914, the Papers of Woodrow Wilson, the Library of Congress; hereinafter cited as the Wilson Papers.

[4] W.W. to the Emperor of Austria-Hungary, June 29, 1914, *Papers Relating to the Foreign Relations of the United States, 1914,* p. 25; hereinafter cited as *Foreign Relations, 1914.*

[5] The Secretary of State to the Ambassador of Austria-Hungary, June 30, 1914, *ibid.*

eign Offices) could see that the fuse to the powder keg was already sputtering. Indeed, there were so few obvious signs of a developing crisis during the days that followed the Sarajevo murders that Colonel House could continue his negotiations in London and conclude that he was on the verge of success. And Wilson could write hopefully on July 9: "I . . . hurry this note off to send you affectionate messages not only but renewed congratulations on the way you are serving the country we love and the peace of the world. It is perfectly delightful to read your letters and to realize what you are accomplishing."[6]

Soon after these words were written the dangers in the European situation became plain for all to see. With the full support of Germany now secured, the Austrian government presented an ultimatum to authorities in Belgrade on July 23, requiring submission to a long list of demands within forty-eight hours. Emboldened by assurances of assistance from Russia, the Serbs refused on July 25, whereupon Austria ordered mobilization against her southern antagonist. From this time on, reports of preparations for war filled the front pages of American newspapers and poured in to the State Department over the wires from the European capitals. "Minister of War tells me that he considers war between Austria and Russia almost inevitable," the American Chargé d'Affaires in St. Petersburg informed the Secretary of State on July 26, for example. ". . . Russian Government has ordered complete army mobilization to begin immediately."[7]

What could the United States do to avert the threatened calamity? On July 27, two days after the Austrian mobilization and a day after the British Foreign Secretary, Sir Edward Grey, had proposed a general European conference to deal with the emergency, reporters crowded in the White House to inquire if the President planned to tender his good offices or take any other action. Wilson replied almost abruptly that it was not the traditional policy of the United States to "take part" in political affairs outside the Western Hemisphere.[8]

The fuse burned into the powder on the following day, July 28, when Austria-Hungary declared war against Serbia "to end subversive intrigues issuing from Belgrade directed against the territorial integrity [of the] Austro-Hungarian Monarchy." "News of Austrian declaration

[6] W.W. to E. M. House, July 9, 1914, the Papers of Edward M. House, Yale University Library; hereinafter cited as the House Papers.

[7] Chargé Wilson to the Secretary of State, July 26, 1914, *Papers Relating to the Foreign Relations of the United States, 1914, Supplement, The World War*, p. 15; hereinafter cited as *Foreign Relations, 1914, Supplement.*

[8] *New York Times*, July 28, 1914.

of war against Servia just been known and causing great excitement and apprehension," the American Chargé wired from St. Petersburg. ". . . Strongest influences in highest circles being brought upon Emperor to declare war and I greatly fear Russian intervention inevitable."[9] The whole world knew that a Russian attack against Austria would bring Germany and then France into the struggle, and the German and British governments moved as best they could to avert this spreading of the fire. They did not succeed. Under unbearable pressure from his Foreign Minister and military advisers, the Russian Czar ordered a general mobilization on July 29. This provoked German preparations, which in turn set off a French mobilization on July 31 and German mobilization a few minutes later, followed by German declarations of war against Russia on August 2 and France on August 3. Main hostilities in the West began at once as German armies occupied Luxembourg and invaded Belgium. This in turn led to a British declaration of war against Germany on August 4, 1914.

Among all the contemporary accounts, none describes the utter poignancy and madness of these events better than the following letter from Ambassador Walter H. Page to the President, written from London only a few days after the British declaration of war:

"The next day the German Embassy was turned over to me, I went to see the German Ambassador at three o'clock in the afternoon. He came down in his pajamas—a crazy man. I feared he might literally go mad. He is of the anti-war party and he had done his best and utterly failed. This interview was one of the most pathetic experiences of my life. The poor man had not slept for several nights. . . .

"Upon my word, if one could forget the awful tragedy, all this experience would be worth a life-time of commonplace. One surprise follows another so rapidly that one loses all sense of time: it seems an age since last Sunday.

"I shall never forget Sir Edward Grey's telling me of the ultimatum [demanding that the Germans withdraw from Belgium]—while he wept; nor the poor German Ambassador who has lost in his high game—almost a demented man; nor the King as he declaimed at me for half-an-hour and threw up his hands and said, 'My God, Mr. Page, what else could we do?' Nor the Austrian Ambassador's wringing his

[9] Chargé Wilson to the Secretary of State, July 28, 1914, *Foreign Relations, 1914, Supplement*, p. 17.

hands and weeping and crying out "My dear Colleague, my dear colleague.' "[10]

These last days before Armageddon were like an extended nightmare for the President of the United States. Stunned by events in Europe, he walked the lonely corridors of the White House not knowing where to turn or what to do to halt the descent into the inferno. And beyond the tragedy abroad there was the greater pain of having to see death steal upon his beloved. When she died on August 6 the dissolution of his world was complete.

Was there ever any chance that the President might have intervened at some decisive moment to save the peace? A few men thought, at least hoped, that there was. The first suggestion came in a dramatic personal message to the White House from the American Ambassador in Paris, Myron T. Herrick. "Situation in Europe is regarded here as the gravest in history," he wrote in a cablegram on the same day that Austria declared war on Serbia. "It is apprehended that civilization is threatened by demoralization which would follow a general conflagration. . . . There is faith and reliance on our high ideals and purposes, so that I believe expression from our nation would have great weight in this crisis. My opinion is encouraged at reception given utterances of British Minister for Foreign Affairs. I believe that a strong plea for delay and moderation from the President of the United States would meet with the respect and approval of Europe and [I] urge the prompt consideration of this question."[11]

Herrick's message arrived at the State Department at 7:30 in the evening of July 28. It must have been delivered to the President and Secretary of State at once, for Bryan responded, certainly with Wilson's approval, a few hours later by asking the American Ambassador in London whether he thought there was any likelihood that the good offices of the United States "would be acceptable or serve any high purpose in the present crisis."[12] Page relayed the inquiry to the Foreign Secretary, Grey, on the morning of July 29 and returned to the Foreign Office in the afternoon of July 31 for a longer conference. "I am just come from a talk with Sir Edward Grey," he reported after the second meeting. "He again expressed his great gratitude for the suggestion of offering the good offices of the United States in case they could be

---

[10] W. H. Page to W.W., August 9, 1914, Wilson Papers.

[11] Ambassador Herrick to the Secretary of State, "To be communicated to the President," July 28, 1914, *Foreign Relations, 1914, Supplement*, pp. 18-19.

[12] The Secretary of State to Ambassador Page, July 28, 1914, *ibid.*, p. 19.

used. . . . Grey asked me if the United States has offered its good offices at Vienna or Saint Petersburg or Berlin, about which, of course, I have no information."[13]

On the same day that the distraught Foreign Secretary made this indirect appeal, Colonel House, who had returned to the United States only a short time before, added a gentle suggestion of his own. "What I particularly want to say to you," he wrote to Wilson on July 31, "is that if either now or at any time soon you feel that you may be able to use me to advantage in this trouble, I shall be, as always, entirely at your command. Both Germany and England know that I hold your confidence, and I would perhaps understand better how to proceed than one new to the situation." "The great danger," he added the following day, "is that some overt act may occur which will get the situation out of control. Germany is exceedingly nervous and at high tension and she knows that her best chance of success is to strike quickly and hard, therefore her very alarm may cause her to precipitate action as a means of safety."[14]

Grey's suggestion afforded the opportunity for American action, and House's advice about the necessity of alleviating the German alarm was sound, but from the White House and State Department there came no further word or deed, no bold attempt to turn the tide from war to peace. A man with a more intimate knowledge of the European situation and a more impulsive nature—like Theodore Roosevelt— might perhaps have tried. But it was not possible for Wilson to move quickly or decisively. Like most other Americans, he looked passively upon the swirl of events abroad, understanding their evil import and yet not knowing what to do. Would it have mattered if he had? Could events beyond the control of the British and German governments have been brought under the command of the President of the United States? It seems doubtful.

To say that the outbreak of war in Europe in 1914 came as a rude surprise and awakening to the American people is to state both an exaggeration and an obvious truth. Only a handful of thoughtful Americans had been aware of the forces and events that had threatened the peace of the world since the 1890's; they were not altogether surprised when pent-up tensions exploded into actual fighting. To the great majority of Americans, who hitherto had either ignored the

---

[13] Ambassador Page to the Secretary of State, July 31, 1914, *ibid.*, pp. 24-25.

[14] E. M. House to W.W., July 31 and August 1, 1914, Wilson Papers.

European scene or else had not been able to read the signs of the approaching catastrophe, the coming of the war was a shock of indescribable proportions. This was true especially of the men and women who had participated in the general world-wide peace movement and of a large group of hopeful idealists who had been persuaded that western man had finally evolved beyond the barbarism of war.

Whatever their level of political sophistication, most Americans, like most Europeans, were dazed by the suddenness of events in late July and early August. Without fully knowing why, they seemed intuitively to understand that the peaceful and morally secure world of the nineteenth century had come to an end, and that mankind was entering a new epoch of unknown violence and peril. "This dreadful conflict of the nations," a North Carolina congressman wrote to his brother, the American Ambassador in London, "came to most of us like lightning out of a clear sky. The horror of it all kept me awake for weeks, nor has the awfulness of it all deserted me, but at first it seemed a horrid dream. Now the grim reality of it stuns you."[15] "I can hardly sleep," another sensitive American wrote, "and in fact have had many broken nights when I have waked up with thoughts of this war, as one has the impression of a horrid nightmare."[16]

The main purpose of this chapter is to show how American reactions to the World War took shape during the first eight or nine months of hostilities, before the crisis in German-American relations over the conduct of submarine warfare caused a significant alteration in official and public opinion. The goal, actually, is almost unattainable. It would be a fairly simple matter if we could be content with easy generalizations—for example, that most Americans, except for the so-called hyphenate fringe, were unthinkingly pro-Allied in sympathies, that the Germans never had a chance to present their side, or that British propagandists warped and controlled American thinking about the war. The trouble with the simple explanations is that they are completely true and completely false, and that the truth does not necessarily lie somewhere in between. Reactions in the United States were as uniform and diverse and as naive and sophisticated as the American people themselves; and this was as true of the administration in Washington

[15] R. N. Page to W. H. Page, November 12, 1914, the Papers of Walter H. Page, Houghton Library, Harvard University; hereinafter cited as the Page Papers.

[16] O. G. Villard to Katharine Mayo, September 9, 1914, the Papers of Oswald Garrison Villard, Houghton Library, Harvard University; hereinafter cited as the Villard Papers.

and of the men who helped to shape public opinion in all walks of life as it was of the so-called masses of people across the American continent.

We must try, however, even though we are bound to fail fully to know and understand the range and character of American thinking about the war in Europe during this early period. This is true not only because the subject deserves a reappraisal after all the mishandling it has received; it is true as well because of the role that public opinion played in American political life in 1914 and afterward. To a large degree it built the framework or set the limits in which President Wilson and his advisers had to operate in forming policies toward the belligerents. It controlled the voting of congressmen and the drafting of party platforms. It helped determine the response that the government in Washington made to British and German efforts to control the seas.

Given their national origins, their past history, and their political and international ideals, it was inevitable that a very large number of Americans should have wanted the Allies (Russia aside, for most Americans did not associate Russia with the cause of the western Allies) to win. So much has been written on the background of American sympathy for France, and particularly for Great Britain, that we do not need to labor this point. It will be enough to say that for various reasons perhaps a majority of thoughtful Americans believed that the future of mankind would be brighter if the liberal British and French democracies controlled Europe, and that it would be dark indeed if brash, ambitious, and autocratic Imperial Germany should triumph. In mid-1914 this was the fundamental predisposition of editors and publicists almost everywhere in the United States.[17]

Thus predisposed, many Americans did react in an almost blind partisanship during the confusing period when the declarations of war were being issued, especially after Germany invaded Belgium and Britain entered the war on August 4. "Germany has run amuck . . . ," exclaimed Frank Cobb in the New York *World*, for example. "The issue is now joined. Either German autocracy must be crushed, or

---

[17] See, for example, the revealing poll of the press published in the *Literary Digest*, a weekly magazine devoted to the analysis of public and editorial opinion, "American Sympathies in the War," *Literary Digest*, XLIX (November 14, 1914), 939-941, 974-978. For scholarly confirmation of this exhaustive contemporary survey, see Edwin Costrell, *How Maine Viewed the War, 1914-1917*; Cedric C. Cummins, *Indiana Public Opinion and the World War, 1914-1917*; and John C. Crighton, *Missouri and the World War, 1914-1917*.

European democracy will be obliterated. There is no middle course. . . . Wantonly and deliberately the Kaiser has plunged his sword into the heart of civilization."[18] "If ever a war occurred in which the cause of civilization was represented by one side to the controversy, the present war furnishes an example," the venerable Senator Elihu Root of New York affirmed.[19] "The war," the editor of a prominent weekly agreed, "is not merely one of race against race. It is the war of a modern people against a mediaeval autocracy."[20]

The significant fact about the great body of pro-British and pro-French opinion in the United States was not its existence or strength at the outbreak of hostilities but the course of its development in the following months. Actually, what occurred was a division of pro-Allied sentiment into two fairly distinct and sometimes irreconcilable groups.

The first, whom we will call moderates, constituted the large majority of the pro-Allied group. They continued to prefer the Allies over the Central Powers, to be sure; but by the late autumn of 1914 they had ceased to be either frantic or blind in their partisanship—by believing, as they had before, that Germany was solely responsible for the war, or that all right was on one side and all wrong on the other. By the end of 1914 most pro-Allied Americans understood that the origins of the war were deep and the immediate causes complex; many of them were beginning, besides, to suspect that Allied objectives were not altogether pure. This was a momentous shift in opinion, and the reasons for it are, fortunately, not entirely obscure. The first and most important was the German propaganda in every conceivable form that flooded the United States during the autumn of 1914.[21] It converted few pro-Allied partisans into outright friends of Germany, but it did make some of the documents on the German side available, and it forced many Americans to admit that there were two sides to the question of war guilt. The second factor is harder to define. It might be called the general political sophistication of the average well-in-

---

[18] New York *World*, August 5, 1914.

[19] Draft of an interview between William H. Short and Senator Root, enclosed in Hamilton Holt to E. Root, August 7, 1914, the Papers of Elihu Root, Library of Congress; hereinafter cited as the Root Papers.

[20] New York *Outlook*, cvii (August 15, 1914), 892-893. For samples of similar comment, which abounded during the week of August 4, 1914, see "Blaming Germany for the War," *Literary Digest*, xlix (August 22, 1914), 292-295, and "The Real Crime Against Germany," New York *Nation*, xcix (August 13, 1914), 181-182.

[21] See below, pp. 31-36.

formed American, which enabled him to recover his balance and impelled him to seek a clear and objective understanding once the first
angry emotional reactions had subsided.

The manifestations of this change in sentiment abound in the private
and public writings of Americans in all sections and walks of life. One
revealing example occurred early in the conflict. On August 6, only
two days after Britain had declared war on Germany, Charles W.
Eliot, former president of Harvard University, addressed a startling
letter to President Wilson, urging him to propose the immediate formation of an alliance of the United States, Britain, France, Russia, Italy,
and Japan for the purpose of punishing Germany and Austria-Hungary.[22] It was, as Wilson wrote in reply, "a momentous proposal" of
"great importance";[23] and yet Eliot hastened to withdraw it only two
weeks after he had said it was desperately urgent. He gave his chief
reason for this action frankly, as follows: "We apparently do not
possess full information on the real purposes and objects of either
Russia or Germany; at least the thinking American public does not
possess this information, and therefore cannot justly fix on Germany
the chief responsibility for the present cataclysm. The extreme rashness
of Germany's action cannot but suggest that elements of the situation,
still unknown to the rest of the world, were known to her. I do not
feel the confidence I then felt in the information accessible when I
wrote my letter to you of August 6th."[24]

Over and again we find American leaders like Eliot trying to rise
above a blind emotional partisanship for England and France. There
was the editor of the *Saturday Evening Post*, for example, who early
rejected the argument that the war was simply a contest between monarchy and democracy. The fundamental causes of the war, he wrote,
were "national jealousy, suspicion and hatred—carefully nursed and
exploited everywhere for the military class and the noisy few who find
a profit in war."[25] Or the editor of the Philadelphia *Public Ledger* who
affirmed and the editor of *The Presbyterian* who agreed that "Germany
is not responsible, Russia is not responsible, nor Austria, nor France,
nor England. . . . All, in a mad stampede for armament, trade, and
territory, have sown swords and guns, and nourished harvests of death-

22 C. W. Eliot to W.W., August 6, 1914, Wilson Papers.

23 W.W. to C. W. Eliot, August 14 and 19, 1914, *ibid.*

24 C. W. Eliot to W.W., August 20, 1914, *ibid.*

25 *Saturday Evening Post*, CLXXXVII (August 29, 1914), 20.

dealing crops."[26] Or the moderately pro-Allied president of the University of California, who wrote: "In the last days of July and the first of August Europe seems . . . to have been in a state of nerves. The Powers glided one after another into war as chips are swept over Niagara. I have just been reading the documents of the crisis as presented by His Majesty's Government to Parliament. I have read also a similar German publication. . . . I cannot for a moment believe that the German Government desired the war, and surely the Kaiser did not. I cannot believe that England desired it."[27]

Even more impressive examples of this kind of thinking can be found in the public utterances of two of the most distinguished Americans of the time, George Harvey and Theodore Roosevelt. As editor of the *North American Review*, Harvey in a sense reflected the thinking of two groups who were almost unanimously pro-Allied in sentiment, the eastern literary elite and the business and financial leadership of New York. In September 1914 he published an analysis of the causes of the war that was as dispassionate and almost as accurate as any historian could write today. "Europe," Harvey said, "has long been sick—perhaps sick unto death. The forty years' peace has been no peace, only a feverish truce wherein national rivalries and racial hatreds have intensified and deepened until the day of reckoning was bound to come."[28] Theodore Roosevelt tried equally conscientiously to be understanding and fair during the first months of the war. Although he ardently desired an Allied victory for emotional and large strategic reasons, he could write in the national weekly magazine that served as his journalistic medium, "The causes of any such great and terrible contest almost always lie far back in the past," and he could proceed to analyze these causes with astonishing impartiality and insight.[29]

To be sure, the reactions of the moderate pro-Allied group were in constant flux. Some individuals, like Harvey and Roosevelt themselves, later reverted to a more or less intense attachment under the impact of English propaganda and developments in the war. Yet in the last

[26] Philadelphia *Public Ledger*, cited in *The Presbyterian* (Philadelphia), LXXXIV (September 30, 1914), 3.

[27] Benjamin Ide Wheeler to Lord Bryce, October 1, 1914, the Papers of James, Viscount Bryce, the Bodleian Library, Oxford University; hereinafter cited as the Bryce Papers.

[28] G. Harvey, "Europe at Armageddon," *North American Review*, CC (September 1914), 322.

[29] T. Roosevelt, "The World War: Its Tragedies and Its Lessons," New York *Outlook*, CVIII (September 23, 1914), 169.

analysis it seems accurate to say that the most important development in the American reaction to the war before the spring of 1915, and probably afterward, was the dilution of pro-Allied sentiment that has just been described. It meant that the largest and most influential body of opinion in the United States would refuse—for the most part, actually, until early 1917—to translate diffuse and general emotional reactions into any consistent or realistic reckoning of the vital interests of the United States in the outcome of the war. It meant, in other words, that these Americans wanted the Allies to win, but not strongly enough to sanction measures that would directly involve their own government in the conflict.

The second group of pro-Allied Americans—let us call them extremists for want of a better term—were, obviously, less numerous and influential than the moderates. Scattered throughout the country but concentrated in the East, they did not form an organization to speak for their entire group until December 1915. However, they had strong individual spokesmen among the newspapers and magazines like the *New York Tribune*, the *New York Times*, the Louisville *Courier-Journal*, *The Nation*, *Harper's Weekly*, *World's Work*, and *Outlook*, and among a literary circle that included William Dean Howells, William Roscoe Thayer, and Booth Tarkington. They also had powerful voices among business and financial leaders and lawyers, especially those with connections in Britain and France, like J. P. Morgan and Robert Bacon of the House of Morgan, Frederic R. Coudert and James M. Beck, attorneys of New York and Philadelphia, and Henry L. Higginson, an investment banker of Boston. Even more outspoken were the extremists among the intellectual and academic circles like the architect Ralph Adams Cram, the publisher George Haven Putnam, the university president John Grier Hibben of Princeton, and the professors Franklin H. Giddings of Columbia and Albion W. Small of Chicago. There were, finally, some ardent but usually silent Allied supporters among the political leaders of the East and to a lesser degree of the South, like former President William H. Taft, former Secretary of War Henry L. Stimson, and Senators Henry Cabot Lodge of Massachusetts, Elihu Root of New York, and John Sharp Williams of Mississippi; and a few men favored the Allies on grounds of national interest.[30]

[30] The reader can find a cross-section of the extremists and their opinions in *Sixty American Opinions on the War*, edited by two Englishmen, "S. R. H." and "J. F. M.," in 1915, "to show how many friends we have in America." The Bryce Papers, previ-

The deepest fountainhead of the feelings of this entire group, except for the few devotees of *Realpolitik* among them, was the conviction that the war was in essence a supreme battle between right and wrong. It was a conflict between democracy and autocracy, freedom and slavery, peace through international cooperation and terror through unrestrained militarism. Germany, the bully of Europe, had carefully prepared for and then launched the war in order to destroy a rising democracy within the German Empire and to establish her absolute mastery of the continent. The degree of the intensity of these convictions of course varied, but that intensity often burned at white heat. It was revealed in private letters, like the one written by an American statesman to an English friend:

"I can see already the dawning of a vague hope that it [the war] means the beginning of a new era, the passing away of the old military dynasties, an immense extension of the principles of popular government, and the establishment of international relations on the basis of a peace which is something more than a military truce. Of course all such hopes are pinned upon the success of your arms."[31]

In the strident stanzas of a contemporary poet:

Ride, Cossacks, ride! Charge, Turcos, charge! The fateful hour
 has come.
Let all the guns of Britain roar or be forever dumb.
The Superman has burst his bonds. With Kultur-flag unfurled
And prayer on lip he runs amuck, imperilling the world.

The impious creed that might is right in him personified
Bids all creation bend before the insatiate Teuton pride,
Which, nourished on Valhalla dreams of empire unconfined,
Would make the cannon and the sword the despots of mankind.

....

O world grown sick with butchery and manifold distress!
O broken Belgium robbed of all save grief and ghastliness!
Should Prussian power enslave the world and arrogance prevail,
Let chaos come, let Moloch rule, and Christ give place to Baal![32]

---

ously cited, are particularly useful for revealing the private views of ardent American supporters of the British cause.

[31] Elihu Root to Lord Bryce, September 23, 1914, Bryce Papers.

[32] Robert Grant, "The Superman," New York *Nation*, xcix (October 29, 1914), 521.

Or in the eloquent words of a great novelist:

"After these nine months of the manifold murder in Europe begun by Germany, we who hold her guilty of all the harm that can flow from the largest evil ever let loose upon the world may fitly take stock of our reasons and convictions, not so much as against Germany as in favor of England and France, and especially England. Why do we still believe as powerfully in her cause as at the first? It is easy to say because it is the cause of liberty, of humanity, of Christianity; that it is something like a last hope of mankind; that if it fails civilization will no longer be free in Europe or America, but will become the dismal condition of soldier-slaves enthralling and enthralled. But to say this does not seem enough. One wishes to count and recount one's convictions, to repeat again that the party of the Allies is the party, above everything, of peace, the party of hope, of the equal right to life, liberty, and the pursuit of happiness, of everything endeared by the Declaration and guarded by the Constitution."[33]

Feelings varied, and some extremists might have said that the poet and the novelist, if not the politician, went too far. However, on one issue and its supreme significance, the German invasion of Belgium in violation of treaty pledges, all extremists (and many other Americans as well) were of a single mind. It laid bare to them in all its ugly nakedness what they thought was the essential immorality of German militarism; it symbolized perfectly the character of the German assault against the western community. "That an innocent nation in no way involved in the quarrel of these nations should thus be made the battlefield and offered as a sacrifice on the altar of German militarism," one editor exclaimed, "is the tragedy of the twentieth century. History will

[33] William Dean Howells, "Why?" *North American Review*, cci (May 1915), 676. For other such reactions of the extreme pro-Allied spokesmen, see *Sixty American Opinions on the War*, already cited; Samuel Harden Church, *The American Verdict on the War*; James M. Beck, *The Evidence in the Case*, a widely read summation of the official documentary series on the origins of the war published late in 1914, which pointed the finger of guilt at Germany; Beck's later volume, published in 1917, *The War and Humanity*; William Roscoe Thayer, *Germany vs. Civilization*; Frederick W. Whitridge, *One American's Opinion of the European War, An Answer to Germany's Appeals*; Norman Hapgood, "The Prussian Menace," *Harper's Weekly*, lix (September 19, 1914), 273-274; "The Real Crime Against Germany," New York *Nation*, xcix (August 13, 1914), 181-182; "British 'Lies' and American Sentiment," *ibid.*, November 26, 1914, pp. 621-622; "Why the World Is Against Germany," *World's Work*, xxx (June 1915), 135A-135F; the surveys of press opinion in "Blaming Germany for the War," *Literary Digest*, xlix (August 22, 1914), 293-295, and "American Sympathies in the War," *ibid.*, November 14, 1914, pp. 939-941, 974-978; and the editorials cited in E. Costrell, *How Maine Viewed the War, 1914-1917*, pp. 33-41.

look long with angry countenance on this crime and follow it with its nemesis. The world will not forgive it."[34] Senator John Sharp Williams voiced the same sentiments privately in another way: "I don't know how you feel about it, but I have felt ever since the invasion of Belgium as if I no longer understood men and things. I don't think I have been happy one minute since it took place, except during the minutes when I was not thinking about it at all. The mental epidemics of the middle ages are as nothing compared. God knows I thought it was a phase of human development that was so far behind us that it was worthy of no consideration. The spring of militarism at the throat of civilization was, candidly, as unexpected to me as my springing at the throat of my brother, or his springing at mine would have been."[35]

Pondering Belgium's fate, some extremists were ridden by guilt and shame because their own government had failed to utter even a mild protest when the Germans marched across the little kingdom's frontiers. Certain Republican leaders raised the issue as part of a broad attack against President Wilson's allegedly weak diplomacy in late 1915 and early 1916. But it came out first in the autumn of 1914, and then only quietly and as a manifestation of authentic distress.

How this occurred can be clearly seen in the reactions of Theodore Roosevelt. In his initial public comment on the Belgian issue, made in an article published on September 23, 1914, the former President tried to be fair to Germany and to say nothing that would embarrass the Wilson administration. The German invasion of Belgium, he wrote, was certainly indefensible from a moral point of view; and yet it was precisely the kind of deed that all great powers, including the United States, had done when they believed that their vital interests compelled them to such action. Moreover, Roosevelt added, "it would be folly to jump into the gulf ourselves to no good purpose; and very probably nothing that we could have done would have helped Belgium. We have not the smallest responsibility for what has befallen her."[36] Such sentiments, if they were ever genuine, did not survive for long. By early October Roosevelt was writing privately that he would have taken strong steps to prevent Germany's invasion of Belgium if he had been President when it occurred, and that the deed was symptomatic

[34] *Presbyterian Banner*, ci (November 5, 1914), 713.

[35] J. S. Williams to W.W., October 28, 1915, Wilson Papers.

[36] T. Roosevelt, "The World War: Its Tragedies and Its Lessons," New York *Outlook*, cviii (September 23, 1914), 172-173.

of German ruthlessness.[37] On November 8, 1914, he broke his public silence on Belgium in an article in the *New York Times*; but he did so cautiously, by suggesting that the United States should protest Germany's alleged violations of the Hague conventions by its methods of warfare in Belgium, and not the violation of Belgian neutrality itself.[38]

Deeper still was the shame that other extremists (it would be fair to say that for various reasons Roosevelt had moved into the extreme pro-Allied camp by this time) felt by the autumn of 1914. Robert Bacon, Ambassador to France during the Taft administration and a partner in the Morgan firm, and Senator Elihu Root conferred at some time in late October. "You have given me great comfort and your clear vision has brought courage," Bacon wrote soon afterward to the old Roman, urging him to speak out on Belgium. " 'If I had been Secy of State,' you said in effect, 'I think I would have made a vigorous protest.' 'If I had not been ill & tired at home I think I should have made the protest in the Senate' and you added, thinking aloud musing 'It is probably too late now.' Oh, Elihu, it isn't too late if it's right & you in your wonderful modesty can not quite appreciate what that word would mean to those kindred souls out there, with their question, generally unasked, trembling on their lips, 'How *do* you stand over there!' Meaning our ideals, our principles, our standards, which my poor intellect & imagination pictures [*sic*] as having grown & developed over here since Cromwell's time."[39]

Few among the extremists, however, were willing yet to join an organized movement for an official American protest, or even to voice their sentiments publicly. Bacon did, on the eve of his departure for France, where he went to take charge of private American relief work.[40] So also did Roosevelt's editorial organ, *The Outlook*.[41] But Root and most other advanced supporters of the Allied cause refused to support the demand publicly,[42] and the movement to give official expression to the extremist view quietly collapsed at this time.

[37] T. Roosevelt to C. A. Spring Rice, October 3, 1914, and to Hugo Münsterberg, October 3, 1914, Elting E. Morison *et al.* (eds.), *The Letters of Theodore Roosevelt*, VIII, 821, 823.

[38] T. Roosevelt, "The International Posse Comitatus," *New York Times Magazine Section*, November 8, 1914.

[39] R. Bacon to E. Root, October 29, 1914, Root Papers.

[40] New York *Outlook*, CVIII (November 18, 1914), 625-626.

[41] *ibid.*, pp. 627-628.

[42] Ambassador Walter Page, among others, tried to persuade Root to lead a movement for an American protest. For Page's efforts and Root's refusal, see W. H. Page to

Besides the pro-Allied extremists whose sentiments were shaped by emotion and by ethical considerations there were the much smaller number of men who wanted the Allies to win chiefly for strategic reasons— because they believed, for example, that British sea power defended American economic and strategic interests almost as much as the British, or that a triumphant Germany would threaten the Monroe Doctrine or imperil American security in other ways. Few in number at the outset, this group exercised little direct influence upon American opinion before the submarine controversy broke out, and perhaps never a decisive influence before 1917.[43] This is not to say, however, that fears of a German victory played no part in helping to shape initial American reactions to the war. Such forebodings underlay much extremist thinking and were manifested from time to time.[44]

Looking back over the responses and activities of the various pro-Allied spokesmen during the formative period of American neutrality, the historian is impressed both by their strength in numbers and by their failure to exert any direct influence upon official American policies toward the belligerents. This was true in part, perhaps, because they did not try. Not a single leader in any section (except C. W. Eliot, who, as we have seen, withdrew his suggestion almost as soon as he had made it) called for the adoption of any measures that would be even of weak assistance to the Allies or for any deviation from a strict official neutrality during the first eight or nine months of the war. Indeed, not many did until it had become obvious that American participation could not be avoided anyway.

This singular absence of any interventionist sentiment during the early period of the war, and of any important interventionist sentiment during almost the entire period of American neutrality, can be ascribed

---

C. P. Anderson, February 4, 1915, the Papers of Chandler P. Anderson, Library of Congress, hereinafter cited as the Anderson Papers; C. P. Anderson to W. H. Page, February 18, 1915, *ibid.*; the Diary of Chandler P. Anderson, Library of Congress, February 18, 1915, hereinafter cited as the Anderson Diary.

[43] Among the men who thought in strategic terms at this time were Alfred T. Mahan, the naval historian; Lewis Einstein, a career diplomat; and George Louis Beer, an historian. For an excellent survey and analysis, see Robert E. Osgood, *Ideals and Self-Interest in America's Foreign Relations*, pp. 125-130.

[44] e.g., H. L. Higginson to E. M. House, September 1, 1914, House Papers; Henry Van Dyke to W.W., September 10, 1914, Wilson Papers; "Are We Neutral?" *Collier's*, LIII (September 12, 1914), 16; W. H. Page to E. M. House, September 22, 1914, House Papers; Stuart H. Perry, "After the War," *North American Review*, cc (November 1914), 732-741; "Germany and the Monroe Doctrine," New York *Outlook*, cviii (November 4, 1914), 521-524.

to only one cause, namely, that the great mass of pro-Allied Americans believed that a course of neutrality was wise and right for their government. It goes almost without saying that these were the sentiments of the majority of Americans who were, for one reason or another, substantially neutral in viewpoint. But it was true as well of most of the ardent supporters of the Allies. With a few exceptions, they applauded the President's appeal for impartiality in thought as well as in deed as enthusiastically as did the neutral majority.[45] Many of the very same editors and spokesmen who warned that a German victory would be a major calamity for civilization, if not a direct menace to the United States, were as warmly commendatory of Bryan's ban on loans to belligerents, which was bound to operate to the disadvantage of the Allies, as were the editors of church weeklies who thought that the Secretary of State had struck another blow for righteousness.[46]

There is no need to labor this point, for an even more important task remains: to explain why people who felt as strongly as the pro-Allied Americans did should have been so impressively neutral as far as policy was concerned. Such an explanation has the merit of shedding light on certain salient aspects of *all* American thinking about the war, for the attitudes and assumptions that produced this result were shared in large measure by most Americans.

To begin with, until early 1917 (and even beyond) virtually all Americans assumed as a matter of course that the Allies would win. This was a governing assumption among the pro-Allied extremists as well; few of them were willing to advocate American participation in a ghastly war solely on grounds of sentiment.

Secondly, few Americans even in the extreme pro-Allied camp thought that the United States had sufficient interests in the outcome of the war to justify the costs of participation, or the risks of participation that would come from executing policies directly beneficial to the Allies. As one British observer put it: "The great bulk of Americans simply do not believe that the present conflict, whatever its upshot, touches their national security or endangers their power to hold

---

[45] e.g., C. W. Eliot to W.W., August 20, 1914, Wilson Papers; W. H. Taft to T. R. Lounsbury, September 6, 1914, the Papers of William Howard Taft, Library of Congress, hereinafter cited as the Taft Papers; W. H. Taft to C. W. Baker, September 19, 1914, *ibid.*; New York *Outlook*, cvii (August 15, 1914), 893-894.

[46] e.g., New York *Nation*, xcix (December 3, 1914), 644; E. C. Stokes to W.W., August 18, 1914, Wilson Papers; *The Financial World*, xxiii (August 22, 1914), 1-2; *The Independent*, lxxx (October 26, 1914), 117-118; *America*, xi (August 22, 1914), 438-439; *The Standard, a Baptist Newspaper*, lxi (August 29, 1914), 1543.

fast to their own ideals of politics and society and ethics. They have been brought up to believe in the invulnerability of their country, in the completeness of its separation from the feuds and ferment of the Old World, and in the wisdom of the tradition that has prescribed for them a policy of non-interference as the logical corollary to their fortunate geographical remoteness. That they should forfeit these advantages for any cause less urgent than the existence or safety of the Commonwealth seems to many millions of Americans a counsel of suicidal insanity."[47]

Thirdly, many of the pro-Allied champions among the intelligentsia were either sheer idealists or idealistic pacifists. They could be eloquent and impassioned in denouncing German militarism, but the thought of America's intervening or even of having anything to do with the war was as abhorrent to them as was the specter of German militarism itself. Perhaps the best example of this type was Oswald Garrison Villard, owner and publisher of the New York *Nation* and the *New York Evening Post*. He believed that the insolent Prussian *Junkerthum*, "which slashes lame cobblers and bends the nation to its own imperious will," was responsible for the war,[48] and that, as he said in a widely read tract published early in 1915, "Americans who believe in self-government and democracy can take but one stand against absolutism and arbitrary power."[49] Villard's influential magazine and daily newspaper were two of the most ardent supporters of the Allied cause in the western world. And yet he, like so many other pro-Allied idealists, fiercely opposed any and all diplomatic measures that remotely implied the use of force, and even the most ineffective preparation for possible war. To him and to men of his mind America's mission was to stand courageously for righteousness, but by the spirit and not by the sword.

Finally, the few genuinely pro-Allied extremists among the *political* leadership of the country never dared to let their sentiments become publicly known, much less to give any effective direction to the pro-Allied forces, so powerful were the countervailing opinions among their constituents and the great majority of the leaders of the country. As they saw it, their only possible role was that of watchdog over American policies, to make certain that their government committed no unneutral act against the Allies.

[47] "The Growth of American Pacifism," London *Nation*, xviii (October 2, 1915), 10.
[48] e.g., E. W. Hilgard to O. G. Villard, September 11, 1914, and O. G. Villard to E. W. Hilgard, September 18, 1914, both in the Villard Papers.
[49] *Germany Embattled*, p. 29.

At the other extreme among the American people stood the partisans of Germany and Austria-Hungary. Although probably less numerous than the broad group of pro-Allied supporters, they were vastly noisier and more industrious in their efforts to influence American opinions and policies. Drawing support from several powerful groups and institutions, they were in certain ways more formidable than their opponents on the other side.

The most important element in this coalition were of course the German Americans, that is, the American citizens who had been born in the Fatherland or one or both of whose parents were of German birth. Vast in number—there were more than eight and a quarter million of them in the United States in 1910—they were heavily concentrated in the eastern cities south of New England and in the Middle West. Generally well educated and highly respected for their industry and good citizenship, they had an aggressive and able press and were extraordinarily well organized on all levels—from local *vereins* to the National German-American Alliance, which claimed 2,000,000 members in 1914, and the branches of the Lutheran Church and the dioceses of the Roman Catholic Church that were primarily German in membership.

Unlike pro-Allied reactions, which ranged far and wide, German-American thinking about the war was, so far as one can tell, uniform and unsophisticated. Indeed, it does not seem farfetched to say that the German Americans were as united in support of the Fatherland as were the Kaiser's most loyal subjects. In personal correspondence, editorials, articles, pamphlets, and books they all preached the same doctrine, that Germany was fighting a defensive war to save Europe from Slavic despotism, that France and England had joined the war only for revenge and profit, and that Germany had had no alternative but to invade Belgium.

"While Germany has declared the war, she is not the aggressor," explained the *New Yorker Staats-Zeitung*, in a typical editorial expression of the German-American point of view. "Germany has been the defendant ever since she claimed her place among the nations. Germany's revilers and evil-wishers have made life miserable for her for decades by calumnies and malicious public utterances against her. . . . The Gordian knot has been cut and Emperor William has requested the people to pray that victory may come to the German arms. With the German battalions marches the good German conscience which has been mobilized with the troops."[50]

"England," the editor of a Lutheran weekly exclaimed, "may succeed in stabbing to the heart the people that, under Herman the Cheruskian, set bounds to imperial Roman aggression, and, under Luther, to papal Roman aggression. But history shall show that this is the world's and England's loss; for the downfall of the German eagle means the triumph of the Russian bear!

"O God of battles! Now that the earth is shuddering from the shock of armies, and the sea is black with wrath, remember in mercy and protect in might the land of Luther, for the sake of Luther's Christ. Amen."[51]

Such love and loyalty could not be content with merely verbal expression. German-American groups—above all, the National German-American Alliance—raised hundreds of thousands of dollars for German war relief, bought the Imperial government's war bonds by the millions of dollars, and brought heavy pressure upon pro-Allied newspapers and movie producers to give a fair showing to the German side. Working with German officials, they formed a Literary Defense Committee in New York that distributed more than one million propaganda pamphlets during the first year of the war. "German-language newspapers sold pictures of the Kaiser, official German casualty lists, '*War Albums*,' American and German flags, watch-fobs, souvenir spoons of the Kaiser, the Kaiserin and General Paul von Hindenburg, new war postcards from Germany, and 'Iron Cross' watches."[52] Finally, these partisans of the Central Powers were equally active in the political arena, in a way and with results that we will later describe. As the British Ambassador wrote, somewhat exaggeratedly, of the German-American organization and activity: "Now at last it is clearly visible that inside the American organization there is

[50] Cited in the *Literary Digest*, XLIX (August 22, 1914), 300.

[51] *Lutheran Youth*, cited in the *Lutheran Church Work*, III (October 1, 1914), 9.
For an excellent survey of German-American press opinion on the broad issues of the war, see Carl Wittke, *German-Americans and the World War*, pp. 3-21. For typical articles, editorials, and books, see Walter Rauschenbusch, "Be Fair to Germany," *The Congregationalist and Christian World*, reprinted in the *Lutheran Church Work*, III (November 19, 1914), 8-10, and partially in the *Literary Digest*, XLIX (November 7, 1914), 892-893; J. L. Neve, "Who Is Responsible for This War?" *Lutheran Church Work*, III (September 3, 1914), 8-9; "Lessons of the War: The German-Americans," *The Open Court*, XXVIII (December 1914), 747-751; Kuno Francke, *A German-American's Confession of Faith*.

[52] Carl Wittke, *German-Americans and the World War*, p. 31.

a foreign one, carefully & systematically organized, spreading to every department of politics, finance, journalism, education, administration, & business: that this has its own ends & its own means—that it is far the best & most powerful of all the organizations and is supported by one or two of the strongest of the others."[53]

The German cause found allies nearly as loyal if not quite as numerous among other so-called hyphenate groups. The most prolific and influential of these were the Irish Americans, 4,500,000 strong in 1914, who were heavily concentrated in the eastern and midwestern cities, and who exercised a political power probably greater than that of the German Americans. As their thinking about the war was largely predetermined by their bitter memories of alleged English oppression in the home country, they were an important center of pro-German strength. Probably a majority of their rank and file were anti-Allied, for no other reason than because "perfidious Albion" was the chief of the Allied powers.[54] Certainly among the majority of their leaders— the men and organizations who were encouraging, subsidizing, and helping to organize the Nationalist movement against British rule in Ireland[55]—hopes for a German victory were as sincere as they were widespread.[56] Carrying on a propaganda that was unceasing,[57] they

[53] C. A. Spring Rice to Lord Bryce, January 5, 1914 [1915], Bryce Papers.

[54] The division in Irish-American opinion was certainly close during the first eighteen months of the war. The British Ambassador reported to the Foreign Office in early June of 1915, for example: "The majority of the Irish are with the Allies, mainly because of the settlement of the Home Rule question." Ambassador Spring Rice to the Foreign Office, June 8, 1915, copy in the Papers of Herbert Asquith, Bodleian Library, Oxford University; hereinafter cited as the Asquith Papers. There can be no doubt, on the other hand, that Irish-American opinion turned massively and savagely against Great Britain after the Irish Rebellion in April 1916. In his excellent study, C. C. Cummins found that the Irish Americans in Indiana were throughout virtually unanimous in their desire for England's defeat. C. C. Cummins, *Indiana Public Opinion and the World War*, pp. 56-57.

[55] The two leading Irish-American organizations in the United States at this time, the Ancient Order of Hibernians and the United Irish-American Societies, had long been identified with this movement and were directly involved in it during the period leading up to the Irish Rebellion. In addition, many of the leading Irish-American newspapers, including the New York *Irish World*, the New York *Gaelic-American*, the Boston *Hibernian*, the Minneapolis *Irish Standard*, and the San Francisco *Leader*, were active in the propaganda of the Nationalist movement in the United States. See C. C. Tansill, *America and the Fight for Irish Freedom, 1866-1922*.

[56] This, all observers agreed, was true from the beginning of the war. "The Irish leaders and organisation here have been captured by the Germans," Ambassador Spring Rice reported in his dispatch to the Foreign Office of June 8, 1915, cited above. "The Clan-na-gael have captured the majority of the New York Irish although not

worked hand in glove with German agents and in return, one must assume, received generous financial assistance from the German Embassy in Washington for their intrigues.[58]

Less openly committed than the German Americans and their Irish allies but for the most part ranged with them were the Jewish Americans, three to four million of them congregated in New York City and to a lesser degree in other metropolitan centers. Whether they were among the high-born minority of German origin or belonged to the Yiddish-speaking majority who had come from Poland and Russia during the past decade and a half, they were nearly unanimous in their sentiments toward the belligerents. That is to say, virtually all of them were ardently anti-Allied in feeling—the Yiddish-speaking Jews because an Allied victory would mean the triumph and extension of Russian despotism and anti-Semitism, the German-American Jews because they were in fact as strongly pro-German as they were anti-Russian.[59]

Finally, there were the Swedish Americans, nearly two million of whom lived in Minnesota and adjoining North Central states, who had a historic hatred of Russia and friendship toward Germany. Although the Swedish-American newspapers were about evenly divided in support of the Allies and the Central Powers, all of them were ardently

---

Tammany," he added some months later. "The St. Patrick's day procession showed that the Redmondites are a small minority. Hatred of England and German gold have carried the day and the organised Irish are against us with many high church dignitaries. It is a melancholy fact but it is a fact. I do not see what more can be done." C. A. Spring Rice to Sir Horace Plunkett, March 23, 1916, the Papers of Sir Horace Plunkett, the Horace Plunkett Foundation, London; hereinafter cited as the Plunkett Papers. This letter to Plunkett was written, it should be remembered, before the Irish Rebellion.

[57] e.g., Daniel K. McGuire (a former Mayor of Syracuse, New York), *The King, The Kaiser, and Irish Freedom* and *What Could Germany Do for Ireland?*; the pamphlet issued by the American Truth Society, *A Way to Stop the War* (1915); and the account of a pro-German rally held under this organization's auspices in New York City, in the *New York Times*, April 26, 1915. The American Truth Society, headed by one Jeremiah A. O'Leary, was among the most active pro-German Irish-American propaganda agencies in the East.

[58] See Minister Hohlt in Santo Domingo to the German Minister in Port-au-Prince, January 20, 1915, the Archives of the German Foreign Office, on microfilm in the National Archives, Washington (hereinafter cited as the German F. O. Archives), telling of the participation of the American Minister in Santo Domingo, James M. Sullivan, in these intrigues.

[59] Joseph Rappaport, "Jewish Immigrants and World War I: A Study of American Yiddish Press Reaction," unpublished Ph.D. dissertation, Columbia University Library, is an excellent detailed study.

opposed to American participation in the war before 1917. Moreover, the rank and file of the Swedish Americans were apparently either wholly neutral or pro-German in sentiment, and their spokesmen in Washington were conspicuous supporters of policies—an embargo on the export of munitions, for example—that would have benefited the Central Powers.[60]

Besides these immigrant groups there were other centers and sources of active support of the Central Powers. Reflecting its predominantly Irish- and German-American constituency and the Vatican's friendship for the Hapsburg dynasty, the Roman Catholic Church in the United States—hierarchy, priesthood, and press—tended toward an open partisanship.[61] The chain of newspapers owned by William Randolph Hearst—there were nine of them from Boston to San Francisco—were ostensibly neutral but invariably anti-British and pro-German, and in fact worked effectively to agitate and encourage the pro-German hyphenate groups.[62] In addition, other newspapers like the powerful Chicago *Daily Tribune,* the *Washington Post,* the St. Louis *Globe-Democrat,* and the Milwaukee *Sentinel* could often be found on the German side, although they could not properly be called pro-German. Finally, there were a number of American leaders of the old stock who took up the cudgels for Germany for one reason or another. Several of them were extraordinarily active, indeed were the most

[60] George M. Shephenson, "The Attitude of Swedish Americans Toward the World War," *Mississippi Valley Historical Association Proceedings,* x (1918-1919), Part I, 79-94.

[61] No one has yet made a systematic survey of American Catholic opinion and the World War. Cummins' thorough analysis of public opinion in Indiana reveals that the entire Catholic press in that fairly typical state was controlled by Irish and German Americans friendly to the Central Powers, and that the strongest pro-German newspaper in the state was the influential *Indiana Catholic,* official organ of the Diocese of Indianapolis and Fort Wayne. C. C. Cummins, *Indiana Public Opinion,* pp. 57-58, 65-67. "Roman Catholic circles here," Ambassador Johann von Bernstorff reported early in 1915, "are very warmly disposed toward us but not very active insofar as agitation is concerned. The influence of the Catholic Church could do very much here. For that instructions from Rome very desirable." Ambassador von Bernstorff to the Foreign Office, February 27, 1915, German F. O. Archives.

[62] Commenting on Hearst's opposition to the Anglo-French loan of 1915, the German Ambassador in Washington wrote to the Imperial Chancellor in Berlin: "An exceptionally brilliant financier of the Morgan group [which sponsored the loan] said in public that the loan was without success in the West since Mr. Hearst's influence was against it. . . . Hearst, who, by the way, has always been pro-German, told me that this statement honored him very much." J. von Bernstorff to T. von Bethmann Hollweg, November 3, 1915, *ibid.*

persuasive propagandists that the Fatherland had in the United States.[63]

Standing somewhere (and sometimes ambiguously) in between the two extremes were probably the majority of the American people and their leaders in church and state. They were on the whole neutral, that is, impartial, in their reactions and thinking, because they either did not care about the issues and outcome of the war, or were so mildly pro-Allied or pro-German as to be actually neutral insofar as policies toward the belligerents were concerned, or else made a conscious effort to follow the President's injunction to be impartial in thought as well as in deed.

One is tempted to say that almost a majority of Americans simply did not care. This attitude of unconcern—some critics called it complacency—permeated all sections and classes but was decidedly stronger west of the Appalachians and in small towns and the countryside than in the East and in metropolitan centers. "The general sentiment of the country, so far as I have been able to gauge it," one astute British journalist wrote early in 1915, "still regards the wars and diplomatic disputes of the Old World, even such a war as the present, with a mainly spectacular concern; still desires to have as few dealings as

[63] The most prominent members of this group were rear Admiral French E. Chadwick, U.S.N., Retired, historian of the Spanish-American War, who pleaded Germany's cause in an almost unending stream of letters to individuals in high places; Professor John W. Burgess, historian, political scientist, and former dean of the faculties at Columbia University, who spoke frequently before German-American groups and contributed to their propaganda; George Stuart Fullerton, professor of philosophy at Columbia and Honorary Professor in the University of Vienna; and former Senator Albert J. Beveridge of Indiana, who went to Germany as a war correspondent in 1914 and returned to continue his efforts to strengthen German-American relations.

For examples of Chadwick's many letters, see F. E. Chadwick to W.W., August 23, September 12, December 16, 1914, and February 19 and August 20, 1915, Wilson Papers; F. E. Chadwick to O. G. Villard, January 4, 1914 [1915], Villard Papers. For Burgess' contributions, see his article in the *Boston Evening Transcript*, August 19, 1914; letter to the Editor, printed in the *Newport* (Rhode Island) *Daily News*, September 12, 1914; letter to the *Springfield* (Massachusetts) *Republican*, reprinted in *The Open Court*, xxviii (October 1914), 587-595; "England Twists Decisions of Civil War to Prop Weak Case," *New York Evening Mail*, August 14, 1915; and especially his *The European War of 1914*, published in 1915. Professor Fullerton argued [in "Why the German Nation Has Gone to War," *Lutheran Church Work*, iii (February 4, 1915), 10-13] that Germany had been forced to take up arms, and that Americans would have done the same thing if they had been confronted with the same threats to their existence. In his *Germany of To-Day*, published in 1915, Fullerton pointed up the German achievement in social legislation and attempted to explain what he said was the true, or defensive, character of German militarism. Beveridge's articles, published originally in *Collier's, Saturday Evening Post*, and the New York *Review of Reviews*, were brought out in book form in 1915 under the title *What Is Back of the War*.

possible with foreign Powers, and still shrinks from any course that might conceivably lead to an 'entangling alliance.' . . . It is altogether natural that this should be so. The United States is remote, unconquerable, huge, without hostile neighbors or any neighbors at all of anything like her own strength, and lives exempt in an almost unvexed tranquility from the contentions and animosities and the ceaseless pressure and counterpressure that distract the close-packed older world. Inevitably, therefore, a sober, sustained, and well-informed interest in foreign affairs is a luxury with which the ordinary American citizen feels he can dispense."[64] "The basic facts," the British Ambassador in Washington wrote in substantial agreement, "are that the current feelings in this country are connected with the personal advantage, etc., of American citizens. . . . The point of view of national honour, as to which the U.S. people were thought to be so sensitive, gives place to the point of view in each section, and class, and nationality, that what they have to do in this world is to look after their own skins. For instance, in California there is a complete contempt for the affairs not only of Europe, but of the middle and eastern States. The middle States think in terms of wheat, and the southern States in terms of cotton."[65]

There is abundant evidence to support this view. If the absence in their journals of any serious discussions about the war and the utterances of their spokesmen in Congress meant anything, then most farmers and workers, for example, were not much interested in events in Europe, except as they affected the price of cotton or wheat, or wages and the cost of living. This provincialism and unconcern combined with other deeply rooted attitudes—pacifism and a hostility toward businessmen and bankers, who they thought started wars anyway—to make farmers and workers the most stubbornly neutral and antiwar groups in the United States. Throughout the entire period of American neutrality they made it plain by their opposition to preparedness and all measures of strong diplomacy that they wanted nothing to do with Europe's troubles. Nor, for that matter, were *most* of the members of the great American business community really profoundly concerned. Their primary objective was the largest measure of trade with the belligerents that their government could achieve; whether they were

[64] Sydney Brooks, "The United States and the War: A British View," *North American Review*, cci (February 1915), 237-238.

[65] C. A. Spring Rice to Dominick Spring Rice, September 17, 1915, Stephen Gwynn (ed.), *The Letters and Friendships of Sir Cecil Spring Rice*, ii, 285-286; hereinafter cited as *The Letters of Sir Cecil Spring Rice*.

pro-Allied or pro-German would depend upon the economic interest involved and upon the degree to which the belligerents' sea measures threatened their prosperity.[66]

In addition, there were the American Socialists and assorted groups of independent radicals—advanced progressives, single taxers, devotees of one panacea or another—who were perhaps the most genuinely neutral Americans of all. Except for a peripheral minority, they all viewed the war with bitter detestation as the inevitable outcome of capitalistic exploitation at home and imperialism abroad. "The ghastly carnage in Europe," one Socialist leader wrote, for example, "has no redeeming features. It is not a war for democracy, culture, or progress. It is not a fight for sentiments or ideals. It is a cold-blooded butchery for advantages and power, and let us not forget it—advantages and power for the ruling classes of the warring nations."[67] Such an interpretation, it should be added, was by no means confined to the forces on the Left; it permeated the thinking of millions of non-Socialist farmers and workers and of progressives like Senator Robert M. La Follette of Wisconsin or Senator George W. Norris of Nebraska.

For many Americans, on the other hand, neutrality meant a good deal more than unconcern or trying to save one's own skin. It meant, even for many who were predisposed to favor the Allies, a conscious effort to be fair, stemming in many cases from the conviction that it was impossible to apportion guilt for the war and that it would be a futile thing to do even if it were possible. It meant trying to understand the abnormal behavior of the belligerents in the light of abnormal circumstances. Evidences of such a disposition abound in the private and public writings of leaders in all fields of thought, but most significantly in the statements and admonitions of the leaders of American Protestantism. Feeling a special duty to guide the thinking of their people, they did in fact express most authentically the more judicious and loftier sentiments of the American people.

"The question of neutrality receives much mention," wrote the editor of one Presbyterian weekly. "What other position can those outside the conflict take, in view of the character of the leading nations on either side of the conflict? The human race has produced no finer people than the Germans. . . . On the other hand, the world has never known a nobler empire than the British. . . . These two splendid

---

[66] See Harold C. Syrett, "The Business Press and American Neutrality, 1914-1917," *Mississippi Valley Historical Review*, XXXII (September 1945), 215-230.

[67] Morris Hillquit in the *American Socialist*, January 9, 1915, quoted in David A. Shannon, *The Socialist Party of America, A History*, p. 85.

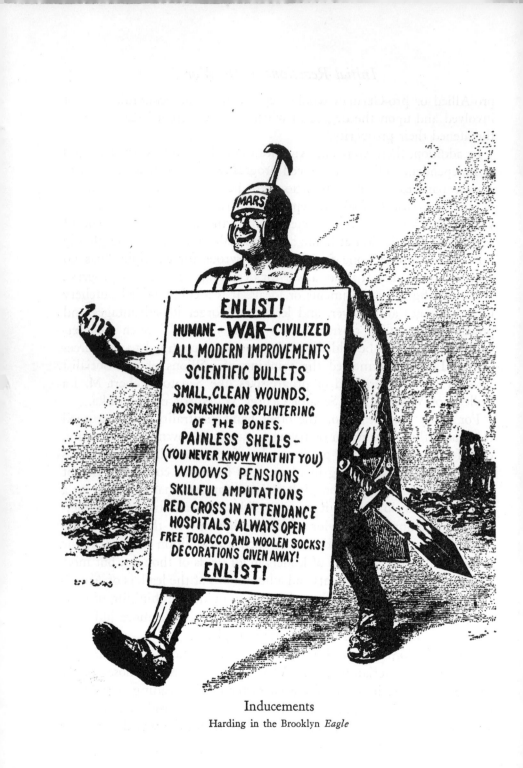

Inducements

Harding in the Brooklyn *Eagle*

people are kindreds of the same noble stock. With these facts and convictions, how can we be other than neutral? How can we do otherwise than deplore and lament this awful conflict? We are not disposed to stop and discuss, blame, locate responsibility, and speculate on the future. We are wholly and profoundly interested in having this war cease, and these people restored to their old faith and obedience toward God and to peace, and fellowship toward each other."[68]

To Americans of this mind, moreover, being neutral meant even more than trying to understand and sympathize. It was the only way that the United States could be true to its ideals and carry out its God-given mission of bringing peace and unity to a warring world. As the Federal Council of the Churches of Christ in America put it in a special appeal to the President: "The Federal Council . . . suggests to the President of the United States, in view of the attempts already made to induce this country to take sides in the present European conflict, that he appeal to the people of the United States, as lovers of their country and of humanity, that neither as individuals nor as groups do they take any action to destroy the complete and absolute neutrality of the United States. We believe that he who would attempt to drag this country into the present war not only sins against patriotism, but would destroy all hope of speedy peace. Only as this nation remains strictly neutral can she offer mediation. If she becomes involved, there is no impartial court left to which the nations may appeal."[69] "Somewhere," the bishops of the Methodist Episcopal Church added later in a pastoral letter, "the song of the angelic host must still be heard. Somewhere the sun of peace must continue to shine, while Europe is in eclipse. From somewhere must blow the kindly currents that shall cool the fever of hate and revenge that is consuming our brothers beyond the sea."[70]

As it often happened, a British observer best understood and most movingly described the idealism that motivated much of American neutralism. His comments deserve to be repeated here:

"The strongest sentiment in the United States of to-day is not anti-German but anti-war, not pro-Ally but pro-peace. There is nothing Americans desire more fervently than to keep out of the present ghastly struggle. They regard Europe as rattling madly back into barbarism,

---

[68] "True Neutrality," *The Presbyterian*, LXXXIV (December 2, 1914), 3.

[69] Shailer Mathews *et al.*, "Appeal to the President," August 18, 1914, Wilson Papers, printed in the Nashville *Christian Advocate*, LXXV (September 4, 1914), 1149, and elsewhere.

[70] New York *Christian Advocate*, XC (May 20, 1915), 677.

while they themselves are the sole depositories of sanity and civilization. They feel the waste and horror and criminality of it all with a physical intensity all the more stark for being devoid of the ennobling consolations which support the actual belligerents. They look down upon us as the victims of dynastic ambitions, diplomatic plots, and an anti-democratic dispensation, and they thank their stars that in America they are exempt from the conditions which have produced so appalling a catastrophe. To remain outside the orbit of its ravages there are very few sacrifices of what in the old phraseology used to be called 'national honor' or 'national self-respect' or 'national interests,' to which they will not consent. They see no obligation of honor or self-respect more stringent, and no interest more compelling, than that of discouraging this war madness and enlisting sentiment on the side of reason and legality. . . .

"We must remember, too, that great fund of American idealism and humanity which their carelessness and affectation of cynicism never quite conceal. They are a fresh and fundamentally wholesome people or medley of peoples, inhabiting a land that is still amazingly under-developed and under-populated, responding eagerly to the needs and opportunities of their environment, but never so absorbed in material things as to be incapable of dreaming dreams and seeing visions. And of all dreams, that which comes nearest to them is the dream of universal peace; of all visions the one they most cherish is of a world freed from the notion that force is the final arbiter in human affairs. It is not a social or a political accident but a deep spiritual conviction that makes the Americans look askance on militarism and all its accessories. . . . In that spacious, unhampered seclusion of theirs, in a society where women and the Churches have taken into their own hands the decision on all questions of ethics, and among a people of such varied extraction and spread over so vast a domain, the reaction against war develops under more favorable circumstances than obtain or are even imaginable anywhere else."[71]

Above all these forces and ideals, not often openly expressed but significant none the less, was the conviction that an aggressive neutralism was the only course capable of holding the centrifugal forces of the American society in check. It was as one observer wrote in early 1916: "By far the most prevalent sentiment in the country seems to be neutralism, which doesn't come from apathy, but is, in my opinion, the present expression of nationalism, & a positive force. People are neutral because they shrink from national division, or, on a lower

[71] "The Growth of American Pacifism," London *Nation*, xviii (October 2, 1915), 9-10.

degree, from splits in their own communities, which, besides being bad for business, would be disagreeable socially, & in some places make life very difficult indeed. One sees this plainly in the smaller towns in the South West, & I hear the conditions are the same elsewhere."[72] Or, as the President himself put it, "We definitely have to be neutral, since otherwise our mixed populations would wage war on each other."[73]

We now come to the most perplexing aspect of this account of American attitudes during their formative period, and that is the question of the degree to which they were shaped by propaganda and propagandists, those special pleaders who worked so industriously to win American sympathies for one side or the other. It would require another volume to describe in detail the mighty war of words that ensued in America after the outbreak of hostilities, and we must be content with a summary view of the matter and its outcome.

The Germans were first in the field and prosecuted the most open campaign during the initial year of the war. Fully aware of the necessity of winning American friends, the Berlin Foreign Office established a propaganda agency in New York in August 1914. Known as the German Information Service, it was headed by a former Colonial Minister, Doctor Bernhard Dernburg, who came to America at the outbreak of the war as the representative of the German Red Cross. Associated with Dernburg were Doctor Heinrich Albert, head of the German Purchasing Commission; Privy Councillor Anton Meyer Gerhard, formerly of the Colonial Office; Doctor Alexander Fuehr, who had recently come from the Imperial Embassy in Tokyo; and George Sylvester Viereck, a young German-American journalist who had already begun editing a weekly called *The Fatherland*. These were the principal operators of the German propaganda machine, but there were others associated with it in various helpful capacities—such as the Ambassador in Washington, Count Johann von Bernstorff, Professor Hugo Münsterberg of Harvard University, and William Bayard Hale, one of the leading American journalists of the day.[74]

The outpouring by these and other spokesmen was a veritable flood that deluged almost every channel of communication in the United States. The German Information Service, which worked under

[72] W. A. Gill to Lord Bryce, February 6, 1916, Bryce Papers.

[73] J. von Bernstorff to T. von Bethmann Hollweg, September 6, 1914, German F. O. Archives.

[74] G. S. Viereck, *Spreading Germs of Hate*, pp. 44-46; J. von Bernstorff, *My Three Years in America*, pp. 33-42.

the general direction of the Foreign Office in Berlin,[75] of course took the lead. It issued daily bulletins and news summaries to the American press and arrranged for the printing and distribution of propaganda materials sent directly from Germany, like the widely read *Truth About Germany, Facts About the War*,[76] or the pamphlet entitled *How the Franco-German Conflict Could Have Been Avoided*.[77] Attempting to justify Germany's invasion of Belgium, the Information Service published documents captured from the Foreign Office in Belgium purporting to prove that the Belgians had long conspired with the British and French for military cooperation in the event of a general war.[78] It subsidized Viereck's German-American weekly and other friendly publications and writers; worked closely with Irish Nationalist leaders; bought control of the New York *International Monthly* in 1915 and the *New York Evening Mail* in 1916 to assure a fair hearing in the largest American city; organized a new press agency, the International Press Exchange, in 1915; and arranged for the publication of German propaganda works by Americans when they could not find regular publishers.[79] Moreover, before he left the United States during the *Lusitania* crisis, Dernburg maintained a drumfire of speeches before German-American audiences and contributed numerous articles to the general periodical press,[80] while Münsterberg and other German professors in America did the same kind of work.[81]

[75] e.g., see Undersecretary Arthur Zimmermann to Ambassador von Bernstorff, December 27, 1914, instructing Bernstorff to ask Münsterberg to answer Theodore Roosevelt on the Belgian question, and A. Zimmermann to J. von Bernstorff, January 16, 1915, sending instructions for the preparation of an anti-Japanese pamphlet to be distributed on the West Coast, both in the German F. O. Archives.

[76] This was an appeal, distributed in the United States by the American News Company, issued under the names of forty-five distinguished German leaders in all walks of life. Included was a statement by Professor Burgess attesting to its "correctness, completeness and veracity."

[77] This pamphlet, issued by the German government for distribution in the United States, was reprinted in the *New York Times*, September 11, 1914.

[78] Bernhard Dernburg, *The Case of Belgium* . . . ; Alexander Fuehr, *The Neutrality of Belgium*. The latter was a detailed analysis of the Belgian documents.

[79] e.g., Charles A. Collman, *The War Plotters of Wall Street*, published by the "Fatherland Corporation" of New York in 1915; S. Ivor Stephen, *Neutrality? The Crucifixion of Public Opinion*, published by the "Neutrality Press" of Chicago in 1916; and Roland Hugins, *Germany Misjudged*, published by the Open Court Publishing Company of Chicago in 1916.

[80] "When Germany Wins," *The Independent*, LXXX (December 7, 1914), 361-362; "Germany and the Powers," *North American Review*, cc (December 1914), 833-846; "The Ties That Bind America and Germany," *World's Work*, XXIX (December 1914), 186-189.

[81] Professor Münsterberg, in a letter to "Most Respected Privy Councillor," dated

This was, however, only a part of the total German effort and the least effective part, at that. The really impressive work was done by the German leaders and people themselves, from the Imperial Chancellor in Berlin and the Ambassador in Washington down to obscure seminary professors in remote parts of the Empire. Day in and day out they filled the pages of American newspapers and magazines in an astounding campaign of direct communication with the people of the United States.[82] These appeals were welcomed by the American press; indeed, American editors, including those who were obviously pro-Allied extremists, often solicited such contributions in their effort to be fair. "Always this deluge of pro-German literature flows on," Oswald Garrison Villard observed in early 1915, "as if the German side were not getting a hearing in the American press."[83]

Not long after hostilities began, for example, the Imperial German Chancellor, Theobald von Bethmann Hollweg, assured Americans that the war was a "life and death struggle between Germany and the Muscovite races of Russia, and was due to the recent royal murders at Sarajevo."[84] A few weeks later he embellished the same theme, described the atrocities that Belgian civilians were allegedly committing against German soldiers, and ended with a personal message from the German Emperor affirming His Majesty's faith in "the justice of the American people, who will not let themselves be hoodwinked by the campaign of lies which our foes are waging against us."[85] Or there was

---

December 4, 1914, German F. O. Archives, gave a detailed report of his propaganda activities to that date. For examples of his contributions, see his "Fair Play!" in the Boston *Herald*, August 5, 1914; H. Münsterberg to W.W., August 5, November 7 and 19, 1914, Wilson Papers; and H. Münsterberg, *The War and America*, published in 1914, and *The Peace and America*, published in 1915. For the propaganda of another professor, see Edmund von Mach, "The German Viewpoint," *Boston Evening Transcript*, December 2, 1914, and *What Germany Wants*.

[82] There were no serious impediments to this kind of communication between Germany and the United States. The British, to be sure, cut the cables linking Germany and the United States on August 5, 1914, but ample channels remained. The mails passed on the whole freely between the two countries (much of the non-urgent diplomatic correspondence between Washington and Berlin moved in this way); normal communication was maintained via the Dutch cables; and two German-built wireless transmitters in the United States provided a channel that was usually reliable.

[83] O. G. Villard, *Germany Embattled*, p. 85; also "German Appeals to America," New York *Nation*, XCIX (October 15, 1914), 455-456.

[84] "Germany's Appeal to America, Chancellor von Bethmann-Hollweg Invites Impartiality," *La Follette's Weekly*, VI (August 29, 1914), 9.

[85] New York *World*, September 23, 1914. See also Bethmann's statement in *World's Work*, XXIX (January 1915), 249-252.

the example of the German Ambassador, appealing for American understanding in a leading weekly magazine,[86] and going out of his way to assure the American public that his government had no intention of expanding in South America if it were victorious in Europe.[87] Or of the Austrian Ambassador in Washington and the Consul in Cleveland patiently attempting to explain why their country had been forced to fight.[88]

Even more eloquent in their messages across the sea were the academic and religious leaders of Germany. "Have faith in us! Believe, that we shall carry on this war to the end as a civilized nation, to whom the legacy of a Goethe, a Beethoven, and a Kant, is just as sacred as its own hearths and homes. For this we pledge you our names and our honour," pleaded ninety-three world-famous leaders of German scholarship, science, music, and art in a broadside that was distributed throughout the United States.[89] "In this," exclaimed the leaders of German Protestantism in a special address to "evangelical Christians abroad," "we know that we are at one with all the Christians among our own people, that we can and must repudiate on their behalf and on behalf of their government the responsibility for the terrible crime of this war and all its consequences for the development of the kingdom of God on earth. With the deepest conviction we must attribute it to those who have long secretly and cunningly been spinning a web of conspiracy against Germany, which now they have flung over us in order to strangle us therein."[90] Statements such as this abounded in the Protestant press in America.[91]

[86] J. H. von Bernstorff, "Germany and the Great War," *The Independent*, LXXIX (September 7, 1914), 333-334.

[87] "German Respect for the Monroe Doctrine," *Literary Digest*, XLIX (November 7, 1914), 871-873. Bernstorff's statement was issued at the instruction of the Foreign Office in Berlin. See A. Zimmermann to the Ambassador in Washington, September 2, 1914, copy in the Page Papers.

[88] K. T. Dumba, "The Austro-Serbian Conflict," *Outlook*, CVII (August 29, 1914), 1028-1030, and "Why Austria Is at War with Russia," *North American Review*, CC (September 1914), 346-352; Ernest Ludwig, *Austria-Hungary and the War*.

[89] *To the Civilized World!*, copy in the Root Papers; see also Ernst Haeckel and Rudolf Eucken, "An Appeal to the Universities of America," *The Open Court*, XXVIII (November 1914), 659-661, and the interview with Professor Hans Delbrück printed in the New York *American*, October 24, 1915.

[90] "A Message from German Churchmen," *Lutheran Church Work*, III (October 8, 1914), 4.

[91] e.g., "An Appeal from Breklum," *ibid.*, pp. 8-9; "A Letter from a German Theologian," *ibid.*, October 1, 1914, pp. 9-11; A. W. Hildebrandt, "About the War," *ibid.*,

Organized and direct German propaganda activity in the United States continued at a high pitch until the spring and summer of 1915, when a series of misfortunes seriously impaired its functioning. One of these was the embittering of German-American relations as a consequence of the submarine controversy, which created an increasingly unfriendly climate for German apologists. A second was the departure, for reasons which we will later see, of two of the key men in the German Information Service, Dernburg and Meyer Gerhard, in May and June of 1915. Still another, and the most serious, was the publication in August 1915 of the contents of a portfolio relating mainly to propaganda activities that Doctor Albert had been foolish enough to leave on an elevated train in New York.

These momentary reversals by no means ended the German propaganda effort. It simply changed and became, many observers believed, more effective than ever before. Without abandoning their propaganda agencies, which continued to function in the United States, the Germans began increasingly to rely upon both more subtle and more open methods of influencing American opinion after the autumn of 1915. In Washington, Ambassador von Bernstorff by assiduous effort won the confidence of the newspapermen and constantly fed them information, most of it actually quite accurate, that portrayed German actions and policies in a favorable light.[92] At the same time, the authorities in Berlin welcomed American correspondents, supplied them with all kinds of "human interest" stories calculated to appeal to the average American reader, and willingly gave interviews on any and all occasions. The result was, as one envious British journalist said while comparing British and German propaganda techniques in early 1916:

"At the present moment two most important papers in New York, the 'New York Times' and the 'New York World,' both pro-Ally in sentiment, are publishing daily two or three articles of major importance from Germany in which all kinds of information favourable to Germany is given out, and interviews appear with German people in

October 15, 1914, p. 8; "Another Message from the German Protestants," *ibid.*, January 28, 1915, pp. 22-23; "An Open Letter from the Methodist Ministers in Germany," New York *Christian Advocate*, xc (May 20, 1915), 686; B. Keip, "The German Social Democracy and the War," *ibid.*, June 3, 1915, pp. 743-744; C. Dippel, "A German View of the War," *The Standard, a Baptist Newspaper*, LXII (October 3, 1914), 102-103; J. G. Lehmann, "A Message from German Baptists," *ibid.*, p. 104.

[92] For a detailed account of Bernstorff's relations with the Washington correspondents, see the New York *World*, March 11, 1917.

Germany like Helferrich, von Hindenburg, von Bethmann-Hollweg, Delbrück, and others. These articles appear not only in the New York papers, but are syndicated all over the country and are read by a large public in every big city in America. The effect of this policy is undoubtedly very great. The articles are not recognised as being German propaganda. From time to time disclosures, such as the 'New York World' made some time ago [of the Albert documents], show that some of these correspondents are in German pay. . . . But as soon as their names appear in such disclosures they are generally dropped and others take their places. All kinds of writers have been used in this way, some consciously and some unconsciously, some paid for their services and others unpaid."[93]

Looking back over the entire period of American neutrality, the historian must conclude that, with certain exceptions (notably during the crisis over the sinking of the *Lusitania*), German propaganda was shrewd, intelligent, even moving at times. As one participant has observed, it "addressed itself primarily to groups from which it could expect a sympathetic response. It sought the old-fashioned American with Revolutionary traditions; the cotton grower of the South, almost bankrupted by the blockade; the Irish with a grudge against England; the Jew with a grudge against Russia; and last, not least, the German American."[94] How effective it all was we will attempt to say in later pages of this chapter.

The British propaganda effort in the United States got under way somewhat later than the German but, as is well known, soon attained an extraordinary efficiency. It began in September 1914, when a member of the Cabinet, Charles F. G. Masterman, organized an official propaganda agency in a London office building named Wellington House, and when Masterman called Gilbert Parker, a Canadian-born Member of Parliament who had traveled widely in the United States, to take charge of the American section.[95] With a small staff of assistants

[93] From a memorandum entitled "Anglo-American Relations and the Press," dated February 18, 1915[6], by an unnamed English journalist of "high standing" in America, printed in a Cabinet paper entitled *Printed for the use of the Cabinet. February 1916. CONFIDENTIAL,* copy in the Asquith Papers.

[94] G. S. Viereck, *Spreading Germs of Hate,* p. 46. For an interesting comment, see Paul Cambon (French Ambassador in London) to General F. Foch, February 16, 1915, Henri Cambon (ed.), *Paul Cambon, Correspondance, 1870-1924,* III, 74-75.

[95] For general surveys of British propaganda work in the United States, see the excellent little volume, James D. Squires, *British Propaganda at Home and in the United States from 1914 to 1917,* and the larger and more detailed H. C. Peterson, *Propaganda*

(among whom, incidentally, was a history don from Oxford, Arnold J. Toynbee), Parker set to work upon the task of retaining or winning American good will for Britain and her allies.

"I need hardly say," Parker afterward wrote in the best summary of his activity that we have, "that the scope of my department was very extensive and its activities widely ranged. Among the activities was a weekly report to the British Cabinet on the state of American opinion, and constant touch with the permanent correspondents of American newspapers in England. I also frequently arranged for important public men in England to act for us by interviews in American newspapers. . . .

"Among other things, we supplied three hundred and sixty newspapers in the smaller States of the United States with an English newspaper, which gives a weekly review and comment of the affairs of the war. We established connection with the man in the street through cinema pictures of the Army and Navy, as well as through interviews, articles, pamphlets, etc.; and by letters in reply to individual American critics. . . . We advised and stimulated many people to write articles; we utilized the friendly services and assistance of confidential friends; we had reports from important Americans constantly, and established association, by personal correspondence, with influential and eminent people of every profession in the United States, beginning with university and college presidents, professors and scientific men, and running through all the ranges of the population. We asked our friends and correspondents to arrange for speeches, debates, and lectures by American citizens, but did not encourage Britishers to go to America and preach the doctrine of entrance into the war. Besides an immense private correspondence with individuals, we had our documents and literature sent to great numbers of public libraries, Y.M.C.A. societies, universities, colleges, historical societies, clubs, and newspapers."[96]

If the effort in Wellington House was immense, the appeal was equally comprehensive. From the very outset of hostilities, British publicists took the offensive in a bold campaign to persuade Americans

for War. The latter work considerably overestimates the influence of propaganda on American opinion.

[96] Gilbert Parker, "The United States and the War," *Harper's Magazine*, cxxxvi (March 1918), 522. J. D. Squires, *British Propaganda*, pp. 86-104, prints a fairly complete list of British propaganda documents that were shipped to the United States. For a larger compilation, which includes English propaganda materials addressed everywhere, see Hermann Wanderscheck, *Bibliographie zur englischen Propaganda im Weltkrieg.*

that Germany and Austria-Hungary were solely responsible for plotting and beginning the war, while Britain had labored for peace during the crisis of July 1914 and had gone to war in great agony only to defend Belgium. "Germany," declared the author of one of the first English propaganda tracts that Wellington House shipped to America, "had meant to fight a war of pure aggression, if not on the Austro-Serbian issue, then on some other; she meant to fight this war either this year or the next, and all her policy was leading up to it."[97] It was an accusation embellished, refined, and repeated many times by British spokesmen in books and broadsides and in direct appeals in the American press.[98] It was also the main theme of the tract, *The Evidence in the Case*, written by the American lawyer James M. Beck, which Wellington House distributed by the thousands of copies throughout the United States in late 1914.

British spokesmen also dwelt at length upon what they said were the mainsprings of the terrible character of Imperial Germany—militarism, ruthlessness that knew no restraints, exaltation of the state, and worship of power and might—and the consequences of the triumph of a nation thus obsessed.[99] To make certain that Americans saw the point, Parker arranged for the translation, printing, and distribution in the United States of the works of extreme German nationalists, militarists, and exponents of *Machtpolitik* like von Treitschke, Nietzsche, and von Bernhardi.[100] While doing this, Parker and his co-workers also made certain that tracts by sympathetic American authors[101] were not ignored by the reading public in the United States.

[97] Ramsay Muir, *Britain's Case Against Germany*, p. 3.

[98] e.g., Douglas Sladen, *The Real "Truth About Germany," Facts About the War*; J. W. Headlam, *England, Germany and Europe*; Herbert Asquith, *Why We Are at War*, and *The War: Its Causes and Its Message*; Gilbert Murray, *The Foreign Policy of Sir Edward Grey*; Oliver Lodge, "The War: A British View," *North American Review*, CCI (January 1915), 45-51; Henry Wickham Steed, "The German Bluff," *Harper's Weekly*, LIX (September 26, 1914), 295-296; "The English Point of View," New York *Outlook*, CVIII (September 2, 1914), 42-44; H. W. Massingham, "British Policy and the War," *Atlantic Monthly*, CXV (January 1915), 116-123; H. W. Massingham, "An Open Letter to the American People," *ibid.*, May 1915, pp. 701-706; Arthur Willert, "Anglo-American Relations—and the War," *World's Work*, XXIX (December 1914), 181-185; Lord Bryce, "Message to the American People," *The Independent*, LXXXI (March 29, 1915), 464.

[99] For an early and eloquent statement along these lines, see J. A. Cramb, *Germany and England*.

[100] e.g., Friedrich von Bernhardi, *Germany and the Next War*, translated by Allen H. Powles.

[101] e.g., F. W. Whitridge, *One American's Opinion of the European War*; S. H.

In addition, much of the British propaganda effort had the practical objective of cementing and improving Anglo-American relations in spite of difficulties over neutral rights. Some of Wellington House's publicists played upon the theme of common ideals and traditions; others sought to win American acquiescence in British methods of maritime warfare by recalling memories of British acceptance of the northern blockade of the South during the American Civil War. Still other British propagandists tried to make it clear that Britain was carrying her load in the Allied war effort. And throughout this literature ran the central theme that the Allies were fighting for American liberties no less than for their own.[102]

Finally, there was the greatest British verbal effort of all during the period under discussion—the vast and growing indictment, enlarged also by the Belgians and French, of the German army for alleged atrocities and barbarities—the destruction of cities and universities, the murder of thousands of helpless civilians, the ravishing of women, and the like—in Belgium and northern France. British war correspondents opened this most awesome part of the propaganda campaign in late August and early September 1914.[103] It was carried forward by the Belgian government, which sent a commission to the United States to lay formal charges before the President and people,[104] and by French officials and publicists a short time later.[105] It was climaxed by the publication in May 1915 of the report of an official British commission of inquiry headed by Viscount James Bryce, former Ambassador to the United States, which collected and confirmed most of the earlier accusations of German bestiality.[106] The so-called Bryce Report was the high point of the atrocity campaign but not the end. Still to follow were recurring agitations against alleged atrocities of German submarine commanders, the execution of the British nurse, Edith Cavell,

---

Church, *The American Verdict on the War*; John Jay Chapman, *Deutschland über Alles, or Germany Speaks.*

[102] J. D. Squires, *British Propaganda*, pp. 69-76.

[103] For its impact upon the American press, see "Darkest Side of the Great War," *Literary Digest*, XLIX (September 12, 1914), 441-443.

[104] "Findings of the Commission of Inquiry," undated MS. in the Wilson Papers; New York *World*, September 17, 1914; James M. Read, *Atrocity Propaganda, 1914-1919*, pp. 51-61.

[105] e.g., Joseph Bédier, *Les Crimes Allemands d'après Témoignages Allemands*; Republic of France, Ministry of Foreign Affairs, *Les Violations des lois de la guerre par l'Allemagne.*

[106] Committee on Alleged German Outrages, *Report of the Committee on Alleged German Outrages.*

the slaughter of Armenians by the Turks, and continuing German crimes in Belgium.[107]

It is a far easier task to describe these rival propaganda campaigns than to determine their impact upon American attitudes and reactions. The historian is tempted to ascribe a decisive importance to propaganda because to do so provides an easy answer to the problem. He is further tempted to ignore the German effort, since the United States did eventually go to war with Germany, and to concentrate upon what seems to have been the successful part of the campaign. But understanding will not come this way, and certainly not by repeating generalizations that have become firmly embedded in American historical literature.

We might begin our own analysis by saying that to a considerable degree the German and British propaganda efforts simply canceled out each other. This was true especially of the propaganda about the origins of the war. By the spring of 1915 most of the evidence had been published by both sides, and there were few thoughtful Americans who would have said that one alliance or the other had alone been guilty of starting hostilities. The generalization about rival propagandas canceling out each other also applies to a large degree to what the Germans and the British had to say about the essential nature of the struggle. The Pro-Allied extremists in the United States who already believed that Germany was militaristic, despotic, and a kind of menace to western civilization were, to be sure, enormously receptive to British propaganda that played upon these themes.[108] On the other hand,

[107] J. M. Read, *Atrocity Propaganda, 1914-1919*, is a magnificent survey; see also Harold D. Lasswell, *Propaganda Technique in the World War*, and Arthur Ponsonby, *Falsehood in War-Time*.

[108] Elihu Root, for example, wrote to a friend in October 1914 that he had just read J. A. Cramb's *Germany and England* and von Bernhardi's *Germany and the Next War*. "They are both being read very widely now and apparently throughout the country," Root continued, "and the effect of Bernhardi seems to confirm the judgment which the American people formed on reading the first British White Paper and the Goschen 'Scrap of Paper' interview. I have never seen anything so extraordinary in the movement of public opinion as the swift and positive judgment which the people of this country formed on reading these papers." E. Root to C. P. Anderson, October 20, 1914, Root Papers. For other direct evidence of the impact of this particular type of British propaganda, see Paul Elmer More, "The Lust of Empire," New York *Nation*, XCIX (October 22, 1914), 493-495, a review of Cramb and Bernhardi; and the series by Norman Hapgood: "Who Made Germany Crazy? I. Bismarck and Von Treitske [*sic*]," *Harper's Weekly*, LIX (October 3, 1914), 316-317; "Who Made Germany Crazy? II. The Kaiser and Von Buelow," *ibid.*, October 10, 1914, pp. 343-345; "Bernhardi and

Americans predisposed toward Germany found ample reinforcement of their views in the German interpretation of the war as a struggle between western culture and Slavic barbarism.

It was much the same with what has usually been regarded as the devastatingly effective Allied atrocity propaganda. At least before the publication of the Bryce Report, the Allied charges were neutralized by German denials and, above all, by American correspondents with the German armies, who time and again denied that the atrocity charges had any substantial foundation.[109] The same correspondents, moreover, contributed detailed and sympathetic accounts of German military operations in Belgium and nothern France to widely read American magazines.[110] The Bryce Report certainly had a profound and shocking impact in the United States; among many Americans the fact that Lord Bryce had signed the document was proof enough of its essential authenticity. However, the evidence indicates that the report was most effective as a propaganda piece[111] among those Americans who were

---

the United States," *ibid.*, October 17, 1914, pp. 367-368; and "Pan-Germanism and the United States," *ibid.*, October 24, 1914, pp. 391-393.

[109] See the statement by Roger Lewis, Irvin S. Cobb, Harry Hansen, James O'Donnell Bennett, and John T. McCutcheon in the New York *World*, September 7, 1914; the statements of an unnamed Associated Press correspondent in Belgium and of John T. McCutcheon, printed in *ibid.*, September 17 and 19, 1914; Joseph Medill Patterson, statement in *ibid.*, September 25, 1914; and Arno Dosch, "Louvain the Lost," *World's Work*, XXVIII (October 1914), D.

[110] I. S. Cobb, "Being a Guest of the German Kaiser," *Saturday Evening Post*, CLXXXVII (October 24, 1914), 14-15, 48-50; I. S. Cobb, "Punitives versus Primitives," *ibid.*, November 14, 1914, pp. 14-15, 37-38; I. S. Cobb, "Johann Schmidt, Private," *ibid.*, January 30, 1915, pp. 13-15, 29-30; Arthur Sweetser, "A Diary from the Front," *World's Work*, XXIX (January 1915), 350-356; A. Sweetser, "With the German Army in Its Dash toward Paris," New York *Outlook*, CIX (January 27, 1915), 186-190.

[111] Perhaps it ought to be said here that Lord Bryce and the distinguished British leaders who served with him on the committee of inquiry regarded their report as being more than a piece of propaganda. There is a great deal of correspondence in the Bryce Papers relating to the inquiry and the preparation of the report. It reveals clearly enough that Bryce and his colleagues tried to be, and thought they were being, judicious and honest in their appraisal. This comes out also in H. A. L. Fisher, *James Bryce*, II, 132-135, and with all the more effect since Fisher had been a member of the committee of inquiry. It should be added, moreover, that careful scholarship has definitely established the fact that the behavior of the German military authorities in the occupied areas was extraordinarily severe, if not brutal, and that the Bryce Report was essentially correct in its major indictment, namely, that the German army used terror as a weapon of intimidation. For example, the Germans executed at least several thousand civilians, many of whom were innocent of any violation of the laws of war. For a detailed survey, see J. M. Read, *Atrocity Propaganda*, pp. 78-103.

already definitely pro-Allied in sympathy[112]—that it, like so much other British propaganda was, as Sir Horace Plunkett said, "mere preaching to the converted"[113]—and that it had no measureable effect at all on the pro-German groups and, insofar as one can see, little on the rank and file of the substantially neutral majority.[114]

It would be just as much a mistake to ignore the achievements of the propagandists as to exaggerate them. Because they never over-estimated the potentialities of ideological warfare and understood the complex motivation of American neutralism, the British leaders used propaganda only to strengthen emotional ties and to promote acquiescence in the British maritime system, not openly to encourage American participation in the war. Their success in gaining these limited objectives was on the whole notable. In one sense, the German propaganda achievement was even more impressive, if not as successful in the long run as the British. Given the pro-Allied predispositions of the large majority of Americans, all that the Germans could expect to accomplish was to neutralize these sentiments to some degree, in the hope that the pro-German groups would offset the pro-Allied extremists.[115] After the beginning of the submarine campaign, German propagandists had a more difficult task, one of persuading substantially neutral America that the German attack upon Allied commerce was legitimate in the circumstances and not an undue infringement of

[112] I do not mean to suggest here that the Bryce Report was unimportant in its impact upon pro-Allied Americans. Coming as it did (quite accidentally) at the time of the sinking of the *Lusitania*, it greatly strengthened the conviction, particularly among the pro-Allied extremists, that Germany was a menace to the civilized international community. For evidence to support this statement, see Harry Brittain to Lord Bryce, May 14, 1915, Bryce Papers; John D. Lawson, Dean of the Law School of the University of Missouri and editor of the *American Law Review*, to Lord Bryce, May 20 and August 3, 1915, *ibid.*; H. C. Lodge to Lord Bryce, May 26, 1915, *ibid.*; C. F. G. Masterman to Lord Bryce, June 7, 1915, *ibid.*; J. H. Choate to Lord Bryce, August 9, 1915; *ibid.*; New York *World*, May 13, 1915; W. H. Taft to G. J. Karger, May 15, 1915, Taft Papers; New York *Nation*, c (May 20, 1915), 553-555; *The Independent*, LXXXII (May 24, 1915), 309-310; New York *Outlook*, cx (May 26, 1915), 150*-151*; *World's Work*, xxx (June 1915), 134; *Collier's*, LV (June 5, 1915), 15; *The Living Church*, LIII (July 17, 1915), 420-421; and the newspaper opinion cited in *Literary Digest*, L (May 29, 1915), 1257-1259.

[113] H. Plunkett to Cecil Spring Rice, April 6, 1916, Plunkett Papers.

[114] Evidence of the impact of the Bryce Report on the majority of Americans who were substantially neutral simply does not exist. Judging from the lack of any pronounced concern in the correspondence of leaders of this group and in media like the farm and labor press, one would have to conclude that the impact was not very profound.

[115] On this point, see J. von Bernstorff, *My Three Years in America*, pp. 47-48.

American national rights. The massive and stubborn resistance to involvement which characterized the American reactions to the submarine controversy down to early 1917 showed how well the Germans succeeded in the face of the most obvious obstacles.

Having said all this, however, the historian must still conclude that propaganda did not play the decisive role in the formation of the fundamental American attitudes toward the war. These took shape very clearly in reaction to certain obvious events and were deeply entrenched long before the propagandists exploited them. And if the Germans came off second best in the war of words, if a majority of the American people were more kindly disposed toward the Allies than the Central Powers at the end of what might be called the formative period of American neutrality, then this was true because German offenses against civilization seemed more egregious than the Allied. As one distinguished American publicist explained in writing to a German who had condemned the partiality of the American press:

"There is much in your complaints of the attitude of the American press that is justified. . . . I am frank to admit that it is no longer possible for the bulk of the papers to deal with judicial minds with the situation; for the bulk of them it has been impossible since Belgium, but I insist that the responsibility rests with Germany alone and that their acts in Belgium, in Louvain and the sinking of the Lusitania readily account for this partisanship of our press. Germany has affronted the moral, neutral sentiment of the world, and that can not be explained away by dismissing our sources of information as English lies, etc. Personally I have read enormous quantities of matter sent out by pro-Germans here and in Germany; I have read attempts to justify the violation of the neutrality of Belgium, and ad infinitum, . . . but when I think of the Lusitania and of our innocent women and children lying at the bottom of the sea as the result of that dastardly crime, I see red; I feel as if my voice and pen must be spurred on anew against those responsible, and yet personally I have always been bitterly hostile to the Russians, and were I in England today, I should be entirely against the war and against the Ministers who have plunged England into such misery."[116]

Meanwhile, what were the attitudes and reactions of the men who would be directly responsible for official policies toward the belliger-

[116] O. G. Villard to Karl Boy-Ed, October 28, 1915, Villard Papers.

ents—the members of the Wilson circle and the President himself?
How ran their hidden thoughts and sympathies during the period when
they were defining American neutrality?

Of all the leaders in Washington the man whose thoughts are easiest
to read was the Secretary of State, William J. Bryan. If any individual in the United States was genuinely neutral, it was he. It was not
that he did not care; on the contrary, he, the great apostle of peace,
was overborne by the tragedy of the war. But he apparently believed
that it was futile to attempt to apportion guilt in the confused circumstances of the time, and his generous heart was filled with compassion for all the suffering peoples of Europe. Thus in Christian love
he uttered no words of condemnation but sought only to understand
and help.

To the Secretary of State, neutrality was a religious duty as much
as a policy of practical wisdom for the United States. As a pacifist he
would accept the status of belligerent only if there were no other choice;
as a statesman he saw no vital American interest involved in the European conflict. "He did not believe there was the slightest danger to
this country from foreign invasion, even if the Germans were successful," Colonel House recorded in his diary after a conversation with
Bryan in November 1914.[117]

To the great Nebraskan neutrality meant more than living by the
letter of the law. It meant acting in the "spirit of neutrality" in an
effort to do substantial justice to both sides, whether in the matter of
loans to the belligerents, or on the question of an arms embargo. To Bryan
neutrality also meant going the second mile and enduring abuses and
insults if this were necessary to avoid engagement. During the submarine controversy, for example, he counseled the President to protest
but then acquiesce in the so-called German blockade measures, just
as he had earlier advised him to accept the British methods of maritime warfare under protest.

In Bryan's mind the supreme justification for neutrality was the
opportunity that it afforded for the United States to take the lead for
peace. Ignoring strategic considerations (indeed, they seem never to
have burdened his mind), he pleaded almost daily with the President
to intervene boldly to stop the fighting. "Now, after appalling losses
on both sides," Bryan wrote in a typical letter to the White House,
"now when all must confess failure to accomplish what they expected;

[117] The Diary of Edward M. House, November 8, 1914, Yale University Library;
hereinafter cited as the House Diary.

now when the cup of sorrow is overflowing and when new horrors are being added daily, it would seem to be this nation's duty, as the leading exponent of Christianity and is [as] the foremost advocate of worldwide peace, to approach the warring nations again and earnestly urge them to consent to a conference with a view to coming to an understanding which will enable them to lay down their arms and begin the work of reconstructing a permanent peace on the basis of justice and friendship."[118] As the following chapters will show in some detail, Bryan never wavered in his faith in neutrality and in his hope that he and the President might be called sons of God.

Standing second in command in the State Department was the Counselor, Robert Lansing. The son-in-law of John W. Foster, Secretary of State under President Benjamin Harrison, Lansing had made a creditable career in the practice of international law before coming to the State Department to succeed Professor John Bassett Moore in April 1914. Immensely learned, he was Bryan's right hand in all matters of law and custom, and his influence in laying the foundations of neutrality was often decisive. Poised, handsome, and formal in dress and manners, Lansing gave the appearance of a dignified and prosperous law clerk. But beneath his bland exterior was a tough mind accustomed to mastering complex data and wrestling with difficult philosophical problems. Strong though he was in moral fiber, he, more than any other man in the Wilson circle, tended to think of foreign policy in terms of strategy and power.[119]

Lansing's reactions to the war during the months before the submarine controversy are not as easily read as Bryan's. This is not because the written records are scanty—the State Department's archives and Lansing's own private papers are filled with his letters and memoranda—but because the Counselor succeeded so well in concealing his private thoughts about the merits of the European conflict. Even so, the historian can see clearly enough the image of a man who was predisposed to favor the Allies but who struggled to keep an open mind and to follow policies so well grounded in the law of nations that they would be safely beyond the reproach of any partisan, and

[118] W. J. Bryan to W.W., December 1, 1914, *Papers Relating to the Foreign Relations of the United States, The Lansing Papers, 1914-1920,* I, 11; hereinafter cited as *The Lansing Papers.*

[119] For a recent appraisal, see Daniel M. Smith, *Robert Lansing and American Neutrality, 1914-1917.*

who in fact believed at this time that neutrality was the wise course for the United States.

This, at any rate, is the impression that one forms after reading the notebook, or diary, in which Lansing set down his innermost thoughts about the war. The entries during the early months are few in number, but they reveal the Counselor's quality of thinking and his effort to understand the behavior of the belligerents.

International law and respect for neutral rights, Lansing wrote in his diary on May 3, 1915, for example, had collapsed completely because technological changes had rendered old rules obsolete and the fierceness of the struggle had made it one of survival among great powers. "Thus neutral rights of trade are ground to powder between the upper and nether millstones." What could a neutral do, unless it were prepared to fight, but protest and reserve all rights? "When a government and people believe that their existence as a nation depends upon their being victorious in a war, can you expect them to weigh carefully the legal rights of neutrals which seem to be obstacles to success? . . . Would you leave a single stone unturned or relinquish a single method of attack for the sole reason that the laws of war directed you to do so?" The answer was obvious: "None of the governments, which are depriving Americans of their rights are going to change its policy because of diplomatic pressure however strong it may be." The neutral could only endure.[120]

At other moments of reflection, Lansing wrestled with the question of why nations broke treaties or committed so-called atrocities. The basic factor in international life, he concluded, was the urge of the nation-state to survive. "It cannot be denied," he once wrote to the Secretary of State, "that national safety may justify a nation in violating its solemn pledges."[121] "No nation at war, whose national safety is menaced," he added at greater length in his diary, "will permit or should be expected to permit obligations of justice, morality, humanity, or honor to interfere with acts which it considers necessary for its self-preservation. . . . I do not recall a case in history in which a nation surrendered its sovereignty for the sole purpose of being right." Since this was true, Lansing continued, "The question of what is and what is not humane conduct would thus seem to resolve itself to this: If military success or advantage can only be gained through the perpe-

---

[120] The Diary of Robert Lansing, Library of Congress, entry dated May 3, 1915; hereinafter cited as the Lansing Diary.

[121] R. Lansing to W. J. Bryan, January 23, 1915, *The Lansing Papers*, I, 194.

tration of acts considered by the civilized world to be cruel, inhuman . . . , a belligerent may be reasonably expected to commit the acts. Furthermore, it is a query how far acts of that character in those circumstances can justifiably be condemned. If, however, the act of a belligerent, which the world condemns generally as cruel, inhuman and reprehensible, has no material effect on the success of military operations, it is stamped with wantonness and is entitled to universal condemnation. . . . The test of guiltlessness in perpetrating an act inhuman under usual conditions, is the *necessity* of that act to the protection of national safety."[122]

These, obviously, were not the conclusions of a sentimentalist whose reason had been deranged by fear or tales of horror. Neither were they the convictions of a man yet wholeheartedly committed to the Allied cause. Such evidence as has been cited—and all the rest available, besides—shows that at least before the late spring of 1915 Lansing believed in the neutrality that he practiced so punctiliously and well.

It was in some ways the same during the early period of the war with Colonel Edward M. House, the President's most intimate if not most frequent adviser on foreign affairs. House was certainly favorably disposed toward the western Allies at the beginning of the war. He knew and trusted many of the English leaders, particularly the Foreign Secretary, Sir Edward Grey, and the British Ambassador in Washington, Sir Cecil Spring Rice, and he looked to Britain as the home and mutual preserver of Anglo-American concepts of government. He feared German militarism and imperialism (then called Pan-Germanism) as a threat to the peace of the world and the safety of the United States. Hence his advice to the President during the early months of the war tended toward a general acceptance of the British methods of warfare and condemnation of the German. Yet House was no ignorant partisan about either the origins or the issues of the war.

"I never believed that Germany was exclusively guilty of starting the War. I now know that she was not," he explained in his unpublished memoirs in the 1930's.[123] "It is clear to me," he wrote in his diary in April 1915, after reflecting upon the origins of the war, "that the Kaiser did not want war and did not actually expect it. He foolishly permitted Austria to bring about an acute controversy with Serbia,

<hr />

[122] "Cruel and Inhuman Acts of War," Lansing Diary, May 25, 1915.

[123] "The Memoirs of Colonel House," unpublished MS. deposited in the papers of George Sylvester Viereck, Yale University Library; hereinafter cited as "The Memoirs of Colonel House."

and he concluded that by standing firm with his ally, Russia would do nothing more than make a vigorous protest, much as she did when Austria annexed Bosnia and Herzigovina [*sic*]. The rattling of the scabbard and the shining armor were sufficient in that case and he thought they would be in this, for the reason that he did not believe Great Britain would go to war concerning such a happening in the Southeast. . . . In this instance he thought Germany's relations with England had improved to such an extent that she would not back Russia and France to the extent of making war on Germany. And he went so far in what might be termed 'bluff' that it was impossible at the last moment to recede because the situation had gotten beyond him."[124]

Nor did House desire a smashing Allied victory. He wanted England and France to win, but to win somehow without destroying Germany or Germany's ability to maintain a strong barrier to Russian expansion, for he feared Russia as much if not more than the Fatherland. "The saddest feature of the situation to me," he wrote to Wilson, acknowledging the difficulty of maintaining the proper balance of European power, "is that there is no good outcome to look forward to. If the Allies win, it means largely the domination of Russia on the Continent of Europe; and if Germany wins, it means the unspeakable tyranny of militarism for generations to come."[125]

In addition to these three principal advisers, there were a number of other members of the Wilson circle who had some influence upon the thinking of the President and the formation of foreign policies. One was the Ambassador in London, Walter H. Page, the one member of the circle who was ardently and openly pro-Allied in sympathy. Another was Cone Johnson of Texas, the Solicitor of the State Department, who became a kind of mouthpiece for the southern cotton growers and other producers who resented Britain's interference with American exports to Germany. A third was Chandler P. Anderson, a special assistant in the Department during the first months of the war and a close friend of Lansing, who countered Johnson's harsh demands by arguing for acceptance of the British maritime measures during the early period of the war. There were also the members of the Joint State and Navy Neutrality Board[126]—James Brown Scott and others—who were inclined to interpret the rules of neutrality rigidly

[124] House Diary, April 15, 1915.
[125] E. M. House to W.W., August 22, 1914, Wilson Papers.
[126] For the establishment and work of this agency, see below, pp. 57-58.

and sometimes to Germany's disadvantage.[127] Finally, there were the rest of the Wilson circle—the President's secretary, Joseph P. Tumulty, the Cabinet members, and all the lesser officials on the high level of the bureaucracy. Some, like the Assistant Secretary of the Navy, Franklin D. Roosevelt, were pro-Allied extremists; others, like Paul M. Warburg of the Federal Reserve Board, were pro-German. Most of them, actually, were as substantially neutral as were the majority of their fellow-countrymen. Regardless of their private sympathies, none of them, not even Page, had any really decisive influence over the man, the President of the United States, who made the important decisions in this area of foreign policy as much as in others.

This brings us to the most important part of our analysis, the reactions and thinking of President Wilson during the early months of the fighting. It need hardly be said that he did not live in a vacuum sealed off from the pressures that constantly weighed upon him. The most important of these was public opinion, which was constantly at work shaping and controlling Wilson's policies and decisions and to a certain degree even his own thinking about the war. Like all other successful Presidents, he knew the role that public opinion plays in the American democracy and the risks that the leader runs when he ceases to speak for the preponderant majority. "The ear of the leader must ring with the voices of the people. He cannot be of the school of the prophets; he must be of the number of those who studiously serve the slow-paced daily need." Thus Wilson had written in 1890;[128] thus he believed and practiced while formulating his policies toward the belligerents. An even more direct influence in the shaping of Wilson's thinking about the war were the attitudes and advices of the men near the throne. Lansing's realistic analyses left their imprint, unconscious though it often was, on the President's mind, just as Bryan's gentler urgings did. Nor was Colonel House without influence.

This does not mean, however, that Wilson was ever a prisoner of public opinion or slavishly followed the counsel of his advisers. He

[127] "The President did me the honor upon the outbreak of the war to appoint me Special Adviser to the Government on questions arising out of it. Otherwise I would tell you how deeply I sympathize with you and your devoted country, and how earnestly I hope that nothing may happen to change its standing in the Society of Nations. But I must not dwell upon this subject if I hope to maintain even the semblance of neutrality. . . . I wish that I could open my heart to you. I cannot. It is a poor bleeding thing, and I am in great distress." James Brown Scott to Lord Bryce, October 10, 1914, Bryce Papers.

[128] Woodrow Wilson, *Leaders of Men*, edited by T. H. Vail Motter, p. 43.

had his own ideals and inner dynamics—the principles and assumptions that governed his general thinking about the international society and America's creative role in the development of mankind.[129] He used his own methods in trying to understand the issues of the European war. And by the end of 1914 he had reached his own judgments and conclusions.

First, however, Wilson went through the shock and confusion that most thoughtful Americans experienced in reaction to the outbreak of hostilities. "The more I read about the conflict across the seas," he wrote on the day that the British government entered the war, "the more open it seems to me to utter condemnation. The outcome no man can even conjecture."[130] "I feel the burden of the thing almost intolerably from day to day," he added a short time later to Colonel House, "I think largely because there is nothing that we can as yet do or even attempt. What a pathetic thing to have this come just as we were so full of hope!"[131]

Like many thoughtful Americans in their turmoil, Wilson also tended to react with emotional sympathy for the Allies at the outset, to resent bitterly Germany's invasion and devastation of Belgium, and to blame the Berlin government for beginning hostilities. He gave some indication of his feeling during an interview with the French Ambassador, Jean Jules Jusserand, on August 27, 1914,[132] and again a short time later, somewhat more indiscreetly, in a conversation with

[129] I have tried to go into Wilson's thinking about international relations in some detail in *Wilson the Diplomatist, a Look at His Major Foreign Policies*, pp. 11-16.

[130] W.W. to C. R. Crane, August 4, 1914, Wilson Papers.

[131] W.W. to E. M. House, August 24, 1914, *ibid*.

[132] "M. Jusserand has been received yesterday by the President of the United States. M. Wilson has spoken to him of the European conflict with an emotion that he did not attempt to hide. . . . If things were as they seemed, the President's expressions were stamped with a real sympathy for France." Raymond Poincaré, *Au Service de la France*, v (*L'Invasion*), 201, summarizing Ambassador Jusserand to the Foreign Office, August 28, 1914. Jusserand added the following significant comment: "Il y a en Amérique d'ardents amis de la France. Mais que pense le grand doctrinaire qui préside actuellement aux destinées des États-Unis? Bien habile qui le pourrait dire, non pas même avec certitude, mais simplement avec vraisemblance." Compare this with the following comment by David Lloyd George, a member of the British Cabinet in 1914 and afterward Prime Minister: "We never quite knew where President Wilson's real sympathies lay. We felt that in the tremendous struggle which was constantly before his eyes, he would have been more than human had his heart not been engaged on one side or the other, whatever his hand might do or his tongue might speak. But his deportment was so studiously unpleasant to both sides that they each suspected him of being antipathetic to their own side." *War Memoirs of David Lloyd George*, ii, 662.

the British Ambassador. "The President sent you warmest greeting and expresses his most sincere sympathy," Spring Rice wrote to Sir Edward Grey soon afterward. "He said: 'Every thing that I love most in the world is at stake,' and later: 'If they succeed, we shall be forced to take such measures of defence here as would be fatal to our form of Government and American ideals.' He spoke of the long trial of the [English] Civil War, and said with deep emotion that he was sure that our country would still show its powers of endurance for a high cause."[133] Colonel House visited the President at his summer home in Cornish, New Hampshire, on August 30, 1914, and recorded the following entry in his diary:

"The President spoke with deep feeling of the war. He said it made him heartsick to think of how near we had come to averting this great disaster. . . . I was interested to hear him express as his opinion what I had written him some time ago in one of my letters, to the effect that if Germany won it would change the course of our civilization and make the United States a military nation. . . . He felt deeply the destruction of Louvain, and I found him as unsympathetic with the German attitude as is the balance of America. He goes even further than I in his condemnation of Germany's part in this war, and almost allows his feeling to include the German people as a whole rather than the leaders alone. He said German philosophy was essentially selfish and lacking in spirituality. . . . He thought the war would throw the world back three or four centuries . . . [and] was particularly scornful of Germany's disregard of treaty obligations, and was indignant at the German Chancellor's designation of the Belgian Treaty as being 'only a scrap of paper.' "[134]

This is all substantial evidence of Wilson's predisposition and of the fact that he reacted in the same way as thousands of other Americans did during the first days of the war—a time, incidentally, when it seemed that the Germans might break through to Paris and end the war in the West quickly.

The important thing was not what the President felt at the outset, but what he thought once he had had an opportunity to view the issues and merits of the European struggle in the light of greater knowledge and perspective. This he was able to do at considerable leisure and under no great stress after the French and British halted

[133] C. Spring Rice to E. Grey, September 3, 1914, printed in George Macaulay Trevelyan, *Grey of Fallodon*, pp. 355-356.
[134] House Diary, August 30, 1914.

the German advance toward Paris during the first Battle of the Marne. He studied the dispatches from the European embassies carefully; he read contemporary scholarly analyses of the origins of the war; he gave studious attention to letters from apologists for both sides; and he could not have avoided seeing some of the official British and German propaganda that was then flooding the country. The more Wilson studied and thought, the more did his sophisticated mental processes assume command and his initial emotional reactions recede. The result by the end of 1914, by which time his settled opinions had fairly crystallized, was a remarkable degree of detachment, impartiality, and understanding.

Fairly abundant evidence reveals this change in a striking way. Early in October 1914 the President visited two dear friends of Mrs. Wilson's and his own in Baltimore. "We discussed the war," one of them later recalled, "and he so obviously felt that all the wrong was not on one side."[135] Colonel House, who was in Washington a short time before and afterward, noted rather petulantly that his friend was much less willing than before to discuss the issues of the war. "I find the President singularly lacking in appreciation of the importance of this European crisis. He seems more interested in domestic affairs, and I find it difficult to get his attention centered upon the one big question," House recorded. "I am sorry to say, as I have said before, that the President does not seem to have a proper sense of proportion as between domestic and foreign affairs. I suppose it is the Washington atmosphere that has gripped him as it does every one else who lives there, and the work of the day largely obscures the tremendous world issues that are now before us."[136] The trouble probably was not that Wilson refused to think about the deep issues of the war, but that he no longer thought the same way the Colonel did. As the President explained at the time, "The whole thing is very vivid in my mind, painfully vivid, and has been almost ever since the struggle began. I think my thought and imagination contain the picture and perceive its significance from every point of view. I have to force myself not to dwell upon it to avoid the sort of numbness that comes from deep apprehension and dwelling upon elements too vast to be yet comprehended or in any way controlled by counsel."[137]

[135] Mary Hoyt, undated memorandum in the Ray Stannard Baker Collection of Wilson Materials, Library of Congress; hereinafter cited as the Baker Collection.

[136] House Diary, September 28, October 22, 1914.

[137] W.W. to W. H. Page, October 28, 1914, Wilson Papers.

The clearest revelation of the course of Wilson's thought came in mid-December 1914, when he gave an off-the-record interview to a reporter for the *New York Times*. "I think that the chances of a just and equitable peace," the President began, "and of the only possible peace that will be lasting, will be happiest if no nation gets the decision by arms; and the danger of an unjust peace, one that will be sure to invite further calamities, will be if some one nation or group of nations succeeds in enforcing its will upon the others."

"It will be found before long," he continued, that Germany is not alone responsible for the war, and that some other nations will have to bear a portion of the blame in our eyes. The others will be blamed and it might be well if there were no exemplary triumph and punishment. I believe thoroughly that the settlement should be for the advantage of the European nations regarded as people and not for any nation imposing its governmental will upon alien peoples. Bismarck was longheaded when he urged Germany not to take Alsace and Lorraine. It seems to me that the Government of Germany must be profoundly changed, and that Austria-Hungary will go to pieces altogether—ought to go to pieces for the welfare of Europe. As for Russia, I cannot help sympathizing with its aims to secure natural outlets for its trade with the world, and a proper settlement should permit this. If the decision is not to be reached wholly by the forces of reason and justice after the trial at arms is found futile, if the decision by arms should be in favor of the nations that are parties of the Triple Entente; I cannot regard this as the ideal solution, at the same time I cannot see now that it would hurt greatly the interests of the United States if either France or Russia or Great Britain should finally dictate the settlement."[138]

Here, then, was the first statement of Wilson's fairly mature conclusions about the European war and its outcome—that the causes of the war were complex and the guilt not all on one side, that the best outcome would be a deadlock and a peace of reconciliation, but that it would not be disadvantageous to the United States if the Allies were able to achieve a decisive victory. Needless to say, this represented only the beginning and not the end of Wilson's reckoning about the war. As time passed, he would grow increasingly less interested in the causes of the war and more concerned about the consequences if it were permitted to continue its ravages.

[138] H. B. Brougham, "Memorandum of Interview with the President, Dec. 14, 1914," in F. Fraser Bond, *Mr. Miller of "The Times,"* pp. 142-143.

Whatever the shades and subtleties of the President's thoughts on these great questions, there was never any doubt in his mind, from the very outset of the war, that an absolute neutrality was the only wise, right, or possible policy for the United States. How strongly he believed this came out in one of his most significant letters from the early months of the war. "Many weeks ago," he wrote in early December, "when the war had just begun, Mr. Eliot wrote me a long and earnest letter arguing that we should actively join the Allies against Germany. I was amazed and distressed then, because I so sincerely respect Mr. Eliot and had thought that he might so confidently be counted on to serve always as part of the balast [*sic*] of the nation, and utter what would be its sober second thought; but that shock has passed. The speeches he makes now add nothing. They come to me like a thing already discounted, an experience that is past and has faded a bit."[139]

Wilson saw the obvious practical grounds for neutrality, but other reasons for avoiding involvement were to him more compelling because they were fundamentally moral in character. Like most Americans of his own generation, he had seen or heard about war and its consequences firsthand during his childhood, and he knew its immorality, malignity, and awful power of corruption. Insane or evil indeed would be the statesman who led his people lightly into the war in Europe, or who *permitted* them to fight unless there were no other way to defend ideals and national rights that could not be compromised! Because he understood the true dimensions of the tragedy that was unfolding in Europe he hoped all the more ardently that America might be privileged to lead the way to peace through mediation. Finally, even at this early stage in the conflict he was beginning to think upon the future and to conceive the hope that he might be able to help build a new and better world order upon the shambles of the old, and he believed that he could do this more successfully as one who had not been involved. The salient aspects of his thinking about the necessities and opportunities of neutrality and the almost Lincolnian quality of compassion that he was beginning to manifest come out in the following excerpts from letters, speeches, and conversations:

"I have been distressed to have to maintain our recent debate with Sir Edward Grey," Wilson wrote to Walter Page, commenting upon the practical necessity of neutrality, "but it was absolutely necessary

[139] W.W. to Mrs. Crawford H. Toy, December 12, 1914, Baker Collection.

that we should discuss the matters Mr. Lansing presented, because not the least part of the difficulty of this war is going to be the satisfaction of opinion in America and the full performance of our utmost duty as the only powerful neutral. More and more, from day to day, the elements (I mean the several racial elements) of our population seem to grow restless and catch more and more the fever of the contest. We are trying to keep all possible spaces cool, and the only means by which we can do so is to make it demonstrably clear that we are doing everything that it is possible to do to define and defend neutral rights. This is in the interest of all the belligerents no less than in our own interest. I mean that if we are to remain neutral and to afford Europe the legitimate assistance possible in such circumstances, the course we have been pursuing is the absolutely necessary course. Please do not suppose that we are not able to see the thing from the point of view of others, but always remember that it is as necessary for them as it is for us that we should present and emphasize our neutral point of view."[140]

In an address at Indianapolis early in January 1915 he voiced the fervent hope that America might show the way to peace:

"Look abroad upon the troubled world. Only America at peace! Among all the great powers of the world, only America saving her power for her own people. Only America using her great character and her great strength in the interests of peace and prosperity.

"Do you not think it likely that the world will some time turn to America and say: 'You were right and we were wrong. You kept your heads when we lost ours. You tried to keep the scale from tipping and we threw the whole weight of arms in one side of the scale. Now, in your self-possession, in your coolness, in your strength, may we not turn to you for counsel and assistance?'

"Think of the deep-wrought destruction of economic resources, of life and of hope that is taking place in some parts of the world, and think of the reservoir of hope, the reservoir of energy, the reservoir of sustenance that there is in this great land of plenty. May we not look forward to the time when we shall be called blessed among the nations because we succored the nations of the world in their time of distress and dismay?

"I for one pray God that that solemn hour may come, and I know the solidity of character and I know the exaltation of hope; I know

140 W.W. to W. H. Page, October 28, 1914, Wilson Papers.

the high principle with which the American people will respond to the call of the world for this service, and I thank God that those who believe in America, who try to serve her people, are likely to be also what America herself from the first intended to be—the servant of mankind."[141]

Finally, he revealed his inchoate thinking about the future in a conversation with his brother-in-law, Stockton Axson, in August 1914.

"It is perfectly obvious," Axson remembered Wilson saying, "that this war will vitally change the relationships of nations. Four things will be essential to the re-establishment in the world after peace is made.

"1. No nation shall ever again be permitted to acquire an inch of land by conquest.

"2. There must be recognition of the reality of equal rights between small nations and great.

"3. Munitions of war must hereafter be manufactured entirely by the nations and not by private enterprise.

"4. There must be an association of the nations, all bound together for the protection of the integrity of each, so that any one nation breaking from this bond will bring upon herself war; that is to say, punishment, automatically."[142]

Such were some of the reactions and conclusions of the man destined to guide the ship of state through the troubled seas of neutrality. If there still be any reasonable doubt that he struggled hard to be impartial in thought as well as in deed, or that he succeeded in this nearly impossible task better than most of his contemporaries, then perhaps the following chapters will shed additional light on the President's fight for neutrality.

[141] *New York Times*, January 9, 1915.
[142] R. S. Baker, "Memorandum of conversations with Stockton Axson on Feb. 8, 10, and 11, 1925," Baker Collection.

CHAPTER II

Wilson and the Establishment of
American Neutrality

FOR Woodrow Wilson the weeks following the outbreak of the war were a time of testing such as he had never known before. These were the days of Ellen Wilson's illness and death, and of the almost unbearable agony of a lonely bereavement. But if the President's emotional turmoil was great, so also was the need for his leadership on the home front, for the war intruded in such a way as to leave little time for a distraught man to contemplate his sorrow.

Among all the urgent problems demanding the attention of the harried leaders in Washington during the early days of August 1914 and following, none was more immediate than the necessity of proclaiming American neutrality and of then establishing it in fact as well as in name. As we have already seen, the President and his colleagues proceeded in the belief that official neutrality was as wise as it was inescapable. Thus the official proclamations, ten of them in all, were issued as a matter of course between August 4 and November 6, 1914. Drafted by the State Department and signed by the President, they made clear what American citizens and foreign nationals and agents would be permitted to do in the United States as long as the war lasted, and what they could not do without risking prosecution and imprisonment or expulsion.[1]

Then during the months following the issuance of the first proclamations, the President and his subordinates worked diligently to apply old rules and devise new ones to establish neutrality in practice. The chain of command in making and executing these policies ran simply and directly. The President of course bore the over-all responsibility and had the final voice in all decisions. His chief adviser was the Secretary of State, who in turn leaned upon the professional international lawyer and Counselor of the State Department, Robert Lansing, for guidance in large matters and the direct execution of most

[1] *Foreign Relations, 1914, Supplement,* pp. 547-551.

routine business. To assist him in deciding technical points, Lansing in mid-August 1914 established the Joint State and Navy Neutrality Board, with James Brown Scott of the Carnegie Endowment for International Peace as chairman.[2] Finally, the responsibility for enforcing laws and regulations on American soil and in American territorial waters fell to the Treasury, Navy, and Justice Departments, assisted from time to time by state and local police officials.

The task of enforcement was usually a routine business of adhering to well-defined custom and law and one facilitated by the rival Ambassadors, Attachés, and Consuls, who were quick to complain of alleged infractions by their enemies. Even the organized German violations, which became the most vexing threat to American neutrality at home in 1915 and which will be discussed in a later chapter, evoked no disputes over domestic law and what the duty of the United States was under the law's provisions.

However, the problem was not always as easy to solve as this might imply. In momentous questions, like the export of munitions, loans to belligerent governments, or the defense of neutral rights at sea, the law of nations was often ambiguous, while considerations of national interest that transcended international law were sometimes involved. Even in some fairly routine matters the law did not furnish a clear guide. It often happened, therefore, that the leaders in Washington had to follow their consciences in choosing between possible alternatives; and this they usually did by attempting to find what the spirit of neutrality commanded when the law failed to speak clearly. They manifested this intention and method in three episodes, among others, during the early weeks of the war.

The first revealed all too clearly that the way of strict neutrality would not always be easy to see. Not long before the war German companies had erected wireless stations at Tuckerton, New Jersey, and Sayville, Long Island, capable of communicating with the homeland. As soon as hostilities began, the German Naval Attaché used both facilities to direct the movements of German warships and merchantmen at sea, thus employing American territory as a base of military operations. Informed of this fact on August 4, 1914,[3] the President issued an executive order on the following day forbidding all radio

[2] For the establishment and personnel of this Board, see J. B. Scott to R. Lansing, August 10, 1914; R. Lansing to W. J. Bryan, August 11, 1914; R. Lansing to J. B. Scott, August 15, 1914; and J. B. Scott to R. Lansing, August 17, 1914, all in the Papers of Robert Lansing, Library of Congress; hereinafter cited as the Lansing Papers.

[3] The British Chargé to the Secretary of State, August 4, 1914, *Foreign Relations, 1914, Supplement,* p. 667.

stations in the United States to transmit any messages of an unneutral character, and directing the Secretary of the Navy to see that the order was obeyed.[4] This the latter did by forbidding the dispatch of any wireless messages in code. At once the German Embassy protested that this ruling was unfair. The British and French, it argued, had free use of cable communications and could send military information to their governments without restraint, while they, the German representatives, had no way other than the wireless of communicating with Berlin, since the British had cut their cable at the beginning of the war.[5]

It was an important matter, and Wilson and Bryan wanted only to be fair to both sides. Would it not be possible, Bryan suggested as a compromise to the British government, to open all cable and wireless facilities to all belligerents on equal terms? "We are not able," he explained, "to find substantial distinction between cable communication and communication by wireless."[6]

When both the British and French governments rejected Bryan's suggestion and again insisted that continued unrestricted German operation of the wireless stations would be a violation of neutrality,[7] the President and Secretary of State had to make a more clear-cut decision. Before doing this, however, they searched the law of nations, the facts, and their own consciences. The law, they soon discovered, was unclear and contradictory. As Counselor Lansing pointed out, one article of the Hague Convention of 1907 forbade a belligerent to erect a wireless station on neutral territory for the purpose of communicating with armed forces on land or sea, and to use any wireless facilities they had erected on neutral territory before the war "for purely military purposes." Another article of the same Convention, on the other hand, declared that a neutral power was not bound "to forbid or restrict the use on behalf of the belligerents of telegraph or telephone cables or of wireless telegraphy apparatus belonging to it or to companies or private individuals."[8]

Nor were the facts altogether clear. In reply to an inquiry from Washington, the German Foreign Office replied that the Imperial gov-

[4] Executive Order of August 5, 1914, printed in *ibid.*, p. 668.

[5] New York *World*, August 13, 1914.

[6] The Secretary of State to Ambassador Page, August 11, 1914, *Foreign Relations, 1914, Supplement*, p. 669.

[7] The French Chargé to the Secretary of State, August 12, 1914; the British Chargé to the Secretary of State, August 14, 1914, *ibid.*, pp. 671-673.

[8] "*Memorandum by the Counselor for the Department of State . . . ,*" dated August 12, 1914, *The Lansing Papers*, I, 152-156.

ernment was not connected "directly or indirectly" with the wireless stations "in any business or other relations whatsoever" and did not use them to communicate to its armed forces "directly or indirectly."[9] Yet the Justice Department reported that there was good reason to believe that the German Foreign Office had had a large interest in the construction at least of the station at Sayville.[10] Moreover, it was certainly true, as Lansing argued, that unrestricted German operation of the stations would inevitably mean the use of American territory for the direct communication of military information, and that cable communication was of a different character because information transmitted via this medium could be sent to armed forces only from the territory of the belligerent itself.

In the end the decision demanded by the spirit of neutrality seemed clear enough to Wilson and Bryan. It was to maintain control of the wireless stations at Tuckerton and Sayville to prevent the Germans from using them for military purposes. On the other hand, all belligerents should be permitted to use the stations and to send messages in code, provided that they furnished copies of both messages and codes to the American government.[11] Consequently, the President took official possession of the stations on September 5, 1914, and directed the Navy Department to operate them or to oversee their operation.[12]

The second episode was one that tested the American government's policy on the sale and export of munitions and other contraband of war—a matter of vital significance to all belligerents. At the outbreak of the war and time and again thereafter, the State Department took

[9] Ambassador Gerard to the Secretary of State, August 30, 1914, *Foreign Relations, 1914, Supplement*, p. 677.

[10] Charles Warren, memorandum for the Attorney General, dated August 19, 1914, Wilson Papers.

[11] New York *World*, September 4, 1914.

[12] He took this action under authority of the Radio Act of 1912. For the President's Executive Order of September 5, 1914, see *Foreign Relations, 1914, Supplement*, p. 678.

Actually, the Navy Department did not operate both stations at first but merely issued the regulations under which they might function and maintained censors at them to enforce compliance. On July 8, 1915, however, the Navy Department assumed the direct operation of the Sayville station, the capacity of which had recently been greatly increased, on the ground that the Atlantic Communication Company, organized to operate the new transmitter, was under the virtual control of the German government and had recently been employing officers of the German military forces. *New York Times*, July 9, 1915. See also British Embassy, memorandum for the State Department, June 9, 1915, *Papers Relating to the Foreign Relations of the United States, 1915, Supplement, The World War*, pp. 887-888; hereinafter cited as *Foreign Relations, 1915, Supplement*.

the position that it had no authority to interfere in this traffic, and that it would in fact be highly unneutral for it or any agency of the government to do so under ordinary circumstances.[13] When a border-line case arose in early November 1914, however, Wilson and Bryan found that it was not always possible to reconcile traditional practice with the spirit of neutrality.

It began when the State Department somehow learned that the Fore River Company and the Bethlehem Steel Corporation had signed contracts to build submarines to be delivered in sections to the British government. Troubled in conscience, Bryan asked Lansing whether the transaction would be legal under international law. Lansing replied that the sale of assembled submarines or hulls would be unneutral, but that the delivery of submarine parts would be proper.[14] Unpersuaded and still perplexed, the Secretary of State appealed to the President. "I fear," he wrote, "that we would be 'skating on thin ice' if we adopted the rule suggested [by Lansing]. It may be within the rules of neutrality but I am afraid we could not convince the average citizen there was any difference in allowing a vessel to be completed here and allowing the parts to be made so that a complete vessel could be shipped and the parts assembled in another port."[15]

Although he had earlier agreed with Lansing,[16] Wilson now took Bryan's side and held to it in the face of an opinion by the Joint Neutrality Board that there was no legal obstacle to the sale of submarine parts and no authority to punish individuals involved in such a transaction.[17] "As I intimated to you," the President wrote to the Counselor on November 30, "I gave the matter very serious thought when the question of the submarines was brought up. I feel that it is really our duty (in the *spirit*, at any rate, of the Alabama decision) to prevent submarines being shipped from this country even in parts, and I hope that you will find a way of checking and preventing this if it is contemplated."[18]

Lansing, who had earlier advised the attorney for the corporations involved that he personally thought the contemplated transaction was

[13] e.g., the circular that the State Department issued to the press on October 15, 1914, printed in *Foreign Relations, 1914, Supplement*, pp. 573-574.

[14] R. Lansing to W. J. Bryan, November 12, 1914, Wilson Papers.

[15] W. J. Bryan to W.W., November 12, 1914, *The Lansing Papers*, I, 114.

[16] R. Lansing, to W.W., November 28, 1914, *ibid.*, p. 114.

[17] Memorandum of the Joint State and Navy Neutrality Board, November 25, 1914, Wilson Papers.

[18] W.W. to R. Lansing, November 30, 1914, *ibid.*

proper, now had to warn him that the administration regarded the sale of submarines or submarine parts as being contrary to the "strict neutrality which this Government seeks to preserve in the present war," and that it would take "all legal means to prevent the exportation of such craft and manufactured parts."[19] Moreover, when Charles M. Schwab, president of the Bethlehem Steel Corporation, came to the State Department a short time later, Bryan told him that the President "regarded the work as contemplated a violation of the spirit of neutrality." There was, consequently, nothing Schwab could do but yield as gracefully as possible, by promising that his firm would not build any submarines for delivery to belligerents during the war. As the Secretary observed in a statement announcing Schwab's decision, the "submarine incident" was closed.[20]

The third incident revealed best of all the President's and the Secretary of State's honest effort to be neutral in spirit as well as in deed, and the dangers of trying to live by faith instead of by the law. It began a few days after the outbreak of hostilities in Europe, when the French government appointed J. P. Morgan & Company as its American financial agent and requested it to float a loan of $100,000,000 on its behalf in the United States.[21] The New York bankers thereupon asked the State Department whether it would object if they arranged the French loan, as well as another one for the House of Rothschild in Paris.

Bryan at once discussed the matter with Lansing, who explained that private loans to belligerent governments were neither unneutral under international law nor illegal under American statutes. But the Counselor's exposition of traditional law and custom made no impression upon the great apostle of peace. At least since 1907 he had been saying that money was a contraband of war, and that neutral nations should not permit their citizens "to grow rich by encouraging wars between other nations."[22] On August 10, the day of the funeral service for Ellen Wilson at the White House, the Secretary of State addressed a fervent appeal to the President for a new policy in accord with the

[19] R. Lansing to J. H. Hayden, December 1, 1914, *Foreign Relations 1914, Supplement*, p. 577.

[20] *New York Times*, December 8, 1914.

[21] *ibid.*, August 6, 7, and 14, 1914; also Rothschild Frères to J. P. Morgan & Company, August 3, 1914, and Morgan, Harjes et Compagnie to J. P. Morgan & Company, August 4, 1914, printed in 74th Cong., 2d sess., *Senate Report No. 944*, Part 6, p. 11.

[22] Address before the First American Peace Congress, New York City, April 17, 1907, cited in *The Independent*, LXXX (October 26, 1914), 117.

spirit of true neutrality, namely, that the American government would not approve "any loan to a belligerent nation." "Money," he went on, "is the worst of all contrabands because it commands everything else," and the United States should take the lead in outlawing loans and thus hasten the end of hostilities. Moreover, Americans who lent money to the belligerents would inevitably want them to win, thus intensifying national rivalries and antagonisms in the United States. Finally, Bryan said, the American financiers who floated foreign loans would be tempted to use their influence through the newspapers to support the interests of the governments to which they had lent money, and "this influence would make it all the more difficult for us to maintain neutrality, as our action on various questions that would arise would affect one side or the other and powerful financial interests would be thrown into the balance."[23]

Whatever Wilson thought about the question, he was in no mood to resist Bryan's obviously passionate determination to institute a new moral policy, especially since Lansing, after explaining traditional law and practice on the subject, had seemed to support the Secretary's arguments.[24] Moreover, there seemed to be sound economic reasons why the administration should discourage large foreign loans at this time. The European demand for gold and dollars had already totally demoralized the American money market, and further draining in the form of loans might well have intensified the crisis at home. In his public statement justifying the administration's policy, Bryan pointed out another reason why loans to belligerents seemed to him unwise. "If the United States," he said, "were to loan money to the belligerent nations, it would be less able to assist the neutrals. . . . We are under special obligation to render such service as we can to South and Central America; it would be difficult to do this if all of our surplus money was flowing into the war chests of Europe."[25]

The question was settled without further discussion, probably by a telephone conversation on or soon after August 12, 1914, when the President returned from Rome, Georgia, where Mrs. Wilson was buried on August 11. With Wilson's consent, Bryan gave the following statement to the press on August 15:

[23] W. J. Bryan to W.W., August 10, 1914, Wilson Papers; also *The Lansing Papers*, I, 131-132.

[24] As Bryan reported in the letter just cited.

[25] W. J. Bryan, "No Loans to Belligerents," *The Commoner*, XIV (September 1914), 2.

Inquiry having been made as to the attitude of this Government in case American bankers were asked to make loans to foreign Governments during the war in Europe, the following announcement is made:

There is no reason why loans should not be made to the Governments of neutral nations, but in the judgment of this Government loans by American bankers to any foreign nation which is at war is inconsistent with the true spirit of neutrality.[26]

Bryan sealed his victory a short time later in a public editorial in his monthly magazine. Hailing "the President's" decision as a blow for peace, he again invoked the argument that had presumably proved decisive with Wilson: "It IS inconsistent with the spirit of neutrality for a neutral nation [*sic*] to make loans to belligerent nations, for money is the worst of contrabands—it commands all other things."[27]

Events and sober second thinking would soon show that the ban on loans was economically unfeasible—unless the United States were prepared to accept the ruin of its foreign trade and all that this catastrophe would entail—and unneutral in application, because highly prejudicial to the Allies.[28] It was also the product of as unclear thinking as ever confused the councils of the American government. All of Bryan's arguments against money as contraband might just as well have been—in fact, were—used against the export of all kinds of war material, which Bryan consistently defended. As we will see,[29] the ban on loans broke down almost as soon as it was inaugurated and was quietly set aside by its author long before the administration implicitly repudiated it at the time of the first public Allied loan in the United States. Even so, the deep significance of the ban remained: More than any other policy adopted during the formative period of American neutrality it symbolized the administration's quest for neutrality in the spirit of impartiality.

[26] *New York Times*, August 16, 1914.

[27] W. J. Bryan, "No Loans to Belligerents," *loc. cit.*

[28] In fairness to Bryan it must be said that this fact was not at all apparent at the time the ban was announced because none of the Allied powers then had any pressing need for American credits, and it was generally assumed that Germany would be able to maintain a large commerce in noncontraband goods with the United States and would want to borrow money in America almost as much as the Allies. No Allied government protested the ban *when it was announced*, while the influential London *Economist* hailed it as an "honour" to the United States and a "service to the world." "European and American Neutrality," *The Economist* (London), LXXIX (August 22, 1914), 340-341.

[29] See below, pp. 132-136.

That quest went on during the first weeks of the war as Wilson and his advisers sought by advice and example to lead the American people into what they thought was the only solid foundation for neutrality in action, namely, a true impartiality of mind and heart. If this were wise and right, then such leadership had to come quickly and effectively, for it seemed during the first days of the war that the nation might divide into warring camps favoring one alliance or the other, and that policies of neutrality would be impossible to execute amid the din of hostile voices. There was the particular threat that the immigrant millions (nearly one-third of all Americans in 1910 were foreign-born) would forget their loyalty to their adopted flag and espouse the cause of their homelands with such violence as to make civil commotion actually possible, at least on a minor scale.

The dangers of the "present inflamed state of the public mind of this country over the European conflict" and of "utterances by the American people and press which would cause hostile feeling by one or more of the belligerents toward the United States" were alarmingly evident to Counselor Lansing as he surveyed the American scene on August 9, 1914. Setting down his fears in a memorandum for the Secretary of State, he went on to suggest that it might be wise for the President "to publish a public address to the American people urging them to preserve in every way a strict neutrality and to be discreet in public expressions either in the press or otherwise showing bias or sympathy with any one of the countries at war."[30] Bryan sent Lansing's memorandum, with a few verbal changes and his hearty endorsement, to the White House on August 10. The funeral trip to Georgia and the press of business after Wilson's return prevented immediate action. But the President found time to draft an appeal to his "Fellow-Countrymen" in the closing hours of August 17, and he gave it to the press on the following day.

In moving cadences it pleaded for serenity and fair play. Every man who loved America, it began, would act and speak in "the true spirit of neutrality, which is the spirit of impartiality and fairness and friendliness to all concerned." It would be easy, the appeal went on, to excite the passions of various national groups and to divide the country into "camps of hostile opinions, hot against each other, involved in the war itself in impulse and opinion, if not in action."

"I venture, therefore, my fellow-countrymen," the President con-

[30] R. Lansing, *"Memorandum by the Counselor . . . ," The Lansing Papers,* I, 151-152.

cluded, "to speak a solemn word of warning to you against that deepest, most subtle, most essential breach of neutrality which may spring out of partisanship, out of passionately taking sides. The United States must be neutral in fact as well as in name during these days that are to try men's souls. We must be impartial in thought as well as in action, must put a curb upon our sentiments as well as upon every transaction that might be construed as a preference of one party to the struggle before another.

"My thought is of America. I am speaking, I feel sure, the earnest wish and purpose of every thoughtful American that this great country of ours . . . should show herself in this time of peculiar trial a nation fit beyond others to exhibit the fine poise of undisturbed judgment, the dignity of self-control, the efficiency of dispassionate action, a nation that neither sits in judgment upon others nor is disturbed in her own counsels and which keeps herself fit and free to do what is honest and disinterested and truly serviceable for the peace of the world."[31]

During the months to come Wilson rarely missed an opportunity to remind Americans of their duty, as he said, to be "impartial in thought as well as in action." For example, he took personal action at the outset of hostilities to prevent army or navy officers, active and retired, from embarrassing the government by indiscretions or by "public comment of any kind upon the military or political situation on the other side of the water."[32] A short time later he blocked a movement set on foot by the Niagara Section, or chapter, of the New York Peace Society for the appointment of an official commission to investigate and report on the causes of the war because, as Secretary Bryan said, such a commission "would have to locate the blame and it would be impossible to fix the responsibility without arousing protest from the party charged with causing the war."[33] Again, when the President

[31] *New York Times*, August 19, 1914.

[32] W.W. to L. M. Garrison and J. Daniels, August 6, 1914, Wilson Papers. This order was probably prompted by a widely printed statement that Rear Admiral Alfred T. Mahan, Retired, gave to newspapermen on August 3, 1914, in which Mahan had some rather sharp things to say about Austrian and particularly German motives and ambitions. Mahan, moreover, had agreed (before the President's order was issued by the Secretary of the Navy, Josephus Daniels) to write regular articles on the war for the New York *World, Leslie's Weekly*, and *The Independent*. Only one of these, entitled "Sea Power in the Present European War," was ever published. It had been submitted before the President's order was issued and appeared in *Leslie's Weekly* on August 20, 1914. See W. D. Puleston, *Mahan, The Life and Work of Captain Alfred Thayer Mahan, U.S.N.*, pp. 340-342.

[33] See the Niagara Section of the New York Peace Society to W.W., August 20, 1914;

learned that audiences in motion-picture theaters were demonstrating when war films were being run, he drafted the following message to be shown on the screen before the newsreels appeared:

It would be a patriotic act in the interest of the neutrality of the nation and the peace of mankind if the audience in this theatre would refrain during the showing of pictures connected with the present war from expressing either approval or disapproval. Woodrow Wilson.[34]

Or, to cite a final example, he refused over and over to grant interviews about the war to reporters, or to say anything for publication that might conceivably be misconstrued.[35] In short, no man could have tried more earnestly than he did to bar war passions from American shores. As he wrote to a correspondent who had complained of the anti-German bias of some American journals:

"I deplore as sincerely as you do expressions of violent condemnation or violent partisanship with regard to either side in the present dreadful conflict in Europe and have taken every public occasion that opened itself to me to urge upon my fellow-citizens a genuine neutrality of thought as well as of action. But, unhappily, the only thing that the Government can do is to enforce neutrality of action. This it has studiously and at every point been careful to do and will continue to do with the utmost vigilance."[36]

W.W. to W. J. Bryan, August 21, 1914; W.W. to the Niagara Section, August 21, 1914, all in *The Lansing Papers*, I, 6; James H. Rand, secretary of the Niagara Section, to W.W., August 22, 1914, and W. J. Bryan to W.W., September 5, 1914, both in the Wilson Papers.

[34] Enclosed in W.W. to W. J. Bryan, September 11, 1914, *ibid.*

[35] e.g., W.W. to Robert Underwood Johnson, December 14, 1914; W.W. to Isidor Singer, February 1, 1915; W.W. to George T. Lemmon, February 1, 1915; W.W. to F. K. Lane, February 9, 1915; W.W. to John A. Aylward, March 8, 1915; and W.W. to Jane Addams, March 8, 1915, all in *ibid.*

One embarrassing incident in the spring of 1915 revealed how extraordinarily sensitive Wilson was on the matter of the publication of his opinions on *any* matter relating to the war. He received Gabriel Alphaud of *Le Temps* of Paris in company with French Ambassador Jusserand at the White House on March 31, 1915, and in the interview that followed he made some totally innocuous remarks about the purposes of American neutral policies. When *Le Temps* published his remarks on April 1, the President shot back with a statement implying that Alphaud had fabricated the interview, *New York Times*, April 2, 1915. "I regret exceedingly having caused any annoyance to President Wilson," Alphaud replied, ". . . but the truth is the truth. Mr. Wilson was aware of my intention to send to *Le Temps* the statements which he so graciously made to me. . . . I can only formally maintain both the text of my interview and the bona fide authorization which I had to publish the statements of the President." New York *World*, April 3, 1915. Wilson made no further comment.

[36] W.W. to Otto J. Krampikowsky, December 14, 1914, Wilson Papers.

Powerless though they were, as Wilson said, to act when private citizens and the press ignored their appeals for impartiality, the leaders in Washington could and did move early in the war to strike at another source of agitation, foreign diplomats who did not know how to hold their tongues. Such misconduct occurred for the first time on September 8, 1914, when the Turkish Ambassador, A. Rustem Bey, gave an interview to the press denouncing the Russians, British, and French for alleged barbarities and accusing Britain and France of setting a "vulgar trap" to ensnare the United States in war with Turkey. The envoy from the Sublime Porte added in passing that it was hardly fitting for Americans, who lynched Negroes daily and had subjected Filipinos to the water cure, to criticize Turks when they massacred Christians.[37]

A request for an explanation brought Rustem to the Secretary of State's office on September 11, 1914. The records do not reveal how the gentle Bryan handled the Turkish firebrand, but Rustem extended his remarks on the following day in what must have been one of the most grossly insulting letters ever received by an American Secretary of State. After attacking the American press for reviling, mocking, and insulting his people and homeland and the United States government for permitting such attacks to be made, the Ambassador blandly explained that he had given the newspapers his statement, which he admitted had been faithfully reproduced, because he wanted to make a straightforward appeal to the American people themselves. "I am conscious," he concluded somewhat grandiosely, "of having fulfilled my moral duty to Turkey, to the United States and to humanity at large."[38]

To Lansing, Rustem's misconduct had been so egregious and his letter so arrogant that the Washington administration had no alternative but to declare him *persona non grata* and to request his recall.[39] After conferring with the President, Bryan decided, however, to forgive the Ambassador in order to avoid further inflaming sentiment in Turkey, provided he agreed to apologize and mend his ways.[40] "I am, therefore, instructed to inform Your Excellency," Lansing thus advised Rustem, "that, if you feel that your services at this capital

[37] Washington *Evening Star*, September 8, 1914, printed in *The Lansing Papers*, I, 70-71.

[38] A. Rustem to the Secretary of State, September 12, 1914, *ibid.*, pp. 68-69.

[39] R. Lansing to W. J. Bryan, September 14, 1914, *ibid.*, p. 71.

[40] W. J. Bryan to R. Lansing, September 16, 1914; W.W. to R. Lansing, September 17, 1914, *ibid.*, pp. 72-73.

can still be useful to your Government, and that if you are willing to express your regret for your published utterances, which this Government considers to be offensive, the President is disposed to pass over without further comment your public statement and your note and renew the cordial and friendly intercourse between Your Excellency and the Government of the United States, which existed before this unfortunate incident occurred."[41] Still unrepentant, Rustem replied that he could not accept the President's terms, and that he had therefore asked the Sublime Porte to call him home.[42]

A second incident occurred a few days later. On September 23, 1914, Baron Wilhelm von Schoen, a member of the staff of the German Embassy in Washington who had recently come from Tokyo, gave an interview to a reporter from the Washington *Evening Star*. In ominous tones he warned that most Japanese hated the United States and believed that war with America was inevitable. "Should both Japan and England be victorious in this war . . . ," he concluded, "the danger to the United States will be great."[43]

Wilson's jaw must have snapped hard when he read this interview, for reporters at the White House noted that his patience was exhausted, and that he was determined to put an end to all such outbursts by foreign diplomats.[44] Von Schoen hastened to the State Department to explain that he had been misquoted, but Lansing, now the Acting Secretary of State, was unconvinced and asked the President what to do.[45] "I hope that if there is any proper way of opening the matter with the German Ambassador, it may be opened," Wilson replied. "I feel with you that there can be no real doubt about the substantial authenticity of the interview and I think it not only desirable, but imperative, that this gentleman should not remain here."[46] Pressed by Lansing for an explanation, Ambassador von Bernstorff was almost embarrassingly conciliatory in reply.[47] For a moment Wilson was adamant, but eventually he accepted the German Embassy's regrets and assurances that the Baron would never again speak to newspapermen.

[41] R. Lansing to A. Rustem, September 19, 1914, *ibid.*, pp. 73-74.
[42] A. Rustem to R. Lansing, September 20, 1914, *ibid.*, p. 74.
[43] Washington *Evening Star*, September 23, 1914, printed in *ibid.*, pp. 76-77.
[44] *New York Times*, September 24, 1914.
[45] R. Lansing to W.W., September 25, 1914, *The Lansing Papers*, I, 75-76.
[46] W.W. to R. Lansing, September 26, 1914, *ibid.*, p. 77.
[47] R. Lansing to the German Ambassador, September 28, 1914; the German Ambassador to R. Lansing, September 29, 1914; R. Lansing to W.W., September 30, 1914, *ibid.*, pp. 77-79.

The severe disposition of these two cases and the publicity given to them in the press had the precise effect that the President intended to achieve. All at once, as it were, the most loquacious diplomats became immensely taciturn.

The hardest test of the President's determination to avoid even a show of moral commitment came when the leaders of the belligerent governments and certain spokesmen at home tried to draw him into the increasingly bitter controversy over atrocities and illegal methods of warfare.

The Germans opened the campaign first, in an obvious attempt to head off their enemies, by asking the State Department to deliver protests to the French and Belgian governments accusing them of inciting their civilian populations to barbaric attacks against the German armed forces.[48] The Belgians struck back by protesting the German army's burning of Louvain, and by announcing that they were sending an official delegation to Washington to lay the evidence of German atrocities on the President's desk.[49] Not to be outdone, the German government issued a blanket denial of these charges long before the Belgian delegation arrived in Washington, while the German Emperor dispatched a personal telegram to the White House informing President Wilson that French and British soldiers had been using dum-dum bullets in violation of the laws of war. Worse still, the Emperor added, Belgian civilians, encouraged by their government, had gone on such a rampage of murder and terror against German soldiers that his generals had been forced to destroy some villages and the old town of Louvain in self-defense.[50] The German villains, President Raymond Poincaré of France countered in a public rejoinder, were simply trying to reverse the charges that were being deservedly made against them. "In the name of flouted right and out-

[48] The American Chargé in Stockholm to the Secretary of State, August 18, 1914, transmitting the protests from the Foreign Office in Berlin, *Foreign Relations, 1914, Supplement*, pp. 791-792.

[49] Minister Emmanuel Havenith to the Secretary of State, August 28, 1914, Wilson Papers.

[50] Ambassador von Bernstorff to the Secretary of State, September 3, 1914, *Foreign Relations, 1914, Supplement*, p. 793; Ambassador Gerard to the Secretary of State, September 7, 1914, transmitting the Emperor's message to the President dated September 4, 1914, *ibid.*, p. 794. The Emperor's message was printed in the *New York Times* and other American newspapers on September 11, 1914.

raged civilization," he wrote to President Wilson, "I send to Your Excellency an indignant protest."[51]

The leaders in Washington had already wrestled with the question of whether to make formal protest against violations of the Hague Conventions in the specific case of the bombardment of Antwerp, an unfortified city, by a German zeppelin on the morning of August 25, 1914,[52] and the President had decided not to send an open message. "My present judgment is that we do not know in sufficient detail the actual facts," he had written on September 4, "and that we ought to be very slow to make formal protests, chiefly because we shall no doubt be called upon by every one of the belligerents before the fighting is over to do something of this kind and would be in danger of becoming chronic critics of what was going forward."[53] "Of course," he explained again not long afterward, "there are many allegations of breaches of the just laws of war and of atrocities of many sorts, but they come from both sides and it is impossible with the evidence at our disposal to determine what element of truth there is in them or what the real circumstances were under which the acts were committed. I do not see how it will be possible to form a just judgment concerning any part of the matter until the war is over and the evidence is all in."[54]

Obviously, Wilson would have preferred to say and do nothing, but this was no longer possible now that the Belgian delegation was on its way and the messages from the German Emperor and the French President were on his desk. After much discussion in the State Department, he received the Belgians at the White House on September

[51] R. Poincaré to the President of the United States, September 10, 1914, *Foreign Relations, 1914, Supplement*, p. 794.

[52] Counselor Lansing to the Secretary of State, August 28, 1914, enclosing two drafts of a note of protest, *The Lansing Papers*, I, 29-32; W. J. Bryan to W.W., September 3, 1914, *ibid.*, p. 32.

[53] W.W. to W. J. Bryan, September 4, 1914, *ibid.*, p. 33. The President did, however, instruct the American Ambassador in Berlin, James W. Gerard, to seek a conversation with "some member of the government upon whom you are likely to make the deepest impression" and to say to him, "unofficially, merely as a voluntary act of personal good will and friendship," that the German bombings of unfortified cities was having an unfavorable, "not to say fatal," effect upon American opinion. "I am deeply interested in maintaining a real neutrality of public opinion here and a scrupulous fairness of judgment," Wilson added, "but my efforts are being wholly nullified, I fear, by these occurrences and will be so long as the present use of bombs where they can be of no possible military service continues." W.W. to J. W. Gerard, October 19, 1914, *ibid.*, p. 35.

[54] W.W. to Mrs. Laura Fay-Smith, November 26, 1914, Wilson Papers.

16 and listened attentively while their spokesman, Minister of Justice Carton de Wiart, told of unspeakable atrocities committed against his fellow-countrymen by the German army. Then, after de Wiart had presented a voluminous document containing what purported to be proof of the charges, Wilson turned to the Belgians and, having thanked them for their expressions of friendship, said:

"You will, I am sure, not expect me to say more. Presently, I pray God very soon, this war will be over. The day of accounting will then come when I take it for granted the nations of Europe will assemble to determine a settlement. Where wrongs have been committed, their consequences and the relative responsibility involved will be assessed. The nations of the world have fortunately by agreement made a plan for such a reckoning and settlement. What such a plan can not compass the opinion of mankind, the final arbiter in all such matters, will supply. It would be unwise, it would be premature, for a single government, however fortunately separated from the present struggle, it would even be inconsistent with the neutral position of any nation which like this one has no part in the contest, to form or express a final judgment."[55]

On the same day Wilson replied in identic language to the German Emperor, adding in conclusion, "I feel sure that such a reservation of judgment until the end of the war, when all its events and circumstances can be seen in their entirety and in their true relations, will commend itself to you as a true expression of sincere neutrality."[56] And three days later he wrote in the same vein to President Poincaré: "The time will come when this great conflict is over and when the truth can be impartially determined. When that time arrives those responsible for violations of the rules of civilized warfare, if such violations have occurred, and for false charges against their adversaries, must of course bear the burden of the judgment of the world."[57]

This was the position to which Wilson stubbornly adhered until an outraged American public opinion finally forced him to speak out in the autumn of 1916 against the deportation of Belgian civilians to Germany for forced labor.

It was not easy to maintain one's silence in the face of the demands of spokesmen like Theodore Roosevelt for a formal protest, and in

[55] *Foreign Relations, 1914, Supplement*, p. 796; New York *World*, September 17, 1914.
[56] Text printed in the *New York Times*, September 17, 1914. The text printed in *Foreign Relations, 1914, Supplement*, p. 797, varies slightly.
[57] W.W. to President Poincaré, September 19, 1914, *ibid.*, p. 798.

the face of the fear that failure to speak would incite denunciations on Capitol Hill and embitter public opinion against the United States in the Allied countries.[58] It was not easy to ask them to desist, as Wilson and Lansing felt they had to do, when the Belgian Minister began to solicit money for the relief of his countrymen and members of the Belgian delegation joined the propaganda battle on the American front.[59] But what else, the President asked, could a fair-minded person do? And how else could he maintain his own impartiality and encourage a spirit of true neutrality among his people? To Wilson the answer was clear: Someone had to "hold excitements at arm's length and escape their contagion. *Somebody* must keep cool while our people grow hotter with discussing the war and all that it involves!"[60] For if he, the moral leader of the people, did not show the way toward calm understanding, then the tide of hatred and alarm would engulf America and unfit her for the tasks of reconciliation that lay ahead.

[58] R. Lansing to W.W., November 23, 1914, and W.W. to R. Lansing, November 26, 1914, *The Lansing Papers*, I, 35-37.

[59] See R. Lansing to W.W., September 25, 1914, and W.W. to R. Lansing, September 26 and 28, 1914, Wilson Papers.

[60] W.W. to Mrs. Crawford H. Toy, December 12, 1914, Wilson Papers.

CHAPTER III

Crises at Home

THE tasks of defining and defending American neutrality were difficult enough, but they intruded less clamorously during these weeks than did problems of domestic adjustment to the disruption of the European community that ensued in the wake of the declarations of war. For a time it seemed as if America's economic life were itself threatened with ruin. No one in Washington could stand still for a moment, not even a man who in his personal sorrow might have preferred withdrawal. For Wilson the challenges were unavoidable. The question was not whether he would meet them, but whether he would meet them with accustomed boldness—whether he would find himself again in service to the people in their time of need.

First there was the problem of caring for the thirty thousand American tourists stranded and helpless on the Continent and in England. The confusion caused by the temporary closing of European banks, the interruption of foreign exchange, and the canceling of steamship sailings seemed at the outset altogether overwhelming to the American Ambassadors on the scene. "God save us! What a week it has been! . . . Those first two days, there was, of course, great confusion," wrote Ambassador Page, describing the scene in London just before England entered the war. "Crazy men and weeping women were imploring and cursing and demanding—God knows it was bedlam turned loose. . . . Men shook English banknotes in my face and demanded United States money and swore our Government and its agents ought all to be shot. Women expected me to hand them steamship tickets home."[1] It was the same in Berlin. "Letters and telegrams from Americans in different parts of Germany pour in at the rate of a hundred or more daily, asking for information as to how to leave the country, how to secure money, etc., etc. . . ," the American Ambassador in the German capital reported. "There appear to be over 3,000 Americans in Berlin itself and more than 10,000 in Germany

[1] W. H. Page to W.W., August 9, 1914, Burton J. Hendrick, *The Life and Letters of Walter H. Page*, I, 303-305.

desiring transportation to the United States."[2] In Paris the panic was apparently worse. As the American Ambassador there remembered the scene: "It was the height of the tourist season, and upon the declaration of war, from every quarter of Europe when they could escape, [American] travelers poured into Paris on their way to the channel ports of France and England. . . . They expected that their troubles would be over when they reached Paris, when in fact they had often only begun."[3]

In Washington, Wilson and Bryan discussed the emergency in a conference at the White House on August 3 and agreed that they should authorize the Embassies in Europe to countersign letters of credit, traveler's checks, and the like, and that the American government must furnish whatever direct relief might be necessary. On the same day, consequently, the President sent a special message to Congress asking for an appropriation of $250,000 "for the relief, protection, and transportation of American citizens," and the legislators voted the money almost within the hour.[4] It was soon obvious that this would not suffice, and Wilson appealed again on August 5 for an additional $2,500,000.[5] Congress again acted quickly, and the cruisers *Tennessee* and *North Carolina* sailed for Europe on August 6 and 8 with nearly $8,000,000 in gold from the Treasury and New York banks.[6]

The arrival of the gold and the efficient work of the relief committees appointed by the Ambassadors eased the plight of the stranded Americans, but the problem of getting them home still remained. The most obvious solution was to use a number of the German passenger liners lying in refuge in American and Italian ports, and Secretary Bryan set about to make the necessary arrangements. The Germans offered the use of their ships, and the British promised to permit them to sail unmolested, provided they were operated by American crews, flew the American flag, and returned to their neutral berths when their relief task was completed. The French government, however, at first categorically refused to grant free passage; later, when the Paris authorities indicated that they might cooperate under certain conditions, the Secretary of State was no longer interested in pushing the

[2] Ambassador Gerard to the Secretary of State, August 18, 1914, *Foreign Relations, 1914, Supplement*, p. 95.

[3] T. Bentley Mott, *Myron T. Herrick, Friend of France*, p. 125.

[4] *New York Times*, August 4, 1914.

[5] *ibid.*, August 6, 1914.

[6] *ibid.*, August 7 and 9, 1914. The Assistant Secretary of War, Henry Breckinridge, sailed aboard the *Tennessee* as director of this relief expedition.

project.[7] This was true because British, French, and Italian transatlantic liners had meanwhile resumed their scheduled sailings, and the problem was well on the way to a happy solution. By mid-September of 1914 it no longer existed in a serious form.

At home the storm out of Europe had broken with a fury that threatened ruin for the national economy. It struck first at the financial structure in a double-barreled assault upon the New York Stock Exchange and the banks, as European bankers, caught unprepared by the onset of hostilities, turned panic-stricken to America to demand funds to reinforce their own fast-dwindling reserves.

The stock market, first hit, was most vulnerable to external pressures since Europeans in July 1914 owned American stocks and bonds with a total market value of about $2,500,000,000. Heavy European selling on the New York Stock Exchange began on July 30, producing the greatest losses in a single day since October 1907 and widespread demands that the Exchange be closed. Meeting at the offices of J. P. Morgan & Company in Wall Street in the late afternoon, the president of the Exchange and pre-eminent bankers of the city agreed that the situation was not yet threatening enough to warrant any desperate action. "So long as there are buyers there is a market . . . ," one of the bankers explained while announcing that the Exchange would open on the following day. "We have had today a very active market and plenty of purchasers. The question of closing shop must only be considered when there are no buyers."[8]

Such confidence soon evaporated in the face of news that threatened stark disaster. In the early morning of July 31 word came that the London Stock Exchange, which for the past four or five days had been the only major European securities market still in operation, had just closed its doors. At the same time, cables from Europe, instructing brokers and bankers to sell huge blocks of shares, came pouring into Wall Street offices. Permitting the Exchange to open, the leaders in the financial district agreed, could mean only the collapse of the market with catastrophic consequences for banks and other institutions. A few minutes later, at nine thirty, their spokesman, J. P. Morgan, Junior, called Secretary of the Treasury William G. McAdoo in Washington and put the decision up to him. It was to close the Exchange.

[7] For the correspondence bearing upon these negotiations, see *Foreign Relations, 1914, Supplement*, pp. 474-485.

[8] *New York Times*, July 31, 1914.

Thus the anxious traders who gathered on the floor at ten o'clock heard not the gong signaling the beginning of business for another day but an announcement that the governors had closed the Exchange until further notice. The final words of the statement were not heard, so loud was the cheering from the floor.[9]

Panic disappeared, but a new danger developed in late October 1914. It was that bankers holding notes with securities as collateral would have to demand payment of these loans,[10] and that this would cause wholesale dumping on the Curb, a final demoralization of prices, which had already declined from 20 to 30 per cent in what was called "outlaw" trading since July 31, and the bankrupting of thousands of individuals and brokers. The administration moved quickly once this danger was apparent. On October 26 John Skelton Williams, Comptroller of the Currency and McAdoo's chief assistant in the Treasury Department, instructed national bank examiners to approve all loans secured by listed stocks at their value as of July 30, 1914, thus in effect putting a floor under security prices.[11] Within a day prices rose, and the Curb market virtually disappeared.[12]

As relatively normal conditions returned to the financial district in the late autumn of 1914, the New York Stock Exchange reopened on November 28 for trading in bonds and on December 12 for dealings in securities under severe restrictions. In spite of considerable industrial stagnation during the next three months, prices held well above the minimum levels set for trading by the Board of Governors of the Exchange. Then Allied orders for munitions and heavy goods started pouring in for the first time in a substantial way during the late winter and early spring of 1915. And when the governors removed all restrictions on trading on April 1, the pent-up pressure produced the wildest bull market that Wall Street had seen since the early 1900's.[13]

The stock market crisis was only the most visible sign of the difficulties that beset the American financial structure during the first weeks of the war. The Stock Exchange might be closed, but there was no way to halt the enormous demands of European creditors

[9] New York *World*, August 1, 1914; William G. McAdoo, *Crowded Years, The Reminiscences of William G. McAdoo*, p. 290; Alexander D. Noyes, *The War Period of American Finance, 1908-1925*, pp. 56-60.

[10] They totaled $1,036,976,740 on June 30, 1914. *Annual Report of the Secretary of the Treasury on the State of the Finances for the Fiscal Year Ended June 30, 1914*, p. 494.

[11] *New York Times*, October 27, 1914.   [12] *ibid.*, October 28, 1914.

[13] *ibid.*, April 10-17, 1915.

for the payment of short-term and demand notes in gold. Secretary McAdoo estimated that American bankers and merchants at the outset of the war owed approximately $450,000,000 to London in obligations the last of which would mature by January 1, 1915.[14] British bankers began to demand payment of a part of this debt even before their country entered the war. In the ensuing panic, despite the shipment of $11,025,000 to Europe on July 31, the pound rose from $4.89 to $7 and the franc from 19⅓ cents to 23½ cents in New York on August 1. On that day the New York bankers imposed an extra-legal embargo on gold exports. The gravest peril, however, was not the disruption of the system of international exchange, which of course did momentarily occur, but the likelihood that fear would seize the public, provoking runs by depositors and the calling in of loans by banks. This would have led inevitably to the failure or near-failure of banks everywhere, for the Federal Reserve System, with its facilities for the issuance of currency and the mobilization of reserves, had not yet gone into operation.

August 2, the day when the crisis was at its worst, fortunately fell on a Sunday, thus affording a brief respite. Early that morning the presidents of all the leading New York and Philadelphia banks met at the Hotel Vanderbilt in New York City to prepare for the panic that seemed inevitable when business resumed on the following day. Calling Secretary McAdoo by telephone, they warned that they must have additional currency, and they urged the Secretary to come to New York at once. Before he left Washington, McAdoo made arrangements to ship $100,000,000 in the "emergency" currency authorized by the Aldrich-Vreeland Act of 1908[15] to Wall Street. Arriving at the Vanderbilt in the evening, he soon learned that this relief would not suffice for long. The basic trouble, the bankers declared, was the Aldrich-Vreeland Act itself; they simply could not get sufficient currency under its severe provisions. Promising that he would do the best he could, McAdoo left the conference for Washington soon after

[14] *Annual Report of the Secretary of the Treasury . . . 1914,* p. 17.

[15] The Aldrich-Vreeland Act authorized the Secretary of the Treasury to issue up to $500,000,000 in so-called "emergency" currency to national banks that organized "National Currency Associations" for the purpose of receiving such funds. Secured by United States bonds, commercial paper, and municipal and state bonds, this currency was an obligation of the banks, not the United States, and was subjected to a tax that increased to 10 per cent six months after it was issued. Fortunately, the Treasury had already printed the full $500,000,000 in the new currency when the financial crisis hit in late July 1914. A. D. Noyes, *The War Period of American Finance,* pp. 77-79.

midnight. We may be sure that he slept little on the trip southward, and that his fertile brain had worked out all details of what would be the administration's plans for meeting the crisis by the time that his train reached the capital.[16]

Those plans were set in motion as soon as the government began its business on Monday morning, August 3. The President, prepared by McAdoo during a conference held probably at breakfast, led off at his regular news conference by appealing for help from the reporters and announcing that there was no cause for alarm.

"Gentlemen," he declared, "before you question me I want to say this: I believe it is really unnecessary, but I want to tell you what is in my mind. It is extremely necessary, it is manifestly necessary, in the present state of affairs on the other side of the water that you should be extremely careful not to add in any way to the excitement. Of course, the European world is in a highly excited state of mind, but the excitement ought not to spread to the United States.

"So far as we are concerned, there is no cause for excitement. There is great inconvenience, for the time being, in the money market and in our Exchanges, and, temporarily, in the handling of our crops, but America is absolutely prepared to meet the financial situation and to straighten everything out without any material difficulty. The only thing that can possibly prevent it is unreasonable apprehension and excitement.

"If I might make a suggestion to you gentlemen, therefore, I would urge you not to give currency to any unverified rumor, to anything that would tend to create or add to excitement. I think that you will agree that we must all at the present moment act together as Americans in seeing that America does not suffer any unnecessary distress from what is going on in the world at large. . . .

"I know from my conference with the Secretary of the Treasury, who is in very close touch with the financial situation throughout the country, that there is no cause for alarm. There is cause for getting busy and doing the thing in the right way, but there is no element of unsoundness and there is no cause for alarm. The bankers and business men of the country are cooperating with the Government with a zeal, intelligence, and spirit which make the outcome secure."[17]

[16] The foregoing is based upon W. G. McAdoo, *Crowded Years*, pp. 290-292, and upon accounts in the New York *World*, August 2 and 3, 1914, and the *New York Times*, August 3, 1914.

[17] *New York Times*, August 4, 1914.

At the same time, the Comptroller of the Currency and two members of the Federal Reserve Board, William P. G. Harding and Charles S. Hamlin, were on hand when the banks opened in New York on Monday, August 3, to supervise the distribution of "emergency" currency from the United States Sub-Treasury and to approve a plan for using certificates instead of cash in the settlement of daily balances at Clearing Houses throughout the country. Moreover, the moment that congressmen gathered on Capitol Hill, McAdoo was in the office of Senator Robert L. Owen of Oklahoma, chairman of the Senate banking committee, with a bill for the liberalization of the Aldrich-Vreeland Act. Congress acted so quickly that the President could sign the measure on the following day, August 4. It permitted "National Currency Associations" to receive at least an additional billion dollars in "emergency" currency beyond the $500,000,000 limit set by the Aldrich-Vreeland Act.[18]

It was a spectacular display of leadership, and it saved the day. Depositors had made substantial withdrawals during late July and the first days of August—$80,000,000 from New York banks alone—but after Wilson's and McAdoo's work on August 3 and 4 there were no runs at all, few extraordinary withdrawals, and only five minor bank failures. Consequently, the forty-three "National Currency Associations" organized throughout the country had received only $256,-170,000 in "emergency" currency by September 8, and only $363,632,-080 by the third week in October.[19] From this point on the volume steadily declined until November 1914, when the "emergency" banknotes were supplanted entirely by the new Federal Reserve currency.

The final task in the liquidation of the financial crisis was the reestablishment of the system of international exchange, disrupted by London's extraordinary demand for gold and dollars and by the New York bankers' embargo on their export. McAdoo called leading bankers and exporters to the Treasury on August 7 to consider the problem. Probably a majority of the conferees favored an indefinite suspension of gold payments, but the spokesmen of Morgan & Company and of Kuhn, Loeb & Company, the two largest private banking firms, were adamant in opposition. The upshot was the appointment of a committee to find a remedy. Announced a month later, it was the formation of a nation-wide gold pool of $150,000,000 (soon reduced to $100,-000,000) to be subscribed by the banks and used in meeting external

[18] *ibid.*, August 4 and 5, 1914.
[19] *ibid.*, September 11, 1914; A. D. Noyes, *The War Period of American Finance*, p. 80.

gold obligations when they fell due. McAdoo and the Federal Reserve Board gave their approval on September 21, and the gold fund was soon oversubscribed.[20]

Actually, only $10,000,000 of the gold was ever transferred to the account of the Bank of England, and the pool committee went out of business entirely on January 22, 1915, because it had nothing more to do. Meanwhile, the system of exchange between New York and London had been firmly re-established, and without any strain upon American gold resources. This was true in the beginning because most English creditors extended the American notes that they held once they were assured of payment; and between August and the end of December 1914 a total of only $104,900,000 in gold was exported from the United States. More importantly, the exchange problem gradually and quietly solved itself when the British and other Allied governments began to place large war orders in the United States in the closing months of 1914. Indeed, by late October the exchange situation had already begun to reverse, and the New York bankers were beginning to discuss the necessity of extending short-term credits abroad.[21]

The European storm was no less devastating in its impact upon American foreign trade than upon the financial structure. Foreign commerce, which totaled more than $4,250,000,000 in 1913, was the lifeblood of the American economy in the years before the war. It was the channel through which farmers and many manufacturers disposed of their surpluses and the means by which American bankers obtained credits for the settlement of international balances. Upon its uninterrupted rhythm depended the price that the southern planter would receive for his cotton and the western farmer for his wheat, the capacity at which steel mills would operate, indeed, whether the entire economy would prosper or decline.

For a nation so dependent upon maritime commerce, the United states was dangerously vulnerable to such a crisis as erupted in the summer of 1914. It simply had no overseas merchant marine worthy of the name. Of the 45,400,000 gross tons of shipping on all the waters of the world at the outbreak of the war, 5,427,636 were of American registry. But of this total, 4,702,652 tons were in use on the Great Lakes,

[20] *Annual Report of the Secretary of the Treasury . . . 1914*, pp. 71-74; A. D. Noyes, *The War Period of American Finance*, pp. 81-84.

[21] See below, pp. 133-134.

in river traffic, or in the coastwise trade, and a smaller amount was engaged on routes to South America and the Philippines. Only fifteen American ships, aggregating 153,526 tons, were in active service on transatlantic and transpacific routes, and all but six were passenger liners that carried little or no cargo.[22]

The dangers of this situation became painfully apparent during the period of the issuance of the war declarations in Europe from July 28 to August 4, 1914. Almost at once maritime commerce ceased to operate, as German and Austrian ships (aggregating nearly 5,500,000 tons) sought refuge in home or neutral ports and as British, French, and neutral European shipping lines canceled sailings. The Chargé at the German Embassy in Washington described the impact on the American economy in a few words: "The paralysis of ocean transportation, especially the total elimination of German merchant ships, has resulted in a complete congestion of the export trade. The docks are overcrowded with goods for export, for which no transportation can be found. Should it prove to be impossible to overcome this situation, America will not be able to bring to the European market this year's record crops on which great hopes were pinned."[23]

Of course, the paralysis was caused as much by the closing of the commodity markets abroad and the disruption of the system of international exchange as by the flight of ships from the sea lanes. And once Britain were in the war her navy would sweep the seas of German raiders and eventually make the routes of maritime commerce again secure. "All our plans," an unidentified high-ranking American official explained on August 3, the day before the British declared war, "are resting on the expectation that England will take her stand with France. That would preserve to us connection with Eastern Europe and give us an outlet for our big grain crop."[24] But it might be months before international trade had revived, and the American economy would meanwhile be prostrated.

Calling Democratic congressional leaders to the White House on July 31, the President described these dangers. The Austrian declaration of war against Serbia would, he said, probably lead to a general

---

[22] *Increased Ocean Transportation Rates, Letter from the Secretary of the Treasury and the Secretary of Commerce*, 63d Cong., 3d sess., Senate Document 673, Part 1, pp. 3-5; hereinafter cited as *Increased Ocean Transportation Rates*.

[23] Edgar K. Haniel von Haimhausen to the Foreign Office, August 8, 1914, German F. O. Archives.

[24] *New York Times*, August 4, 1914.

war that it would "require the blood of the whole world to extinguish." For six or eight months, until the British navy had done its work, German raiders would frighten British and other European shipping from the seas. Meanwhile the great American harvests would "waste in the warehouses," if they did not "rot in the fields." "My object in calling you gentlemen," Wilson went on, "was to lay before you the circumstances and to ask you to provide ships [to] . . . carry our commerce to all ports of the world." The upshot of the conference was agreement that Congress should adopt legislation as soon as possible to encourage foreign ships to register under the American flag, as the first step toward building an American merchant marine.[25]

Representative Oscar W. Underwood of Alabama, Democratic majority leader in the House, took charge of the matter and went at once to the Department of Commerce. There he and the Commissioner of the Bureau of Navigation drafted a new Ship Registry bill. It repealed the existing requirement that foreign-built ships be no more than five years old at the time they were admitted to American registry, and it authorized the President to suspend certain regulations governing the crew and the inspection of ships in the foreign trade of the United States.[26] Approved by Wilson, the bill was introduced in the House on August 3 and adopted unanimously following a brief debate on the same day.[27] The Senate added several important amendments,[28] but it then receded under strong pressure from the President[29] and approved the House version on August 17 by a vote of forty to twenty. The President signed it the next day.[30] "By this act," exulted the New York *World*, "many fine ships of foreign construction already owned by Americans may come under our flag at once without question. Taking advantage of its terms, some of the greatest merchantmen of the world, now useless by reason of war, may be lawfully added to our fleet by bonafide purchase. . . . We have stricken shackles from our commerce which can never be restored."[31]

[25] William C. Adamson, undated memorandum in the Baker Collection; New York *World*, August 1, 1914.

[26] *Congressional Record*, 63d Cong., 2d sess., p. 13173.

[27] *ibid.*, p. 13190; *New York Times*, August 4, 1914.

[28] The most important of these required that at least a majority of the stock of shipping firms seeking American registry for foreign-built vessels be owned by American citizens.

[29] W.W. to Senator Willard Saulsbury, August 15, 1914, Wilson Papers.

[30] *New York Times*, August 18 and 19, 1914.

[31] New York *World*, August 18, 1914. An important supplement to the Ship Registry Act was the measure proposed in the first instance by Secretary McAdoo to create a

What the *World's* editor predicted did in fact take place to a limited degree. Between August 18 and December 23, 1914, the American owners of 104 vessels totaling 372,488 gross tons, most of which had heretofore sailed under British and German flags, took advantage of the Ship Registry Act and hoisted the American ensign.[32] But what Wilson, McAdoo, and virtually all administration and congressional leaders hoped most would happen—either that American firms would purchase the 500,000 tons of German ships riding at anchor in American ports, or that their German owners would take out American registry for them—did not occur. The Allied governments would have confiscated any German-owned ships flying the American flag on the high seas, and the owners of the German vessels lying in American harbors were never so foolhardy as to send them out under a technical American registry. In the final reckoning, moreover, neither the British nor the French government would permit American citizens to purchase German ships for use in the general European trade.

This latter fact, however, was not at all clear while the Ship Registry bill was under debate in Congress.[33] Administration spokesmen in both houses time and again declared that no diplomatic difficulties could ensue, and the British government uttered no contradictory word. Consequently, almost everyone assumed that American firms or citizens would purchase the German ships as soon as the Ship Registry bill had become law. Indeed, officials of the Hamburg-American Line made the necessary legal arrangements to sell that company's fifteen ships lying in New York and Boston harbors, including the *Vaterland*, the largest passenger ship afloat, and they began negotiations with undisclosed persons looking toward the sale on August 15.[34]

Newspaper reports of this development stirred rumblings of protest

---

Bureau of War Risk Marine Insurance in the Treasury Department for the purpose of insuring American ships and cargoes whenever private companies refused to do so at reasonable rates. With the President's strong support, a bill appropriating $5,000,000 to put the Bureau of War Risk Marine Insurance into operation encountered little opposition in Congress and was approved on September 2, 1914. The Bureau operated throughout the period of American neutrality and participation in the war, collected premiums totaling $47,000,000, and made a net profit of about $17,000,000. W. G. McAdoo, *Crowded Years*, pp. 297-298.

[32] *Increased Ocean Transportation Rates*, pp. 17-19.

[33] Although the French government lodged a provisional warning against the transfer of German ships on August 4, 1914. Chargé Clausse to the Secretary of State, August 4, 1914, *Foreign Relations, 1914, Supplement*, p. 485.

[34] *New York Times*, August 15 and 16, 1914; New York *World*, August 16, 1914.

in London[35] and an indirect warning from the British government, relayed to the President through J. P. Morgan, that it would not hesitate to capture any former German ship flying the American flag, even one purchased in good faith by American citizens.[36] Wilson was astounded. "Surely if Mr. Morgan's information is correct as stated in the enclosed letter," he wrote to Lansing, asking for legal advice on the whole question of ship transfers during wartime, "the British Government is in danger of taking a very unjustifiable and high-handed action."[37]

It soon became evident that the British leaders were determined either to block the sale of the German ships entirely, or to make certain that they would never be used for Germany's benefit, but to do so as politely as possible and to avoid giving any offense at a time when other more serious difficulties with the United States impended. Thus Sir Edward Grey, the Foreign Secretary, intimated on August 21 that Great Britain would not object should the United States *government* purchase the ships and guarantee that they would never be used to supply Germany with noncontraband commodities like food, even through neutral ports. Indeed, Grey continued, the British government had itself been contemplating purchasing the German ships in American harbors, but it would gladly yield if the Washington authorities were determined to proceed on their own.[38] It was a clever counterstroke—reasonable on its face yet certain to achieve Grey's objectives. It avoided the direct issue of the purchase of German ships by American citizens, about which the British were not yet prepared to make a fight; best of all, from Grey's point of view, it suggested an alternative that was sure to avoid difficulties and serve British interests at the same time.

Wilson apparently did not read the messages conveying Grey's counterproposal; and Lansing, in telling the President that the British would not object to the sale under certain conditions of the German vessels to the United States or to American *citizens*, somewhat misinterpreted the dispatches.[39] Thus Wilson could write happily on Au-

[35] *New York Times*, August 17, 1914.

[36] J. P. Morgan to W.W., August 21, 1914, Wilson Papers.

[37] W.W. to R. Lansing, August 22, 1914, *ibid.*

[38] Ambassador Page to the Secretary of State, August 21, 1914, *Foreign Relations, 1914, Supplement*, pp. 489-490; E. Grey to Chargé C. Barclay, August 21, 1914, Wilson Papers.

[39] R. Lansing to W.W., August 24, 1914, *The Lansing Papers*, I, 101-103. Lansing's mistake was a natural one in view of the fact that the London government, because

gust 25, "I think that the situation is clearing up in a very satisfactory way."[40]

Actually the President's optimism did not seem unjustified, because only a few days earlier he had espoused a measure that would have averted entirely any diplomatic controversy over the transfer of the German ships to *private* American citizens. This was the Ship Purchase bill for the immediate formation of a large federally owned merchant fleet—the administration's boldest remedy for the revival of American foreign trade.

Proposals for some such action had been made and widely discussed ever since the outbreak of the war,[41] but it was McAdoo who conceived the administration's plan and took the initiative. At a conference with business and financial leaders at the Treasury on August 14 the Secretary listened to pleas that the government do something quickly to relieve the shipping crisis.[42] "One morning at dawn [probably on August 15]," McAdoo afterward remembered, "I was lying in bed, thinking about the matter, when it occurred to me that I might as well write out a tentative draft of a shipping bill which would embody the idea of a government-owned corporation. . . . In the course of the day I submitted this skeleton draft to the President and discussed its main features with him. He was favorably impressed with the idea, but said that he wanted to think it over for a day or so. He remarked that the government ownership of merchant ships, no matter how desperate the need . . . , would arouse the hostility of every reactionary in the United States. . . . When I saw the President again, he was strongly in favor of the plan that I had submitted. He handed me back the draft of the bill and said, with a smile, 'We'll have to fight for it, won't we?' 'We certainly shall,' I replied. 'Well, then, let's fight,' he said."[43]

---

of Britain's utter dependence upon its merchant fleet, had traditionally taken a liberal attitude toward ship transfers during wartime.

[40] W.W. to R. Lansing, August 25, 1914, *ibid.*, p. 103.

[41] On August 1, 1914, for example, Representative James M. Curley of Massachusetts urged the President to recommend the appropriation of $50,000,000 for the purchase of a fleet of fifty merchant vessels. J. M. Curley to W.W., August 1, 1914, Wilson Papers. Moreover, the Senate on August 3 had approved a bill introduced by John W. Weeks of Massachusetts authorizing the use of twenty-two naval transports for the temporary relief of the shipping crisis. New York *World*, August 4, 1914.

[42] *Annual Report of the Secretary of the Treasury . . . 1914*, pp. 4-8; New York *Sun*, August 15, 1914.

[43] W. G. McAdoo, *Crowded Years*, p. 296.

Wilson opened the campaign by summoning his party leaders and the committee chairmen in Congress who were immediately concerned[44] to the White House on August 19, 1914. McAdoo led off by describing the present paralysis of America's foreign trade. A great wheat crop was being harvested, he said, and some 50,000,000 bushels were already piled up in elevators and freight cars because of the lack of ocean shipping, while the railroads had placed an embargo on the shipment of any further grain to the congested ports of Galveston and New Orleans. The situation, moreover, would grow worse when the cotton crop began to move to market. It was, McAdoo concluded, a "radical situation that required heroic treatment"— immediate federal action to put ships on the seas. At the President's urging, the conferees approved McAdoo's plan, and the Secretary polished his draft of the Ship Purchase bill and sent it to the House and Senate commerce committees on the following day. It authorized the chartering of a corporation with a capital stock of $10,000,000, empowered to raise additional funds up to $30,000,000 through the sale of Panama Canal bonds. The corporation, which would be controlled by a Shipping Board composed of the Secretary of the Treasury, the Postmaster General, and the Secretary of Commerce, should purchase vessels and operate them in trade with Latin America "and elsewhere."[45]

Opposition broke out on Capitol Hill even before the bill could be formally introduced, on the ground mainly that federal operation of merchantmen would inevitably provoke grave international difficulties. As one editor put it, echoing these fears, "A fleet of government-owned merchant ships on the high seas means a daily and deadly tinder box for war."[46] Calling his congressional leaders back to the White House on August 21 and 22, Wilson assured them that such fears were groundless and then virtually demanded that they put the Ship Purchase bill through.[47] But the Democratic leaders, notably Representatives Joshua W. Alexander of Missouri and Oscar W. Underwood of Alabama, balked again, while undisclosed congressmen tried to relieve the pressure from the executive by telling reporters that the Pres-

[44] Senators James P. Clarke of Arkansas and Furnifold M. Simmons of North Carolina, and Representatives Oscar W. Underwood of Alabama and Joshua W. Alexander of Missouri.

[45] *New York Times*, August 20, 21, and 25, 1914.

[46] *Chicago Evening Post*, August 25, 1914.

[47] New York *World*, August 22 and 23, 1914.

ident was willing to wait to see whether private capital could fill the
need for shipping.[48] Wilson lashed back angrily in his press conference on the following morning. The report that he had sidetracked
the Ship Purchase bill was completely untrue, he asserted; on the contrary, he expected to see the measure approved within the next three
weeks.[49] He expressed the same determination a few days later in a
letter to a friend who had warned him of the dangers of the bill:

"I appreciate, I think, almost as keenly as you express them the difficulties and doubts about the ship purchase proposal, and yet sitting
here and hearing all sorts and varieties of suggestions it becomes
clearer to me day by day that private capital is not going to undertake
this thing on an adequate scale or in the most serviceable way without
asking for the very kind of government backing and support to which
I feel the deepest objection on principle not only, but because of some
interests that would be necessarily involved. The idea in the proposal
is not that the government should permanently embark in these
things, but that it should do the immediate and necessary thing."[50]

The pressure from the White House was too strong to be resisted,
and Representative Alexander, chairman of the House committee on
the merchant marine, and Senator James P. Clarke, chairman of the
Senate commerce committee, introduced the Ship Purchase bill in their
respective houses on about August 24, 1914. Spurred by the President,
Alexander's committee reported the measure favorably to the lower
house on September 8. During the ensuing two weeks Postmaster General Albert S. Burleson and other administration leaders threatened
and cajoled, but they could not persuade the House Democrats to consider the bill, much less to pass it. In the face of a warning that he
would split the party if he pushed any harder, Wilson finally relented
near the end of the session, but only after giving notice that he would
renew the fight when Congress reconvened in December. Meanwhile,
the Senate commerce committee had steadfastly refused to report the
Ship Purchase bill.[51]

Wilson failed in this opening round of what was destined to become
one of the hardest legislative battles of his career because he never succeeded in quieting public and congressional fears that the operation
of a merchant fleet by the Washington government, especially one

[48] *ibid.*, August 23, 1914.   [49] *New York Times*, August 25, 1914.
[50] W.W. to O. G. Villard, September 4, 1914, Wilson Papers.
[51] The foregoing is based upon accounts in the *New York Times*, August 31, September 3 and 26, 1914, and in the New York *World*, September 9 and 29, 1914.

consisting for the most part of former German vessels, would involve the United States in grave diplomatic complications with all the major belligerents. Although he had seemingly obtained Britain's approval of the purchase of the German ships, he could not divulge this apparent fact without violating the confidence of the London authorities; and he therefore had to rely upon the rather vague assurance to Congress and the public that there would simply be no diplomatic difficulties if the Ship Purchase bill went into operation.

Actually, it seems highly doubtful that Wilson gave much thought to the serious potentialities for international trouble of the measure that he was pushing so hard. British consent to the American operation of the German ships had been given on the explicit condition that they should never be used in any commerce with Germany, even through neutral European ports like Rotterdam. The British Ambassador in Washington stated his government's point of view succinctly, as follows:

"The President is in favour of a plan by which the Government will keep control over the ships acquired and will see to it that they do not perform unneutral services. . . . If the Government is responsible, then we can act directly through him in order to prevent infractions of neutrality. Thus I think on the whole that it is in our interest that the Government itself, and not individuals, should take the ships over; but we should, I think, make it very clear that we are making a concession, and that the President who professes entire neutrality is really rendering a great service to our enemy. In return for our concession he should show a real desire to prevent the unneutral use of the ships, and we should, I think, make a written statement of the conditions which we should object to."[52]

The scanty evidence that we possess indicates that Wilson accepted the consent without either comprehending or agreeing to the vital condition. Perhaps he did think that it would be possible to operate the federal shipping line (and the former German vessels) in trade only with neutral countries and the Allies. If so, then he was closing his eyes to inevitable difficulties with the German government and to the likelihood of nearly irresistible pressures at home for using the government's ships to carry noncontraband goods to Germany.

It seems likely that the President had not thought this far ahead, and that he was simply refusing to face what were the almost certain

[52] C. Spring Rice to E. Grey, August 25, 1914, *The Letters of Sir Cecil Spring Rice,* II, 219-220.

perils of his program. One is led to this conclusion by the way in which he ignored protests and opinions that would have jolted anyone sensitive to the international issues involved. When Jusserand, the French Ambassador, delivered a sharply worded verbal warning against the purchase of German ships at the White House on August 27, for example, the President only replied that there was food for thought in what Jusserand had said.[53] Then, when the Ambassador added an almost ominous formal protest a few days later,[54] the President apparently made no comment at all until early November 1914, when he mentioned the French objections in a letter to Secretary McAdoo.[55] Nor, presumably, was he disturbed when the Joint Neutrality Board, in an opinion rendered for Counselor Lansing on September 16, 1914, fully vindicated the French argument. Ambassador Jusserand's allegations, the Board declared, could not be refuted, as the Ship Registry Act of August 18 itself violated traditional law, and the purchase of German vessels by the United States would be an even graver infraction of neutrality.[56]

A second and more important reason for the failure of the first Ship Purchase bill was the fact that the shipping crisis disappeared while the congressional committees were considering McAdoo's measure. By mid-August the British navy had swept most German raiders from the seas, and by about the first of September there were no unusual impediments to commerce in the North Atlantic, except, of course, to Germany. Serious obstacles to the revival of American foreign trade still remained, but lack of shipping was not one of them. On the contrary, by September there were more bottoms than cargoes in American ports, and maritime transportation rates had returned

[53] "Ce que vous me dites va être pour moi l'occasion de bien sérieuses réflexions," Wilson said to Jusserand. R. Poincaré, *Au Service de la France*, v, summarizing Ambassador Jusserand to the Foreign Office, August 28, 1914.

[54] "The President of the United States," the note concluded after arguing that purchase of German ships would constitute a flagrant breach of America's neutrality, "in a memorable proclamation urged upon his fellow countrymen the most absolute neutrality in deed, in speech, even in thought. He cannot possibly approve a transaction so contrary to the views legitimately expressed by himself and allow his country *thus to take sides against us* in the solemn hour when the fate of France and also the fate of the ideas that France personifies are at stake." Ambassador Jusserand to the Secretary of State, September 3, 1914, *Foreign Relations, 1914, Supplement*, pp. 490-492; italics added.

[55] W.W. to W. G. McAdoo, November 8, 1914, Wilson Papers.

[56] Joint State and Navy Neutrality Board, "Note to the French Ambassador Concerning Purchase of German Merchant Ships," dated September 16, 1914, copy in the Anderson Papers.

to normal levels or below.[57] Thus the onward rush of events had deprived McAdoo and the President of their only effective argument for the Ship Purchase bill. Wilson admitted as much when he gave up the fight near the end of September.[58]

Over the broad reaches of the American continent the European storm broke with greatest fury in the South, spreading economic havoc in that fair region and stirring a controversy in Congress that was to culminate in a near rebellion against the President's leadership.

The South was in travail during the late summer and early autumn of 1914 because of the war-borne disasters that befell King Cotton, still the reigning monarch of the southern economy. Since 1897 Southerners had lived in a happy world of insatiable demand and rising prices for cotton. The crop of 1913 of a little more than 14,000,000 bales, the largest in American history to that date except for one year, had brought the excellent average price of 13½ cents a pound for the middling grade. Southerners had planted an even larger crop in the spring of 1914 (it would be the largest in American history) and had gone confidently into debt to finance it. The fate, not only of the four million people engaged directly in cotton production, but of almost every economic interest in the South, depended upon the fortunes of this crop. And those fortunes depended directly upon the export of some 9,000,000 bales abroad.

Disaster struck quickly and overwhelmingly with the outbreak of hostilities. The German and Austrian markets, which had taken 2,500,000 bales during the preceding year, disappeared as suddenly as the German merchant fleet fled from the seas; and there was no likelihood that American or neutral ships could be found soon to carry cotton to the Central Empires, even though the British government pledged that it would not interfere with such traffic and honored its promise at least for a time.[59] Worse still, within a week after the outbreak of the war the cotton exchanges in the Allied countries closed their doors because of the disruption of international exchange, thus barring a market that had purchased nearly 4,500,000 bales in the preceding twelve months. And when the exchanges in New York and New Orleans closed almost simultaneously, the normal market for cotton

[57] See the analysis in the New York *Journal of Commerce*, December 9, 1914, and the tables of monthly rates printed in *Increased Ocean Rates*, pp. 23-30.

[58] New York *World*, September 30, 1914.

[59] See below, p. 131.

simply ceased to exist. "A condition," one authority has written, "seemed to be foreshadowed for midwinter in which more than half of our 16,000,000-bale crop of 1914 would be left unsold and unsalable on the hands of producers who were in debt for the money spent to raise and harvest it."[60] In consequence, the price of cotton fell from 12½ cents a pound in July to between 6 and 7 cents a pound in mid-October 1914—when buyers could be found. For the South as a whole this meant a potential loss of half the value of the cotton crop, a total loss estimated by most contemporaries at $500,000,000 or more.[61]

Leaders in this section reacted vigorously with plans for action on the home front and appeals to Washington. E. J. Watson, Commissioner of Agriculture of South Carolina and president of the recently organized Southern Cotton Congress, took the lead on August 3, 1914, by inviting the President, the Secretaries of the Treasury and of Agriculture, and southern governors, senators, congressmen, bankers, and businessmen to meet in Washington on August 13 and 14—"The date fixed," Watson added, "is at the time when cheap round trip excursion rates are on sale"—to discuss means of coping with the crisis.[62] On the day following this call, the leaders of the southern delegations met in the Capitol to map political strategy.[63] The outcome of these initial maneuvers was the convening by Secretary McAdoo of a cotton conference to meet in the Pan-American Building in Washington on August 24.[64]

Panic had already seized the South and stimulated inchoate demands for unprecedented federal support of the cotton market by the time the so-called cotton conference opened. But it seemed that McAdoo, surrounded as he was by an impressive array of high administration officials and big-city bankers, had firm control as the 200-odd delegates assembled on August 24. "We will probably have to carry 4,000,000 bales of the cotton crop," he warned as he outlined his plan for meeting the crisis: the issuance of a sufficient quantity of "emergency"

[60] A. D. Noyes, *The War Period of American Finance*, p. 65.

[61] A. S. Link, "The Cotton Crisis, the South, and Anglo-American Diplomacy, 1914-1915," in J. C. Sitterson (ed.), *Studies in Southern History in Memory of Albert Ray Newsome*, p. 122.

[62] E. J. Watson, "To the People of the Cotton Belt," August 3, 1914, copy in the Papers of Daniel A. Tompkins, University of North Carolina Library; hereinafter cited as the Tompkins Papers.

[63] New York *World*, August 5, 1914.

[64] *ibid.*, August 19, 1914.

currency to southern national banks to enable farmers to carry the surplus until the market had revived.[65]

Spokesmen of the farmers held their tongues while McAdoo outlined his remedy but countered strongly on the following day, August 25. Frank B. Hayne of Louisiana led off by demanding that the Washington government valorize[66] the price of cotton at 8 cents a pound or $40 a bale. Denouncing McAdoo's plan as inadequate, Representative Thomas U. Sisson of Mississippi added an impassioned plea that state banks be permitted to issue currency based on warehouse receipts. Speaker after speaker rose to support this demand. Waiting until the furor had subsided, McAdoo now struck hard at the rebels. Valorization, he declared bitingly, was "a perfectly wild and ridiculous expedient and should not be resorted to in any circumstances." Nor could any responsible person contemplate the issuance of state bank notes. It would ruin the country, and it was unnecessary in any event, as the national banks could obtain more than enough "emergency" currency to meet the needs of the South. Finally, the Secretary of Agriculture, David F. Houston, an economist trained in the most orthodox school, rose to remind the cotton spokesmen that they lived under a government of laws, and that it would be folly for the federal authorities to attempt to determine the price of any commodity.[67]

Confidence momentarily returned to the South in the wake of McAdoo's assurances. It was buoyed in mid-September by a slight resumption of English buying, and by an increase in the price of cotton to 8 and 8½ cents a pound from the mid-August low of 6½ cents.[68] It was further encouraged by a "buy a bale of cotton" movement that

[65] *New York Times*, August 25, 1914; New York *Journal of Commerce*, August 25, 1914.

[66] This was a term that was much used during the cotton crisis. It means to maintain the price of a commodity at an arbitrary level, usually by governmental action.

[67] These proceedings are best reported in the *New York Times*, August 26, 1914, and the New York *Journal of Commerce*, August 26, 1914.

McAdoo outlined his relief plan in explicit detail in a public statement, which was also sent to the national banks, two days after the end of the cotton conference. He would issue "emergency" currency under the authority of the Aldrich-Vreeland Act to "National Currency Associations" in the South on a basis of four-month notes secured by warehouse receipts for cotton or tobacco, at 75 per cent of the face value of the notes. *Annual Report of the Secretary of the Treasury . . . 1914*, pp. 11-12. A special committee appointed by the Secretary recommended that national banks lend to farmers on a basis of 8 cents a pound for cotton. *ibid.*, p. 64.

[68] *New York Times*, September 22, 1914.

began in the South around September 1 and spread northward soon afterward.[69] "There is no reason, in my opinion," McAdoo announced reassuringly on September 21, "for pessimism in the South about cotton. The assistance which the Federal Government is extending to the banks . . . has already greatly improved the situation, and if the banks, the merchants, and the manufacturers throughout the South will quit taking counsel of fear and will go forward with confidence, the situation will, I believe, improve still further."[70]

Even while the Secretary spoke the crisis was nearing its severest stage. The harvesting of the crop was getting into full swing, and the inadequacy of McAdoo's measures was being clearly revealed. The basic cause of discontent was prices that failed even to cover the costs of production; it was compounded by the failure of the Aldrich-Vreeland Act's rather cumbersome currency machinery to provide sufficient credit. For one thing, loans of "emergency" currency secured by warehouse receipts had to be redeemed within four months—obviously too short a time for moving a cotton crop.[71] More important, most of the banks that served southern farmers and merchants could not join "National Currency Associations" and receive "emergency" currency because they were state-chartered institutions. And state banks often found it simply impossible to borrow "emergency" currency from the larger national banks.[72]

Fear revived and panic spread as cotton overflowed the warehouses for want of buyers. "It seems to me that unless we are given relief and that in short order," one South Carolina country banker wrote to the White House, "the whole south will be put into bankruptcy and ruin."[73] "This is a simple but pathetic echo of the ruin now running riot in the South," a Texas senator added. "May God in his infinite wisdom point us some path to safety."[74] "The deliberate judgment of our most capable thinkers," a group of bankers in Austin, Texas, warned, "is [that] without prompt and substantial help from

[69] New York *World*, September 9, 1914; *New York Times*, September 25, 1914.

[70] *ibid.*, September 22, 1914.

[71] As Governor Oliver B. Colquitt of Texas pointed out in O. B. Colquitt and C. H. Terrell to R. L. Henry, September 12, 1914, the Papers of Carter Glass, University of Virginia Library; hereinafter cited as the Glass Papers.

[72] As the editor of the *Progressive Farmer*, the most influential farm paper in the South, pointed out with telling effect, Clarence Poe to Josephus Daniels, October 5, 1914, Wilson Papers.

[73] J. W. Hamer to W.W., October 8, 1914, *ibid.*

[74] M. Sheppard to W.W., October 29, 1914, *ibid.*

the national government Texas will soon confront a condition of general bankruptcy. The condition grows more threatening every day."[75]

Something, southern leaders agreed, had to be done quickly, not by private groups or even by the states, for they were incompetent to deal with a crisis so overwhelming, but by the federal government itself. And when no new plan came from Washington, the National Farmers' Union, the organization representing most southern farmers, offered one on September 18 that seemed to promise definitive relief. It was to have the newly organized Federal Reserve Banks purchase three to four million bales of cotton at 12 cents a pound and Congress impose a tax of 10 cents a pound on all cotton grown in 1915 in excess of half the crop of 1914.[76] The Farmers' Union plan, with variations on the details, at once became the South's solution, and southern pressure for action along its lines began to mount in Washington.[77]

Controversy broke out on Capitol Hill near the end of September, when Secretary of Agriculture Houston, speaking presumably for the President, attempted to head off a cotton bloc then being formed in Congress by announcing that of course the administration could not approve any plan to support the price of cotton. Having done all it could do in the crisis, the federal government, Houston said, could not single out cotton growers for special benefits. And besides, he went on, federal price supports and any public regulation, whether state or federal, of cotton acreage would be unconstitutional. "It is not a question of sympathy—the cotton growers have the sympathy of the whole world in their distress—but a question of sound business and good government."[78]

Ignoring this reprimand, the cotton spokesmen in Congress, reinforced by representatives from the tobacco-growing districts, opened their offensive during the first week in October. The most articulate member of the group, Representative Robert L. Henry of Texas, a southern agrarian with strong cheap-money tendencies,[79] led off on October 2 by urging Secretary McAdoo to sell $200,000,000 worth of

[75] W. R. Hamby *et al.* to E. M. House, October 13, 1914, House Papers.

[76] S. G. McLendon to W.W., September 18, 1914, Wilson Papers.

[77] See, e.g., the resolutions adopted by the conference of southern governors and congressmen on September 29, *New York Times*, September 30, 1914; C. Poe to J. Daniels, October 5, 1914, cited above; and W. R. Hamby to E. M. House, October 14, 1914, House Papers.

[78] *New York Times*, September 29, 1914.

[79] For a characterization and an account of Henry's earlier leadership of the agrarian elements in Congress, see A. S. Link, *Wilson*, II, 218-222, 424.

Panama Canal bonds and deposit "several hundred million dollars" in southern banks. "In one short week," Henry promised, "he can rescue the South from ruin and a wild orgy of bankruptcies soon to ensue."[80] Then on October 7 and 8 representatives and senators from most of the southern states met in the House caucus room in the Capitol and formally organized a cotton-tobacco bloc, appointed a committee on strategy with Henry as chairman,[81] and drafted a relief bill, which Henry introduced on October 9. It instructed the Secretary of the Treasury to deposit $250,000,000 (to be raised either by the issue of Treasury notes or the sale of Panama Canal bonds) "in national banking associations and State banks situated in States producing cotton or tobacco, or both . . . to be advanced to the producers of cotton or tobacco, or owners of lands upon which the same was produced, . . . at a rate of interest not exceeding four per centum per annum."[82]

No longer could the President, who had taken no part in the public debate to this point, stand aside and speak only through his Cabinet officers. In an interview with a delegation from North Carolina on October 7 he announced his implacable opposition to all such emergency measures as the southern agrarians were pressing. There was already ample currency to meet every need, Wilson said, and the cotton crisis would have to be solved with the head and not the heart, "within the limitations of economic law and safe finance," and in such a way as not to disturb the "fabric" of the country's currency system.[83] The following day, moreover, the President told a group of Georgians that he did not favor plans to reduce cotton acreage in 1915. Such

[80] R. L. Henry and the Committee, "MEMORANDUM FOR THE PRESIDENT," October 2, 1914, Wilson Papers; also printed as R. L. Henry to W. G. McAdoo, October 2, 1914, *Congressional Record*, 63d Cong., 2d sess., pp. 16069-16070.

[81] The other members of the committee were Representatives E. W. Pou of North Carolina, K. D. McKellar of Tennessee, H. D. Stephens of Mississippi, D. E. Finley of South Carolina, E. W. Saunders of Virginia, D. M. Hughes of Georgia, T. H. Caraway of Arkansas, Scott Ferris and W. H. Murray of Oklahoma, J. J. Russell of Missouri, J. B. Aswell of Louisiana, and A. W. Barkley of Kentucky.

[82] R. L. Henry to C. Glass, October 9, 1914, Glass Papers, telling about the organization of the cotton-tobacco bloc and enclosing a copy of the bill; *New York Times*, October 10, 1914. Actually, the southern bloc's bill was offered as a substitute for a measure that Representative Henry had introduced on August 31, 1914, and which the House banking committee had tabled on October 8. Henry's first bill had instructed the Secretary of the Treasury to issue $500,000,000 in legal-tender notes to southern banks, to be lent to cotton producers at 3 per cent interest against the security of cotton valued at 10 cents a pound. For the text of this bill and a fervid defense by its author, see the *Congressional Record*, 63d Cong., 2d sess., pp. 16204-16208.

[83] *New York Times*, October 8, 1914.

plans, he said, had to be uniform and universal in order to succeed, and he did not see how they were possible.[84]

Thus the battle between the administration and the southern agrarians was clearly joined by the time that Representative Henry introduced the southern bloc's relief bill on October 9. The rebels made the halls of Congress ring during the next three weeks,[85] and spokesmen in the South added their voices to the rising din.[86] When Henry failed to win approval of his bill by the House banking committee, a group of senators led by Hoke Smith of Georgia[87] entered the fray on October 14 by introducing a cotton relief bill[88] as an amendment to the administration's emergency war revenue measure then pending before the Senate. Warning that they would not permit the latter bill to pass unless their cotton relief measure were also approved, they filibustered for several days but then finally surrendered. "We have made every effort that we can make," Senator Clarke of Arkansas exclaimed in the next to the final day of the session. ". . . The die has been cast. We are at our rope's end. . . . Nothing is to be gained by this sham battle."[89] Meanwhile, on October 21, Representative Henry had succeeded in forcing the House to consider his own bill, and it had failed of passage by a vote of ninety-one to 123.[90]

For all their effort the Southerners fought a losing battle from the beginning because they stood alone, without any support from the other sections. Worse still, for their cause, the administration not only was firm in opposition but also countered all their moves with greater strength. When Henry issued his first appeal on October 2, for example, McAdoo replied in a scathing public letter intended to expose

[84] *ibid.*, October 9, 1914.

[85] For the final phase of the controversy, see the running debates printed in *Congressional Record*, 63d Cong., 2d sess., Volume 51, Part 16, *passim*.

[86] e.g., the *Progressive Farmer* to "Dear Sir," form letter dated October 12, 1914, copy in the Glass Papers.

[87] In addition to Hoke Smith, this group included E. D. Smith of South Carolina, L. S. Overman of North Carolina, J. P. Clarke and J. T. Robinson of Arkansas, J. K. Shields of Tennessee, Morris Sheppard of Texas, J. K. Vardaman of Mississippi, and F. S. White of Alabama.

[88] It instructed the Secretary of the Treasury to issue $250,000,000 in bonds, to be exchanged directly with cotton planters for up to 5,000,000 bales of cotton valued at 10 cents a pound. It also imposed a tax of 2 cents a pound on all cotton produced in 1915 that exceeded 50 per cent of the crop of 1914. *Congressional Record*, 63d Cong., 2d sess., pp. 16594-16595.

[89] *ibid.*, p. 16960; also the New York *World*, October 18 and 23, 1914, and *New York Times*, October 23, 1914.

[90] *New York Times*, October 22, 1914.

the absurdity of the cotton bloc's plan.[91] Or again, when it seemed that Southerners on the Senate finance committee might vote to table the war revenue bill if it did not include their amendment for cotton relief, Postmaster General Burleson rushed to the Capitol to turn the tide in favor of the administration.[92] Looking back, we can see that the southern spokesmen did not exaggerate the dimensions of their region's plight, and that their plans for price supports and crop controls were by no means ridiculous, although they were the first of their kind. But it was not possible for a President and an administration still guided to a considerable degree by *laissez-faire* concepts to act in the only way that could have met the need effectively.

Something had to be done to allay the bitterness that was swelling in the South and to ease the deep and genuine concern that Wilson and McAdoo both felt. Neither could look upon the South's distress without remembering that its people were his own, and that it was the cornerstone of Democratic strength.[93] "I have spent more sleepless nights thinking about cotton than anything else with which I have had to deal since I took charge of the Treasury Department," McAdoo wrote on October 14, 1914.[94] "The thing that is giving us the greatest concern just now," Wilson added on the following day, "is the situation of the South in view of the tremendous curtailment of the market for her one marketable crop, the cotton. For a little it looked like bankruptcy, and that is among the disturbing possibilities yet."[95]

During the first two months of the cotton crisis, the administration, as we have seen, depended mainly upon its general measures for the strengthening of the financial structure and upon a revival of international trade for the relief of southern distress. There was, besides, one early supplementary measure—a bill prepared by Secretary Houston and sponsored by A. F. Lever of South Carolina in the House and Hoke Smith in the Senate, to establish federal inspection and licensing of agricultural warehouses and thus to facilitate borrowing

[91] W. G. McAdoo to R. L. Henry, October 9, 1914, printed in *ibid.*, October 10, 1914.

[92] New York *World*, October 18, 1914.

[93] Unlike the investment banker of Boston, Henry L. Higginson, who observed: "The cotton men can stand low prices perfectly well, and any sensible man will tell you that men do not need to make money every year." H. L. Higginson to W.W., October 22, 1914, Wilson Papers.

[94] W. G. McAdoo to J. Daniels, October 14, 1914, the Papers of Josephus Daniels, Library of Congress; hereinafter cited as the Daniels Papers.

[95] W.W. to Mrs. Crawford H. Toy, October 15, 1914, Baker Collection.

by farmers against warehouse receipts.[96] The bill passed the Senate on August 24 and then ran afoul the opposition of eastern representatives and of the embittered southern agrarians in the lower house. Combining with the Easterners, the Southerners on October 5 defeated a motion to suspend the rules and put the Smith-Lever bill on the calendar.[97] All the pressure that the administration could apply, including a personal appeal from President Wilson,[98] failed to budge the cotton rebels from their determination to have their own bill or none at all.

Meanwhile, the President and his friends had found a plan that seemed to promise a sure and safe remedy. It was the suggestion, first made by Festus J. Wade, president of the Mercantile National Bank of St. Louis, on October 5, 1914, that private bankers combine to create a fund of $150,000,000 to be lent to southern farmers so they could hold their cotton for at least a year.[99] It was the first ray of hope that administration leaders had seen on the southern horizon, and they hastened to make the cotton-loan plan the cornerstone of their program for southern relief. As Colonel House explained to the President, "This is an emergency matter of the greatest importance and the ordinary technicalities and niceties should not be allowed to stand in the way. The South feels that a calamity has come upon them much as a flood, fire or any other such devastating element and they can never be made to believe that the Government should not in some way come to their relief. If this plan goes through, they will be satisfied that the Administration has met the emergency."[100]

The necessary arrangements were, therefore, quickly made. High-level discussions began in Washington on October 9, while Colonel House set to work on the same day to insure the participation of his

[96] For the text, see *Congressional Record*, 63d Cong., 2d sess., pp. 16189-16190.

[97] The motion, which required a two-thirds majority, was lost by the narrow margin of 164 yeas to 109 nays, with southern agrarians like Henry, Sisson of Mississippi, and Sam Rayburn of Texas cast the deciding votes against immediate consideration. *ibid.*, p. 16210.

[98] "The passage of the cotton warehouse bill," the President wrote to Representative Henry, "seems to me an essential measure for the relief, or partial relief, of the South. It is one of the concrete things that we can do and should do. May I not urge that you use every endeavor to promote its immediate passage?" W.W. to R. Henry, October 22, 1914, Wilson Papers.

[99] New York *Journal of Commerce*, October 6, 1914.

[100] E. M. House to W.W., October 14, 1914, Wilson Papers.

friends in Wall Street.[101] Four days later he won their promise of a $50,000,000 subscription to the cotton-loan fund.[102] The Federal Reserve Board gave its blessing on October 24 and agreed to administer the fund, while the Attorney General two weeks later affirmed that the arrangement would be legal in every way.[103] "If this cotton Loan fund can be put through," Wilson wrote soon afterward in support, "I shall feel that we are on the high road to a real recovery and re-generation of our business."[104]

In response to pleas like this one, bankers everywhere except in New England[105] rallied in support; the cotton-loan fund, the amount of which had meanwhile been reduced to $135,000,000, had been raised by November 17, 1914; and the plan went into operation on November 30. "We believe," McAdoo exulted in a public statement on the day the full amount of the fund was raised, "that the carrying out of this plan is going to be beneficial, not only in helping the cotton situation and the foreign exchange situation, but also by promoting the general prosperity of the country, which now has such a happy impulse that it would be difficult to retard it."[106]

McAdoo's hopes were, unfortunately, never realized. Never did a project launched with such fanfare and expectation fail more resoundingly or quickly than the cotton-loan fund of 1914. This was true because the Central Committee, composed of the members of the Federal Reserve Board, which set the terms upon which the money might be

---

[101] *New York Times*, October 10, 1914; E. M. House to W.W., October 9, 1914, Wilson Papers.

[102] E. M. House to W.W., October 14, 1914, *ibid.*, House Diary, October 13, 1914.

[103] *New York Times*, October 25, 1914; T. W. Gregory to W.W., November 6, 1914, Wilson Papers.

[104] W.W. to H. L. Higginson, November 16, 1914, *ibid.*

[105] New England bankers and manufacturers were not only unwilling to abet any plan to maintain or increase the price of raw cotton but also tried in various ways to thwart the completion of the cotton-loan fund. Boston banks subscribed only $2,085,-000 to the fund, as compared with the $53,000,000 subscribed by banks in New York, the $13,000,000 by banks in Chicago, and the $11,500,000 by banks in Saint Louis. "The success of this plan has at no time been in doubt," McAdoo declared in a public statement announcing the completion of the fund, "but its completion has been delayed by the selfish opposition of certain textile manufacturers and local interests who have tried to defeat it." *New York Times*, November 18, 1914. For evidence of the New England opposition to which McAdoo was referring, see Josiah Quincy to E. M. House, October 28 and November 9, 1914, House Papers; *Financial Age*, xxx (November 14, 1914), 917; St. Louis *Star*, November 16, 1914; New York *Sun*, November 16, 1914; and Boston *Transcript*, November 19, 1914.

[106] *New York Times*, November 18, 1914.

borrowed, acted as if it were determined that none of it should ever be used. Announced on November 30, these terms permitted loans to farmers against warehouse receipts for cotton that would run for one year and might be renewed for an additional six months. Such loans were to be made against cotton valued at 6 cents a pound, but with a margin of 20 per cent above the face value of the loan. This meant that the farmer in the end could borrow only 5 cents a pound on cotton.[107] For all the tightness of credit, southern farmers could get better terms than these through ordinary banking channels, especially after the Federal Reserve System went into operation on November 16, 1914. By the time the cotton-loan fund went out of existence on February 1, 1915, consequently, the Central Committee had approved only seven loans totaling $28,000.[108]

Actually, the failure of the project had no catastrophic consequences, for other developments, notably the resumption of English and German buying, were bringing an end to the worst phase of the crisis in the closing months of 1914. But the failure did leave a residue of bitterness in the South and a lingering suspicion that the administration in Washington and bankers in the North had never intended that the cotton-loan fund should succeed. "There is no doubt," one of President Wilson's strongest friends in Texas complained, for example, "but what the cotton loan plan is badly balled up and has produced a very acute situation. . . . It is a matter of common rumor in banking circles in Texas that bankers in the North and East have stated that it was not intended by at least some of the subscribers to the fund that the money subscribed should be actually used; that the condition should be made so onerous and unworkable that it would not be used, and that in this way it would serve the purpose of 'jollying the South,' without really giving them any financial relief."[109] Or, to cite a second example, there was the following volley fired by the Governor of Texas, Oliver B. Colquitt: "The President stood in the road and condemned the South, which made him, to heavier loss and more widespread misery than it has known in three generations. He vindicated

[107] *New York Times*, December 9, 1914. In all fairness to the Central Committee it should be pointed out that these were the terms upon which the New York bankers had insisted at the time they agreed to subscribe to the cotton-loan fund. Frank A. Vanderlip, president of the National City Bank, had originally suggested lending on cotton valued at 4 cents a pound! House Diary, October 13, 1914.

[108] *New York Times*, February 3, 1915.

[109] Thomas B. Love to E. M. House, December 13, 1914, House Papers; for additional revealing comment, see the *Financial Age*, xxx (November 21, 1914), 943.

an obsolete theory of political economy but he mighty near ruined the country by doing it."[110]

Meanwhile, the President and Secretary McAdoo had been hard at work in all the furor of the cotton crisis on a solution of the last of the major domestic crises created by the war—the somewhat dire plight of the federal Treasury in August and September of 1914. This occurred because the federal government then depended upon customs receipts for about two fifths of all its general revenues; and they declined so sharply in the wake of the disorganization of international trade that overnight the administration was confronted with the prospect of a deficit of from sixty to one hundred million dollars for the coming fiscal year. Either the government would have to borrow the money or raise it by new taxes, and the latter choice was not particularly appealing to congressmen and senators about to go before the voters for re-election.

Wilson made the decision himself soon after his return from Mrs. Wilson's funeral in Georgia. Calling the chairmen of the tax-raising committees of Congress, Representative Underwood and Senator Furnifold M. Simmons of North Carolina, to his office on August 17, he declared that he would insist upon new taxes, and that he would take personal responsibility for legislation to raise them.[111] Then on September 4 he went briefly before a joint session to describe the emergency and suggest a remedy. "Conditions have arisen which no man foresaw," he declared as he read from the small sheets upon which he had typed the message. "They affect the whole world of commerce and economic production; and they must be faced and dealt with." The answer, he went on, lay neither in using the Treasury's surplus funds, for that would mean calling in federal deposits scattered in banks throughout the country, nor in borrowing, for that would also deplete banking resources and was unnecessary in any event. The proper remedy, he maintained, was the imposition of internal taxes to assure an additional revenue of $100,000,000.[112]

McAdoo, Underwood, and Simmons had already agreed upon a draft measure that relied exclusively upon new excise taxes to meet the deficit, but the southern agrarian majority took control when the Dem-

[110] Fort Worth *Star-Telegram*, December 27, 1914.

[111] New York *World*, August 18, 1914.

[112] Ray S. Baker and William E. Dodd (eds.), *The Public Papers of Woodrow Wilson, The New Democracy*, I, 160-163; hereinafter cited as *The New Democracy*.

ocratic members of the House ways and means committee assembled on September 7 to prepare a tax bill. The South had suffered enough, they asserted in an open display of sectional bitterness; let the industrial North and the grain-producing states, which stood to profit from the war, carry the burden. Following such sentiments, they proceeded to draft a bill to raise $100,000,000, one third from increased income taxes, one third from additional levies on beer and wines, and one third from a new impost on railroad freight bills.[113]

It was the beginning of a controversy that would not end until Congress had adjourned on October 24, 1914. Calling Underwood and Simmons back to the White House on the morning after the ways and means committee had completed its bill, the President announced that the provision for increased income taxes would have to be deleted. The government needed immediate revenue, he said, and income taxes could be collected only in June and July of 1915. "We will have to start all over again," Underwood told reporters as he left the White House.[114] It was quickly done. Meeting on September 10, the Democratic members of the ways and means committee eliminated the income tax provision and nearly doubled the tax on railroad freight.[115] But this stirred such protest that the war revenue bill seemed destined to defeat even before Underwood's committee could report it to the House. So overwhelming was the opposition, in fact, that its leaders had no trouble in obtaining enough signatures of Democratic members for a petition to force the calling of a party caucus.[116]

The President met this challenge cheerfully, as he did not particularly care where the revenue came from so long as it came quickly. Conferring with Underwood, Simmons, McAdoo, and Burleson at the White House on September 15, before the House caucus met, he agreed to yield the tax on freight shipments and to accept a bill that the majority of House Democrats would approve. As described by Underwood, it levied additional taxes of $40,500,000 on beer and domestic wines; new taxes on tobacco manufacturers and dealers and on gasoline, to raise $24,000,000; a special impost on bankers and brokers, to yield $5,800,000; and a stamp tax on bonds, bills of sale, drafts, mortgages, and the like, to bring in some $35,000,000. Aimed as it was at "wet" northern and midwestern big cities and at the business com-

[113] *New York Times,* September 8 and 9, 1914.
[114] New York *World,* September 10, 1914.
[115] *New York Times,* September 11, 1914.
[116] *ibid.,* September 12, 13, 15, 1914.

munity, the new measure was enthusiastically approved by the House caucus on September 15, and it passed the House by the huge majority of 234 to 135 on September 25. Only eleven Democrats voted against the bill; seven of them were still-disgruntled southern agrarians.[117]

The Southerners, however, had not yet completed their sectional refinements. Taking charge when the Senate Democratic caucus considered the war revenue bill on October 6, they added amendment after amendment that made the measure even more discriminatory than it was when it passed the House. Thus they struck out the provision for a tax on gasoline, because southern farmers presumably also drove automobiles; raised the tax on tobacco manufacturers sharply; increased the tax on beer and wines and added a new one on brandies, which Southerners allegedly did not drink; and added taxes on patent medicines, cosmetics and perfumes, and places of amusement. The caucus completed its work on October 7, but the administration leaders in the Senate were unable to obtain action by the upper house itself until ten days later because the leaders of the cotton bloc were still trying to add amendments for relief of the South.[118] The conference committee, meeting on October 20 and 21, accepted all the important Senate changes except the further increase in the tax on beer and the new tax on rectified spirits.[119] Both houses approved the conference report on October 22, 1914, and Wilson rushed from the golf course to the President's room in the Capitol to sign the measure at 5:45 p.m. on the same day.[120]

Thus did the American people and their leaders meet the problems and crises provoked in their own land by the outbreak of Armageddon. And so did the man who carried the heaviest burdens fight through his overwhelming personal sorrow to renewed leadership in time of national trouble.

[117] *ibid.*, September 16 and 26, 1914; *Congressional Record*, 63d Cong., 2d sess., p. 15772.

[118] *New York Times*, October 7, 8, and 18, 1914.

[119] The conference report is printed in *Congressional Record*, 63d Cong., 2d sess., pp. 16906-16909.

[120] *New York Times*, October 23, 1914.

CHAPTER IV

Accepting the British Maritime System

FOR Woodrow Wilson and the men in the State Department who advised him, the primary objective in foreign policy once the war in Europe had begun was to win the largest possible freedom of trade with all belligerents for American citizens, within the bounds of neutrality. It could not have been otherwise in view of the political and economic pressures at home for the unfettered export of American raw materials and manufactured goods and the right of American ships to sail where they pleased, to say nothing of the Washington government's determination to pursue policies that were strictly impartial. Such demands and determinations soon collided with an equally powerful force, namely, the resolution of the British government to use its great fleet, protector of the realm and empire, to cut off the flow of life-giving supplies to the Central Powers. In those troubled times Britain was mistress of the seas in fact as well as in name; with one arm of her fleet she could keep the Imperial Germany Navy at bay and with the other exercise a watchful control over all the sea lanes from the New World to western Europe.

For Wilson and his colleagues, then, the first external problem of neutrality was the easily stated but awesomely difficult one of finding the line where the rights of British sea power under international law and custom ended and the rights of American trade began. The trouble was that the proper relation between belligerent pretensions and neutral claims could not always be clearly defined by appealing to international law. Although it had been partially codified by various international conferences and scholars, it remained ambiguous on the most important points of potential conflict. Worse still, its essential principles governing blockade and warfare at sea, having been adopted during the eighteenth and nineteenth centuries, would be difficult if not impossible to apply in an age when technology had rendered many of the old methods obsolete.

These difficulties were oppressively apparent to the men in Washington during the first days of the war. How could the United States

obtain the greatest freedom of trade possible and avoid the controversies that were inevitable if it based its claims upon the contradictory body of international law? To the learned and practical Counselor Lansing, the answer came almost as soon as Great Britain entered
the war: there would be few disputes over trade if only the belligerents would agree to adopt the body of rules known as the Declaration
of London as their code of maritime warfare. As Lansing wrote afterward, the Declaration "seemed available in the emergency and most
probable of unanimous acceptance by the maritime powers involved
in or affected by the war. The Government felt that by the general
adoption of the Declaration, the differences of opinion as to the rights
and duties of nations in time of war, which have heretofore been the
cause of controversy long after a war ended, would be in large measure
removed in the present conflict."[1]

What Lansing wrote was unquestionably true insofar as it went.
The Declaration, which had been drafted and approved by an international conference in London in 1908-1909, did provide an elaborate
and specific set of rules. But an even greater advantage from the American point of view was the fact that these rules were immensely beneficial to neutral rights of trade during wartime. To be sure, they confirmed the right of belligerents to capture the two categories of contraband goods, absolute and conditional,[2] when neutrals carried them
to the enemy. However, they set up a long so-called free list of essen-
tail raw materials, including cotton, rubber, wool, and copper, which
could never be transferred to the contraband list; threw numerous
safeguards around neutral ships at sea; and cast grave doubt upon the
right of a belligerent to capture conditional contraband consigned to
neutral ports, even though its eventual destination was an enemy country, thus perhaps negating the old doctrine of continuous voyage.[3] The
advantages that would have accrued to American and other neutral
trade from the adoption of these limitations upon sea power are at

[1] R. Lansing, "THE NEGOTIATIONS FOR THE ADOPTION OF THE DEC-
LARATION OF LONDON . . . ," memorandum dated February 1, 1915, *The Lansing
Papers*, 1, 268.

[2] Absolute contraband consisted of goods obviously destined for the armed forces
of a belligerent, such as munitions and raw materials used primarily for war production. Conditional contraband consisted of goods or commodities that might be used by
armed forces, such as foodstuffs, clothing, and the like.

[3] For the text of the Declaration of London, see *Papers Relating to the Foreign Relations of the United States, 1909*, pp. 318-333.

once apparent: it would have meant the virtual abrogation of all controls over neutral trade except traffic in obvious contraband.

We do not know how the decision was made (probably Lansing first suggested it on August 4 or 5 and Wilson and Bryan approved at once), but on August 6, 1914, the Secretary of State dispatched a note to the principal belligerents asking if they would agree to follow the rules of naval warfare laid down by the Declaration of London.[4] The German and Austrian Foreign Offices, naturally delighted by the prospect of so easily obtaining such restraints on the sea power of their enemies, replied eagerly, saying that their governments had already put the Declaration into force and would continue to observe it if their enemies followed suit.[5] Everything, of course, depended upon the reply from London. It arrived over the State Department's wire in Washington on August 26. His Majesty's Government, the British Foreign Office declared, had decided to follow the rules of the Declaration of London in general, but would have to make certain modifications "which they judge indispensable to the efficient conduct of their naval operations." Among these were new regulations, which had been specified in an Order in Council on August 20, providing for the capture of neutral ships on the high seas when their enemy destination could be inferred "from any sufficient evidence," and permitting the capture of conditional contraband consigned to a neutral port when it was destined ultimately for the Central Powers.[6]

Given the compelling necessity, as the British saw it, of throttling neutral trade in strategic materials to the Central Powers, the reply from London was the only one that was possible. No government that promised to concede virtual freedom of the seas could have survived for an hour at Whitehall. But in refusing to be bound fully by the Declaration of London, the leaders in the British Cabinet were acting not merely inevitably but also well within the bounds of accepted practice. The Declaration might have embodied the most humane and liberal concepts of naval warfare at the time, but it had never been ratified by the British and American governments, and, except as it codified accepted statutes, it was not a part of the body of international law. Even had it been, the British probably would have

---

[4] The Secretary of State to Ambassador Page and to other Ambassadors, August 6, 1914, *Foreign Relations, 1914, Supplement*, p. 216.

[5] Ambassador Gerard to the Secretary of State, August 10, 1914; Ambassador Penfield to the Secretary of State, August 13, 1914, *ibid.*, pp. 216-217.

[6] Ambassador Page to the Secretary of State, undated, transmitting a note from the Foreign Office dated August 22, 1914, *ibid.*, pp. 218-220.

violated it because it gave such an enormous advantage to the land-locked Central Powers.[7]

Lansing pondered the British reply and the response that should be made during late August and early September of 1914. He discussed some aspects of the problem with the Joint Neutrality Board and certain legal authorities, including, perhaps, Cone Johnson, Solicitor of the State Department. But insofar as we can tell, he did not discuss the matter with the President; nor could he confer with the Secretary of State, for Bryan was on the hustings in various parts of the country during these busy weeks of the congressional campaign of 1914. We know, however, that the Counselor was profoundly disturbed by the prospect of endless and potentially dangerous Anglo-American controversies and, moreover, felt a heavy pressure from American public opinion, from domestic producers and exporters, and from the German government, which on September 2 had sent a strong protest against recent French and British violations of the Declaration of London.[8] Some action, it seemed, had to be taken, for as Ray Stannard Baker has written, "The British not only stood upon the alterations and exceptions they had already announced, but on September 21st added a number of raw materials to the list of conditional contraband, chief among them copper, one of Germany's principal needs and an important American export. A number of cargoes on their way to neutral ports were stopped, and a fresh clamour arose among American business men. The situation was daily becoming more difficult; many of the complaints of the cotton, copper, and other producers and exporters were sent directly to the President."[9]

During the last week in September Lansing must have decided that further efforts to persuade the British to follow the Declaration of London were futile and that the time had come for a vigorous assertion of American neutral rights and a sweeping denunciation of the emerging British system of maritime warfare. With a memorandum prepared by James Brown Scott of the Joint Neutrality Board

[7] As Sir Edward Grey, the British Foreign Secretary at the time, has intimated. Viscount Grey of Fallodon, *Twenty-Five Years, 1892-1916,* II, 106.

[8] Ambassador Gerard to the Secretary of State, September 2 (received September 16), 1914, *Foreign Relations, 1914, Supplement,* pp. 224-225.

[9] R. S. Baker, *Woodrow Wilson: Life and Letters,* v, 204-205. For the British action putting copper, rubber, and other raw materials on the list of *conditional* contraband, see Ambassador Page to the Secretary of State, September 30, 1914, *Foreign Relations, 1914, Supplement,* p. 236.

as a guide,[10] Lansing set to work on his own and completed the draft of a long note of protest and warning on September 26. It reviewed the State Department's unsuccessful efforts to obtain mutual adoption of the Declaration of London, accused the British of establishing a paper blockade and of threatening to disregard neutral rights altogether in the matter of conditional contraband, and reserved all rights which the United States enjoyed under international law respecting any losses that American citizens might suffer in consequence of British procedures. Concluding, the Acting Secretary of State struck a distinctly ominous note, as follows:

"It is a matter of grave concern to this Government that the particular conditions of this unfortunate war should be considered by His Britannic Majesty's Government to be such as to justify them in advancing doctrines and advocating practices which in the past aroused strong opposition on the part of the Government of the United States, and bitter feeling among the American people. The Government feels bound to express the fear, though it does so reluctantly, that the publicity, which must be given to the rules which His Majesty's Government announce that they intend to enforce, will awaken memories of controversies, which it is the earnest desire of the United States to forget or to pass over in silence. This Government in view of these considerations ventures to suggest in no unkindly spirit and with the sole purpose of preserving the mutual good will which now exists between the people of the United States and the people of Great Britain, that the British Government may find it possible to modify their intention before it has been put into practice, as its realization seems fraught with possible misunderstandings which the United States desires at all times to avoid."[11]

On the following day, September 27, Lansing laid the entire matter before the President by sending to the White House a huge package that contained a copy of his draft note, nearly one hundred and fifty pages of documents relating to the recent British maritime measures, which Page had sent from London, and memoranda by the Joint Neutrality Board and an American legal scholar. "I am sorry to disturb you today," the Acting Secretary of State wrote in a covering letter, "but I think it very desirable that the enclosed enstruction [*sic*]

[10] Charles C. Tansill, *America Goes to War*, p. 141, prints an excerpt from this memorandum.

[11] The Acting Secretary of State to Ambassador Page, September 26, 1914, *Foreign Relations, 1914, Supplement*, pp. 225-232.

to Mr. Page at London, if it meets with your approval, should go forward by tomorrow's pouch, which closes at 2 P.M. . . . I cannot but feel that the action of the British Government calls for unqualified refusal of this Government to acquiesce in its legality and that our objections should be clearly and firmly stated. The British Order in Council will suggest to you, I think, the obnoxious Orders in Council of the Napoleonic Wars, and will, if its provisions are called to public attention in this country, cause severe criticism in the press."[12]

Almost as if Fate had decreed it to happen, Colonel House arrived in Washington at about the same hour that Lansing was completing this letter to the President, and Wilson, House, and the McAdoos were enjoying a quiet after-dinner conversation when Lansing's package arrived at the White House. "This was the signal for . . . the family to leave," House recorded in his diary, "and the President and I immediately got down to work." House, at least, was shocked by the severity of the language in Lansing's draft note, perceived the significance of sending such a protest to London at this time, and urged Wilson not to permit it to be sent. Obviously tired and in no mood for controversy, the President called the Acting Secretary of State by telephone and asked him to prepare a briefer dispatch to Page and to delay sending his long protest. "I then suggested," House further related, "that he permit me to have a conference with Sir Cecil Spring-Rice and get at the bottom of the controversy. He expressed warm approval of this plan. After this we went to bed, pretty tired and somewhat worried."[13]

Events moved swiftly on the following day toward the adoption of a milder method of confronting the British maritime system. Colonel House met the British Ambassador at ten o'clock and permitted him to read Lansing's draft note. "He was thoroughly alarmed over some of the undiplomatic expressions," House wrote soon afterward. "One paragraph in particular [the last, probably] he thought amounted almost to a declaration of war. He said that if that paper should get into the hands of the press, the headlines would indicate that war with Great Britain was inevitable, and he believed one of the greatest

[12] R. Lansing to W.W., September 27, 1914, the Papers of the Department of State, the National Archives; hereinafter cited as the State Department Papers.

[13] House Diary, September 27, 1914. Compare this account with the highly embellished and excited one that House related to the British Ambassador, in which House said that Wilson had been astonished by Lansing's draft and had declared that it "could not go at once." See C. Spring Rice to E. Grey, October 1, 1914, *The Letters of Sir Cecil Spring Rice*, II, 233.

panics the country ever saw would ensue, for it was as bad or worse than the Venezuelan incident."[14] What Spring Rice was desperately eager to avoid was any public protest at all by the American government, but particularly one that would, when published, make Washington's essential acceptance of the British maritime system virtually impossible. As House told the story:

"We discussed the best ways and means of getting out of the difficulty, which he said would never have arisen if the State Department had talked the matter over with him frankly in the beginning. His Government's attitude had been known at the State Department for a month, and yet not a word of objection had been raised. If he had known what the feeling of this country was he would have taken it up with his Government, and their attitude would have been modified. As it was, they had already published their intention of doing the things to which our Government objected, and it would be difficult to handle it now in a way to save the *amour propre* of his Government."[15]

House rushed from this conference to the White House to report to the President. It was then, probably, that Wilson agreed that Lansing should send no open formal protest to the Foreign Office,[16] but should, instead, begin private conversations with the London government to see if some agreement could be found. House left shortly after eleven, and Lansing came to talk about the brief telegram that the

[14] House Diary, September 28, 1914. This, undoubtedly, is what Spring Rice told House. Actually, however, the Ambassador was not quite as upset as he was careful to give the impression of being. He related the episode to the British Foreign Secretary as follows: "I had suspected for some time that something was up among the lawyers in the State Department, but I could extract no hint of what was intended. The only indication was a rather unfriendly atmosphere. I received one day a sudden message from a friend of yours here [House], who said he wished to see me. . . . I saw it [Lansing's draft note] and was really astonished at the tone in *one or two of the sentences*. I *merely* remarked that if it went off as it was, there would be a big catastrophe equal to, or worse than, that brought on by Cleveland's Venezuelan despatch." C. Spring Rice to E. Grey, October 1, 1914, *The Letters of Sir Cecil Spring Rice*, II, 223; italics added.

[15] House Diary, September 28, 1914.

[16] Lansing sent his draft note of September 26 to Secretary Bryan on September 29 and, undoubtedly with the approval of the President, mailed a copy to Page on October 1, with the instruction that Page should read the note only for his own information and should not present it to the Foreign Office until he was specifically directed to do so. See R. Lansing to W. J. Bryan, September 29, 1914, *The Lansing Papers*, I, 249, and the Secretary of State to Ambassador Page, October 1, 1914, *Foreign Relations, 1914, Supplement*, p. 239.

President had asked him to prepare. Lansing wrote his draft soon afterward and forwarded it to Wilson for his approval, probably in the mid-afternoon. The President made a number of changes in the text, and Lansing sent it to Page in London by wire at nine o'clock in the evening of the same day, September 28. It follows as Wilson edited it, with the deletions that he made in Lansing's text enclosed within brackets and his own additions printed in italics:

"Strictly Confidential. You will immediately see Sir Edward Grey and state to him informally *and confidentially* that this Government [has given careful consideration to] *is greatly disturbed by* the intention of the British Government to change the provisions of the Declaration of London by the Order in Council of the twentieth August and to adopt the Declaration thus changed as the code of naval warfare for the present war. This Government [as the result of its examination,] feels grave concern at all of the proposed changes, especially those in Articles three and five of the Order in Council, which so materially affect the rights of neutral commerce. If the proposed rules are *sought to be* put into force and the matter becomes the subject of public discussion in this country, as it undoubtedly will, it is to be [feared] *confidently expected* that it will arouse a spirit of resentment among the American people toward Great Britain, which this Government would extremely regret but which it would be unable to prevent. You will also point out that the enforcement of these rules by the British Government would furnish to those inimicable to Great Britain an opportunity, which they would not be slow to seize, *and which they are already using in our press upon the mere publication of the Order.*

"Paragraph. You will further say that the President *earnestly* desires [, if possible,] to avoid a formal protest to those proposed rules and their enforcement and hopes that the British Government will [carefully] *be willing to* consider the advisability of modifying [the objectionable] *these* features of the Order in Council, which possess such latent possibilities. [of disturbing the existing relations between the peoples of the two countries.]

"You will impress upon Sir Edward Grey the *President's conviction of the* extreme gravity of the situation and [the] *his* earnest wish [of the President] to avoid *even* causes of irritation and controversy between this Government and the Government of his Majesty.

"In presenting the substance of this instruction to Sir Edward Grey you will assure him [that it is done in the most friendly spirit.] *of the earnest spirit of friendship in which it is sent. The President is anxious*

*that he should realize that the terms of the Declaration of London
represent the limit to which this Gov't could go with the approbation
and support of its people.*

"Telegraph result of interview as soon as possible."[17]

This entire affair, from the framing of Lansing's note of protest
of September 26 through the sending of the telegram of September
28, has been rightly regarded as an important milestone in the official
American response to the British maritime system. But its significance
has never been correctly understood, mainly because it has been assumed, even by his most hostile critics, that Colonel House succeeded
materially in weakening the firm position that Lansing had proposed
that the Washington government should take.[18]

As we have seen, House did prevent the dispatch of Lansing's note
of September 26—assuming, of course, that Wilson would have permitted the note to go to London if House had not intervened as he
did. If this assumption is correct, then House's role was not inconsequential, for he thus averted what might well have become a fairly
sharp Anglo-American crisis over neutral trade once the note were
published, one in which the Washington authorities would have been
hard pressed to find sound arguments to support their accusations and
claims.

Even if it is true, this point is irrelevant to the main question of
whether House's intervention had the result of substantially weakening
the force of the note that actually went to London on September 28.
Following House's own account of the part that he played, scholars
have concluded that the Colonel and the British Ambassador were
chiefly responsible for drafting the telegram of September 28.[19] A
perusal of the files of the State Department will soon show that this
conclusion is incorrect. Colonel House and Ambassador Spring Rice
may have outlined some kind of a note themselves and edited a copy
of the telegram, as House related at the time.[20] But the records clearly

[17] *"Proposed Telegram,"* dated September 28, 1914, State Department Papers. The
Acting Secretary of State to Ambassador Page, September 28, 1914, *Foreign Relations,
1914, Supplement,* pp. 232-233, is the printed version of the message as sent. It varies
slightly from the text printed above.

[18] e.g., C. C. Tansill, *America Goes to War,* pp. 145-146, and R. S. Baker, *Woodrow
Wilson,* v, 206-207.

[19] See, particularly, Charles Seymour (ed.), *The Intimate Papers of Colonel House,*
I, 308, and C. C. Tansill, *America Goes to War,* pp. 145-146.

[20] "We [Spring Rice and House] outlined a despatch for this Government to send
to Page, and then we outlined the despatch which we thought he [Spring Rice] should
send Sir Edward Grey." House Diary, September 28, 1914, printed in C. Seymour

reveal that it was Lansing who drafted and Wilson who edited the telegram that was sent. Moreover, there is no evidence to substantiate House's claim that he and the President "softened" Lansing's draft; on the contrary, the changes that Wilson made actually increased the force of the document.

Now that we have seen who its authors were, we can finally ask whether the Wilson-Lansing note of September 28 was in fact weaker than the note that Lansing had drafted two days before. The answer is not as obvious as it might seem at first glance. Although it was somewhat abrupt and vaguely ominous in its conclusion, Lansing's note did no more than assert the traditional American view of neutral rights of trade, declare that the United States could not compromise its neutrality by acquiescing in or submitting to Britain's measures, and reserve all rights under international law. The Wilson-Lansing telegram of September 28 was briefer and used language rather less blunt, and it opened the way for negotiations instead of stating the American position in public terms. However, it said much the same thing that Lansing's note had said, and almost as emphatically. Indeed, by adding the sentence to the effect that the American people would insist upon the observance of an unmodified Declaration of London by the British government, Wilson took a more advanced position than Lansing had done.

Events following the affair of September 26-28 soon revealed that although the President was eager to negotiate in a friendly way in order to avoid a public controversy with the British government, he had no intention of retreating from his advanced position. It must be said at the outset that the differences between the two governments at this time were still largely theoretical and not very great. No one in Washington denied the right of British cruisers to stop American

(ed.), *The Intimate Papers of Colonel House*, I, 308. "I had the good fortune to be there [in Washington] at a time when the discussion of the Declaration of London had reached a critical stage. Bryan was away and Lansing, who had not mentioned the matter to Sir Cecil, prepared a long communication to you which he sent to the President for approval. The President and I went over it and I strongly urged not sending it until I could have a conference with Sir Cecil. I had this conference the next day without the knowledge of anyone excepting the President, and had another the day following. . . . At the President's suggestion, Lansing then prepared a cablegram to you. This, too, was objectionable and the President and I together softened it down into the one you received." E. M. House to W. H. Page, October 3, 1914, printed in B. J. Hendrick, *The Life and Letters of Walter H. Page*, I, 378-379.

ships carrying unquestionable contraband to Germany. The one important issue was whether the British could treat raw materials like foodstuffs, copper, oil, and cotton as conditional contraband and seize them when they went to Germany through neutral ports.

It seems fairly obvious that it was political and economic necessity and the hope of averting conflict, rather than any principled conviction, that drove Wilson to high ground on this issue. We are entitled to infer from what followed that the President realized from the beginning that in a showdown he could not deny the British right to capture strategic raw materials, even those on the unratified Declaration of London's free list, when they were destined for military uses. At the same time, he was overborne by fear of the consequences of the unchallenged assertion of a theoretical right. The panic of the South would, he knew, become uncontrollable if the British attempted to hamper the export of cotton to Central Europe. To the southern demand for retaliation would be added the clamor of other outraged interests. Worse still, wholesale British interference with American commerce would arouse a latent but fierce national pride in all sections and provide a perfect opportunity for demagogues. Could he control it if such a situation did ensue? Might not the result be a violent break, the very thing he wanted to avoid, instead of a gradual accommodation to legitimate British sea controls?

"When we were discussing the seizure of vessels by Great Britain," Colonel House wrote, recording a conversation with the President on September 30, "he read a page from his 'History of the American People,' telling how during Madison's Administration the War of 1812 was started in exactly the same way as this controversy is opening up. The passage said that Madison was compelled to go to war despite the fact that he was a peace-loving man and desired to do everything in his power to prevent it, but popular feeling made it impossible. The President said: 'Madison and I are the only two Princeton men that have become President. The circumstances of the War of 1812 and now run parallel. I sincerely hope they will not go further.' "[21] House passed on this grim remark to Spring Rice; he in turn relayed it to Sir Edward Grey, adding the following significant comment on the President's mood: "The President is very much impressed by the gravity of the question because it touches the pockets and the prejudices of so many of the people. It happens to be just

[21] House Diary, September 30, 1914.

the sort of question which takes the popular fancy and also enlists the monied people as well."[22]

Negotiations to find a way of avoiding such pitfalls began in Washington between Lansing and Spring Rice on September 28, 1914, and in London between Grey and Page, assisted by Page's legal adviser, Chandler P. Anderson, on the following day. They continued at a confusing pace for nearly three weeks. For their part, the British were obviously determined to intercept all American exports of raw materials and other commodities that might be used to sustain the German war machine, and above all to refuse to accept the Declaration of London unmodified.[23] At the same time, the British made it clear that they were grateful for the American willingness to negotiate; that they were eager to avoid any public controversy with Washington; and that they would go to extreme lengths to meet what they considered to be any reasonable American objections.

Indeed, conciliation of America was perhaps the Foreign Office's chief concern at this early juncture in the war. As Grey later stated the basic assumption of his policies toward the United States, "blockade of Germany was essential to the victory of the Allies, but the ill-will of the United States meant their certain defeat. After Paris had been saved by the battle of the Marne, the Allies could do no more than hold their own against Germany; sometimes they did not even do that. Germany and Austria were self-supporting in the huge supply of munitions. The Allies soon became dependent for an adequate supply on the United States. If we quarrelled with the United States we could not get that supply. It was better therefore to carry on the war without blockade, if need be, than to incur a break with the United States about contraband and thereby deprive the Allies of the resources necessary to carry on the war at all or with any chance of success. *The object of diplomacy, therefore, was to secure the maximum of blockade that could be enforced without a rupture with the United States.*"[24] "Considerations of this kind," one of his subordinates in the Foreign Office afterward remembered, "were always in Grey's mind, and throughout the blockade controversies with America he never lost

[22] C. Spring Rice to E. Grey, October 1, 1914, *The Letters of Sir Cecil Spring Rice,* II, 233.

[23] e.g., Ambassador Page to the Secretary of State, September 29, 1914, *Foreign Relations, 1914, Supplement,* p. 233; the Foreign Secretary to Ambassador Spring Rice, September 28, 1914, *ibid.,* pp. 236-237; C. Spring Rice to W.W., September 30, 1914, Wilson Papers.

[24] Grey of Fallodon, *Twenty-Five Years,* II, 107; italics added.

sight of them. To him, though it was very important to make our economic pressure as effective as possible, yet the continuance of American friendship was even more so."[25]

In private conversation and direct warnings to subordinates and the British press, the Foreign Secretary made it plain that he would not permit any group to endanger or to force him to endanger Britain's most vital connection.[26] What was more important, few men in the government dared to challenge him, so great was his influence and power.[27] As the British Ambassador in Paris, who wanted a more ruthless policy, put it ruefully, "It is fear of the United States, who see fine opportunities for driving a roaring trade with Germany, that prevents us from asserting ourselves. We would snap our fingers at the other States such as Italy, Spain, Norway, Sweden, Denmark and Holland."[28]

Grey's position is easy to understand, but the historian can never be certain that he fully comprehends Lansing's motives and purposes as he reads the long conversations and communications that were exchanged during the Anglo-American discussions. The more one studies the documents, however, the more the conviction grows that Lansing had decided (even before he drafted his ill-fated note of September 26) that the United States would have no alternative in the circumstances but to accept the basic features of the British maritime system, because they were to such a large extent grounded in law and custom. At the same time, he was obviously desperately eager to find a way of accommodation that would be acceptable to American opinion and, if possible, afford no ground for legitimate complaint by the Central Powers.

The main problem, of course, was to find a way by which the British could prevent the entry of strategic raw materials into Germany through neutral ports without exercising such naked control over neutral commerce as to incite American opinion. The Counselor

[25] From a memorandum by Lord Robert Cecil, printed in G. M. Trevelyan, *Grey of Fallodon*, pp. 351-352.

[26] e.g., see the memorandum by Alwyn Parker of the Foreign Office recalling what Grey told the officials of the Contraband Department soon after the establishment of that body, printed in *ibid.*, pp. 347-349; and Amy Strachey, *St. Loe Strachey, His Life and Paper*, p. 326, paraphrasing the warning that the Foreign Office sent to British editors.

[27] On this point, see Ernest R. May, *The World War and American Isolation, 1914-1917*, pp. 7-9.

[28] Lady Algernon Gordon Lennox (ed.), *The Diary of Lord Bertie of Thame, 1914-1918*, I, 55.

suggested one method to the British Ambassador at the outset of the negotiations: let the British rescind their Order in Council of August 20; at the same time, the British might both put vital raw materials on the list of *absolute* contraband and proceed with their negotiations aimed at persuading the Netherlands government to place an embargo on the passage of such commodities through Holland into Germany.[29]

When the Foreign Office snapped up this suggestion and promised to issue a new Order in Council and publish a new list of absolute contraband,[30] Lansing came back with a second proposal. It was that the British government accept the Declaration of London without change but use its rights under the Declaration to add those commodities obviously destined for the German war economy to the list of absolute contraband. "Now the point I am driving at is just this," he wrote to Spring Rice. "Do not the powers conferred upon a belligerent by Articles 23 and 25 [of the Declaration] furnish sufficient means to protect the interests of your Government without modifying the declaration at all? If I understand your main object it is that you are seeking to apply the doctrine of 'continuous voyage' to certain articles now listed as conditional contraband, but which you consider munitions of war. If such articles can be treated as absolute contraband upon notice, what is the use of modifying the articles of the declaration?"[31] "This Government," the Acting Secretary of State further explained to Ambassador Page, "would view with eminent satisfaction British acceptance of declaration without change in order that for the present war uniform set of rules of naval warfare could be put in force defining relations between neutrals and belligerents. It would also quiet public unrest, which is increasing, as to present British action."[32]

Ignoring Lansing's second suggestion, Grey replied to his first on October 9 by sending the draft of a new Order in Council and new lists of absolute contraband. "It is draft, and will not be issued," Page explained, "till it has been discussed, and, he hopes, approved by you."[33] Knowing full well how much depended upon the American response, Page, Grey, and Spring Rice all appealed directly to the President in

[29] "Memorandum by the Acting Secretary of State," dated September 29, 1914, *Foreign Relations, 1914, Supplement*, pp. 233-235.

[30] Ambassador Page to the Secretary of State, September 30, 1914, *ibid.*, p. 235; the Foreign Secretary to Ambassador Spring Rice, September 30, 1914, *ibid.*, pp. 237-238.

[31] R. Lansing to Ambassador Spring Rice, October 2, 1914, *ibid.*, pp. 240-241.

[32] The Acting Secretary of State to Ambassador Page, October 4, 1914, *ibid.*, p. 244.

[33] Ambassador Page to the Secretary of State, October 9, 1914, enclosing Grey's "Draft Contraband Order in Council," *ibid.*, pp. 244-246.

the hope that he would take control out of Lansing's hands and seal a far-reaching acquiescence by his own approval. "The question seems wholly different here from what it probably seems in Washington," Page wired in an urgent personal message to the White House. "There it is a more or less academic discussion. Here it is a matter of life and death for English-speaking civilization. It is not a happy time to raise controversies that can be avoided or postponed. Nothing can be gained and every chance for useful cooperation for peace can easily be thrown away and is now in jeopardy. In jeopardy also are our friendly relations with Great Britain in the sorest time of need in her history. . . . [Chandler P.] Anderson and [Irwin] Laughlin [Counselor of the Embassy] agree with me emphatically."[34] "In the life and death struggle in which we are now engaged," Spring Rice wrote, "it is essential to prevent war supplies reaching the German armies and factories."[35] "We are most anxious to come to an agreement with United States Government," Grey added, "for otherwise we shall have to choose between a dispute with United States Government or giving up all attempts to prevent Germany from getting free supplies for her army and materials for all munitions of war: either alternative would or might be fatal to our chance of success and insure ultimate German victory and disappearance of Great Britain as a fully independent Power in Europe."[36]

Wilson was deeply moved by this outpouring. "The tone of it," he wrote to Lansing about Spring Rice's message, "is so candid and sincere, and so earnest that I am sure you will wish to send our reply at once." But he and Lansing had apparently already decided on the night before these appeals arrived that they could not possibly give open approval to the proposed new Order in Council. To begin with, as Lansing pointed out soon in a formal reply to London, such acceptance "might be construed by the enemies of Great Britain to be contrary to that strict neutrality which it is the earnest wish of the President to preserve throughout the present war." But more important, as the Counselor said in a memorandum for the President and afterward in his formal reply, the proposed Order in Council was actually less acceptable to the United States than the one it would replace, because the new Order imposed even more sweeping controls over neutral trade than the earlier one had done.

[34] Ambassador Page to the Secretary of State, "for the President," October 15, 1914, *ibid.*, pp. 248-249.

[35] Ambassador Spring Rice to W.W., October 15, 1914, *The Lansing Papers*, I, 250.

[36] The Foreign Secretary to Ambassador Spring Rice, n.d., *ibid.*, p. 252.

For the record, Lansing dispatched a note embodying these objections to Page at three p.m. on October 16, 1914.[37] Much more important was an urgent message that the Counselor had sent to London two hours before. It so fully revealed his own and the President's purposes that it is printed virtually in full, as follows:

"Strictly confidential and personal. To be deciphered by the Ambassador himself. . . .

"The desire of this Government is to obtain from the British Government the issuance of an order in council adopting the declaration [of London] without any amendment whatsoever and to obtain from France and Russia like decrees, which they will undoubtedly issue if Great Britain sets the example. Such an adoption by the allied Governments will put in force the acceptance of the Declaration of London by Germany and Austria, which will thus become for all the belligerent powers the code of naval warfare during the present conflict. This is the aim of the United States.

"It cannot be accomplished if the declaration is changed in any way as Germany and Austria would not give their consent to a change.

"In the frequent informal and confidential conversations which have taken place here and in the admirable frankness with which Sir Edward Grey has stated the reasons for the action which Great Britain has deemed it necessary to take in regard to the declaration, this Government feels that it fully understands and appreciates the British position, and is not disposed to place obstacles in the way of the accomplishment of the purposes which the British representatives have so frankly stated.

"The confidence thus reposed in this Government makes it appreciate more than ever the staunch friendship of Great Britain for the United States, which it hopes always to deserve.

"This Government would not feel warranted in offering any suggestion to the British Government as to a course which would meet the wishes of this Government and at the same time accomplish the ends which Great Britain seeks, but you might in the strictest confidence intimate to Sir Edward Grey the following plan, at the same time stating very explicitly that it is your personal suggestion and not one for which your Government is responsible.

"Let the British Government issue an order in council accepting

---

[37] The Acting Secretary of State to Ambassador Page, October 16, 1914, *Foreign Relations, 1914, Supplement*, pp. 250-252.

the Declaration of London without change or addition, and repealing all previous conflicting orders in council.

"Let this order in council be followed by a proclamation adding articles to the lists of absolute and conditional contraband by virtue of the authority conferred by Articles 23 and 25 of the declaration.

"Let the proclamation be followed by another order in council, of which the United States need not be previously advised, declaring that, when one of His Majesty's Principal Secretaries of State is convinced that a port or the territory of a neutral country is being used as a base for the transit of supplies for an enemy government a proclamation shall issue declaring that such port or territory has acquired enemy character in so far as trade in contraband is concerned and that vessels trading therewith shall be thereafter subject to the rules of the declaration governing trade to enemy's territory.

"It is true that the latter order in council would be based on a new principle. The excuse would be that the Declaration of London failing to provide for such an exceptional condition as exists, a belligerent has a right to give a reasonable interpretation to the rules of the declaration so that they will not leave him helpless to prevent an enemy from obtaining supplies for his military forces although the belligerent may possess the power and would have the right to do so if the port or territory was occupied by the enemy.

"When the last-mentioned order in council is issued, I am convinced that a full explanation of its nature and necessity would meet with liberal consideration by this Government and not be the subject of serious objection.

"I repeat that any suggestion, which you may make to Sir Edward Grey, must be done in an entirely personal way and with the distinct understanding that this Government is in no way responsible for what you may say."[38]

This, undoubtedly, was the President's proposal as much as Lansing's. We cannot determine the exact authorship of the above lines,[39] but many of them bear the certain mark of Wilsonian phrasing. Moreover, Wilson left no doubt about his own position when he sent the following urgent message to Page a few hours after the secret message had

[38] The Acting Secretary of State to Ambassador Page, October 16, 1914, from the original copy in the Page Papers and the printed text in *Foreign Relations, 1914, Supplement*, pp. 249-250.

[39] The only copy of this message that survives in the State Department files is the typed copy of the final draft that was sent.

gone over the wire: "Beg that you will not regard the position of this Government as merely academic. Contact with opinion on this side the water would materially alter your view. Lansing has pointed out to you in personal confidential despatch of this date how completely all the British Government seeks can be accomplished without the least friction with this Government and without touching opinion on this side the water on an exceedingly tender spot. I must urge you to realize this aspect of the matter and to use your utmost persuasive efforts to effect an understanding, which we earnestly desire, by the method we have gone out of our way to suggest, which will put the whole case in unimpeachable form."[40]

If there were any merits to Wilson's and Lansing's plan, they were only faintly seen in London. To start with, Page burned with shame and rage as he read the Acting Secretary of State's telegram on the morning of October 17, 1914. At first glance—and this, obviously, is all the attention that he gave it—it seemed as if all the painful negotiations of the preceding weeks had been in vain. After appearing to come close to the British view, here was Lansing still talking about His Majesty's Government adopting the Declaration of London unmodified, and (as Page thought) with a dishonest reservation added besides!

Halfheartedly and plainly embarrassed, the Ambassador went to the Foreign Office on October 17 to lay the proposal before Sir Edward Grey. Although he afterward reported that he had followed his instructions "literally," Page's persuasive power must surely have been at low ebb. "I did not tell him whose idea it is," he wrote to the President soon after the interview, "but only that I was discussing the subject informally. I must be spared from saying that anything is my *'personal suggestion and not one for which my government is responsible,'* when this is not true. . . . Still I tried for the fourth time to persuade Sir Edward to accept . . . [the Declaration of London] *in toto*—such were my instructions—and then to issue another proclamation as explained in Mr. Lansing's dispatch."[41]

[40] W.W. to W. H. Page, October 16, 1914, *Foreign Relations, 1914, Supplement*, pp. 252-253. The original copy of this dispatch—a note written in longhand by the President—may be found in the State Department Papers.
"*STRICTLY CONFIDENTIAL AND PERSONAL*," Lansing wired to Page on October 19, 1914 (*ibid.*), "The confidential and personal telegrams to you from the President and myself dated October sixteenth, together with this telegram, must not be placed in files of Embassy but be held by you personally in greatest secrecy."
[41] W. H. Page to W.W., October 21, 1914, Wilson Papers. I have transposed the above sentences.

Grey thought no more of the plan than Page did. "Do you mean," he asked almost petulantly, "that we should accept it [the Declaration], and then issue a proclamation to get around it?" Wearily, the Foreign Secretary explained again why his government could not adopt the Declaration of London, even with such modifications to protect its control over the flow of contraband through neutral ports as Lansing had suggested. To begin with, he said, "A simple acceptance of the Declaration of London would in effect bind us to carry out every detail of an instrument which we have never ratified and to which objection has been taken in Parliament."[42] More important, Sir Edward went on, acceptance of the Declaration, even with the reservation regarding the flow of contraband through neutral ports to Germany, would mean the loss forever of any control over the raw materials which the Declaration had stipulated should never be removed from the free list. As Page explained in his letter to the President, "Now the Declaration itself distinctly forbids the addition of copper and iron ore and rubber and hides to the contraband list," articles which, as Grey pointed out, "are now used in Germany exclusively or mainly for purposes of war." This, the Foreign Secretary intimated, would have to be his final word on the Declaration of London. As Page reported to the State Department, "This finally ends all hope of his acceptance of the declaration entire. He is courteous, appreciative, and willing to go to any length he can to meet us, but he will not accept the declaration for the reasons given."[43] "The interview ended," Page added in his letter to the President, "with a feeling on my part that I had lost ground and really been put on the defensive by my insistence on his acceptance of the Declaration for the fourth time—coupled now with a proposal that could not be made to appear wholly frank and friendly."[44]

[42] The Foreign Secretary to Ambassador Spring Rice, October 17, 1914, *Foreign Relations, 1914, Supplement,* p. 254.

[43] Ambassador Page to the Secretary of State, October 19, 1914, *ibid.,* p. 253.

[44] W. H. Page to W.W., October 21, 1914, Wilson Papers. "The Foreign Office doubts our wisdom and prudence since Lansing came into action," Page wrote to Colonel House, somewhat more frankly, soon afterward. " . . . God knows I have tried to keep this confidence intact and our good friendship secure. But I have begun to get despondent over the outlook since the President telegraphed me that Lansing's proposal would settle the matter. I still believe he did not understand it—he couldn't have done so. Else he could not have approved it. But that tied my hands. If Lansing again brings up the Declaration of London—after four flat and reasonable rejections—I shall resign. . . . It would be too asinine an act ever to merit forgiveness or ever to be forgotten. I should blame myself the rest of my life. It would grieve Sir Edward more

In the circumstances, Grey concluded, his government would have to proceed to its own solution, but not, however, without considerable regard for neutral trade. Ironically, in view of the indignation with which Page and Grey had greeted Lansing's secret proposal of October 16, the Foreign Secretary's own plan differed very little from the one that the Counselor had suggested. It provided, simply, that the London government should accept the Declaration of London as its rule for economic warfare on the high seas, subject only to two amendments safeguarding control over contraband and the right to stop cargoes of contraband consigned to unnamed persons or firms in neutral countries but evidently destined for the Central Powers. "He proposes," Page explained, "to issue a proclamation to the foregoing effect, repealing all preceding proclamations. He does not ask our acceptance of this proclamation, but he hopes we will not protest against it, and that we will be content to declare that we reserve all rights under international law and usage if in its execution any harm be done to our commerce, and that we will take up cases of damage, if any occur, as they arise."[45]

What, indeed, could the Washington leaders do but tacitly agree? As Lansing pointed out to the President, it was useless to talk any more about obtaining mutual adoption of the Declaration of London. "We must, therefore," the Counselor went on, "stand on the rules of international law which have been generally accepted without regard to the Declaration."[46] The decision was made at a conference at the White House on October 21, and the note, approved beforehand by the President and read by the British Ambassador,[47] went to London on the following day. "Inasmuch as the British Government consider that the conditions of the present European conflict make it impossible for them to accept without modification the Declaration of London," the new instructions to Page read, "you are requested to inform His Majesty's Government that in the circumstances the Government of the United States feels obliged to withdraw its suggestion that the Declaration of London be adopted as a temporary code of

---

than anything except this war." W. H. Page to E. M. House, October 22, 1914, B. J. Hendrick, *The Life and Letters of Walter H. Page*, I, 383-384.

[45] Ambassador Page to the Secretary of State, October 19, 1914, *Foreign Relations, 1914, Supplement*, pp. 253-254; also the Foreign Secretary to Ambassador Spring Rice, October 19, 1914, *ibid.*, p. 255.

[46] R. Lansing to W.W., October 20, 1914, *The Lansing Papers*, I, 255-256.

[47] It was shown to Spring Rice at Wilson's suggestion. W.W. to R. Lansing, undated note in longhand, but written October 21, 1914, in the State Department Papers.

naval warfare to be observed by belligerents and neutrals during the present war; that, therefore, this Government will insist that the rights and duties of the United States and its citizens in the present war be defined by the existing rules of international law and the treaties of the United States irrespective of the provisions of the Declaration of London; and that this Government reserves to itself the right to enter a protest or demand in each case in which those rights and duties so defined are violated or their free exercise interfered with by the authorities of His Britannic Majesty's Government."[48]

It was exactly what Grey wanted most to hear from Washington. "I am very glad," he wrote to Spring Rice, "that the United States Government no longer insist upon the declaration of London in its entirety: this decision will smooth the path very much."[49] The Foreign Secretary, Page reported to the State Department on October 23, "understands that you will not make formal protest against new order in council and list of contraband and conditional contraband but reserve all rights under international law and usage. . . . On this understanding he expressed great satisfaction and assured me that His Majesty's Government will endeavor to cause the United States and citizens of the United States the very least trouble that the exigencies of a great war will permit, and that he will meet us in a friendly spirit in all cases that come up for consideration or controversy."[50]

Thus confident of American acquiescence, Grey could now proceed to the final arrangements for the institution of the new maritime system. It was put into effect by a royal proclamation and an Order in Council, both dated October 29, 1914. The proclamation published a revised list of absolute and conditional contraband, the most notable feature of which was the addition of unwrought copper, iron ore, aluminum, rubber, and gasoline and oil to the list of *absolute* contraband. The Order in Council affirmed the continued British adherence to the Declaration, subject, first, to the changes in the contraband lists already announced and, second, to certain provisions designed to prevent neutral ships from carrying contraband to neutral ports when its ultimate destination was the Central Powers.[51] This done, Grey called

---

[48] The Acting Secretary of State to Ambassador Page, October 22, 1914, *Foreign Relations, 1914, Supplement*, pp. 257-258.

[49] E. Grey to C. Spring Rice, October 24, 1914, *The Lansing Papers*, I, 257.

[50] Ambassador Page to the Secretary of State, October 23, 1914, *Foreign Relations, 1914, Supplement*, p. 258.

[51] The proclamation and Order in Council are printed in *ibid.*, pp. 261-263.

the officials of the newly established Contraband Department of the Foreign Office to his study for a special warning. As one of the officials present later recalled, he "emphasised the vital importance of our relations with America. He recalled that in 1812 questions of neutrality had actually involved us in war with the United States, and that the surest way to lose this war would be to antagonise Washington, since, apart from all other considerations which he dwelt on, Lord Kitchener [Secretary of State for War] was dependent on munitions from America for his new Army. 'Mind, therefore, you keep a sense of proportion.' "[52]

At this point, the biographer is tempted to proceed to an account of how events worked out under the new British maritime system. To do this, however, would be to leave unanswered some important questions that have long troubled historians of this period and have undoubtedly occurred to the reader as well. First, why did the President and his advisers, after beginning by insisting so emphatically upon a full-fledged British observance of the Declaration of London, end by accepting a new maritime system that contravened the Declaration in several vital particulars? Clearly, willingness to adopt such a compromise was the meaning of all of Lansing's suggestions aimed at facilitating a seeming British acceptance of an unmodified Declaration. It was also the clear meaning of Wilson's decision to make no formal protest against the proclamation and Order in Council of October 29, 1914. Second, did the acquiescence of the leaders in Washington contradict the neutrality in which they believed and were attempting to practice in numerous ways?

It is easy enough to understand why the President and his advisers concluded that they would have to abandon their campaign for the mutual observance of the Declaration of London. That instrument was not a part of the body of international law. The leaders in Washington knew well enough, therefore, that they had no right to *demand* that the British government follow its rules and obey its limitations. In fact, they never made any such demand; their advocacy of the Declaration was based throughout upon expediency, not right. When the British refused to yield, they had no alternative within the recognized bounds of neutrality and friendly intercourse but to fall back upon international law, unsatisfactory recourse though that was. It would have been unneutral in the highest degree for them to have

[52] Alwyn Parker, memorandum printed in G. M. Trevelyan, *Grey of Fallodon*, p. 347.

compelled the British to accept a code of naval warfare that was highly beneficial to their enemies.

There remains, then, the question why Wilson and Lansing went even further and tacitly approved the main features of the maritime system that the British substituted for the Declaration of London. The answer is simply that the Washington leaders, given their determination to be neutral, had no other choice but to acquiesce. The maritime system that the British government inaugurated on October 29, 1914, was in all its main features based soundly upon international law and practices which, though not formally sanctioned, enjoyed a near legality through custom and usage by all maritime powers, including the United States. British sea power, it is almost needless to say, was one of the important facts of international life in 1914. The American leaders could not have been substantially neutral, that is, as impartial as circumstances would permit, and deny that the British had a right to stop the flow of supplies and raw materials that were obviously essential for the easy functioning of the German war economy. Moreover, they could not have been substantially neutral and make a determined challenge to British sea power merely because the British used methods, like applying the doctrine of continuous voyage, that had never been sanctioned by international conferences but had been used to a large extent by the United States government itself in the past, notably during the Civil War of 1861-1865.

In a letter written for the Secretary of State for the enlightenment of the American people, Counselor Lansing once explained why all this was true, and why it was often extremely difficult to find the point at which the rights of British sea power ended and American neutral rights began. Lansing's commentary, still one of the best ever written on this subject, follows in part:

"The fact that the commerce of the United States is interrupted by Great Britain is consequent upon the superiority of her Navy on the high seas. History shows that whenever a country has possessed that superiority our trade has been interrupted and that few articles essential to the prosecution of the war have been allowed to reach its enemy from this country. . . .

"There is no Hague convention which deals with absolute or conditional contraband, and, as the Declaration of London is not in force, the rules of international law only apply. As to the articles to be regarded as contraband, there is no general agreement between nations. It is the practice for a country, either in time of peace or after the outbreak of war, to declare the articles which it will consider as absolute or conditional contraband. It is true that a neutral government is seriously affected by this declaration, as the rights of its subjects or citizens may be impaired. But the rights and interests of belligerents and neutrals are opposed in respect to contraband articles and trade and there is no tribunal to which questions of difference may be readily submitted.

"The record of the United States in the past is not free from criticism. When neutral, this Government has stood for a restricted list of absolute and conditional contraband. As a belligerent, we have contended for a liberal list, according to our conception of the necessities of the case. . . . It will be recalled . . . [moreover] that American courts have established various rules bearing on these matters. The rule of 'continuous voyage' has been not only asserted by American tribunals but extended by them. They have exercised the right to determine from the circumstances whether the ostensible was the real destination. They have held that the shipment of articles of contraband to a neutral port 'to order,' from which, as a matter of fact, cargoes had been transshipped to the enemy, is corroborative evidence that the cargo is really destined to the enemy instead of to the neutral port of delivery. It is thus seen that some of the doctrines which appear to bear harshly upon neutrals at the present time are analogous to or outgrowths from policies adopted by the United States when it was a belligerent. The Government therefore cannot consistently protest against the application of rules which it has followed in the past, unless they have not been practiced as heretofore."[53]

Wilson's and Lansing's acquiescence was greatly facilitated, moreover, by the very manner and language that Sir Edward Grey employed to plead his government's case. Throughout the negotiations preparatory to the promulgation of the new maritime system on October 29, Grey was, to be sure, firm, but he was also intimate and appealing and never marred the image that Wilson had formed of him. By contending that the British government had no desire to injure American trade, by talking as much in terms of international law as Wilson himself, and by appearing to be, as he undoubtedly was, as regardful as possible of American neutral rights, Grey succeeded in giving a purely legal character to the differences between the two

[53] Printed in *Foreign Relations, 1914, Supplement*, p. ix. I have transposed the above paragraphs.

governments and entirely avoided permitting the issues of sovereignty and inviolable national rights to be raised.

Finally, Wilson and Lansing could not have ignored the obvious practical reasons for accepting the British sea measures in the autumn of 1914. To begin with, most American foreign trade was carried on with the Allied world; forcing a break or imperiling good relations with the Allies over highly dubious neutral rights of trade would, therefore, have been of questionable wisdom from a sheerly practical point of view. Moreover, Wilson could not have been unaware of the political results that would have flowed from an effective American challenge to British sea power—the wrecking of American friendship with the two great European democracies, the possible victory of the Central Powers, and the sure ending of all hopes of American mediation—all without a single compensating gain for the interests and security of the American people and the future welfare of mankind.

Once the great decision was made, the tasks of the State Department during the months immediately following the issuance of the Order in Council of October 29, 1914, until about the end of January 1915, consisted in the main of helping the American business community to adjust to the British maritime system and of watching to make certain that the Admiralty in London honored the Foreign Office's promises about respecting American trading rights within the framework of the Anglo-American understanding.

The adjustment was, actually, a relatively painless one. Most American exports went as a matter of course to Allied ports; about them there were no disputes at all. Nor were there any difficulties about the shipment of obvious contraband like munitions, for no American exporter (insofar as this writer knows) was ever willing to risk the almost certain capture of such cargoes by shipping them to Germany; and the State Department could not have protested anyway if the British had seized them. Thus the important American interests adversely affected by the British maritime system, those whose rights of trade could be a matter of dispute in any event, were few in number during this period. They were the producers and exporters of copper, illuminating oil, and some foodstuffs and meat.

To be sure, the files of the State Department bulged with angry protests from the representatives of these interests when the British seized their ships and cargoes; and the State Department, busier than

ever before, conducted vigorous negotiations in their behalf.[54] But in
actual fact these negotiations now involved matters of detail and rarely
questions of principle, and there was no great tension between the two
governments over these commodities. To begin with, the American
authorities conceded that the British had the right to treat them as
contraband when they could prove that their ultimate destination was
Germany. And in applying their controls to these commodities the
British were, on the whole, extraordinarily careful to avoid unnecessary injury to American interests. For example, they confiscated few
cargoes and in all doubtful cases paid full value for the cargoes they
did not release. Moreover, by negotiating agreements (they were coercive, to be sure) with Holland and the Scandinavian neutrals to prevent the passage of strategic materials through their ports into Germany, the British made it certain that most American trade with the
European neutrals could be carried on in a normal way, without
threatening the integrity of their maritime controls.[55] Finally, the British went to the extreme length of concluding private agreements at
least with the major American copper producers and meatpackers, and
perhaps also with the oil companies. They were in part coercive, but
they served their purpose by assuaging discontent because they offered
a guaranteed market at going prices to American producers in return
for promises to refuse to sell to German buyers.[56]

In the final analysis, the British succeeded in averting dangerous

[54] See, e.g., the documents printed in *ibid.*, pp. 270-356.

[55] For an excellent analysis of this matter, see Marion C. Siney, *The Allied Blockade
of Germany, 1914-1916*, pp. 33-59, 75-122.

[56] For a detailed account of the negotiation of the agreement between the British
and the copper producers, see F. Leverton Harris, Adviser in Commerce to the Trade
Division of the Admiralty, *Control of American Copper Exports, Printed for the use
of the Cabinet. March 1915*, memorandum dated March 3, 1915, Asquith Papers; also
David Lloyd George, *War Memoirs*, II, 664-665. For the negotiations between the
British and the American meatpackers, which were much more protracted, see the New
York *World*, January 13, March 6, July 16, and September 17, 1915; *New York Times*,
July 15, September 17, October 3, 7, and 12, 1915; and April 14, 1916; Ambassador
Spring Rice to Chandler P. Anderson (who managed the negotiations for the meatpackers), December 13 and 18, 1915, Anderson Papers; C. P. Anderson, memorandum
of a conference with representatives of the meatpackers in Chicago, dated December 19,
1915, *ibid*; Anderson Diary, January 12, 16, and 18, February 8, 1916; copy of agreement between Eyre A. Crowe, Assistant Undersecretary of State for Foreign Affairs
and C. P. Anderson, and between Lloyd C. Griscom and W. F. Archer, dated London,
April 13, 1916, Anderson Papers; F. L. Harris to the Prime Minister, February 26,
1916, enclosing a memorandum entitled "Negotiations with the American Packing
Houses," Asquith Papers.

trouble with the United States during the period under discussion because they were careful not to offend the wrong American economic interests or too many of them all at once. To put the matter somewhat crudely, it was politically safe for the British to stop the shipment of American oil to Germany, for the chief American exporter, the Standard Oil Company of New Jersey, had no votes and little influence in Congress. It was more dangerous for the British to treat foodstuffs, meat, and copper as contraband, but not fatally so, for the shipment of the first two commodities to Germany was small, and most American copper was mined in sparsely populated states with few representatives in Congress.

The question of cotton, however, was of an altogether different character. An ingredient of gunpowder and a basic staple of military uniforms, cotton was as essential a war material as copper, and the Foreign Office could certainly have made an excellent legal case for treating it as contraband. However, Sir Edward Grey, resisting strong pressure from the Admiralty, from public opinion at home, and from the French Foreign Office, not only refused to make cotton contraband; he took the unusual step of announcing on October 26, 1914, that "cotton is not contraband and so far as the British Government is concerned will not be."[57] As a consequence, American cotton flowed in huge quantities—perhaps 1,750,000 bales in all—to Germany via neutral and even German ports between October 1914 and March 1915.[58] The point is that Grey's policy toward cotton was not motivated by any special tenderness for the staple but exclusively by fear that any open affronting of the southern senators and congressmen would incite them to join forces with pro-German groups to adopt some retaliatory measure like an embargo on the export of munitions.

Two developments in the autumn of 1914 gave additional evidence of the Washington government's willingness to live with and to accept the economic consequences of British control of the seas.

The first of these was the refusal of the American leaders to protest when the British drastically extended their maritime system by mark-

[57] Ambassador Page to the Secretary of State, October 24, 1914, Page Papers; the British Ambassador to the Acting Secretary of State, October 26, 1914, *Foreign Relations, 1914, Supplement*, p. 290. These assurances were published in the American press, e.g., the *New York Times*, October 26 and 27, 1914.

[58] Edwin J. Clapp, *Economic Aspects of the War*, pp. 116-118. Twenty American freighters laden with cotton entered Bremen or Bremerhaven between January 2 and March 22, 1915, alone.

ing out the entire area of the North Sea as a zone of war. The background of this measure is somewhat involved, but it may be briefly summarized. Since the early days of the war the German navy had been laying submarine mines in various parts of the North Sea off the British coast. Charging that their enemies were violating the rules by scattering mines indiscriminately, the British Admiralty countered by planting a large mine field of its own in the southern waters of the North Sea on October 2, 1914. Then, when the Germans renewed their allegedly illegal mine laying, the British Admiralty went the whole way in retaliation on November 2, by announcing that after November 5 the entire North Sea would be a zone of military operations. "Within this area," the announcement said, "merchant shipping of all kinds, traders of all countries, fishing craft, and all other vessels will be exposed to the gravest dangers from mines which it has been necessary to lay and from warships searching vigilantly by night and by day for suspicious craft." Neutral vessels could still traverse the area, the announcement made clear, but they could do so safely only by following certain stipulated safety lanes.[59] The effect of this measure was not to close the North Sea, as some writers have said, but to give the British Admiralty an almost absolute control over neutral commerce entering and leaving this broad zone.

The State Department received the announcement with silence. Apparently both Bryan, who was now back at his desk after his long absence, and Lansing thought that the British action was not sufficiently important from the American point of view (since virtually no American ships traveled in the North Sea) to warrant any discussion, for there is no evidence that they laid the matter before the President or even gave it much attention. The leaders in the State Department also might well have concluded that in any event they had no good legal or practical grounds for complaint, since the British had taken careful pains to safeguard neutral shipping in the new war zone. They simply let the announcement pass without comment at first and then afterward refused to join the Scandinavian neutrals in a joint protest.[60]

The second development was the change in the administration's attitude toward the extension of private loans or credits to belligerent governments that occurred, or began to occur, at the very time that

---

[59] *New York Times*, November 3, 1914.

[60] e.g., the Secretary of State to the Minister in Norway, November 10, 1914, *Foreign Relations, 1914, Supplement,* p. 466.

the decision was made to acquiesce in the new British maritime system. This, it might be said at the outset, did not mean that the administration's determination to follow the path of neutrality was any weaker than before. On the contrary, it signified that the President and his advisers were simply learning to accept the most important economic consequence of neutrality, which was the development of a large war trade between the United States and Allied countries. Ironically, initiative in this change of policy was taken by none other than the author of the ban on loans himself, Secretary Bryan. An account of how this occurred will shed some light on the Nebraskan's curious mental processes,[61] as well as upon the problem itself.

It all happened so informally, at least in the beginning, that the facts were never embodied in the American documentary record and came to light only years later. Undaunted by their earlier failure to obtain a loan through the Morgan firm, French officials struck out upon a new course in September 1914 by opening negotiations with the National City Bank of New York for a credit of $10,000,000 to the French government. It would be a crucial test, and the French Ambassador himself sought out the Secretary of State on one of the rare occasions when he was in Washington during late September. Jusserand argued earnestly that Bryan's ban was generally prejudicial to the Allies and a major impediment to the French government in particular. Severely shaken, Bryan replied that he might consider his attitude.

The way thus prepared, Roger L. Farnham of the National City Bank followed Jusserand to the Secretary's office, probably in early October. It was clever strategy, for Farnham had worked intimately with officials on Haitian policy and, more important, enjoyed Bryan's complete respect and trust. He explained that the National City Bank wanted to arrange for the provision of a banking credit of $10,000,000 to the French government. He must have emphasized that this would be no conventional loan through bonds offered to the public, but only a banking credit that would be expended entirely in the United States for American products. And we may be sure that he mentioned the difficulties of the exchange situation and how this transaction was

---

[61] "He struck me, when I had dealings with him," Lord Bryce wrote not long afterward about Bryan, "as being almost unable to *think* in the sense in which you and I would use that word. Vague ideas floated through his mind but did not unite to form any system or to crystallise into a definite practical proposition." Lord Bryce to Henry White, July 7, 1915, Bryce Papers.

essential to the maintenance of exports to France. We do not know what thoughts ran through Bryan's mind—whether he had simply forgotten his earlier statement about money being the worst form of contraband, whether he had concluded that the ban on loans was actually unneutral, or whether he was simply eager to please a friend. Farnham's arguments, at any rate, sufficed. There was a difference, Bryan must have agreed, between a private commercial credit and a public loan that would agitate the people and sway their affections. He would approve the transaction, he told Farnham, provided that "no advertisement of the forthcoming issue of French Treasury bonds [which were to serve as collateral for the "credit"] be published in the press."[62]

The documentary record does not reveal what ensued immediately, but Bryan almost certainly informed the President and Counselor Lansing of his action just before he left Washington again for the hustings in early October. Perhaps this was what prompted Lansing, in order to prepare the way for the change of policy, to issue his circular, mentioned earlier, to the press on October 15, asserting that the federal authorities had no legal right to prevent the export of "any article of contraband."

In any event, the appearance of this statement at once set off the very kind of public discussion that Bryan had been eager to avoid and, as we will see, a second round of discussions on the high level. Reporters probably heard rumors of Bryan's decision and, reading between the lines of the State Department's circular on October 15, they must have concluded that the administration had lifted or was about to lift the ban on loans. At the regular White House press conference on that day one of the correspondents asked the President whether this were true. Refusing to make a statement for publication, Wilson gave the following as a confidential opinion: "My own information is that loans stand in the same case as anything else,—loans from private individuals."[63]

[62] The preceding two paragraphs are based upon the 74th Cong., 2d sess., *Senate Report No. 944*, Part 6, pp. 17-19, printing the testimony of Frank A. Vanderlip, former president of the National City Bank of New York, before the Special Committee on Investigation of the Munitions Industry; and Charles A. Beard, "New Light on Bryan and War Policies," *The New Republic*, LXXXVII (June 17, 1936), 177-178, printing a letter from Maurice Léon, who had acted as representative of the French government in the negotiation of the "credit."

[63] Memorandum of a press conference of October 15, 1914, in the Papers of Charles L. Swem, Princeton University Library; hereinafter cited as the Swem Papers.

The fat was in the fire when the newspapermen picked up the cue and reported that "it was admitted in a high authoritative quarter today that shipments of gold to belligerent countries and loans by American bankers to bankers or other persons in belligerent countries were to be regarded as included in the shipments of contraband articles."[64] This gave rise to so much speculation that the President felt compelled to offer a word of clarification. The administration, he told reporters on October 19, had not changed its position on the question of *loans*; it still regarded loans to the belligerents as being contrary to the spirit of "true neutrality."[65]

What Wilson said was of course technically true, but the bankers involved in the impending transaction failed to see the subtleties of the explanation. In some consternation, we may assume, Samuel McRoberts, vice president of the National City Bank, called upon Acting Secretary of State Lansing during the morning of October 23 and made it plain that his bank had to know whether the administration had any objection to the proposed French credit.[66]

In Bryan's absence Lansing could not make the decision, and he went to the White House during the evening of the same day for guidance. Wilson apparently did not hesitate to confirm Bryan's change of policy. "There is a decided difference between an issue of government bonds, which are sold in open market to investors," he replied in substance, "and an arrangement for easy exchange in meeting debts incurred in trade between a government and American merchants. The sale of bonds draws gold from the American people. The purchasers of bonds are loaning their savings to the belligerent government, and are, in fact, financing the war." Trade with belligerents, he went on, was entirely proper; it was, therefore, "desirable that obstacles, such as interference with an arrangement of credits or easy method of exchange, should be removed." Lansing might tell anyone entitled to know that these were his *impressions* of the President's views, Wilson concluded; however, he added, Lansing should make it plain that he had "no authority to speak for the President or the Government," since "the question of an arrangement of this sort

[64] *New York Times,* October 16, 1914; New York *World,* October 16, 1914.

[65] *ibid.,* October 20, 1914; memorandum of a press conference of October 19, 1914, Swem Papers.

[66] Samuel McRoberts to the Acting Secretary of State, October 23, 1914, recapitulating their conversation on the same date, *The Lansing Papers,* I, 136-137.

ought not to be submitted to this Government for its opinion, since it has given its views on loans in general."[67]

Lansing conveyed the substance of Wilson's statement to Willard Straight of the House of Morgan on October 24 and to Farnham of the National City Bank two days later. It was not hard to read between the lines, and the latter institution proceeded to extend the $10,000,000 credit to the French government.[68] It was followed in January 1915 by the granting of a $12,000,000 trade credit to the Russian government by J. P. Morgan & Company, and in March 1915 by a nine-month loan of $10,000,000 to Germany by a banking syndicate headed by Chandler & Company of New York and a one-year loan of $50,-000,000 to France by the Morgan firm and other New York banks.[69]

These credits sufficed to keep the channels of exchange open during these months of expanding foreign trade. It was, therefore, easy for the administration to adhere to the policy of condoning short-term bankers' credits while still condemning outright loans.[70] Of course, what Wilson and Bryan said about the difference between a loan to belligerents that was sold publicly and short-term credits arranged privately was true. The real test of the administration's exceptional virtue on this matter would come later, when war trade with the Allies had grown to such huge dimensions as to demand more drastic measures of financial support in the United States.

[67] "*Memorandum by the Acting Secretary of State of a Conversation with President Wilson, October 23, 1914, 8:30 p.m.,*" *ibid.*, p. 140.

[68] *New York Times*, October 30, 1914.

[69] *ibid.*, January 19, March 27 and 31, 1915.

[70] See the representation of the President's views as given in the New York *World*, October 31, 1914; Bryan's statement, contained in a public letter of January 8, 1915, to Senator W. J. Stone, to the effect that the administration still strongly disapproved granting loans to belligerent governments, *Foreign Relations, 1914, Supplement*, p. xii; and Bryan's statement of March 31, 1915, publicly approving short-term credit arrangements while still maintaining the ban on public war loans, *New York Times*, April 1, 1915.

CHAPTER V

Toils and Troubles:
Congress and the German Americans

THE six weeks following the adjournment of the second session of the Sixty-Third Congress in mid-October 1914 had given Wilson and his advisers a respite from domestic concerns during which to conduct their first important negotiations with the British government. Even so, it was apparent that this political quietude could not long survive once the lame duck session convened in early December. This would have been true, to be sure, in the ordinary course of events, but the war had created unusual problems and stimulated popular demands for action that could be confronted only in the open political arena.

To begin with, the President, under heavy pressure from Secretary McAdoo,[1] had decided to revive the Ship Purchase bill and to make this measure the main item in his legislative program for the lame duck session.[2] This decision alone made a long and bitter political struggle inevitable. In the second place, Wilson and the men on Capitol Hill would have to face a movement for the drastic enlargement of the nation's military forces. It had begun on a fairly modest scale during the first months of the war as a consequence of the concern mainly of the professional military and naval leaders and their periodical spokesmen. Between October and early December it gained considerable momentum as Senator Henry Cabot Lodge and his son-in-law, Representative Augustus P. Gardner of Massachusetts, raised the demand for a special congressional investigation into the state of the nation's defenses. Theodore Roosevelt, his journalistic organ, *The Outlook*, and other newspapers and magazines, and the service organizations, the Army League and the Navy League, joined the outcry for preparedness. And an imposing group of leaders formed a nonpartisan organization, the National Security League, on December 1 to rally

[1] W. G. McAdoo to W.W., November 7, 21, and 28, 1914, Wilson Papers.
[2] As he told reporters on December 1, *New York Times*, December 2, 1914.

public opinion behind the movement.[3] It would not be possible for the President either to ignore or to scoff at these demands, as he had earlier done,[4] once they were voiced in the halls of Congress. Finally, there was the problem posed by the German Americans and other anti-British groups, who were daily growing more indignant at the administration's acquiescence in the British maritime system. By the beginning of December they were mounting a powerful campaign for the adoption of an arms embargo, and their demands were sure to provoke a hard fight once Congress assembled.

Congress convened on December 7, 1914; and the President went before the joint session on the following day to deliver his second Annual Message. Ignoring the German-American demand, he dealt first with the necessity for constructive conservation legislation and endorsed a measure then pending to give a larger degree of self-government to the Filipinos. The preliminaries over, he faced the two remaining major issues without equivocation. The country's most pressing need, he said, was an adequate merchant marine to carry its surpluses to distant markets, especially ones in Latin America. "Hence the pending shipping bill, discussed at the last session but as yet passed by neither House. In my judgment such legislation is imperatively needed. . . . I very earnestly hope that the Congress will be of this opinion, and that both Houses will adopt this exceedingly important bill." There were a few faint rounds of applause, but most congressmen and senators were obviously not moved as the President spoke these words and then went on to mention other less controversial but peripheral matters. The atmosphere, however, changed suddenly when Wilson announced that he was taking "leave to mention . . . the subject of national defense."

Forthrightly he replied to the preparedness champions and condemned their agitation. Of course America, he said, was not prepared to "put a nation in the field, a nation of men trained to arms"; she would never be prepared to do this so long as she retained her "pres-

[3] William H. Harbaugh, "Wilson, Roosevelt, and Interventionism, 1914-1917," unpublished Ph.D. dissertation, Northwestern University Library, gives an excellent survey of the early phases of the preparedness movement.

[4] On October 19, 1914, for example, Wilson laughingly referred to the discussion over preparedness as "good mental exercise," adding that talk of this kind had been going on ever since he was a boy of ten. *New York Times*, October 20, 1914. Again, on November 30, he referred to the movement for a special congressional investigation as "untimely." *ibid.*, December 1, 1914.

ent political principles and institutions." With obvious emotion he continued:

"Allow me to speak with great plainness and directness upon this great matter and to avow my convictions with deep earnestness. I have tried to know what America is, what her people think, what they are, what they most cherish and hold dear. I hope that some of their finer passions are in my own heart,—some of the great conceptions and desires which gave birth to this Government and which have made the voice of this people a voice of peace and hope and liberty among the peoples of the world, and that, speaking my own thoughts, I shall, at least in part, speak theirs also, however faintly and inadequately, upon this vital matter.

"We are at peace with all the world. No one who speaks counsel based on fact or drawn from a just and candid interpretation of realities can say that there is reason to fear that from any quarter our independence or the integrity of our territory is threatened. . . . We are the champions of peace and of concord. And we should be very jealous of this distinction which we have sought to earn. Just now we should be particularly jealous of it, because it is our dearest present hope that this character and reputation may presently, in God's providence, bring us an opportunity such as has seldom been vouchsafed any nation, the opportunity to counsel and obtain peace in the world and reconciliation and a healing settlement of many a matter that has cooled and interrupted the friendship of nations. This is the time above all others when we should wish and resolve to keep our strength by self-possession, our influence by preserving our ancient principles of action."

America would do in the future what she had done in the past. She would rely for her defense, not upon a standing army, nor yet upon a reserve army, but "upon a citizenry trained and accustomed to arms." "More than this," Wilson went on, "carries with it a reversal of the whole history and character of our polity. More than this, proposed at this time, permit me to say, would mean merely that we had lost our self-possession, that we had been thrown off our balance by a war *with which we have nothing to do, whose causes can not touch us,* whose very existence affords us opportunities of friendship and disinterested service which should make us ashamed of any thought of hostility or fearful preparation for trouble. . . . But I turn away from the subject. It is not new. There is no new need to discuss it.

We shall not alter our attitude toward it because some amongst us are nervous and excited."[5]

These deeply felt sentences were repeatedly interrupted by applause, and congressmen stood cheering as the President concluded. But there were many long faces in the crowd even among the Democrats, and all observers knew that the life of the short session was bound to be a stormy one.[6]

The fight over preparedness broke out first, as Representative Gardner and Senator Lodge introduced resolutions for a special investigation of the national defenses on December 7 and 8, 1914. They evoked a scattered support among the newspapers[7] and set off a flurry of activity among the advocates of military expansion. But it was evident almost from the beginning that the movement had no chance of succeeding. The President, of course, stood squarely opposed. Only a few days before, he had made it plain that he would do everything he could to block the resolution if Gardner introduced it;[8] he had even called the Massachusetts representative to the White House on December 7 to ask him to abandon his project.[9] And when Gardner ignored this appeal, Wilson hit back angrily on December 8 by hinting accusingly that some lobby was responsible for the preparedness agitation.[10] Only a public demand of the most gigantic proportions could have persuaded Democratic leaders in Congress that it was necessary to defy the resolute man in the White House. But the fact was plain for all to see that the President spoke for the overwhelming majority of the country. The outpouring of approval that followed his Annual Message left no doubt about the sentiments of the American people on this score.[11]

[5] From the version of this address printed in *Foreign Relations, 1914*, pp. xi-xix; italics added.

[6] *New York Times*, December 9, 1914.

[7] See the *Chicago Tribune*, December 9, 1914; *New York Tribune*, December 11, 1914; New York *Outlook*, cviii (December 16 and 30, 1914), 865-866, 986-988; and the editorials cited in "Should We Prepare for Attack?" *Literary Digest*, xlix (December 12, 1914), 1159-1161, and "Our Government's Attitude Toward National Defense," *ibid.*, December 19, 1914, pp. 1205-1207.

[8] *New York Times*, December 1, 1914; New York *World*, December 2, 1914.

[9] *New York Times*, December 8, 1914.   [10] *ibid.*, December 9, 1914.

[11] e.g., S. S. Wise to W.W., December 8, 1914; Hamilton Holt to W.W., December 9, 1914; C. S. Osborn to W.W., December 9, 1914; E. M. House to W.W., December 11, 1914; L. W. Nieman to W.W., December 11, 1914; Church Peace Union to W.W., December 16, 1914; Andrew Carnegie to W.W., January 29, 1915, and hundreds of

This did not mean that the President and Congress could avoid the issue entirely, for the short session would have to make some decisions on broad military policy when it considered and adopted, as it would have to do eventually, the appropriation bills for the two armed services. But there was no doubt from the beginning what those decisions would be. Thus, with the approval if not at the suggestion of the President, the House committees on military and naval affairs began cursory and carefully controlled hearings of their own into the state of the army and navy on December 9, 1914. Secretary of the Navy Daniels and two admirals friendly to the administration, Frank F. Fletcher, commander of the Atlantic Fleet, and Charles J. Badger, a member of the General Board, assured the congressmen that the navy was in splendid shape—"ship for ship . . . as good as the navy of any other nation," as Badger put it.[12] Before the military affairs committee, moreover, two hand-picked generals, Hugh L. Scott, Chief of Staff, and William Crozier, Chief of Ordnance, were also reassuring.[13] Many an old-line officer in both services must have snorted in derision, but the two among them who dared to speak out and say that the nation's defenses were dangerously inadequate—General Leonard Wood, former Chief of Staff, and Admiral Austin M. Knight, president of the Naval War College—were quickly warned by their civilian superiors to keep silent.[14]

---

other such letters in Series ii and Series vi, Box 467, Wilson Papers; Louisville *Courier-Journal*, December 8, 1914; *Chicago News*, December 9, 1914; New York *Nation*, xcix (December 10, 1914), 679; *The Independent*, lxxx (December 14, 1914), 392; *The Standard*, xlii (December 19, 1914), 441; New York *Christian Advocate*, xc (January 14, 1915), 43-44; Church Peace Union to W.W., printed in *ibid.*, January 21, 1915, p. 74. It ought to be said, however, that apparently a majority of the big-city newspapers believed that the nation's defenses were inadequate and should be increased. At least so the *Literary Digest* reported in January 1915 after making a nation-wide poll of the press. "Nation-Wide Press Poll on Army and Navy Increase," *Literary Digest*, l (January 23, 1915), 137-138, 162, 164-169.

[12] *New York Times*, December 10 and 11, 1914, and the *Literary Digest*, xlix (December 19, 1914), 1206-1207, for a summary of their testimony. There is some doubt whether their reassurances were altogether well-grounded. See A. F. Nicholson, senior member of the General Board of the Navy, to the Secretary of the Navy, September 9, 1914, Wilson Papers, reporting that the efficiency and morale of the Atlantic Fleet were at a very low ebb.

[13] For a review of their testimony, see the *Literary Digest*, xlix (December 19, 1914), 1206.

[14] General Wood's indiscretion consisted in telling the Merchants' Association of New York on December 15, 1914, that the United States was wholly unprepared for war with a first-class power. *New York Times*, December 16, 1914. He received a private reprimand from Secretary of War Lindley M. Garrison, who acted at President Wilson's

"To Arms! To Arms!"
Kirby in the New York *World*

So complete was the administration's control that there was virtually no controversy at all during the ensuing weeks while the military and naval appropriation bills were being hammered out on Capitol Hill. At the outset of the discussions there was general agreement that the navy should receive approximately the same appropriations as it had the year before, and that the army should be given a moderate increase in manpower.[15] But the President, warned by House Majority Leader Underwood that a deficit impended, insisted at first upon reductions in the ordinary expenditures.[16] He later relented and permitted some increases for both services, but they were so small as to be insignificant.[17]

Thus ended in defeat the first drive of the gathering preparedness movement. Thus did the President and all who agreed with him that the United States had no need of great military power in the foreseeable future have their way.

At the outset of the short session it did not seem likely that Congress could escape the necessity of yielding to the presidential will on another subject, legislation to provide federal operation of merchant ships, on which Wilson's determination was equally strong. On December 9, 1914, Senator William J. Stone of Missouri introduced a Ship Purchase bill that was virtually identical with the measure that

---

request. W.W. to L. M. Garrison, December 21, 1914, and L. M. Garrison to W.W., December 21, 1914, both in the Wilson Papers. Admiral Knight made the mistake of criticizing the administration's naval policies at a public meeting in New York City on January 25, 1915. "I desire you, Mr. Secretary," the President told Secretary Daniels at a Cabinet meeting the next day, "to convey to the Admiral . . . that he should confine his remarks to questions asked him by committees of Congress." Daniels transmitted the presidential rebuke to Knight on the same day, January 26. The Diary of Josephus Daniels, Library of Congress, January 26, 1915; hereinafter cited as the Daniels Diary.

[15] This was the tentative agreement of a conference of the defense secretaries, the chairmen of the House and Senate committees on military and naval affairs, and Representative Underwood on January 5, 1915. *ibid.*, January 5, 1915; *New York Times,* January 7, 1914.

[16] Daniels Diary, January 22, 1915.

[17] In 1914 Congress appropriated $102,017,112 for the military establishment for the coming fiscal year; in 1915 it appropriated $110,313,751. The strength of the Regular Army was 4,701 officers and 87,781 men on June 30, 1914, and 4,834 officers and 97,248 men on June 30, 1915.

In 1914 Congress appropriated $144,868,717 for the naval establishment for the coming fiscal year; in 1915 it appropriated $149,661,865. Enlisted personnel in the navy totaled 52,667 on June 30, 1914, and 52,974 on December 1, 1915.

had been reported to the House of Representatives during the preceding session. After considering it dutifully if hastily, the commerce committee issued a favorable report on December 30. In recommending the measure to the Senate's friendly consideration, the committee simply echoed what Secretary McAdoo and Secretary of Commerce William C. Redfield had said in a special communication on the problem on December 29—that the shortage of ships had caused a spectacular increase in ocean transportation rates since mid-October and now threatened to cripple American foreign trade. As the two cabinet members put it:

"The general situation shows a large and universal advance in transportation rates, the lowest seeming to be that of 10 per cent to Asia, a general shortage of tonnage available to carry American goods, and a substantial embargo upon the commerce of the United States at a time when the opportunities for that commerce were never so large. The whole commercial world reaches out to us for goods to-day and we have not the facilities with which to deliver them. The goods are here in abundance; the buyers are yonder in abundance; but the means of transit are not sufficient. . . . The growers of cotton and wheat, the manufacturers of goods in a hundred forms, are at the mercy to-day of the shipowner, and almost wholly of the foreign shipowner, who reaps his harvest of freight receipts without regard to the interests of American commerce."[18]

The solution, the commerce committee concluded in its own report, was the immediate creation of a federally owned and operated merchant marine. It alone could force ocean transportation rates to a reasonable level and provide the bottoms for a potentially rich commerce with Latin America and with Germany in cotton and other noncontraband commodities.[19] Concurring, more or less under presidential pressure, the Democratic majority of the Senate voted on January 4, 1915, to call the Ship Purchase bill up for immediate debate.

These were only superficial promises of speedy Senate approval; underneath the portents augured ill. To begin with, there were signs

[18] *Increased Ocean Transportation Rates*, pp. 14-15. McAdoo and Redfield came back with a supplementary report on January 25, 1915, pointing to further increases in ocean freight rates and alleging that these charges were imposing an intolerable burden on the American economy. See *Increased Ocean Transportation Rates, Letter from the Secretary of the Treasury and the Secretary of Commerce*, 63d Cong., 3d sess., Senate Document 673, Part 2.

[19] *New York Times*, December 31, 1914, has a long summary of the commerce committee's report.

that the Republican leaders were preparing for a determined stand, perhaps a filibuster. Three Republican elders, Lodge, Root, and Jacob H. Gallinger of New Hampshire, the minority leader, opened a broad attack with bitter remarks on January 4, while Theodore E. Burton of Ohio led off with what he said would be a ten-day speech when the Senate began formal debate on the Ship Purchase bill on January 7.[20] Even more disturbing to the President and his managers, Stone and Duncan U. Fletcher of Florida,[21] were indications of revolt within the Democratic ranks. It was clear to all observers that few Democratic senators really favored the measure; some of them were even threatening to oppose it on the ground that it was socialistic in principle.

Sensing the danger, President Wilson struck hard at the dissidents in both camps in a rousing partisan Jackson Day address at Indianapolis on the afternoon of January 8, 1915. After affirming the absolute necessity for more American bottoms,[22] he lashed out at the Republicans who were threatening to talk the Ship Purchase bill to death. "Who commissioned them, a minority, a lessening minority?" he cried. ". . . These gentlemen are now seeking to defy the nation and prevent the release of American products to the suffering world, which needs them more now than it ever needed them before." He then added a word of warning to his brethren in the Senate: "The Democratic Party is still on trial. . . . This country is not going to use any party that cannot do continuous and consistent team work. If any group of men should dare to break the solidarity of the Democratic team for any purpose or from any motive, theirs will be a most unenviable notoriety and a responsibility which will bring deep bitterness to them. . . . If a man will not play in the team, then he does not belong to the team."[23]

[20] *ibid.*, January 5, 1915; New York *World*, January 8, 1915.

[21] Stone was chairman of the foreign relations committee; Fletcher, a ranking Democratic member of the commerce committee.

[22] "Only America among the great powers of the world is free to govern her own life," he said, "and all the world is looking to America to serve its economic need, and while all this is happening what is going on? Do you know, gentlemen, that the ocean freight rates have gone up in some instances to ten times their ordinary figure, and that the farmers of the United States, those who raise grain and those who raise cotton—these things that are absolutely necessary to the world as well as to ourselves—cannot get any profit out of the great prices that they are willing to pay for these things on the other side of the sea because the whole profit is eaten up by the extortionate charges for ocean carriage. . . . The merchants and farmers of this country must have ships to carry their goods, and just at the present moment there is no other way of getting them than through the instrumentality that is suggested in the Shipping bill."

[23] New York *Times*, January 9, 1915.

It reminded observers of a remark that the President had reputedly made in October 1913: "The Democrat who will not support me is not a Democrat. He is a rebel."[24]

["The whole speech was not only angry but cheap," Senator Lodge observed somewhat sourly to his friend Theodore Roosevelt, "and the natural cheapness of the man has come out. I live in hopes that he will be found out by the people of the United States for what he really is."[25] "Of course you did not like the Indianapolis speech," Wilson wrote to a friend a short time later; "(that palpable lapse of taste, 'Woodrow etc.'[26] was only a silliness of the moment; was not in the notes; was produced by the psychology of the stump, no doubt, and admits of no excuse); I instinctively knew that you would not: any more than you would like a real fight, or anything that wore the aspect of partisanship."[27]]

It was irresistible pressure, and the President's managers in the Senate moved quickly to whip their "team" into line by calling a caucus of the Democratic members of the upper house. They held a number of stormy sessions between January 18 and 23 in an atmosphere supercharged by the accusation of the administration's editorial organ, the New York *World*, that the shipping interests were conducting a powerful and improper lobby to defeat the President and wreck his leadership.[28] Wilson's spokesman in the caucus, Senator Stone, finally drove his colleagues to a vote on January 23 by telling them that they would have to choose between the President and the Republican party. "There can be no middle ground," the Missourian exclaimed. "Either you are with the Administration or against it. The issue is clear cut. It is a fight between the people on the one side and special interests on the other." Thus confronted, the thirty-seven Democrats present in the caucus room voted unanimously to approve an amended Ship Purchase

[24] A. S. Link, *Wilson*, II, 230.

[25] H. C. Lodge to T. Roosevelt, January 15, 1915, the Papers of Theodore Roosevelt, Library of Congress; hereinafter cited as the Roosevelt Papers.

[26] While defending his Mexican policy, Wilson had said: "With all due respect to editors of great newspapers, I have to say to them that I seldom take my opinion of the American people from their editorials. So that when some great dailies not very far from where I am temporarily residing thundered with rising scorn at watchful waiting, Woodrow sat back in his chair and chuckled, knowing that he laughs best who laughs last—knowing, in short, what were the temper and principles of the American people."

[27] W.W. to Mrs. Crawford H. Toy, January 31, 1915, Baker Collection.

[28] New York *World*, January 21 and 22, 1915; *New York Times*, January 19, 22, and 23, 1915.

bill[29] and to make it a party measure binding upon all Democrats.[30] The President, reporters noted, was elated by the outcome. He could not, however, have failed to discern the ominous fact that sixteen Democratic senators had refused to attend the final session of the caucus or the sullen character of much of the support that he had received.[31]

Meanwhile, the entire Republican membership of the Senate, except for four midwestern insurgents,[32] had conferred and pledged themselves to an all-out opposition to the Ship Purchase bill by systematic and prolonged debate.[33] John W. Weeks of Massachusetts commenced with an all-day speech on January 21, and the Republican outpouring continued thus uninterrupted until near the end of the month, with Lodge and Root managing the affair and hammering hard themselves in periodic attacks.

The Republicans pressed the main lines of a searching criticism consistently and fiercely. They attacked the Ship Purchase bill first on grounds of principle, alleging that it would commit the government to public ownership, with all that such a commitment would imply for the future political economy of the United States. Senator Root expressed these fears in a private letter as follows: "The great fundamental vice in the bill is that it is a measure of state socialism which, if established, will inevitably destroy individual liberty. It is wholly unrepublican, un-American, and destructive of the principles upon which our free government has been built up and maintained."[34] Republican senators next met Wilson's and McAdoo's arguments that increased costs of ocean transportation were a burden upon American producers and merchants by replying that it was the European purchaser and not the American shipper who paid the freight charges. Thirdly, they admitted that there was some shortage of shipping; but they argued that competition and private enterprise would solve the problem more rapidly and efficiently than the government could ever do. Finally, day in and out they pressed the charge that the

[29] The amendments adopted by the caucus enlarged the membership of the Shipping Board to include three appointees outside the government, stipulated that the proposed federal shipping corporation should be incorporated under the laws of the District of Columbia, limited the capital stock of the corporation to $20,000,000, and provided that all ships owned by the corporation might be operated in the coastwise trade.

[30] *New York Times*, January 24, 1915; New York *World*, January 24 and 25, 1915.

[31] *New York Times*, January 25, 1915.

[32] Robert M. La Follette of Wisconsin, Moses E. Clapp of Minnesota, William S. Kenyon of Iowa, and George W. Norris of Nebraska.

[33] *New York Times*, January 22, 1915.

[34] E. Root to C. W. Wilson, February 4, 1915, Root Papers.

Administration intended to purchase German ships lying in American harbors, that the Allied governments would not recognize the legality of such a transfer, and that violent conflict was bound to ensue when the shipping board sent the former German ships to sea and Allied cruisers captured or sank them. Root and Lodge, for example, advanced this argument with special vigor on the Senate floor on January 30, charging also that the Allied governments had already filed strong protests against the contemplated American purchase of the disputed vessels.[35]

This was an authentic fear that drove the two Republican leaders to desperate resistance and Lodge, at least, even to false accusations. "You cannot be more at a loss than I am to account for the President's strange insistence upon the Ship Purchase bill," Root wrote. ". . . The purpose apparently is to buy belligerent ships, and in that case the international situation would immediately become very grave."[36] For his part, Lodge was certain that war with England was possible if the measure passed; moreover, he had somehow concluded that McAdoo was party to a corrupt deal for the purchase of the German ships. He wrote to Roosevelt on January 15, voicing all his fears and suspicions:

"The ship purchase bill . . . is one of the most dangerous things internationally—I say nothing of its viciousness economically—which could be imagined. The plan is to buy the German ships. If this is done and the Allies refuse to recognize the transfer of the flag—which France and Russia certainly will do . . . —we shall find ourselves with Government-owned ships afloat, which the Allies regard as German ships and therefore good prize and which are liable to be fired on and sunk. . . . I do not think that the force behind it is the desire to help Germany by relieving her of these ships, which is an unneutral act and almost an act of hostility. I think the force is a much worse one. McAdoo is closely connected with Kuhn-Loeb & Co., who are, if I am rightly informed closely connected with the German steamship lines. . . . The indications all point to a job in which McAdoo and some other of the President's close friends are involved.

[35] Louis Seibold in the New York *World*, January 31, 1915.

[36] E. Root to Lawrence Godkin, January 16, 1915, Root Papers. In the same vein, see H. L. Higginson to E. M. House, January 13, 1915, House Papers; C. W. Eliot to D. F. Houston, January 19, 1915, the Papers of David F. Houston, Houghton Library, Harvard University, hereinafter cited as the Houston Papers; F. R. Coudert to E. Root, January 29, 1915, Root Papers; A. Carnegie to W.W., January 31, 1915, Wilson Papers; W. H. Taft to Mabel Boardman, February 1, 1915, Taft Papers.

Whether proof of this can be obtained is another question,[37] but there is little doubt here of this sinister influence which is behind this business. If they should buy the ships, and if the powers should refuse to recognize the transfer and treat them as German ships, this incompetent Administration may flounder into war, just as they blundered and floundered into bloodshed at Vera Cruz."[38]

At any time during this early stage of the debate the President could have allayed such fears and perhaps assured adoption of the Ship Purchase bill if he had only done what Root and Lodge were challenging him and the Democrats to do—accept an amendment offered by the latter forbidding the shipping board to purchase any ships owned by belligerents. By accepting such an amendment, Wilson also could have quieted the extraordinary fear then current in England that he meant to challenge the British maritime system with his fleet of former German vessels.[39]

It all seemed transparently simple to Secretary Bryan, who had no idea that the President intended to permit the shipping board to purchase the ships. "If you said—or authorized me to say," Bryan suggested on January 22, " 'To avoid misunderstanding and misrepresentation of the Government's purpose, the press is informed that in case the shipping bill is passed the corporation authorized by that bill being partly owned by the Government will not, in the purchase of ships, acquire any vessel whose purchase would raise any international question or issue.'—I believe it would do much to calm the fears across the ocean and it would also remove one of the objections which is made against the shipping bill by its opponents in Congress. As we could not afford and, therefore, have no intention of raising an issue

---

[37] Eventually this charge against McAdoo came out into the open, when Senator Burton of Ohio introduced a resolution calling upon the Secretary of the Treasury to inform the Senate of the arrangements that he had made for the possible purchase of ships. Advised by McAdoo that he had nothing to hide, the Democrats adopted Burton's resolution on February 15, 1915, but with an amendment instructing a committee of investigation (T. J. Walsh of Montana, F. M. Simmons, J. A. Reed of Missouri, J. W. Weeks, and Burton) to determine the degree to which private shipping interests had attempted to defeat the Ship Purchase bill. New York *World*, February 15, 1915; *New York Times*, February 16, 1915. The special committee held brief hearings, beginning on February 17, and found no evidence whatever of any improper activity on the part of the Secretary of the Treasury or, for that matter, by the so-called "shipping trust." See 64th Cong., 1st sess., *Senate Report 25*, Part 1, for this testimony.

[38] H. C. Lodge to T. Roosevelt, January 15, 1915, Roosevelt Papers. Also H. C. Lodge to T. Roosevelt, January 20 and 26, 1915, *ibid.*, and H. C. Lodge to John T. Morse, Jr., January 28, 1915, the Lodge-Morse Correspondence, Massachusetts Historical Society.

[39] See below, pp. 179-182.

by purchasing German ships, would it not be worth while to remove the fears that are based upon the possibility of such a purchase?"[40]

The President, alas, could not give any such assurances. To begin with, he and McAdoo did intend to purchase German vessels (and British and French ships, too, if they could be found), as there simply seemed to be no other way to assemble a merchant fleet quickly.[41] Precisely what Wilson proposed to do with the ships once he got them—that is, whether he intended to use them in the European trade or only in commerce with Latin America—is not at all clear.[42] Wilson would not heed Bryan's suggestion, in the second place, because he believed that the United States had a right in international law to purchase belligerent ships, and that it would be unneutral for him publicly to abandon the right. "My difficulty in this whole matter," he explained to a friend, "has been this: Our rights as neutrals in the matter of the purchase of ships from citizens of belligerent countries is, I believe, susceptible of clear establishment in any impartial tribunal. Just now the United States stands as the chief custodian of neutral rights and I do not think that any branch of the Government should say anything officially that would seem to be equivalent to even a temporary renunciation of those rights."[43]

The really compelling reasons why the President would not accept the Lodge amendment ran much deeper than this. By the end of January 1915 Wilson obviously believed that the struggle over the Ship Purchase bill had become a crucial test of his leadership, of the Democratic party's devotion to the people, and of the country's confidence in his own integrity. It was, he now thought, a battle between democracy and special privilege, between himself and those sinister spokesmen of reaction, Root and Lodge. To yield on the Lodge amendment at this point, moreover, would be tantamount to confessing that he, Wilson, might involve the country in serious difficulties abroad if the

[40] W. J. Bryan to W.W., January 22, 1915, *The Lansing Papers*, I, 110. Bryan repeated this advice in a letter to Wilson on the following day (*ibid.*, p. 111), saying that he thought a simple announcement by the President would be preferable to the Lodge amendment to prohibit the shipping corporation to purchase belligerent ships.

[41] From the evidence now at hand there can no longer be any doubt on this point. See, e.g., W. G. McAdoo to W.W., November 7 and 21, 1914, Wilson Papers; W.W. to R. Lansing, November 23, 1914, *The Lansing Papers*, I, 107.

[42] W.W. to C. W. Eliot, February 23, 1915, Wilson Papers, indicates that Wilson was thinking, at least when he wrote this letter, of using the former German ships exclusively in trade with Latin America.

[43] W.W. to C. W. Eliot, February 18, 1915, *ibid.*

amendment were not adopted. He expressed these convictions and poured out his deep personal feelings in his letters at this time:

"There is a real fight on. The Republicans are every day employing the most unscrupulous methods of partisanship and false evidence to destroy this administration and bring back the days of private influence and selfish advantage. I would not, if I could, imitate their tactics; but it is no time for mere manners. The barriers of taste may be overstepped in stating the truth as to what is going on; it must be displayed naked. . . . The struggle that is on, to bring about reaction and regain privilege is desperate and absolutely without scruple. It cannot be met by gentle speeches or by presidential utterances which smack of no bias of party. A compact and fighting party must be led against them. I think you cannot know to what lengths men like Root and Lodge are going, who I once thought had consciences but now know have none. We must not suffer ourselves to forget or twist the truth as they do, or use their insincere and contemptible methods of fighting; we must hit them and hit them straight in the face, and not mind if the blood comes. It is a blunt business, and lacks a certain kind of refinement, but so does all war; and this is a war to save the country from some of the worst influences that ever debauched it. Please do not read the speeches in which I use a bludgeon. I do not like to offend your taste; but I cannot fight rottenness with rose-water. . . .

"As for the shipping bill, it does, as you perceive, permit us to commit blunders, fatal blunders, if we are so stupid or so blind; but it is not a blunder in itself, and, if we use ordinary sense and prudence, it need lead us into no dangers. The only dangers it involves have already been created by the ship registry bill and the war risk insurance measure, for which the Republicans hastened to vote, some coming back to Washington to advocate what the shipping interests wanted who had been absent from their seats for weeks. But the shipping interests do not want this bill. They will do nothing themselves without a subsidy, unless, that is, they are given government money out of the taxes to use as they think best for themselves; if they cannot get that, and of course they cannot, they do not mean to let the development take place, because the control of ocean carriage and of ocean rates will pass out of their hands. We are fighting as a matter of fact the most formidable (covert) lobby that has stood against us yet in anything we have attempted; and we shall see the fight to a finish; trying, when we have won, to act like men who know very familiarly the dangers of what they are about to undertake. . . . One would suppose that this was a bill to authorize the government to buy German ships. There would be just as stiff a fight against it, and from the same quarters, if it merely conferred the power to build ships.

"The path is indeed strewn with difficulties at every turn, in this and in many other matters, and God knows I have no serene confidence in my own judgment and discretion; but of one thing I am resolved, to break the control of special interests over this government and this people."[44]

"I am realizing now, as I have not realized before, even during the fight on the currency bill, that the influences that have so long dominated legislation and administration here are making their last and most desperate stand to regain their control. They are mustering every force they have in this very fight on the shipping bill. It is a very grim business, in which they will give no quarter and in which, so far as I am concerned, they will receive none. If they cannot be mastered, we shall have to have a new struggle for liberty in this country, and God knows what will come of it. Only reform can prevent revolution."[45]

"Alas, I am afraid that there is nothing anyone can do outside the Senate to remedy the present condition there which threatens the prestige and success of the party more, perhaps, than anything that has happened."[46]

Who could yield if the stakes were so high? Privately Wilson assured his friends that of course he knew what the potential international difficulties were; they would, he said, simply have to trust him to avoid them.[47] Publicly he said the same thing, not directly, but through his spokesmen in the Senate. "I have thought," he explained, "that the only course open to us was to ask the public to trust us on the principle that no administration that had not lost its head would be likely to do anything that would bring extraordinary risks to the country itself and add to the perplexities and hostilities of a terrible season of war like this."[48]

The fight in the Senate reached a desperate stage on Friday and

[44] W.W. to Mrs. Crawford H. Toy, January 31, 1915, Baker Collection.
[45] W.W. to Mrs. C. H. Toy, February 4, 1915, *ibid.*
[46] W.W. to D. F. Malone, February 5, 1915, Wilson Papers.
[47] e.g., W.W. to H. L. Higginson, February 1, 1915, *ibid.*
[48] W.W. to C. W. Eliot, February 18, 1915, *ibid.*

Saturday, January 29 and 30, 1915, when the Democratic leaders, boasting that they had the votes and would break the now-obvious Republican filibuster, kept the upper house in continuous session for thirty-seven hours. While senators dozed on cots and couches in the cloak rooms, Reed Smoot of Utah held the floor for eleven hours and thirty-five minutes from Friday night until Saturday morning. He was back again on the floor at midnight, Saturday evening, threatening to talk until he collapsed. At this point the Democratic leaders yielded to the alleged religious scruples of certain senators and permitted the house to adjourn over Sunday, January 31.[49]

When the Senate reconvened on Monday, February 1, the Democratic leaders warned that they would not permit it to adjourn again until it had approved the Ship Purchase bill. William Alden Smith, Republican of Michigan, droned on for six hours through the late morning and afternoon. He was followed by James P. Clarke, Democrat from Arkansas and President Pro Tempore of the upper house. Rising ponderously and remarking that the country needed a rural credits measure more than it needed ships, he moved to send the Ship Purchase bill back to the commerce committee. Stunned momentarily by such high treason, the Democratic leader Stone struck back by attempting to table Clarke's motion. But this effort failed because seven Democratic senators[50] defected in the showdown; and the regular Democrats themselves had to filibuster to prevent a vote on Clarke's motion to recommit until the Senate agreed to adjourn. Later in the evening reporters discovered that the dissident Democrats had met earlier in the day and planned their strategy under the tutelage of the Republican managers, Root, Lodge, and Gallinger.[51]

The Senate Democratic leaders, joined by the President himself, worked desperately during the following day, February 2, to regain

[49] *New York Times*, January 30 and 31, 1915; Louis Seibold in the New York *World*, January 31, 1915.

[50] Clarke, John H. Bankhead of Alabama, Johnson N. Camden of Kentucky, Thomas W. Hardwick of Georgia, Gilbert M. Hitchcock of Nebraska, James A. O'Gorman of New York, and James K. Vardaman of Mississippi. Most of them opposed the Ship Purchase bill out of a sincere conviction that the government should not participate in such an enterprise as running a shipping corporation. In addition, some of them were undoubtedly eager to teach the President a lesson in the separation of powers; most of them feared that diplomatic complications would ensue should the measure pass; and Hitchcock, Camden, and Vardaman, at least, were taking this opportunity to repay the administration for having allegedly slighted them in distributing the patronage.

[51] *New York Times*, February 2, 1915; New York *World*, February 2, 1915.

control. The Democratic caucus met early in the morning; but the seven rebels refused to attend, and the caucus instructed three consummate politicians—Duncan U. Fletcher of Florida, Furnifold M. Simmons of North Carolina, and Thomas S. Martin of Virginia—to see if some compromise could be found. Vardaman replied that he would vote against the Ship Purchase bill in any form. The remaining six at first indicated that they might return to the party fold if the President accepted certain amendments to the bill;[52] but they all reneged later in the day when word came from the White House that Wilson was willing to concede most of their demands.

While these futile negotiations were proceeding the President had also been at work along a different line. He had invited three midwestern insurgent Republican senators who had kept aloof from the struggle—George W. Norris of Nebraska, Moses E. Clapp of Minnesota, and William S. Kenyon of Iowa—to the White House to see if there was any possibility that the Ship Purchase bill might be amended so as to win their support. Clapp made it clear that he would never vote for the measure,[53] but Norris and Kenyon were encouraging, as was Robert M. La Follette of Wisconsin, who did not take part in the White House conferences but indicated that he might cooperate with the President.[54] So close was the division in the Senate that their three votes would turn the tide even if the seven rebels stayed off the reservation. Wilson felt safe again, as the following interchange with reporters on this day of great maneuvering indicated:

"Mr. President, can you say anything about the shipping bill?"

"That needn't bother you."

"It does."

"Well, you must not let it."

"It doesn't bother us, Mr. President, we just want to know about it."

"It is going through all right."

"With some changes, Mr. President?"

[52] These provided that the Secretaries of the Treasury and of Commerce should be eliminated from the membership of the proposed shipping board and sought to make it crystal clear that the establishment of a federally operated merchant marine was an emergency measure, that no belligerent ships should be purchased, that the government's ships should be sold or leased after the war had ended, and that the shipping board should give major attention to the development of trade with Latin America. New York *World*, February 3, 1915.

[53] As he had already indicated in M. E. Clapp to T. Roosevelt, January 25 and 28, 1915, Roosevelt Papers.

[54] Louis Seibold in the New York *World*, February 3, 1915; *New York Times*, February 3, 1915; W. S. Kenyon to W.W., February 3, 1915, Wilson Papers.

"No changes of any sort that is [*sic*] not consistent with the principle of the bill."[55]

The situation cleared somewhat on the following day, February 3, when the seven Democratic rebels met and pledged themselves to spurn all overtures from the White House. It was obvious now that the fate of the Ship Purchase bill rested in the hands of the insurgents. Norris and La Follette were willing to support the measure if it provided unequivocally for governmental operation of the merchant fleet and (as Norris insisted) against the purchase of any belligerent ships. Willing at this point to make nearly any concessions, the President agreed almost eagerly. But Kenyon wavered, and the Democrats still lacked a majority in the Senate.[56]

During the next few days, however, the Democratic leaders devised a plan to break the impasse. It was to filibuster to prevent approval of Clarke's motion to recommit until two absent Democrats, Francis G. Newlands of Nevada and Ellison D. Smith of South Carolina, could return to Washington. Then, with Vice President Thomas R. Marshall voting to break the tie, the Democrats would command a majority without Kenyon and could instruct the commerce committee to report the Ship Purchase bill with the amendments upon which Norris and La Follette had insisted. For added safety, they would also concentrate upon winning Kenyon's vote.[57]

For a brief time it seemed that this strategy would succeed. Newlands and Smith returned to the Senate chamber on February 8; and the Democrats with the help of Norris and La Follette defeated a motion to adjourn by a vote of forty-eight to forty-seven, with only the still-wavering Kenyon not voting. It was the signal for the resumption of a continuous session and the Republican filibuster. Elated by this sudden turn, the President joined the fight again on the following day, February 9, by telling reporters that he hoped his friends in the Senate would "fight it out to the finish."[58] At the same time, he moved quickly to secure the victory by winning Kenyon to the Democratic side. Senator Lodge described the President's maneuver in an unfriendly but not entirely inaccurate way on February 11, as follows:

"Yesterday the Administration did something which, for what [Sen-

[55] Transcript of a press conference on February 2, 1915, MS. in the Swem Papers.
[56] *New York Times*, February 4, 1915.
[57] *ibid.*, February 5, 1915.
[58] *ibid.*, February 9 and 10, 1915; New York *World*, February 10, 1915.

ator William E.] Borah calls a brutal disregard to decency, I have never seen surpassed. They sent in the name of Kenyon's brother-in-law for postmaster at Fort Dodge [Iowa], where Kenyon lives. Of course it is one of those things that no explanation on Kenyon's part would ever cover and leaves the impression on the public mind that he is bought, which I believe to be wholly untrue. Of course there is no possible means of his overcoming such an impression except by voting steadily against the Administration, which I think he understands. There is a coarse cynicism about such an act as this which it is difficult to comprehend. They have been using patronage in this way with little concealment."[59]

The Massachusetts senator did not misjudge the fatal consequences to the President of this stratagem. On the same day that Wilson sent the nomination for the postmastership of Fort Dodge to the Senate, Kenyon announced that the fight over the Ship Purchase bill had gone far enough. And when Senator James A. O'Gorman moved for adjournment late in the afternoon (the Senate had been in session for fifty-five hours), Kenyon and Norris, who must have also been alienated by the President's move, joined the opponents of the bill to carry the motion for adjournment by a vote of forty-eight to forty-six.[60]

It was, actually, the end of the fight in the upper house.[61] But the President was too deeply involved, too convinced that he had the country behind him,[62] to accept defeat without yet another effort. Some

[59] H. C. Lodge to T. Roosevelt, February 11, 1915, Roosevelt Papers.

[60] *New York Times*, February 11, 1915.

[61] As Senator J. R. Thornton of Louisiana bluntly pointed out to the President. J. R. Thornton to W.W., February 12, 1915, Wilson Papers.

[62] In fact, Wilson did have strong support from those groups, concentrated in the South and West, who were interested in the easy export of farm products and other raw materials, as well as from those newspapers closely identified with the Democratic party. On the other hand, most of the business and financial interests of the East and West Coast and most eastern newspapers and weekly periodicals were violently opposed to the Ship Purchase bill.

For evidences of the kind of support that the President received, see R. O. Johnston *et al.* of the City Club of Memphis to W.W., January 5, 1915, Wilson Papers; Edward N. Hurley to J. P. Tumulty, January 20, 1915, *ibid.*, reporting that the directors of the Illinois Manufacturers' Association had unanimously endorsed the Ship Purchase bill; J. M. Price, for the National Lumber Exporters Association, to W.W., January 25, 1915, *ibid.*; Sidney St. John Eshleman, president, Southern Hardware Jobbers Association, to W.W., February 7, 1915, *ibid.*; *New York Times*, February 4, 1915, reporting the endorsement of the National Grange and the National Farmers' Alliance.

For typical newspaper and periodical support of the measure, see the *St. Louis Republic*, January 22 and February 6, 1915; *Birmingham News*, February 2, 1915; *Springfield* (Massachusetts) *Republican*, January 28, 1915; the editorials cited in "The

way must be found to save the party from disgrace and to re-establish his own leadership. Thus driven at this juncture, he took personal command. Summoning the Democratic leaders in the House of Representatives to his study on February 10, he warned that he would call Congress into special session if the Ship Purchase bill were not approved before the life of the lame duck session had expired on March 4, 1915. At the same time he outlined a new strategy to his visitors—to have the lower house adopt a shipping bill in such a form and by so emphatic a majority that the Senate would not dare to reject it. During the evening of the same day, moreover, the President took the unprecedented step of calling at the home of the Speaker of the House of Representatives, Champ Clark of Missouri, to seek advice and support.[63]

Not daring to defy the President in his present mood, the House leaders quickly complied. They pushed an amended[64] Ship Purchase bill through the House Democratic caucus on February 15 and then rammed it through the lower chamber at 1:25 a.m. on February 17 by a vote of 215 to 122.[65] "The President is not to be weakened," wrote the German Ambassador, who had been ardently hoping that the Ship Purchase bill would succeed,[66] "and has already decided to

---

President's Plan for a Commercial Navy," *Literary Digest*, L (January 16, 1915), 81-83; and *Harper's Weekly*, LX (February 13, 1915), 162.

Evidence of the sentiment of the business and financial communities may be found in H. L. Higginson to E. M. House, January 13 and 15, 1915, House Papers; Francis L. Leland, president, New York County National Bank, to E. Root, January 23, 1915, Root Papers; the Merchants' Association of New York, circular letter to the members of Congress dated January 28, 1915, the Papers of William Kent, Yale University Library; Shipowners' Association of the Pacific Coast to W. Kent, January 26, 1915, *ibid.*; Daniel M. Barringer to W.W., February 2, 1915, Wilson Papers.

For samples of eastern newspaper and periodical opinion, which was almost unanimously opposed to the Ship Purchase bill, see the *New York Evening Post*, January 26, 1915; New York *Journal of Commerce*, January 25, 1915; the editorials cited in the *Literary Digest*, L (January 16, 1915), 81-83; New York *Nation*, C (January 28, 1915), 94; New York *Outlook*, CIX (January 20, February 3, 1915), 119-120, 256-257; *New Republic*, II (February 13, 1915), 29; *Collier's*, LIV (February 27, 1915), 16.

[63] *New York Times*, February 11 and 20, 1915; C. Clark to W.W., February 11, 1915, Wilson Papers.

[64] The amendment provided that the federal shipping board should wind up its affairs and that the government's merchant fleet should be turned over to the navy for use as auxiliary vessels within two years after the end of the war.

[65] *New York Times*, February 13, 14, 16, and 17, 1915; New York *World*, February 14, 1915.

[66] See Ambassador von Bernstorff to the Foreign Office, January 25 and February 3, 1915, German F. O. Archives.

call an extra session, as well as to go to the country himself in order to make the ship-purchase bill palatable to public opinion. It is possible that Wilsonian autocracy will lead to mutiny within the Democratic party. Signs of this are already appearing."[67]

It was, indeed, a futile gesture of defiance, one born of desperation and despair. The rebellious Democratic senators were no less intransigent than before, while the three insurgent Republicans, La Follette, Norris, and Kenyon, were now totally alienated by the provision in the House bill for a definite end to the government's shipping activities after the war. Meeting at the office of Senator Martin of Virginia during the afternoon of February 17, the Democratic leaders in the upper house surveyed the dismal scene and agreed that there was nothing left to do but end the hopeless fight.[68] They so informed the President the following day. And with his approval they sealed an agreement with the Republican leaders to take up immediate consideration of the various appropriation bills and meanwhile to send the Ship Purchase bill to a conference committee for decent burial.[69] "I think it is dead," Lodge wrote soon afterward. "We have such assurances from the Democrats—from the honorable ones among them —that if they do take it up in the last hours we are wholly prepared and will talk it over noon on March 4th without difficulty. All we fear is a trick, or strong arm methods, and on that they have given us absolute promises,—I mean the responsible men. . . . I do not wonder that you feel warlike with this Administration. I never expected to hate any one in politics with the hatred which I feel towards Wilson. I was opposed to our good friend Grover Cleveland, but never in any such way as this."[70]

The Democrats tried no such tricks or strong-arm methods as Lodge feared[71] but instead permitted the Senate to devote the last days of the short session to the appropriation bills. Wilson, meanwhile, had made it plain that he would not call a special session of Congress,[72]

---

[67] Ambassador von Bernstorff to T. von Bethmann Hollweg, February 17, 1915, *ibid.*
[68] *New York Times*, February 18, 1915.
[69] *ibid.*, February 19, 1915.
[70] H. C. Lodge to T. Roosevelt, March 1, 1915, Roosevelt Papers.
[71] In spite of intimations that the Democratic leaders would try to force the Ship Purchase bill through the upper house in the last few days of the short session that would end on March 4, 1915. New York *World*, February 27, 1915.
[72] On this point he yielded to the urgent advice of the Democratic leaders in Congress, most of whom were vehemently opposed to an extra session. See the *New York Times*, February 27, 1915; J. R. Thornton to W.W., February 12, 1915, Wilson Papers; J. P. Tumulty to W.W., February 26, 1915, *ibid.*

and he had even taken steps to pacify certain House Democrats who had voted against the Ship Purchase bill.[73] But his anger at the Republicans and particularly at the seven rebellious Democratic senators had not diminished; and on about March 3 he prepared a long statement for the press throwing responsibility for what he said was the dire shortage of shipping upon them.

"The shipping bill," he wrote, "has failed because the Republican Senators and their unexpected allies from the Democratic side were unwilling to permit the business of the country to be served and relieved at a time of extraordinary crisis and necessity,—when all the rest of the world needed what America produces, and America was ready to supply the need,—when the whole foreign trade of the country was threatened with a disastrous congestion and the fortunes and opportunities of thousands of her people put at jeopardy. . . .

"Seven Democratic Senators united with the Republican Senators to defeat the plan by filibuster when they realized the weakness of debate, and they have achieved their object. The members of that ill-omened coalition must bear the whole responsibility for it, the very grave responsibility for infinite damage to the business of the United States, to farmers, to laborers, to manufacturers, to producers of every class and sort. They have fastened the control of the selfish shipping interests on the country and the prospect is not a little sinister. Their responsibility will be very heavy, heavier and heavier as the months come and go; and it will be very bitter to bear.

"I shall not call an extra session of Congress. I have promised the country that there should be as long a period as possible of accommodation to the new conditions which have been created by recent important legislation. Unless circumstances arise which I cannot at present foresee, I cannot in good faith deny the business of the country this time of adjustment in many large matters, even to remedy the perhaps irremediable damage this unnatural and unprecedented alliance has brought upon our business. Their opportunity to rectify their grievous disloyalty has passed."[74]

[73] e.g., W.W., to R. N. Page of North Carolina, February 23, 1915, *ibid.*

[74] "Statement about the shipping bill," MS. in *ibid.* Wilson soon afterward explained more fully what he probably meant by applying the charge of "grievous disloyalty" to the seven Democratic rebels. One of them, Thomas W. Hardwick, of Georgia, wrote to the President on March 11, 1915 (*ibid.*), saying that he had opposed the Ship Purchase bill out of deep personal conviction, and that he hoped that he had not lost Wilson's friendship and respect by thus following the dictates of his conscience. Wilson replied on March 15, 1915 (*ibid.*), with one of the most illuminating expositions of

For some reason, perhaps because he concluded on second thought that nothing could be gained by further exacerbating the division in the Democratic ranks, Wilson decided not to issue this statement. Instead, he went in seeming good temper to the President's Room in the Capitol on the last day of the short session, March 4, 1915, where he greeted all Democrats with unfailing cordiality. Then, returning to the White House, he issued the following statement on the work of the Sixty-Third Congress, which had given the country the most comprehensive and perhaps the most constructive reform program in its history:

"A great Congress has closed its sessions. Its work will prove the purpose and quality of its statesmanship more and more the longer it is tested.

"Business has now a time of calm and thoughtful adjustment before it, disturbed only by the European war. The circumstances created by the war put the nation to a special test—a test of its true character and of its self-control.

"The constant thought of every patriotic man should now be for the country, its peace, its order, its just and tempered judgment in the face of perplexing difficulties. Its dignity and its strength alike will appear not only in the revival of its business, despite abnormal conditions, but also in its power to think, to purpose, and to act with patience, with disinterested fairness, and without excitement, in a

his views on party responsibility and leadership in the presidential-congressional system that he ever penned, as follows:

"You are right in thinking that differences of opinion upon public questions cannot alter my personal feeling towards men whom I respect and with whom it is a pleasure for me to work [Wilson could not in truth say that Hardwick was one of these!] and I thank you for judging me so truly. I must in frankness say, however, that the recent situation in the Senate distressed and disturbed me not a little. I do not see how party government is possible, indeed I can form no working idea of the successful operation of popular institutions, if individuals are to exercise the privilege of defeating a decisive majority of their own party associates in framing and carrying out the policy of the party. In party conference personal convictions should have full play and should be most candidly and earnestly presented, but there does not seem to me to be any surrender either of personal dignity or of individual conviction in yielding to the determinations of a decisive majority of one's fellow workers in a great organization which must hold together if it is to be serviceable to the country as a governing agency.

"This conviction on my part lies back of and supports every conclusion that I have come to in years of study not only, but in recent years of experience, with regard to the feasibility and efficiency of party government, and I beg, my dear Senator, that you will allow me to press this view upon you with the earnestness of a conviction which underlies all others."

spirit of friendliness and enlightenment which will firmly establish its influence throughout the world."[75]

Long before the epic struggle over the Ship Purchase bill had reached its climax, the President had to fight to head off a challenge to his leadership on yet another front. It was a virtual rebellion of the German Americans and their allies against the administration's policies of neutrality that culminated in a loud campaign to force Congress to enact and the President to approve a measure imposing an embargo on the export of munitions to the European belligerents.

Hatred of Wilson, which would drive the German Americans and Irish Americans to ferocious assaults against the administration in 1915 and 1916, developed first in a serious way in the autumn of 1914, as it became increasingly apparent that neutrality as the President practiced it meant American acquiescence in British control of the seas and the outpouring of munitions and war supplies from the United States to the Allied countries. Virtually all German Americans and their anti-British cohorts said they wanted their government to follow only a course of true neutrality. What they meant by neutrality was doing everything possible to prevent the British from enjoying the advantages that accrued to dominant sea power. As Secretary Bryan observed, noting how the growing German-American hostility to the administration had manifested itself in a specific way during the congressional elections in early November 1914, "There is a great deal of feeling among the German-Americans because we allow the sale of contraband. The fact that Germany can*not* take advantage of this opportunity enables those friendly to Germany to appeal to those who sympathize with that country. We lost a good many votes on this account in German-American communities."[76] "As the statistics prove," the German Ambassador reported to Berlin, "the Democratic party was beaten in the last elections in all districts where the German and Irish votes were the decisive factors."[77]

Having earlier ignored the extreme German-American propagandists, probably because he did not think that they spoke for the rank and file of their compatriots,[78] Wilson was somewhat startled when he received a letter from Professor Hugo Münsterberg of Harvard

---

[75] *New York Times*, March 5, 1915; New York *World*, March 5, 1915.
[76] W. J. Bryan to W. H. Page, December 14, 1914, Page Papers.
[77] Ambassador von Bernstorff to the Foreign Office, January 12, 1915, German F. O. Archives.
[78] e.g., W.W. to R. Lansing, October 28, 1914, *The Lansing Papers*, I, 159.

immediately after the November elections, warning that German Americans and Irish Americans were turning against the Democratic party on account of the President's allegedly pro-British policies.[79] "I have received and read with a great deal of surprise your letter of November seventh," Wilson hastened to reply. "Certainly no administration ever tried more diligently or watchfully to preserve an attitude and pursue a line of conduct absolutely neutral. I would consider it a favor if you would point out to us what are considered the unneutral acts of which this administration is thought to have been guilty. If we have done anything contrary to our professions, I should certainly wish to correct the mistake if it were possible to do so. We have acted in strict accordance with international law, so far as we know."[80]

Münsterberg replied in a long letter on November 19, making it plain that he spoke not for himself or the German government, but only for the "masses of voters" who believed that "the State Department subordinates its decisions to the wishes of England." The German Americans, he reported, resented the government's obvious acquiescence in the British maritime system and above all the export of munitions, which was prolonging the war and benefiting the Allies exclusively.[81] Wilson was deeply impressed. "Here at last," he wrote to Lansing, asking for his comments, "is a very definite summing up of the matters upon which German anti-administration feeling in this country is being built up. . . . The case they make out is *prima facie* very plausible indeed." Perhaps it would be wise, Wilson added, to take "very serious notice" of the complaint.[82]

Submitting a long memorandum answering Münsterberg's indictment,[83] Lansing replied that he doubted the wisdom of sending an official communication to "a German subject, in fact an agent of the German Government," and Wilson agreed.[84] But German-American denunciations of the leaders in Washington reached a new crescendo in late November and early December 1914, on the eve of the meeting

[79] H. Münsterberg to W.W., November 7, 1914, Wilson Papers.

[80] W.W. to H. Münsterberg, November 10, 1914, *ibid.*

[81] H. Münsterberg to W.W., November 19, 1914, *ibid.*; printed in *The Lansing Papers*, I, 161-165.

[82] W.W. to R. Lansing, December 1, 1914, *ibid.*, p. 161.

[83] "Memorandum by the Counselor for the Department of State . . . ," *ibid.*, pp. 167-179.

[84] R. Lansing to W.W., December 9, 1914; W.W. to R. Lansing, December 10, 1914, *ibid.*, pp. 166, 179.

of Congress.[85] Some answer, Lansing now admitted, had to be made: "However unjustified the complaints may be, there can be no doubt of their political effect. Thousands of former friends of the Administration are being converted into bitter adversaries."[86] Discussions ensued, and the upshot was an agreement that Senator Stone, as chairman of the foreign relations committee, should address a letter to the Secretary of State simply reporting the charges of unneutrality that were then being made, and that Bryan should reply with a definitive explanation. The letters, prepared for the most part by Lansing, were published in the press on January 25, 1915.[87] Point by point Bryan (or Lansing) answered the German-American indictment; frankly and fully he explained why the United States could not make any effective challenge to British sea power or place an embargo on the export of munitions without acting in flagrant unneutrality.

A sharp increase in the German-American resentment was the principal result of this forthright and, one must add, cogent defense of American neutrality. Bryan's name was hissed, for example, at numerous rallies of the friends of the Fatherland from this time until his resignation as Secretary of State. A more immediate result was the gathering of all the distinguished leaders of the German-American community in Washington on January 30. There in the center of national political power they formed the National German-American League for direct action, warning that they would "support only such candidates for public office, irrespective of party, who will place American interests above those of any other country, and who will aid in eliminating all undue foreign influences from official life."[88] Another immediate result of the State Department's pronouncement was to spur the German Americans to frenzied activity in their now most important undertaking—a gigantic campaign for an arms embargo.

There had been sporadic protests against the traffic in arms almost from the beginning of the war,[89] but the organized movement for an

[85] Clifton J. Child, *The German-Americans in Politics, 1914-1917*, pp. 47-48.

[86] R. Lansing to W. J. Bryan, December 26, 1915, *The Lansing Papers*, I, 184.

[87] e.g., the *New York Times*, January 25, 1915; the exchange was afterward printed in *Foreign Relations, 1914, Supplement*, pp. vi-xiv.

[88] New York *World*, February 2, 1915; Ambassador von Bernstorff to the Foreign Office, February 1, 1915, German F. O. Archives; "What the German-Americans Are Organizing For," *Literary Digest*, L (February 13, 1915), 299-301.

[89] e.g., G. F. Sherwood *et al.*, for the Salem, Oregon, Local of the Socialist Party, to W.W., August 23, 1914, Wilson Papers; Albert Worltem, for the Fort Wayne Local of the Socialist Party, to W.W., August 25, 1914, *ibid.* J. H. Schiff to W.W., November 19, 1914, *ibid.*

embargo did not get seriously under way until December 1, 1914. On that day some 16,000 German and Irish Americans met in Chicago and formed the German-Irish Central Legislative Committee for the Furtherance of American Neutrality, the sole objective of which was the adoption of an embargo measure by the impending Congress.[90] Then, as soon as the short session convened on December 7, Senator Gilbert M. Hitchcock of Nebraska and Representatives Richard Bartholdt of Missouri, Henry Vollmer of Iowa, and Charles O. Lobeck of Nebraska all introduced embargo bills. "Before Congress and the House of Representatives," the German Ambassador reported to Berlin a short time later, "are the Hitchcock and Vollmer resolutions, concerning prohibitions on the export of arms, munitions, etc. . . . On account of the great importance of the matter, I took it upon myself to give financial support to the movement, and provisionally supplied the 5,000 dollars requested from responsible quarters."[91]

During the following weeks German Americans, leaders and followers alike, rallied loyally for what they hoped would be an irresistible campaign. A lobby representing the German-Irish Central Legislative Committee was on hand in Washington to greet congressmen arriving for the short session; and new pleaders for peace and neutrality descended upon the Capitol when the House foreign affairs committee held brief hearings on the Vollmer and Bartholdt bills on December 30 and 31, 1914, and January 4, 1915.[92] "By this time," as one historian has written, "the agitation had spread far beyond the House Committee on Foreign Affairs, and there was work to be done in a much broader field. Petitions in support of the embargo were coming in from all parts of the country, some of them spontaneous, but many more prompted by the [German-American] Alliance and the German-language newspapers. Huge bundles, said to contain the signatures of two million citizens were wheeled into the Capitol at Washington. Mass meetings were held in most of the large cities, often with pro-German congressmen and state governors on the platform.

[90] Horace L. Brand, chairman, form letter to E. Root, December 9, 1914, Root Papers, enclosing "Resolutions Adopted by the German-Irish Demonstration at Chicago, December 1st, 1914."

[91] Ambassador von Bernstorff to the Foreign Office, December 16, 1914, German F. O. Archives.

[92] New York *World*, December 16, 1914, and January 5, 1915; C. J. Child, *The German-Americans in Politics, 1914-1917*, pp. 49-51, for a summary of the testimony before the House committee. For a survey of the propaganda of the German-American newspapers, see the *Literary Digest*, L (January 2, 1915), 3.

The German Evangelical Synod of North America telegraphed its support."[93] It would be an exaggeration to say that the country was convulsed, but the excitement was considerable.

By themselves, the German- and Irish-American leaders could not hope to exert enough pressure to bend Congress and the administration to their will. The important question at this point was whether

"Neutral" German Americans
Robinson in *Harper's Weekly*

they would win enough support from the uncommitted majority to put their measure across. There were many signs that the anti-munitions propaganda was making a strong appeal to the humane consciences of the rank and file of Americans. *The Survey*, spokesman of the organized social workers, voiced what was by now a widespread feeling in announcing its support of an arms embargo, as follows: "The simple and appalling consideration which should control our decision is that if the cannon, armor plate, copper, powder, motor cars, and gasoline with which the war is carried on, are supplied by this

[93] C. J. Child, *The German-Americans in Politics, 1914-1917*, p. 51.

country, we are responsible for its continuance. We might easily find ourselves literally more responsible for it than any nation engaged on the battle field."[94] Probing American press opinion on the issue in late January 1915, the editors of the *Literary Digest* found much agreement with these sentiments. Out of a total of 440 editors who replied, 244 opposed and 167 favored an arms embargo, while twenty-nine were noncommittal. But the advocates of the measure were probably a majority among midwestern editors and spoke as well for perhaps a majority of editors in small towns throughout the entire country.[95] It was no sure sign of public opinion, but it gave striking proof that the response to the German-American appeal was genuinely national in character.

It was small wonder, then, that the British Foreign Office and the friends of the Allies were profoundly disturbed. As we have seen, Sir Edward Grey's policy toward cotton at this time had the sole objective of pacifying the South in order to avoid driving the powerful southern Democrats into alliance with the German Americans. In addition, Sir Edward took the unusual step of lodging an informal protest against the Hitchcock bill even though it had not been reported by the foreign relations committee.[96] And friends of the Allies throughout the United States repeated, publicly and privately, what Grey had said, that the imposition of an arms embargo would destroy American neutrality and range the United States squarely on the side of the Central Powers. Moreover, they answered the idealists and moralists on their own ground. As the *New Republic*, for example, argued:

"There is a catchy reasonableness about the German-American argument that our neutrality is unreal unless we forbid the export of arms. Germany having lost command of the sea, American traffic in war supplies helps the Allies. . . . Partisans aside, there is, we believe, a growing body of pacifist opinion . . . which insists that American manufacturers are 'capitalizing carnage,' making profits out of murder, and that in decency and in humanity this nation ought to have nothing to do with the European crime. But what would be the consequences of so pure a stand? It would 'stop the war,' we are told, but where? With Germany in possession of Belgium and the richest part of

[94] *The Survey*, xxxiii (January 2, 1915), 387.

[95] "Press Poll on Prohibiting the Export of Arms," *Literary Digest*, l (February 6, 1915), 225-226, 274-283.

[96] Ambassador Page to the Secretary of State, December 11, 1914, *Foreign Relations, 1914, Supplement*, pp. 578-579.

France. And the lesson to England and France? It would be that militarism pays, that God is on the side of the big ready battalions, that a nation which dreams, plans, and organizes war can impose its will on the less military nations. Such an embargo would be regarded by the Allies as the most desperate treachery, as an arbitrary reversal of all international law, not in time of peace but in the midst of a terrible crisis. We should by the embargo which Mr. Bartholdt and others propose neutralize at one stroke a large part of British naval superiority; we should be doing as much for Germany as if we established a fairly good blockade in the Atlantic. And if we ourselves ever faced a life-and-death struggle, we should have established a precedent which might prove fatal. The proposal is a piece of thoughtless morality, a bit of good intention with unconsidered consequences. As a method of warring against war it belongs with incantations, spells, and the sacrificing of goats."[97]

In these circumstances of a nearly even division in public opinion, the fate of the embargo bills depended in large measure upon what the President did and said. There is no reason to think that he considered himself bound by the State Department's circular of October 15, 1914, about contraband, which he had approved.[98] It had, anyway, merely affirmed that Americans had the legal right to sell contraband and that the President possessed no authority *under existing legislation* to interfere with such commerce.[99] Whether or not to impose the same kind of ban on the shipment of arms as he had on the granting of loans was not an easy question for Wilson, and he struggled hard, one might even say prayerfully, during the late autumn of 1914 for the right answer. We may be sure that his conscience was revolted as much as any man's by the thought of American arms killing Germans by the tens of thousands, and that he also knew that Germans would

[97] *New Republic*, 1 (January 9, 1915), 3. See also Paul Fuller, Senior, Benjamin F. Tracy, and Frederic R. Coudert to W.W., December 8, 1914, *The Lansing Papers*, 1, 180; New York *Outlook*, cviii (December 23, 1914), 903-904; *The Public*, xviii (January 22, 1915), 74; W. H. Taft to E. von Mach, January 26, 1915, Taft Papers; *The Churchman*, cxi (February 6, 1915), 166; *Harper's Weekly*, lx (March 13, 1915), 242; and the editorial opinion against an arms embargo cited in the *Literary Digest*, l (February 6, 1915), 225-226, 274-283.

[98] As R. S. Baker, *Woodrow Wilson: Life and Letters*, v, 217, implies: "In the meantime, on October 15th, the American government had, in its circular giving definite sanction to the munitions traffic, thrown away its best bargaining asset [with Great Britain]—that of a possible—or impossible!—embargo."

[99] *Foreign Relations, 1914, Supplement*, pp. 573-574.

kill British and French soldiers by the tens of thousands if the latter had to fight without American arms.

The more he pondered the dilemma the more hesitant he became to render a clear-cut decision, as he revealed in an interchange with Jacob H. Schiff, head of the New York investment firm of Kuhn, Loeb & Company. Schiff, a prominent German American, had urged the President to issue a public appeal to American munitions manufacturers not to contribute to the European carnage.[100] Wilson replied three weeks later, saying that he had waited so long to answer because he had needed time to wrestle with the problem. "Not," he continued, "that it was the first time that I had tried to think it out, for it is one of the most perplexing things I have had to decide. The law standing as it does, the most I can do is to exercise influence, and in the case of the lending of money I was directly applied to for advice and approval. There my duty was clear. It was my duty to discourage the loans to belligerents. In the matter of sales of goods of all kinds, however, the precedents of international law are so clear, the sales proceed from so many sources, and my lack of power is so evident, that I have felt that I could do nothing else than leave the matter to settle itself."[101]

Surely these were not the words of a man on solid moral ground. Nor, apparently, was he as confident of his legal position as this letter seemed to imply. This he revealed two days later. Three distinguished international lawyers had sent a telegram to the White House asserting that the enactment of an embargo bill would be an "absolute violation of neutrality."[102] Wilson sent the telegram on to Lansing with the significant question, "Are these gentlemen right in the position they take, do you think?"[103]

He probably knew the answer that would come from the State Department, for all along Lansing had held that it would be unneutral for the United States to deny the Allies the right to purchase arms unless there were good political reasons for doing so. "I think these gentlemen are entirely right in the general principle asserted," the Counselor replied to Wilson's direct query. "Any change in our statutes by amendment or repeal would undoubtedly benefit one or the

[100] J. H. Schiff to W.W., November 19, 1914, Wilson Papers.

[101] W.W. to J. H. Schiff, December 8, 1914, *ibid.*

[102] P. Fuller, Senior, B. F. Tracy, and F. R. Coudert to W.W., December 8, 1914, *loc. cit.*

[103] W.W. to R. Lansing, December 10, 1914, *The Lansing Papers*, 1, 179.

other of the belligerents."[104] Nor did Bryan, who always tried as hard as Wilson to make right decisions, have any doubt about the matter. To him, the meaning of an arms embargo was as plain as daylight: "Any action looking to interference with the right of belligerents to buy arms here would be construed as an unneutral act, not only because the effect of such action would be to assist one party at the expense of the other, but also because the *purpose* of the [Bartholdt] resolution is plainly to assist one party at the expense of the other."[105]

There was, actually, little likelihood that the President would contradict what his two chief advisers on foreign relations were saying, because he obviously believed that they were right. There remained, then, only the question of how best to resist and repel the German-American pressure upon Congress. This Wilson and Bryan did in several ways. When the members of the House foreign affairs committee asked the Secretary of State for the administration's opinion of the Bartholdt embargo bill, Bryan replied bluntly in the words quoted above; and Wilson authorized him to tell the committee that he agreed entirely.[106] As a consequence, the committee reported none of the embargo bills that had been referred to it. The two leaders met the issue even more squarely in Bryan's public letter to Senator Stone. (It was, Wilson said, "the best way to clear away the mists that have been accumulating around this subject."[107]) The President of the United States, Bryan (or Lansing) declared, had no power to prevent the sale of munitions to belligerents; and international law imposed no duty upon a neutral to restrict the trade in arms. Indeed, the letter to Stone continued, making its most telling point, the German government itself had affirmed, in a memorandum dated December 15, 1914, that the arms traffic was entirely legal and proper.[108]

For added emphasis Wilson seized an opportunity a few days later to make certain that the American people understood where he personally stood. On February 4 he received Doctor Frederick Bente of the Concordia Lutheran Theological Seminary at the White House and heard the usual argument for an arms embargo. When his visitor had finished, the President rebuked him, saying that all Americans should think only of their own country and should not embarrass

[104] R. Lansing to W.W., December 10, 1914, *ibid.*, p. 180.
[105] W. J. Bryan to W.W., January 6, 1915, Wilson Papers.
[106] W.W. to W. J. Bryan, January 7, 1915, *ibid.*
[107] W.W. to W. J. Stone, January 7, 1915, *ibid.*
[108] *Foreign Relations, 1914, Supplement*, pp. x-xi.

their government by "seeking to influence it away from pursuing a course of the strictest neutrality."[109] He repeated the same admonition to a group of ladies who came to the Executive Mansion on February 18 to present a large petition for an arms embargo.[110]

By the middle of February 1915 it was clear that the German-American campaign had foundered on the rocks of presidential and public opposition.[111] Indeed, up to this point the advocates of an arms embargo had failed even to obtain a show of hands in the two houses of Congress, for the embargo resolutions had meanwhile been carefully buried by the House and Senate committees. Then quite without warning on February 18, in the middle of the Senate debate over the Ship Purchase bill, Senator Hitchcock introduced his arms embargo bill as an amendment to the shipping bill. Senator Fletcher at once moved to table the amendment, thus preventing any discussion on the embargo itself. The motion to table carried by a majority of fifty-one to thirty-six, but only because most Democrats voted to uphold the administration and nine out of eleven eastern Republicans joined them to make a majority. If the midwestern senators had had their way, the Hitchcock amendment would have been considered and probably adopted.[112] It was an astounding revelation both of the power of the anti-munitions appeal to the American conscience and of the German-American vote in a great region.

The advocates of an arms embargo made no more futile forays in the closing days of the Sixty-Third Congress. As events would later reveal, however, the defeat of the Hitchcock amendment marked only the end of the first phase of the German-American campaign. The pressure for an arms embargo would increase, not diminish; and battles more severe than the one through which they had just passed would engage the President and his friends in the future.

[109] New York *World*, February 5, 1915.

[110] *ibid.*, February 19, 1915.

[111] Actually, this fact had been obvious long before then to acute observers like the German Ambassador. See Ambassador von Bernstorff to the Foreign Office, December 31, 1914, and February 3, 1915, German F.O. Archives.

[112] *Congressional Record*, 63d Cong., 3d sess., p. 4016. If we define the Middle West as composing the twelve states from Ohio to the tier of Plains states, including Missouri and excluding Oklahoma, then the midwestern division on the Fletcher motion was as follows: fifteen votes against tabling, seven in favor of tabling, and two not voting. Of the seven midwestern senators who voted to table, at least four (Pomerene of Ohio, Kern and Shively of Indiana, and Stone of Missouri) were loyal administration Democrats.

CHAPTER VI

The President and the First Crises with Great Britain

WHILE the President and Congress were deeply mired in the toils and troubles of the lame duck session, relations between the United States and Great Britain took a sudden turn, only mildly disturbing at first but then worsening, until a state of near crisis developed. Or so it seemed as several lines of conflict converged suddenly in late December 1914 and early January to produce an outpouring of recrimination.

Trouble developed first as a consequence of the seeming severity with which the British Admiralty began to enforce the Order in Council of October 29, 1914. The greatest irritant was British treatment of American copper after that commodity was put on the list of absolute contraband by royal decree. Between late October and early November the British navy fell upon a number of ships carrying American copper to Swedish, Dutch, and Italian ports and escorted them to naval stations in Great Britain and Gibraltar for action by the Prize Court.[1] There the vessels and cargoes stayed, often for months at a time, as it turned out, without court hearing and sometimes without any notification to the owners.

The State Department sent a stream of specific protests to London in November, but the rising tide of complaints, mainly from the copper producers and shippers and their political representatives,[2] convinced Secretary Bryan and his colleagues in the State Department that some general public protest would have to be made. Cone Johnson, the Solicitor, completed the first draft with Lansing's help on about December 16, 1914.[3] It was, Johnson explained, "intended to be

[1] The New York *World*, January 25, 1915, prints a list of these ships and their cargoes, together with information about their sailings, their destinations, and the dates when they were captured.

[2] For some of these, see *Foreign Relations, 1914, Supplement*, pp. 278-284; also Samuel Untermyer to J. P. Tumulty, November 10, 1914, and John D. Ryan to J. P. Tumulty, December 24, 1914, both in the Wilson Papers.

[3] C. Johnson to R. Lansing, December 16, 1914, State Department Papers.

temperate in tone, but vigorous in the presentation of our explicit objections to the course being pursued by Great Britain which, if not materially changed, will result in the destruction of our commerce with the neutral countries of Europe."[4] A fairly temperate indictment of current British practices, it was also wordy, unclearly written, and in a few places provocative in tone.[5]

Bryan sent the proposed note to the White House on December 17. "I think, in view of the increasing tension there is on the subject," he advised the President, "it is well for us to put this Government's views in definite form so that in case inquiry is made as to what has been done it will be manifest that we have exerted ourselves to the utmost to bring about a lessening of the hardships imposed upon neutral countries. It is a matter of such importance, however, that we are anxious to have you go over it carefully and suggest any changes in phraseology or any additions or subtractions that you may think wise."[6]

Wilson did not receive the draft note in good humor. Colonel House, who seemed to have an uncanny way of being in Washington when notes of protest to Great Britain were being prepared, was at the White House on December 18 when the proposed instructions arrived. Reading the document, Wilson observed that it was crudely written; obviously, he said, he and House would have to rewrite it. Before he had gone through the first paragraph, the President threw down his pencil and exclaimed, "It is not right to impose such a task upon me. They have not written good and understandable English, much less writing it in a way to avoid offense."[7] He thereupon sent the draft back to the State Department with the observation that it was "too abrupt" and the request that it be rewritten.

The President must have made his irritation plain in other ways, for Lansing carefully redrafted the note and submitted it to Bryan on December 21. The two men went over this draft together, and Lansing worked it over again on Christmas Eve.[8] "Mr. Lansing went over the text a second time," Bryan explained as he sent the draft to the White House, "and smoothed out such harsh places as he dis-

---

[4] C. Johnson to R. Lansing, December 14, 1914, *ibid.*

[5] C. Johnson, "Draft of a Proposed Instruction to the Ambassador at London," dated December 16, 1914, *ibid.*

[6] W. J. Bryan to W.W., December 17, 1914, *The Lansing Papers*, I, 257-258.

[7] House Diary, December 18, 1914.

[8] "Redraft of Instructions to American Ambassador at London," December 21, 1914, State Department Papers; "Second Redraft of Instruction to American Ambassador at London," December 24, 1914, *ibid.*

covered and then I went over it after him, making some other modifications. . . . We have tried to soften the expression without modifying or impairing the strength of our protest."[9] "This paper is much improved," Wilson replied as he sent the draft back with a few minor changes on December 26, "and I am glad to give it my sanction."[10]

A short time afterward Wilson gave an amusing and somewhat embellished account of this episode to a group of friends. "Bryan," he related, "brought me that note in an entirely rough and unliterary form, threatening, too. I drew my pen through certain offensive passages, wrote out new statements on the margin and between the lines, handed it back to him and suggested that he should re-write it. Three days passed and I was wondering what had become of that note when Bryan brought it to me exactly in the form in which I had given it to him and pointing to the marginal notes *made in my own hand-writing* said that he had made those corrections, and was I now satisfied. Nothing else had been done." "What did you say," one of his listeners asked. "Nothing," Wilson replied. "What *was* there to say!"[11]

Meanwhile, at Wilson's request Colonel House had told Ambassador Spring Rice that a note of protest was being drafted, and that it would be well for the British government to release ships and cargoes as quickly as possible.[12] The Foreign Office being thus properly forewarned, the note was put on the State Department's wire at four p.m. on December 26 and presented to Sir Edward Grey two days later. In strong and measured terms it conveyed the growing American concern at British seizures of ships and cargoes. "It is needless to point out to His Majesty's Government, usually the champion of the freedom of the seas and the rights of trade," it said in its key statement, "that peace, not war, is the normal relation between nations and the commerce between countries which are not belligerents should not be interfered with by those at war unless such interference is manifestly an imperative necessity to protect their national safety, and then only to the extent that it is a necessity." "It is with no lack of appreciation of the momentous nature of the present struggle in which Great Britain is engaged," the note continued, ". . . that this Government is

[9] W. J. Bryan to W.W., December 24, 1914, *ibid.*

[10] W.W. to W. J. Bryan, December 26, 1914, *The Lansing Papers*, I, 258.

[11] Mrs. Crawford H. Toy, "Second Visit to the White House," diary entry dated January 3, 1915, MS. in the Baker Collection. One regrets spoiling a good story, but the truth is that the President made only four minor alterations in words and phrases and no "marginal notes" when he edited the final copy.

[12] House Diary, December 18, 1914.

reluctantly forced to the conclusion that the present policy of His Majesty's Government toward neutral ships and cargoes exceeds the manifest necessity of a belligerent and constitutes restrictions upon the right of American citizens on the high seas which are not justified by the rules of international law or required under the principle of self-preservation." Then followed a detailed indictment of what the note implied was the capricious British treatment of copper and of conditional contraband like foodstuffs. "Not only is the situation a critical one to the commercial interests of the United States, but many of the great industries of this country are suffering because their products are denied long-established markets in European countries. . . . Producers and exporters, steamship and insurance companies are pressing, and not without reason, for relief from the menace to transatlantic trade which is gradually but surely destroying their business and threatening them with financial disaster." The American government was confident, the note concluded, that the British authorities would refrain from all unnecessary interference with neutral trade, for if the present situation continued very long it might well "arouse a feeling contrary to that which has so long existed between the American and British peoples."[13]

It was as unoffending and unthreatening as any American protest could have been in the circumstances. But what was more important, its whole language and tone implied unmistakably that the leaders in Washington were concerned only with details and had no thought of challenging the basic legality of the British maritime system. "I cannot believe," Lansing wrote to a Canadian friend in explanation, ". . . that this correspondence will in any way affect the friendly relations between the two countries. There is no doubt that our commerce along certain lines has suffered greatly by the interferences which have taken place. Naturally we seek to relieve our exporters as far as possible from restrictions, which appear to be unnecessarily severe. It does not seem to me that our note goes further than that or that we could say less. . . . Certainly the temper of it is amicable and not defiant; and you may be sure, unless something unforeseen occurs, the same spirit will be manifested in the continuance of the discussion. . . . The whole thing is a matter of mutual trust. I am sure that we will come at least half way."[14] Page and the British lead-

[13] The Secretary of State to Ambassador Page, December 26, 1914, *Foreign Relations, 1914, Supplement,* pp. 372-375.

[14] R. Lansing to Sir Charles Fitzpatrick, January 9, 1915, Lansing Papers.

ers understood and were immensely pleased. "It is an admirable paper, & it is a pleasure to present it. . . . It will have a good effect and will supplement and strengthen the work that I have been trying to do," Page wrote from London, in one of the few kind letters that he ever addressed to Secretary Bryan.[15] Spring Rice was equally commendatory: "It seems to me a very fair just courteous and firm presentment of the case to which no objection whatever could be raised on the ground of its form. I am sure that it will create a very lasting impression."[16]

There was, however, momentary excitement when the American press, on December 29, 1914, published a very abbreviated version of the note with headlines blazoning the news that the President had called on England to lift her "embargo."[17] Letters commending what one correspondent called this new Declaration of Independence filled the White House mail bags,[18] and reporters noted that the Democratic members of Congress were greatly relieved.[19] Thinking that a crisis impended, British newspapers featured the news of the protest on their front pages in large headlines. British editors generally withheld comment, but there was a strong undercurrent of opinion to the effect that the note was proof of the influence of German propaganda in the United States.[20]

In an attempt to repair the damage, Wilson called in reporters and told them that the recent note, although it had of course been meant in all seriousness, contained no threats or suggestions of any action that might conceivably lead to a break in relations. The administration, he took special pains to make clear, did not intend to force an issue with Great Britain that would cause serious trouble.[21] Further to allay popular alarm, the State Department and the Foreign Office gave the full text of the note to the press on either side of the Atlantic for publication on January 1, 1915.

[15] W. H. Page to W. J. Bryan, December 28, 1914, *The Lansing Papers*, I, 259.

[16] C. Spring Rice to E. M. House, c. December 31, 1914, House Papers.

[17] e.g., *New York Times*, December 29, 1914. According to William Phillips of the State Department, Tumulty was responsible for the leak. House Diary, December 30, 1914.

[18] S. T. Everett to W.W., December 29, 1914, Wilson Papers; also, e.g., E. M. Kolb to W.W., C. J. Plankenhorn to W.W., W. P. Deppé to W.W., all dated December 29, 1914, *ibid.*, and the Longview, Texas, Chamber of Commerce to W.W., December 30, 1914, *ibid.*

[19] *New York Times*, December 30, 1914.

[20] *ibid.*; Ambassador Page to the Secretary of State, December 30, 1914, Page Papers.

[21] *New York Times*, December 30, 1914.

The atmosphere of apprehension cleared at once. A few extreme pro-Allied spokesmen in the United States and a coterie of anti-American editors in England exploded, to be sure, because any protest at all had been made. "Belgium suffered, and we said nothing," Theodore Roosevelt's editorial organ cried; "our trade suffers, and we speak. On questions of honor and obligation we keep silence; we raise our voice only when dollars are involved."[22] "In an underhand way he [President Wilson] has been trying to help Germany," Senator Lodge added privately. "He has cut off the French loan; he has prevented Schwab from exporting parts of submarines. He has remained silent in regard to the violation of Belgium's neutrality by Germany; . . . and then he suddenly finds his voice in a protest to England, one of the Allies, about interference with our trade."[23] "It is unfortunate," a London weekly agreed, "that the American Government, acting admittedly under a purely commercial pressure, should have protested against the action of the British Fleet, and said not a word about the conduct of the German Army."[24] But these spokesmen, like the German-American and Hearst newspapers, which protested bitterly that the note was not severe enough, reflected the opinions only of extremists. The great majority of Americans and Englishmen agreed with the London editor who declared:

"It would be absurd to speak of the American protest as to the searching and detention of her ships as a 'crisis.' It is not so at all. It is simply a frank and precise declaration by the American Government of the delay, inconvenience, and loss to the American trader involved in the necessary policing of the sea by Great Britain. . . . On the one side is Great Britain, with command of the sea, resolved as a belligerent that the enemy shall not be strengthened and supported by the sea. On the other side is America desiring to get as freely as possible into her usual markets. The two points of view are directly in conflict, but that does not mean that America and Great Britain are bound to quarrel. . . . The conflict . . . is not a conflict of temper or principle, but simply of interest."[25]

[22] "The American Protest to Great Britain," New York *Outlook*, CIX (January 6, 1915), 10.

[23] H. C. Lodge to T. Roosevelt, January 15, 1915, Roosevelt Papers.

[24] *The Spectator*, CXIV (January 2, 1915), 7.

[25] *The Saturday Review*, CXIX (January 2, 1915), 3. See also the London *Nation*, XVI (January 2, 1915), 432-433; *New Republic*, I (January 9, 1915), 8-9; *Montreal Gazette*, January 18, 1915; the survey of British and American press opinion in "Our Warning to Great Britain," *Literary Digest*, L (January 9, 1915), 37-39; and Armin Rappaport, *The British Press and Wilsonian Neutrality*, p. 19.

"Obstructing Traffic, Your Honor"
Kirby in the New York *World*

In strong agreement with these views, President Wilson was determined that the denouement of the episode should be a happy one. Sir Edward Grey replied to the American protest with some "preliminary observations" on January 7, 1915. He pointed to the swelling of American exports to the European neutrals since the autumn of 1914 as proof that the British navy had not suppressed any legitimate American trade. But the note was in no way contentious, and Grey made it clear that he agreed in principle with the Washington government.[26] And when Lansing submitted a long and disputatious com-

[26] Ambassador Page to the Secretary of State, January 7, 1915, *Foreign Relations, 1915, Supplement*, pp. 299-302.

mentary on Grey's reply,[27] Wilson made it plain that he wanted no new controversy over mere details. "The two governments being apparently in substantial agreement about the principles involved," he wrote in comment on the Counselor's memorandum, "it would seem to me best that the whole argument should be directed to practicable methods of handling the whole matter with the least possible delay, unfairness, or friction, and with a view to bringing the British practices to some basis of uniformity and consistency upon which our merchants could reckon. My feeling is that it is not worth while debating details with them."[28]

A further revelation of Wilson's thoughts came at about the same time that the above words were written. On January 9 Chandler P. Anderson, who had recently returned to Washington after serving as a special adviser to Ambassador Page in London, had a long conversation with the President. Anderson explained the British point of view on matters of neutral trade. "The President," Anderson wrote in his diary immediately afterward, "said that on my presentation of the situation there were no very important questions of principle involved in the differences between the two Governments because our objections were directed chiefly against the manner in which Great Britain was interfering with neutral trade rather than against the right of Great Britain to exercise the supervision which she claimed over commerce with the enemy." Where the differences were merely legal, as was now the case, Wilson continued, then all the American government could do was to submit them to judicial decision; and, he added, he had already reminded the British authorities that they were building up a large bill for damages. Anderson conceded that this was true but said that the United States should reserve all these questions for future decision and not attempt to impose its point of view at a time when Britain was fighting for her life. "The President apparently agreed to all of this, and said that although he had not been able to devote his personal attention to the details of carrying out the policy of this Government, he felt that the policy he had laid down was exactly in accordance with the views I had expressed."[29]

Soon after these interchanges, Bryan and Lansing, in deference to the President's obvious wishes, prepared a brief and friendly acknowl-

[27] R. Lansing to W.W., January 11, 1915, *The Lansing Papers*, I, 261-265.
[28] W.W. to W. J. Bryan, January 14, 1915, *ibid.*, p. 266.
[29] Anderson Diary, January 9, 1915.

edgement of Grey's preliminary note.[30] And when the Foreign Secretary sent his definitive formal reply on February 10, 1915—it was a long and eloquent defense of the legality and execution of the British maritime system[31]—the leaders in the State Department did not even suggest the drafting of an answer. In view of the apparent Anglo-American agreement over general principles and Wilson's determination to avoid useless bickering over details, there was little that Bryan or Lansing could have said or done.

Not the least important reason for the President's refusal to permit a disputatious correspondence with the London Foreign Office was the fact that relations between the two governments had recently taken a sharp and bitter turn, not, as we have already pointed out, over trade, but over the issue of the transfer of German ships to the American flag. In the background had been the British fear of the Ship Purchase bill and of what might happen if the United States government did in fact buy German ships and use them to carry cotton and other non-contraband to Germany. However, the immediate *cause célèbre* of the Anglo-American crisis of January and early February 1915 was a case involving a hitherto obscure American citizen living in Michigan and an equally obscure German vessel named the *Dacia*. Upon the outcome of the case the future relations of the two governments seemed for a time to depend.

It all began when Edward N. Breitung, a mining operator of Marquette, Michigan, conceived the idea of making some quick dollars by purchasing German steamers in American ports and using them to carry cotton to the Central Powers. On about December 28, 1914, he purchased the steamship *Dacia*, 3,545 tons, then at Port Arthur, Texas, from the Hamburg-American Line and transferred her to American registry on January 4, 1915. It was merely the beginning of what Breitung hoped would soon become a flourishing enterprise. "It is no use denying it," he told reporters some time later, "for the fact of the matter is that had we been able to operate the Dacia under our flag it was our intention to purchase many, if not all, of the interned German liners now in American harbors."[32] "If the Dacia as an American vessel is permitted . . . to carry Southern cotton to Eu-

---

[30] The Secretary of State to Ambassador Page, January 12, 1915, *Foreign Relations, 1915, Supplement*, pp. 305-306.

[31] E. Grey to the American Ambassador, February 10, 1915, *ibid.*, pp. 324-334.

[32] *New York Times*, November 13, 1915.

rope," Breitung's lawyer declared at the time the ship was transferred to American registry, "a solution of the cotton export problem will have been made."[33]

Events moved rapidly as Breitung loaded the *Dacia* with some 11,000 bales of Texas cotton and asked the State Department to clear the way with the British government for the ship to sail to Bremen or Rotterdam. Inquiries addressed to the British Ambassador elicited only vague warnings and a general statement of British policy on ship transfers during wartime.[34] Consequently, on January 14, 1915, the Secretary of State instructed Ambassador Page to lay the matter before the Foreign Secretary himself. "Vessel will go direct to Rotterdam," Bryan explained, "not touching at any enemy port, and return this country, agreeing to detention for examination of cargo. . . . Seek to have British Government consent not to raise question of transfer for this particular voyage on conditions above stated, neither Government waiving any principle involved and case not to serve as precedent hereafter."[35]

At this point the diplomatic pot began to boil. Spring Rice, who now had full instructions, informed Bryan on January 15 that his government was determined to seize the *Dacia* and bring her into Prize Court if she sailed. "This ship," he averred, "has been now for five months in port to evade capture. She has been transferred to the American flag in order that she may come out without risk. . . . The British Government . . . feel that if they recognize the transfer of the *Dacia* it will clearly be followed by the wholesale transfer of German ships to neutral flags to the enormous relief of Germany and the greatest prejudice to British interests."[36] The following day, moreover, the French Ambassador, prompted, probably, by his colleague, addressed a solemn note to the State Department declaring that the transfer of any German vessels to American registry would be "an act of assistance" to the enemies of the French Republic.[37]

Actually, these protests in Washington were only mild reverberations of the anti-American feeling that was by now sweeping through the British Isles in wake of the news of the transfer of the *Dacia* and

---

[33] *ibid.*, January 5, 1915.

[34] Ambassador Spring Rice to the Secretary of State, January 12, 1915, *Foreign Relations, 1915, Supplement*, pp. 676-677.

[35] The Secretary of State to Ambassador Page, January 14, 1915, *ibid.*, pp. 678-679.

[36] The British Ambassador to the Secretary of State, January 15, 1915, *ibid.*, p. 680.

[37] The French Ambassador to the Secretary of State, January 16, 1915, *ibid.*, pp. 681-682.

of the Washington administration's determination to force the adoption of the Ship Purchase bill by Congress. British editors were up in arms, denouncing the transfer of the *Dacia* as a German trick, demanding that their government take a firm stand against any ship transfers, and venting a very obvious spleen against the proper neutral on the other side of the water.

"Englishmen who love and admire America," one distingished spokesman exclaimed, ". . . cannot help feeling at this moment acute anxiety and alarm at the way in which we are drifting towards the danger of a collision with the United States. The force of circumstances may at any moment undo all the good done since the Treaty signed at Ghent one hundred years ago."[38] The *Dacia* case, another editor declared, "is a matter so essential to our safety and success that no compromise upon it is possible."[39] "If the Dacia transfer were permitted," a third editor agreed, "similar transfers might be made of all German ships in America."[40]

In moving language Page described the causes and relentless progress of this anti-American feeling: "There is a steadily deepening and spreading feeling throughout every section of English opinion that the German influence in the United States has by this temptation to buy these interned ships won us to the German side. The old criticism of the President for not protesting against the violation of the Hague Treaty by Germany when she invaded Belgium is revived with tenfold its first earnestness. This is coupled with our protest against shipping as showing an unfriendly spirit. But both these criticisms were relatively mild till the DACIA was transferred to the American flag. That transfer added volume and vehemence to all preceding criticisms and is cited in the press and in conversation everywhere as proof of our unfriendliness. They regard the DACIA as a German ship put out of commission by their navy. She comes on the seas again by our permission which so far nullifies their victory. If she comes here she will, of course, be seized and put into the Prize Court. Her seizure will strike the English imagination in effect as the second conquest of her [—] first from the Germans and now from the Americans. Popular feeling will, I fear, run as high as it ran over the TRENT affair; and a very large part of English opinion will regard us as enemies. If another German ship should follow the DACIA here I

[38] *The Spectator,* cxiv (January 23, 1915), 101.
[39] London *Standard,* January 16, 1915.
[40] London *Westminster Gazette,* January 16, 1915.

do not think that any Government could withstand the popular demand for her confiscation; and if we permit the transfer of a number
of these ships there will be such a wave of displeasure as will make
a return of the recent good-feeling between the two peoples impossible
for a generation. There is no possible escape from such an act being
regarded by the public opinion of this Kingdom as a distinctly unfriendly and practically hostile act. . . . For the first time I have felt
a distinctly unfriendly atmosphere. It has the quality of the atmosphere just before an earthquake. . . . I can not exaggerate the omi-
nousness of the situation. The case is not technical but has large human
and patriotic and historic elements in it."[41]

Official echoes of the British alarm came when Page saw Sir Edward
Grey at the Foreign Office on January 18. "My inquiry whether British
Government would object to purchase and transfer of German interned
ships . . . ," the Ambassador reported by wire, "brought from Sir
Edward Grey the most ominous conversation I have ever had with
him." In tones that grew increasingly severe, the Foreign Secretary
made it plain that he was disturbed as much by what might happen
if the Ship Purchase bill passed as by the *Dacia* case itself. "If the
United States," Page went on, "without intent to do Great Britain an
injury, but moved only to relieve the scarcity of tonnage, should buy
these [German] ships it would still annul one of the victories that
England has won by her navy. . . . He spoke earnestly, sadly, ominously, but in the friendliest spirit."[42]

Two days later the Foreign Secretary was more specific in avowing
his government's intentions regarding the *Dacia*. The British would
not harm the cotton on the vessel but would either purchase it at the
contract price or reship it to Rotterdam at their own expense. But,
he continued, the *Dacia* could not be permitted to pass. "This voyage
of the 'Dacia' is being looked to as a test case," Grey went on in a
pointed reference to the possible purchase of German ships by the
American government. "If we do not interfere . . . there will at once
be a wholesale purchase real or colourable of German merchant ships
and a transfer of them to a neutral flag (at prices, if the purchase is
real, giving a huge profit to German ship-owners) to escape capture
and to carry on German trade. It is impossible for us to concede this

[41] Ambassador Page to the Secretary of State, January 18, 1915, Page Papers; also
Foreign Relations, 1915, Supplement, pp. 682-683.
[42] Ambassador Page to the Secretary of State, January 18, 1915, *ibid.,* p. 682.

point and if the 'Dacia' is captured we must submit the vessel as apart from the cargo to the Prize Court."[43]

Grey was so distraught by the gloomy prospect that he took the unusual step of making a direct personal appeal to the American leaders. In a long dispatch to Ambassador Spring Rice on about January 20, he reported all the bitter feelings that were causing opinion in Britain to turn against America. Englishmen, he wrote, were beginning to wonder whether the United States was really neutral after all, or whether its policies toward the belligerents were not being largely dictated by the German Americans. The American government had, among other things, prevented a banking house from making a loan to an Allied government. It had forbidden the export of submarine parts to Great Britain. Worse still, it was now using all its power to force a measure through Congress to make possible the purchase of German ships. Moreover, a committee of Congress had under consideration a bill sponsored by "the German members of Congress under the open direction of the German Ambassador" to prohibit the export of arms, and "the United States Government has taken no public steps to discourage it." Finally, "Prospects are held out that the United States on whom as all other neutrals the indirect consequences of the war in some ways bears hardly, will cut off the supplies of munitions of war upon which the Allies are in need and at the same time insist that the door be kept open for supplies of contraband to Germany, with the object of bringing the war to an end by the complete victory of the latter." This was what the British people were beginning to believe. "Should people in England," he concluded, "come to believe that the dominant influence in United States politics is German, it would tend to create an untoward state of public opinion which we should greatly regret."

It was an extraordinary message, all the more significant because it so obviously reflected the thinking of the British Cabinet. Spring Rice delivered it in slightly varying form—to Colonel House on January 22 (and through him to the President) as a confidential message from the Foreign Secretary,[44] and to the Secretary of State on January

---

[43] E. Grey to C. Spring Rice, January 20, 1915, Page Papers. Spring Rice transmitted the substance of this message to the State Department in a note dated January 21, 1915, and printed in *Foreign Relations, 1915, Supplement*, pp. 687-688.

[44] It may be found in the House Papers as E. Grey to C. Spring Rice, January 22, 1915. The Ambassador's son delivered this version to Colonel House in New York on January 22, and House immediately sent a copy to the President, as Spring Rice of

21 or 22 in the form of a report on British press opinion on American neutrality.[45]

It happened that Wilson and Bryan had been working on a personal message to Grey at the very time that the Foreign Secretary was putting his own on the wire to Washington. The two American leaders were as much disturbed as Grey, and about the same problems.[46] Bryan wrote out a rough draft, "hurriedly and only in the form of suggestions for consideration," on about January 20, and Wilson edited this copy and returned it to the State Department on January 22. Before putting the message into cipher, Bryan urged the President to consider a final important addition. "Mr. Lansing and I," he wrote, "have been conferring in regard to the general situation, and we are inclined to think that it would go a long way toward relieving the fear that is expressed in Great Britain if an announcement was made by the authorities that the Government had no thought of purchasing German ships under the authority which the shipping is intended to confer. I believe that a large part of the alarm in Great Britain arises over the fear that if the *Dacia* sale is allowed to stand the Government would expect to use it as a precedent and proceed to buy the German ships. That was [Ambassador] Jusserand's fear and you remember how agitated he was at the time."[47] For reasons that we have already seen,[48] Wilson refused thus to mollify either his British critics or his opponents in the struggle over the Ship Pur-

course expected him to do. It is printed *in part* in C. Seymour (ed.), *The Intimate Papers of Colonel House*, I, 347-349.

[45] "I am enclosing a personal statement from the British Ambassador which I think you will find interesting," Bryan wrote as he sent Spring Rice's letter to the President on January 23. "I was talking with him the other day and he asked me if I would like to know what the British papers were saying and I told him I would—and this letter is intended to furnish the information." W. J. Bryan to W.W., January 23, 1915, *The Lansing Papers*, I, 111. This version, printed as the British Ambassador to the Secretary of State, January 21, 1915, *Foreign Relations, 1915, Supplement*, pp. 777-779, was even more ominous in tone than the one handed to Colonel House.

[46] Actually, the two messages nearly crossed each other in transit. Apparently neither Bryan nor Wilson saw Grey's dispatch in any form before they had completed the draft of their own on January 22, although they might have seen the version that the British Ambassador handed to Bryan before they sent their message to London on January 23. For all practical purposes, however, Wilson's and Bryan's message may be regarded as being a direct reply to Grey's, for they responded to questions that Page and the Foreign Secretary had earlier raised and which Grey had merely repeated in his long confidential telegram of about January 20, 1915.

[47] W. J. Bryan to W.W., January 22, 1915, *The Lansing Papers*, I, 110.

[48] See above, pp. 150-151.

chase bill that was reaching its violent peak at this very time. The message went to Page on January 23, 1915, unaccompanied by any such soothing statement as Bryan had suggested.

"The President directs me to send the following," the Secretary of State wrote by way of introduction to the main body of the message, which opened with a paragraph about the German Americans and their role in American politics. They were a large and important element in the American population, the note conceded, and they were understandably pro-German in viewpoint; but they did not determine American policies, and there was no chance that the measures that they were advocating, like an arms embargo, would be adopted. On the contrary, Bryan (or Wilson) continued, the great majority of Americans were trying sincerely to be neutral. They also had a cordial feeling toward Great Britain. But there was considerable irritation in the South and West on account of cotton and copper and among the German Americans and Irish Americans because of the export of munitions to the Allies. This was a fact that the British leaders should face realistically, for the irritation would become dangerous if the American people ever believed that the British were damaging their legitimate commerce. The *Dacia* case, the message went on, need not cause any trouble at all between the two governments. As far as the State Department knew, Breitung had bought the vessel in entire good faith. Of course the British could seize her and take her into the Prize Court; but the American government would expect that tribunal to release the *Dacia* if the evidence proved Breitung's good faith in transferring the ship to the American flag. Historically, the United States and Great Britain had recognized the rightfulness of such transfers during wartime, and it would be a clear violation of "a well-settled rule" if the British government refused to recognize a *bona fide* sale. Then Bryan (using Wilson's words) confronted the larger question of ship transfers and the Ship Purchase bill, as follows:

"The point which should be made very clear to the British authorities as our view and purpose in the whole matter, if such purchases are made, is that as a matter of actual fact such purchases do not constitute a restoration of German commerce to the seas. Such ships would not and could not be used on the former routes or with the former and usual cargoes and would serve as German commerce in no particular. They would serve only the trade of the United States with neutral countries and within the limits necessarily set by war and all its conditions. . . . They would be used on new routes and for the release of American merchandise to new ports. . . . America must have ships and must have them for these uses. She will build them if she cannot find them for sale. The legitimate restoration of American commerce may be delayed but it cannot be prevented. . . . Already provision has been made for the transfer and register of foreign bottoms and Congress is considering a measure authorizing the Government to take part in a corporation for the operation of ships. These measures have been the outgrowth of six months of war. Is it not worth while to consider the possibilities of the future? If this Government must undertake the building of enough ships to carry its commerce while idle ships lie in its harbors will there not be an excess of ships when the war is over?"

The President wanted Sir Edward Grey to know, Bryan's message concluded, that the American government would adhere "conscientiously to its course of neutrality." Since the two governments agreed so nearly on matters of principle, surely practical methods could be found to keep trade and shipping disputes to a "negligible minimum." If such methods could be found, then the English government could be "thus assured of compliance with all its just regulations and of freedom from even the risk of friction and hostile sentiment as between the two nations."[49]

This was easily the most important commentary that the President composed during the early period of the war, for it shed clear light on his thinking about all the problems of Anglo-American relations before the German submarine campaign submerged old quarrels and raised a host of new and more difficult ones. As Wilson made clear, the United States would not challenge the British maritime system so long as it remained, as it essentially was at this time, moderate and limited in its pretensions. Nor would the American government deviate from a strict neutrality in the matter of the export of munitions. At the same time, it would not compromise on the *Dacia* case, or yield on the larger question of ship transfers, or abate its determination to put a merchant fleet of its own on the seas.

Ironically, Page never presented the President's message formally to Grey. But he must have conveyed its burden, and the Foreign Secretary must have decided that it was necessary to avoid any conflict with the Washington government over the *Dacia*. The easy solution was an obvious one—to let the French navy seize the ship and bring her

[49] The Secretary of State to Ambassador Page, January 23, 1915, *Foreign Relations, 1915, Supplement*, pp. 684-687.

into the French Prize Court, which could then apply the historic severe French rule against the transfer of any belligerent ships during wartime. Page made such a suggestion himself,[50] but it would be naïve to assume that the idea had not already occurred to Grey. Indeed, he had probably already made the necessary arrangements with the French authorities by the time Page spoke to him about the matter.

In any event, a French cruiser seized the *Dacia*, which had sailed from Galveston on January 31, 1915, as she entered the English Channel on February 27 and escorted her to Brest. The French government purchased the ship's cargo of cotton, but the French Prize Court condemned the vessel in August 1915.[51] Renamed the *Yser*, she put to sea under the French flag and was sunk by a German submarine in the Mediterranean on about November 9, 1915. Meanwhile, upon the advice of the State Department, Breitung had appealed the ruling of the Prize Court to the French civil courts. Eventually, on November 30, 1916, decision was rendered in favor of the French government; by this time, however, the whole question of ship transfers had long since become completely academic as far as the American public and government were concerned.

Thus ended anticlimatically the *Dacia* affair which, as Page had warned, had all the makings of a first-class Anglo-American crisis. The question of ship transfers never rose again to threaten relations between the two governments. This was true, first, because the French seizure of the *Dacia* made the purchase of German vessels too risky an enterprise for individuals to undertake. It was true, more importantly, because after the failure of the Ship Purchase bill there was simply no chance that the United States government itself would ever be directly involved in conflict over former German vessels.

A week before the *Dacia* left Galveston on its ill-fated voyage, a second American ship left New York harbor in a new challenge to the British maritime system. She was the *Wilhelmina*, an American vessel (not a recent German one) loaded with foodstuffs for Germany. Her sailing might have provoked a new crisis in Anglo-American relations if peculiar developments had not intervened.

The *Wilhelmina* affair had its origins in the plan of a group of German Americans and of Doctor Heinrich Albert, head of the German Purchasing Commission in New York, to test British policy con-

[50] B. J. Hendrick, *The Life and Letters of Walter H. Page*, I, 394-395.
[51] *New York Times*, August 5 and 17, 1915.

cerning the neutral export of food to Germany. Since the early weeks of the war the British had in theory defined foodstuffs as conditional contraband; in practice, however, the British Admiralty had seized all the food bound for Germany that it could lay its hands upon, on the ground that it was inevitably destined for the use of the armed forces. The State Department had accepted this practice in fact if not in principle. It was for the purpose of exposing the British suppression of all neutral exports of food to Germany and of forcing the Washington government to raise a challenge that the *Wilhelmina* project was conceived.

In early January 1915 the Southern Products Trading Company of Saint Louis purchased the *Wilhelmina,* and the W. L. Green Commission Company, also of Saint Louis, contracted to ship a cargo of foodstuffs to Germany on board the vessel. The president of the former was one Simon, a German American who, according to reports of agents of the Justice Department, had recently lived in the Fatherland and had received the money for the purchase of the *Wilhelmina* from a bank in Germany.[52] The W. L. Green Commission Company was an old Saint Louis firm that had long shipped food products to Germany through its office in Hamburg. Taking careful pains to make an airtight case, officers of the company filed an affidavit with customs officials in New York promising that the *Wilhelmina's* cargo would be sold only to civilian firms; indeed, they offered to give bond to guarantee that none of the cargo would go to the German armed forces.[53] At the same time, unknown to the State Department and the British government, Doctor Albert insured the cargo so as to remove any risk of loss if it were captured.[54]

All signs seemed to indicate that the *Wilhelmina,* which sailed for Hamburg on January 22, might succeed in opening a hole in what was in fact the British food blockade of Germany. Having assured the W. L. Green Commission Company of the propriety of its shipment, the State Department was apparently prepared to defend it vigorously before the British authorities. In London, Sir Edward Grey was in a considerable dilemma. If he let the *Wilhelmina* and her cargo pass, he would stir the opposition of the Admiralty and of British public opinion, which was already beginning to clamor for all-out

[52] Anderson Diary, February 22, 1915.

[53] New York *World,* January 23, 1915; Hays, Kaufman, and Lindheim to the Secretary of State, January 22, 1915, *Foreign Relations, 1915, Supplement,* pp. 313-314.

[54] Johann von Bernstorff, *My Three Years in America,* p. 77.

economic warfare against the enemy. On the other hand, if he permitted the Admiralty to seize the *Wilhelmina*, he would run the risk of being repudiated by the British Prize Court and of provoking serious controversy with the United States. He apparently concluded that the danger abroad was greater than at home; at any rate, he told Page later that his "first intention" had been to do nothing about the *Wilhelmina's* cargo.[55]

Then the German authorities gave Grey an excuse to act. On January 25, while the *Wilhelmina* was still in the North Atlantic, the Bundesrat, or Federal Council of the German Empire, issued a decree forbidding private transactions in major food staples and appropriating all stocks of corn, wheat, and flour for governmental distribution after February 1, 1915.[56] The Berlin government quickly assured the State Department that the decree would not apply to any foodstuffs imported from abroad; and it even offered to permit the American Consul in Hamburg to distribute the *Wilhelmina's* cargo, as a guarantee that it would go only to civilians.[57] But the damage, from the German point of view, was done. Sir Edward Grey informed Page on January 27 that the *Wilhelmina* would be stopped. "The military powers of the German Government," he explained, "have now officially taken over the use and distribution of all food in the Empire so that . . . all food in effect belongs to the army." Since the *Wilhelmina* had begun her voyage before the Federal Council's decree was issued, Grey continued, the British government would purchase her cargo to avoid throwing any loss upon its owners.[58] British officials, consequently, seized the *Wilhelmina* when she reached Falmouth on February 11, 1915.[59]

The matter was far from being at an end, and the President and the Secretary of State were afterward much involved. By the time that these later negotiations were proceeding, however, the case of the *Wilhelmina* and her cargo had ceased to be an issue only between the United States and Great Britain and had become, instead, a pawn in

---

[55] Ambassador Page to the Secretary of State, January 27, 1915, *Foreign Relations, 1915, Supplement*, p. 317.

[56] New York *World*, January 27, 1915.

[57] Ambassador Bernstorff to the Secretary of State, January 28, 1915, *Foreign Relations, 1915, Supplement*, pp. 317-318; Ambassador Bernstorff to the Foreign Office, February 3, 1915, German F. O. Archives; *New York Times*, February 7, 1915.

[58] Ambassador Page to the Secretary of State, January 27, 1915, *Foreign Relations, 1915, Supplement*, p. 317.

[59] New York *World*, February 12, 1915.

a death struggle between Great Britain and Germany for control of the seas. We will, therefore, come back to the *Wilhelmina,* but not until we have seen the way in which Wilson and his advisers confronted other problems almost as important during the first period of American neutrality.

CHAPTER VII

The Beginnings of Wilsonian Mediation

No sooner had the war commenced than men began to talk of peace, and nowhere was the talk more unending than in the United States, where humanitarianism and self-interest combined to maintain a steady pressure upon the American government to take leadership in projects of mediation. Not that the President and his Secretary of State needed much prompting to play the blessed role. The hope of leading hostile statesmen to the conference table burned brightly in both men during the first months of the war and, in part, justified a posture of resolute neutrality.

They made their first move—a formal offer of American good offices—even before England went to war. Ambassador Walter Page had wired from London only the day before that there was no chance that such an offer would be accepted,[1] but the Washington leaders decided to make the effort anyway. As Wilson said, the risks were small and such a move could, "at least, do no harm."[2] Thus at seven p.m. on August 4, 1914, the State Department sent the following personal message from the President to the Emperors of Germany, Russia, and Austria-Hungary, to the King of England, and to the President of France:

"As official head of one of the Powers signatory to The Hague Convention, I feel it to be my privilege and my duty under Article Three of that Convention, to say to you in a spirit of most earnest friendship that I should welcome an opportunity to act in the interest of European peace, either now or at any other time that might be thought more suitable, as an occasion to serve you and all concerned in a way that would afford me lasting cause for gratitude and happiness."[3]

It was not long, as Bryan ruefully noted, before the spokesmen of the principal belligerents began to make excuses all with one accord. The President of France replied that his country loved peace and had

[1] Ambassador Page to the Secretary of State, August 3, 1914, *Foreign Relations, 1914, Supplement*, p. 37.

[2] W.W., to E. M. House, August 5, 1914, Wilson Papers.

[3] *New York Times*, August 6, 1914.

gone to war only after it was attacked.[4] The aged Hapsburg Emperor assured the President that his government would accept American mediation "at such time as the honor of the flag will permit and when the objects of the war shall be attained."[5] The British Foreign Secretary, Sir Edward Grey, promised that his government would welcome Wilson's mediation "whenever a favorable time comes."[6] Russia, her Foreign Minister Sergei Sazonov declared, had done everything possible to avert hostilities, but, he added, "from the moment this war was imposed upon her she cannot fail to defend her rights by force of arms."[7] The German Emperor sent the most elaborate reply of all. It was a personal message for President Wilson that reviewed the steps leading to hostilities and, needless to say, absolved the Berlin government of any responsibility.[8] As the Secretary of State further pointed out while reviewing these replies, "Each one declares he is opposed to war and anxious to avoid it and then lays the blame upon someone else."[9] The outlook, obviously, was not at all encouraging, even to so inveterate an optimist as the Apostle of Peace.

Still determined to let no opportunity pass, Bryan was busy preparing a new campaign, one aimed at limiting the spread of the war in the Far East, even while the replies were coming in from the European chancelleries. Much more was involved in this undertaking than the mere desire to be helpful. At stake, potentially, was the balance of power in the Far East, for Europe's preoccupation had created unparalleled, perhaps irresistible, opportunities for Japanese expansion throughout the entire Pacific area and above all in China. The United States stood committed by historic policy to a defense by all peaceful means of the territorial integrity and political independence of China. But in early August 1914 it stood alone, the only great power actually capable of confronting possible Japanese ambitions, although Japan and Great Britain were bound by a treaty of alliance and the London Foreign Office would undoubtedly lay a restraining hand upon its Oriental ally.[10]

---

[4] Ambassador Herrick to the Secretary of State, August 6, 1914, *Foreign Relations, 1914, Supplement*, p. 48.

[5] Ambassador Penfield to the Secretary of State, August 7, 1914, *ibid.*, pp. 49-50.

[6] Ambassador Page to the Secretary of State, August 7, 1914, *ibid.*, p. 50.

[7] Chargé Wilson to the Secretary of State, August 26, 1914, *ibid.*, pp. 78-79.

[8] Ambassador Gerard to the Secretary of State, August 14, 1914, *ibid.*, pp. 60-61.

[9] W. J. Bryan to W.W., August 28, 1914, *The Lansing Papers*, I, 7.

[10] For an account of this entire episode, see Ernest R. May, "American Policy and

The Japanese hesitated during the first days of hostilities in Europe before striking out upon any course, and their delay gave the leaders in Washington a breathing space in which to deliberate upon what should and could be done. Fearful of a Japanese *démarche*, the Chinese government urgently suggested that the United States join it in trying to prevent the spread of hostilities to the foreign concessions and leased territories occupied by the European powers in China.[11] Then there was an alternative, one much more ambitious than the policy suggested by the Peking authorities—a vigorous American diplomatic campaign to avert the outbreak of any hostilities at all in the Far East.

Bryan and Lansing pondered these possibilities alone during August 6 and 7, for the President had withdrawn in mourning for his wife. The Counselor argued that any suggestion for neutralizing the entire Far East was bound to be rejected by certain belligerents, and that it would consequently serve American and Chinese interests better to seek only what might be obtained: the neutralization of so-called treaty ports and assurances of respect for Chinese neutrality and the preservation of the *status quo* in the new republic of the East. "To ask more," he went on, "would I believe endanger all and would, in any event, so delay an international arrangement as to seriously impair its value when obtained. . . . I believe that the preservation of the *status quo* to be the most important to American interests."[12] Bryan, obviously, did not agree entirely. Breaking Wilson's seclusion, the Secretary sent Lansing's comments to the White House on August 8. "While I approve of his suggestions," Bryan wrote, adding his own, "I believe it might be well to go even further, that is, we might suggest in our representations (1) an agreement that hostilities *be not extended to the Far East*, and (2) if that is not agreeable to the contending powers, an agreement as to the neutralization of treaty ports, respect for Chinese neutrality and preservation of the status quo in China."[13]

No record of Wilson's reply has survived, but he apparently agreed with Bryan, before he left Washington for Mrs. Wilson's funeral in Georgia on August 10, that some ambitious effort should be made.

Japan's Entrance into World War I," *Mississippi Valley Historical Review*, XL (September 1953), 279-290.

[11] Chargé MacMurray, from Peking, to the Secretary of State, August 3, 1914, 5 p.m., and August 3, 1914, 11 p.m., *Foreign Relations, 1914, Supplement*, pp. 161-162.

[12] "*Memorandum by the Counselor for the Department of State on Course To Be Pursued To Preserve the 'Status Quo' in China*," dated August 7, 1914, *The Lansing Papers*, I, 1-3.

[13] W. J. Bryan to W.W., August 8, 1914, Wilson Papers.

As they discussed the situation on August 8 or 9, however, the two leaders must also have agreed to move cautiously and without any show of force. By this time it seemed almost certain that Japan would enter the war against Germany as an ally of Great Britain but had no intention of undertaking any general campaign throughout the far eastern area. The main threat, therefore, was a Japanese attack against the German leasehold of Kiaochow on the Shantung Peninsula, and what such an attack would portend for the future of China. At this time Wilson and Bryan had no reason to believe that the Japanese contemplated anything more than limited military action against the German naval base at Tsingtao in the Kiaochow leasehold. Given these circumstances, they must have agreed that nothing could be lost by a friendly effort to neutralize the Far East, but that there was not sufficient danger to American or Chinese interests to justify stern representations to Tokyo.

Thus during the next few days Bryan and Lansing sounded out the British and German governments on the possibility of "circumscribing the area of hostilities and maintaining the *status quo* in the Far East."[14] But they made it plain that they were making inquiries and not proposals, and they did not even raise the issue with the Imperial Japanese government. Instead, the American leaders simply waited to see how events developed. These soon moved quickly toward their climax. On August 15 the Japanese Foreign Office informed the State Department that the Imperial government intended to force the Germans to withdraw from the Shantung Peninsula. Japan, the Foreign Minister Takaaki Kato emphasized, "was not animated by any selfish purpose but was acting strictly in pursuance of the alliance with Great Britain and would not seek any territorial aggrandizement or selfish advantage in China and would carefully respect all neutral interests." In seizing the German leasehold at Kiaochow, Kato promised, the Japanese government contemplated returning the territory eventually to China.[15] Three days later word arrived from London that the British and Japanese governments had agreed that Japan should come into the war. Both governments would respect the independence and integrity of China, the British Foreign Office's announcement continued, and Japanese military operations would be of a very limited nature.[16]

[14] The Secretary of State to Ambassador Page, August 11, 1914; the Secretary of State to Ambassador Gerard, August 11, 1914, *Foreign Relations, 1914, Supplement,* pp. 166-167.

[15] Ambassador Guthrie to the Secretary of State, August 15, 1914, *ibid.*, pp. 170-171.

[16] The British Chargé to the Secretary of State, August 18, 1914, *ibid.*, p. 171.

This news stirred a mild excitement in the United States, mainly among the German Americans. On August 17, 1914, Representative Fred A. Britten of Illinois, speaking for a heavily pro-German constituency, introduced a resolution in the House of Representatives requesting the Secretary of State to inform the Japanese government that any attack against Kiaochow would be a cause of grave concern to the American government. At the same time, Doctor C. J. Hexamer, president of the National German-American Alliance, appealed to the President to protect the peace of the Far East. But Wilson rebuffed all such appeals coldly. "The President," a statement given to reporters on August 17 read, "feels it incumbent upon himself to express no opinion whatever on the attitude of Japan or any other country."[17]

It was obvious to Wilson and his advisers that there was nothing they could do to affect the immediate course of events in the Far East.[18] To be sure, these developments had certain portentous possibilities. They meant that Japan would be entrenched on Chinese soil; they also meant, perhaps, the beginning of a concerted Japanese campaign for control of the Chinese government. Wilson, Bryan, and Lansing could not have failed to recognize the likelihood of this, but the Japanese and British governments had made the decision to extend the war to the Pacific area, and the Washington authorities could not interfere without seeming to act on Germany's behalf. Besides, the Japanese had acted with entire propriety as far as their obligations to the United States were concerned. All that the Washington authorities could do was to accept the Japanese assurances at face value and to reaffirm their own continuing concern for the independence and territorial integrity of China. Thus on August 19 the State Department addressed the following note to Tokyo:

"The American Government, while regretting that differences have arisen between the Imperial Japanese Government and the Imperial German Government which may eventuate in war, . . . notes with satisfaction that Japan, in demanding the surrender by Germany of the entire leased territory of Kiaochow, does so with the purpose of restoring that territory to China, and that Japan is seeking no territorial aggrandizement in China in the movement now contemplated. . . . Should disturbances in the interior of China seem to the Japanese Government to require measures to be taken by Japan or other powers

---

[17] *New York Times*, August 18 and 19, 1914.
[18] As Wilson implied in a note to Bryan on August 17, 1914, *The Lansing Papers*, I, 5.

to restore order, the Imperial Japanese Government will no doubt desire to consult with the American Government before deciding upon a course of action."[19]

The talk of peace did not diminish after the failure of President Wilson's offer of good offices and Secretary Bryan's efforts in the Far East; if anything, such talk increased. Nor did the American leaders lose hope during the late summer and autumn of 1914 that some opportunity for their mediation might arise. Their first failures had shown, perhaps, that the time was not yet ripe for any further public efforts, but this fact was not discouraging to men nobly fired with zeal for service to mankind. They would not permit any seeming opportunity to pass.

The first occurred less than two weeks after Japan declared war on Germany. During the evening of September 5, Count Johann von Bernstorff, the German Ambassador, had dinner with Oscar S. Straus, a former American Ambassador to Turkey, James Speyer, a prominent investment banker with intimate German connections, and others at the Speyer home in New York. Inevitably, the conversation turned to the subject of peace. Straus asked the Ambassador if he thought the German Emperor would consider a mediation offer favorably if the President extended one. Bernstorff replied that he could not speak officially but that he had reason to believe, on the basis of what the Imperial Chancellor had told him before he returned to the United States, that the Emperor would accept mediation if his enemies were also willing.[20] In great excitement, Straus rushed to Washington on the midnight train; arriving in the capital on the following morning, Sunday, September 6, he went straight to Bryan's home to tell the good news. Bryan immediately informed the President, who agreed that the Secretary should ask Bernstorff for permission to report the conversation to the German Foreign Office, and that Straus, meanwhile, should talk with the British and French Ambassadors in Washington about the matter.[21]

[19] The Secretary of State to Ambassador Guthrie, August 19, 1914, *Foreign Relations, 1914, Supplement*, p. 172.

[20] The Secretary of State to Ambassador Gerard, September 7, 1914, *ibid.*, p. 98. The following is Bernstorff's own report of the conversation: "Oscar Straus felt me out about an American mediation action by way of an ambassadorial conference in Washington. He believes the moment for it has come, since France has been defeated, and it would be advisable to prevent the destruction of Paris." Ambassador von Bernstorff to the Foreign Office, September 7, 1914, German F. O. Archives.

[21] The above is based in part upon the detailed account in the *New York Times*,

Great activity ensued in Washington on September 7. Bryan saw Bernstorff in the morning and obtained his consent to a report to the Foreign Office in Berlin. (Bernstorff did not dare to refuse, as he believed that Straus had been acting under instructions from the President and Secretary of State.) Then in the early afternoon the Secretary sent his cable to Berlin telling about Straus's conversation with Bernstorff and adding the following instructions to Ambassador James W. Gerard: "You will . . . please deliver a paraphrase of this despatch to the Emperor at once and say to him that upon receipt of a favorable reply the President will make similar inquiry of the other governments and that he will be much gratified if he can be the means of bringing the parties into conference with a view to the adjustment by them of their differences."[22]

Without waiting for any reply from Berlin, Bryan called the British and French Ambassadors, Spring Rice and Jusserand, to the State Department on the same day. "Bryan insisted," Spring Rice reported to London, "that we should give any proposal of the sort a favourable reception to this extent, namely that we should not refuse to say what we were fighting for and on what terms we would make peace."[23] Then the following day the Secretary of State informed the American Ambassadors in London and Paris of these developments, adding:

"We do not know, of course, what reply the German Emperor will make but this war is so horrible from every aspect that no one can afford to take the responsibility for continuing it a single hour. The British and French Ambassadors fear that Germany will not accept any reasonable terms but even a failure to agree will not rob an attempt at mediation of all its advantages because the different nations would be able to explain their attitude, the reasons for continuing the war, the end to be hoped for and the terms upon which peace is possible. This would locate responsibility for the continuation of the war and help to mold public opinion."[24]

September 13, 1914, and Oscar S. Straus, *Under Four Administrations, From Cleveland to Taft*, pp. 378-380.

[22] The Secretary of State to Ambassador Gerard, September 7, 1914, *Foreign Relations, 1914, Supplement*, p. 98.

[23] C. Spring Rice to E. Grey, September 8, 1914, *The Letters of Sir Cecil Spring Rice*, ii, 222. Jusserand's report, which was received by the French Foreign Office on September 9, 1914, is paraphrased in Raymond Poincaré, *Au Service de la France*, v, 272-273.

[24] The Secretary of State to Ambassadors Page and Herrick, September 8, 1914, *Foreign Relations, 1914, Supplement*, p. 99.

Events of the next few days revealed, tragically, that the American effort had not the slightest chance of succeeding. Not a single responsible leader of any belligerent nation was willing to permit peace discussions to reach a serious stage at this time. Statesmen in both alliances had already persuaded themselves that their enemies had been responsible for the war; already they were all snared by the delusion that they could end it on terms that would guarantee their nations' security for generations to come. The President of France stated this determination eloquently in a public speech on November 26, 1914, as follows:

"An indecisive victory and a precarious peace would expose the creative French spirit anew to insults of this refined [German] barbarity. . . . In the sacred union of her children and with the unflagging assistance of her allies, France will persevere to the end in the work of European liberation which has begun. And when her efforts have been crowned, she will find, under the auspices of her dead, a deeper life in glory, concord, and security."[25]

All the leaders in the foreign offices realized, however, the dangers that would flow from giving the American government and people the impression that they wanted war while their enemies wanted peace. Some way, they knew, had to be found to prove that their own burning desire for peace was being frustrated by hostile lust and greed.

From the outset, the dangers and necessities of the situation were clear to the British and German Ambassadors in Washington. "As regards our position here," Spring Rice warned Sir Edward Grey, "it is important to bear in mind that probably the peace negotiations will take place in this country and American popular opinion will be a useful factor. Now nothing would tend to win over the public here [to the German side] so much as the belief that we had refused a fair offer for peace which the Germans had made us, or had refused to listen to a peaceful suggestion of the United States Government. I have consulted some of our friends here and they have advised a course of action. It is that we should at once declare that the allies are anxious for peace with guarantees of permanency."[26] Bernstorff was equally concerned. "Here everyone desires peace," he wired the German Foreign Secretary. ". . . I, therefore, did not reject the offer, since I wanted to leave the odium of rejection to our enemies. . . .

[25] R. Poincaré, *Au Service de la France*, v, 454.

[26] C. Spring Rice to E. Grey, September 8, 1914, *The Letters of Sir Cecil Spring Rice*, II, 222-223.

As I see the situation here, I feel obliged to recommend to Your Excellency the acceptance of Mr. Wilson's propositions, which he will give to you through Mr. Gerard, since public opinion here, which has already been strongly influenced by England, will definitely turn against the belligerent whom they consider to be responsible for prolonging the war."[27]

Such advice was transparently sound, and the rival Foreign Ministers did not find it hard to devise the right answers. Sir Edward gave his to Page on September 9. He had done everything possible to avoid this war which Germany had deliberately planned, he said. Even so, he was willing to come to any honorable agreement at any time. Everything would of course depend upon the terms. Great Britain would insist upon the destruction of German militarism—that "armed brute power in central Europe which violates treaties"—and reparation to ruined Belgium. Furthermore, Grey went on, he would gladly cooperate if the American leaders could devise any means "that would bring this war to an end and prevent another such war being forced on Europe." Meanwhile, he could only await the German Emperor's reply to the Secretary of State's inquiry.[28]

The Undersecretary of the Foreign Office on the Wilhelmstrasse in Berlin, Arthur Zimmermann, gave Germany's preliminary reply to Ambassador Gerard on the same day that Grey spoke to Page. Eager to help, Gerard suggested that the time for mediation would soon come, when Paris had been captured: then the German government could impose a large indemnity upon France and take as many French colonies as it wanted. The matter, Zimmermann replied, was not so simple, there had to be a settlement also with Russia and England. The German people wanted peace, to be sure, but one that would endure; and the Imperial government would be willing to talk only when its enemies asked for mediation and would make overtures through the Washington government.[29] Gerard did not report this conversation to his superiors, but the Imperial Chancellor, Theobald von Bethmann Hollweg, gave a formal reply to Bryan's inquiry on September 12. The war, he affirmed, had been forced upon Germany.

[27] Ambassador von Bernstorff to the Foreign Office, September 7, 1914, German F. O. Archives.

[28] E. Grey to C. Spring Rice, September 9, 1914, Page Papers; Ambassador Page to the Secretary of State, September 10, 1914, *Foreign Relations, 1914, Supplement*, pp. 100-101; Ambassador Jusserand to the Foreign Office, two telegrams, September 10, 1914, R. Poincaré, *Au Service de la France*, v, 277.

[29] A. Zimmermann, memorandum dated September 9, 1914, German F. O. Archives.

Therefore, he went on, America "would first have to get our enemies to propose peace to us. We can accept a peace only that promises to be really permanent and protects us from new aggressions by our enemies. If we accept America's mediation offer now it would be interpreted by our enemies as a sign of weakness and not understood by our people at all, for the people who have made such sacrifices demand guarantees of security and peace."[30]

The receipt in Washington of the German Chancellor's message on September 16, 1914, brought an end to the first stage in these initial discussions. The second stage began immediately afterward, on September 18, when Colonel House took charge of the negotiations, if one may call them such. Discussions during the first stage had been managed almost exclusively by Bryan and conducted under the glare of extraordinarily full and accurate publicity.[31] The Secretary of State left Washington on about September 18 for a vacation in Asheville, North Carolina; until early November 1914, moreover, he was on the stump in various parts of the country as the Democratic party's chief spokesman in the congressional and senatorial campaigns then in progress. But the President, encouraged by Bethmann's reply and Bernstorff's assurances that Germany really wanted peace, was determined that the discussions begun by Straus should proceed. He obviously thought that Bryan was thoroughly incompetent to manage the affair; and he probably seized the opportunity afforded by the Secretary's trip to North Carolina to call in the man he so completely trusted, Colonel House. Hereafter, Wilson managed by one ruse or another to exclude the Secretary of State from participation in any serious peace talks.

Thus occurred early in the war a profoundly important change in the control of a major aspect of American foreign policy. The importance of the shift from Bryan's management to House's stemmed not so much from differences in personality or ability to play the role as

[30] T. von Bethmann Hollweg to the Foreign Office, September 12, 1914, *ibid.*; transmitted in Ambassador Gerard to the Secretary of State, September 14, 1914, *Foreign Relations, 1914, Supplement*, p. 104.

[31] The newspapers published detailed accounts of every single step in the negotiations, from the dinner at Speyer's home to the receipt of the Imperial German Chancellor's note. The latter, for example, was published almost verbatim in the *New York Times* on September 18, 1914. Only the Secretary of State could have given *all* the details to the reporters. Perhaps it was a deliberate attempt to force peace discussions into the open and compel the belligerents to avow what they were fighting for.

from fundamental differences in their thinking about the timing and purposes of American mediation.

Bryan believed simply that the American government should do everything that it could to end the war as soon as possible. It should not wait until the rival alliances were evenly balanced, for he doubted that such a time would ever come. Nor should it assume that any of the belligerents would take the initiative for peace, for he believed that each coalition wanted to crush the other and impose a settlement; and if this happened, Bryan argued, a reasonable peace would be impossible. Believing that any settlement at this time would have to be a compromise, the Secretary of State was not particularly concerned about terms. He was concerned only about stopping the fighting. Thus over and over he pleaded for bold action—that the President demand that the belligerents at least avow what they were fighting for and the terms upon which they would make peace, or that he convene a conference of all neutral and belligerent nations in Washington at which statesmen would have to speak frankly.[32]

Bryan expressed these views and revealed the depth of his passion in a conversation with Ambassador Spring Rice in early November 1914. "Bryan spoke to me about peace as he always does," the Ambassador reported to his superiors. "He sighs for the Nobel Prize, and besides that he is a really convinced peaceman. He has just given me a sword beaten into a ploughshare six inches long to serve as a paperweight. It is adorned with quotations from Isaiah and himself. No one doubts his sincerity, but that is rather embarrassing for us at the present moment, because he is always at us with peace propositions. This time, he said he could not understand why we could not say what we were fighting for. The nation which continued war had as much responsibility as the country which began it. The United States was the one great Power which was outside the struggle, and it was their duty to do what they could to put an end to it. . . . He said that all the Powers concerned had been disappointed in their ambitions. Germany had not taken Paris. France had not retaken Alsace, England had not cleared the seas of the German navy. The last month had made no appreciable difference in the relative positions of the armies, and there was now no prospect of an issue satisfactory to any

---

[32] The above paragraph is a summary of the thoughts and proposals expressed in W. J. Bryan to W.W., September 19, October 7, December 1, and December 17, 1914, all in the Wilson Papers. Bryan's letters of October 7 and December 1, 1914, are printed in *The Lansing Papers*, I, 9-11.

Power. Why should they not make peace now, if they had to make peace a year hence after another year's fruitless struggle. It would be far wiser if each said what it was fighting for and asked the United States to help them in arriving at a peaceful conclusion."[33]

House was neither so obsessed by the dream of mediation nor so hopeful of its prospects as was the Secretary of State. The Colonel, who was to some degree Machiavellian in his thinking about the war, did not believe that the belligerents would consent to mediation until they had lost all hope of forcing a military decision, or unless they were sure that American mediation would help them to achieve their objectives. House, moreover, had very definite ideas about the kind of peace settlement that American mediation should be used to attain. He did not either at this early stage of the war or later desire the crushing defeat of Germany; indeed, he regarded this possibility with mild abhorrence. But he did want a limited Anglo-French victory, one sufficiently conclusive to make possible the removal of what he regarded as the cancer of German militarism, and then general disarmament throughout Europe.[34] Hoping for this kind of settlement, House would never consent to forcing the Allies to participate in a peace project if it were likely to serve only German interests. He would be willing to use mediation only to serve English and French interests, or, more precisely, *what he interpreted English and French interests to be.*

In choosing House over Bryan as his spokesman in peace discussions, Wilson was of course manifesting his confidence in the one's ability and discretion and his distrust of the other's. But the significance of the choice ran deeper than this. It also meant that he shared House's view of the really narrow possibilities of American action at this stage in the war. As the President put it early in the autumn of 1914, "My own expectation is that the matter does not lie with us. I do not think we will be called upon to choose which nations shall participate in the mediation or that we shall be at liberty to invite others to participate."[35] He was more fearful than Bryan of making an abortive move, of doing or saying something which, "in the present state of passion

---

[33] C. Spring Rice to Sir Arthur Nicolson, November 13, 1914, *The Letters of Sir Cecil Spring Rice*, II, 240.

[34] House, it should be added, was not actually anti-German in this desire. He believed that the Kaiser and the civilian leaders of the German Empire had not wanted the war, and that they would cooperate gladly in building a new Europe once they were freed from the domination of the militarists.

[35] W.W. to W. J. Bryan, October 8, 1914, Wilson Papers.

on the other side of the water," would only exasperate the belligerents and hence prevent any real progress.[36] Wilson's choice meant, finally, that he shared for the most part House's view of the uses to which American mediation should be put. At this particular juncture in the war, at any rate, he expected and probably desired a limited Allied victory; certainly, it seems safe to say, he would not be willing to participate in any peace movement that seemed likely to promote a German triumph.

At Wilson's direction, and also at Bernstorff's urging, Colonel House began informal and secret negotiations looking toward a meeting of the German, British, and French Ambassadors for an exchange of views on peace. The Colonel's first move was to invite Ambassador von Bernstorff to his apartment in New York on September 18, 1914. House was in his best form—warm, intimate, and encouraging—but he assumed, curiously, that Bernstorff had come as a supplicant, and he was somewhat condescending. England, House said, dominated the Allies at this time. It was so clearly in her interest not to crush Germany totally, he continued, that he hoped some peace move might be initiated at once. Would Bernstorff be willing to confer with Spring Rice? he asked. The Ambassador hesitated and then agreed when House promised that no one but the President would know about the encounter.[37] "If we can get these two together," the Colonel wrote to Wilson on the same day, "we can at least make a start. . . . England . . . would probably be content now with an agreement for general disarmament and an indemnity for Belgium. Germany, I think, would be glad to get such terms. Shall I go on?"[38]

Wilson read House's letter the following morning, September 19, with some excitement and sent a reply by wire, urging his friend to see Spring Rice without delay.[39] The British envoy arrived by invitation in New York on September 20 and went to House's apartment for a long talk. House was friendly but emphatic. England, he said, could probably get peace now on the basis of the disarmament of Germany and compensation for Belgium, and that, he added, was all she

[36] W.W. to H. A. Bridgman, January 6, 1915, *ibid.*

[37] House Diary, September 18, 1914.

[38] E. M. House to W.W., September 18, 1914, Wilson Papers.

[39] The following paragraph is based upon the House Diary, September 20, 1914; C. Spring Rice to E. Grey, September 22, 1914, *The Letters of Sir Cecil Spring Rice,* II, 224-227; and E. M. House to W.W., September 20, 1914, Wilson Papers.

could properly expect.[40] "He told me," Spring Rice reported to Sir Edward Grey, "that he wished very much to communicate with you on the subject of the war and American mediation, and that the President had consulted him on the subject. . . . He warned me that although for the present American sympathy was strongly with the Allies, this attitude might be modified by two eventualities. The first was if it could be asserted with any show of reason that Germany was willing to make peace, but that the Allies were determined on war at all hazards. The other was that the real object of the Allies should prove to be not the restoration of the balance of Europe, but its destruction by the entire elimination of Germany."

House then told Spring Rice about his conversation with Bernstorff and asked the British Ambassador whether he would be willing to meet the German envoy. Spring Rice replied with a tirade against his hostile colleague; in any event, he went on, he could not meet Bernstorff alone, as the British were bound by treaty not to negotiate without the knowledge and consent of their allies. "House said he fully understood," Spring Rice further reported, "but he thought it a good thing for us and the Allies and we should not adopt a *non possumus* attitude as to negotiations, and that it could be only to our advantage that Germany should be forced to show her hand. The reason why it was desirable to begin conversations now, or rather not to stop them, was that if we waited, either Germany or Russia would gain a great preponderance, and this would so much alter the situation in every way as to make terms of peace which might be possible now wholly out of the question. It would certainly much alter the attitude of the President and the American people."

The upshot of this conversation was an agreement that Spring Rice should convey House's thoughts and suggestions at once by telegram to Sir Edward Grey. This Spring Rice did the following day, September 21, after he had returned to the British Embassy in Washington.[41]

---

[40] In addition, House described what he called his own peace program. Together with the two points about German disarmament and restitution to Belgium, it included the division of Alsace-Lorraine between Germany and France, France taking Alsace and Germany keeping Lorraine; the establishment of an independent Poland; the formation of a strong Balkan confederation that would include the non-German and non-Magyar portions of the Hapsburg Empire; and the neutralization of the Dardanelles. House Diary, September 20, 1914. House must have made it clear that these were only his personal views, as Spring Rice did not report them to the Foreign Office in London.

[41] There is a copy of this telegram in the House Papers. It is printed with a few

During the following week or ten days, Bernstorff, eager to make the most of Spring Rice's refusal to confer, maintained a steady pressure on Colonel House, assuring him that Germany wanted peace and would give "full cooperation" in negotiations, and even suggesting that House might go direct to England and Germany to get formal talks under way.[42] However, there was nothing much the President or Colonel House could do until they received some word from London. Grey did not hasten to reply, and neither Spring Rice nor Page gave any encouragement.[43] House explained the situation to the President during a conversation on September 28, 1914. Wilson did not think well of Bernstorff's suggestion that House go to London and Berlin but suggested, instead, that he write to Grey, warning him of the danger of postponing peace negotiations. "If Germany and Austria are entirely crushed," House wrote in his Diary, "neither of us could see any way by which Russia could be restrained. He thought I should bring this strongly to Sir Edward Grey's attention."[44] This House did in a letter to Page on October 3, one that fully revealed the Washington leaders' thinking about the problems of peace at this time. It follows in part:

"The attitude, I think, for England to maintain is the one which she so ably put forth to the world. That is peace must come only upon condition of disarmament and must be permanent. I have a feeling that Germany will soon be willing to discuss terms. I do not agree that Germany has to be completely crushed and that terms must be made either in Berlin or London. It is manifestly against England's interest and the interest of Europe generally for Russia to become the dominating military force in Europe, just as Germany was. The dislike which England has for Germany should not blind her to actual conditions. If Germany is crushed, England cannot solely write the terms of peace, but Russia's wishes must also largely prevail.

"With Russia strong in militarism, there is no way by which she could be reached. Her Government is so constituted that friendly conversations could not be had with her as they might be had even with

---

editorial changes in Charles Seymour (ed.), *The Intimate Papers of Colonel House*, I, 328-329.

[42] E. M. House to W.W., September 22, 1914, Wilson Papers, reporting a conversation with Bernstorff on the previous day; House Diary, September 26, 1914, summarizing what Bernstorff had told House's friend, Hugh C. Wallace, on September 25, 1914.

[43] e.g., House Diary, September 29, 1914.

[44] *ibid.*, September 28, 1914.

such a power as Germany and the world would look forward to another cataclysm and in the not too distant future.

"When peace conversations begin, at best they will probably continue many months before anything tangible comes from them. England and the allies could readily stand on the general proposition that only enduring peace will satisfy them and I see no insuperable obstacle in the way. . . .

"I am writing this to you with the President's knowledge and consent and with the thought that it will be conveyed to Sir Edward. There is a growing impatience in this country because of this war and there is constant pressure upon the President to use his influence to bring about normal conditions. He does not wish to do anything to irritate or offend any one of the belligerent nations, but he has an abiding faith in the efficacy of open and frank discussions between those that are now at war."[45]

The eager peacemakers received small encouragement during the two months following the dispatch of House's letter to Page on October 3. Bernstorff was perpetually pacific—indeed, he and other German spokesmen in the United States were conducting a systematic propaganda to persuade the American public that Germany wanted peace—but he had no support from his superiors, while the British leaders made obvious efforts to fend off any serious American intervention. Grey did not even reply to House's letter, and Page reported that the British leaders and people were preparing for a protracted war. "A long luncheon talk to-day with Sir Edward Grey," he wrote on November 18, "revealed the state of mind of the Government, namely, that peace cannot be thought of and will not be discussed till Germany will agree to pay for the full restoration of Belgium, and he does not think that Germany will agree to this till she is thoroughly exhausted."[46] Spring Rice, moreover, added the intimation that his government would regard any American peace move as an unfriendly act. As Colonel House pointed out to the President in reporting the Ambassador's warning, "It is very clear therefore that what is best is to do nothing at present, but to keep in touch with the situation as you are doing and be ready when the hint is given. Sir Cecil thinks

[45] E. M. House to W. H. Page, October 3, 1914, House Papers.
[46] Ambassador Page to the Secretary of State, November 18, 1914, *Foreign Relations, 1914, Supplement,* p. 132.

that this time will arrive, but just when, he is not now prepared to say."[47]

These sharp warnings caused House to doubt that a mediatory effort should be undertaken at all—certainly not, he thought, if it imperiled Anglo-American friendship, without which all American peace moves were bound to fail. He had a long and revealing talk about the problem with Wilson on December 3, 1914. The President read a recent letter from the Secretary of State, suggesting that he, Wilson, move boldly by calling upon the belligerents to state their war aims.[48] "I was certain," House wrote in his Diary, "it would be entirely footless to do this, for the Allies would consider it an unfriendly act, and further it was not good for the United States to have peace brought about until Germany was sufficiently beaten to cause her to consent to a fundamental change in her military policy. . . . When Germany was pushed back within her own borders I thought it would be advisable for me to go there and see the Kaiser and endeavor to get his consent to two conditions [indemnification of Belgium and general European disarmament]. . . ." Wilson agreed but thought it would be difficult for the German Emperor to consent to such terms because of the opposition of his entourage.

Then there was the danger that Bryan might have to be brought into any serious peace discussions. "The President," House continued in his record of the conversation, "said that he, Mr. Bryan, did not know that he, the President, was working for peace wholly through me, and he was afraid to mention this fact for fear it would offend him. He said Mr. Bryan might accept it gracefully, but not being certain, he hesitated to tell him. . . . The President had a feeling that I could do more to initiate peace unofficially than anyone could do in an official capacity, for the reason I could talk and be talked to without it being binding upon anyone."[49]

It all now depended upon Colonel House, as the President said, and by mid-December House was about ready to abandon the mediation project altogether. On the day after his conversation with the President, House wrote to Ambassador Page, telling him that Wilson meant to begin peace parleys at "the very earliest moment," and asking the Ambassador to sound out Sir Edward Grey on terms.[50] On

---

[47] E. M. House to W.W., October 8, 1914, Wilson Papers.
[48] This was W. J. Bryan to W.W., December 1, 1914, *ibid.*
[49] House Diary, December 3, 1914.
[50] E. M. House to W. H. Page, December 4, 1914, House Papers.

December 14, however, House sent a cable asking Page to ignore the letter. "I did this," he explained, "for the reason that . . . I [have] concluded it would not do to unduly press the British Government at this time to consent to the President's offer of mediation. I feel they are determined to make a complete job of it while they are in it, and I also feel in my heart that it is best for Germany, best for Europe and best for the world, to have the issue settled now for all time to come."[51]

Then occurred an unforeseen event that suddenly revived all of Wilson's and House's ebbing hopes. It was the receipt by Colonel House on about December 15 or 16 of a letter from the German Undersecretary of State for Foreign Affairs, Arthur Zimmermann, inviting the President to take the lead in a new peace effort. As Zimmermann's suggestion set off a chain of events that would culminate in the first really serious intergovernmental peace discussions, it might be well to see what the Germans had in mind.

Colonel House had, he thought, established an intimate relationship with Zimmermann during those days in the late spring of 1914 when House was in Berlin talking so hopefully of an Anglo-American-German *entente*. An opportunity to strengthen the relationship had come when Zimmermann wrote at the outbreak of the war, lamenting the failure of House's good efforts.[52] With the President's approval, House had replied at once, saying that the President's recent offer of good offices had not been an empty one. "Now that His Majesty has so brilliantly shown the power of His army," House had continued, "would it not be consistent with His lifelong endeavor to maintain peace, to consent to overtures being made in that direction? If I could serve in any way as a medium it would be a great source of happiness to me, and I stand ready to act immediately upon any suggestion that Your Excellency may convey, or have conveyed confidentially to me."[53]

This letter, which House sent through Bernstorff, did not arrive in Berlin until October 20, six weeks after Bryan addressed his peace inquiry to the German Foreign Office at the time of the discussion begun by Oscar S. Straus. Coming as it obviously did from the President of the United States himself and being (so the Germans understood) a new offer of personal good offices of mediation, House's let-

---

[51] House Diary, December 14, 1914.

[52] A. Zimmermann to E. M. House, August 1, 1914, House Papers.

[53] E. M. House to A. Zimmermann, September 5, 1914, handwritten copy in the German F. O. Archives.

ter set off the first really serious German discussions about the possibilities of American mediation. We have no record of the oral discussions during the following weeks among the Imperial Chancellor, the Foreign Secretary, Gottlieb von Jagow, and the Undersecretary. There is, however, much evidence to indicate that the Emperor and his civilian advisers were not at all optimistic about Germany's military prospects and would have been happy to conclude the war on a basis of the *status quo ante bellum.*[54] The truth was, unhappily, that the Chancellor could not seriously contemplate opening negotiations on a basis that could possibly succeed. Any German peace move at all would have provoked the violent opposition of most of the leaders in the army and navy; worse still, it would have affronted all those elements in the German population, particularly among the parties of the Right, who were beginning to dream of annexations and indemnities, thus shattering the unity upon which the successful prosecution of the war seemed to depend. Thus Bethmann's hands were fairly tied in any event.[55] In addition, German public opinion was by now so aroused against the export of American munitions to the Allies that Bethmann could hardly have dared to turn to President Wilson for mediation, even if he had wanted to do so.

In a long letter written at Supreme Headquarters on November 23, 1914, Bethmann explained the hidden dangers of the situation and conveyed his decision to the Foreign Secretary. He agreed with von Jagow, Bethmann began, that it would not be wise to think in terms of outright rejection of the President's offer. "We have to avoid the appearance of favoring, in principle, the continuation of the war." Yet, he went on, he could not foresee any practical success from American mediation, mainly because it would be extraordinarily difficult to persuade the British to stop fighting. "Furthermore," Bethmann continued, "I see a certain danger in an American mediation move because it would probably lead to an international congress, and our position in such a congress—two great powers against three—would be an unfavorable one. . . . And from the American side we would have to expect Mr. Wilson's and Mr. Bryan's known do-good tendencies and the injection of a lot of questions (disarmament, arbitration, and world peace) which, the more utopian they are, the more they make practical negotiations difficult." House's proposals were, Bethmann went

[54] e.g., Theobald von Bethmann Hollweg, *Considérations sur la Guerre Mondiale*, II, 168-171.

[55] On this point, see E. R. May, *The World War and American Isolation*, pp. 102-106.

on, all dictated to such an extent by "an unpractical peace-swooning" that it would be difficult for a realist to give a precise answer. "If the luck of battle is favorable to us, it is highly improbable that we would renounce all idea of booty, as point One [disarmament] seems to contemplate. Point Two [arbitration] would always remain an empty formula, and on the execution of point Three [world peace] I have as much doubt as Your Excellency."

The point was, of course, the Chancellor emphasized, that Germany could not reject an American mediation proposal in principle. How, then, should Zimmermann reply? By finding a form of answer which, without going into any detail on specific points, conveyed the impression of a sympathetic reception to House's offer. How this could be done Bethmann then revealed in the draft of a reply to Colonel House, which he said he would ask Zimmermann to send.[56]

The Chancellor's reply, which went to Colonel House in the form of a personal letter from Zimmermann on about December 3, 1914, sought first to convey a sincere longing for peace and then to shift the onus of refusing to negotiate on to the Allies. "We have greatly appreciated the President's and your own good offices," the letter read. ". . . Germany has always desired to maintain peace, as she proves by a record of more than forty years. The war has been forced upon us by our enemies and they are carrying it on by summoning all the forces at their disposal, including Japanese and other colored races. This makes it impossible for us to take the first step towards making peace. The situation might be different if such overtures came from the other side. I do not know whether your efforts have been extended in that direction and whether they have found a willing ear. But as long as you kindly offer your services in a most unselfish way, agreeing to act upon any suggestion that I convey to you, so it seems to me worth while trying to see where the land lies in the other camp."[57]

Zimmermann's letter must have reached Colonel House on December 15, for he left for Washington that evening, carrying the precious document with him, and went straight to the White House on the following day. Both the President and his adviser were plainly excited by Zimmermann's suggestion—the first clear call for peace discussions that had yet come from any belligerent government. House, Wilson declared, should go to Europe as soon as possible to begin the con-

[56] T. von Bethmann Hollweg to G. von Jagow, November 23, 1914, German F. O. Archives.

[57] A. Zimmermann to E. M. House, December 3, 1914, House Papers.

versations; meanwhile, he should see Bernstorff at once to prepare the way.[58] The Colonel, consequently, had a long and frank conversation with the German Ambassador on the following day, December 17. Elated by the sudden turn in events, Bernstorff promised that House would find the Germans eager to begin peace talks if he could persuade the Allies to cooperate. "I replied," House recorded in his Diary, "that there was no use taking it up with the Allies excepting upon a basis of evacuation and indemnity of Belgium and drastic disarmament which might ensure permanent peace." There would be "no obstacle in that direction," Bernstorff said. "I congratulated him upon this position," House further recorded, "and . . . I asked him to confirm this by cabling to his Government."[59]

The Colonel relayed the gist of Bernstorff's assurances to Ambassador Spring Rice soon afterward, on December 18. Warning that the Allies would be severely compromised if they refused to consider peace upon these terms, House asked Spring Rice to inform Sir Edward Grey and get an answer from him as soon as possible.[60]

It would not be accurate to say that Grey was alarmed by the news from Washington, but he understood the dangers of his predicament and was not unconcerned. He had no confidence in the sincerity of the German overture and believed that it was designed merely to drive a wedge between America and the Allies. Moreover, he knew that the German maneuver might succeed, for the Allies had no intention of making peace upon the basis of *general* disarmament and the restoration of Belgium. Allied war aims had by no means crystallized, but they were already so ambitious that they could be achieved only by a dictated peace. It would, as the British Ambassador in Paris put it, be "disastrously foolish" for the Allies to think of peace at this time.[61] Or, as Georges Clemenceau, the French politician and editor, added while "pooh-poohing" the idea of American intervention, "peace must be the concern of the belligerents only with no outside mediation or interference."[62] Besides, from Grey's point of view this was the worst possible time for peace talks, for he and the other Allied leaders were at this very moment working desperately to bring Italy, Greece, and Rumania into the war by dangling the bait of Austrian, Hungarian, and Turkish territories. Finally, Grey knew that a negative

---

[58] House Diary, December 16, 1914.   [59] *ibid.*, December 17, 1914.
[60] *ibid.*, December 18, 1914.
[61] Lady Algernon G. Lennox (ed.), *The Diary of Lord Bertie of Thame*, I, 73.
[62] *ibid.*, pp. 81-82.

response to Washington would only incite the Germans to greater pressure for peace discussions and might well leave the Allies precisely where their enemies wanted them, that is, in a position of opposing any and all efforts for peace. Such an eventuality, obviously, had to be avoided somehow.

Thus in responding to House's inquiry of December 18, Grey maneuvered to give the impression of willingness to consider peace on the two-point basis without committing his government to such a program. Spring Rice conveyed Grey's reply to House on December 20. "He had word from Sir Edward Grey concerning our peace proposals," the Colonel wrote in his Diary, "and thought it would not be a good thing for the Allies to stand out against a proposal which embraced indemnity to Belgium and a satisfactory plan for disarmament. Sir Edward wished me to know that this was his personal attitude." House returned to the White House to report the good news. Wilson was so encouraged that he asked whether the Colonel could go to Europe as early as the coming Saturday, December 26.[63]

House must have told Spring Rice of the President's reaction, for the Ambassador wired to London on the same day in such a way as to elicit a second, more chilling message from Grey. The Foreign Secretary, Spring Rice said, was still personally agreeable to peace talks on a basis of the two-point program. But he also wanted the American leaders to know certain other facts—that he had not discussed the matter with the British Cabinet, much less with the Allied governments, and that French and Russian objectives would depend largely upon "the progress of the war." House was neither surprised nor discouraged. It was futile, he replied, to go into the details of the settlement at this point; the Kaiser and his civilian leaders knew that the war was a failure and would be glad to "get out of it whole now."[64]

Confronted thus with an obvious American determination to proceed, Grey now went the whole length in attempting to discourage discussions in the near future and to prepare for them diplomatically should they still occur. Toward the end of December he called in Chandler P. Anderson, who was leaving for the United States after a tour of duty in the American Embassy, and asked him to convey certain statements orally to the President. He did not believe that the

[63] House Diary, December 20, 1914.

[64] *ibid.*, December 23, 1914. Grey's telegram to Spring Rice, dated December 22, 1914, is printed in G. M. Trevelyan, *Grey of Fallodon*, pp. 356-357.

time had come for peace overtures or even for the discussion of possible terms, Grey began, but he wanted the President to know that the Allies would insist upon certain terms if they were in a position to do so at the end of the war. These included reparation for Belgium, the return of Alsace-Lorraine and the payment of an indemnity to France, and Russian acquisition of Constantinople and the Dardanelles. Anderson conveyed the message to Wilson on January 9 and to Colonel House a short time later, adding on his own that Japan and Italy, if the latter came into the war, as now seemed likely, would also have to be satisfied in the final reckoning.[65]

Grey added a final word a few days after his conference with Anderson. House had told the British Ambassador that there was no chance that the Washington government would "countersign" any postwar agreement for the preservation of peace. "If this is so," Grey warned, "it is difficult to see how a durable peace can be secured without complete exhaustion of one side or the other." "For the moment," he went on, "I cannot help feeling from all indications that reach me that Germany is not prepared to make peace on terms that will concede what is just now and give us security for the future." Moreover, he added gloomily, "President's friend must not forget that France and Russia have to be consulted about European peace and that I could not open discussion with them unless very sure of the ground respecting Germany's real disposition."[66]

Knowing that even the sternest warnings might go unheeded, Grey also set to work to inform the French and Russian governments of the discussions that had occurred, and to prepare them for all potential unpleasant necessities. After summarizing what he had already told the Washington authorities, he went on in explanation of his own attitude, as follows:

"Sir E. Grey is far from a desire to discourage any overture made in a sincere manner, which offers a promise of leading to the conclusion of a satisfactory peace; and if any satisfactory assurance at all is given that Germany truly shows a desire for peace, Sir E. Grey would then observe that conditions would have to be agreed upon by the

---

[65] Anderson Diary, January 9 and 14, 1915. Wilson made no comment except to say that he had anticipated that the Dardanelles would either be neutralized or else given to Russia, and that he believed that Britain's traditional policy of preventing Russian access to the Mediterranean was based on theoretical rather than practical dangers to British interests.

[66] E. Grey to C. Spring Rice, January 2, 1915, G. M. Trevelyan, *Grey of Fallodon*, pp. 357-358.

Allies. In this case Great Britain would discuss this with Japan . . . as well as with France and Russia. . . . The information which has come to His Majesty's Government from neutral sources concerning the true opinion of official circles in Berlin does not testify to its peaceful character. Sir E. Grey is of the opinion that so long as this state of mind persists, the continuation of the war with the greatest possible zeal is the only subject about which there is any useful purpose to be served by discussion."[67]

Meanwhile, Wilson and House had received no more encouragement from the leaders in Berlin than from the British Foreign Secretary. On December 17, 1914, House had asked Bernstorff to obtain confirmation from his government of his assurances that Germany stood ready to make peace on a basis of the two-point program. No such confirmation had come by early January 1915.[68] House, therefore, wrote again to Zimmermann on January 3, saying that his discussions had led him to believe that peace conversations might begin at once if the belligerents could agree upon an indemnity to Belgium and a settlement that would insure permanent peace. "If you could give me any assurances in this direction," the Colonel added, "I would leave immediately for England where I have reason to believe I would get a sympathetic hearing. I stand ready to start at any time upon receipt of either a letter or a cable from you indicating that Germany would be willing to begin the discussions upon such terms."[69]

Even as he wrote these words, Colonel House expected an evasive reply. It was obvious, he thought, that he and the President were at a dead end, and that nothing remained but to confront the rival leaders in person. Going to Washington on January 12, he discussed the situation briefly with the President before dinner that evening. "We had exactly twelve minutes' conversation before dinner," he wrote in his Diary, "and during those twelve minutes it was decided that I

[67] Sir George Buchanan to Sergei Sazonov, January 12, 1915, as printed in E. R. May, *The World War and American Isolation*, p. 86.

[68] There is no evidence in the files of the German Foreign Office that Bernstorff ever sent the cable, or that he ever told his superiors about the assurances that he had given on the two-point program. "There has never been any talk of the conditions of peace in my conversations with House," the Ambassador later told the Foreign Office untruthfully. "The matter was only that I told him that he would be well received in Berlin." Ambassador von Bernstorff to the Foreign Office, March 2, 1915, German F. O. Archives.

[69] E. M. House to A. Zimmermann, January 3, 1915, *ibid.*

should go to Europe on January 30. I had practically decided before I came to Washington that this was necessary, and I was certain, when I gave my thoughts to the President, he would agree with me it was the best thing to do." They had gone as far as they could go with the Ambassadors in Washington; it was time to deal directly with the principals. "I had a feeling we were losing ground and were not in as close touch with the Allies as we had been, and that it was essential to take the matter up directly with London and afterward Berlin."[70]

The decision thus firmly made, House now set about to prepare the way. He conveyed the news to Spring Rice the following morning. The British Ambassador was in a testy mood at first but was relieved by the Colonel's assurances that the American leaders were interested only in obtaining a "permanent settlement" and would not meanwhile insist upon an armistice.[71] At Spring Rice's insistence, House also met the French and Russian Ambassadors in company with their British colleague late in the afternoon. The French and Russian envoys bluntly warned that their governments would never accept a negotiated peace and predicted that House's mission would be utterly fruitless. But House pacified them—at least so he thought—by suggesting (speaking with his tongue in his cheek) that it would be well to "find out how utterly unreliable and treacherous the Germans were, by exposing their false pretenses of peace to the world."[72] Then on the following day, January 14, the Colonel informed Bernstorff of his impending trip and asked him to suggest that his government cease senseless raids by zeppelins and warships against noncombatants while the peace talks were proceeding—a suggestion that he repeated to the German Ambassador on January 20.[73] Bryan, obviously, also had to be told,

[70] House Diary, January 12, 1915.

[71] Sir Edward Grey sent word a short time later that he would welcome Colonel House and talk to him freely. "Of course," Grey added, "he understands that all that can be promised here is that if Germany seriously and sincerely desires peace, I will consult our friends as to what terms of peace are acceptable." E. Grey to C. Spring Rice, January 22, 1915, House Papers. This was the opening paragraph of Grey's confidential dispatch of January 22, which Spring Rice's son brought to House's apartment on the same day. For the remainder of this letter, see above, p. 183.

[72] House Diary, January 13, 1915. For the Russian Ambassador's account of this conversation, see the dispatch printed in E. R. May, *The World War and American Isolation*, pp. 79-80.

[73] House Diary, January 14 and 20, 1915; Ambassador von Bernstorff to the Foreign Office, January 15 and 23, 1915, German F. O. Archives. "House is definitely favorably inclined towards us," Bernstorff wrote to the Foreign Office on January 15. "He has no further ambition in this trip than to get both camps started speaking openly to each other."

and House rather than Wilson broke the news to him on January 13. The Secretary of State was visibly upset, saying that he had planned to go to Europe himself; however, he added quickly, House was certainly the best possible choice if the mission were to be undertaken by a private individual.[74]

There now remained only the final essential preparations. Wilson and House went to work together during the evening of January 13, devising a code for cable messages and agreeing upon the outline of a letter of commission and instructions. Written only for the eyes of Sir Edward Grey and the German Foreign Secretary,[75] it was a prolix document replete with gracious phrases. "We have no thought," it said in its key passage, "of suggesting, either now or at another time, the terms and conditions of peace. . . . Our single object is to be serviceable, if we may, in bringing about the preliminary willingness to parley which must be the first step towards discussing and determining the conditions of peace. If we can be instrumental in ascertaining for each side in the contest what is the real disposition, the real wish, the real purpose of the other with regard to a settlement, your mission and my whole desire in the matter will have been accomplished."[76] The day after he sent this letter to House in New York, Wilson drafted another, which the Colonel was to use if he ever needed to give some public excuse for his presence in Europe. It commissioned him as the President's unofficial representative to study American war relief in Europe.[77]

[74] The President, Colonel House recorded in his Diary, was much disturbed by Bryan's reaction and said that he believed that the Secretary of State would prefer not to have peace if he could not bring it about himself. Then he corrected himself, saying that this statement was unfair. What he should have said, Wilson went on, was that Bryan was simply obsessed with the idea of mediation. He would permit Bryan to resign, he added, before he would let him undertake such a delicate mission, for which he was unfitted. House Diary, January 13, 1915.

[75] At least, so House told Bernstorff as he let him read the letter. Ambassador von Bernstorff to the Foreign Office, January 23, 1915, German F. O. Archives.

[76] W.W. to E. M. House, January 17, 1915, Wilson Papers.

[77] W.W. to E. M. House, January 18, 1915, *ibid.* Insofar as this writer knows, House never had to use this second letter, perhaps because the President, at an early stage in House's mission, put an effective end to reporters' inquiries about the purpose of the Colonel's journey. Rumors had come from London to the effect that House was in Europe to sound out the belligerents on the prospects of peace through American mediation. The White House reporters, on February 9, 1915, asked Wilson if this were true. According to the correspondent for the *New York Times*, the President "discouraged" this rumor. Colonel House, he said, did not carry any *credentials* from him or from the United States government. The Colonel, he further explained, usually

House returned quietly to Washington on January 24 and 25 for a final word with the President. "He asked me," House recorded, "to tell Sir Edward Grey his entire mind, so he would know what his intentions were about everything, and he wished me to mention his relations with Mr. Bryan and the conduct of the State Department under him. He said, 'Let him know that while you are abroad, I expect to act directly through you and to eliminate all intermediaries.' He approved all I had in mind to say to Sir Edward and to the Germans. He said, 'There is not much for us to talk over, for the reason we are both of the same mind and it is not necessary to go into details with you.' "[78]

Then came the time for farewell. House describes the scene far better than the biographer can: "The President's eyes were moist when he said his last words of farewell. He said: 'Your unselfish and intelligent friendship has meant much to me,' and he expressed his gratitude again and again, calling me his 'most trusted friend.' He declared I was the only one in all the world to whom he could open his entire mind. I asked if he remembered the first day we met, some three and a half years ago. He replied, 'Yes, but we had known one another always, and merely came in touch then, for our purposes and thoughts were as one.' . . . He insisted upon going to the station with me. He got out of the car and walked through the station and to the ticket office, and then to the train itself, refusing to leave until I entered the car."[79]

"Good-bye, dear friend," House wrote the day before he sailed, "and may God sustain you in all your noble undertakings. When I think of the things you have done, of the things you have in mind to do, my heart stirs with pride and satisfaction. You are the bravest, wisest leader, the gentlest and most gallant gentleman and the truest friend in all the world."[80]

House sailed from New York on January 30, 1915, aboard the reigning queen of the Atlantic, the *Lusitania*. The voyage was unevent-

---

went abroad at this season, and in making this journey he had no *official* message of any kind. He carried letters of identification, Wilson added, but no *formal* letters. *New York Times*, February 10, 1915. It was a superb example of what House once called Wilson's method of "grazing the truth," that is, of saying something that was literally true but conveyed a false impression.

[78] House Diary, January 24, 1915.

[79] *ibid.*, January 25, 1915.

[80] E. M. House to W.W., January 29, 1915, Wilson Papers.

ful except for a brief violent storm off the Grand Banks and for the captain's action in running up the American flag as the ship approached the Irish coast.[81] Only the day before, February 4, the German Admiralty had announced its intention to begin submarine warfare against Allied shipping within the waters surrounding the British Isles, and the *Lusitania's* captain was taking all precautions.

Arriving in London on February 6, House had his first conference with Sir Edward Grey on the following morning. It was a long meeting, and, House reported to the President, "We discussed the situation as frankly as you and I would have done in Washington, and, as far as I could judge, there was no reservation." Grey, however, was obviously taking House's measure. He was willing, he said, to work with the President, but there were certain difficulties ahead. The Allied negotiations with Italy and Rumania were not going well; there was the problem of French and Russian territorial ambitions; finally, there was the question of American support for the peace settlement. Although he did suggest that perhaps the best solution of the problem of Alsace-Lorraine was the neutralization of the province, House was generally noncommittal in reply, saying not much more than that the President and he desired only to bring the belligerents together, not to suggest terms of peace.[82]

House met Grey again three days later, on February 10, at a luncheon attended also by Ambassador Page and Grey's secretary, Sir William Tyrrell. The Foreign Secretary began by repeating what he had said many times before, that the German peace overtures were not sincere. House strongly disagreed. Then Grey raised again the question that was evidently beginning to assume large dimensions in his mind, the possibility of American participation in the peace conference and support for whatever security system that assemblage might devise. Page described Grey's germinating idea: "The uncertain thing is whether it [the war] will end as a drawn battle or be prolonged to a decisive defeat. Nobody can yet tell that. And here this idea comes in: If it were definitely known by England that in the discussion that must follow the laying down of arms, all the moral power of the world—our power in particular—wd be actively and strenuously exerted for the making of a programme of forcible security for the future—in that event England might consent to end the war as a drawn contest and trust to the subsequent discussion and world-

[81] House Diary, February 5, 1915.
[82] E. M. House to W.W., February 8 and 9, 1915, Wilson Papers.

wide agreement to secure safety for the future."[83] It was, insofar as this writer knows, the first official proposal of a postwar league of nations made during the war. House emphatically repudiated the suggestion,[84] saying that noninvolvement in European affairs was an unwritten American law and that the most the United States would be able to do would be to sign a postwar convention recodifying the rules of war.

But there was the more immediate problem of how to get peace discussions under way. What could be done? Grey apparently replied at once with a clear declaration. As Page reported it: "The Allies will not *propose* peace till they have won some more convincing military victory; but they will listen now to any proposal from the other side and England at least will heartily welcome any sincere proposal wh. will include the restoration of Belgium and security for the future. All other conditions are details. These two are the English essentials. The other Allies, of course, will demand something—the Black Sea, Alsace-Lorraine, etc., but presumably nothing insuperable."[85]

To this House replied with equal forthrightness. "I told Sir Edward Grey," he wrote, "that I had no intention of pushing the question of peace, for in my opinion, it could not be brought about, in any event, before the middle of May or the first of June. I could see the necessity for the Allies to try out their new armies in the Spring, and I could also see the necessity for Germany not to be in such an advantageous position as now, for the reason she would be less likely to make terms that would insure permanent peace."[86]

This was, altogether, a momentous declaration, one that changed the character of House's mission at the very outset. No wonder Grey received it cordially, for at one stroke it removed all British fear of immediate American pressure and, together with what House had already said about peace terms, assured the Foreign Secretary that the Washington government would use its influence to achieve only a settlement acceptable to the Allies. No wonder, too, that Grey at once saw in the Colonel a man whom he could trust, and that he could later

[83] W. H. Page to W.W., February 10, 1915, *ibid.* For another statement of Grey's hopes, see the Diary of Sir Horace Plunkett, February 6, 1915, the Plunkett Foundation, London (hereinafter cited as the Plunkett Diary), and Margaret Digby, *Horace Plunkett, An Anglo-American Irishman*, p. 180.

[84] He was somewhat irritated when Page contradicted him. House Diary, February 10, 1915.

[85] W. H. Page to W.W., February 10, 1915, Wilson Papers.

[86] House Diary, February 11, 1915.

write while reminiscing, "I found combined in him in a rare degree the qualities of wisdom and sympathy. In the stress of war it was at once a relief, a delight, and an advantage to be able to talk with him freely. . . . He had a way of saying 'I know it' in a tone and manner that carried conviction both of his sympathy with, and understanding of, what was said to him."[87]

It is possible that House said more than he meant to say. He did not record this part of his conversation in his Diary on the day that it took place but added it the following day, deciding, perhaps as an afterthought, that it must go in. Moreover, he did not report his statement accurately to the President,[88] for the Colonel well knew that it fell short of expressing Wilson's purpose, which was to press for a beginning of peace discussions in all earnestness. Making this statement may, then, have been an accident that House, having once made, did not know how to repair. But if this conclusion is accurate, it seriously impeaches his skill as a negotiator.

It is, of course, also possible that House spoke deliberately. We know that he believed that the United States could not really take any strong initiative but could move only when the Allies, or, for that matter, the Germans, were ready. By the time he talked to Grey and Tyrrell on February 10, House surely must have understood that the Allies were far from ready for serious peace discussions; and he had no certain knowledge that the Germans were any more eager. He may simply have decided, therefore, that the wisest thing to do was to relieve Grey's obvious anxiety and to hope that a favorable reply from Germany would afford an opportunity for reopening the matter with the British leaders. This interpretation does not, to be sure, explain House's deception of the President; it is possible that he did not want to disappoint him by telling the whole truth.

House's conversations with Grey and other English leaders, including the Prime Minister, Herbert Asquith, proceeded at a notably relaxed pace during the week following the crucial conference on February 10. Most of the talk during these days was inconsequential, except for

---

[87] Grey of Fallodon, *Twenty-Five Years*, ii, 124-125.

[88] This is all he wrote to Wilson in reference to his statement that he had no intention of "pushing the question of peace": "I think the Allies will not consent to final peace terms until they have had a try at Germany during the coming spring. I explained to Grey, however, that it was not too early to get the machinery in order and that if it developed that Germany would give now terms that would be acceptable, it would be foolish to sacrifice so many useful lives." E. M. House to W.W., February 11, 1915, Wilson Papers. I have decoded the foregoing.

one new suggestion that Grey offered first on February 13, that House should postpone his contemplated trip to Germany until the fate of the new German campaign in Poland against the Russians had been decided.[89] It was prompted by House's receipt of a letter from Zimmermann on February 12, written in reply to House's letter of January 3. The Undersecretary was by no means discouraging. The German leaders, he said, stood ready to do their share in ending the war and were eager to talk to House in Berlin; on the other hand, he added, House's suggestion of a German indemnity to Belgium was hardly feasible.[90] To Grey this was only further proof of German treachery, and he and Asquith again urged House to stay in England, adding that there would be little point anyway in a visit to Berlin unless the Germans consented beforehand to the essential points of the restoration of Belgium and postwar disarmament.[91]

House described the situation in a series of letters and cablegrams to the White House that made his agreement clear. Wilson's hopes for peace, however, having been fed by Bernstorff and Ambassador Gerard in Berlin, had meanwhile increased. He replied impatiently on February 20: "Your dispatch of the 17th received. It will of course occur to you that you cannot go too far in allowing the English Government to determine when it is best to go to Germany because they naturally desire to await some time when they have the advantage because of events in the field or elsewhere. If the impression were to be created in Berlin that you were to come only when the British Government thought it the opportune time for you to come, you might be regarded when you reached there as their spokesman rather than as mine. Do you think that we can frankly state this dilemma to Grey? He will doubtless realize how very important it is to learn Germany's mind at the earliest possible moment. No one can be sure what a single day may develop, either in events or in opinion. The whole atmosphere may change at any moment."[92]

In a cablegram on February 22 and then in a long letter to Wilson on the following day, House finally described in all its stark reality the hopelessness of prospects for American mediation at this time. Up to this point, he wrote, all anyone knew was that the Germans had refused either to say that they would indemnify Belgium or to make

[89] House Diary, February 13, 1915.
[90] A. Zimmermann to E. M. House, Wilson Papers.
[91] House Diary, February 17, 1915.
[92] W.W. to E. M. House, February 20, 1915, Baker Collection.

any proposals at all. Even if they were willing to meet the minimum British demands, France and Russia would not make peace on any such terms. Indeed, the truth was, House went on, that a majority of the British Cabinet and the rank and file of the British people were determined to fight on to the bitter end, if that were necessary to achieve a lasting settlement, and would not approve a peace based only on the two-point program. "It is almost as important to us to have the settlement laid upon the right foundations as it is to the nations of Europe. If this war does not end militarism, then the future is full of trouble for us," House continued. "If there was any reason to believe that Germany was ready to make such terms as the Allies are ready to accept, then it would be well to go immediately [to Berlin]; but all our information is to the contrary and the result of my visit there now would be to lose the sympathetic interest which England, and through her the Allies, now feel in your endeavors and without accomplishing any good in Germany. . . . Asquith told Page yesterday that he sincerely hoped that I would not make the mistake of going just now. That simply means, if I do go they will probably cease to consider you as a medium." He had written to Zimmermann again,[93] and he would go to Germany if the Undersecretary replied. "But it will accomplish nothing for the moment, for he will not now go further; and the Allies will not be willing to begin parleys upon such a basis [as the evacuation of Belgium and postwar disarmament]."[94]

It was all very convincing, provided one accepted House's suppositions, as Wilson did. "Your cables," the President replied, "enable me to understand the situation in all its phases. I greatly appreciate them. I am, of course, content to be guided by your judgment as to each step."[95]

House stayed on in London during the next two weeks, dining and talking with leaders in every segment of English public life and thought. His fertile mind began to conceive new plans for postwar security, and the British leaders, seeing an opportunity to deflect his concern from the problems of the immediate future, were encouraging in their comments. Indeed, by this time the London authorities had ceased altogether to worry about Colonel House. Peace talk, and

[93] This was E. M. House to A. Zimmermann, February 17, 1915, German F. O. Archives, in which House asked whether the German government would be willing to talk on a basis of the evacuation of Belgium and postwar security if the issue of an indemnity to Belgium were waived for the moment.

[94] E. M. House to W.W., February 23, 1915, Wilson Papers.

[95] W.W. to E. M. House, February 25, 1915, Baker Collection.

presumably House's peace talk, the Prime Minister told Page in early March 1915, was "the twittering of a sparrow in a tumult that shakes the world."[96] Thus Grey was not alarmed when House, on hearing again from Zimmermann in a more encouraging way,[97] revived the idea of a trip to Berlin. On the contrary, the Foreign Secretary was so certain that all danger had passed that he even agreed that the time had come for House to go.[98]

"Just a last word to say that I leave everything here in admirable shape. It could not be better," House wrote to the President on March 9, 1915.[99] Two days later he left London for the Continent, going first to Paris for brief but discouraging conversations with the French Foreign Minister, Théophile Delcassé, other officials in the Foreign Office, and the British Ambassador in Paris.[100] Traveling to Berlin by way of Switzerland, he arrived in the German capital in a snowstorm on March 19 and went almost at once to the Foreign Office for a conference with Zimmermann.

The Undersecretary must have felt some trepidation as he greeted this still enigmatic American. The German Foreign Office had, after all, stimulated the peace talks in the first instance. What if House should demand to know the terms upon which the Imperial government would make peace? How, then, could the German leaders reply without disclosing that their objectives (like the Allies') could be won only by rifles and cannon?

These fears, if they actually existed, quickly receded once House approached the main subject. He had concluded that it was obviously futile to talk peace to the Germans on a basis merely of the two-point program. Some other formula had to be found to break the Anglo-German impasse and at the same time bring the American government more actively into the picture. And that formula, House had

[96] The Diary of Walter H. Page, March 11, 1915, Houghton Library, Harvard University; hereinafter cited as the Page Diary.

[97] A. Zimmermann to E. M. House, March 2, 1915, House Papers.

[98] E. M. House to W.W., March 5, 1915, Wilson Papers; House Diary, March 7, 1915.

[99] E. M. House to W.W., March 9, 1915, Wilson Papers.

[100] E. M. House to W.W., March 14 and 15, 1915, *ibid.* Noting in his Diary on March 16, 1915, that he had just dined with Colonel House, the British Ambassador, Sir Francis Bertie, added, "He is, I understand, looking around to see what opportunity the President may find for proposing peace, and so securing the German vote for a second Presidential Election. I had some conversation with him, but nothing worth noting." Lady Algernon G. Lennox (ed.), *The Diary of Lord Bertie of Thame*, I, 130.

already decided before he left London, was the freedom of the seas—
a vital German and American interest.

Peace, House told Zimmermann, would ultimately have to be made
by Britain and Germany; and he went on to explain the kind of terms
that the British and French had in mind. However, House added
quickly, he had no intention of pushing peace negotiations on anyone.
Much relieved, Zimmermann replied that he thought it was quite
impossible to discuss terms at this time because the German people
would never accept any such settlement as the western Allies contemplated. At this point, House gently shifted the discussion to his new
ground. Saying that there were questions upon which Germany and
the United States could agree—the limitation of British naval power
and the protection of neutral trade during wartime—he expressed the
hope that the two nations could work together to achieve these objectives after the war was over. Zimmermann, House noted, "was
exceedingly sympathetic with this thought, and I think it will have
a tendency to put us on a good footing here."[101]

The Colonel saw many German leaders during the following week,
but in all his conversations he sought only to build foundations for
German-American cooperation and mutual confidence, and he assiduously avoided giving any impression of being interested in specific
and immediate peace discussions. In a brief meeting with the Foreign
Secretary, von Jagow, on March 23, for example, House voiced the
hope that Germany would join the United States after the war in
establishing new international rules to protect the freedom of trade.
Of course Germany would do this, von Jagow replied. Then the Foreign Secretary gingerly broached the matter of specific peace proposals, saying that he could not comment on them without knowing
what they were. House cut off this phase of the conversation quickly
by replying that the President was not now in a position to make
specific proposals. Von Jagow then raised the issue that was most important to the German army and people, that of the export of American munitions to the Allies. House was both conciliatory and promising in reply. The United States, he said, depended upon private
munitions factories to supply her army in the event of war, and the
President would ruin the munitions industry and raise grave perils
for the future if he now forbade the export of munitions. However,

---

[101] E. M. House to W.W., March 20, 1915, Wilson Papers; House Diary, March 19,
1915. Perhaps it is significant that House did not inform the President that he had
told Zimmermann that he did not intend to push peace negotiations upon anyone.

he continued, the President was considering the possibility of nationalizing the munitions industry, and if this were done he could prohibit the export of weapons without endangering the nation's security. If Wilson did not make such a proposal, House added, it would be only because he was convinced that Congress would not approve.[102]

In a long and intimate second conversation with Zimmermann on the following day, March 24, House made it even clearer than before that he thought it was pointless to go into discussion of peace prospects. The Undersecretary, House noted in his Diary, "frankly said that if peace parleys were begun now upon terms that had any chance of acceptance, it would mean the overthrow of the Government and the Kaiser. I understood this, and did not mean to press matters or to say anything further about it, for it was not the President's purpose to insist upon something that was not at the moment desired."[103] And in his most important conference of all in Berlin, with Chancellor von Bethmann Hollweg on March 27, the Colonel went the whole way before the chief civilian official of the German Empire in his strategy of laying new foundations for American mediation. Here is House's account of the meeting, printed for the first time:

"The Chancellor came in immediately and was exceedingly cordial and delightful. I told him I knew he was busy and would be as brief as possible. He replied that his time was entirely at my disposal and he hoped I would not be hurried. I showed him the President's letter. He read it slowly and with more care than anyone had yet done. He said it was fine and he appreciated the President's motives and wished I would tell him so. . . .

"I gave him in detail what I had done since the beginning of the war, of my visit to England, to France and to Germany. He listened attentively. I was aware of public opinion in Germany and of how impossible it was to discuss peace parleys now upon a basis that would have any chance of success.[104] I outlined my suggestion as to the freedom of the seas, and of my purpose to take it up with the British Government and fight it out with them. . . .

[102] G. von Jagow, memorandum dated March 23, 1915, German F. O. Archives; House Diary, March 23, 1915.

[103] House Diary, March 24, 1915.

[104] House apparently said more than this. In a brief report of this meeting that the Foreign Office sent to the Embassy in Washington there were the following sentences: "House himself did not think that the time for peace had yet come. In France they are totally wild, in England somewhat less." G. von Jagow to Ambassador von Bernstorff, March 31, 1915, German F. O. Archives.

"The Chancellor spoke of my plan as being the first thread to be thrown across the chasm which would finally have to be bridged. He was enthusiastic over the situation and bade me Godspeed, asking me to keep him informed. He was courteous, he was kind, and he impressed me as being one of the best types of German I have met."[105]

Colonel House described the situation that he had found and explained what he was trying to accomplish in a series of summary reports to the President just before he left Berlin. They follow, in part:

"The situation of Germany is this: Peace is desired generally, but not having actual facts given them, the people would overthrow the government and . . . the throne if parleys should now be commenced on the basis of having any chance of success. The civil government would listen to proposals based on evacuation of Belgium and France, and about half the military government would consent to this; but the people generally would not permit it. The problem is to save the face of the authorities, and to enlighten the people. I have proposed a way to do this and it was cordially received by von Bethmann-Hollweg and Zimmermann. In substance it is for us to try to induce England to consent to the freedom of the seas as one of the peace conditions. If they yield, as we have reason to believe they will, then Germany can say to the people that the great cause they have been striving for has been won, and there is no need to retain Belgium and her coast in order to be in a position to wage a more successful maritime war at some future time; that to hold an alien people would be a source of weakness rather than strength and would bring future trouble."[106]

"I have drawn particularly upon our desire for the freedom of the seas, and how in the second convention [that is, the treaty to be written by all the neutral and belligerent powers to guarantee international security after the peace settlement itself had been made] they would find us standing firmly by Germany to bring about the desired result. I have said that our thought went far beyond the Declaration of Paris, or the proposed Declaration of London, and that we have in mind the absolute freedom of commerce in future warfare, and that navies should be used almost wholly for protection against invasion. This thought has been enthusiastically received and it has done more to

[105] House Diary, March 27, 1915.
[106] E. M. House to W.W., March 29, 1915, Wilson Papers.

bring about a better feeling than anything that has been said or done."[107]

"I have sown this thought of the Freedom of the Seas very widely since I have been here, and already I can see the results. . . . I believe I can show England that, in the long run and looking at the matter broadly, it is as much to her interest as it is to the other nations of the earth. The Chancellor seems to think, and so does Zimmermann, that I have offered in this suggestion the best idea as a peace beginning. . . . I leave here fairly satisfied with the situation, as we now have something definite to work on and as the warring nations have tentatively accepted you as their Mediator."[108]

Would the freedom of the seas, then, be the new formula of peace? Was its magic strong enough to break the Anglo-German impasse? At least the ever hopeful man in the White House thought that it might be. "The suggestion you are to carry to London," he wired to House soon after his departure from Berlin, "seems to me very promising and may afford the opening we are looking for. . . . I warmly admire the way in which you are conducting your conferences at each stage. You are laying the indispensable groundwork and sending me just the information I need."[109]

Leaving Berlin on about March 30, 1915, House went to Nice and Biarritz in France for incidental conferences with the American Ambassadors at Rome and Madrid, Thomas Nelson Page and Joseph E. Willard, on April 2 and 8; thence he journeyed to Paris on about April 10. Spring had come to Europe, and new hopes of victory on the battlefields. In the East a combined German and Austrian army was beginning a campaign that would drive the Russians beyond the Carpathians to the Dniester River. The British had begun an amphibious operation against the Turkish-held Dardanelles, and a large British expeditionary force was nearing the Ottoman domain for an ill-fated campaign on Gallipoli at the very time that House turned northeastward toward Paris. The British and French diplomatic efforts to persuade Italy to come into the war against the Hapsburg monarch were on the verge of success. Altogether, the immediate situation was not promising, the itinerant peacemaker must have thought as he en-

[107] E. M. House to W.W., March 26, 1915, *ibid.*
[108] E. M. House to W.W., March 27, 1915, *ibid.*
[109] W.W. to E. M. House, April 1, 1915, Baker Collection.

tered the French capital, for obviously new excursions and a greater din, not talk of peace, were the order of the day.

House did not, therefore, dare to pose as a would-be mediator in Paris. He saw Delcassé on April 13 and removed his fears of American meddling with the assurance that it was not his or President Wilson's intention to insist upon any peace negotiations. House also promised the Foreign Minister that no amount of pressure would force the President to accept an arms embargo. Delcassé was delighted. "He," House recorded, "was good enough to express his satisfaction at the way negotiations have been carried on up to now."[110]

For the balance of House's visit the French leaders exuded a Gallic kind of cordiality. House had a long conference with President Raymond Poincaré on April 16. House had been warned that *monsieur le président* was cold and austere, but House found him affable. Wilson had sent a personal message conveying his warm gratitude for the fact that the French were "so generous as to receive our offers of friendship in just the spirit in which they are offered and with such full and sympathetic comprehension of the part we wish to play."[111] Poincaré was visibly pleased. "I can see from my interview," House wrote in his Diary immediately afterward "not only with Delcassé and Poincaré but with others, that I would have made a mistake if I had attempted to talk peace at this time. France as a whole has an idea that the President is not altogether in sympathy with the Allies and that he is inclined to be pro-German, and that it is for that reason he has tried to push peace measures and in order to save Germany's face."[112]

In response to an urgent secret message from Ambassador Gerard, which he received via an American courier on about April 21, House did, however, break his silence on the subject of peace. Gerard reported that he had just talked with von Jagow, and that the Foreign Secretary had said that Germany might be willing to make peace on the basis of German retention of Namur, Liège, and the valley of the Meuse in Belgium, an indemnity from France, and German acquisition of part of the Congo.[113] "While I was sure there was no chance of a

---

[110] House Diary, April 13, 1915; E. M. House to W.W., cablegram dated April 13 and letter dated April 14, 1915, both in the Wilson Papers. Again House did not report his statement to the effect that the American government had no intention of pushing peace negotiations to President Wilson. It appears only in his Diary.

[111] W.W. to E. M. House, April 15, 1915, Baker Collection.

[112] House Diary, April 16, 1915.

[113] E. M. House to W.W., April 22, 1915, Wilson Papers, summarizing Gerard's message.

beginning along these lines," House afterward explained to the Ambassador, "I thought it was worth while to try the matter out."[114] Actually, he did not go to much effort. Handing Gerard's message to Delcassé on April 22, House said that he simply wanted him to understand what was in the mind of the German government, and that he thought von Jagow's suggestion was absurd. Delcassé replied that surely the German Foreign Secretary must be joking. As for the indemnity, he said, "Let them come and get it." The whole encounter ended cordially, with Delcassé agreeing that England, France, and the United States should cooperate to rewrite international law after the war had ended.[115]

It was, House thought, all parry and thrust with the leaders in Paris, and a game not to be taken too seriously in any event. His thoughts were now concentrated on the plan for an Anglo-American-German *démarche*, and even while he was in Paris he wrote to prepare Grey for the discussion that would ensue once he, House, had returned to London.[116] "What I want to do," he explained to the President, "is to get Sir Edward's consent to what might be termed a paper campaign. If he agrees to this I will write to him even though in London, and have him reply. Copies of this correspondence will be sent to either the German Chancellor direct, or to him and Zimmermann through Gerard. This will necessitate replies, and we may have them talking to one another before they realize it. If this plan fails, then I think it would be well for you to write me concerning the second convention and its purposes. I will send copies of your letters to both Sir Edward and to the Chancellor, and ask for such additions or eliminations as may occur to them. This correspondence will at first necessarily be far flung, but we will narrow it from time to time, until again we will have them discussing terms of peace. I feel sure that your thoughts upon that subject and the felicity with which you express them, will help beyond measure to convince these warring peoples."[117]

Back in London on April 28, House went two days later to the Foreign Office to lay the matter before Sir Edward Grey. "My argument," the Colonel wrote in his Diary, "was that Great Britain had all the territory she desired, and it was now merely a question of holding it. With the freedom of the seas as I defined it, her position in

[114] E. M. House to J. W. Gerard, April 26, 1915, House Papers.
[115] House Diary, April 22, 1915.
[116] E. M. House to E. Grey, April 12, 1915, House Papers.
[117] E. M. House to W.W., April 12, 1915, Wilson Papers.

the future would be secure. I called his attention to the dangers of a world-wide coalition against her; of the dangers of the submarine, aircraft, and other means of warfare against which no navy was a protection." Then, his excitement growing, House went on to describe his plan to begin immediate correspondence between London and Berlin, how he would organize the peace conference, and how Britain and America could unite there to work unselfishly for the welfare of mankind.

One can only wonder what thoughts ran through Grey's mind as his friend proceeded. He surely must have thought that the good Colonel had left some of his reason in Berlin to be talking so seriously about peace, which, he had been plainly told in the three belligerent capitals, was at present completely out of the question. One is entitled to wonder, moreover, what Grey really thought of the Colonel's plan for the future paralyzing of England's indispensable offensive weapon. Whatever his thoughts, he replied by evading gently—by saying that he agreed personally but would have to discuss the matter with his colleagues in the Cabinet. Moreover, he added, Britain's approval would in any event be contingent upon German evacuation of Belgium and France and upon the consent of *all* the Allies. "He suggested," House wrote, "that I discuss it with [Arthur] Balfour, Austen Chamberlain and [Andrew] Bonar Law. He thought I would find Law and Chamberlain with narrow views, but they had too much influence to be ignored. He said if Great Britain accepted the doctrine of the freedom of the seas, she would demand in return the freedom of the land, so that Germany or other nations could not make an aggressive war."[118]

House was far from being discouraged. He must have thought that coming events on the battlefields and on the seas would soon create a situation in which he might move successfully. He apparently took it for granted that the Dardanelles campaign would succeed; he knew that Italy would soon enter the war against Austria-Hungary; and he must have assumed that the coming autumn would find the Central Powers in desperate straits, eager to negotiate. This would be the time when American mediation could succeed if only he could lay the groundwork in a firm Anglo-American understanding—when both sides would be sick of the mass killing, when the French might be inclined to compromise on Alsace-Lorraine, and when the civilian leaders in Germany might have a chance of taking firm control.

[118] House Diary, April 30, 1915; E. M. House to W.W., May 1, 1915, Wilson Papers.

House was so hopeful after his conference with Grey on April 30 that he sent a full report of it to Zimmermann on the following day. "If the belligerents," he went on, "really desire to make an honorable peace that will be of far reaching good, not only to themselves, but to the entire world, I think the opportunity will soon be here. If you will give me some assurance that you consider these questions [post-war security on land and sea and the evacuation of Belgium and France] at least debatable, it will go a long way to aid us in our endeavors. I shall understand that no commitments are made, either directly or indirectly, and that everything is unofficial, but this seems to me to be the most promising starting point. It will take a long while to make a successful campaign in England in regard to the freedom of the seas, but we will undertake it with both pleasure and enthusiasm, provided our efforts are cordially seconded by the other Nations at interest."[119]

Exactly a week after House wrote the above letter his mission of peace was abruptly if momentarily changed into a mission of war by the sinking of the *Lusitania* and the violent explosion of the submarine issue between Germany and the United States, one which the Colonel had not even mentioned in Berlin and had virtually ignored in all his conversations with the European statesmen.

It was the end, for many months, of all talk of American mediation and the beginning of a period of high German-American tension that seemed for a time bound to culminate in the entry of the United States into the conflict. House stayed on in London for nearly a month afterward, growing more and more belligerent as the days passed. When he sailed for home on June 5, 1915, the epitaph on his first peace mission, which Page had written a short time before, seemed fitting. As Page put it, "Peace-talk, therefore, is yet mere moonshine— House has been to Berlin, from London, thence to Paris, thence back to London again—from Nowhere (as far as peace is concerned) to Nowhere again."[120]

[119] E. M. House to A. Zimmermann, May 1, 1915, House Papers.
[120] Page Diary, April 30, 1915.

CHAPTER VIII

Mexico: Wilson and the Rise and Fall of Villa

To Americans in the summer of 1914 the triumph of General Venustiano Carranza and his Constitutional forces in Mexico appeared as the one sign of hope in the otherwise dreadful vista of the world beyond their borders. The tyrant, Victoriano Huerta, was in exile; his government and army, in shambles. The Revolution begun so haltingly by the martyred Francisco Madero was now triumphant and full of the promise of a better day for the downtrodden masses of Mexico.

To American observers it was all the more gratifying because the result had been accomplished in such large measure by their own President. He it was who had prevented American financial interests and the European powers from succoring Huerta; he it was, moreover, who had maintained a relentless diplomatic pressure against the usurper, strengthened his opponents, the Constitutionalists, and finally made open war at Veracruz upon Huerta's regime.[1] "The President's Mexican policy," exclaimed Wilson's leading editorial spokesman, ". . . has triumphed. A constitutional government is to be established. There will eventually be peace at home and peace with the United States. . . . The triumph is ours as well as Mexico's. . . . Thanks to Woodrow Wilson, a great country and an oppressed people are upon the threshold of a new epoch."[2] Such prophecies might in fact come true, Wilson believed. "The final working out of the situation in Mexico is still a little blind," he wrote to a Georgia congressman who had offered congratulations, "but we have certainly cleared the stage and made a beginning and with the support of thoughtful men it would be possible to hold things steady until the process is finally complete."[3]

But what would Mexico's "new epoch" and "the final working out of the situation" be like? It was not easy for an informed observer

---

[1] For an account of these events, see A. S. Link, *Wilson*, II, 347-416.

[2] New York *World*, July 16, 1914; see also W. C. Adamson to W.W., July 16, 1914, Wilson Papers; W. H. Page to W.W., July 19, 1914, *ibid.*; *The Public*, XVII (July 24, 1914), 697-698; New York *Nation*, XCIX (July 23, 1914), 91.

[3] W.W. to W. C. Adamson, July 20, 1914, Wilson Papers.

in Washington or Mexico City to give an answer. It was all tremendously grand—the sight of Carranza riding through the streets of the capital, and the thunderous sounds of cheering crowds, ringing cathedral bells, and fanfare of trumpets. Yet few conquerors ever rode more uneasily than this bearded hero of Coahuila. He held the executive power in a country prostrated by more than a year and a half of civil turmoil. He was the leader of the Revolution, but his leadership was at the mercy of self-seeking generals who were scheming for the supreme power. In addition, he faced the difficult problem of getting on with a powerful neighbor to the north who had already demonstrated his determination to have a large hand in Mexico's future. How to control his rivals, bring peace to the land, and establish a constitutional government that could carry out a reform program free from the dictation of the Washington authorities—these were the awesome problems that would confront the First Chief in the months that lay ahead.

As it turned out, Mexico in August 1914 did stand on the verge of a "new epoch," but unhappily it was not the epoch of peace and rebuilding that so many hopeful Americans then foresaw. It was for Mexicans a time of renewed bloodshed at home, one marked by rising tensions with the United States that would culminate nearly two years hence in fighting and the threat of full-scale war between the two countries. And for Wilson and his advisers it was a time of constant trial and confusion as they sought to devise policies to meet changing circumstances and lead the Mexican people into the way of peace. But we are ranging far ahead of our immediate story. It concerns the course of the Mexican Revolution from the late summer of 1914 to the early part of 1915 and what the American President and his advisers did to try to affect its outcome.

Mexico in the midsummer of 1914 was like a volcano about to erupt. To the south and southeast of Mexico City, principally in the State of Morelos, Emiliano Zapata, the agrarian revolutionary, and his Army of Liberation, defied Carranza's authority by the same kind of armed independence of Mexico City that they had maintained during the rule of Madero and Huerta. Everywhere throughout the country discontent was mounting in direct proportion to the economic distress caused by the war. But the greatest source of potential trouble lay far to the north in the State of Chihuahua. There the General of the Division of the North, Francisco Villa, called Don Pancho by his followers, and a coterie around him were plotting to gain control of the revolutionary movement.

Among the whole company of new and violent leaders whom the Revolution spawned in 1910, Villa was the most remarkable. Born Doroteo Arango of peon parents in the State of Durango on October 4, 1887, Villa had been a cattle rustler and an outlaw in the northern states during his youth. Joining the *Maderista* revolt against Porfirio Díaz in 1911, he had thrown in his lot with the Constitutionalists after Madero's murder in 1913. As General of the Division of the North he had been a bold and dashing military leader—the real force behind the Constitutionalist revolt in the northern states. Of all Carranza's chieftains he was now, in the summer of 1914, the most powerful.

"Physically," wrote one reporter who was friendly to Pancho, "Villa is a superb animal. His bullet-shaped head is set closely on a pair of heavy shoulders, which are not, however, out of proportion with the rest of his anatomy. . . . He is dark for a Mexican, and of a smooth darkness that makes the talk of a strain of Negro blood seem not improbable. His most distinguishing features are his cruel mouth which can smile most unctuously, and his eyes, bloodshot, protruding, and piercing. A reporter who saw them blazing at Torreon describes them as 'the eyes of a man who will some day go crazy.' "[4]

Although ignorant, naïve, and almost illiterate, Pancho possessed considerable native intelligence and a certain shrewdness, and these qualities combined with an impulsive nature and unbounded courage to make him a commanding leader of men. He was not without personal charm and the ability to give the appearance, at least, of complete sincerity. But his saving qualities, if he had any, were more than offset (most contemporaries agreed) by a total amorality, a primeval cruelty, and a violent temper. He was, in fact, almost the prototype of the "natural" man—passionate and wild, who thought no more of killing a man than of eating a meal. "He has hunted throughout almost the length of his whole life his fellow men, and they have hunted him," wrote one American who had occasion to know Villa well. "He has lived with the back of his hand against every man who stood for law and order since boyhood. The stern necessities of his peculiar life bred in him daring, cunning, animal craftiness and alertness. . . . The change in circumstances has not changed his heart; he is to-day the

---

[4] Gregory Mason, "With Villa in Chihuahua," New York *Outlook*, CVII (May 9, 1914), 75.

same brutal, overbearing and untamed savage that he was when first he took up the trade of highwayman."[5]

Apparently convinced that Carranza was a mere *caudillo*, nursing grievances real and imagined, and consumed with ambition, Villa began careful preparations during the spring and summer of 1914 for the coup that would make him master of Mexico. To begin with, independently of the First Chief he established his own authority in Chihuahua and the surrounding area under his personal control. "There," one informed observer wrote in early August 1914, "Gen. Villa holds an imperium in imperio. He has installed his own officials and has by force thrown out the Carranzista occupants of office; he collects not only the State and Municipal revenues but also the Customs revenues at El Paso. He is a law unto himself. Through his agent, Felix Sommerfeld, and the instrumentality of Flint & Co., of New York, he is making extensive purchases of arms and ammunition, no small quantity of which is even now being openly directed to El Paso, in absolute confidence that it will find its way across the border. He is enlisting hundreds of peons in his division, notwithstanding the fact that there is no longer serious armed opposition to the Constitutionalist cause."[6]

In the second place, Villa redoubled his efforts, begun in the early months of 1914, to win the approval and support of the authorities in Washington. At all times and in all places he said what he thought President Wilson and Secretary Bryan wanted to hear. Was it loyalty to Carranza that Washington demanded? Then Pancho was the First Chief's most loyal lieutenant![7] Was it protection for foreigners and foreign property that the American government now desired, or observance of the rules of civilized warfare? Villa was eager to afford all guarantees and to comply.[8] Was it recognition of his own incom-

[5] Marion Letcher to the Secretary of State, February 21, 1914, State Department Papers; see also Herman Whitaker, "Villa—Bandit—Patriot," *The Independent,* LXXVIII (June 8, 1914), 450-452; Joseph R. Taylor, " 'Pancho' Villa at First Hand," *World's Work,* XXVIII (July 1914), 265-269; George Marvin, "Villa," *ibid.,* pp. 269-284; James Hopper, "Pancho Villa," *Collier's,* LVII (April 29, 1916), 8-10, 43 ff.; George Pattulo, "The Enchanted Captain," *Saturday Evening Post,* CLXXXIX (January 20, 1917), 6-7, 73-74, 77.

[6] Herbert J. Browne to W. J. Bryan, August 4, 1914, the Papers of William J. Bryan, the National Archives; hereinafter cited as the Bryan Papers, National Archives.

[7] G. C. Carothers to the Secretary of State, January 1, February 3, 1914, State Department Papers.

[8] F. Villa to G. C. Carothers, February 1, 1914, *ibid.;* G. C. Carothers to the Secretary of State, February 18, 1914, *ibid.;* T. C. Hamm to the Secretary of State, April 19, 1914, *ibid.*

petence and admission of Mexico's need for American guidance in solving the problems of political and economic reconstruction that Wilson required of him? Then Villa was the first to agree.[9] Did Carranza bitterly resent the American attack against and the occupation of Veracruz and even threaten armed resistance to such violation of Mexican soil? Then it was Villa himself who personally prevented an open rupture and assured President Wilson that there would be no war.[10]

The main question in Mexican affairs during the late spring and early summer of 1914 was whether Villa would raise the standard of revolt before Huerta was overcome, or whether he would wait to make a supreme bid for power once the field was free. There was a sharp and violent flare-up between Carranza and Villa in early June over plans for a campaign against Zacatecas; and for a moment it seemed that the Constitutionalists would divide even before they could occupy Mexico City.[11] But the breach was healed by American agents and above all by Mexican generals on both sides, who persuaded Carranza and Villa to accept a truce known as the Torreón Agreement. Signed on July 8, 1914, this document compromised immediate differences and provided that a convention of revolutionary generals should meet in Mexico City soon after the Constitutionalists had occupied the capital to make arrangements for the establishment of a new constitutional regime.[12]

Under extraordinary pressure from the State Department, Villa remained at Torreón while other Constitutionalist generals pressed the campaign against Mexico City. But once Huerta had fled and victory was assured, Don Pancho proceeded with his final preparations for a showdown. As early as July 25 the American Consul in Chihuahua reported that he was recruiting men and scouring the countryside for horses.[13] "Villa is recruiting many men," the United States Collector at El Paso also warned a few days later, "has been and is smuggling

---

[9] e.g., New York *World*, February 28, 1914.

[10] A. S. Link, *Wilson*, II, 403.

[11] M. Letcher to the Secretary of State, June 4, 1914, State Department Papers; Z. L. Cobb to the Secretary of State, June 12, 1914, transmitting G. C. Carothers to Cobb, June 10, 1914, *ibid.*; Z. L. Cobb to the Secretary of State, June 16, 1914, *ibid.; New York Times*, June 17, 1914; New York *World*, June 18, 1914.

[12] G. C. Carothers to the Secretary of State, June 18, 1914, State Department Papers; *New York Times*, June 18, 1914; G. C. Carothers to the Secretary of State, July 9, 1914, *Foreign Relations, 1914*, pp. 559-560.

[13] M. Letcher to the Secretary of State, July 25, 1914, State Department Papers.

much ammunition in spite of preventive efforts . . . , has bought large quantity of hospital supplies for future use, is buying and shipping coal, sent twelve trains containing quantities of supplies south to Chihuahua yesterday, and has an army distributed along the railway fully equipped and ready for action, probably sufficient to overpower Carranza and other leaders."[14]

Villa, actually, was preparing for hostilities only as a last resort and was maneuvering to seize power peacefully if possible, and with the approval of the American government. He saw the State Department's special agent assigned to his headquarters, George C. Carothers, at Chihuahua City on July 26, 1914, explained his plans, and asked Carothers to go at once to Washington to convey the following message to the President and Secretary of State:

He would remain in Chihuahua, Villa said, and make no effort to prevent Carranza from entering Mexico City. On the other hand, he had no intention of permitting the First Chief to occupy the National Palace very long. He would insist that the convention of revolutionary generals meet in the City of Mexico, as the Torreón Agreement provided, as soon as the Constitutionalists entered the capital. He had increased the size of his own army to 60,000 men, so that it was now as large as the other Constitutionalist divisions combined. Thus under the formula for representation in the convention stipulated by the Torreón Agreement—one delegate for every 1,000 soldiers—he would control half the convention, and with his friends in the other divisions he would easily command a majority of the delegates. He had no personal ambitions, Villa further explained, but he would insist upon agrarian reform and would support his artillery chieftain, General Felipe Angeles, for the presidency. All would go well provided Carranza honored the Torreón Agreement, but there would be fighting if the First Chief did not. Therefore, the American government could best serve the cause of peace in Mexico by bringing enough pressure to bear upon Carranza to force him to permit the convention of revolutionary generals to meet on schedule. Meanwhile, Villa promised, he would make no further move until he had heard from the American leaders.[15]

Carothers went immediately to El Paso and caught the first train

---

[14] Z. L. Cobb to the Secretary of State, August 1, 1914, *ibid.*

[15] G. C. Carothers to the Secretary of State, July 27, 1914, *ibid.*; W. J. Bryan to W.W., August 2, 1914, Wilson Papers, giving a detailed account of Bryan's conference with Carothers of August 1, 1914.

for Washington. Arriving at the capital on August 1, he went straight to the State Department and there transmitted Villa's message orally to Bryan.[16] Much, the President and Secretary of State now knew, might depend upon them during the next few weeks.

The arrival of Villa's message must have convinced Wilson and Bryan that the time had come for the American government to play a more active role in Mexican affairs than had earlier been possible when they had dealt only with the First Chief, that suspicious guardian of Mexican sovereignty. The correspondence of the leaders in Washington indicates that they discussed the Mexican situation at some length between August 2 and August 5, 1914, and that they came to some agreement on their response to Villa's bid. No record of their conversation and no full and direct evidence of the policy that they agreed upon have survived, but other evidence points to the following conclusions:

In the first place, they evidently agreed to support Villa's demand for a revolutionary convention and the speedy establishment of a new constitutional government in Mexico. Secondly, they apparently made plans to encourage what seemed to them to be the already obvious disintegration of Carranza's power. Finally, they were prepared to accept, if not actually to promote, Villa's ascendancy in the new regime. These are, admittedly, somewhat cryptic statements, but their meaning will perhaps become clearer as we proceed to examine the execution of the Wilson administration's subsequent Mexican policies in detail.

Before we do this, however, we must digress briefly to try to answer the most important and puzzling question of all about Wilson's and Bryan's thinking on Mexican affairs in the midsummer of 1914, namely, how they could ever have seriously contemplated lending any support at all to Villa's plans and ambitions. It is fair to say that Pancho had already given ample demonstration by this time of his utter tempera-

[16] Carothers also gave the Secretary a vivid description of Villa. "I questioned him about Villa," Bryan wrote in his report to the President on August 2. "He says that he is a mixture of Spanish and Indian and that there may be some trace of African blood. He says he can barely write his name. If you will remind me when I see you I will tell you about his domestic relations. Carothers says Villa has a great deal of natural sense and the elements of leadership. His soldiers idolize him and he claims to have no ambition whatever except to see these reforms carried out. He is a teetotaler and does not gamble except at cock-fights. He is very fond of cock fighting, and attends a cock-fight every Sunday when they have one and bets on his favorite rooster; but Carothers says it is not for the purpose of winning so much as to help along the fight."

mental incapacity to govern in his own right or to work in harness with the First Chief. By now it was also clear that Villa was fast becoming the tool of some of the most predatory elements in the revolutionary movement. It is perhaps understandable why the President and Secretary of State chose to ignore the clear warnings on these points of the American Consul at Chihuahua, Marion Letcher, of other American observers in northern Mexico, and of Carranza himself, for these men might have been regarded as hostile witnesses. But it is difficult to understand how Wilson and Bryan could have failed to recognize what was so clear to all disinterested observers, that Villa was essentially violent and destructive and therefore incapable of giving leadership to a great people.

The historian cannot be dogmatic in trying to explain why Wilson and Bryan decided in early August 1914 that they had no choice but to look to Villa as the new leader of Mexico. He can only suggest that the following are possible and perhaps probable answers:

To begin with, the American leaders may have decided to support or accept Villa because they personally wanted to, and because they thought such a policy would best implement their own purposes for Mexico. Wilson, at any rate, was clearly intrigued by Villa and not averse to thinking that he might become the bright hope of the Mexican Revolution. "General Villa," he wrote in April 1914, "certainly seems capable of some good things and often shows susceptibilities of the best influences. He is hard to understand, however."[17] A short time later, after Villa had come to Wilson's defense during the Veracruz crisis, the American President was talking about Pancho as representing the "forward movement" in Mexico.[18] And by the end of July 1914 Wilson obviously believed, as one correspondent put it, that "Villa, a crude and cruel barbarian in many ways, is playing square, and is the only man in this troubled situation that is looking out for the welfare of his country," and that the time would come when Villa would be recognized as "the greatest Mexican in his generation."[19]

It is clear, also, that Wilson had concluded by midsummer that Villa, not Carranza, represented the best hope for a lasting settlement of the

[17] W.W. to H. L. Scott, April 16, 1914, Wilson Papers.

[18] House Diary, April 27, 1914.

[19] William Kent to W.W., June 29, 1914, Kent Papers. "I share your view of Villa," Wilson wrote in reply to Kent, "and deeper than everything else in my mind lies the passionate desire to see something come out of this struggle which will redound to the permanent benefit of at least partial emancipation of the great body of the Mexican people." W.W. to W. Kent, June 30, 1914, *ibid.*

agrarian problem in Mexico. "The thing which seems to me most important now with regard to the Mexican business," he explained to Ambassador Page in London, "is that the people over there should get a more just and correct view of Villa. Carranza I believe to be an honest but a very narrow and rather dull person whom it is extremely difficult to deal with but who can be counted upon no doubt to try to do the right thing by those [the *Villistas*?] who are now centering their hopes in him for working out a decent solution of the economic problem which underlies the situation in Mexico. . . . A landless people will always furnish the inflammable material for a revolution. There is an article on Villa . . . appearing in this week's number of the (American) Outlook, which . . . contains an intimate estimate of Villa which I think it would be worth your while to look [into] and to filter into London society."[20] The author of this article depicted Villa as "the man of the hour in Mexico"—a genuine reformer and the only man strong enough to "save Mexico from herself."[21]

Wilson's attitude must have been profoundly influenced, furthermore, by the fact that Villa would apparently welcome American guidance in the political and economic reconstruction of Mexico and that Carranza obviously would not. Indeed, the First Chief had made it plain from the beginning of the Constitutionalist revolt against Huerta that he and his administration not only would not accept but would forcibly resist any attempted American interference. To Wilson this posed both a personal and a political problem. Personally, he wanted ardently to help the Mexicans in their struggle toward democracy. Politically, he was deeply responsible for future events in Mexico, both to the American people[22] and to the British government, to which he had made large promises about the protection of *all* foreign interests under a Constitutionalist regime.[23]

There was the additional fact that Wilson knew that a policy of support of Villa would be acceptable to a large segment of public

[20] W.W. to W. H. Page, June 4, 1914, Wilson Papers.

[21] Gregory Mason, "The Mexican Man of the Hour," New York *Outlook*, CVII (June 6, 1914), 292, 301-306.

[22] As former President Taft noted, in W. H. Taft to Gus J. Karger, July 20, 1914, Taft Papers.

[23] The British Foreign Secretary, Sir Edward Grey, did not permit the President to forget these promises. See W. H. Page to the Secretary of State, May 6, 1914, State Department Papers; W. J. Bryan [actually W.W.] to W. H. Page, May 9, 1914, *ibid.*; W. H. Page to the Secretary of State, May 11, 1914, *ibid.*; E. Grey to C. Spring Rice, May 20, 1914, *ibid.*; W.W. to W. H. Page, June 1, 1914, Wilson Papers.

opinion in the United States. Pancho had enjoyed a friendly press in that country, particularly among progressive circles, since the early months of 1914. By the middle of the year he was being almost universally hailed as a Robin Hood-like protector of the downtrodden, a good friend of the United States, and incomparably the strongest man in Mexico. As one distinguished weekly put it, "There is no doubt that Villa has become a popular hero in America. He has proved himself a great soldier, a marvelous strategist, a military genius of the first rank."[24]

These were all important factors shaping Wilson's (and presumably Bryan's) thoughts about future policy in Mexico, but there was another consideration that was even more compelling. It was the assumption, which now seemed to be correct beyond any doubt, that Carranza's day was over—he had no army of his own and had to lean upon generals of dubious loyalty—and that Villa, with his large, disciplined, and well-equipped Division of the North, was bound to triumph in a test of arms. Colonel House recorded the President's convictions on this point somewhat cryptically after a conversation at Cornish, New Hampshire, in late August 1914. "We went into the Mexican situation carefully," the Colonel wrote, "and agreed that Villa is the only man of force now in sight in Mexico. We are afraid Carranza is not equal to the situation."[25] Since this was true, the President might well have reasoned, then he had no choice but to try to make the most of the facts of Mexican political life by working with and through the man who seemed so eager for American guidance. That is to say, the one alternative of all-out support of Carranza could not have seemed very attractive in the circumstances that apparently prevailed in Mexico in the summer of 1914, if for no other reason than because it might have meant actual military participation in the Mexican civil war. And this Wilson was determined to avoid if possible. As he had earlier explained to the British Foreign Secretary, his policy toward the Con-

[24] *Harper's Weekly*, LIX (July 18, 1914), 50; also the New York *World*, April 28, 1914; *Harper's Weekly*, LVIII (June 6, 1914), 3; New York *Outlook*, CVII (June 6, 1914), 277; *The Public*, XVII (June 12, 1914), 554; especially the articles by John Reed, originally published in the *Metropolitan Magazine* and then printed as *Insurgent Mexico* in 1914, and the friendly newspaper comment cited in "The Rise of Villa's Star," *Literary Digest*, XLVIII (April 18, 1914), 889, and "Shall We Join Hands with Villa?" *ibid.*, May 23, 1914, pp. 1235-1238.

[25] House Diary, August 30, 1914.

stitutionalists was simply to recognize the leader who came out on top.[26]

The President wasted no time in taking the first step in a new course after he had received Villa's message from Carothers. "Mr. Browne," Wilson wrote to Bryan on August 5, 1914, "who wrote the enclosed very interesting letter which I am returning,[27] of course, does not know that he was speaking our own opinion in wishing that some men of first-rate capacity could be sent down to be present and exercise what influence he [*sic*] can during the present happenings in Mexico." John Lind, the former Minnesota Governor who had served as special adviser on Mexico during the Huerta regime, would not do, Wilson continued, "because of the violent prejudice that has been formed against him by the representatives of the Roman Catholic church, whom we are at present trying to protect in Mexico." But there was Paul Fuller, Senior, a partner in the New York law firm of Coudert Brothers, who "would serve us admirably in this case if he were willing to go to Mexico." Fuller, the President went on, "is a Democrat, is in full sympathy with the purposes of the administration, and is accustomed by long habit to deal with our friends in Latin-America. I hope that this suggestion commends itself to you."[28]

Bryan agreed, and Wilson sent a call to Fuller to come to Washington as soon as possible. At the White House on August 9 the President explained his present purposes for Mexico. He did not, Wilson presumably told Fuller, desire to dictate the terms of a political settlement. But he was convinced that the differences between Villa and Carranza were not as deep as they seemed to be; and he would insist that the hostile factions avoid open fighting and come to some agreement for the early establishment of a constitutional government. Would Fuller go at once to Villa, Wilson asked, and convey such a message, warning above all that nothing but catastrophe could ensue if Villa opened hostilities at this time?[29] The new Special Agent of course agreed and

[26] "As for what might follow the success of the forces at the north," Wilson had written in May 1914, "we of course have no favourites and no individual personal choice of our own. We shall merely try to secure an orderly reorganization of the government of Mexico and a choice of president by the Mexicans themselves as nearly as may be in accordance with the provisions of the national constitution." W. J. Bryan to W. H. Page, May 9, 1914, State Department Papers.

[27] H. J. Browne to W. J. Bryan, August 4, 1914, Bryan Papers, National Archives.

[28] W.W. to W. J. Bryan, August 5, 1914, Wilson Papers.

[29] No record of this conversation can be found. This reconstruction is based upon

left Washington so hurriedly that he took with him only a small suit-case with one change of clothing,[30] along with a personal letter from President Wilson to the Mexican chieftain.[31]

Arriving at El Paso on August 12, Fuller made the necessary ar-rangements for travel in northern Mexico and set out for Chihuahua on August 14. Villa was on the move and hard to find, but Fuller finally tracked him down at Santa Rosalia, about six hours' distance from Chihuahua City by slow train, and conferred with him there on Sunday morning, August 16, 1914.

The meeting was obviously entirely congenial to both men. "Villa," Fuller reported, "is an unusually quiet man, gentle in manner, low voiced, slow of speech, earnest and occasionally emotional in expres-sion but always subdued, with an undercurrent of sadness." After hand-ing Wilson's letter to the general, Fuller "explained the intense interest of the President in the preservation of peace in Mexico and the avoid-ance of any possible conflict among the Constitutionalists at the very threshold of the new government which this successful struggle had made possible." Villa was warmly appreciative. He had, he said, only one desire—to see real democracy in Mexico and the uplifting of the masses from serfdom. He dreaded the possibility of a new dictatorship under Carranza, and he demanded only that a new government truly representative of the people be established at once. If the American government would withhold recognition from Carranza, Fuller asked in a leading question, would Villa give assurances of peace in northern Mexico? Of course, Pancho replied, adding that he had no personal ambitions, wanted no office, and desired only to serve the cause of political and agrarian reform in his country.[32]

At Fuller's suggestion, Villa and his advisers prepared a long state-ment for President Wilson that enumerated their demands for a set-

---

what Fuller later told Villa and upon a letter that Wilson wrote two days later for Carothers to take back to the general. For the latter, see the Secretary of State to Special Agent Carothers, August 11, 1914, *Foreign Relations, 1914*, p. 584.

[30] At least so a reporter wrote in the New York *World* on August 18, 1914, in an otherwise highly inaccurate article.

[31] Wilson must have written this letter on his own typewriter without making a carbon copy, for no copy has survived. From Villa's reply we know that the President's letter was dated August 9, 1914.

[32] Special Agent Fuller to the Secretary of State, n.d., received August 17, 1914, State Department Papers; Paul Fuller, Sr., "Memorandum for the President," dated "On train from El Paso, 20th Aug. 1914," *ibid*. The latter document, badly out of place in the Mexican file in the State Department's archives, may be located under its file number, 812.00/15013.

tlement in specific detail. It began with a blast at Carranza for assuming and exercising dictatorial power. "The Division of the North," the statement then continued, "representing the interests of the largest body of people in arms, which has contributed more than any to the triumph of the Revolution, deems itself justified in asking Mr. Carranza or whoever may be appointed during the interim to govern the Republic, that he shall during this interim term of power furnish assurances that such procedure as he may deem necessary shall be carried out so as to effectively put in operation a true democratic government and assure the peace of Mexico based upon justice and the satisfying of national needs." The Division of the North would support the interim government, however, provided only that Carranza agree not to become a candidate for any public office, give the *Villistas* large representation in the provisional government, and, in effect, concede Villa's sovereignty over the Division of the North.[33]

In Washington, meanwhile, Wilson and Bryan had been greatly cheered by Fuller's first telegraphic report from Santa Rosalia[34] on August 16 or 17. "We feel," Bryan wrote (using the President's words) to Villa's agent in Washington on about August 17, "that it might prejudice the whole process of settlement if suggestions seem to come from outside sources, and we feel moreover that we are not competent here to judge of the feasibility of that part of the plan that deals with the matter and manner of selecting the provisional President. But we desire to compliment Villa upon the *moderation and reasonableness* of the program of reform and we feel reassured as to the spirit with which he is approaching the subject."[35]

Soon afterward the American leaders were further heartened by the results of a *démarche* they had pursued at the same time that they sent Fuller to Chihuahua. This was to send Carothers back to Villa's territory with instructions to promote good relations between Villa and General Álvaro Obregón, commander of the Division of the Northwest and one of the men upon whom Carranza leaned most heavily for support. Was this the beginning of an effort to drive a wedge be-

---

[33] F. Villa to W.W., August 18, 1914, and "Statement by General Villa of the purposes and intentions of his Division of the North with reference to the new government in Mexico, August 18, 1914," both in the Wilson Papers.

[34] It was written at Santa Rosalia but actually sent from Campargo, Mexico.

[35] Note added to the copy of P. Fuller, Sr., to the Secretary of State, received August 17, 1914, in the Wilson Papers, under the caption by Bryan, "This is reply made to Villa's representative here"; italics added.

tween Obregón and Carranza and to form an Obregón-Villa axis? The records do not yield an answer. But with Carothers as a kind of chaperon, the two generals made a joint "pacifying" tour through Sonora in the last week in August, and with results that seemed to signify that a new union might be in process of formation.[36]

Fuller returned to Washington on August 22 and submitted his report and Villa's letter. Wilson read them carefully and then, on August 26, called Bryan and the Special Agent to the White House. Again, unfortunately, no record of their conversation has survived, if ever one was made. But they must have discussed all aspects of the Mexican situation and agreed that the time had come to move as effectively as possible for a final settlement in Mexico City. At Wilson's suggestion, no doubt, Fuller agreed to go at once to the Mexican capital to work for this objective. We do not know from any direct evidence what instructions, oral or written, the President gave the Special Agent. But there is no reason to doubt the explanation of the purpose of his mission that Fuller later made to a group of friends. "We also had," one of them wrote in his diary, "an interesting description by Mr. Fuller of his recent trip to Mexico as the special representative of the President. He stated confidentially that the object of his mission was conciliation and mediation between the hostile elements, directed chiefly to bringing about a convention which would place Villa in control."[37]

In any event, accompanied by his wife Fuller went at once to Galveston, where they boarded a ship for Veracruz. Arriving in that port, still occupied by American troops, on September 3, 1914, the Fullers were met by the Foreign Minister in Carranza's provisional govern-

[36] Z. L. Cobb to the Secretary of State, September 1, 1914, State Department Papers; Á. Obregón to Z. L. Cobb, September 1, 1914, *ibid.*, also printed in *Foreign Relations, 1914*, p. 593.

[37] Anderson Diary, February 20, 1915. One reporter close to the White House offered another explanation. Fuller was going to Mexico City, this reporter wrote, to tell Carranza that he must hold early elections for a constitutional government, and that he could never obtain recognition by the American government if by chance he were elected to the Mexican presidency. New York *World*, August 31, 1914. The report might well have been inaccurate, for, as it turned out, Fuller told the First Chief no such thing. On the other hand, it is possible that Wilson did authorize his Special Agent to convey such a message and that Fuller afterward decided to withhold it. There is one indication that the *World's* story conveyed at least part of the truth, namely, in what the President told Colonel House about the Fuller mission. "He," House reported Wilson as saying at the very time that Fuller was on his way to Mexico City, "is letting Carranza know that he will not be recognized unless he maintains himself *as he should*, and non-recognition means failure." House Diary, August 30, 1914; italics added.

ment, Isidro Fabela, who rode with them to Mexico City. During the steep railway ascent, Fuller lectured his companion on democracy but seemed to make little impression. Arriving at the capital on September 5, Fuller found no atmosphere of tension, for only a brief time before Carranza had issued a call for the meeting of the convention of revolutionary generals provided for by the Torreón Agreement, thus satisfying Villa's chief demand; and news had come that Obregón and Villa had reached an understanding. Obviously, Fuller must have concluded, it was no time for stern warnings to anyone!

He was, therefore, almost cordial at his first conference with Carranza at the National Palace in the morning of September 5. Presenting a letter from President Wilson,[38] Fuller said that he wished to emphasize the President's earnest desire for a perfect union of the Constitutionalist factions and the earliest possible realization of their avowed purpose to form a permanent constitutional regime. The First Chief replied that he agreed entirely; he had, he said, convoked the meeting of the generals precisely for this reason. "I want every element of the party to be convened and consulted," he went on, "so that none can complain and all will submit to the common will and none may be able to say that I exercised undue influence towards the result." There was dissension in the North, he added, but the convention should eliminate all the present difficulties.[39]

Even more encouraging was a conversation that Fuller had two days later, on September 7, with Angel de Caso, a personal representative of Villa, who had arrived from the North the night before with General Obregón. Villa and Obregón, de Caso told the Special Agent, had come to complete agreement on a program for civil reconstruction. It provided for the immediate appointment of Carranza as Provisional President, with the further stipulation that he should be ineligible to succeed himself as constitutional President. The agreement also provided that representation in the revolutionary convention should be apportioned according to the formula specified in the Torreón Agreement, and that the governors of the twenty-seven Mexican states, whom Carranza had included in his list of delegates, should be excluded. It meant, in other words, that Obregón and Villa had agreed that the latter should control the convention, and that the First

[38] It was a letter of introduction, no copy of which can be found.

[39] J. R. Silliman to the Secretary of State, September 5, 1914, transmitting Fuller's message of the same date, State Department Papers; Paul Fuller, Sr., "Memorandum for the President," dated September 18, 1914, Wilson Papers.

Chief should have virtually no voice at all. Fuller understood and approved. "New program should be carried out and will so tell Carranza at interview," he wired to the State Department. Indeed, before he saw the First Chief again, Fuller sought out General Obregón at the request of two of Villa's advisers then in Mexico City and told him that he hoped Obregón's agreement with Pancho would be speedily carried out.[40]

In a farewell conference with Carranza on September 8, the Special Agent reiterated the advice that he had just given Obregón. The recent Villa-Obregón agreement, Fuller said with some emphasis, was in line with President Wilson's own views, and its early realization would evoke the sympathy and approval of the American people. Just as Fuller was about to say good-by, Carranza turned solemnly and said that there was one remaining matter that ought to be discussed—the question of Veracruz. American occupation of that port now that Huerta was gone was, the First Chief said ominously, "without justification and intolerable." The Mexican people could regard it only as an act of hostility; moreover, it might lead to a conflict that he, Carranza, would be unable to control. To this remonstrance Fuller replied rather lamely, saying that there was not even a provisional Mexican government to which the United States could transfer the port and that, in any event, he was not competent to deal with the question since his mission was limited "to friendly counsel & admonition as to the necessity for complete union among the constitutionalists and the earliest possible organization of a constitutional Government capable of furnishing the guarantees to . . . [foreign] property which such a Government imparts." But he did promise to transmit the First Chief's message to the President, and the Fuller mission ended on this note of subtle tension.[41]

We have no record of what the Special Agent reported orally to the President after he returned to Washington in late September. A newspaperman close to the State Department later wrote that Fuller had said that Carranza was a petulant old man, obsessed with hatred for Americans, who would never be able to re-establish order in Mex-

[40] J. R. Silliman to the Secretary of State, September 7, 1914, transmitting Fuller's message of the same date, State Department Papers; P. Fuller, Sr., "Memorandum for the President," dated September 18, 1914, Wilson Papers.

[41] P. Fuller, Sr., "Memorandum for the President," dated September 18, 1914, Wilson Papers; J. R. Silliman to the Secretary of State, September 8, 1914, transmitting Fuller's message of the same date, State Department Papers.

ico.[42] This report may have been false, but we are certainly entitled to doubt that Fuller's remarks about the First Chief were complimentary.

Hopes for a final end to the vexing problem of Mexico ran high in Washington during the days immediately following the end of the Fuller mission. Wilson was determined not to haggle over Veracruz. Indeed, when Carranza, Villa, and Obregón all sent personal messages to the White House urging the President to withdraw the American forces,[43] he welcomed this demonstration of accord as an excuse for ending what had by now become a pointless occupation. On September 15, 1914, he requested the Secretary of War to issue orders and make preparations for the immediate withdrawal of the troops from Veracruz. "In view of the entire removal of the circumstances which were thought to justify the occupation," Wilson explained, "it seems to me that the presence of the troops there is no longer necessary."[44] And when all the Mexican leaders, informed of the American government's intention, responded gratefully, the President was almost pious in commendation. "He hopes," the State Department replied to one of them, Villa, "that the withdrawal will be regarded by the Mexican people as another evidence of this Government's desire to lend its aid to bring about the speedy establishment of a truly just and representative government in Mexico."[45]

Alas, the chain of events that would plunge Mexico into a new civil war had already been set in motion by the time that Acting Secretary of State Lansing sent the dispatch quoted above. The initiator was Villa himself. Fearing that Carranza intended as he, Villa, did to pack the revolutionary convention scheduled to meet in Mexico City on October 1, 1914, Pancho announced that the Division of the North would not attend unless the First Chief gave guarantees that elections would be called and a civil government would be established without

[42] New York *World*, November 14, 1914.

[43] V. Carranza to W.W., handwritten letter dated September 7, 1914, Wilson Papers; J. R. Silliman to the Secretary of State, September 11, 1914, transmitting Á. Obregón to F. Villa, September 9, 1914, State Department Papers; J. R. Silliman to the Secretary of State, September 12, 1914, transmitting F. Villa to Á. Obregón, September 11, 1914, *ibid.*

[44] W.W. to L. M. Garrison, September 15, 1914, Wilson Papers; see also the *New York Times*, September 16, 1914.

[45] The Acting Secretary of State to Special Agent Carothers, September 22, 1914, *Foreign Relations, 1914*, pp. 602-603.

delay.[46] At about the same time Villa revealed his hand more fully in an encounter with General Obregón at Chihuahua City on September 17. Obregón, who had just arrived from Mexico City in the company of Carothers and another American agent, Leon J. Canova, met Villa at his headquarters to discuss plans for the coming convention. Carothers had gone on to El Paso by the time the meeting occurred, but Canova was on hand and later described the affair:

"On Thursday morning I met General Villa and he asked that I come to see him at 4 P.M. I went at that hour but he was in conference with General Obregon. While I was in the inner court, next to the office of General Villa's secretary, one of the clerks rushed out and excitedly called the corporal of the guard, telling him to bring a picket of soldiers in a hurry 'for they are screaming at one another.' The man left the house running. I was then asked to take a seat in the ante room. In there I could hear, but not distinguish the excited conversation going on between Villa and Obregon. Both were walking up and down, Villa stopping occasionally to whack the table with his fist. He was laying down the law. It was about Carranza in general and particularly about his forces under General Hill, over in Sonora. Not wishing to appear eavesdropping I went out and sat in the coach I had in waiting. No sooner had I seated myself than a squad of sixteen soldiers came at double quick, assuming stations on the front porch of the house. This occurred at 4:25 and the soldiers were held there until 5:50."[47]

It came out later that Villa had demanded that Obregón order the *Carrancista* forces under the command of General Benjamin Hill to withdraw from the neighboring State of Sonora (the withdrawal of Hill's troops would have given Villa undisputed control of northern Mexico); that Obregón had refused; and that Villa had threatened to shoot his erstwhile ally on the spot.[48] Obregón stood his ground, and Villa's passion subsided, but it was several days before Canova or anyone else knew whether Villa would kill Obregón or let him go. Eventually Pancho relented and permitted Obregón to return to Mexico City, but only after he had promised to try to persuade Carranza to

[46] G. C. Carothers to the Secretary of State, September 19, 1914, State Department Papers, and L. J. Canova to G. C. Carothers, September 18, 1914, quoted in Carothers' dispatch just cited.

[47] L. J. Canova to W. J. Bryan, September 22, 1914, State Department Papers.

[48] G. C. Carothers to the Secretary of State, September 19, 1914, *ibid.*

consent to the holding of immediate elections in order to avert bloodshed.[49]

Villa and his advisers left no doubt as to their intentions during and immediately following these tense days when Obregón was a prisoner in Chihuahua City. To state the matter briefly, they meant to force Carranza's immediate retirement, even before the revolutionary convention could assemble, to dominate the convention, and to control the new government of Mexico. They would do this without open fighting if possible; but they were prepared to march at once to Mexico City if that were necessary.[50] Disclosing this intention partially, Villa gave a statement to reporters on September 23 that was tantamount to a declaration of war. "In view of the attitude of Venustiano Carranza," it read, ". . . we have been obliged to renounce him as Commander-in-Chief of the Constitutionalist Army . . . , and we have declared hostilities, being disposed to fight until the last—until he is forced to abandon his power and place."[51]

Events now moved rapidly toward an open rupture. Fighting broke out near Nogales, in the State of Sonora, between *Villistas* and *Carrancistas* on September 25, 1914, while Villa's forces occupied Zacatecas and San Luis Potosí far to the south, in south central Mexico, on September 27.[52] A day later the generals of the Division of the North demanded that the First Chief turn over the executive power to Fernando Iglesias Calderón, the leader of the old Liberal Party of Mexico.[53] On September 29 Villa sealed an agreement with commissioners from Zapata's headquarters for cooperation against Carranza.[54] And finally, on September 30, Pancho issued a "Manifesto to the Mexican People" justifying his recent actions on the ground that Carranza meant to dominate the revolutionary convention and thereby perpetuate his power. The Manifesto, moreover, promised that neither Villa nor any of his generals would seek or accept the presidency of the Republic,

[49] L. J. Canova to the Secretary of State, September 24 and 25, 1914, *ibid.*

[50] As Z. L. Cobb to the Secretary of State, September 21, 1914, *ibid.*, put it.

[51] *New York Times*, September 24, 1914. For expressions of similar sentiments by Villa, see L. J. Canova to the Secretary of State, September 23 and 25, 1914, State Department Papers.

[52] *New York Times*, September 26, 1914; New York *World*, September 28, 1914.

[53] General Luis Aguirre Benavides *et al.* to V. Carranza, September 28, 1914, quoted in J. W. Belt to the Secretary of State, September 28, 1914, State Department Papers.

[54] New York *World*, September 30, 1914.

and it called upon all Mexicans to join the Division of the North in re-establishing a constitutional regime.[55]

In Mexico City, meanwhile, Carranza had received the news from the North quietly if somewhat sadly. Earlier, or at least so John R. Silliman, the American consular agent accredited to the First Chief, was told, Carranza had resolved not to interfere with the work of the revolutionary convention and to accept its decisions loyally. But after Villa's imprisonment of Obregón, the First Chief concluded that any kind of agreement with the Division of the North was impossible.[56] And, although he declared publicly that he would gladly retire if the convention so demanded,[57] Carranza must have resolved at this time to ignore the convention if the *Villistas* controlled it and to accept the challenge to arms when fighting could no longer be avoided.

In Washington, on the other hand, President Wilson and Acting Secretary of State Robert Lansing viewed events in Mexico during the last week in September with little surprise and no alarm. Indeed, "high officials of the administration" told reporters that they were optimistic about the prospects for peace. Villa, they said, did not really want to begin a new revolution and was only insisting that Carranza obey the letter and spirit of the Torreón Agreement. The First Chief, a reluctant reformer at best, might not want to comply; but he would have to accede to Villa's demands simply because Pancho commanded overwhelming military power in Mexico. In these circumstances, these unnamed administration spokesmen added, the United States government would not attempt to interfere but would look on while the factions settled their differences among themselves.[58]

That this was also the President's own view was confirmed by the well-informed Washington reporter for the Louisville *Courier-Journal*. "I want to advise you what you doubtless have already gleaned from the events in Mexico," he wrote to his editor on September 28, "that the President has been, and is, fully advised of all Villa's movements, secretly encourages and supports them, is in constant communication with the General and believes that Villa will succeed, in a very few

[55] Printed in *Foreign Relations, 1914*, pp. 607-608.

[56] J. R. Silliman to the Secretary of State, September 22, 1914, State Department Papers.

[57] New York *World*, September 30, 1914.

[58] *New York Times*, September 25, 1914.

days, in eliminating Carranza from the government down there. He also believes the consummation will make for reasonably permanent peace in Mexico and has little faith in a government of Carranzistas. What I told you in May about the entente between Wilson and Villa is being well borne out."[59]

Nor is there any reason to doubt that General Hugh L. Scott, a military adviser close to the White House, reflected President Wilson's opinions when he wrote: "I will tell you the way I look on Villa. Carranza has climbed to what power he has on Villa's shoulders and is trying to kick him down—he has no real power of his own. Villa is the real force of Mexico and has caught Carranza by the neck each time he has broken his agreements and put him back on the track until now when it has arrived at such a stage in the game that his falsity can be stood no longer. . . . Villa . . . does not want to be dictator himself which he could make himself with ease but is determined on a constitutional government & the uplift of the peon so far as it is possible in such a country. . . . I don't look for any real resistance from Carranza."[60]

Events in Mexico during early October 1914 seemed completely to justify these expectations. There was no public sign that Carranza intended to resist and no indication that he could possibly succeed if he did. Indeed, everything seemed to point to a bloodless triumph by Villa. Carranza's generals were apparently divided and helpless. Eager to avoid any new carnage, many of them including Obregón, met Villa and his chieftains in a so-called peace conference at Zacatecas on September 30, 1914, and there conceded virtually all of Pancho's demands. They agreed upon the promulgation of an immediate armistice and the cessation of troop movements, which, in view of Villa's recent thrusts both north and south, was distinctly advantageous to the Division of the North. More important, they agreed that the revolutionary convention should meet only briefly in Mexico City on October 1 and should then adjourn to meet in regular session at Aguascalientes, which was declared to be a neutral zone, on October 10. Although the documents do not reveal the fact, the *Carrancistas* must also have conceded

[59] Arthur Krock to Henry Watterson, September 28, 1914, the Papers of Henry Watterson, Library of Congress; hereinafter cited as the Watterson Papers.

[60] H. L. Scott to Mary M. Scott, September 26, 1914, the Papers of Hugh L. Scott, Library of Congress; hereinafter cited as the Scott Papers.

Villa's demand that most of Carranza's civil appointees should be excluded from the convention.[61]

Events proceeded smoothly according to this plan. The convention assembled at Mexico City on October 1 and 2, effected a temporary organization, and adjourned to Aguascalientes.[62] In that resort city some 350 miles northwest of the capital, the revolutionary chieftains began to gather on and after October 5, 1914. Meeting in a theater on October 10, the convention proceeded forthwith to adopt a rule for the qualification of delegates that virtually assured Villa's supremacy. It specified that no delegate would be seated unless he commanded at least one thousand men, or was a general or a governor, *and* had fought in the revolutionary army before the capture of Zacatecas.[63] The approval of the latter qualification debarred most of Carranza's personal appointees.[64] When the convention met again on October 12, the *Villistas* moved to reinforce their control by demanding that General Zapata be invited to send delegates to Aguascalientes. There was a brief heated debate the following day, but Obregón supported the demand, and Carranza's spokesman, General Eduardo Hay, withdrew his objections.[65] It was no wonder that Villa could write on the 14th that all was going well at the convention, and that Carranza's doom was sealed.[66]

From this point on there never was any doubt where the convention was heading. On October 14 it declared its sovereignty, thus repudiating all of Carranza's claims to rightful power, while the delegates pledged their loyalty to the new authority both by oath and by writing their names upon a large Mexican flag.[67] To signalize his triumph Villa came to Aguascalientes on October 16 and went before the convention on the following morning. "Pandemonium ensued," the American agent on the scene reported, "while Villa and Obregon embraced each other and continued while Villa took the oath and

---

[61] For reports of the Zacatecas conference, see G. C. Carothers to the Secretary of State, September 30, 1914, and the *New York Times*, October 2, 1914.

[62] J. W. Belt to the Secretary of State, n.d., received October 2 and 3, 1914, State Department Papers; *New York Times*, October 3, 1914.

[63] L. J. Canova to the Secretary of State, October 10, 1914, State Department Papers.

[64] For Villa's reactions, see G. C. Carothers to the Secretary of State, October 11, 1914, *ibid*.

[65] L. J. Canova to the Secretary of State, October 12 and 13, 1914, *ibid*.; New York *World*, October 13, 1914.

[66] F. Villa to F. Sommerfeld, October 14, 1914, copy in the Scott Papers.

[67] L. J. Canova to the Secretary of State, telegram and letter both dated October 14, 1914, State Department Papers.

signed his name on the flag as all the others had done. The convention although in secret session became boisterous [with] joy. The chairman made a rich eulogistic speech in which he dwelt upon Villa's greatness in war but that his military achievements were as nothing compared to this act of his in our presence today."[68] Then, following Villa's departure, the convention established the framework of a provisional government by naming a commission to assume the duties ordinarily performed by the Secretaries of War, Foreign Affairs, the Interior, Justice, the Treasury, and Communications.[69]

The following two weeks saw the convention hard at work on the remaining and most important problems. One was the task of channeling the hitherto aloof movement of Emiliano Zapata into the mainstream of the Revolution. This was quickly if not too well done after the arrival and seating of Zapata's twenty-six delegates on October 28. Zapata demanded approval of the Plan of Ayala, a program for land distribution among the peons, as the price of his cooperation. In a conference with the *Zapatistas* before they attended the convention, Villa gladly conceded their demand; and the convention sealed the bargain on October 28 by adopting *in principle* the Plan of Ayala as the program of agrarian reform for Mexico.[70]

The second problem—how to persuade Carranza to surrender the leadership of the revolutionary movement and submit to the convention's sovereignty—was considerably more urgent and difficult. In an effort to force his hand, the convention on October 19 sent a delegation headed by General Obregón to Mexico City to invite the First Chief to come to Aguascalientes. He replied by moving some 20,000 troops of the Division of the Northeast under General Pablo Gonzáles to Querétaro, not far from where the convention was meeting, and by sending a written message back to the convention by the delegates who had visited him.[71] Read to the delegates on October 29, the First Chief's reply was forthright and explicit. He would gladly relinquish command of the army and the executive power of the nation, indeed, he would leave Mexico altogether, Carranza promised, but only provided that Villa and Zapata would resign their commands and agree to leave Mexico if the convention decided that he, Carranza, must go.

[68] L. J. Canova to the Secretary of State, October 17, *ibid.; New York Times*, October 20, 1914.

[69] L. J. Canova to the Secretary of State, October 20, 1914, State Department Papers.

[70] L. J. Canova to the Secretary of State, October 25, 26, and 28, 1914, *ibid.; New York Times*, October 30, 1914.

[71] L. J. Canova to the Secretary of State, October 20, 21, 24, and 25, 1914.

However, the First Chief warned, under no circumstances would he accept a dictatorship by Villa; and he was firmly resolved to go on fighting "if the only thing desired is to remove me from the leadership so that personal ambitions or reaction may find the way cleared."[72]

The convention responded the following day, October 30, by adopting a peace plan drafted by a joint committee of generals and civilians. It deposed Carranza as First Chief in charge of the executive power and Villa as Chief of the Division of the North, and called for the election of a Provisional President who should carry out the decrees of the convention until a constitutional government could be established. The important provision of the plan was the sixth article, which specified that Villa should remain in the army as a "Chief of Division," subordinate to the Secretary of War.[73] Shortly afterward, in the early hours of November 2, 1914, the convention elected General Eulalio Gutiérrez, Governor of the State of San Luis Potosí and a former *Carrancista*, as Provisional President of the Republic of Mexico. Villa at once sent a telegram to Gutiérrez, reiterating his allegiance to the convention and placing himself at the new President's command. "Truly," the State Department's observer at Aguascalientes exulted, "the Republic of Mexico was born again last night by the selection of a man upon whom all factions and elements could center without discord."[74]

The choice of accepting a provisional government dominated by *Villistas* or plunging Mexico into civil war now depended upon Carranza. And Carranza's choice and his hopes for ultimate victory depended upon the loyalty of his leading generals—General Cándido Aguilar, commander of troops in the State of Veracruz; General Luis Blanco, commander of the 15,000 cavalrymen in Obregón's division or army; General Obregón, commander of the Division of the Northwest; and above all General Pablo Gonzáles, commander of the Divi-

[72] L. J. Canova to the Secretary of State, October 29, 1914, *ibid.* The *New York Times*, October 31, 1914, prints Carranza's message to the convention. In a conversation with John R. Silliman on October 31, Carranza declared that his offer had been very seriously meant. If Villa accepted his proposal, Carranza said, then the convention could work out its program unhindered and uninfluenced. But if Villa refused to retire, civil war would probably ensue. J. R. Silliman to the Secretary of State, October 31, 1914, State Department Papers.

[73] L. J. Canova to the Secretary of State, October 30, 1914, *Foreign Relations, 1914,* p. 615; *New York Times*, November 1, 1914; New York *World*, November 2, 1914.

[74] L. J. Canova to the Secretary of State, November 2, midnight, 1914, *Foreign Relations, 1914,* p. 617; L. J. Canova to the Secretary of State, November 2, 1 p.m., 1914, State Department Papers; *New York Times*, November 3, 1914.

sion of the Northeast. Aguilar, Blanco, Gonzáles, and a number of lesser chieftains lost no time in affirming their loyalty to the First Chief. Obregón, however, hesitated. Perhaps he sincerely wanted, as he said, to do everything possible to avoid hostilities; perhaps he remembered the incident at Chihuahua City and wondered whether the man who had nearly killed him could be entrusted with the fate of Mexico; or perhaps he had political ambitions himself and was simply waiting to join the strongest side. Whatever his motives, Obregón cast his lot with Carranza on November 10, 1914. The realignment of the Constitutionalist army was now fairly complete. The convention had the support only of the powerful Division of the North, of the recently created Central Division under General Panfilo Natera, and of scattered small units. Carranza had all the rest—a clear majority of the Constitutionalist forces.[75]

Carranza's boldness grew in direct proportion to the accretion of his military power. Moving his headquarters from Mexico City to the less exposed City of Puebla on about November 3, he announced that since the convention had not complied with his terms regarding his own and Villa's retirement, he would continue to exercise the executive power of the nation.[76] And when the convention replied with an ultimatum giving the First Chief until six p.m., November 10, to yield the provisional presidency to Gutiérrez, Carranza shot back on November 9 with a manifesto ordering his delegates to withdraw from the convention and all generals in the Constitutionalist army to take charge of their commands.[77]

Despite such threats and counterthreats, it was obvious that no one wanted the responsibility for civil war. The convention declared Carranza a rebel at six p.m. on November 10, 1914,[78] but there was no major fighting during the next few days because the *Carrancistas* made an earnest effort to avoid it. The First Chief's generals, including Gonzáles, Blanco, and Eduardo Hay, dispatched a telegram to the

[75] The above paragraph is based upon L. J. Canova to the Secretary of State, November 3, 4, 9, and 10 (two telegrams), 1914, State Department Papers; J. R. Silliman to the Secretary of State, November 4 (two telegrams) and 10, 1914, *ibid.; New York Times*, November 5 and 10, 1914.

[76] *ibid.*, November 4, 1914.

[77] L. J. Canova to the Secretary of State, November 5 and 9, 1914, *Foreign Relations, 1914*, p. 618; L. J. Canova to the Secretary of State, November 6, 1914, State Department Papers; *New York Times*, November 9 and 10, 1914.

[78] L. J. Canova to the Secretary of State, November 10, 7 p.m., 1914, State Department Papers; G. C. Carothers to the Secretary of State, November 11, 1914, *ibid.*

convention on November 11 pledging their personal honor that Carranza would leave Mexico if Villa also went into exile, and warning that "if for any cause our demand that General Villa be retired absolutely and in fact is not complied with, we who subscribe hereto pledge ourselves to fight him until he is reduced to submission."[79] Obregón added his support by sending a similar message to Villa and the Division of the North.[80] Gutiérrez replied by naming Villa commander in chief of the convention's forces, and Villa by calling upon all Mexicans to take up arms.[81] Under pressure from his generals, particularly Gonzáles, Carranza came back on November 16 with a new proposal—that he resign his command to Gonzáles; that he, Carranza, and Villa leave Mexico immediately and go to Havana by November 25; that the convention reassemble in Mexico City and elect a new Provisional President for the entire preconstitutional period; and that Gonzáles and Gutiérrez then deliver their forces to the new government.[82] Villa's response was that he would gladly leave Mexico, but only after Gutiérrez had been firmly installed in Mexico City as head of the Republic.[83]

To the generals around the First Chief it was the final proof of Villa's treachery and perfidious ambitions and the end of all hopes for a peaceful settlement. "I consider useless anything except armed force," Obregón, then in Mexico City, declared on the day after Villa gave his reply to Carranza's final offer. ". . . I am proud to say that fortunately the Army of the Northwest, which I command, is prepared to enter the contest in defense of the principles for which the Mexican people have been fighting during the last four years."[84]

The portentous consequences of the rupture were not at all apparent to President Wilson and Secretary Bryan as they observed events in Mexico from early October to mid-November 1914 with an attitude of calm detachment and near disinterest. To be sure, Bryan was absent from Washington during most of this period, and Wilson was engrossed in more pressing diplomatic problems. But their unconcern

[79] Quoted in L. J. Canova to the Secretary of State, November 11, 1914, *ibid.*

[80] J. R. Silliman to the Secretary of State, November 12, 1914, *ibid.*

[81] L. J. Canova to the Secretary of State, November 11, 1914, *ibid.; New York Times,* November 12, 1914.

[82] J. R. Silliman to the Secretary of State, November 16, 1914; L. J. Canova to the Secretary of State, November 16, 1914, both in *Foreign Relations, 1914,* p. 623.

[83] New York *World,* November 18, 1914.

[84] *New York Times,* November 19, 1914.

stemmed also from certain assumptions and convictions about the future course of events in Mexico and the role that the United States should play.

In the first place, they still must have assumed, as they apparently had before, that even if war came again it would not be long before Villa subdued the remnants of Carranza's army. Before mid-November, at least, there were certainly plenty of reasons for believing that this would happen, especially in view of the reports that their Confidential Agent, Leon J. Canova, was sending to Washington during these weeks from Aguascalientes.[85] Two quotations from these dispatches will illustrate the opinions and advice that Canova was pressing upon his superiors in Washington.

"While it has been very apparent, since August 24th," he wrote on November 12, 1914, "that General Villa is the only individual who can put the country on a peaceful footing and establish confidence, the revelations of the past twenty days emphasises [*sic*] this conclusion. The mention of his name puts the fear of God into the hearts of many, while he is respected and admired throughout the land. Now, with his very perfect understanding with the Zapata element, his ability to restore order is unquestioned. . . . Were he to leave the country at this time, or before a duly elected Administration is inaugurated in office, Mexico would witness, and be the victim of, a reign of anarchy. . . . In the Convention, and what it represents, the country must rest its hope. All else is futile, misleading, and must prove fatal to the realization of the principles of the revolution."[86]

"Sometimes it is necessary that a painful surgical operation has to be undergone in order that a body may return to good health," Canova

[85] Canova was another of the "Special Agents" through whom Wilson and Bryan seemed to prefer to do diplomatic business in Mexico. He was a Floridian formerly engaged in newspaper work in Havana and apparently a political friend of the Secretary of State. He was appointed a Special Agent for the State Department (the records seem to indicate that it was the President who took the initiative in making the appointment) in June 1914 to work with Carothers and make an exhaustive study of conditions in Mexico. (W.W. to W. J. Bryan, June 5, 1914, Wilson Papers; W. J. Bryan to L. J. Canova, June 19, 1914, State Department Papers.) After spending most of the summer of 1914, from early July to early September, at Carranza's headquarters in Saltillo and Mexico City, Canova joined Villa in Chihuahua and went from there to the Aguascalientes convention as the State Department's observer. Originally friendly to Carranza, he seems to have fallen under Villa's spell during his association with him in Chihuahua in September; and by the time the revolutionary convention met, he was easily Villa's strongest supporter among all the American representatives in Mexico.

[86] L. J. Canova to W. J. Bryan, November 12, 1914, State Department Papers.

wrote a few days later, at the end of the Aguascalientes convention, "and while I regret to say it, a clash of arms will be, in the end, the best thing for the country, for it will clarify the political atmosphere."[87] For, as he had put it earlier, "I think one good fight will settle the question, and Carranza will find himself with scant forces and will have to flee the country, and if he can, he will be fortunate."[88]

Certain signs seemed to indicate that the President was contemplating some kind of active policy favorable to Villa and the convention. He had a long conference about Mexico with Secretary Bryan on November 13, and on that day a reporter for the New York *World* sent in an apparently inspired dispatch saying that the administration, expecting Villa to make short work of Carranza's forces, would lend its moral support to the convention government in the weeks ahead.[89] When the Conventionist Provisional President, Gutiérrez, sent a long message to Secretary Bryan announcing his assumption of office and voicing a desire for friendly relations with the American government, Wilson was extraordinarily cordial in reply. "You may say to General Gutiérrez," Bryan wrote on November 16, "that I have taken pleasure in bringing his telegram of November 13 to the attention of the President, and add that this Government appreciates the sentiments expressed therein and that it hopes that he will do everything in his power to bring about lasting peace in Mexico."[90] A week later the New York *World's* correspondent reported that the President, having lost all confidence in Carranza, would put his weight behind Villa's efforts to establish Gutiérrez' government as the ruling power in Mexico.[91]

These newspaper reports, which presumably came direct from the White House and the State Department, may have been accurate insofar as they went. But they ignored one fact that was more important than the administration's apparent desire for Villa's triumph. It was Wilson's own determination to avoid doing anything that might conceivably mean active involvement in the Mexican civil war at this time. It was easier now to follow such a course than it had ever been before. The threat of independent British intervention, which had

---

[87] L. J. Canova to W. J. Bryan, November 16, 1914, *ibid.*
[88] L. J. Canova to W. J. Bryan, October 21, 1914, *ibid.*
[89] New York *World*, November 14, 1914.
[90] The Secretary of State to Special Agent Canova, November 16, 1914, *Foreign Relations, 1914*, p. 622.
[91] New York *World*, November 23, 1914.

earlier been a powerful stimulus to preventive action by the President, was now entirely gone. Moreover, there were as yet no strong pressures from public opinion at home; indeed, that opinion had been almost completely quiescent since Carranza's entry into Mexico City. Finally, it is possible that Wilson, presumably unlike Bryan, was not entirely deceived by Canova's predictions about the inevitability of Villa's triumph. He might well have gleaned the truth from Silliman's dispatches that told how Carranza still commanded the loyalty of the larger portion of the Constitutionalist forces. If this was true, then it would help to explain the President's obvious decision to go slowly in giving outright recognition to the convention government.

One indication of his cautious attitude came two weeks after the end of the Aguascalientes convention, in the way in which he responded to a suggestion from Secretary Bryan. "The situation," the Secretary of State wrote on December 2, 1914, "seems to be clearing up in Mexico. Villa and Zapata are working in harmony and Gutierrez seems to be about to assume authority over most of the country. The occupation of Carranza is not likely to last long." Bryan then went on to suggest that inasmuch as Gutiérrez would be "the head of the government" it might be well to send him "a strongly worded representation" emphasizing the necessity for protecting religious workers and property and the rights of foreigners. Wilson replied that he was "heartily glad to see things clearing up, as they seem to be, in Mexico," and that he prayed "most earnestly" that it "may indeed be the beginning of the end." He would be glad, he continued, to convey such a message as Bryan had suggested confidentially and unofficially. But, he added, "I feel that there is very considerable embarrassment involved in sending what might seem to be official communications to the new government before it has got *a little more firmly in the saddle.*"[92]

Wilson's determination to avoid any open show of commitment to either side had been further indicated only a short time before the above words were written, by his withdrawal of American troops from Veracruz at a time when such withdrawal meant handing over the city to the First Chief. It will be recalled that the American President had earlier decided upon the evacuation, and that this decision had been announced on September 15, 1914. The evacuation was delayed, to begin with, by negotiations between the State Department and Carranza's Foreign Secretary over certain problems arising out of the

[92] W. J. Bryan to W.W., December 2, 1914, Wilson Papers; W.W. to W. J. Bryan, December 3, 1914, *ibid.*; italics added.

American occupation of the port and the manner in which the provisional government would deal with Mexicans who had collaborated with the occupation forces. The President, obviously, was determined to avoid pressing Carranza too hard on these points. "I am clear in the judgment," he wrote to Bryan on October 2, "that we ought not to linger in our departing. I think it would make a very bad impression not only in Mexico, but in Latin-America generally. . . . My wish is to get out at the very earliest possible date."[93]

Then there was further delay after the Aguascalientes convention met, because the State Department negotiated both with Carranza and with the convention about the guarantees it was seeking, and because the American leaders seemed to be on the verge of recognizing the convention's claim that it alone was entitled to accept Veracruz from the Americans. On November 6 Acting Secretary of State Lansing instructed Carothers to ask Villa whether the American authorities should turn over the port to General Cándido Aguilar, whom Carranza had appointed to receive it, or whether they should wait until an officer had been named by the convention. "This Department," Lansing explained, "is doubtful as to course to pursue since the duty to enforce the guarantees of the convention, if Vera Cruz is delivered to Aguilar, would seem to fall on a general who has not recognized the authority of the convention to give such guarantees."[94] Villa of course advised that the American government should surrender Veracruz only to an officer named by President Gutiérrez.[95]

The trouble with following Villa's wishes was that such a policy was a risky one for the United States. There was simply no way to deliver Veracruz to the convention government, for the *Carrancistas* were strongly entrenched in the entire triangular area from Mexico City to Tampico and Veracruz. It might be a long time before the *Villistas* could occupy the region. Meanwhile, there would be the constant danger of hostilities between Carranza's forces and American troops around Veracruz; indeed, according to the American Secretary of War that danger was acute by early November.[96]

Wilson was not willing to run the risk *merely* to strengthen the Conventionist government. On about November 11 the State Depart-

[93] W.W. to W. J. Bryan, October 2, 1914, *ibid.*

[94] Acting Secretary Lansing to G. C. Carothers, November 6, 1914, State Department Papers.

[95] G. C. Carothers to the Secretary of State, November 10, 1914, *ibid.*

[96] L. M. Garrison to W.W., November 4 and 5, 1914, Wilson Papers.

ment received word that Carranza had conceded all its demands for guarantees.[97] Taking policy into his own hands two days later, the President typed out and dispatched to the Department a statement that he wanted sent "by wire to-night" to Carranza and "Guiterez." It was a simple announcement that read: "Both General Carranza and the Convention at Aguascalientes having given the assurances and guaranties we requested, it is the purpose of the administration to withdraw the troops of the United States from Vera Cruz on Monday, November 23. All persons there for whose personal safety this Government had made itself responsible have now left the city. The priests and nuns who had taken refuge there[98] and for whose safety fears were entertained are on their way to this country."[99]

In other words, as the President made it clear through the newspapers, the United States would not surrender Veracruz to anyone; it would simply withdraw its forces.[100] Villa could have the city if he could get to it before November 23, as Wilson may at first have expected him to do; if not, then Carranza would have to be permitted to occupy it.[101] This, too, was the meaning of the orders for the evacuation that were sent to the commanding general in Veracruz, General Frederick Funston: "Do not make any arrangements with local Mexicans or with Mexican representatives from outside the city that could make it seem that you are recognizing the right of Carranza to jurisdiction over the city. It is merely desired that you get out in the best

[97] The Brazilian Minister to Mexico to the Secretary of State, November 10, 1914, transmitting a message from Acting Foreign Secretary I. Fabela of the same date, *Foreign Relations, 1914,* pp. 618-620.

[98] Secretary of War Lindley M. Garrison had earlier reported that from 220 to 500 priests and nuns were estimated to have sought refuge in Veracruz. L. M. Garrison to W.W., October 7, 1914, Wilson Papers.

[99] W.W. to W. J. Bryan, November 13, 1914, State Department Papers. Actually, Wilson was mistaken in saying that all the refugee priests and nuns had left Veracruz. General Frederick Funston, commanding general at the port, reported on November 14 that forty-nine priests and eleven nuns remained. The War Department at once sent a transport to Veracruz to evacuate them. New York *World,* November 15, 1914.

[100] *New York Times,* November 14, 1914.

[101] The New York *World* reported on November 15, 1914, that the President had set the date for the evacuation on November 23 in order to give Villa, who had already launched a campaign against Tampico, time in which to capture Veracruz before the American withdrawal occurred, and that General Funston would be directed to withdraw his troops slowly if Villa had any difficulty in reaching Veracruz by the appointed date. This report may not have been entirely inaccurate, for at the time it was written Carranza seemed to be tottering on the brink of ruin. By November 23 the military situation in Mexico had changed so drastically to the First Chief's advantage that there would have been no point in delaying the American withdrawal.

practical fashion, leaving things in as good shape as possible and making no declaration that could be interpreted as committing this Government to the recognition of the authority of any individual or faction."[102]

That is the way it was done. At nine o'clock in the morning of November 23 the American troops in the outposts around Veracruz began to retire to the center of the city. Meanwhile, General Funston's 5,000 troops and marines had begun boarding the eight transports in the harbor. By one o'clock in the afternoon the embarkation was complete, and the transport fleet sailed out to open sea. Immediately afterward, the Constitutionalist forces under General Aguilar came down from the hills and reclaimed the sacred soil of Veracruz for Mexico.[103]

While Wilson was thus enforcing his decision for extrication, events in Mexico raced toward Villa's seeming triumph. Dangerously exposed in Mexico City, the *Carrancista* troops there under Obregón and Blanco executed a gradual withdrawal eastward from November 20 to November 24, while Carranza established his own headquarters in Veracruz on November 26. Meanwhile, Zapata's Army of Liberation, which had encamped to the south of Mexico City, entered its suburbs as Blanco withdrew his remaining troops during the evening of November 24. Zapata arrived unostentatiously three days later and set up headquarters in a modest hotel to await the coming of his allies from the North.

Villa had meanwhile divided the Division of the North into three columns and sent them plunging toward Guadalajara, Tampico, and Mexico City in what he thought would be the knockout blow. Villa and Gutiérrez accompanied the 25,000 troops that moved without opposition and with lightning speed toward the capital, which they reached on November 30. Gutiérrez moved into the National Palace on December 3, and Villa went to the ancient town of Xochimilco, eighteen miles south of Mexico City, for his first encounter with Zapata on the following day. Meeting in the narrow streets of the town at noon, the two chieftains embraced and then went with their respective entourages to the municipal school to make arrangements for the formal occupation of the capital. Canova, who was on the

[102] The Acting Secretary of War to General Funston, November 20, 1914, *Foreign Relations, 1914*, p. 625.

[103] *New York Times*, November 24, 1914.

scene, has left an almost ecstatic account of this memorable encounter: There was "General Villa,—tall, robust, weighing about 180 pounds, with a complexion almost as florid as a German, wearing an English helmet, a heavy brown sweater, khaki trousers, leggings and heavy riding shoes. Zapata to his left, with his immense sombrero sometimes shading his eyes so that they could not be seen, dark complexion, thin faced, a man very much shorter in stature than Villa and weighing probably 130 pounds. He wore a short black coat, a large light blue silk neckerchief, pronounced lavender shirt. . . . He had on a pair of black, tight-fitting, Mexican trousers with silver buttons down the outside seam of each leg. Villa did not have a sign of jewelry on, nor any color in any of his personal adornment. Sitting in the semi-circle as we were, and watching every play of his and Zapata's countenance, I could not but measure Villa as the highest type of a warrior, a man of great energy and unbounded self-confidence. . . . One wonders in looking at . . . [Zapata], where his qualities of a leader are hidden, but it seems to have been his honesty of purpose, his constancy to the interests of his people and his unfailing kindness to them, which have made him the great leader he is."[104]

Two days later, on Sunday morning, December 6, 1914, Villa and Zapata signalized their victory by riding at the head of their combined troops, some 30,000 strong, through the broad avenues of the City of Mexico to the National Palace, where President Gutiérrez and the diplomatic corps received them.[105]

It was a showy beginning, but ensuing events did not fulfill Villa's gaudy promises of a new reign of peace and justice. On the contrary, Villa behaved as only he knew how, irresponsibly, dissolutely, and despotically. Gutiérrez, who seems to have believed that Villa actually meant to establish a responsible civilian regime, soon discovered that he was a virtual prisoner in the National Palace, and that Pancho expected him to be a good puppet. The so-called Provisional President looked on in horror while Villa gave a free hand in the municipal administration to two of his more bloodthirsty lieutenants, Generals Rodolfo Fierro and Tómas Urbina, who began executing political prisoners and personal foes by the score.[106] And when Gutiérrez sent

[104] L. J. Canova to the Secretary of State, December 8, 1914, State Department Papers.

[105] *ibid.*

[106] L. J. Canova to the Secretary of State, December 14, 15, and 16, 1914, State Department Papers.

a strong remonstrance and threatened to resign if the assassinations did not cease, Villa threw his own guard around the National Palace and told the Provisional President that he would not be permitted to quit.[107] The situation, from Gutiérrez' point of view, worsened drastically soon afterward, when the convention reassembled in Mexico City on January 1, 1915, and proceeded to consider—and later to adopt— a plan for the government of Mexico. It provided that Gutiérrez should retain the presidency until the end of the year, but under conditions that made the Provisional President and his so-called Cabinet figureheads of the convention.[108]

It was all more than poor Gutiérrez could endure. After secretly and vainly negotiating with Obregón and Aguilar for the formation of a new government,[109] he fled Mexico City by night on January 15, 1915, taking with him to Carranza's camp three so-called Cabinet ministers, some 5,000 troops, and whatever hard money he could lay his hands upon. His successor, named at once by the convention, was Roque González Garza, a *Villista* general from Chihuahua, who had been Minister of the Interior in Madero's first Cabinet.[110]

Gutiérrez' defection was an indication of the way the political wind was blowing in Mexico. More than any other event during this period, it reflected the conviction that was growing among the responsible elements that it was fatuous to expect constructive leadership from Villa. The reorganized convention had bold plans for reconstruction and included some idealistic elements in the revolutionary movement,[111] but its fate was bound entirely to Villa's military fortunes. On the surface his military supremacy seemed assured at the beginning of 1915. His armies occupied most of northern Mexico, a large section of the rich interior from Mexico City in the South to Guadalajara in the West and Aguascalientes in the North, and, together with the *Zapatistas*, the capital and the State of Morelos to the south of it.

---

[107] Vice Consul Silliman to the Secretary of State, December 29, 1914, *Foreign Relations, 1914*, pp. 634-635.

[108] Vice Consul Silliman to the Secretary of State, January 14, 1915, *Papers Relating to the Foreign Relations of the United States, 1915*, p. 644; hereinafter cited as *Foreign Relations, 1915*.

[109] See Eliseo Arredondo to W.W., January 19, 1915, State Department Papers, enclosing E. Gutiérrez to Á. Obregón and C. Aguilar, January 7, 1915; Á. Obregón to E. Gutiérrez, January 12, 1915; and "Translation of Manifesto which Gutiérrez promised to publish should Generals Obregon and Aguilar accept his proposals."

[110] J. R. Silliman to the Secretary of State, January 16, 17, and 18, 1915, State Department Papers; *New York Times*, January 18 and 21, 1915.

[111] See Robert E. Quirk, *The Revolutionary Convention of Aguascalientes, passim.*

Actually, Villa's military weaknesses, unapparent to casual observers, were staggering. He was outnumbered by the *Carrancistas*, while his enemies controlled the east and west coasts and all the important northern port towns except Juaréz. Moreover, Villa's command system was essentially chaotic and greatly inferior to Carranza's. Worse still, Villa's line of supply, stretching as it did from Juaréz to Mexico City, was fearfully overextended. For political reasons he had to try to hold the capital, but the very effort was bound to be fatal.

Visible proof of Villa's inherent weakness came in the first real test of strength in battle. On January 5, 1915, Obregón hit Puebla, some seventy miles southeast of Mexico City, with a well-trained army of 30,000 men. Hundreds of Conventionist troops were penned in the narrow streets and slaughtered by Obregón's machine guns; a thousand others, together with troop trains and artillery, were captured.[112] Under relentless pressure from Obregón's approaching army, Villa withdrew his forces northward from the capital on January 27, and Obregón occupied the city on the following day. The *Zapatistas* and the convention fled to Cuernavaca, Zapata's stronghold in Morelos, while Villa himself went to Chihuahua City and there established a government that was expected to function until the sovereignty of the convention could be re-established.[113]

These events constituted a humiliating blow for Villa and, as the future would reveal, the first turning point in the military fortunes of the civil war. But it was not the end of the internecine struggle, for Pancho in defeat was still Pancho in power through broad areas of central and northern Mexico. That struggle would grow in ferocity and in the process multiply the perplexities of the men in Washington who had so confidently assumed that their troubles in Mexico were at an end. Before we go on with this story, however, we must give some attention to other and direr crises that were forming at this time in Asia and in Europe.

[112] *New York Times,* January 6, 1915.

[113] *ibid.,* January 28 and 29, 1915; G. C. Carothers to the Secretary of State, February 6, 1915, State Department Papers; the Confidential Agent of the Conventionist Government to the Secretary of State, March 8, 1915, enclosing "Manifesto to the Mexican Nation by General Francisco Villa," dated January 31, 1915, and "Decree of General Villa assuming political power and creating provisional departments of government," dated February 2, 1915, *Foreign Relations, 1915,* pp. 662-664.

CHAPTER IX

Wilson, Bryan, and the Far Eastern Crisis of 1915

AT the very time that the President and Secretary of State were once again being drawn into the whirlpool of Mexican factional politics and maneuvering for mediation in the European war, a grave crisis was coming to a head in the Far East and was raising new and even more perplexing difficulties for the leaders in Washington. In brief, it seemed that the tide of Japanese imperialism was threatening to inundate the Chinese mainland. Whether to commit American influence and power in a bold effort to stem the tide, whether to attempt merely to moderate it, or whether to do nothing in the face of the Japanese challenge to the now almost sacrosanct ideal of the Open Door—these were the choices that Wilson and Bryan pondered as the crisis developed during the early months of 1915. In making their decision, they were forced, for the first time, to give some searching thought to the fundamental aspects of the far eastern policy of the United States.

The cauldron began to boil as soon as the Japanese government entered the war against Germany on August 23, 1914. Landing an invading force on the southern coast of the Shantung peninsula on September 3, the Japanese soon invested the German naval base at Tsingtao in the Kiaochow leasehold and eventually forced its surrender on November 7. Meanwhile, on the pretext of military necessity they had also occupied the main line of the Shantung Railway some two hundred miles into the interior, all the way to Tsinan, the capital of the province. It was the first step, Chinese authorities believed, in Tokyo's grand design for control of the entire Shantung Province and, eventually, of northern China as well.

The leaders in Washington viewed these events on the other side of the globe with only mild interest and certainly no great alarm. Lansing made this fact plain enough in the only general statement of policy concerning China that came out of the State Department during these months, and particularly by the way in which he made it. Doctor

V. K. Wellington Koo of the Chinese Foreign Office had sought out the American Chargé d'Affaires in Peking, J. V. A. MacMurray,[1] on August 27, 1914, and suggested that the United States had a right under the so-called Root-Takahira Agreement of 1908 to expect Japan to seek American approval before undertaking any military operations in Shantung Province outside the German leasehold at Kiaochow. It was a distortion of the meaning of the Agreement as well as an obvious attempt to draw the American government into an active role as China's protector, and MacMurray did not take the suggestion seriously. Indeed, not until September 10 did he inform the State Department of the conversation and ask for instructions; and then he sent his dispatch by mail, so that it did not arrive in Washington until October 20.[2]

Lansing, then in charge as Acting Secretary of State, took no pains to send an early reply. Apparently without consulting the President, he finally answered on November 4, saying that the State Department regretted that the war had spread to the Far East but was not surprised. Then, in a concluding paragraph, he made it plain that the American government had no intention of becoming entangled, even in defense of historic policies. He wrote:

"With respect to other questions raised in the despatch you are instructed that, while the Department desires, of course, to safeguard all American rights in China, to protect all legitimate interests there and to promote by all proper methods the development of American trade, it is at the same time anxious that there shall be no misunderstanding of its aims by the Chinese Government. The United States desires China to feel that American friendship is sincere and to be assured that this Government will be glad to exert any influence, which it possesses, to further, by peaceful methods, the welfare of the Chinese people, but the Department realizes that it would be quixotic in the extreme to allow the question of China's territorial integrity to entangle the United States in international difficulties."[3]

Events, however, were conspiring to involve the Washington administration even as Lansing wrote this disclaimer. Signs that Japan was planning some bold new *démarche* in China were already evident by

[1] The American Minister to China, Paul S. Reinsch, was on vacation and absent from Peking at this time.

[2] Chargé MacMurray to the Secretary of State, September 10, 1914, *Foreign Relations, 1914, Supplement*, pp. 186-189.

[3] The Acting Secretary of State to Minister Reinsch, November 4, 1914, *ibid.*, pp. 189-190.

late November 1914;[4] they were unmistakably clear by the end of the year. For one thing, the Japanese Foreign Minister, Baron Takaaki Kato, had intimated in a speech in the Diet on December 9 that the Imperial Cabinet was considering measures to strengthen Japan's position in South Manchuria and Inner Mongolia; at the same time, he denied that the Foreign Office had made any promises to anyone to return the former German leasehold to China.[5] For another, the Tokyo authorities were demanding that the Chinese government replace the German subjects employed in the Tsingtao customs office with Japanese collectors chosen by the Imperial government—a demand that threatened to disrupt the entire Maritime Customs Service of China.[6] But more ominous still were reports of Japanese troop movements in Manchuria and the beginning of what the American Minister at Peking believed to be a systematic Japanese campaign to discredit American enterprise throughout China.[7]

The climactic play in the unfolding Japanese strategy came not long afterward, when the Japanese Minister at Peking, Eki Hioki, sought a private interview with the Dictator-President of China, Yüan Shih-k'ai, at night on January 18, 1915, and handed him a draft treaty embodying a series of demands and "requests" of China by the Imperial Cabinet in Tokyo. They were twenty-one in number, arranged in five groups. The first group related exclusively to Shantung Province and included demands for Chinese approval of the transfer of all German rights to Japan and for assurance that China would not lease any territory in the province to a third power. The second group was designed to strengthen Japan's position in South Manchuria and to open Inner Mongolia to Japanese penetration. Its demands included the extension of the Japanese-owned concessions for the Kwantung leasehold and the South Manchuria Railroad for an additional ninety-nine years; freedom of trade and settlement for Japanese businessmen and colonists and virtually exclusive Japanese control over the mines and railroads of South Manchuria and Inner Mongolia; and the promise that China would consult Japan before it sent political,

---

[4] P. S. Reinsch to the Secretary of State, November 28, 1914, State Department Papers.

[5] The text of his address is printed in *Foreign Relations, 1914, Supplement*, pp. 206-207.

[6] Minister Reinsch to the Secretary of State, December 18 and 23, 1914, *ibid.*, p. 204; W. J. Bryan to W.W., December 16, 1914, State Department Papers; W.W. to W. J. Bryan, December 29, 1914, *ibid.*

[7] P. S. Reinsch to the Secretary of State, December 22, 1914. *ibid.*

financial, and military advisers into the two regions. In the third group the Japanese sought to strengthen their control over the Han-Yeh-P'ing Iron and Coal Company located in central China, an important source of supply for the ore-hungry steel industry of Japan, by demanding that this company, which was a Chinese-controlled concern heavily in debt to Japanese capitalists, be reorganized as a joint Sino-Japanese enterprise, and that the company be given a monopoly on the operation of mines "in the neighborhood." The single demand in Group IV had as its objective (as the Japanese later explained) the establishment of an undisputed Japanese sphere of interest in the Province of Fukien, which lay directly to the west of the Japanese colony of Taiwan, or Formosa. It was a guarantee that China would not cede or lease any harbor, bay, or island along the coast of China to a third power.

Then followed certain miscellaneous "requests" in Group V that were by far the most sweeping and important of all the Japanese proposals. They specified that the Chinese central government should employ "influential" Japanese as political, financial, and military advisers; appoint Japanese to the police departments "in localities (in China) where such arrangements are necessary"; permit Japanese hospitals, temples, and schools in the interior of China to own land; agree either to purchase 50 per cent or more of its munitions supply from Japan or to join the Imperial government in building an arsenal that would use materials purchased in Japan; grant concessions to Japanese capitalists for the construction of three railroads to connect the middle Yangtze region with the southern Chinese coast; agree to consult Japan if it (the Chinese government) needed foreign capital for the development of Fukien Province; and permit Japanese subjects to carry on missionary work in China.

"As regards the proposals contained in the fifth group," read the instructions that Baron Kato had handed to Minister Hioki on December 3, 1914, "they are presented as the wishes of the Imperial Government. The matters which are dealt with under this category are entirely different in character from those which are included in the first four groups. An adjustment, at this time, of these matters, some of which have been pending between the two countries, being nevertheless highly desirable for the advancement of the friendly relations between Japan and China as well as for safeguarding their common interests, you are also requested to exercise your best efforts to have our wishes carried out."[8]

Interpreting these instructions liberally, the Japanese Minister made no distinction between the demands in the first four groups and the "requests" or "wishes" in Group V when he presented the proposed treaty to President Yüan. At the same time, Hioki enjoined absolute secrecy "on pain of serious consequences"; and he went on to hint that Yüan's continued rule in Peking and the peace of his country depended upon the Chinese government's speedy acquiescence in all the demands and "requests."[9] In this manner was launched the boldest and most portentous diplomatic campaign in Japan's history to this time, one aimed at nothing less than transforming China from a ward of all the powers into very nearly a protectorate of Japan.

It is not difficult at this late date to understand the forces and ambitions that impelled the statesmen of the island empire into so pretentious a *démarche*. The exigencies of internal Japanese politics—for example, the need of an insecure ministry for some triumph to show for the lives and money lost in the campaign against the Germans in the Kiaochow leasehold—were in part responsible.[10] But the basic compulsions ran much deeper than this. They stemmed in part from feelings of frustration and wounded national pride, from the fact that the European powers had heretofore succeeded in preventing any significant Japanese penetration into their spheres of interest in China south of the Great Wall. Thus many of the so-called twenty-one demands (like the ones for railroad concessions in central China and the conversion of the Han-Yeh-P'ing Company into a Sino-Japanese concern with monopolistic privileges) sought simply to give Japan the same kind of rights in China proper that the European powers had long enjoyed.

These compulsions also stemmed from a haunting sense of insecurity about the area in which Japanese interests were already concentrated and which the Japanese people regarded as their most important

[8] From the text of the instructions and ensuing demands and "requests" as printed in *Foreign Relations, 1915*, pp. 159-161.

[9] Paul S. Reinsch, *An American Diplomat in China*, pp. 129-130.

[10] A ministry headed by Count Shigenobu Okuma had come to power on April 15, 1914, succeeding an unpopular and short-lived one headed by Admiral Gombei Yamamoto. The Okuma ministry lacked majority support in the Japanese Diet and was under heavy pressure from extremist elements for a "decisive" policy toward China after the outbreak of the war in Europe. Smimasa Idditti, *The Life of Marquis Shigenobu Okuma, A Maker of New Japan*, pp. 359-372.

strategic frontier—South Manchuria. Japanese treaty rights in this area were severely limited, to begin with, and only recently the American government had made a bold if futile attempt to open the area to exploitation by American investors. Thus in the eyes of the Japanese the most urgent of their demands were the ones designed to seal off Southern Manchuria as an exclusive Japanese preserve. Moreover, the Tokyo government's fear that the safety of Formosa was menaced by the threat of foreign and particularly American penetration of Fukien Province seems to have been very real.

The most powerful compulsions driving the Japanese leaders to this extraordinary campaign of imperialism were the deeply felt needs and ambitions that stemmed from the dynamics of Japan's recent past— the need for resources, markets, and an outlet for a rapidly growing population, and the ambition that the entire Japanese people shared for the leadership of the Far East, an ambition not entirely unlike the one that the American people had already realized in the Western Hemisphere. The "requests" listed in Group V revealed these ambitions in an unmistakable fashion.[11]

One can also understand why the Japanese moved against China when they did. In the ordinary course of events the fulfillment of what they believed to be their national destiny could have occurred only in the far distant future, if at all. The outbreak of war in Europe presented an opportunity that the leaders of the Empire could not resist. The European powers with interests in China were in no position to prevent Japan from realizing her destiny, and the United States, so the Japanese leaders undoubtedly believed, would not try. Minister Hioki stated the matter plainly if somewhat crudely to the American Minister in Peking when he said that his government "could not be expected to forego the advantages of [the] extraordinary opportunity opened to it in China in consequence of the war in Europe."[12] Or, as one American scholar has written in summary: "Western interventionists had repeatedly thwarted Japan in her pursuit of what, to her, was not only a just but vitally essential policy. This time she would profit by experience. She would strengthen her foothold

[11] For the above discussion I have leaned heavily upon Thomas E. La Fargue, *China and the World War*, pp. 28-48, which explains the motivation for the twenty-one demands in much greater detail than I have done; Marius B. Jansen, *The Japanese and Sun Yat-sen*, pp. 179-183; and Roger F. Hackett's forthcoming biography of Prince Aritomo Yamagata, to be published by Harvard University Press.

[12] P. S. Reinsch to the Secretary of State, February 20, 1915, State Department Papers.

in Manchuria and Mongolia, and make that in Shantung secure. . . . She would establish access to China's raw materials, to the financial, industrial and commercial privileges which she considered indispensable to her existence as a modern industrialized state. . . . Finally, she would make the contract so binding that it could not be broken on European council tables once the war freed Europe's attention."[13]

For several days after the Japanese Minister presented the twenty-one demands on January 18, 1915, the Chinese authorities were so stunned that they did not know what to do or where to turn. Obviously, the only hope for China in the ensuing negotiations lay in exposing the full truth to the outside world and in appealing to America and Britain for diplomatic support. Consequently, one of the Chinese ministers divulged the nature of the demands to the American envoy in Peking, Paul S. Reinsch, on January 22. "He finally confided to me, almost with tears," Reinsch afterward recalled, "that Japan had made categorical demands which, if conceded, would destroy the independence of his country and reduce her to a servile state. He then told me in general terms their nature, saying: 'Control of natural resources, finances, army! What will be left to China!'"[14]

It was China's good fortune that President Wilson had played an active role in the appointment of the new American Minister to Peking in early 1913, and that the President's intervention had resulted in the selection of Reinsch instead of the kind of deserving Democrat whom Bryan liked to name as head of a Legation. A distinguished legal historian and one of the few far eastern experts in the United States, Reinsch had left a professorship at the University of Wisconsin to accept the President's call to service. As a student of Oriental institutions and culture, he was by no means anti-Japanese in point of view; on the contrary, he looked to Japan to give leadership in the Far East in westernization and industrialization.[15] But his love for the Chinese people and his conviction that the United States had an appointed mission to protect China against any outside aggression were too profound for him ever to be a disinterested or impartial observer in the event of conflict between China and Japan. Thus in the far eastern crisis of 1915 he played a dual role, as a defender of his own govern-

[13] A. Whitney Griswold, *The Far Eastern Policy of the United States*, pp. 188-189.
[14] P. S. Reinsch, *An American Diplomat in China*, p. 131.
[15] P. S. Reinsch, "Informal Memorandum on China and Japan Submitted at the suggestion of the Secretary of State," dated August 27, 1914, State Department Papers.

ment's interests, and as a personal adviser and spokesman of the Chinese authorities. As he later explained:

"It was my personal opinion that America had a sufficiently vital interest to insist on being consulted on every phase of these negotiations. The Chinese had hoped that America might lead Great Britain and France in a united, friendly, but positive insistence that the demands be settled only by common consent of all the powers concerned. But the situation was complex. The state of Europe was critical. The most I could do, and the least I owed the Chinese, was to give a sympathetic hearing to whatever they wished to discuss with me, and to give them my carefully weighed opinion. Our own national interests were closely involved. It was my positive duty to keep close watch of what was going on."[16]

Reinsch sounded the general alarm to the State Department in two telegrams dispatched during the evening of January 23, 1915. "The Japanese Minister," he wrote in the first, "has submitted a long list of demands. . . . [They] are stated to be such as could not be granted without abandoning entirely the open-door policy as well as independence in political and industrial matters." It was, he added in the second, "the greatest crisis yet experienced in China. The independence of China and equal opportunity of western nations are at stake." As the British Legation in Peking was much perturbed, the American government should exchange views with the Foreign Office in London at once.[17] Three days later the Minister could report some of the specific Japanese demands.[18] Then on February 1 he was finally able to tell the State Department about the "requests" in Group V, which heretofore had been unknown to him, and to offer the following advice to his superiors in Washington:

"The concession of these and other similar demands would make China politically and in a military sense a protectorate of Japan and establish a Japanese monopoly in the commercial resources of China most requisite for military purposes.

"With respect to these demands [in Group V] the Japanese authorities are attempting to stifle publicity. . . . In view of these efforts to escape or prejudice the public opinion of other countries it is a question whether the United States ought not in its own interests as well as

[16] P. S. Reinsch, *An American Diplomat in China*, p. 144.

[17] Minister Reinsch to the Secretary of State, January 23, 1915, 7 p.m., and January 24, 1915, 2 a.m., *Foreign Relations, 1915*, pp. 79-80, and State Department Papers.

[18] P. S. Reinsch to the Secretary of State, January 26, 1915, State Department Papers.

in those of China which it has hitherto loyally championed to assume the possibility of asking the Chinese Government to disregard the injunction of secrecy and make it officially cognizant of the facts in this regard of the substance of which it is already advised in order that the American Government may be enabled to adopt such measures as may be appropriate for the protection of its interests guaranteed by existing international agreements. I believe that the Chinese Government would readily make such a communication if assured that the Government of the United States would assume moral and consequent political responsibility for insistence upon the disclosure of matters affecting its rights.

"In my opinion such a direct application to the Chinese Government would constitute a supplement to an understanding with Great Britain for the purpose of influencing Japan towards a course of moderation and equity. All aspects of the crisis indicate that the British Government holds the key of the situation. . . . Should the British Government take the position which we would seem warranted in anticipating the result would almost certainly be a quietus upon the present Japanese designs which could not be carried out without the acquiescence of her Ally. In the alternative Japan would risk an estrangement possibly leading to the dissolution of that [Anglo-Japanese] Alliance. In either case, the Alliance would be purged of the danger of being employed as a means of nullifying any moderating influence which Great Britain might otherwise bring to bear in the event of Japan's desiring for any reason to impose upon the United States the military ascendancy which would have been made feasible by a command of the immense material resources of China and encouraged by success in a policy of aggression."[19]

It was startling advice urgently given, but it arrived in Washington at a time when the President and Secretary of State were deeply concerned about what seemed to be a much more serious crisis that was then developing with Germany over submarine warfare. This crisis not only diverted Wilson's and Bryan's attention from the Far East; it also made them understandably reluctant to rush into a conflict with Japan. E. T. Williams, head of the Far Eastern Division in the State Department and the officer chiefly responsible for advising the Secretary on developments and policy in that area, had no such qualms.

[19] P. S. Reinsch to the Secretary of State, telegram, February 1, 1915, *ibid.* and Wilson Papers. The extract printed in *Foreign Relations, 1915*, pp. 81-82, is drastically abbreviated.

A former Chargé of the Legation in Peking, Williams was a leader of that small but powerful group in the Foreign Service who believed that America's great economic opportunity in the future lay in the development of Chinese railroads and resources and in the exploitation of the potential Chinese market for American industrial products. Alert and ever suspicious of Japanese motives and ambitions, he was the man who set off the first discussions in Washington in response to Reinsch's alarums.

After reading the Minister's early dispatches, Williams addressed three urgent memoranda to Bryan on January 25, 27, and 28, warning that a "serious crisis in Far Eastern affairs" threatened "not only China's peace but America's interests." "In our own interest and in that of the powers who have at our request entered into the 'Open Door' agreements," he wrote, for example, on January 27, "it seems to be our duty to ask explanation from Japan and *insist firmly upon our rights.* . . . Our present commercial interests in Japan are greater than those in China, but the look ahead shows *our interest* to be *a strong and independent China* rather than one held in subjection by Japan. China has certain claims upon our sympathy. If we do not recognize them, as we refused to recognize Korea's claim, we are in danger of *losing our influence in the Far East* and of adding to the dangers of the situation."[20]

The receipt of Reinsch's long and urgent telegram of February 1 confirmed all of Williams' darkest fears; and from a sick bed at home he appealed to his superior for stern and resolute resistance to Japanese pretensions. American security in the Far East, to say nothing of Chinese independence, was, he wrote to Bryan on February 2, in gravest peril. "With such beginnings," he continued in reference to the proposals in Group V, "it is not difficult to foresee the course which events are likely to take, and with control of . . . [Chinese] resources, Japan, which is not restrained by the scruples of the West, and which declines to enter into peace pacts, becomes a greater menace than ever to the U. S. She has given us fair warning that she will not tolerate what she considers race discrimination against her people. I suggest that we ought to call the attention of the Chinese Government to the published reports of demands that affect our interests and

[20] E. T. Williams to the Secretary of State, January 25, 1915; E. T. Williams, "MEMORANDUM. THE CRISIS IN CHINA," January 27, 1915; E. T. Williams, "Comment on telegram of January 26, 8 p.m., page 2," all in State Department Papers; italics added.

our Treaty Rights and protest against the grant of concessions that violate those rights. To assure ourselves that nothing of the sort is intended China ought to make public the demands that all the world may judge. Great Britain probably has her blind eye on the telescope and does not desire to see the danger signal. Nevertheless, if we can get the demands made public, she will undoubtedly be glad and aid in bringing about a modification of them." Nor was this all the American government should do. "If we can succeed in reducing the demands," Williams concluded in the most revealing suggestion of all, "it seems to me that we ought to insist upon China's putting her house in order and making herself able to defend herself. We *can* and *ought* to assist her in this, and in so doing we shall be building up *a strong defence for ourselves.*"[21]

One can only wonder what the President and Secretary of State thought as they read all these dire warnings. Certainly they must have been troubled by forebodings, for we find Wilson writing on January 27 that he was worried about Japan's "present attitude and intentions in China and her willingness or unwillingness to live up to the open door in the East."[22] But it was not Wilson's method, or Bryan's, either, to decide upon the merits of a question when they had evidence on only one side, or to rush headlong into controversy even when they knew all the facts. Their first reaction, therefore, was to reserve judgment and to appeal to London and Tokyo for information.[23] Their second, probably, was to ask themselves how far they should go in defense of China if reports from Peking were accurate. From all that followed we may surmise that they never seriously contemplated adopting any provocative policies that carried the risk of war, such as Williams was suggesting. They obviously believed that American interests in China did not justify taking any such chances; had they been tempted to think otherwise, the threat of serious difficulty with Germany at this time would alone have induced a high degree of caution. In short, they could not do much until they had all the facts, and they might not be able to do much even then. As Wilson wrote to Reinsch on February 8:

"I have thought a great deal about the present situation in China,

---

[21] E. T. Williams to W. J. Bryan, February 2, 1915, Wilson Papers; italics added.

[22] W.W. to W. J. Bryan, January 27, 1915, Bryan Papers, National Archives.

[23] W. J. Bryan to Minister Reinsch, January 28, 1915, State Department Papers, asking Reinsch to repeat his, Reinsch's, telegram of January 26, 1915, to the Embassy in Tokyo; the Secretary of State to Ambassador Page, February 2, 1915, *Foreign Relations, 1915*, p. 82.

in view of the Japanese demands, and have been doing what I could indirectly to work in the interest of China. I have had this feeling, that any direct advice to China or direct intervention on her behalf in the present negotiations would really do her more harm than good, inasmuch as it would very likely provoke the jealousy and excite the hostility of Japan, which would first be manifested against China herself. I have been trying to play the part of prudent friend by making sure that the representatives of Great Britain realized the gravity of the situation and just what was being attempted. For the present, I am watching the situation very carefully indeed, ready to step in at any point where it is wise to do so."[24]

Events of the next two weeks did not deflect Wilson and Bryan from their policy of waiting watchfully while seeking to learn the truth about Japanese intentions. The London Foreign Office did not respond to the State Department's query of February 2 until eleven days later, and then in a cryptic way that yielded no information.[25] But in the interim there was some encouragement from Tokyo, for the Japanese Foreign Office finally broke its silence and seemed to be willing to take the interested powers into its confidence. On February 8 the Japanese Ambassador in Washington, Viscount Sutemi Chinda, delivered to Bryan a memorandum which listed most of the demands in the first four groups. The following day, moreover, the Imperial Foreign Minister, Baron Kato, called the American Ambassador, George W. Guthrie, to his office for their first conversation about the Sino-Japanese negotiations. He wanted the Secretary of State to know the true nature of the "propositions," the Foreign Minister said, and that they were "not contrary to China's integrity or to the rights and interests of other nations."[26] Not a word did Viscount Chinda's memorandum or Baron Kato say about the proposals in Group V.

This was the aspect of the situation that most baffled the Secretary of State. Had the Japanese government ever made such demands on China as Reinsch had reported, and if it had, what were their specific terms? It was difficult for Bryan to know what to believe. On February 11 Ambassador Guthrie wired from Tokyo that he had been confidentially informed that the Japanese memorandum had

[24] W.W. to P. S. Reinsch, February 8, 1915, Wilson Papers.

[25] Ambassador Page to the Secretary of State, February 13, 1915, *Foreign Relations, 1915*, p. 88.

[26] The Japanese Embassy to the Department of State, n.d., but February 8, 1915; Ambassador Guthrie to the Secretary of State, February 9, 1915, *ibid.*, pp. 83-85.

omitted some demands; and Minister Reinsch sent a message the following day confirming the accuracy of his earlier reports.[27] As E. T. Williams at the Far Eastern desk pointed out on February 15, it all seemed to indicate that "the Japanese memorandum was intentionally misleading."[28] In spite of this evidence, Bryan was not convinced. He put the question of additional demands directly to Chinda on February 16; and when the Ambassador emphatically denied the truth of the reports from Peking,[29] Bryan was apparently satisfied. "I think they [Reinsch and others] are mistaken," he wrote in comment at the bottom of Williams' memorandum of February 15. "I trust the Japanese Ambassador."

Bryan's faith was severely shaken and the far eastern crisis moved into a new stage in consequence of developments that occurred during the following week. On February 18 and 19 the American newspapers published long dispatches from correspondents in Peking listing all the demands that the Japanese Minister was pressing upon the Chinese government, including the ones in Group V.[30] At about the same time the Chinese authorities were emboldened to reveal their plight to the world. Using the submission of the memorandum by the Japanese Foreign Office as an excuse, the Chinese Foreign Office transmitted to the powers the full text of the Japanese demands and so-called "requests" on February 18.[31]

The truth was presumably in the open at last, and Bryan, after discussing these developments with the President at a Cabinet meeting during the morning of February 19, hastened to smoke out the Foreign Office in Tokyo by dispatching two telegrams to Ambassador Guthrie. The first was a note for delivery to the Foreign Office. After repeating the "requests" or demands in Group V as they had been published in the newspapers, it went on to say that the American authorities had been much relieved to find that the Japanese memorandum had not mentioned any such demands, and that they therefore assumed that of course the newspaper reports must be false. The sec-

[27] Ambassador Guthrie to the Secretary of State, February 11, 1915; Minister Reinsch to the Secretary of State, February 12, 1915, both in *ibid.*, pp. 87-88.

[28] E. T. Williams to W. J. Bryan, February 15, 1915, State Department Papers.

[29] W. J. Bryan, memorandum dated February 16, 1915, *Foreign Relations, 1915*, p. 92.

[30] *New York Times*, February 18 and 19, 1915.

[31] Minister Reinsch to the Secretary of State, February 17, 1915, 7 p.m., State Department Papers; *New York Times*, February 19, 1915; the Chinese Minister to the Secretary of State, n.d., but February 18, 1915, *Foreign Relations, 1915*, pp. 93-95.

ond was a confidential message for the American Ambassador explaining that the publication of the demands by the press "enables us to comment upon them without coming into conflict with the announced position of Japan which, we assume, is fully stated in the [Japanese] memorandum handed us."[32]

It was uncommonly shrewd diplomacy for the Great Commoner (indeed, one is tempted to assume that it was the President who devised the method), and it yielded quick results. Baron Kato saw Guthrie on February 21 and tried to extricate himself from the trap into which he had blundered. The Japanese memorandum, the Foreign Minister explained, had included all the "demands" upon which his government would insist "and refusal of which without good grounds would be a serious matter." It *was* true, Kato went on reassuringly, that the Foreign Office had made certain other proposals to China, but they were merely "requests" or "wishes" of which "friendly consideration was desired." "He asked me," Guthrie added in his report of this conversation, "to forward this information to you confidentially. He was particularly anxious that you should understand that the reason for confining the statement sent you strictly to Japan's 'demands' was that the other items were 'requests' and were so designated when presented to China."[33] In Washington the following day, moreover, Viscount Chinda handed Bryan a memorandum listing all the "requests" in Group V.[34]

The receipt of Baron Kato's message and the new Japanese memorandum marked the end of confusion and uncertainty in Washington and the beginning of a new phase in which the President and his advisers would play an increasingly active role in the far eastern crisis. The American authorities could not have avoided some participation even had Kato's assurances been sincerely meant, or if the Japanese had withdrawn Group V altogether at this time. The necessity for some kind of action became inescapable to Wilson and Bryan when it soon grew apparent that the Foreign Minister's explanation had been only technically correct, and that the Japanese government was still pressing as hard for Chinese acceptance of the "requests" as of

[32] W. J. Bryan to Ambassador Guthrie, two telegrams, February 19, 1915, State Department Papers.

[33] Ambassador Guthrie to the Secretary of State, February 21, 1915, *Foreign Relations, 1915*, p. 96.

[34] Printed in *ibid.*, p. 97.

the demands.[35] There was nothing left to do, the President and the Secretary of State agreed, but to force their way into the controversy with a strong representation. The very integrity of historic policies seemed to be at stake; besides, as Reinsch made clear in a personal message to the President, the Chinese depended upon American support in defending their independence and freedom.[36] "It is evident that things are being pressed at Peking . . . ," Wilson wrote, therefore, to Bryan on February 25. "I fully approve of taking advantage of the opening to present to Japan very frankly our views on her 'suggestions' or 'requests.' I think those views can be made very weighty and conclusive. We shall not have uttered a more important state paper."[37]

But where should the American government stand, and what should it do? It was not possible to answer these questions without first making a more searching reappraisal of American far eastern policy than the leaders of the Wilson administration had ever made before. Such a reconsideration began on the same day that Ambassador Chinda delivered the second Japanese memorandum to the State Department, when Bryan addressed his first extended comments on the twenty-one demands to the President. The Secretary of State was obviously not eager to rush defiantly into the fray as an antagonist of Japan. He had almost certainly concluded that most of the demands in the first four groups, except the demand for special policing rights in Manchuria, implied no threat to the Open Door and were therefore unobjectionable. Moreover, he was not prepared to deny the Japanese claims to special privileges in Manchuria. "I am not sure," Bryan wrote, indeed, "but that it would be worth while for China to agree to the cession of Manchuria to Japan if, by doing so, she could secure freedom as to the rest of the country." But he recognized that the Chinese would never accept any such proposal, and acquiescence in most of the demands in the first four groups was, therefore, as far as the Secretary of State was willing to go. To him it was clear that most of the "requests" in Group V menaced China's political integrity and infringed Japan's agreements with the United States for the Open Door of eco-

[35] As Reinsch reported, among other times, two days after Baron Kato gave his assurances to Ambassador Guthrie. Minister Reinsch to the Secretary of State, February 23, 1915, *ibid.*, p. 97.

[36] P. S. Reinsch to the Secretary of State, for the President, February 20, 1915, State Department Papers.

[37] W.W. to W. J. Bryan, February 25, 1915, *The Lansing Papers*, II, 407. I have transposed these sentences.

nomic opportunity, and that the State Department should soon address a note embodying these views to Tokyo.[38]

Nor, it soon became apparent, were Bryan's principal advisers clamoring for all-out opposition to Japanese claims. The head of the Far Eastern Division, E. T. Williams, had lost most of his earlier belligerence now that he found himself impelled into a general reappraisal of far eastern policy. In a memorandum to the Secretary of State on February 26 about the proposed note to Japan, Williams argued that one simply had to admit that Japan had "special interests" in Manchuria and Inner Mongolia in view of the fact that more than 80,000 Japanese had settled in these areas. It was necessary, also, to understand that continued Japanese emigration to Manchuria was, from the American point of view, preferable to Japanese emigration to California. Did not the present crisis, Williams suggested, offer an opportunity for a definitive settlement of the still-smoldering dispute between the two countries over the California alien land law of 1913?[39] It might be possible, he added, to obtain Japan's acceptance of the California law in return for American acquiescence in her demands relating to Manchuria and Inner Mongolia.[40] Reading Williams' memorandum, Counselor Lansing was much impressed. "If a bargain along these lines could be struck," he wrote to Bryan on March 1, "it would relieve us of the vexatious California land controversy, and prevent in large measure future disputes which seem almost inevitable if the 'demands' of Japan are permitted at the present time to pass unchallenged. In any event can there be any harm in attempting to reach a reciprocal understanding?"[41]

These discussions must have proceeded orally in the State Department and between the President and the Secretary of State during the first ten days of March 1915; and Williams, assisted perhaps by Lansing, must also have begun drafting a note to Japan during the same period. At some point the proposal for a bargain was abandoned— perhaps at the insistence of the President, who may have recoiled at the suggestion of a deal at China's expense. Then, while the Washington leaders were still engaged in their leisurely proceedings, news of

[38] W. J. Bryan to W.W., February 22, 1915, *ibid.*, pp. 405-407.

[39] For an account of this controversy, see A. S. Link, *Wilson*, II, 289-304.

[40] E. T. Williams to W. J. Bryan, February 26, 1915, State Department Papers.

[41] R. Lansing to W. J. Bryan, March 1, 1915, *The Lansing Papers*, II, 407-408. For an extended analysis, see Burton F. Beers, "Robert Lansing's Proposed Bargain with Japan," *Pacific Historical Review*, XXVI (November 1957), 391-400.

threatening developments in the Sino-Japanese negotiations came from Peking. Irritated by Chinese resistance, especially to the "requests" in Group V, the Japanese Minister informed the Chinese authorities that his government might use means "outside of diplomacy" if they did not make "important concessions" by March 12.[42] Obviously, this was no time for bargains and trades; as the President pointed out, a general statement of the American position had to go to Tokyo at once.[43]

The note was completed on about March 11, approved by the President with minor editorial changes on the following day, and delivered to the Japanese Ambassador in Washington on March 13, 1915. A summary was also telegraphed to Reinsch on the same day.[44] It revealed clearly enough what the records fail precisely to tell us, that is, the direction that official American thinking about the twenty-one demands had taken during the interval between the beginning of the reappraisal and the completion of the note.

The note began by voicing gratification over the fact that the Japanese government had made the proposals in Group V as "requests" and not demands, and by saying that the American government understood that the "requests" were "not to be pressed if the Chinese Government should decline to consider them." It then proceeded to review Secretary of State John Hay's negotiation of the Open Door notes in 1899 and 1900 and to emphasize how the Japanese government had formally affirmed on numerous occasions its support of the principles of the political and territorial integrity of China and of equality of commercial and industrial opportunity for all foreigners in that country. Then followed a brief history of American activities in China, with a specific review of the Sino-American treaties that confirmed "broad and extensive" rights and privileges that the American government was bound to uphold. "While on principle," the note continued in a momentous qualification, "and under the treaties of 1844, 1858, 1868 and 1903 with China the United States has ground upon which to base objections to the Japanese 'demands' relative to

[42] Minister Reinsch to the Secretary of State, March 8, 1915, *Foreign Relations, 1915,* p. 103.

[43] W.W. to W. J. Bryan, March 10, 1915, State Department Papers.

[44] Wilson also asked Bryan to send copies of the note to the British, French, and Netherlands governments if this could be done without running the risk of leakage of the contents. W.W. to W. J. Bryan, March 16, 1915, *ibid.* The President and Secretary of State must have decided that the risk was too great, for the records of the State Department contain no evidence that the note was ever transmitted to the above governments.

Shantung, South Manchuria, and East Mongolia, nevertheless the United States frankly recognizes that territorial contiguity creates special relations between Japan and these districts." The United States government was, therefore, not disposed to raise any objections to the Japanese demands in Groups I and II relating to these provinces. Nor did the American government see any "special menace" to its rights in the demand in Article IV for a Chinese pledge of nonalienation of its coast and in certain of the "requests" in Group V.[45] The note, curiously, said nothing about the demands in Group III relating to the Han-Yeh-P'ing Company. Coming to the remaining demands and "requests," it suddenly hardened in tone. Asserting that they clearly infringed the Open Door and American treaty rights, it declared in words that could not be misunderstood:

"These proposals, if accepted by China, while not infringing the territorial integrity of the Republic, are clearly derogatory to the political independence and administrative entity of that country. . . . It is difficult for the United States, therefore, to reconcile these requests with the maintenance of the unimpaired sovereignty of China, which Japan, together with the United States and the Great Powers of Europe, has reaffirmed from time to time during the past decade and a half in formal declarations, treaties and exchanges of diplomatic notes. The United States, therefore, could not regard with indifference the assumption of political, military or economic domination over China by a foreign Power, and hopes that your excellency's Government will find it consonant with their interests to refrain from pressing upon China an acceptance of proposals which would, if accepted, exclude Americans from equal participation in the economic and industrial development of China and would limit the political independence of that country. The United States is convinced that an attempt to coerce China to submit to these proposals would result in engendering resentment on the part of the Chinese and opposition by other interested Powers, thereby creating a situation which this Government confidently believes the Imperial Government do not desire."

The note resumed its cordial tone in its concluding paragraph. The American government, it said, had only "friendship and esteem" for Japan's aspirations in the Far East, was in no way jealous of Japan's leadership or of intimate cooperation between Japan and China for

---

[45] These concerned the right of Japanese hospitals, churches, and schools in the interior of China to own land; certain railway concessions; and the right of Japanese subjects to carry on missionary activities in China.

their mutual benefit, and had no desire to influence China in opposition to Japan. "On the contrary," it ended, "the policy of the United States, as set forth in this note, is directed to the maintenance of the independence, integrity and commercial freedom of China and the preservation of legitimate American rights and interests in that Republic."[46]

It was, as Wilson had predicted it would be, a memorable state paper with enormous significance for the future. This was true both for what it yielded and for what it held fast to. The admission of the claim, long advanced by the Japanese, that "territorial contiguity" created special relations between Japan and South Manchuria and Inner Mongolia was far-reaching in implication. It was also badly worded. What the authors of the note had meant to say was that the Japanese had "special interests" in these provinces because of their extensive colonization and investment there.[47] But the note said something quite different, and the Japanese would later use the term "territorial contiguity" to justify their claim to special interests in all of China. On the other hand, the enunciation of the traditional American position on the political independence of China and the Open Door could hardly have been more forthright. Whether it would have any important impact upon the Japanese government, only the future could reveal. At least the lines were finally being drawn.

The sending of the note of March 13 accomplished one of its major objectives almost immediately. It forced the Foreign Office in Tokyo into direct conversations with Washington, which was tantamount to admission that the United States had legitimate concern in the Sino-Japanese negotiations. Baron Kato's initial reaction was to suspect that the State Department had acted at the instigation of China,[48] but American assurances apparently satisfied him on this point. He gave a partial answer to Guthrie on March 21;[49] then, after the Imperial Cabinet had given its approval on March 19, he sent a long and responsive reply to Washington, which Ambassador Chinda delivered orally and in the form of a memorandum to the Secretary of State

[46] The Secretary of State to the Japanese Ambassador, March 13, 1915, *Foreign Relations, 1915*, pp. 105-111.

[47] This is certainly what Williams and Lansing meant in their memoranda of February 26 and March 1, 1915, cited above.

[48] Ambassador Guthrie to the Secretary of State, March 17, 1915, *Foreign Relations, 1915*, p. 112.

[49] Ambassador Guthrie to the Secretary of State, March 21, 1915, *ibid.*, pp. 113-115.

on March 22. After expressing "unfeigned gratification" at the American government's "frank recognition of Japan's special position in South Manchuria, Eastern Mongolia and Shantung," Kato went on to point out what was thus far true, that American concern was on the whole limited to four proposals in Group V concerning the appointment of Japanese advisers at Peking, the question of China's munitions supply, Japanese participation in the policing of China, and the Province of Fukien. The Imperial government, Kato continued, had no intention of forcing the Chinese to accept Japanese advisers. This request had been "formulated with a sincere hope and expectation that it would, if carried out, result in the improvement of the domestic administration of China." The Imperial government regarded its proposal that China purchase half its munitions from Japan as "a pure and simple business proposition" and not one that conflicted with the principle of equal opportunity, since in the past the Chinese had bought all their arms from Germany and Austria anyway. Moreover, the proposal for joint policing applied only to Manchuria and possibly to Inner Mongolia in certain contingencies. On these three points, Kato's communication implied, the Japanese and American governments could not be far apart.

However, the Foreign Minister went on, the "request" concerning the Province of Fukien to which the United States had objected (that China first consult with Japan before permitting foreign capitalists to develop mines or build railways and harbor facilities in the province) was a matter of very serious import to Japan. Fukien Province was not many miles removed from Taiwan. Ever since the time of Secretary Hay there had been rumors that the United States desired a naval station on the Fukien coast; only recently the newspapers had published reports that the Bethlehem Steel Company was negotiating with the Chinese government for the improvement of the harbor of Fukien. "To state frankly," the Foreign Minister continued, "any intrusion of foreign influence in Fukien would lead the people of Japan to entertain fear that the defence of Taiwan would thereby be directly or indirectly menaced." The Japanese government might be willing to withdraw the request in deference to the wishes of the Washington authorities, Kato added, but "in that contingency the Japanese Government will have to desire that the American Government enter into an engagement to make the citizens of the United States refrain from any undertaking in Fukien which may directly or indirectly cause the above-indicated fear on the part of the Japanese people, and that the engagement be strictly and effectively carried out."[50]

Bryan was delighted by this seeming progress toward understanding. Sending a copy of Guthrie's telegram of March 21 and the Japanese Ambassador's memorandum of March 22 to the President, he added an extended comment that revealed that he was willing to accept Baron Kato's explanations about the first three controverted "requests" and eager to allay Japanese apprehensions about Fukien. The latter, he explained, might be simply done—by a formal statement that the United States did not desire a naval station anywhere along the coast of Fukien Province, and by an agreement between China and Japan forbidding *all* foreign naval bases and investment in harbor works along that coast.[51]

Wilson's reply, written on March 24, revealed that his suspicions about Japanese intentions now ran deeper than Bryan's. He was, the President wrote, eager to clear away the Japanese fears about Fukien.[52] "The other matters," he continued, "give me more trouble. Frankly, I do not think that the explanations of the other 'requests' which are offered in Ambassador Chinda's note are convincing, and I hope that a candid discussion of them by the two governments may result in putting them in a more satisfactory light. I quite understand the motives disclosed. I do not feel like criticising the Japanese Government in regard to them. But I think that the remedies and safeguards proposed in the 'requests' go too far. Whatever the intention, they do, in effect constitute a serious limitation upon China's independence of action, and a very definite preference of Japan before other nations, to whom the door was to be kept open. I shall look forward with

[50] "Unofficial Memorandum left by Ambassador Chinda Mch 22—1915 at my [Bryan's] request after he had delivered its contents as an oral communication," Bryan Papers, National Archives. There is a copy of this memorandum in the Archives of the Imperial Japanese Foreign Office, Tokyo; hereinafter cited as Japanese F. O. Archives.

[51] W. J. Bryan to W.W., March 22, 1915, *The Lansing Papers*, II, 409-411.

[52] This Bryan did on March 26, in a message to Guthrie instructing him to inform the Japanese Foreign Office that the United States had no desire for a naval station on the coast of Fukien and would have not the "slightest objection" to a Sino-Japanese agreement "looking toward the withholding of any concession to any foreign Power which contemplates the improvement of any harbor on the coast of Fukien or the establishment of a coaling station or naval base along said coast by any foreign Power." The Secretary of State to Ambassador Guthrie, March 26, 1915, *Foreign Relations, 1915*, pp. 116-117. Bryan also handed a copy of this note to Ambassador Chinda on March 30, 1915.

pleasure to discussing these points with you when we get Japan's direct and official reply to our note of inquiry."[53]

The Secretary of State, however, was neither disheartened nor able to suppress the compulsion to be helpful to both sides. "As Japan and China must remain neighbors," he told the President on March 25, "it is of vital importance that they should be neighborly, and a neighborly spirit cannot be expected if Japan demands too much, or if China concedes too little."[54] He expressed the same convictions a short time later: "The thing that disturbs me most in this eastern trouble is the feeling of suspicion on both sides—a feeling that does not give assurance of peace. These two nations must remain neighbors and unless they deal with each other in the spirit of friendship there is no way of avoiding great antagonism."[55]

On the same day, March 26, that he sent the note about Fukien to Tokyo, therefore, Bryan (with Wilson's approval) dispatched a second one suggesting a neighborly compromise on the three crucial "requests." On the question of advisers, Bryan urged, let China agree that she would not discriminate against the Japanese in their appointment; on the issue of the Chinese munitions supply, let China agree not to discriminate against Japan in making purchases; as for the employment of Japanese police, let China agree that this might be done, but only in Manchuria and eastern Mongolia, where a number of Japanese resided.[56]

Rarely has a diplomatic effort so well meant turned out so badly in the end. Instead of paving the way for a friendly compromise, it set off a violent explosion which, when combined with other events in late March and early April, caused an important shift in American policy in the far eastern crisis. It was, in short, a sort of turning point, one that marked the end of Bryan's nearly exclusive direction of far eastern affairs in general and of policies of friendly mediation based upon assumptions of Japanese good faith, and the beginning of Wilson's increasing participation in the making of far eastern policy and a rapid movement toward a posture of opposition to the Japanese.

The aftermath of Bryan's venture helped set the change in motion. After receiving the Secretary's note of March 26 conveying the compromise proposals, the Embassy at Tokyo had telegraphed a copy in

[53] W.W. to W. J. Bryan, March 24, 1915, *The Lansing Papers*, II, 411.
[54] W. J. Bryan to W.W., March 25, 1915, *ibid.*, p. 413.
[55] W. J. Bryan to W.W., April 6, 1915, *ibid.*, p. 415.
[56] The Secretary of State to Ambassador Guthrie, March 26, 1915, *ibid.*, p. 414.

a routine way to the Legation in Peking. Scarcely able to believe what he read, Reinsch could not conceal his indignation and feeling of shame as he wired in protest to Washington:

"From my knowledge of the attitude of the Chinese government and people I feel it my duty to inform you that the compromises suggested in that instruction are such as the Chinese feel would irrevocably derogate from the principle of administrative independence and, with no return even in the form of an assurance that they had bought peace by such concessions, would definitely set a term to the existence of China as a free country. Should they become aware that the American government favors an adjustment by which China would forego its freedom to choose advisers whom it trusts, to buy munition according to its needs and without foreign supervision of its military organization and to exercise police functions independently in the territory still under its sovereignty, I fear that such knowledge would produce in the minds of the Chinese a conviction that [the] United States had betrayed its historic friendship and its moral responsibility in respect to [the] principles of China's administrative integrity and the Open Door.

"If it is not the policy of the United States to take any preventive action in the present crisis I beg to submit that it would at any rate be more expedient to follow a course of passive acquiescence rather than to intervene in such a manner as could scarcely fail to cause [a] revulsion of Chinese feeling against the United States and put an end to our influence here and our opportunities either of assisting the Chinese government or of preserving our own rights in China.

"I therefore beg to urge that if there is still time [the] Embassy at Tokyo be instructed to make no use of the suggestions referred to which if once communicated to the Japanese government would serve to render its attitude towards China more inexorable and could not of course be prevented from coming eventually to the knowledge of the Chinese."[57]

This telegram arrived at the State Department in the early afternoon of March 30 with a shattering impact. In immense consternation and confusion, and not at all in the anger that many men would have felt after reading Reinsch's accusations, the Secretary of State drafted his reply. The compromise proposals, he explained to the Minister, "were not to be volunteered by Ambassador Guthrie but only to be

[57] Minister Reinsch to the Secretary of State, March 30, 1915, State Department Papers.

made in the case of inquiry"; anyway, he had suggested them only for the purpose of removing friction between China and Japan. "We are very sorry," Bryan went on, "if the advice that we have given in a spirit of friendship to both nations should prove unacceptable, but, being given as advice it is no more binding upon China than upon Japan."[58]

It was of course no answer at all to the questions that Reinsch had raised, but it was the best that Bryan could do. Perhaps he agreed that Reinsch was right at least in saying that the effect of his attempt at mediation would be to encourage the Japanese and demoralize the Chinese at a critical point in the negotiations in Peking. Unfortunately, there was no way to repair the damage, for Bryan had given a partial summary of the note to Ambassador Chinda orally on March 27;[59] Guthrie had delivered its contents to the Foreign Office in Tokyo on March 29;[60] and Bryan had handed a copy to Chinda only a few hours before Reinsch's telegram reached the State Department.[61] Needless to say, Bryan did not inform the Minister in Peking of these facts. Nor did he tell the President of his predicament. He simply sent copies of Reinsch's telegram and of his reply to the White House without comment on March 31[62] and pulled his note to the Japanese Ambassador from the official files and buried it in his private papers!

The effect of this episode was to put a sudden end to Bryan's unhappy efforts at mediation, except on the Fukien issue, on which he was already firmly committed.[63] This was the first stage in the change in American policy in the far eastern crisis of 1915. The second occurred between April 1 and 15 as a consequence mainly of developments in Peking. The negotiations there had not been going at all

[58] W. J. Bryan to Minister Reinsch, April 1 [March 31], 1915, *ibid.*

[59] Viscount Chinda to Baron Kato, Telegram No. 103, March 28, 1915, Japanese F. O. Archives.

[60] Baron Kato, memorandum of a conversation with Ambassador Guthrie, March 29, 1915, *ibid.*

[61] W. J. Bryan to Viscount S. Chinda, March 30, 1915, Bryan Papers, National Archives.

[62] W. J. Bryan to W.W., March 31, 1915, *ibid.* Wilson's reply indicated that he also had been upset by Reinsch's telegram. "I had read Reinsch's message, in the flimsy sent me," he wrote, "and it had given me a good deal of concern. I sincerely hope that this telegram [Bryan's reply to Reinsch] will set the matter in the right light alike in Reinsch's mind and in the mind of the Chinese, when they learn of our interchange of views with Japan." W.W. to W. J. Bryan, March 31, 1915, *ibid.*

[63] Minister Reinsch to the Secretary of State, April 7, 1915; the Secretary of State to Minister Reinsch, April 9, 1915, both in the State Department Papers; W. J. Bryan to W.W., April 9, 1915, Bryan Papers, National Archives.

satisfactorily for the Japanese. The Chinese representatives, skilled in the tactics of obstruction and delay, had offered surprisingly effective resistance, while the Chinese people had joined the struggle by boycotting Japanese merchants and goods. The Japanese Minister, consequently, intensified his pressure, especially for Chinese acceptance of *all* the "requests" in Group V, warning that further talk was useless and that China must be prepared to accept the consequences of refusal.[64]

Reinsch's reports of these proceedings were disquieting enough to the American leaders, but the event that produced the sharpest reaction in Washington was the arrival of two dispatches from Peking on April 13 and 14. The first was a letter that Reinsch had put in the mail on March 6, enclosing a verbatim copy of the treaty that the Japanese government was seeking to impose on China ranged alongside a copy of the demands which the Japanese Minister had given to Reinsch on February 14, 1915.[65] A quick comparison of the treaty with the text of the demands as the Japanese government had stated them yielded seemingly astonishing results. The comparison proved, Williams of the Far Eastern Division asserted, that "the Japanese Government has systematically and deliberately sought to deceive the American Government by concealing the most serious items in the demands."[66]

The second dispatch, a telegram marked "STRICTLY CONFIDENTIAL," was even more jarring. It reported that the Japanese Minister had lately been warning the Chinese negotiators that they would be foolish to expect any support from the United States, since the American government had approved the Japanese demands. As evidence that this belief was beginning to spread through China, Reinsch cited an article in the *Tientsin Times*, which quoted a "prominent Japanese" as declaring that the United States would do nothing to help China because "the Secretary of State is so much under the influence of Baron [*sic*] Chinda that he is not saying a word against the wishes of Japan," and which commented bitterly that the facts seemed to confirm this statement. "It is to be feared," Reinsch concluded, "that unless our Government unmistakably dissociates itself from the ap-

[64] e.g., Minister Reinsch to the Secretary of State, March 31 and April 5, 1915, *Foreign Relations, 1915*, pp. 118-122.

[65] Minister Reinsch to the Secretary of State, March 6, 1915, with enclosures, *ibid.*, pp. 98-103.

[66] E. T. Williams to the Secretary of State, April 13, 1915, State Department Papers.

pearance of acquiescence in the unconscionable demands of Japan, persistent flagrant misrepresentations of its motives, such as cited above, will embitter Chinese public opinion against it. With a view to offsetting such propaganda, I beg to request authorization to give informally, impersonally and unofficially, publicity to the view that the American Government has not abandoned either its material interests or its moral obligation in respect to China and, while of course, awaiting the results of the present negotiations in confident expectation that these rights and obligations will remain unimpeachable, it may be expected to take appropriate action if that belief should prove likely to be disappointed."[67]

We can only guess what thoughts ran through Bryan's mind as he read this message. He probably agreed that the time had come to cease dealing exclusively with Japan[68] and to make a firmer assertion of American rights as they were affected by the Japanese demands. On the other hand, Bryan certainly had no desire to make any such bold defense of China as Reinsch had been urging so passionately. This was true in part because he had apparently not lost faith in the Japanese leaders;[69] it was true, more importantly, because Bryan, remem-

---

[67] Minister Reinsch to the Secretary of State, April 14, 1915, 7 p.m., State Department Papers. In an earlier telegram dated April 12, 1915 (*ibid.*), Reinsch had reported that the Japanese in Peking were trying to give the impression that China could not "build any hopes upon the attitude of the United States."

[68] We find the Secretary writing to Wilson on April 15 as follows:

"The Chinese Minister was here yesterday and inquired very confidentially whether we had consented to China's proposals in regard to Fukien. I told him that we had no objection to an agreement between China and Japan [such as the Chinese had proposed] that would exclude concessions to *any* foreign power, but that we had not surrendered any treaty rights that we had. I suggested to him that his Government might say to Japan that wherever we were quoted as favoring or consenting to anything, China should claim the privilege of communicating with us directly in order to avoid any possible misunderstanding.

"Japan could hardly object to China inquiring of us in regard to any matter concerning which Japan presumes to quote us.

"In other words—Japan could not expect to speak for us in dealing with China. China would expect to speak to us and have our position directly from us." W. J. Bryan to W.W., April 15, 1915, Bryan Papers, National Archives.

[69] There is some evidence that this was true in the matter-of-fact way in which Bryan commented on the alleged disparity between the versions of the demands and "requests" that the Japanese Minister had presented to China and to Minister Reinsch. "You will notice," Bryan wrote to Wilson, "that there is some discrepancy." He was apparently disturbed only by the discrepancy in the demand concerning the Han-Yeh-P'ing Iron and Coal Company. The Japanese memorandum (given to both Reinsch and the State Department) had included only a single demand regarding this company,

bering that his government was on record in its note to Japan of March 13 as not objecting to most of the Japanese demands, must have concluded that such a radical change of policy would not be possible in any event.

It was, therefore, with a keen memory of previous American commitments and concessions that the Secretary of State carefully prepared a reply to Reinsch's telegram of April 14 and sent it to the President for his approval. A simple statement of American interest and concern, it authorized the Minister in Peking to make an informal statement in the following sense: "The American Government has not surrendered any of its treaty rights in China or abated one iota of its friendly interest in all that concerns the industrial and political welfare of China. It is awaiting the results of the present negotiations in the confident expectation that the rights and obligations of the United States will not be affected or its interests impaired."

This, precisely, was the juncture at which the President first began to take hold of far eastern policy in a decisive way. All along he had been more suspicious of the Japanese than Bryan;[70] now, obviously, he was determined to have an end to Bryan's policy of neutral mediation and to strike out upon a new course. As he explained in two letters to the Secretary of State:

"I am very uneasy about what is going on, as reported by Mr. Reinsch, and must frankly admit that I do not credit the assurances

---

namely, that Japanese subjects be given an equal share in its ownership and operation. The full text revealed that the Japanese had also demanded that the Chinese government grant a monopoly on mining operations to the newly constituted Sino-Japanese concern in "the neighborhood" of the mines owned by the company. The newspapers had reported this demand two weeks before, and Bryan had already sent an inquiry to Tokyo on April 2. See the Secretary of State to Ambassador Guthrie, April 2, 1915, *Foreign Relations, 1915*, p. 119.

Actually, Bryan was right in his conclusion, stated to the President, that the discrepancies between the two versions of the Japanese demands were not very great. As he pointed out to Wilson, most of them arose from the fact that the copy of the Japanese memorandum with which Reinsch had compared the full text of the treaty had not included the "requests" in Group V, about which the American government had long since been informed. W. J. Bryan to W.W., April 16, 1915, State Department Papers.

[70] Wilson's fears must have been greatly intensified by the long telegram that he received on about April 12 from the American political advisers and certain American missionary leaders in Peking. This was a violent denunciation of Japan's allegedly rapacious imperialism and militarism and a fervid appeal to the President to throw the full support of the American government behind the Chinese cause. Charles F. Hubbard *et al.* to W.W., "Peking: Memorial to the President," April 8, 1915, Wilson Papers.

the Japanese have sought to give us. I wish that you might find an opportunity to express to the Japanese ambassador the grave concern we feel at hearing that his government is insisting upon the acquiescence of the Chinese government in the 'Requests,' because they are so clearly incompatible with the administrative independence and autonomy of the Chinese Empire [*sic*] and with the maintenance of the policy of an open door to the world.

"In short, I feel that we should be as active as the circumstances permit in showing ourselves to be the champions of the sovereign rights of China, now as always, though with no thought of seeking any special advantage for ourselves. In this way only can we make good this [Bryan's proposed] message to Reinsch."[71]

"The aspects of this matter between Japan and China change so often as our information grows more complete that I am convinced that we shall have to try in every way practicable to defend China. . . . We shall have to be very chary hereafter about seeming to concede the reasonableness of any of Japan's demands or requests either, until we get the whole of the situation in our minds by hearing from Peking as well as Tokyo."[72]

This was strong language to begin with, but it assumed a new and almost extraordinary meaning when Wilson went on, in the first letter quoted above, to comment on the draft of Bryan's note to Reinsch affirming the concern of the American government for its treaty rights in China and for that country's "industrial and political welfare." He hoped, the President wrote, that the Secretary would send the telegram, but he wondered whether Reinsch had been told definitely that it was not true that the State Department had "acquiesced in *any* of Japan's demands," as Count Okuma, the Japanese Premier, had been quoted by the newspapers as saying. Obviously, Wilson had simply forgotten the sweeping concessions implied in certain fateful sentences of the note to Japan of March 13, sentences that he had read and approved.[73] Obviously, he was ready to begin anew, as if the preceding negotiations with Japan had not occurred.

[71] W.W. to W. J. Bryan, April 14, 1915, Bryan Papers, National Archives.

[72] W.W. to W. J. Bryan, April 16, 1915, State Department Papers.

[73] They are important enough to bear repetition here: "While on principle and under the treaties of 1844, 1858, 1868 and 1903 with China the United States has ground upon which to base objections to the Japanese 'demands' relative to Shantung, South Manchuria, and East Mongolia, nevertheless the United States frankly recognizes that territorial contiguity creates special relations between Japan and these districts. This Govern-

It was not, however, so easy for Bryan to wipe out the past. The records do not tell us whether he reminded the President of the compromising parts of the note to Japan of March 13 or pointed out in some other way the difficulty of making any such denial to Reinsch as Wilson had suggested. In any event, when Bryan sent his statement to Peking on April 15 he added the following sentence: "For your own information you will say that you have received copies of all our communications from which you will see that we have not acquiesced in anything that violates China's rights or disregards this Nation's interests."[74] This was something like the President wanted Bryan to say, even if it did stretch the truth.

The main problem confronting the Secretary of State during the last two weeks of April and the early part of May was the difficult one of shifting American policy to an open defense of China without seeming to repudiate past concessions to the Japanese and without giving the appearance of gratuitous meddling at this late stage in the Sino-Japanese negotiations. In a telegram on April 24, 1915, Reinsch suggested a method and provided the opportunity for entering the controversy in a really serious way. Pointing to the recent manifestations of British alarm, particularly at the threat posed by the Japanese demand for railroad concessions in the Yangtze Valley, the British sphere of influence in China, the Minister suggested that the British and French might welcome a circular note from the Washington government calling upon all the powers to renew their allegiance to the principles of Chinese integrity and the Open Door. Indeed, Reinsch added, "from such reports as have come to me in regard to the attitude and apprehensions of [the] British Legation here I have inferred that the British Government might welcome such a proposal as a means of determining the disposition and intentions of Japan with respect to the [Anglo-Japanese] alliance."[75]

---

ment, therefore, is disposed to raise no question, at this time, as to Articles I and II of the Japanese proposals."

It should perhaps be said that only a pettifogging legalist would argue that the phrase "at this time" was an important qualification to the concessions that the preceding sentences had made.

[74] The Secretary of State to Minister Reinsch, April 15, 1915, *The Lansing Papers*, II, 417.

[75] Minister Reinsch to the Secretary of State, April 24, 1915, State Department Papers.

It is likely that the London Foreign Office had instructed the British Minister in Peking, Sir J. Jordan, to make such an intimation personally and informally to Reinsch. One cannot be certain that this was true until the correspondence between the Foreign

Wilson and Bryan discussed Reinsch's suggestion, perhaps on April 25, and agreed that Bryan should draft a preliminary note of warning to Japan. Completed and submitted to the President on April 27, it was filled with assurances of friendship but left no doubt that the

---

Office and the British Legation in Peking is opened to view, but the documents in the Archives of the Imperial Japanese Foreign Office reveal that the British Foreign Office had become seriously alarmed by the twenty-one demands and had already taken steps by mid-April to restrain the Japanese government. Since so little has been known heretofore concerning the role that the British played in the far eastern crisis of 1915, the following review of the early discussions between London and Tokyo might be in order:

The British Foreign Office first learned officially of the twenty-one demands in early February, when the Japanese Foreign Office handed a copy of its first memorandum on the demands to the British Embassy in Tokyo. (British Embassy to the Japanese Foreign Office, February 6, 1915, transmitting a telegram from Sir E. Grey dated February 5, 1915, Japanese F. O. Archives.)

On February 22 the British Foreign Secretary, Sir Edward Grey, sent his first important comment on the twenty-one demands to Tokyo, saying that he was confident that the Imperial government would be ready to discuss the question whether the demands upon China conflicted with British economic interests and concessions, and adding: "I am very anxious that the Japanese Government should refrain from advancing any demands which could reasonably be considered to impair the integrity or independence of China, as I should find myself in a difficult position if I were to be asked to explain how it was possible to reconcile such demands with the terms of the Alliance between England and Japan." (Memorandum handed by the British Ambassador to Baron T. Kato, February 22, 1915, *ibid.*)

The British Ambassador, Sir W. C. Greene, presented this note to Baron Kato on February 22 and supplemented it with an additional memorandum concerning the question of Japanese railroad development in the Yangtze Valley on March 10, 1915. (The British Ambassador to Baron Kato, March 10, 1915, *ibid.*) At the same time, Grey made it clear in a separate note that the British Foreign Office regarded the question of Japanese economic penetration into the British sphere of influence as a "minor point." "What causes me anxiety," he added, "is the possibility of general political developments arising out of the Japanese negotiations with China. . . . I have heard in one Japanese quarter, though not an official one, there has been entertainment of a forcible occupation of Peking by Japan with object of obtaining a controlling influence over all China. I hope that Japan will be patient in negotiations with China for I cannot believe that China will be so unreasonable as to resist all the Japanese demands. At the same time I trust Japan will not press demands which will impair present regime in China. My desire is to be able to say, if other Powers approach me, that there is nothing in Japanese action which conflicts with Anglo-Japanese Alliance and that I am therefore prepared to justify Japanese action, or, if required, to support it. . . . I recognise that there must be an expansion of Japanese interests and influence in China as there has been in case of other Powers, and that Japan naturally expects to see this increased but I am most anxious situation should not arise at this moment involving conflict between Japan and China and all the complications that might ensue." (Telegram from Sir E. Grey, March 9, 1915, handed to Baron Kato on March 17, 1915, by the British Ambassador, *ibid.*)

American government was about to enter the far eastern crisis in an active, public way. After indirectly rebuking Japan for increasing the number of its troops in China, failing to honor its promise that it would not attempt to force the "requests" in Group V upon China, and attempting to gain control of Chinese iron and steel resources, the note concluded with a pointed warning. "The embarrassment caused to both our Government and yours," it read, "by the privacy of our representations to Japan and by the fact that we have not felt free to confer with China regarding matters covered by treaty between the United States and China raises the question whether it might not be better for all parties for us to make our views public. Your Government has felt it necessary to give out statements from time to time and our silence has invited speculation and misrepresentation."[76]

Wilson's comment revealed again that he was eager to move further and faster than his Secretary of State, and specifically that he was now contemplating some kind of a circular note to the powers. He thought, Wilson wrote, that Bryan's draft was excellent and said things that ought to be said. "But I was thinking," he added, ". . . that the real weakness of our influence in the matter lay in the *privacy* of our representations to Japan with regard to it. I think, therefore, that it would be wise to say to the Japanese Ambassador that our position with regard to these important matters, of which treaties with China as well as our general interest in the position China is to take in the economic development of her resources give us a right to speak, has been so generally misunderstood and so misleadingly speculated about that we feel that it may become immediately necessary to make our views public, *perhaps* in conjunction with other nations whose interests and sympathies are equally involved. . . . This, I am convinced, is the only means we have of reassuring China, our own people, and other governments at present less free than we to protest.

"I think, too, that we ought to instruct Reinsch to assure the Chinese government that it has our sympathy in resisting any demands which too seriously impinge upon its sovereignty, its administrative independence, or its territorial integrity."[77]

Bryan seems to have agreed but suggested that it might be wiser to add the warning about the circular note orally to the Japanese Am-

[76] W. J. Bryan to Viscount S. Chinda, April 27, 1915, Bryan Papers, National Archives.

[77] W.W. to W. J. Bryan, April 27, 1915, *The Lansing Papers*, II, 417-418.

bassador. Wilson concurred,[78] and Bryan then apparently forgot the oral postscript when he presented his note to Viscount Chinda at the State Department on April 29. Chinda was evidently greatly agitated by the note. Saying that he feared that the reference to the increase of Japanese military forces in China would be particularly embarrassing to his government, Chinda appears to have asked whether the Secretary would be willing to redraft his communication without reference to this matter. Bryan must have agreed.[79]

The Japanese Ambassador was probably playing for time in the hope that events in Peking would remove the pretext or opportunity for any American intervention by way of an appeal to the powers. The fact was that the Sino-Japanese negotiations had already reached a climax by the time that Bryan and Chinda had their conference on April 29. The Japanese Minister in Peking had presented a new draft treaty to the Chinese authorities only three days before, warning at the same time that it was the Imperial government's final offer.

Chinda apparently did not have an exact copy of the "amended project," as the Japanese called their new proposals, when he talked with Bryan on April 29. Perhaps, however, the Ambassador knew enough to intimate what would become evident once a copy had reached Washington—that the Japanese authorities had made an earnest effort to meet almost all important American objections to the original twenty-one demands. The "amended project" included all the original demands in Groups I and II relating to Shantung, South Manchuria, and Inner Mongolia, which the Washington government had tacitly approved in its note of March 13. The new treaty added a promise to return the former German leasehold at Kiaochow to China under certain conditions, but offset it with certain new minor

---

[78] "I dare say you are quite right," Wilson replied on April 28 to a letter from Bryan, a copy of which cannot be found. "Perhaps what I had in mind might be better accomplished by your handing this communication [Bryan to Chinda, April 27, 1915] to the Ambassador in person and taking occasion to say to him that, inasmuch as the subject matter of the relations of China to the rest of the world had more than once been the subject of correspondence between the United States and the chief European powers, it might become our duty to make our position clear (and invite comment) by means of a circular note. I mean, just to intimate this to him as something we had in mind as possible." W.W. to W. J. Bryan, April 28, 1915, Bryan Papers, National Archives.

[79] As Bryan seems to have intimated in W. J. Bryan to W.W., May 3, 1915, *The Lansing Papers*, II, 421-422. Chinda reported the gist of this conversation, however, without waiting to receive the revised note, in Viscount Chinda to Baron Kato, Telegram No. 139, received on May 2, 1915, Japanese F. O. Archives.

demands for extraterritorial rights for Japanese subjects in South Manchuria. It was in the balance of the new treaty that the success of Bryan's efforts and, it must be added, the restraining influence of the British Foreign Office, could be most clearly seen. In the revised Group III the Japanese still sought to gain a large share in the control of the Han-Yeh-P'ing Company, but they dropped their demand that this company be given a monopoly on the operation of all mines in the neighboring area. As for Group IV, the Japanese accepted the Chinese government's pledge that it would not alienate any part of its coast to *any* foreign power. Finally, the new draft treaty reiterated the "requests" in Group V,[80] but they had been softened in an effort to make them unobjectionable to the United States and Great Britain.[81]

Ambassador Chinda delivered a memorandum detailing the revised demands to the Secretary of State on April 30, at the very time that Bryan was preparing a second draft of his note to the Tokyo government. As he indicated in a long letter to the President, Bryan was immensely pleased by the Imperial government's efforts to meet American objections. But either Bryan did not realize how much he had already achieved or else, as seems more likely, his own attitude toward Japan had severely hardened. In any event, in his letter to the President he suggested objecting to every single remaining and new Japanese proposal that seemed to infringe Chinese sovereignty, even the proposal for certain extraterritorial rights for Japanese subjects in South Manchuria. Indeed, Bryan's letter revealed that he, like Wilson, was also prepared virtually to ignore some of the earlier concessions embodied in the note of March 13, and that he was even beginning to think in terms of using American capital to neutralize Japan's modified "request" for the construction of railroads in central and southern China.[82]

With Wilson's entire approval Bryan redrafted his note to Tokyo in this new spirit on May 4, 1915. Aiming it specifically at the provisions of the "amended project" dealing with extraterritoriality in South Manchuria, the Han-Yeh-P'ing Company, and the revised "requests," the Secretary of State made it clear that his government would soon

[80] Except for the "requests" concerning Fukien Province, upon which agreement had already been reached, and joint policing, which was entirely withdrawn.

[81] Minister Reinsch to the Secretary of State, April 27, 1915, State Department Papers; undated memorandum handed to the Secretary of State by the Japanese Ambassador on April 30, 1915, *Foreign Relations, 1915*, pp. 128-130; "The Amended Japanese Proposals," *ibid.*, pp. 163-166.

[82] W. J. Bryan to W.W., May 3, 1915, *The Lansing Papers*, II, 418-422.

have to make a public pronouncement. "Our silence," he wrote, "has been misinterpreted and our position misunderstood. The papers, according as it suited their purpose, have represented us as agreeing to proposals submitted, or as objecting to demands made. We are convinced that a frank statement of this Nation's position will contribute to a solution of the problems involved, and that the time has come when we must make such a statement."[83]

Bryan delivered this note to the Japanese Ambassador on May 5.[84] On the following day he gave his threatened statement, which the President had read and approved,[85] to the newspapers for publication on May 7 and sent copies to Peking and Tokyo. In clear and ringing terms it announced the new policy of no concessions to Japan to the world:

> In order that there may be no misunderstanding of the position of the United States in reference to the negotiations pending between Japan and China the following announcement is made:
>
> At the beginning of negotiations the Japanese Government confidentially informed this Government of the matters which were under discussion and accompanied the information by the assurance that Japan had no intention of interfering with either the political independence or territorial integrity of China, and that nothing that she proposed would discriminate against other Powers having treaties with China, or interfere with the "Open Door" policy to which all the leading nations are committed.
>
> This Government has not only had no thought of surrendering any of its treaty rights with China, but it has never been asked by either Japan or China to make any surrender of these rights. There is no abatement of its interest in the welfare and progress of China and its sole interest in the present negotiations is that they may be concluded in a manner satisfactory to both nations, and that the terms of the agreement will not only contribute to the prosperity of both of these great Oriental empires but maintain that cordial relationship so essential to the future of both, and to the peace of [the] world.[86]

Bryan's note to Chinda of May 5 and his public statement of the following day came too late to have any direct effect on the final stage of the negotiations in Peking and deliberations in Tokyo. The

[83] W. J. Bryan to Viscount S. Chinda, May 5, 1915, Bryan Papers, National Archives.
[84] For the copy in the Japanese Foreign Office Archives, see Viscount S. Chinda to Baron T. Kato, Telegram No. 144, received May 7 [May 6, Washington time], 1915.
[85] W.W. to W. J. Bryan, May 5, 1915, Bryan Papers, National Archives.
[86] As printed in *Foreign Relations, 1915*, p. 143.

Chinese authorities responded to the revised Japanese treaty on May 1 by accepting most of the demands in the first four groups, rejecting some of them, and refusing to consider the revised "requests" in Group V, except the one relating to Fukien Province.[87] When Japanese newspapers reported on May 4 that the Imperial Cabinet had voted to present an ultimatum,[88] however, the Chinese leaders, panic-stricken, offered to make substantial concessions on the "requests."[89] But the ultimatum which the Japanese Minister presented on May 7 demanded Chinese acceptance, by six p.m. on May 9, only of the first four groups of the "amended project" and the "request" concerning Fukien. It declared specifically that the Imperial government, "prompted by the desire to bring the present negotiations to a satisfactory close and avoid the development of any serious complication in the situation," was willing to withdraw the balance of the revised "requests" in Group V and to reserve them for future discussion.[90]

The decision to abandon Group V and the ambitions that it embodied was a major concession, and the reasons for it are now not hard to find. It came only after a hard struggle between Baron Kato and the extraconstitutional body of four men known as the *Genro* or Elder Statesmen, who acted as advisers to the Emperor on all important matters of state. At the outset the *Genro* had consented to the inclusion of Group V among the demands to be presented to China.[91] Relations between the Elder Statesmen and Kato had become severely strained by early May, however, because Kato had been attempting to establish the complete independence of the Foreign Office and the *Genro* resented this fact, and particularly because the *Genro* feared Kato's aggressiveness in foreign policy and had been upset at the way in which he had dealt with the great powers during the negotiations with China.

The showdown came on May 4, at a joint conference of the *Genro* and the members of the Imperial Cabinet which had been called to obtain

[87] Minister Reinsch to the Secretary of State May 3 and 4, 1915, *ibid.*, pp. 130-131, 137-141; "The Final Amended Project of the Chinese Government," handed to Minister Hioki on May 1, 1915, *ibid.*, pp. 166-168.

[88] e.g., Tokyo *Yomiuri*, May 4, 1915.

[89] Minister Reinsch to the Secretary of State, May 17, 1915, *Foreign Relations, 1915*, p. 149.

[90] Minister Reinsch to the Secretary of State, May 7, 1915, *ibid.*, p. 144; "Japan's Ultimatum to China," handed by Minister Hioki to the Chinese Minister of Foreign Affairs, May 7, 1915, *ibid.*, pp. 168-170.

[91] T. E. La Fargue, *China and the World War*, pp. 73-74, summarizing M. Ito, *Kato Takaaki Den* (Biography of *Count Takaaki Kato*), II, 198.

the permission of the Elder Statesmen for the dispatch of an ultimatum to China after the Cabinet had approved the sending of the ultimatum and the inclusion of Group V in the terms to be demanded. Objecting, the *Genro* pointed to the recent diplomatic dispatches and the signs of warning that they conveyed. There was, to begin with, a message from the Japanese Ambassador in London hinting darkly of impending severe trouble with America if the Imperial government pressed its demands on China too hard.[92] Even more alarming were two recent messages from the British Foreign Secretary, Sir Edward Grey. The first, dated April 29, was a preliminary comment on the Japanese "amended project" of April 26 and a general warning against any rupture over Group V.[93] The second, dated May 3, by implication accused the Japanese government of duplicity and threatened a rupture of the Anglo-Japanese Alliance if war ensued over Group V. It read:

"Sir Edward Grey believes that the only question of the Japanese demands now outstanding is Group 5, and, if this is so, he hopes most earnestly that there will not be a rupture between China and Japan. The group in question was not even included in the first information given to His Majesty's Government, and its contents were described as 'wishes.' Some doubt appears to exist as to what is the exact meaning of these demands. The demand respecting the appointment of Japanese advisers, according to the wording given to us, appears reasonable but it is said to be construed at Peking as meaning that the Japanese are to have a majority of all new foreign advisers, that is to say more than all foreign countries put together. This would be but little removed from a protectorate over China.

"The construction placed on the demand respecting supply of arms and ammunition is also that the right of exclusive supply in future is being secured to Japan. If any ground existed for ascribing a rupture between Japan and China to the latter having declined to accept the demands which were open to this construction, it would in the eye of public opinion in England be impossible to reconcile the position thus erected with the terms of the Anglo-Japanese Alliance.

"Sir Edward Grey hopes therefore either that Japan will refrain from insisting on these points or that she will make it clear that the

[92] Ambassador Inoue to Baron Kato, Telegram No. 269, May 4, 1915, Japanese F. O. Archives.

[93] Sir E. Grey to Sir W. C. Greene, April 29, 1915, handed by the British Embassy to the Imperial Foreign Office, May 2, 1915, *ibid.*

construction which is being placed on the demands in some quarters is erroneous.

"The question of railways is rather one of adjusting special British and Japanese commercial interests than of general policy and I will telegraph separately on this subject."[94]

To the Elder Statesmen, who had helped to build Japanese foreign policy upon the foundation of cooperation with Great Britain, these words were inexpressibly painful. One of them, Prince Matsukata, even went so far as to accuse Foreign Minister Kato of disgracing Japan's good name by trying to keep Group V secret from its ally.[95] The meeting adjourned soon afterward, with the *Genro* declaring

[94] Sir E. Grey to the British Embassy, Tokyo, May 3, 1915, delivered to the Japanese Foreign Office, May 4, 1915, *ibid.*

This telegram was the outgrowth of discussions that had taken place in the British Foreign Office during late April following the receipt from the Japanese Ambassador in London of an *aide-mémoire* on the "amended project" of April 26, which, after explaining the new proposals in the "amended project," went on to say that failure of Japan's negotiations with China "might even render it difficult for us to fulfil our share in the realisation of the objects of the Anglo-Japanese Alliance."

Studying the *aide-mémoire*, officials in the British Foreign Office were both alarmed and outraged. "This is hypocrisy," they agreed at a staff meeting on April 30, 1915 "Japan's action in connection with the demands throughout has been calculated precisely to break the peace and destroy the objects of the Alliance. The excuse [is] that the refusal of the present terms may break up the Alliance and that they are well aware that this will be contrary to the spirit and text of the Alliance, but that they are ready to sacrifice the Alliance to gain their ends." "I cannot help thinking," one of the members present at this meeting added, "that Baron Kato's allusion to Alliance is bluff, to get us to give in over the Yang-tsze railway questions, and to agree that the rest of the modified proposals are reasonable—some of which infring[e] the open door, sovereign rights, and the integrity of China in a barefaced manner." "The situation as between Japan and China is becoming serious," Sir Edward Grey and Arthur Nicholson, the Permanent Undersecretary of State for Foreign Affairs, commented later as they laid the entire matter before the Cabinet, "and the question of our Alliance threatens to become also a debatable point. The question altogether is of such seriousness, especially in regard to possible developments, that it emerges from being a departmental one." The foregoing is based upon and taken from *Japanese Demands on China*, a Cabinet paper initialed by E. Grey and dated May 1, 1915, a copy of which is in the Asquith Papers. It contains the following: (1) the Japanese *aide-mémoire* of about April 27, 1915; (2) a translation of a telegram sent by the Imperial Foreign Office to the Japanese Minister in Peking on April 22, 1915; (3) "Minutes" of a Foreign Office meeting of April 30, 1915; (4) a memorandum on the far eastern crisis by "W. L."; and (5) a concluding note by Grey and Nicholson.

It might be added that Grey did lay this whole matter before the Cabinet on May 6, 1915, and that the Cabinet approved the Foreign Office's position. See the Prime Minister to the King, May 7, 1915, *ibid.*

[95] Iichiro Tokutomi, *Koshaku Matsukata Masayoshi Den (Biography of Prince Masayoshi Matsukata)*, II, 919-920.

that they would not give their consent to the proposed ultimatum. Conferences among the Japanese leaders ensued during the evening of May 4, until the deadlock was broken by the suggestion of Home Minister Oura that the Imperial Foreign Office should withdraw Group V from the ultimatum, and that the *Genro* in turn should approve the sending of the ultimatum in this amended form. Thus it was decided by the Cabinet that same evening and confirmed by the *Genro* at a joint conference on the following day.[96] As has already been said, the ultimatum was dispatched to Peking on May 7, 1915.

Meanwhile, rumors that the Japanese Cabinet were preparing an ultimatum arrived in Washington on May 4, just as Bryan and Wilson were discussing the new draft of Bryan's note to Tokyo concerning the Japanese "amended project." The Secretary of State voiced his alarm to Ambassador Chinda when he presented the note on May 5.[97] At the same time, without the faintest notion of the contents of the impending Japanese ultimatum, Bryan hurriedly dispatched a message to Peking, urging the Chinese to continue the negotiations "in a spirit of patience and friendliness";[98] a personal appeal to Premier Okuma;[99] and, an hour later, an urgent invitation to the British, French, and Russian governments to join the Washington authorities in a "friendly but earnest appeal to Japan and China to continue their negotiations in the spirit of patience and friendship until a satisfactory conclusion is reached."[100]

This outburst of activity certainly did no good even if it did no real harm. The appeal to the powers fell completely flat. The French and Russian governments apparently did not even deign to reply. Sir Edward Grey responded on May 7 by giving Ambassador Page a copy

[96] Iichiro Tokutomi, *Koshaku Yamagata Aritomo Den (Biography of Prince Aritomo Yamagata)*, II, 931. See also Marius B. Jansen, *The Japanese and Sun Yat-sen*, pp. 183-184, and particularly Professor Hackett's biography of Prince Yamagata, previously cited, which contains the fullest account in the English language of the memorable meetings of May 4 and 5, 1915.

[97] I infer this from W. J. Bryan to W.W., May 4, 1915, and W.W. to W. J. Bryan, May 5, 1915, both in the Bryan Papers, National Archives, in which the Secretary of State and the President discussed what Bryan should say to the Japanese Ambassador.

[98] The Secretary of State to Minister Reinsch, May 6, 1915, *The Lansing Papers*, II, 422.

[99] The Secretary of State to Chargé Wheeler, May 6, 1915, *ibid.*, pp. 422-423.

[100] The Secretary of State to Ambassador Page, May 6, 1915; the same, *mutatis mutandis*, to the American Ambassadors in France and Russia, *ibid.*, p. 423.

of his own appeal for a continuation of peaceful negotiations,[101] and by saying that now that Japan had withdrawn Group V—definite news of the Imperial Cabinet's ultimatum had meanwhile come to the West—he was urging the Chinese government to comply with the final Japanese demands.[102] The leaders in Tokyo were not only irritated but also fearful lest Bryan's last-ditch effort embolden the Chinese to reject their ultimatum.[103] Count Okuma returned a waspish reply to Bryan's personal message, intimating that the Japanese government had thus far made the largest concessions, and that the United States could best serve the cause of peace in the Far East by letting the Chinese know that they would receive no further support from Washington.[104] Acting by instruction of the Imperial Foreign Office, Viscount Chinda, on May 8, lodged an official protest against Bryan's invitation to the powers.[105]

It is possible that even Bryan felt a little foolish as events unfolded on the day after the dispatch of his peace appeals. A telegram from Reinsch in Peking arrived at the State Department on May 7, probably during the morning. It described the terms of the Japanese ultimatum as being "in fact almost identical with those conceded by China as reported in my telegram of May 3 . . . and on the surface less exigent than those which this [the Chinese] Government informally offered to concede yesterday," and telling of the withdrawal of Group V.[106] Then later in the day came confirmation from London, together with the news that Sir Edward Grey was advising the Chinese government to accept the ultimatum.[107] Surprised and enormously relieved by the Japanese government's moderation, the Secretary of State was almost effusive when the Japanese Ambassador came to his office on May 8 to deliver Count Okuma's reply to Bryan's personal message. "I told him," the Secretary informed the President, comment-

[101] It was a copy of a memorandum that Grey had handed to Ambassador Inoue on May 6, 1915, and is printed in *ibid.*, p. 425.

[102] Ambassador Page to the Secretary of State, May 7, 1915, *ibid.*, pp. 424-425.

[103] As Ambassador Chinda told Bryan on May 6, Viscount Chinda to Baron Kato, Telegram No. 147, received May 8, 1915, Japanese F. O. Archives.

[104] Count Okuma to the Secretary of State, May 8, 1915, transmitted in Ambassador Chinda to W. J. Bryan, May 9, 1915, Bryan Papers, National Archives.

[105] Baron Kato to Viscount Chinda, Telegram No. 85, May 8, 1915; Viscount Chinda to Baron Kato, Telegram No. 152, received May 9, 1915, both in the Japanese F. O. Archives.

[106] Minister Reinsch to the Secretary of State, May 7, 1915, *Foreign Relations, 1915*, p. 144.

[107] See above, fns. 101 and 102.

ing on Okuma's suggestion that the American government might do well not to interfere, "we were not contemplating sending *any* advice to China & that our information was to the effect that terms would be accepted by China. I expressed gratification that group five had been withdrawn." It was a great relief "at such a time as this" (news of the torpedoing of the *Lusitania* had come only the day before), Bryan added, to know that the matter was thus "all settled."[108] "We consider the Japanese concession, especially the withdrawal of Group V," Chinda reported Bryan as saying, "as having been due to your Government's taking our wishes into account. We appreciate it very much."[109]

Bryan, obviously, was eager to leave well enough alone, particularly after the Chinese submitted to the Japanese ultimatum without ado on May 9, 1915.[110] In view of the American note to Japan of March 13 and the subsequent Japanese-American agreement over the Fukien question, American silence now would be tantamount to acquiescence in the Sino-Japanese settlement, except for the several relatively minor points to which Bryan had objected in his note of May 5, and for the somewhat vague reservation of American treaty rights made in Bryan's public statement of May 6. This reservation of rights would be useful if Japan attempted any further *démarches* in the future, but Bryan was certainly not inclined to regard it as constituting a withdrawal of concessions already made.

It was, however, considerably different with the man in the White House. He was presumably relieved like Bryan at the peaceful outcome in Peking. But his suspicions of Japanese intentions had deepened;[111] he felt no gratitude to the Imperial government for its efforts to meet American and British wishes; and he was now more than ever determined to repudiate American approval of any part of the Sino-Japanese settlement that impaired the Open Door. He would do this, he informed the Secretary of State, by publishing a statement that Lansing had prepared *at the time when it seemed that Japan was*

[108] W. J. Bryan to W.W., May 8, 1915, *The Lansing Papers*, II, 424. I have transposed these sentences.

[109] Viscount Chinda to Baron Kato, Telegram No. 152, received May 9, 1915, Japanese F. O. Archives.

[110] Minister Reinsch to the Secretary of State, May 9, 1915, *Foreign Relations, 1915*, p. 145.

[111] As Wilson put it in a letter to Bryan on May 10, 1915 (*The Lansing Papers*, II, 426), "The whole suspicious business has lost *for the time being* its critical character." Italics added.

preparing to impose Group V upon China, by war, if necessary.[112]
The President announced this intention in the following letter to Bryan
on May 10:

"In view of the situation as a whole (I mean the situation of the
world, politically) I think that it would be wise to file such a caveat
as Mr. Lansing suggests. It will not do to leave any of our rights indefinite or to seem to acquiesce in any part of the Japanese plan which
violates the solemn understandings of the nations with regard to China.

"It may favourably affect the Japanese official mind with regard to
the wisdom of postponing the discussion of Group V for a very long
time indeed."[113]

On the following day Bryan (whether reluctantly or cheerfully, we
do not know) put Lansing's statement on the wires to Tokyo and
Peking and gave it to the newspapers for publication. It follows:

> Please call upon the Minister for Foreign Affairs and present to him
> a note textually as follows:
> "In view of the circumstances of the negotiations which have taken
> place and which are now pending between the Government of Japan
> and the Government of China, and of the agreements which have been
> reached as a result thereof, the Government of the United States has the
> honor to notify the Imperial Japanese Government that it cannot recog-
> nize any agreement or undertaking which has been entered into or which
> may be entered into between the Governments of Japan and China,
> impairing the treaty rights of the United States and its citizens in China,
> the political or territorial integrity of the Republic of China, or the inter-
> national policy relative to China commonly known as the open door
> policy."[114]

What, in fact, did it mean? The answer all depended upon how
statesmen chose to interpret these words, both at the time they were
written and in the future. Wilson obviously meant the note to be,
as he said, a warning against any Japanese attempts to revive the "requests" in Group V at some future date. One might also *surmise* that
he intended the note of May 11 to be interpreted as withdrawing
American approval of the Japanese demands relating to South Manchuria and Inner Mongolia that clearly infringed the Open Door and
Chinese sovereignty in these areas, as some of them did.

[112] See R. Lansing to the Secretary of State, May 7, 1915, *ibid.*, p. 424.
[113] W.W. to W. J. Bryan, May 10, 1915, *ibid.*, p. 426.
[114] The Secretary of State to Ambassador Guthrie, May 11, 1915; the same, *mutatis
mutandis*, to the American Legation in China, *Foreign Relations, 1915*, p. 146.

Bryan, on the other hand, not only viewed the note of May 11 in a somewhat different light but, what was more important, also committed the Washington government to his own interpretation. This happened in the following manner: Puzzled by the wording of the note and alarmed by its possible implications, Ambassador Chinda on May 13 asked Bryan directly whether it meant that the American government intended to object to some particular points in the Sino-Japanese settlement. No, Bryan replied; the American leaders had had "no other intention than to clarify their position just as a *precaution*."[115]

Actually, the question whether the note of May 11 repudiated earlier American concessions to Japan was not important. The Japanese would proceed to consolidate their position in South Manchuria and Inner Mongolia, and to do so with the silent consent of the government in Washington. What was important was the fact that the note of May 11 did commit the American government to stern resistance to any further Japanese encroachments against China. In this sense, it was the historic document that historians have generally described it as being.

There is this final word to be said: The decision to play an active role as China's defender in the far eastern crisis of 1915 was made by President Wilson almost alone. Left on his own, Secretary Bryan probably would have approved a settlement (assuming that the Japanese had imposed it in the face of British opposition) that would have provided for a large increase in Japanese political influence over the central Chinese government. As we have seen, it was Wilson who intervened to reverse Bryan's policy of accommodation and who, at the end, set the American government implacably against any further Japanese expansion in China. In view of the future course of events in the Far East, the President was assuming a far larger responsibility than he knew.

[115] Viscount Chinda to Baron Kato, Telegram No. 159, received May 14, 1915, Japanese F. O. Archives.

CHAPTER X

The Challenge of the Submarine and Cruiser

AT the very moment that Wilson and Bryan were being drawn into the crisis in the Far East, new difficulties were mounting in the West. The landlocked Germans, using an untried weapon to strike at Britain, were loosing a submarine campaign against ocean-borne trade that threatened American ships and lives at sea. In retaliation, the British were severely tightening their already firm controls over neutral commerce, thus further abridging the ill-defined freedom of the seas. It was not a situation that made for restful nights in Washington—or in London or Berlin. It was one that would test the endurance and wisdom of the President and his advisers as they had never been tested before.

The German decision to launch a submarine war against maritime commerce—the *Handelskrieg mit U-Booten*—was exclusively responsible at the outset for the challenge to American peace that arose in the mid-winter of 1915. This is not to say that German-American relations were more than formally cordial during the early months of the war. Indeed, signs of tension on both sides had already become evident by the beginning of 1915.

There was on the German side first the bitterness that leaders and people felt on account of the export of American munitions to the Allies. Even though this traffic was still in its infancy, the German military and newspapers were pointing accusing fingers at the United States and commencing to stir the populace to what would soon become a high pitch of indignation. "Since my last [letter]," the American Ambassador in Berlin wrote on January 25, 1915, "the 'hate' campaign against America is assuming great proportions. *Zimmermann*, usually so quiet, when I went to see him the other day about some routine matter, was loaded and waiting for me. He showed me long list of firms and supplies going to the Allies from America, evidently from an effective spy system.[1] . . . He said that if he gave out the list

---

[1] Ambassador von Bernstorff and Captain Franz von Papen, the German Military Attaché who had offices in New York City, sent such reports frequently to Berlin. e.g., Ambassador von Bernstorff to the Foreign Office, December 14 and 22, 1914, and F. von Papen to the War Office, February 11, 1915, German F. O. Archives.

here it would cause war and he spoke of 500,000 trained Germans in America joining the Irish and starting a revolution to upset our present Government!!!"[2]

In addition, the suspicion was growing among the German leaders, particularly in the navy, that the Wilson administration neither intended nor wanted to make any effective challenge to the British maritime system, because such an effort might imperil the burgeoning war trade with the Allies and hence American prosperity and profits. This suspicion was first prompted by the American government's failure to respond to a German protest against alleged British violations of the Declaration of London.[3] It was reinforced in the official German mind when the Washington authorities refused to join the Danish government in denouncing the British mine decree of November 2, 1914, and sent their mild note of general protest to London afterward on December 28.[4]

A much more serious impediment, on the German side, to good relations between the two countries was the failure (one is tempted to say refusal) of most Germans to make any effort to understand the American people—their traditions, institutions, and national ideals —and the difficulties that the Washington government faced in trying to be neutral. The prevailing German image of America reflected all the worst features of its life—the crudities of the national culture, the materialism of the people, and so on—and almost none of the nobler ones. The American people, most Germans thought, were concerned only for profits and their own safety; and the high-flown idealism of their President was nothing more than a hypocritical veneer on policies designed to advance material interests.

On the American side there were also deeply rooted causes for distrust. In an earlier chapter we have seen the causes for the popular anti-German sentiment, which the leaders in Washington shared to

[2] J. W. Gerard to E. M. House, January 25, 1915, House Papers; also J. W. Gerard to W.W., January 24, 1915, Baker Collection.

[3] The German memorandum, dated October 10, 1914, is printed in *Foreign Relations, 1914, Supplement,* pp. 263-265. For comment on the failure of the American government to respond (actually, no one in Washington thought that the German government expected a reply), see Arno Spindler, *La Guerre Sous-Marine,* I, 41; hereinafter cited as Spindler, *La Guerre Sous-Marine.*

[4] Minister Rantzau, Copenhagen, to the Foreign Office, November 7, 1914; Ambassador von Bernstorff to the Foreign Office, November 12, 1914, both in the German F. O. Archives; "Memorandum of the Foreign Office concerning German Countermeasures . . . ," printed in Alfred von Tirpitz, *Politische Dokumente von A. von Tirpitz,* II, 290-292; hereinafter cited as Tirpitz, *Politische Dokumente.*

some degree.[5] In addition, the President and his advisers grew increasingly suspicious that the German government was directly encouraging the German Americans in their campaign for an arms embargo and that the Imperial authorities were anti-American in personal feeling.[6] Although Wilson, Bryan, and other officials in Washington usually made an honest effort to understand the problems and point of view of the German government, they could not escape these suspicions.

It must be said, finally, that relations between the two countries were not much strengthened by the men who served the President in Berlin and the Emperor in Washington on the eve of the greatest crisis in the history of German-American relations to this time. The Imperial Ambassador, Count von Bernstorff, was a trained diplomat of the old school, outwardly correct and proper; but he was far too wily and imperiously Prussian in appearance and manner ever to gain the President's intimacy, and he had the typical German opinion of the government to which he was accredited. Even so, Bernstorff fairly shone in comparison with his American counterpart in Berlin, James W. Gerard. This former dilettante in Tammany politics was an authentic international catastrophe. At a time when circumstances demanded tact, understanding, and wisdom from the American representative in Berlin, Gerard could offer only ineptitude, ignorance, and folly. The history of his gaucheries and blunders is too long to recount here.[7] Fortunately for the good relations of their countries, both the German and American authorities eventually took Gerard's measure and came more and more to rely upon the Counselor of the Embassy, a young career diplomat named Joseph C. Grew.

These irritants were, to be sure, like malign growths; they would have sunk their roots deeper as the war progressed and left a heritage of mutual bitterness for the future even if the submarine controversy

[5] Above, Chapter I, *passim*.

[6] Sending a copy of Gerard's letter reporting Zimmermann's alleged statement about a German and Irish uprising in America to Colonel House, the President commented, for example, "Is not the last paragraph amazing?" W.W. to E. M. House, January 28, 1915, Baker Collection. "Zimmermann's outbreak," House replied, "indicates the necessity of our holding to the friendship of England." E. M. House to W.W., January 29, 1915, Wilson Papers.

[7] Some of them are related by August Stein of the *Frankfurter Zeitung* to Undersecretary Zimmermann, September 1, 1914, German F. O. Archives, and by Henry White, a distinguished American diplomat (in response to the President's request that he investigate and report upon Gerard's behavior in Germany), in H. White to W.W., December 5, 1914, and April 5, 1915, Wilson Papers.

had not occurred. By themselves, however, they almost certainly would not have strained German-American relations to the breaking point. They were important, therefore, not for the immediate dangers that they posed but rather because they made mutual understanding and adjustment immensely difficult to achieve when the one issue capable of threatening the German-American peace, the issue of submarine warfare, did arise.

The decision to launch a submarine war against commerce originated in discussions that took place and plans that were made a few months before the fateful step was taken. The German navy entered the war with but twenty-eight submarines in service, and only twenty-five of these were capable of sailing the high seas. Fifteen were driven by gasoline-fired engines and were of limited range and endurance. The other ten were new long-range models powered by diesel engines, but they had not been thoroughly tested, and no one yet knew their remarkable capacities. From such a small force the leaders of the German navy did not expect great things in ordinary operations against enemy warships; no one in the Navy Ministry or the Admiralty had given any thought to the use of submarines as commerce destroyers.[8]

Altogether, the submarine proved to be almost totally valueless as an offensive weapon against enemy naval craft during the first months of hostilities. But two events occurred during this period that fired the imagination of the German public and planted the seeds of what would eventually become a U-boat obsession. The first was the sinking of the English cruiser *Pathfinder* by the *U21* on September 5, 1914; the other, the lucky destruction of three aged English cruisers, *Aboukir, Hogue,* and *Cressy,* by the old gasoline-driven *U9* on September 22. These were the sole tangible results of submarine operations during the first two months of the fighting.

There was, however, one intangible result that would soon change the course of history—the birth and spread of the idea of a submarine war against maritime commerce. Sailing on their futile cruises in the North Sea and the English Channel, submarine captains saw through their periscopes hundreds of slow-moving merchantmen, easy marks

[8] Nor had anyone in the navy at large, except for one Lieutenant Blum, judge advocate at the Submarine Station at Kiel, whose report of June 1914 suggesting the use of submarines in a future war against British commerce was buried until after the World War was over. The above discussion is based upon Spindler, *La Guerre Sous-Marine,* I, 187-214.

for their torpedoes. Inevitably they thought how simple it would be to sink them; and most of them returned home to argue for the inauguration of a submarine blockade. Not long afterward, on October 8, 1914, the head of the submarine fleet, one Captain Bauer, reiterated these arguments in a formal report to the commander of the High Seas Fleet, Admiral Friedrich von Ingenohl. Citing alleged British violations of international law as a good excuse for German reprisals, Bauer suggested sending submarines to stations off the eastern and western coasts of England, there to sink merchantmen without warning.[9] Von Ingenohl, who had earlier ignored the talk of the submarine skippers, forwarded Bauer's report to the head of the Admiralty, Admiral Hugo von Pohl, with an emphatic endorsement.[10] "Since England pays no attention to international law," von Ingenohl urged, "we need not limit ourselves by international law. . . . The more energetically the war is carried on, the more quickly will it be brought to a conclusion."[11]

At first von Pohl rejected the proposal on the ground that British practices did not justify such an extreme reprisal, but he quickly changed his mind after the British issued their mine decree of November 2, 1914. Writing to the Imperial Chancellor, Bethmann Hollweg, from Supreme Headquarters on November 7, the chief of German naval operations announced his alignment with the champions of the

[9] *ibid.*, pp. 12-19, 215-216.

[10] Perhaps a word about the German system of naval command would be helpful at this point. Ultimate authority lay with the Emperor as Supreme War Lord, whose adviser on naval affairs among his intimate entourage was an official known as the Chief of the Naval Cabinet. Directly responsible to the Emperor was the Imperial Chancellor who, although head of the civilian government, might exercise control through the Emperor when naval operations affected domestic or foreign policies. The Naval Ministry and its head, the Secretary of State for Naval Affairs, were responsible for nonoperational administration and constitutionally subordinate to the Imperial Chancellor. However, the Naval Secretary, Grand Admiral Alfred von Tirpitz, enjoyed influence and power far beyond the ordinary—the right, among others, of direct access to the Emperor, which the latter had granted at the outbreak of the war. Responsible for all planning and operations were the Admiralty and its head, who was in effect the chief of naval operations and whose orders went to the Chief of the High Seas Fleet and through him to commanders of divisions, stations, flotillas, etc. The head of the Admiralty was ordinarily responsible directly and only to the Emperor. At the outbreak of the war, however, the Emperor had commanded that the head of the Admiralty should confer with von Tirpitz and come to agreement with him on important operational policies.

[11] The Chief of the High Seas Fleet to the Head of the Admiralty, October 10, 1914, Tirpitz, *Politische Dokumente*, II, 281-282.

submarine and enclosed for the Chancellor's consideration the draft
of a proposed declaration of submarine blockade.[12]

From this point on until the end of January 1915, von Pohl pushed
an increasingly determined campaign for an early inauguration of a
Handelskrieg mit U-Booten. He bombarded the Foreign Office with
memoranda, requested the Chief of the High Seas Fleet, the commander of the submarine flotilla, and other naval officers to prepare technical reports on the possibilities of and plans for an underseas campaign, and appealed to Grand Admiral Alfred von Tirpitz, Secretary
of State for Naval Affairs and father of the German navy, to use his
great influence with the Emperor and the political leaders on behalf
of the navy's new cause. Excitement spread rapidly through the fleet
in the wake of von Pohl's crusade. To men who could have no real
hope of ever challenging Britain's dominion of the seas, the appeal
of the submarine was irresistible. It offered a means of getting the
navy into the war; it could hit the hated English where it hurt most;
more important, it was (so von Pohl and others now argued) the one
hope of victory. Although his embittered mind burned with malice
toward the mistress of the seas, von Tirpitz was not yet wholly de-
luded by false hopes. Time and again during November and December of 1914 he replied discouragingly to von Pohl, warning that the
navy did not have enough submarines for an effective blockade of
England, and urging caution upon the Admiralty and High Seas
Fleet.[13] Finally, however, on January 6, 1915, the Grand Admiral gave
his approval in principle, advising at the same time that the submarine campaign be inaugurated gradually and cautiously.[14]

The submarine fever had begun to spread also through the German
press and populace, a consequence, ironically, of Tirpitz's own boasting. On November 21, 1914, the Admiral had given an interview for
publication in the American press to Karl H. von Wiegand, head of
the United Press Bureau in Berlin. During a violent diatribe against
Britain and Japan, von Tirpitz had exclaimed: "America has not raised
her voice in protest and has taken little or no action against England's
closing of the North Sea to neutral shipping. What will America say

[12] The Head of the Admiralty to the Imperial Chancellor, November 7, 1914, *ibid.*,
pp. 283-285.

[13] e.g., A. von Tirpitz to H. von Pohl, November 9, 1914, *ibid.*, pp. 285-286, and the
marginal notes and letters printed in Spindler, *La Guerre Sous-Marine*, I, 53-54.

[14] A. von Tirpitz to H. von Pohl, January 6, 1915, Tirpitz, *Politische Dokumente*,
II, 296.

if Germany declares submarine war on all the enemy's merchant ships? Why not? England wants to starve us. We can play the same game. We can bottle her up and torpedo every English or allies' ship which nears any harbor in Great Britain."[15] Published in the German press on December 21, 1914,[16] these words by a public idol set German hopes ablaze. As Bethmann later remarked, "From this moment it was not possible to tear the submarine war from the heart of the nation."[17] Indeed, by early January the agitation in the press was already too strong for the Foreign Office to subdue it by censorship.[18]

It raised a host of problems for the men entrusted with responsibility for the foreign policy of the Empire, and above all for the Imperial Chancellor who, as the Emperor's personal spokesman, presumably had the final word in all questions with political ramifications. From the outset of the submarine discussions, the Foreign Office and the Chancellor took the stand that Germany had the undoubted right under the law of reprisal to institute an underseas campaign against *British* commerce, and that neutral governments had no just ground for complaint since they had acquiesced in Britain's violations of international law.[19] The political leaders were, however, enormously concerned about the reaction of the neutrals, particularly Italy and America.[20] The time for his submarine offensive, Foreign Secretary von Jagow told von Pohl early in December 1914, simply was not ripe. But the Admiralty chief came back more urgently on December 19, proposing a definite date, the end of January 1915, for the inauguration of the campaign. "In agreement with Your Excellency," he added, "I would not choose the form of a declaration of blockade,

[15] New York *World*, December 23, 1914.

[16] Actually, by a mistake of the Foreign Office. Von Wiegand submitted the transcript of the interivew to the Navy Ministry for approval. Officials there consented to publication provided the Foreign Office did not object, whereupon von Wiegand gave a copy to the censor of the Foreign Office on December 19, 1914, requesting permission to publish the interview in the German press. Thinking mistakenly that the interview had already appeared in the United States, the censor passed it for publication at home. See G. von Jagow to T. von Bethmann Hollweg, March 19, 1915, German F. O. Archives, and "Appendix I: The Wiegand Interview," Tirpitz, *Politische Dokumente*, II, 621-623.

[17] T. von Bethmann Hollweg, *Considérations sur la Guerre Mondiale*, II, 244.

[18] As Foreign Secretary von Jagow ruefully observed to Undersecretary Zimmermann in a letter dated January 17, 1915, German F. O. Archives.

[19] e.g., the Foreign Office to the Imperial Chancellor, November 30, 1914, printed in Spindler, *La Guerre Sous-Marine*, I, 60-61.

[20] The Imperial Chancellor to the Foreign Office, November 27, 1914; the Foreign Office (Zimmermann) to the Imperial Chancellor, November 30, 1914, *ibid.*, pp. 71-73.

since the formalities that are required by international law for a blockade cannot be fulfilled, but, following the British method, I would
choose the declaration of a certain war zone—in this case the English
Channel and all the waters that wash the English and Irish coasts—
and warn against sailing in these waters."[21]

The more the pressure mounted, the more did Bethmann know
that he would have to take a firmer stand. He had no high hopes
for the success of a submarine effort; indeed, he must have thought
it would have no good military results and only make reconciliation
with England more difficult. But he could not avow such sentiments
before the military chieftains, because he was already suspect as the
leader of a group who had worked for understanding with England
in the prewar period. In opposing the submarine campaign, he had
to sound very much like the Pan-Germans themselves.

From Supreme Headquarters at Charleville in France, on December
27, 1914, the Imperial Chancellor sent his decision to the Foreign
Office for transmittal to the Admiralty. In making plans for the speedy
termination of the war, he wrote, one had to discard all considerations
for England. The trouble was that the proposed U-boat blockade would
affect neutrals as well as the enemy. If the neutrals did nothing to
stop English terrorism at sea, then Germany should not hesitate to
use power and fear in dealing with them.[22] "The question for us now,"
he went on, "is at what point the resistance of the neutrals would become dangerous for us, and how far the advantages that we expect
to gain from the submarine war will outweigh the disadvantages
stemming from the resistance of the neutrals. . . . Thus the question
is whether dangers could arise from this [neutral] irritation which
would seriously threaten our position in the war." Because of her lack
of military power, America would hardly declare war. She would,
however, undoubtedly do everything possible to encompass Germany's

[21] H. von Pohl to the Foreign Secretary, December 19, 1914, German F. O. Archives.

[22] Bethmann qualified this somewhat stark statement in a subsequent paragraph, as
follows: "That the neutrals, by subjecting themselves to English policies, make themselves guilty of the English breach of international law, might be correct theoretically.
In actual fact, however, their attitude is determined by realistic facts. They cannot
fight against England; at least they believe that they cannot. The longer English
terrorism lasts, the more resentment against English rule of the seas will grow. And
this irritation will bear its fruits for us after the war, if we win it. Already England
has had to free cotton imports out of consideration for American interests. In the
three Scandinavian kingdoms (meeting at Malmö), the seeds of resistance to the
English yoke have been planted."

defeat. Moreover, Italy, Holland, and the Scandinavian neutrals would probably join the United States in a trade boycott against Germany, and English hopes of a complete economic blockade of the Central Powers would then be realized. "Under these conditions would we be in a position to endure a longer war?"

"The concern of the Foreign Office," Bethmann wrote in conclusion, "about the contemplated submarine blockade is, therefore, not of a legal nature but stems from considerations of a military and political nature. The question is not *if* but *when* the measures could be taken without harming our situation. In the East a decision has not been reached. In the West it has been brought to a standstill for more than two months. . . . A measure such as the submarine blockade, which would embitter the neutrals, can, according to our opinion here, be employed without dangerous consequences only if our military position on the Continent is so secure that the ultimate decision could be taken for granted and the danger of the neutrals going over to our enemies would be considered out of the question. Today this moment does not seem to have come."[23]

Like a man possessed, von Pohl drove on defiantly, for he now had seemingly conclusive proof to clinch his argument—a technical report on the possibilities of an underseas campaign by Captain Bauer, the commander of the submarine fleet. Bauer reported that it would indeed be possible to maintain an effective blockade of England with the small number of submarines on hand, provided they were permitted to sink merchantmen without warning and *without having to take undue pains to spare neutral shipping*. Going over the Chancellor's head, as he had a right to do, von Pohl appealed to the Emperor on January 7, 1915. Acknowledging Bethmann's objections, the admiral went on to answer them and to urge, "Nevertheless, we have in our versatile submarines a means in hand of cutting England's life line by means of a declaration of commercial blockade against her coasts and by hindering the commerce from which she gains her power of resistance and her superiority."[24]

Caught in the cross fire, the Emperor summoned von Pohl and

[23] "The Declaration of the Imperial Chancellor," December 27, 1914, German F. O. Archives; also printed in Tirpitz, *Politische Dokumente*, II, 292-295. Bethmann sent a copy of this statement to the head of the German General Staff, General Erich von Falkenhayn.

[24] Spindler, *La Guerre Sous-Marine*, I, 55-58; H. von Pohl, "The More Detailed Draft for the Memorandum Concerning the Further Use of Naval Forces," January 7, 1915, *ibid.*, pp. 78-79; Tirpitz, *Politische Dokumente*, II, 297-298.

Bethmann to his headquarters at Charleville on January 9. The admiral was emphatic, but the Chancellor stood his ground and had his way easily. "In that which affects the submarine war," William told von Pohl, "it is necessary to wait until the real uncertainty of the political situation has been removed. The approval of His Majesty must be solicited anew. While waiting, one should prepare the submarines for a war against commerce."[25]

Unrelenting, von Pohl redoubled his pressure on Bethmann and the Foreign Office, pleading that submarines could prevent the transport of the Argentine wheat harvest to England, that the neutral states of northern Europe were eager for the beginning of an underseas campaign, that America would offer no resistance out of fear of civil war at home if trouble with Germany ensued, and the like.[26] At the same time, pressure from the newspapers and populace for war to the death against England was daily mounting. On January 26, for example, a group of distinguished professors appealed to the Chancellor, the head of the Admiralty, and the commander of the High Seas Fleet to use all means at their disposal "in reply to the plan to starve the German people, which our enemies plot contrary to international law."[27]

Bethmann held out stubbornly for a few days. In a conference with von Pohl, General Erich von Falkenhayn, chief of the Great General Staff of the Army, and von Jagow on January 23, the Chancellor complained bitterly that he had been isolated by the navy's propaganda.[28] Talking with von Tirpitz four days later, he renewed his warning that America and Italy would retaliate against an underseas campaign that disturbed their commerce.[29] However, Bethmann's resistance was

[25] From the notes taken at the conference by Admiral Georg A. von Müller, Chief of the Naval Cabinet, printed in Spindler, *La Guerre Sous-Marine*, I, 80-81; Also A. von Tirpitz to the Crown Prince, January 14, 1915, Tirpitz, *Politische Dokumente*, II, 298.

[26] H. von Pohl to the Imperial Chancellor, January 20, 1915, German F. O. Archives.

[27] Cited in Spindler, *La Guerre Sous-Marine*, I, 92; for an example of the newspaper pressure, see the *Frankfurter Zeitung*, January 16, 1915, reprinting an article from the *Kölnische Zeitung*.

[28] H. von Pohl, memorandum dated January 23, 1915, Tirpitz, *Politische Dokumente*, II, 300.

[29] A. von Tirpitz, "Conference with the Imperial Chancellor on 27 January 1915," *ibid.*, pp. 300-303. Tirpitz agreed with Bethmann about postponing the submarine campaign until the coming spring or summer, but he did not share the Chancellor's fears of neutral countermeasures. "As far as North America is concerned," the Grand Admiral wrote in the memorandum cited above, summarizing what he told Bethmann, "it was primarily a matter of maintaining the burgeoning weapons business. I did not believe that America would declare war because of this. Moreover, such a

nearing its end. Von Pohl, who was about to relieve von Ingenohl as commander in chief of the High Seas Fleet, came to Berlin during the end of January in order to turn his office at the Admiralty over to his successor, Vice Admiral Gustav Bachmann. Determined to crown his tour of duty in the operational office by winning the objective that overshadowed all others in his mind, von Pohl obtained a final conference with the Chancellor on February 1, one attended also by General von Falkenhayn, Undersecretary Zimmermann, and Clemens Delbrück, Secretary of the Interior. Although no records were made at the time of the discussion that followed, there is good reason to believe that these leaders went over familiar ground; that von Pohl argued convincingly that there would be little difficulty from the neutrals, since neutral shipping would avoid the war zone in sheer fright; and that the admiral scored heavily with Bethmann by emphasizing the dangers of continuing to resist the public clamor for the U-boat campaign. Whatever the reasons, the Chancellor "caved in," as von Pohl afterward put it; on the following morning, moreover, he called the Admiralty by telephone to convey his consent to the inauguration of the submarine campaign.[30]

For von Pohl there now remained only the necessity of obtaining the Emperor's approval. This was easily done by this determined sea dog. In collaboration with the Chancellor and the Foreign Office, von Pohl first hastily drafted a "Declaration of a War Zone," while the Foreign Office prepared an explanatory note to be sent to the neutral governments. Next von Pohl sent a brief note to Admiral von Tirpitz informing him of the decision, knowing at the same time that von Tirpitz would not see the letter because he had just left Berlin for Wilhelmshaven.[31] Then on February 3 von Pohl set out for Wilhelmshaven, where he was to join the Emperor in a grand review and take command of the High Seas Fleet. The admiral chose his moment well on the following day. Waiting until the Imperial party was aboard a launch crossing the port of Wilhelmshaven and the

declaration could possibly be meaningless for us, since the English, French, and Russian fleets are already strong enough in their opposition to us, and the Americans would not send over troops."

[30] Spindler, *La Guerre Sous-Marine*, I, 102-110.

[31] H. von Pohl to A. von Tirpitz, February 2, 1915, Tirpitz, *Politische Dokumente*, II, 304. Having arranged the conference of February 1 so as to exclude von Tirpitz, von Pohl sent this formal notification the following day in order to comply with the letter of an Imperial order of July 30, 1914, specifying that the Grand Admiral's advice must be sought on all important questions relating to the conduct of naval warfare.

entourage had gone below, von Pohl cornered the Emperor on the bridge and presented the war zone declaration to him, saying that the Chancellor had approved it. Hearing no dissent, William signed the declaration at once.[32]

Von Pohl must have telephoned the good news to Berlin soon afterward, for the Admiralty issued the declaration of a war zone on the same afternoon, February 4. "The waters around Great Britain, including the whole of the English Channel," it read, "are declared hereby to be included within the zone of war, and after the 18th inst. all enemy merchant vessels encountered in these waters will be destroyed, even if it may not be possible always to save their crews and passengers.

"Within this war zone neutral vessels are exposed to danger since, in view of the misuse of the neutral flags ordered by the Government of Great Britain on the 31st ultimo and of the hazards of naval warfare, neutral vessels cannot always be prevented from suffering from the attacks intended for enemy ships.

"The routes of navigation around the north of the Shetland Islands in the eastern part of the North Sea and in a strip thirty miles wide along the Dutch Coast are not open to the danger zone."[33]

Two days later, on February 6, the Foreign Office sent its explanatory note to the neutrals. It began with a long indictment of alleged British crimes against international law and a rebuke to the neutrals for acquiescing in them. The British had pleaded the necessity of protecting vital interests as justification, and the neutrals had accepted the plea. "Germany," the note continued, "must now appeal to these same vital interests to its great regret. It therefore sees itself forced to military measures aimed at England in retaliation against the English procedure." Thus after February 18 German submarines would destroy all enemy merchantmen found in the war zone. Submarine commanders had instructions to avoid violence to neutral vessels; but neutral ships could find safety only by staying out of the war zone or by using the safe lanes marked out by the war zone declaration.[34]

News of the German proclamation of February 4 came almost like a bolt out of the blue to Washington. Gerard had cabled an intimation on February 2, but for some reason his telegram did not arrive at the

---

[32] The above paragraph is based upon Spindler, *La Guerre Sous-Marine*, I, 111-122.

[33] As printed in the *New York Times*, February 7, 1915.

[34] "Memorandum of the German Government . . . ," dated February 4, 1915, *Foreign Relations, 1915, Supplement*, pp. 96-97.

State Department until the morning of February 4. Moreover, the Ambassador's telegram conveying the text of the decree did not reach Washington until late in the evening of February 5, so that the President first learned the news when he read the newspapers on the morning of that same day. Coming as it did, coldly and starkly, it must have made a shocking impression. Wilson discussed the matter with the Cabinet at their regular weekly meeting in the morning and apparently then asked Lansing, who had come to the meeting in the place of the momentarily absent Secretary of State, to prepare a draft note of reply.[35]

It was, as the Counselor told the President, "a most delicate situation," and Lansing set to work in the afternoon with a heavy heart. To him the legal and political issues raised by the implied German threat to destroy American shipping in violation of the laws of cruiser warfare were crystal clear; and the draft note that he completed and sent to the White House on the following day, February 6, was stern, even peremptory, in word and meaning. Defining the destruction of neutral merchant ships without visit and search as a "wanton act unparalleled in naval warfare," it warned that any such destruction of American ships would be regarded as "a flagrant violation of neutral rights, as one offensive, if not hostile," for which the American authorities would hold the German government to "strict accountability." Wilson went over the draft, polishing its language but softening its tone only slightly if at all.[36]

This was all done tentatively in anticipation, with no intention of acting without full knowledge. Up to this point Wilson and Lansing had read only the brief paragraphs of the war zone declaration. Then the newspapers published the text of the Foreign Office's explanatory memorandum, which they had received by wireless, on the morning of February 7. "The memorandum," Lansing wrote to the White House after reading it, "impresses me as a strong presentation of the German case and removes some of the objectionable features of the declaration, if it is used without explanitory [sic] statements. In my opinion it makes the advisability of a strong protest, or of any protest at all, open to question."[37]

Discussing the German memorandum with Lansing on February 7 or 8, the President must have agreed that it changed the situation

[35] *New York Times*, February 6, 1915.
[36] Lansing's draft, with Wilson's alterations, is in the Wilson Papers.
[37] R. Lansing to W.W., February 7, 1915, *ibid.*

considerably. He understood well enough why the Germans felt that they were driven to extreme reprisals; he was not inclined to make any protest against the submarine campaign insofar as it affected only Allied shipping. Even so, he decided to make a firm but friendly defense of American rights on the sea without delay. Thus on February 8 he drafted a revised note on his own typewriter, adding a paragraph in reply to the German memorandum, a sentence at the end saying that a note of protest against the British misuse of the American flag had already gone to London, and a somewhat cordial tone to the entire note. For example, he took out altogether his own (not Lansing's) earlier ominous warning that the United States would regard German destruction of American ships and lives in the war zone as a "deliberately unfriendly" act. Moreover, even more than Lansing had done, he directed the burden of the note to the issue of American ships and American citizens traveling on them in the war zone. We do not know what discussions ensued during the next two days. Bryan had returned to Washington by February 8. He certainly read Wilson's revised draft and probably discussed it with him when he saw the President at the White House on the morning of February 9; and Wilson must have insisted upon sending it at once. At any rate, it went to Berlin in the early afternoon of February 10 over Bryan's signature and with his tacit approval.

Opening with a brief review of the German war zone proclamation and particularly that part of it relating to neutral shipping, the President added that it was the duty of the American government to warn the Imperial authorities that a critical situation might arise should the German naval forces destroy American ships or cause the death of American citizens while carrying out the Admiralty's orders. It was not necessary, he continued, to remind the German government that it had certain obligations toward neutral vessels, "unless a blockade is proclaimed and effectively maintained, which this Government does not understand to be proposed in this case." Simply to sink vessels without warning "would be an act so unprecedented in naval warfare that this Government is reluctant to believe that the Imperial Government of Germany in this case contemplates it as possible." The accusations against neutral governments for acquiescing in illegal British measures, Wilson went on, obviously did not apply to the United States. Coming to the heart of the matter, he warned:

"If the commanders of German vessels of war should act upon the presumption that the flag of the United States was not being used in good faith and should destroy on the high seas an American vessel or the lives of American citizens, it would be difficult for the Government of the United States to view the act in any other light than as an indefensible violation of neutral rights which it would be very hard indeed to reconcile with the friendly relations now so happily subsisting between the two Governments.

"If such a deplorable situation should arise, the Imperial Government can readily appreciate that the Government of the United States would be constrained to hold the Imperial German Government to a strict accountability for such acts of their naval authorities and to take any steps it might be necessary to take to safeguard American lives and property and to secure to American citizens the full enjoyment of their acknowledged rights on the high seas.

"The Government of the United States, in view of these considerations, which it urges with the greatest respect . . . , expresses the confident hope and expectation that the Imperial German Government can and will give assurance that American citizens and their vessels will not be molested by the naval forces of Germany otherwise than by visit and search, though their vessels may be traversing the sea area delimited in the proclamation of the German Admiralty."[38]

It was easy for the casual reader to miss the important implication of these words: the American government was simply demanding protection for "American citizens and their vessels,"[39] without challenging the right of the Imperial authorities to invoke the law of reprisal in undertaking a ruthless campaign against *enemy* merchant shipping. This crucially significant fact was further underlined by the note that the State Department dispatched to London a short time before it sent the "strict accountability" note to Berlin. The note to London was a vigorous protest against the way in which British ship captains, acting under authority of an Admiralty order of January 31, 1915, had been hoisting the American flag as a *ruse de guerre* when they thought they were in danger.[40] But the burden of the American com-

---

[38] The Secretary of State to Ambassador Gerard, February 10, 1915, *Foreign Relations, 1915, Supplement*, pp. 98-100.

[39] It is just possible that Wilson and Lansing were being deliberately ambiguous at this point so as not to exclude future negotiations for the defense of American citizens in the war zone, whether they traveled on neutral or belligerent ships. The fact remains, however, that the main burden of their warning was aimed at protecting American citizens on American ships.

[40] See the *New York Times*, February 7 and 8, 1915. In its reply the Foreign Office (correctly) defended the practice as one long used by belligerent vessels to protect

plaint was that it would be a "serious and constant menace to the lives and vessels of American citizens" if U-boat commanders could not reliably distinguish between American and British ships, and that part of the responsibility for the loss of American vessels would fall upon the London government if British masters did not stop misusing the American flag. "You may add," the instruction to Ambassador Page concluded, "that this Government is making earnest representations to the German Government in regard to the danger to *American vessels and citizens* if the declaration of the German Admiralty is put into effect."[41]

Published in the American press on February 12, the two notes of protest evoked overwhelming approval among thoughtful spokesmen. Most American editors had greeted the issuance of the war zone proclamation with an outburst of jingoism.[42] On second thought, most responsible publicists agreed that the President had said the right thing, and that the Germans could not be really serious in their threats anyway. "It is," remarked the editor of the New York *World* in a typical comment on the note to Germany, "a firm, temperate, courteous statement of what is in the minds and hearts of the American people, and if Germany accepts it in that spirit, nothing is likely to occur to disturb . . . amicable relations."[43]

Virtually all dispatches to the German Foreign Office during the following week brought disquieting news about the violent reaction of the neutral world to the submarine decree. It was, however, the receipt of the "strict accountability" note on February 12, 1915, and of urgent messages from Bernstorff soon afterward, warning that *an extraordinarily serious commotion which could have the worst consequences*" would ensue if submarines sank *American* vessels without

---

neutral passengers aboard or to avoid capture. The Foreign Office declared, however, that the "British Government have no intention of advising their merchant shipping to use foreign flags as general practice or to resort to them otherwise than for escaping capture or destruction." Memorandum of the Foreign Office, transmitted in Ambassador Page to the Secretary of State, n.d., but received February 20, 1915, *Foreign Relations, 1915, Supplement*, pp. 117-118.

[41] The Secretary of State to Ambassador Page, February 10, 1915, *ibid.*, pp. 100-101; italics added.

[42] See the survey of press opinion in the *Literary Digest*, L (February 20, 1915), 357-360.

[43] New York *World*, February 12, 1915; also the New York *Nation*, c (February 11 and 18, 1915), 156, 159, 186; *The Independent*, LXXXI (February 15, 1915), 223.

warning,[44] that sounded the loudest alarm in the Wilhelmstrasse. Indeed, it did considerably more; it forced a heated showdown between the civil and military leaders on relations with the powerful neutrals, a matter that had by no means yet been clarified in German policy.

Some direct reply to the United States had to be made soon, since the President had specifically requested one. The Foreign Office set to work at once on a draft, but it sought to allay American objections even while discussions over the reply proceeded in Berlin. To begin with, the Foreign Office, at the suggestion of the Admiralty, drafted a new memorandum on February 11 explaining that it was the English determination to use armed merchantmen flying the American flag and all other available ruses to destroy submarines that made it impossible for U-boat captains to comply with the ordinary rules while sinking ships in the war zone.[45] More important, the German Foreign Office and Ambassador von Bernstorff both hinted broadly that the Imperial government would be willing to call off its submarines if the British would permit the entry of food for civilian use into Germany;[46] and the deputy head of the Admiralty, Admiral Paul Behncke, issued such an offer formally a few days later.[47]

These suggestions made a profound impression upon Secretary Bryan, who was at this very moment engaged in negotiations with London over the passage of the American food ship *Wilhelmina* to a German port, and who had now obtained assurances from the German government that any food received from the United States would be used exclusively by civilians.[48] Bryan wrote to the President late in the afternoon of February 15, suggesting that they relay to London the alleged German offer to abandon the submarine campaign in return for the free entry of food into Germany. "If we can secure the withdrawal of these two orders [the submarine decree and the British food embargo]," the Secretary of State added, "it will greatly clear the atmosphere and if we cannot do it I believe that we are approaching

[44] Ambassador von Bernstorff to the Foreign Office, February 17, 1915, and one message, No. 287, received February 19, 1915, German F. O. Archives.

[45] The German Ambassador to the Secretary of State, February 15, 1915, *Foreign Relations, 1915, Supplement*, pp. 104-105.

[46] Ambassador Gerard to the Secretary of State, February 12, 1915, *ibid.*, p. 102; *New York Times*, February 14, 1915.

[47] *ibid.*, February 17, 1915.

[48] The German Ambassador to the Secretary of State, February 13, 1915, *Foreign Relations, 1915, Supplement*, pp. 102-103. For the background of the *Wilhelmina* case, see above, pp. 187-190.

the most serious crisis that we have had to meet."[49] Wilson approved, and Bryan sent such a message to Page on the following afternoon.[50] Page replied encouragingly at first, and Bryan came back with an even stronger plea to the British authorities than before.[51]

Meanwhile, the Foreign Office in Berlin had completed the first draft of its reply to the American "strict accountability" note by February 14. In fairly temperate language it reviewed the reasons for resorting to the submarine reprisal and then proceeded in precise terms to answer the main American objections. The submarine campaign was not, the draft note said, in any way aimed against "the just rights of the neutrals." Indeed, it went without saying that "the officers of the Imperial Navy have received precise orders to cause no damage to ships flying neutral flags when it is possible to determine their nationality and that they do not carry contraband." The trouble was, of course, the note went on, that British merchantmen were using American flags to escape attack, and the London Admiralty had armed merchantmen and advised them to attack submarines. Even so, the German government was willing to give a provisional guarantee that ships flying the American flag would not be subject to underseas attack, provided English ships stopped misusing the American flag. It would, moreover, be helpful if the American ships traveled in recognizable convoys.[52]

It was these specific guarantees for American shipping that stimulated the violent disputation between the civil and naval leaders. Bethmann, von Jagow, and the new Admiralty chieftain, Bachmann, discussed the draft note at the Foreign Office on February 14. Bachmann was adamant, saying that the entire submarine campaign would fail if the government gave such guarantees to the neutrals. It simply was not possible for submarines to observe the rules of cruiser warfare or to establish with any reliability the nationality of merchantmen before attacking them. On his part, Bethmann was equally unyielding, for he had obviously been much impressed by the American warning. It was, he said, necessary *at all costs* to avoid serious difficulties with the United States, and he would find agreement somehow. The result

[49] W. J. Bryan to W.W., February 15, 1915, *The Lansing Papers*, I, 353-354.

[50] The Secretary of State to Ambassador Page, February 16, 1915, *Foreign Relations, 1915, Supplement*, p. 107.

[51] Ambassador Page to the Secretary of State, February 17, 1915; the Secretary of State to Ambassador Page, February 19, 1915; *ibid.*, pp. 111-112.

[52] Spindler, *La Guerre Sous-Marine*, I, 142-146, prints the draft note in full.

was a complete impasse, and the antagonists agreed to appeal to the Emperor for a decision. Thus Bethmann sent a copy of the draft note to Supreme Headquarters, now at Lötzen; Bachmann forwarded a copy of a letter to the Chancellor embodying his objections and ending with a taut warning: "I consider it my duty to report to His Majesty that the announced submarine action will be completely without effect in view of the concessions that you propose to make to the United States." Until the Emperor had made his decision, Bachmann agreed, submarine commanders should not attack merchantmen flying neutral flags unless they had definitely ascertained that they were enemy ships. He sent such an order to the fleet on February 14.[53]

Although the lines of battle over the submarine were by no means yet tightly drawn, the pressures for an all-out effort, even at the risk of serious trouble with America, were beginning to mount in Germany, and it was not easy for the Emperor and his advisers to follow the dictates of reason. The naval spokesmen redoubled their appeals and agitations. Grand Admiral von Tirpitz supported Bachmann's demands "in every respect,"[54] not because he believed the submarine campaign would succeed, but because the navy must have its way against timid political authorities. Admiral von Pohl's answer was a simple one: Germany should reply to America by sinking *every* ship in the war zone. "With this order," the commander of the High Seas Fleet telegraphed to Bachmann in comment upon the latter's order of February 14, "any possibility of successfully prosecuting the submarine war is excluded. . . . The prestige of the Navy will, in my opinion, suffer tremendously if an undertaking which has been loudly proclaimed and looked upon with great hope by the people fails. Please convey my sentiments to His Majesty."[55] Moreover, perhaps as a clever bit of blackmail, von Pohl ordered all submarines to remain at their bases, explaining that "existing orders do not permit one to hope for the least success."[56]

The navy's demands were also finding an echo in the German press, which had been stimulated to participate in these discussions by the publication of the "strict accountability" note in the newspapers on

[53] *ibid.*, pp. 142, 146-148; Admiral Bachmann to the Imperial Chancellor, February 14, 1915, Tirpitz, *Politische Dokumente*, ii, 309-310.

[54] As Bachmann said in his letter to Bethmann of February 14, 1915, cited above.

[55] The Chief of the High Seas Fleet to the Head of the Admiralty, February 15, 1915, Tirpitz, *Politische Dokumente*, ii, 311.

[56] The Chief of the High Seas Fleet to the Head of the Admiralty, February 15, 1915, Spindler, *La Guerre Sous-Marine*, i, 149.

February 13 and 14, 1915. Some editors remarked upon the friendly tone of the President's warning, but virtually all agreed that the Imperial government could make no important concessions.[57] And two prominent editorial spokesmen were provocative. "When something does not suit the Yankees," exclaimed one of them, "they are accustomed to adopt as threatening and as frightful a saber-rattling tone as possible."[58] "One cannot escape the conclusion," the foremost naval publicist in Germany added, "that President Wilson and Secretary Bryan, in their communications with the Mexican pretenders and rebel leaders, have accustomed themselves to a tone that is not suitable for communications with the German Empire. The only way to preserve the existing relations between the German Empire and the United States is actual American recognition of the German war zone declaration and regard for the warning expressed therein."[59]

In spite of the navy's pressure and the muted demands of most of the newspapers, the Chancellor carried the day without much difficulty. The crucial discussions occurred at a conference at Lötzen attended by the Emperor, General von Falkenhayn, Admiral Georg A. von Müller, Chief of the Naval Cabinet, and Colonel Karl G. von Treutler, the Foreign Office's envoy at Supreme Headquarters, which began at eleven in the morning on February 15. The conferees went over the draft note of reply and Bachmann's letter to the Chancellor. It was absolutely necessary, von Treutler urged, to meet the Americans halfway, for no one could guarantee that the Washington government would not take serious measures if the German response were a negative one. The stakes were too high to run any risks. Falkenhayn agreed emphatically. American entry into the war at this time, he said, had to be prevented at all costs. Would it not be wise, he suggested, to ask the Admiralty whether it was prepared to guarantee that the submarine blockade could bring England to terms within six weeks, as had been said? The Emperor concurred, adding that he had never believed all the boasts of the navy.

The upshot of these discussions was agreement, first, that the Foreign Office should send its note to Washington in virtually its original

[57] e.g., Berlin *Vossische Zeitung*, morning edn., February 14, 1915; *Berliner Lokal-Anzeiger*, morning edn., February 14, 1915; *Frankfurter Zeitung*, second morning edn., February 14, 1915; *Hamburger Nachrichten*, February 14, 1915.

[58] Berlin *Post*, February 14, 1915.

[59] Count Ernst von Reventlow in the Berlin *Deutsche Tageszeitung*, morning and afternoon edns., February 14, 1915.

form, without making any important concessions to Bachmann, and, second, that von Müller should undertake to subdue the navy.[60] This he did by telegraphing Bachmann immediately, saying that the Emperor had commanded that submarine operations against neutral shipping should not begin until he had given personal orders to that effect. "Further," this telegram continued, "His Majesty wants immediate telegraphic reply to the following question: To what extent will you take responsibility for guaranteeing that England will be ready to give in within six weeks after the beginning of the new war against commerce? The opinion of the Secretary of State for the Navy [von Tirpitz] is to be telegraphed also."[61]

Having won the victory, Bethmann now proceeded to throw it away. At least, so events of the following day, February 16, seemed to indicate. Bachmann's and von Tirpitz's reply to the Emperor's direct query arrived at Lötzen in the morning. "The Secretary of State and the Head of the Admiralty," it read, "are convinced that England will be led to give in six weeks after the beginning of the new war against commerce if all military measures at our disposal are used from the beginning to prosecute this war." The reply was, William remarked to von Müller, "perfectly jesuitical" and full of loopholes. At the same time, a new draft of a note of reply to the United States, one that the Foreign Office and presumably the Chancellor had prepared in collaboration with Bachmann and von Tirpitz during the night before, was telephoned from Berlin. Reading the transcribed copy, the Emperor discovered that the Foreign Office's new draft included none of the concessions that had been embodied in the first version.[62] It was enough to confuse even a wise ruler, which William was far from

---

[60] K. G. von Treutler to the Imperial Chancellor, February 15, 1915, German F. O. Archives.

[61] G. A. von Müller to the Admiralty, February 15, 1915, transmitted in K. G. von Treutler to the Imperial Chancellor, February 15, 1915, *ibid.*

[62] The key concession in the first draft had read: "The German Government . . . expresses the hope that this [American flag] protest will cause England to respect the American flag in the future. In this expectation it agrees for the time being that ships flying the American flag will not be attacked by German submarines." The Emperor had instructed Bethmann on February 15 to make the second sentence read: "In this expectation it will instruct its naval forces for the time being not to attack merchant ships that travel under neutral flags." The sentence in the revised draft sent to Lötzen on February 16 read: "In this expectation the commanders of the German submarines have been instructed, as was already stated in the note of fourth instant, to abstain from violence to American merchant vessels when they are recognizable as such."

being. He approved the new draft—it was given to Gerard on the same day[63] and published in the German press amid the huzzas of the jingoes on February 18[64]—but ordered the Admiralty to delay further any action against neutral shipping and to present to him the instructions that it was preparing for the submarine commanders.[65]

These developments, however, reflected reality only in its superficial appearances. Events of the climactic phase of this first battle over submarine policy from February 17 through February 22, 1915, revealed that Bethmann must have come to some agreement with the admirals that gave the shadow of the victory (no public yielding to the United States) to the navy and saved the substance (a severe limitation on submarine operations in deference to the United States) for himself. The Emperor returned to Berlin on February 17, and Bachmann hastened to the Supreme War Lord to plead once again for the quick inauguration of the underseas campaign. But the admiral now talked much of the necessity for sparing American ships and of new methods of so doing. Concluding, he asked only that His Majesty order the beginning of the submarine war "as soon as negotiations with the neutrals will permit it."[66] At the Emperor's command, Bachmann prepared a new order for the execution of the U-boat war and sent it to the front on February 18, 1915.[67] It directed submarine commanders to sink all enemy merchant ships but to spare hospital ships, ships of the Belgian Relief Commission, and neutral merchantmen, particularly when they traveled in convoys under the protection of warships. The campaign thus decreed, however, would begin "only upon the special order of His Majesty."[68]

The 18th of February was the day appointed and announced for the beginning of the dreadful onslaught against Allied shipping. Only two

[63] Ambassador Gerard to the Secretary of State, February 17, 1915, *Foreign Relations, 1915, Supplement*, pp. 112-115.

[64] e.g., Count E. von Reventlow in the Berlin *Deutsche Tageszeitung*, morning and afternoon edns., February 18, 1915; Berlin *Post*, February 18, 1915; also the *Kölnische Zeitung*, first morning edn., February 18, 1915, and Berlin *Vossische Zeitung*, February 18, 1915, for more moderate opinion.

[65] Admiral von Müller to the Admiralty, February 16, 1915, Tirpitz, *Politische Dokumente*, II, 316.

[66] Spindler, *La Guerre Sous-Marine*, I, 162-165.

[67] It replaced a tentative order, which the Admiralty had sent to the High Seas Fleet on February 2, 1915, directing submarine commanders to sink all ships found in the war zone.

[68] The order of February 18, 1915, is printed in Spindler, *La Guerre Sous-Marine*, I, 165-166.

submarines were at sea, but they were impotent under their present orders. There was, moreover, no chance of putting even the new orders into effect without Bethmann's consent, and Bethmann was now insisting upon further guarantees for American and Italian shipping.[69] Thus Bachmann had to choose between giving up the submarine project entirely, as von Pohl was urging him to do, or undertaking it in a severely limited way. Fearing that the German navy would become the laughingstock of the world if it did not take some action, he chose the second alternative. With the Chancellor's and Foreign Office's explicit approval, he urged the Emperor on February 19 to begin the submarine war in the North Sea and the English Channel, but with additional instructions to U-boat commanders to spare ships sailing under the American and Italian flags unless they were absolutely certain that they were enemy merchantmen. The Emperor approved, and such orders were sent to the front on February 20.[70] Finally, on February 22, again with the consent of the Chancellor and the Foreign Office, the Head of the Admiralty proposed and the Emperor approved the extension of submarine operations to the entire war zone. But yet a further warning accompanied the order of execution that was sent to the front. "His Majesty," it read, "desires that the submarine commanders be expressly informed that, on account of political difficulties which have arisen with the United States and Italy, it is necessary that they act with the greatest circumspection in dealing with ships of these two countries, to avoid sinking one of them by mistake."[71]

Two submarines were already in the war zone; four others followed them on February 24. The *Handelskrieg mit U-Booten*, with all its unknown perils for German-American relations, had at last begun.

In the meantime, the President and his advisers in Washington knew nothing of the struggle proceeding in Germany or its outcome. All that they knew about these developments between the sending of the American note of February 10 and the receipt of the German reply a week later came from Gerard, who was so highly excitable and gullible that he could not (and made no effort to) distinguish between gossip and truth. Inevitably, he missed what any astute envoy with the right connections would have discovered—the impact of his gov-

---

[69] See his handwritten note at the bottom of "Order for the Execution of the Submarine War Against Commerce," dated February 18, 1915, German F. O. Archives.

[70] Spindler, *La Guerre Sous-Marine*, I, 171-172, prints the text of this order.

[71] Admiralty order of February 22, 1915, printed in *ibid.*, pp. 175-176.

ernment's warning upon the men who were making the crucial decisions. And instead of reporting what it was really vital for his superiors to know, Gerard bombarded the State Department with telegrams telling (what was not true) how the German government and press were intensifying what he had earlier called the "hate campaign" against America. "Hear on all sides," he wired on February 14, in one of his most hyperbolic reports, "of possibility of war with America. Belief here that great quantities of munitions are sent from America, thus prolonging the war. German officials confident Germans in America organized by consuls will rise and destroy bridges, arsenals and factories. I assure you the situation is very tense."[72]

It was in the darkness shed by Gerard's reports that the President and the leaders in the State Department had to consider the German note of February 16. Bryan and Lansing read the text for the first time in the *Washington Star* on the afternoon of February 18 (the official text did not arrive from the Embassy in Berlin until the following morning), and Lansing quickly dissected the note and added his own copious comments.[73] The two leaders in the State Department obviously did not regard the German reply as fully reassuring or satisfactory, but they were much encouraged by its hint that the Berlin government might call off its submarines if the United States could persuade the Allies to observe the Declaration of London and permit the flow of food and industrial raw materials to the Central Powers. Bryan had suggested a compromise on food imports to the Foreign Office in London and had received an encouraging response only the day before, on February 17.[74] The next move was obvious, as Bryan wrote immediately to the White House—to propose a formal compromise arrangement by which Great Britain would permit the Germans to import foodstuffs to be distributed exclusively for civilian use under American supervision, Germany would agree not to sow floating mines or use submarines to sink merchantmen except according to the rules of cruiser warfare, and both belligerents would promise that their merchant vessels would not use neutral flags.[75] The President agreed entirely,[76] and Bryan, acting as "a sincere friend desirous

[72] Ambassador Gerard to the Secretary of State, February 14, 1915, *Foreign Relations, 1915, Supplement*, p. 104.

[73] They are printed in *The Lansing Papers*, I, 354-361.

[74] Ambassador Page to the Secretary of State, February 17, 1915, *Foreign Relations, 1915, Supplement*, p. 111.

[75] W. J. Bryan to W.W., February 18, 1915, *The Lansing Papers*, I, 361-363.

[76] W.W. to W. J. Bryan, February 19, 1915, *ibid.*, p. 363.

of embarrassing neither nation involved," sent identic notes to Berlin and London embodying the proposed *modus vivendi* on February 20, 1915.[77]

Received at the Foreign Office in Berlin two days later, Bryan's suggestion met a friendly welcome. Sending a copy of the note to various leaders on February 23, Secretary von Jagow argued that acceptance, perhaps with some modifications (including insistence upon the free entry of raw materials as well as foodstuffs), would place England in a difficult position. "She would," he pointed out, "be forced on her part either to reject it or to admit that her conduct of the war thus far is contrary to international law. Moreover, under the pressure of the submarine threat she would have to announce her intention of abandoning her plan to starve Germany. This would mean a moral victory over England's self-assumed dominion of the seas, and on the other side we would be sure to receive Germany's food supplies."[78] No doubt in collaboration with the Imperial Chancellor, the Foreign Office soon afterward drafted a cordially worded reply along these lines. It accepted the proposed *modus vivendi* with rather profuse thanks, but with the reservations that Germany would continue to use anchored mines for offensive purposes, as international law permitted, that Great Britain should guarantee that the raw materials on the Declaration of London's free list and list of conditional contraband might flow unhindered to the Reich, and that Allied merchantmen should never be armed.

Finding a new opportunity to disagree with the civilian authorities, von Tirpitz and Bachmann objected so violently to the proposed reply[79] that the Chancellor had to arrange for an Imperial conference to settle the matter. It took place at Bellevue Castle in Berlin on February 28 and saw the outbreak of a sharp verbal duel between Bethmann and the Grand Admiral that ranged far beyond the immediate question and went to the heart of their differences over the submarine

[77] The Secretary of State to Ambassador Page and Ambassador Gerard, February 20, 1915, *Foreign Relations, 1915, Supplement*, pp. 119-120.

[78] G. von Jagow to various German leaders, February 23, 1915, German F. O. Archives.

[79] Arguing that British concessions on food and raw materials would be utterly meaningless in view of the shortage of shipping, they demanded that the Foreign Office add a new reservation specifying that Britain must permit the German ships now lying in American harbors to sail to German ports. Only this kind of guarantee, von Tirpitz and Bachmann insisted, would justify the German government in surrendering the threat of the submarine war. Admiral Bachmann to the Foreign Office, February 27, 1915, Tirpitz, *Politische Dokumente*, II, 321-322.

issue. William wavered, and von Tirpitz tried again to draw him to his side. Then Admiral von Müller intervened, and the Emperor deferentially commanded that Bethmann send his note without the further changes that the admirals had demanded.[80] It was given to the American Ambassador a few hours later.[81]

The German reply, obviously, asked more than Bryan's proposed *modus vivendi* had suggested, but it did open the way for negotiations, and it was precisely what the President and Secretary of State expected to hear from Berlin.[82] Upon the response from London, they believed, everything now depended, and Wilson moved at once to bring pressure upon the British Cabinet. "We are sending today," he cabled on February 20 to House, then in London on the first leg of his peace mission, "identical notes to the British and German Governments. Please say to Page that he cannot emphasize too much in presenting the note to Grey the favorable opinion which would be created in this country if the British Government could see its way clear to adopt the suggestions made there."[83]

House consequently did what he could. He urged Ambassador Page to plead strongly with the Foreign Secretary and even garbled the President's message in transmitting it to Page to make it read that Wilson wanted the Ambassador to present the *modus vivendi* to Sir Edward "with all the emphasis in his power."[84] And when Page agreed only reluctantly to comply, saying that he had "no stomach" for the proposal and that he did not "consider its acceptance favorable to the British Government," the Colonel himself sought Grey out on February 24, and again three days later, and urged him to accept the "President's suggestion."[85] His supplications were largely wasted. In response Grey was kind but noncommittal, without being totally discouraging. He personally thought well of the suggestion in principle, he told House and Page, but he would have to discuss the matter with the Cabinet before he could give a definite answer.[86]

[80] "Report of a Conference at Bellevue Castle, February 28, 1915," *ibid.*, pp. 322-326.
[81] Ambassador Gerard to the Secretary of State, March 1, 1915, *Foreign Relations, 1915, Supplement*, pp. 129-130.
[82] As the White House correspondent for the *New York Times* reported on March 4, *New York Times*, March 5, 1915.
[83] W.W. to E. M. House, February 20, 1915, Baker Collection.
[84] House Diary, February 22, 1915.
[85] *ibid.*, February 24 and 27, 1915.
[86] Ambassador Page to the Secretary of State, February 23, 1915, *Foreign Relations, 1915, Supplement*, p. 122; House Diary, February 24 and 27, 1915.

The British answer was announced between the first and middle of March 1915, and in terms that portended new perils for the neutrals. That response was virtually foreordained by the almost unlimited new opportunities that the German war zone decree had opened for the Allied leaders. Pressure on the London Foreign Office for an intensification of economic warfare had been steadily increasing from the Admiralty, certain political leaders, and a segment of the British press since the autumn of 1914. Nor was the French government much less insistent in its demand for unlimited war upon the seas during this same period.[87] Arguing the necessity for caution and concessions to America, Sir Edward Grey had withstood these demands on the whole successfully before early February 1915. The German declaration of February 4, however, provided the opportunity for embarking upon no-quarter policies that Grey himself wanted to undertake and would undoubtedly have approved ultimately, when they were possible without incurring what might be fatal political risks.

All the considerable evidence indicates that Grey and the other British leaders *welcomed* the submarine decree. It was, they knew, largely bluff and no threat at all to their sea-borne commerce at this time; it had the further advantage of being likely to embroil Germany in serious difficulties with the United States; most important, it meant that the British could now proceed to their own severe reprisals on the ground that German criminality had driven them to such an unpleasant course. "The contraband difficulty," Grey told a friend on February 6, "was greatly relieved by Germany's having announced a blockade of England and that she will sink ships trying to run it, drowning the crews! This will enable England to do ditto to Germany but to guarantee not to murder the crews."[88] "England," wrote the President of France in his Diary, reflecting what he had heard from London, "will be in a position to profit by the menace that the Germans pose against neutral shipping by organizing a real blockade of the Central Powers."[89]

The British decision on how to proceed most profitably was made during the two weeks following the issuance of the submarine decree. Winston S. Churchill, First Lord of the Admiralty, apparently made the first suggestion on February 10—to issue a royal proclamation

[87] E. R. May, *The World War and American Isolation*, pp. 21-25, 305-307.

[88] Plunkett Diary, February 6, 1915. In the same vein, see also Winston S. Churchill, *The World Crisis*, II, 296.

[89] Raymond Poincaré, *Au Service de la France*, VI, 65-66.

announcing that hereafter the Royal Navy would stop *all* commerce, contraband and noncontraband alike, to and from the Central Powers. The Cabinet discussed this and other proposals on February 16. "Mr. Churchill & others strongly urged," the Prime Minister reported to the King, "that we should announce our intention to seize & detain all cargoes, under any flag, of food & other useful commodities, as to which there is a presumption of German destination, and also all cargoes of German exported goods in neutral bottoms. This was the prevailing opinion of the Cabinet, but the Prime Minister, Sir E. Grey & Lord Crewe urged very strongly the importance of not alienating & embittering neutral & particularly American opinion, the proposed reprisals being obviously much more injurious to neutral commerce & interests, than the more or less illusory German threat."[90]

We do not know what further discussions and debates occurred during this day and the next, but circumstantial evidence indicates strongly that Grey held out and won his point. It was not that the Admiralty should abstain from instituting the complete embargo that Churchill desired, but that it should proceed with extraordinary caution, in such a way that American commercial interests would suffer no great damage. By February 18, apparently, both the Admiralty and the French government had agreed that this should be the guiding principle of the plans upon which they were now at work.

Precisely when the British and French authorities agreed upon a general plan, we do not know. The receipt of President Wilson's proposed *modus vivendi* in London on about February 22 did, however, cause some delay, not because the British leaders ever seriously considered accepting it, but because they had to go through the motions of discussing it.[91] Then on March 1, 1915, the Prime Minister rose in the House of Commons to read an announcement that the Foreign Office had just sent to the neutral powers. The German government, it said, was obviously determined to conduct a ruthless and illegal underseas campaign against sea-borne commerce to the British Isles.

[90] The Prime Minister to the King, February 17, 1915, Asquith Papers.

[91] For these discussions, see M. P. A. Hankey of the Committee of Imperial Defence to H. H. Asquith, February 25, 1915, *ibid.*; Sir Edmond Slade, Sir Francis Hopwood, and the Director of the Trade Division of the Admiralty, *Observations upon the United States Note of the 22nd February, 1915. Printed for the Use of the Cabinet. March 1915*, a memorandum dated February 28, 1915, and distributed to the Cabinet by W. S. Churchill, copy in *ibid.*; and a Cabinet paper entitled simply *Printed for the use of the Cabinet. February 24, 1915*, copy in *ibid.*, containing memoranda by C. J. B. Hurst, Eyre Crowe, and A. Nicolson.

Britain and France had, therefore, been driven to retaliatory measures, "in order in their turn to prevent commodities of any kind from reaching or leaving Germany," and would "hold themselves free to detain and take into port ships carrying goods of presumed enemy destination, ownership, or origin." However, this would be done without confiscating such vessels or cargoes "unless they would otherwise be liable to condemnation."[92]

Delivered at the State Department at noon on March 1 by the British and French Ambassadors, the declaration could scarcely have occasioned much surprise in Washington. As early as February 20 Page had reported that it was virtually certain that the British would soon adopt severe new maritime measures,[93] and American newspaper correspondents in London had confirmed this report on February 26 and 27.[94] Bryan and Lansing were, however, considerably perplexed by the cryptic terms of the Anglo-French announcement. To the Counselor's precedent-filled mind it made no sense at all. On the one hand, the Allied governments seemed to be talking as if they were preparing to institute a formal blockade of Germany; on the other, as if they would deal with neutral ships and cargoes as though no blockade existed. "The paradoxical situation thus created," he wrote in a letter of comment to the Secretary of State, "should be changed and the declaring powers ought to assert whether they rely upon the rules governing a blockade or the rules applicable when no blockade exists."[95] To clarify the situation, Lansing drafted a brief note to Page instructing him to ask the British Foreign Secretary point-blank whether a blockade existed. If the reply were in the negative, then Page should inquire "under what principle of international law or practice the proposed total interruption of commerce will be enforced."[96] Agreeing, Bryan sent Lansing's letter and draft note to the White House on March 3 with the request that the President edit the draft quickly, if he approved it, so that it could go to London that night.[97]

Wilson, obviously, had already decided that it would be foolish to rush into a new quarrel with the British government before waiting to see how the Foreign Office's announcement would be put into execu-

[92] *New York Times*, March 2, 1915; the British Ambassador to the Secretary of State, March 1, 1915, *Foreign Relations, 1915, Supplement*, pp. 127-128.

[93] Ambassador Page to the Secretary of State, February 20, 1915, *ibid.*, pp. 118-119.

[94] *New York Times*, February 27 and 28, 1915.

[95] R. Lansing to W. J. Bryan, March 2, 1915, *The Lansing Papers*, I, 270-271.

[96] "Draft Telegram . . . ," *ibid.*, p. 272.

[97] W. J. Bryan to W.W., March 3, 1915, *ibid.*, pp. 271-272.

tion. He agreed, undoubtedly, with Page, who wrote on March 3 in a telegram marked "Very confidential. For the Secretary and President":

"In view of the decisive effect of the British reprisals which brings the war into its final stage, in view of the unparalleled power with which the British will be left when peace comes, and in view of this government's courteous regard for us and for our rights, and in view of British public opinion which is more thoroughly aroused and firmly united than ever before in English history, I most urgently recommend the following:

"That we content ourselves for the present with a friendly inquiry how the proposed reprisal will be carried out and with giving renewed notice that we hold ourselves free to take up all cases of damage to our commerce and all unlawful acts on their merits as they occur. This will enable us to accomplish all that we can accomplish by any sort of note or protest."[98]

This was, precisely, what the President wanted to do. The trouble with Lansing's draft, he must have thought, was that it sounded too much as if the Washington government were preparing for a massive resistance. It was, he wrote somewhat testily to Bryan, "abrupt in expression" and, moreover, "a bit difficult to interpret as it stands." Thus he took Lansing's letter of comment and prepared it for transmittal as a note of inquiry.[99] It said the same thing as the draft telegram, but in a much less peremptory and more informal way. It went to London (and Paris, as well) on the following day,[100] and Page handed it to Grey on March 8.

Sir Edward did not reply until he was ready to publish the Order in Council putting the new maritime system into operation.[101] Dated March 11, 1915, it began by invoking the right of His Majesty's Government to resort to reprisal against the illegal and inhuman German submarine campaign. It went on to decree the complete stoppage of all neutral trade to and from Germany, whether through neutral or German ports, in any commodities of any kind. The intention was in ef-

[98] W. H. Page to the Secretary of State, March 3, 1915, Wilson Papers.

[99] W.W. to W. J. Bryan, March 4, 1915, *The Lansing Papers*, I, 273.

[100] The Secretary of State to Ambassador Page, March 5, 1915, *Foreign Relations, 1915, Supplement*, pp. 132-133.

[101] Apparently it was Churchill and his naval advisers in the Admiralty who worked out the practical details of the system once the general principles had been agreed upon. See, e.g., W. S. Churchill to the Cabinet, March 3, 1915, printed in W. S. Churchill, *The World Crisis*, II, 294-295.

fect a complete blockade without any resort to the legal formalities or penalties of one, for the Order made it plain that the British would not ordinarily confiscate neutral ships and noncontraband cargoes that violated its provisions; they would simply not be permitted to proceed to their destinations.[102] As the general instructions that were apparently issued to the Admiralty at this time put it: "The object aimed at should be to induce vessels not to carry goods for Germany. Vessels should therefore be detained long enough to make them feel the inconvenience of carrying such goods, and the advantage of not doing so, but they should be given the benefit of the doubt when the case is not clear. The treatment should gradually grow stricter. Ships of owners who show no indication of conforming to the desires of His Majesty's Government should be dealt with more severely."[103]

Delivering a copy of the Order in Council to Page on March 15, Grey added a note of explanation in response to the American inquiry of March 5. "I can at once assure your excellency," the Foreign Secretary began, "that subject to the paramount necessity of restricting German trade His Majesty's Government have made it their first aim to minimize inconvenience to neutral commerce." Although the British certainly intended to enforce a blockade, Grey went on, they were most reluctant to impose on neutral shipping all the penalties attaching to a breach of blockade. "In their desire to alleviate the burden which the existence of a state of war at sea must inevitably impose on neutral sea-borne commerce," he concluded, "they declare their intention to refrain altogether from the exercise of the right to confiscate ships or cargoes which belligerents have always claimed in respect of breaches of blockade. They restrict their claim to the stopping of cargoes destined for or coming from the enemy's territory."[104]

Page explained British intentions more candidly six days later. The new blockade, he wrote, differed from conventional practice in that it would be maintained by moving cruisers instead of warships stationed off the enemy's coast—a change necessitated by the danger of attack by submarines—and contemplated exempting neutral ships and cargoes from confiscation. The only practical difference that the new

[102] The Order in Council of March 11, 1915, is printed in *Foreign Relations, 1915, Supplement*, pp. 144-145.

[103] *RECOMMENDATIONS AS TO CARRYING THE RETALIATION POLICY INTO EFFECT. Printed for the use of the Cabinet. March 1915*, undated, unsigned Cabinet paper in the Asquith Papers.

[104] Ambassador Page to the Secretary of State, March 15, 1915, *Foreign Relations, 1915, Supplement*, p. 143.

Order in Council would make would be the complete stoppage of American exports of cotton and foodstuffs to Germany. The British leaders, Page went on, expected the American government to protest for the political effect at home. They would receive protests courteously, "pay no further attention to them, proceed to settle our shipping disputes with an effort at generosity and quadruple their orders from us of war materials." "They care nothing," he added, "for our definitions or general protests but are willing to do every practical favor and will under no conditions either take our advice or offend us. They regard our writings as addressed either to complaining shippers or to politicians at home."[105]

In spite of these efforts in London to pave the way, reaction in Washington was sharp when the President and his advisers first read the text of the Order in Council in the morning newspapers on March 16, 1915. Newspapermen who talked with Wilson noted that he was unusually reticent and glum. Asked whether he knew of any precedent for the new British maritime system, he started to reply, stopped himself—did he have United States Civil War precedents in mind?—and then went on to say that he would defer all comment until he had conferred with the State Department. According to one reporter, however, he "indicated broadly" that he was not pleased. Later in the morning the President and the Cabinet went over the situation briefly in a preliminary way.[106] We have no record of their conversation, but we may be sure that they all agreed that some kind of crisis impended, and that the Secretary of State would have to send a protest soon.

This necessity was due to the extremely agitated state of opinion at home, if to no other reason. The American people, as the British Ambassador had observed to Sir Edward Grey only a short time before, would "suffer almost anything rather than go to war." But it was also true, as the Ambassador warned, that "the most peaceable countries are those which often become suddenly the most warlike." An incident might lead to an explosion—"this is what everybody fears."[107]

The first explosion of public opinion had in fact already occurred when the British announced on March 1 that a kind of blockade would

---

[105] Ambassador Page to the Secretary of State, March 21, 1915, *ibid.*, pp. 146-147.
[106] *New York Times*, March 17, 1915.
[107] C. Spring Rice to E. Grey, February 26, 1915, *The Letters of Sir Cecil Spring Rice*, II, 257-258.

soon be instituted.[108] But it was mild compared to the extraordinary outburst that followed the publication of the Order in Council of March 11. "Now, again, after the lapse of more than one hundred years," exclaimed the New York *American*, "this nation is face to face with the same pretensions, the same decrees and orders, the same insolent aggressions, the same intolerable seizure of its peaceful trading ships which roused our fathers to hot indignation and to war."[109] Administration leaders might discount the expletives of the leading Hearst newspaper, but they could not ignore the fact that everywhere throughout the country (except among openly pro-Allied circles in the East) editors spoke in remarkably the same vein.[110] Nor could leaders in Washington well close their ears when powerful Democratic leaders like Senators Thomas J. Walsh of Montana and Hoke Smith of Georgia, speaking for the copper and cotton producers who would presumably be hardest hit by the new British decree, openly demanded retaliation in the form of an embargo on exports to the Allies and said that Congress would adopt embargo legislation if it were in session.[111]

But where should the Washington government stand, and what kind of protest should it send to London? These were the questions to which Wilson, Bryan, Lansing, and other officials involved had to address themselves during the last two weeks of March 1915. In answering them they revealed more clearly than they had ever done before their intimate thoughts about the role that the United States could and should play in defense of neutral rights now that the war at sea was entering a more desperate stage.

The President himself opened the discussions on March 19 by preparing a draft of a note to serve "as a suggestion, and as the basis upon which we may be shaping our thoughts in this important matter."[112] A written version in an incomplete form of what Wilson had said earlier the same day at a Cabinet meeting,[113] the draft made the President's basic position clear at the outset.[114] It revealed that he was

[108] See the review of American press reaction in the *Literary Digest*, L (March 13, 1915), 529-530.

[109] New York *American*, March 18, 1915.

[110] See the survey of press opinion in the *Literary Digest*, L (March 27, 1915), 671-673; also the New York *World*, March 20, 1915, and the *New Republic*, II (March 20, 1915), 163-164.

[111] *New York Times*, March 17 and 27, 1915.

[112] W.W. to W. J. Bryan, March 19, 1915, *The Lansing Papers*, I, 277.

[113] For a long account of this meeting, see the *New York Times*, March 20, 1915.

[114] It is printed in *The Lansing Papers*, I, 278-279.

willing to accept the argument that changed conditions of warfare justified the long-range method of blockade that the Allies had instituted. It *seemed* to reveal, moreover, that he was willing to admit that the British might use their novel measures to prevent all commerce to and from Germany, even traffic in noncontraband through neutral ports. The only issue of serious concern in President's mind, the draft also seemed to indicate, was the right of Americans to engage in trade with the northern European neutrals in noncontraband goods without a German destination.[115] The proposed note met this issue by saying that the American government took it for granted that the British did not intend to stop such commerce.

Additionally, the draft note revealed that the President may have been almost totally naïve about the legal aspects of the problem and even without much understanding of the full implications of the new Order in Council. This was indicated by the title that he gave to his draft—"Note in Reply to Ours Received, Notifying Us of the Establishment of a Blockade of the Coasts of Germany which It Is Intended to Make in All Respects Effective"—and by the concluding sentence of the note: "The Government of the United States, in brief, does not understand His Majesty's Government as claiming the right to set aside any accepted principle of international law, or to plan to act in contravention of any such principle."

It is difficult to know what to make of these curious statements. Was the President really so misinformed and so ignorant of international law that he could say that the British had instituted a blockade "of the coasts of Germany," and that such a blockade as they had actually begun did not violate "any accepted principle of international law"? Or were these statements made for the purpose of making it impossible for the British to refuse to concede the President's modest sole demand—recog-

---

[115] This seemed to be the meaning of the following sentences in the President's draft: "The cordon of blockading ships which it is intended to maintain is, however, of such an extent, the blockade as indicated in the plan announced covers so great an area of the high seas, that it seems that neutral vessels must pass through it in order to approach many important neutral ports which it is not Great Britain's privilege to blockade, and which she of course does not mean to blockade. The Government of the United States takes it for granted, in view of the anxiety expressed by His Majesty's Government to interfere as little as possible with neutral commerce, that the approach of American merchantmen to neutral ports situated upon the long line of coast affected will not be interfered with *when it is known that they do not carry goods which are contraband of war or goods consigned to a destination within the belligerent territory affected.*" Italics added.

nition of the right of Americans to carry on noncontraband trade with the northern neutrals?

Wilson sent his draft to Bryan on March 19, and Bryan turned it over to Lansing, who had already begun to consider the main outlines of a note of protest. The poor Counselor's brain must have spun as he read the President's sentences. He had already meticulously analyzed the British Order in Council and concluded (as any well-trained international lawyer would have done) that the alleged blockade was unknown in law and practice, spurious, and destructive of American neutral rights.[116] He had, moreover, sought and obtained an opinion from the Joint Neutrality Board that affirmed that the Order in Council was "a grave violation of neutral rights," such as had led to war between the United States and Great Britain in 1812, and declared that Germany had a right under the Prussian-American Treaty of 1828 to expect the United States to keep open the channels of German-American commerce.[117]

To Lansing it was plain enough what should be said to the British government. As he made clear in a memorandum prepared for the Secretary of State on March 24, he had no desire or intention to press the issue so hard as to risk any kind of rupture; indeed, he would probably have recoiled from any such suggestion. He simply wanted to make a firm and friendly defense of neutral rights and international law, file a *caveat*, and permit the violation of neutral rights under protest until the end of the war, when a legal settlement could be made. To do less, he thought, would be to stir the resentment of the American people, hand a powerful political issue to the Republican party, and abandon the ground for private legal claims against the British government. Worse still, it would mean renouncing America's chief duty in the war —the defense of neutral rights. As he put it in this same memorandum:

"The United States in the present war is the guardian of neutrality. For the sake of the future it ought to assert firmly the rights of neutrals. I have the impression that Great Britain after the war is over will be glad to recede from certain positions now assumed and admit that the position taken by the United States was legally correct. . . . While the assertion of legal rights may have no practical effect on the present com-

[116] See Lansing's comments upon the newspaper text of the Order in Council, written presumably on March 16, 1915, and his memorandum dated March 20, 1915, printed in *The Lansing Papers*, I, 273-277, 280-281.

[117] James B. Scott *et al.* to the Counselor of the State Department, March 18, 1915, copy in the Anderson Papers.

mercial situation, it will in the future be of extreme value to those who suffer by reason of the Order in Council and to neutrals in general in case of another maritime war."[118]

These were deep convictions, but it was not easy for a man who remembered his place to come out openly against the President of the United States. In his uncertainty, Lansing called in his friend, Chandler P. Anderson, on March 20 for advice and laid the President's draft before him. Anderson was shocked. The President, he said, had given away almost everything; unless the note to Great Britain went further than Wilson's, the American government would fail in its duty as a neutral and in its primary obligation to protect national interests.[119]

His own convictions thus confirmed, Lansing decided that he had no choice but to take the risk of drafting a new note. "As I have approached the subject from an entirely different standpoint from that of the President, who accepts the assertions in the British note that a blockade has been instituted," he explained as he sent his draft to the Secretary of State on March 22, "I have taken the liberty of preparing a suggestion for reply based on the ground that the Order in Council is inconsistent with their statement that a blockade has been established. . . . I hesitate to submit this suggestion on account of the President's memorandum but believe it to be my duty to do so."[120]

In an obviously moderate temper Lansing's draft went straight to the point of the British inconsistency on the legal issues and reminded the London government of the accepted law governing the maintenance of a blockade. Moreover, it rejected the Order in Council's implication that German action justified illegal British retaliation that impaired the rights of neutrals, and it warned that the United States expected the British navy to respect legitimate American commerce with neutral ports. Should illegal interference occur, the draft concluded, the United States government would hold the British responsible for any ensuing loss or damage to American citizens.[121]

Sending the Counselor's draft to the White House on March 22, Bryan put his own point of view into writing for the first time. He was not greatly impressed by Lansing's exegesis of the legal aspects of blockade. The word "blockade," the Secretary wrote, described a method of procedure. "We cannot, I think," he went on, "ignore the change in methods

[118] "Memorandum by the Counselor . . . ," *The Lansing Papers*, I, 290-291.
[119] Anderson Diary, March 20, 1915.
[120] R. Lansing to W. J. Bryan, March 22, 1915, *The Lansing Papers*, I, 281-282.
[121] "Memorandum by the Counselor . . . ," dated March 22, 1915, *ibid.*, pp. 282-285.

of warfare. If we recognize the submarine as a legitimate engine of war, we cannot ignore the change in the location of the blockade line made necessary by the use of the submarine. So far as the blockade of enemy's ports are [*sic*] concerned, I believe the use of the submarine justifies the withdrawing of the cordon to a sufficient distance to protect the blockading ships." What did disturb him, Bryan added, was the British government's announced intention to stop noncontraband goods going to Germany through neutral ports. The President's draft, Bryan pointed out gently, assumed that the British did not intend to interfere with such commerce, but the language of the Order in Council was clear on this point.[122] "In the matter of the blockade," Bryan reiterated in a second letter on the following day, "we can make allowance for the use of new implements of warfare but the changing of conditions does not affect the laws in regard to contraband. Unless a belligerent has a right to add *everything* to the contraband list we cannot concede their right to interfere with shipments through neutral countries of such merchandise as is not contraband."[123]

Whether President Wilson had already concluded that his own first draft had yielded too much on the issue of trade in noncontraband with Germany through neutral ports, or whether he was persuaded by Bryan's analysis, the records do not reveal. In any event, he replied at once in entire agreement with the Secretary of State in a clear and incisive statement of his own second thoughts, as follows:

"These notes by Mr. Lansing are admirable and convincing; but they lead only to debate, and debate with the British Government (which for the time being consists of the War Office and the Admiralty) is at present of no practical avail.

"Inconsistencies in the Order and inconsistencies between the Order and Sir Edward Grey's note accompanying it are neither here nor there, as it seems to me; neither is the lack of the ordinary forms of notice of blockade. We are face to face with *something they are going to do*, and they are going to do it no matter what representations we make. We cannot convince them or change them, we can only show them very clearly what we mean to be our own attitude and course of action and that we mean to hold them to a strict responsibility for every invasion of our rights as neutrals. . . .

"If, then, we speak only to the facts, is not this our right course? Ought we not to say, in effect: You call this a blockade and mean

[122] W. J. Bryan to W.W., March 22, 1915, *ibid.*, pp. 285-286.
[123] W. J. Bryan to W.W., March 23, 1915, *ibid.*, pp. 287-288.

to maintain it as such; but it is obvious that it is unprecedented in almost every respect, but chiefly in this, that it is a blockade of neutral as well as of belligerent coasts and harbours, which no belligerent can claim as a right. We shall expect therefore that the discretion lodged by the Order in Council in the administrative officers and courts of the crown will be exercised to correct what is irregular in this situation and leave the way open to our legitimate trade. If this is not done we shall have to hold you to a strict accountability for every instance of rights violated and injury done; but we interpret Sir Edward Grey's note to mean that this is exactly what will be done. . . .

"I hope that Mr. Lansing will be kind enough to try his hand at a note such as I have indicated, and then we can get together (perhaps all three of us?) and put the thing into a shape that will thoroughly hold water (and exclude it, too, as a maritime paper should)."[124]

It was, of course, the final word, and Lansing set to work on a new draft on March 24, completing it on the following day for delivery to the White House.[125] At some time during the next three days the President worked through Lansing's draft and typed out a new one. "You will see what I have done," he wrote to the Counselor as he sent the draft to him on March 28. "I have recast the note as a statement and interpretation: so that there is no argument involved, but it is meant to mean: We have the Order and the note accompanying it. We cannot understand these as notice of illegal action. We shall assume the contrary until actual things compel us to look upon the matter differently. Then we shall hold the British government responsible in accordance with the well known principles of international law, of which we now remind her, so that she may know just what we understand them to be."[126]

Lansing was satisfied. The note, he thought, now made sufficient reservation of American legal rights, and he sent it back to the President after making minor editorial changes, "being chiefly 'pluralizing'

[124] W.W. to W. J. Bryan, March 24, 1915, *ibid.*, pp. 288-289.

[125] Lansing's first draft was in rough outline form. It was a penciled memorandum entitled "*Notes. Reply to Great Britain on Order in Council of March 15, 1915*," and is in the State Department Papers. His second draft, entitled "Draft Telegram to American Ambassador, London. March 25," *ibid.*, is the one that he sent to the White House and the copy that Wilson used as a basis for the final draft of the note that was actually sent.

[126] W.W. to R. Lansing, March 28, 1915, *The Lansing Papers*, I, 293. Wilson used large portions of Lansing's draft in preparing the final version of the note. His most important change was to convert the Counselor's somewhat contentious arguments about the laws of blockade into statements of fact, and to add that the American government assumed that of course the British authorities accepted these rules.

pronouns relating to the British Government."[127] Wilson then sent the revised copy to Bryan for his comment. The Secretary of State was immensely pleased: "The position which you take is very clearly and strongly stated and yet due consideration is given to the exigencies that call forth the Order in Council and to the promises which they make in regard to its enforcement." With Lansing's approval Bryan made two changes clarifying the President's language and added "a little sweetening" to the concluding paragraph. "I am sure," he further wrote, "you will pardon me for making these suggestions, in compliance with your request."[128] Wilson approved graciously,[129] and the note as thus edited went to London a few hours later—at eight p.m. on March 30, 1915.

It began with the frank observation that the British Order in Council of March 11, if interpreted literally, would constitute a "practical assertion of unlimited belligerent rights over neutral commerce within the whole European area, and an almost unqualified denial of the sovereign rights of the nations now at peace." The American government, the note continued, took it for granted that there was no question what those rights were, for the governments of the United States and of Great Britain had both affirmed them time and again in the past. They included the right to carry on unlimited trade in noncontraband goods with neutral nations and even with an enemy of Great Britain, provided such innocent goods went to or came from enemy territory through neutral ports. The British government had announced the establishment of a new kind of blockade. The Washington administration recognized that changed conditions of modern warfare might justify new methods, but it could not admit the right of any belligerent to blockade neutral traffic in noncontraband goods to or from neutral ports. By no interpretation of international law could the right of retaliation be stretched this far, and the American government confidently anticipated that British naval authorities would not interfere with the approach of American merchantmen to neutral ports when they did not carry "contraband of war or goods destined to or proceeding from ports within the belligerent territory affected."[130] The American government was confident that His Majesty's Government would adjust their practices to the "recognized rules of international law,"

[127] R. Lansing to W.W., March 28, 1915, *ibid.*, p. 294.

[128] W. J. Bryan to W.W., March 29, 1915, *ibid.*, pp. 295-296.

[129] W. W. to W. J. Bryan, March 30, 1915, *ibid.*, p. 296.

[130] That is, unless American ships were trying to force the British blockade by trading directly with enemy ports.

conscientiously avoid imposing illegal hardships upon neutral commerce, and be prepared to make reparation for every violation of American neutral rights. The note then concluded with Bryan's "sweetening" final paragraph. It explained that this statement had been made in a friendly spirit and in accord with the candor which had characterized the close relations of the two governments in the past.[131]

It was, altogether, an extraordinary achievement that reconciled Lansing's determination to affirm and reserve legal rights with Wilson's and Bryan's decision to offer no challenge to the so-called blockade at this time. In certain respects the note of March 30, 1915, was inconsistent, but minor irregularities did not obscure its main meaning: The American government would accept the new British blockade system, novel and unprecedented though it was in law, but only so long as the British kept substantially within the bounds of international law in enforcing it against American commerce.

This, therefore, was the way that the President replied at the outset to the challenge of the submarine and the cruiser—by tacitly accepting both new systems of naval warfare as the inevitable consequence of the prolongation and embittering of the war, and by warning that he meant to hold both the Germans and the British to a strict accountability for the violation of American neutral rights.

There was no guarantee, Wilson knew, that his response would protect American ships from the peril of the torpedo or keep the channels of legitimate commerce to Central Europe open. "Together," as he put it, "England and Germany are likely to drive us crazy, because it looks oftentimes as if they were crazy themselves, the unnecessary provocations they invent."[132] "Both sides," he added three weeks later, "are seeing red on the other side of the sea, and neutral rights are left, for the time being, out of their reckoning altogether. They listen to necessity (and to necessity as they interpret it), not to reason, and there is therefore no way of calculating or preparing for anything."[133]

In these circumstances what more could a responsible leader do than combine expedient yielding with firm attachment to principle, and hope that reason would soon rule the day?

[131] The Secretary of State to Ambassador Page, March 30, 1915, *Foreign Relations, 1915, Supplement*, pp. 152-156.

[132] W.W. to Mary A. Hulbert, February 14, 1915, Wilson-Hulbert Letters, Princeton University Library; hereinafter cited as the Wilson-Hulbert Letters.

[133] W.W. to Mary A. Hulbert, March 7, 1915, *ibid.*

CHAPTER XI

Mounting Tension with Germany

EVENTS following the dispatch of the American note of March 30, 1915, to London soon made plain what President Wilson and his advisers had not yet entirely seen—the difficulty of continuing to steer the ship of state on a safe course by relying for navigation on the sextant of expediency. The trouble was that once Germany had undertaken her own maritime campaign it was no longer possible for the President to formulate policies toward one belligerent without profoundly affecting the policies of the other belligerent toward the United States. The sizable dimensions of this dilemma became quickly apparent once the United States had acquiesced, or, more accurately, had seemed to acquiesce, in the new British blockade.

The most important consequence was the sudden and serious deterioration of German-American relations that occurred during April and early May of 1915. Leaders and public spokesmen in Germany thought that they understood the import of the American note of March 30 as soon as it was published in the German press on April 7. It means, exclaimed the editorial spokesman of the Conservative party, "the far-reaching retreat of America, inasmuch as it permits Great Britain to carry out its 'blockade' measures against American ships even when they carry goods which are not contraband, but come from or go to ports of hostile lands." "It appears to be a note against Germany rather than against England," the usually restrained *Cologne Gazette* agreed. ". . . It affords England certitude that she may continue her illegal blockade of Germany. It is carte blanche for the English war of starvation. . . . America submits to every English act of violence, while at the same time she continues eagerly to supply our enemies with arms and other war material, and even advances them money for these supplies."[1]

The impact upon German public opinion of the American failure to challenge the British blockade was all the more profound because the publication of the note of March 30 took place at the same time

[1] Berlin *Kreuz-Zeitung* and *Kölnische Zeitung*, cited in the New York *World*, April 8, 1915.

when the export of American munitions to the Allies was mounting and beginning to cause a frenzy of bitter comment throughout Germany. "Next to their English cousins," wrote an American correspondent after traveling the length and breadth of the Empire, "the sons of the Fatherland dislike the Americans. . . . The hatred against everything and everybody American has become more pronounced since the allies are said to have commenced to use American arms and ammunition against the Germans."[2]

German bitterness over the twin issues of blockade and munitions was profoundly intensified and official German-American relations were severely jolted by an incident not long after the dispatch of the American note to London. For some months Count Johann von Bernstorff, the German Ambassador in Washington, had been active organizing and inciting sentiment in the United States, particularly among the German Americans, for the adoption of an embargo on the export of munitions. As agitation for the measure had ebbed drastically following the adjournment of Congress in early March, the Ambassador set to work to stimulate a new campaign, which he hoped to inaugurate with an official public protest against the arms traffic by the Imperial Embassy itself.[3] On March 28, 1915, he asked the Foreign Office in Berlin for permission to submit such a statement, saying that he would use as a pretext the American government's refusal to permit German agents to supply coal to German cruisers at sea.[4] The Foreign Office was discouraging,[5] but the Ambassador went ahead, probably on his own initiative,[6] and handed a memorandum dated April 4 to the State Department on April 9, timing the delivery so

---

[2] Gustav C. Roeder in *ibid.*, April 17, 1915.

[3] This statement is based upon circumstantial evidence which will become apparent as this account proceeds.

[4] Ambassador von Bernstorff to the Foreign Office, March 28, 1915, German F. O. Archives.

[5] The Foreign Secretary to Ambassador von Bernstorff, March 31, 1915, *ibid.*

[6] Bernstorff declared at the time and afterward wrote in his memoirs that the Foreign Office had authorized him to present his protest to the State Department. *New York Times*, April 14, 1915; J. von Bernstorff, *My Three Years in America*, pp. 63-64. On the other hand, the files of the German Foreign Office do not contain any evidence to support this statement. The correspondence in these archives shows clearly enough that Bernstorff did not submit his memorandum to the Foreign Office before he handed it to the State Department. He had not yet sent a copy to Berlin as late as April 19, 1915, although the statement had already been published in the newspapers both in America and in Germany.

Neutral America

"Don't think for a moment, Mr. Death, that I wish only to make money.
I sell you these things only because they will bring peace to the world."

Simplicissimus (Munich)

that it occurred just three days after the publication in the United
States of the American note to Great Britain of March 30.

Bernstorff's statement was an extraordinarily bitter, indeed, an almost
insulting, articulation of the rising German feeling. Reviewing the
alleged failure of the Washington government to protect the trade

of its citizens in noncontraband with Germany, it declared accusingly: "The Imperial Embassy must therefore assume that the United States Government acquiesces in the violations of international law by Great Britain." Then followed a denunciation of the arms traffic and the accusation that the United States government was failing to observe "the spirit of true neutrality" by refusing to prevent the export of munitions when such deadly merchandise could go only to one side in the struggle. Finally, as if to rub salt in the wound, the Ambassador cited the President's own statement, made earlier in connection with the Mexican civil war, to the effect that "the true spirit of neutrality as compared with a mere paper neutrality" demanded an embargo on the export of arms to the parties to a conflict.[7]

When the State Department said not a word about the protest to newspapermen, Bernstorff gave a copy to the press on April 11, 1915. And he timed its publication to coincide with the appearance in newspapers throughout the country of "An Appeal to the American People," a full-page petition for an arms embargo which had been signed by the editors and publishers of more than one hundred foreign-language newspapers, not including any in the German language.[8] As the Ambassador explained to his superiors in Berlin, "Our friends here have greeted the memorandum as a fanfare which gave the signal for renewed attack."[9] "From the standpoint of this nation [Germany]," he added a few days later, "the principal value of the Memorandum lies in the fact that it is strengthening the agitation against export of weapons and will serve as a banner around which the advocates of an embargo will gather."[10]

Surveying the damage done to German-American relations by his own cleverness, the Ambassador must have wondered, however, whether the small return justified the great cost, and whether he had not permitted arrogance to carry him beyond bounds. To begin with, the publication of the memorandum set off a nearly unprecedented venting of anti-German spleen throughout the United States. Such epithets as "insulting," "preposterous," "insolent," "offensive and arrogant," and "impudent" "meet the eye again and again as we scan

[7] The German Ambassador to the Secretary of State, April 4, 1915, *Foreign Relations, 1915, Supplement*, pp. 157-158.

[8] For the text of the "Appeal," see the New York *Outlook*, cix (April 14, 1915), 860, and the *Literary Digest*, l (April 17, 1915), 861.

[9] Ambassador von Bernstorff to the Foreign Office, April 16, 1915, German F. O. Archives.

[10] Ambassador von Bernstorff to the Foreign Office, April 19, 1915, *ibid.*

the editorial utterances of the American press on Germany's 'memorandum' to our State Department," reported the editors of the *Literary Digest*. ". . . Even in such centers of German-American population as Milwaukee, St. Louis, and Cincinnati we find vigorous dissent from the German contentions."[11] As one New York editor said, "If the allies were directing the affairs of the German Embassy in Washington they could hardly have hit upon anything more shrewdly calculated to prejudice American opinion against the German cause than the Bernstorff note. If notable service deserves a corresponding reward, Great Britain owes Count von Bernstorff the Garter and France the Grand Cross of the Legion of Honor."[12]

Worse still was the way Bernstorff's note further fanned the flames of anger toward America among his own people when it was published in the German press on April 14, 1915. "Our Foreign Office," one editor exclaimed, for example, "has now found the right language against France, against England, and, without any sort of consideration, against the United States too. With consideration and forbearance we get nowhere. The German people will gradually finish with their open enemies, . . . but behind them stand other enemies who pretend to be neutral . . . but who, none the less, continuously and zealously support our enemies and assist them in their war against us."[13]

There was one further important consequence of this affair—the irreparable damage to his own standing and influence with the American government that Bernstorff's bungling caused. Although the Secretary of State soon replied temperately (in words written for the most part by the President) to the Ambassador's accusations,[14] he made no effort to conceal his and President Wilson's shock and anger at the entire affair.[15] There is no direct evidence to reveal Wilson's own reaction, but it seems reasonable to believe that his really violent antipathy for Bernstorff, which was clearly evident a few months later, had its roots in the episode we have just related.

This poison in the bloodstream of German-American relations would have gained additional potency simply as a consequence of the contin-

[11] *Literary Digest*, L (April 24, 1915), 937.

[12] New York *World*, April 14, 1915.

[13] *Hamburger Nachrichten*, April 14, 1915. For similar if slightly less ominous comments, see the Berlin *Vossische Zeitung*, April 22, 1915, and the *Berliner Lokal-Anzeiger*, morning edn., April 22, 1915.

[14] The Secretary of State to the German Ambassador, April 21, 1915, *Foreign Relations, 1915, Supplement*, pp. 160-162.

[15] New York *World*, April 13 and 20, 1915.

uing agitation of the munitions question, but one particularly unfortunate incident greatly exacerbated German bitterness in the late spring of 1915. It began when the Cleveland Automatic Machine Company published a full-page advertisement in a weekly trade journal on May 6, 1915, displaying an automatic machine that produced a new type of shrapnel shell. The advertisement described the shell, as follows:

"The material is high in tensile strength and VERY SPECIAL and has a tendency to fracture into small pieces upon the explosion of the shell. The timing of the fuse for this shell is similar to the shrapnel shell, but it differs in that two explosive acids are used to explode the shell in the large cavity. The combination of these two acids causes terrific explosion, having more power than anything of its kind yet used. Fragments become coated with these acids in exploding and wounds caused by them mean death in terrible agony within four hours if not attended to immediately.

"From what we are able to learn of conditions in the trenches, it is not possible to get medical assistance to anyone in time to prevent fatal results. It is necessary to immediately cauterize the wound if in the body or head, or to amputate if in the limbs, as there seems to be no antidote that will counteract the poison.

"It can be seen from this that this shell is more effective than the regular shrapnel, since the wounds caused by shrapnel balls and fragments in the muscles are not as dangerous as they have no poisonous element making prompt attention necessary."[16]

The *Frankfurter Zeitung* picked up the advertisement and published its text in full on June 1, 1915. Then on June 26 it printed a facsimile of the advertisement on its front page, along with the following comment: "It is significant that the American man of feeling glories in its manufacture; the struggle of the wounded is especially terrible. To some readers the reported fact was so monstrous that they doubted its veracity. To lay all such doubts, the original is herewith published."[17] Inevitably, other German newspapers followed suit,[18] while the Foreign Office called Ambassador Gerard's attention to the advertisement,[19] and some-

[16] *American Machinist*, XII (May 6, 1915), 27.

[17] *Frankfurter Zeitung*, third morning edn., June 26, 1915.

[18] e.g., Berlin *Deutsche Tageszeitung*, evening edn., June 25, 1915; Berlin *Vossische Zeitung*, evening edn., June 25, 1915; *Kölnische Volkszeitung*, evening edn., June 25, 1915.

[19] *New York Times*, July 8, 1915.

The President about 1915

President Wilson and His Granddaughter, Ellen Wilson McAdoo

Herbert Asquith

Theobald von Bethmann Hollweg

LEADERS OF RIVAL ALLIANCES

Robert Lansing

William J. Bryan

MAKERS OF AMERICAN FOREIGN POLICY

Sir Edward Grey   Colonel House

BUILDERS OF THE ANGLO-AMERICAN PEACE

James W. Gerard

Jules J. Jusserand

Walter H. Page

Sir Cecil Spring Rice

AMBASSADORS ALL

Count Johann von Bernstorff and Hugo Münsterberg

Lusitania Leaving New York Harbor on Her Last Voyage

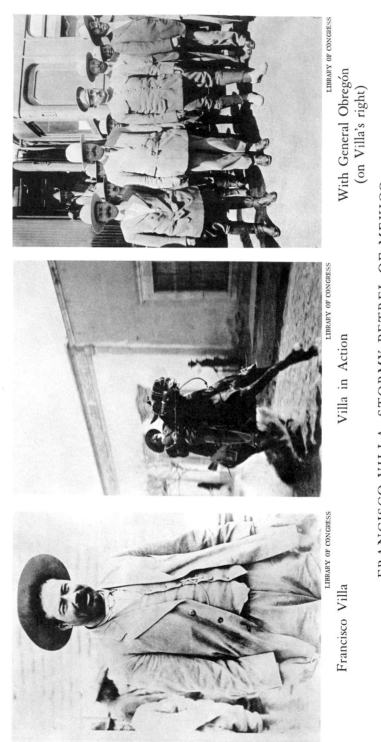

With General Obregón
(on Villa's right)

Villa in Action

Francisco Villa

FRANCISCO VILLA, STORMY PETREL OF MEXICO

one laid a facsimile copy on the desk of every member of the Reichstag.[20]

Such harsh outbursts, such proclamations that the United States must now be numbered among the enemies of the Fatherland, as were evoked by Bernstorff's memorandum, had an indescribably important significance and impact. They reflected convictions and emotions that were shared as much by the leaders as by the people of Germany; above all, they surcharged the German atmosphere at the very time when the leaders of the Empire were being pressed to change the one policy—the conduct of submarine operations—that could threaten the German-American peace.

To say the least, the submarine campaign had not been going well since mid-February. Results to April 1, 1915—a total of 132,000 tons sent to the bottom, according to the German count—were not enough to justify the effort, much less to vindicate the extravagant predictions of the naval spokesmen. To von Tirpitz and Bachmann the solution was simple: remove the chief obstacle to a successful submarine campaign—the Emperor's order compelling U-boat commanders to spare neutral ships. On April 1 Bachmann submitted a report to the Emperor surveying the dismal record and urging an intensification of operations. The submarine war could really be effective, he urged, only if U-boats could attack all ships in the war zone, and could attack them without having to surface and determine their nationality.[21] Tirpitz cornered William at Supreme Headquarters at Charleville on the following day and, reiterating Bachmann's argument generally, emphasized the dangers that submarines encountered by surfacing.[22] Without waiting to consult his political advisers, the Emperor immediately sent two orders

[20] J. W. Gerard to E. M. House, August 24, 1915, House Papers. The incident, it might be added, also stirred up considerable furor in Washington, including discussion of the advertisement at a Cabinet meeting, an investigation to determine whether the offensive piece could be barred from the United States mails, and the sending of a sharp reprimand to the Cleveland Automatic Machine Company by the administration. See J. P. Brophy, vice president and general manager of the Cleveland Automatic Machine Company, to W.W., June 21, 1915, Wilson Papers, File VI, Box 492; W. C. Redfield to W.W., July 12, 1915, *ibid.*; W. C. Redfield to J. P. Brophy, July 12, 1915, *ibid.*; W.W. to E. F. Sweet, July 14, 1915, *ibid.*, Letterbook 22; W. C. Redfield to the Hill Publishing Company, July 12, 1915, *ibid.*, File VI, Box 492; E. F. Sweet to W.W., July 16, 1915, *ibid.*; the Postmaster General to the Secretary of State, *Foreign Relations, 1915, Supplement*, p. 788; the Secretary of State to Ambassador Gerard, July 7, 1915, *ibid.*, pp. 789-790; the Secretary of State to the Postmaster General, July 8, 1915, *ibid.*, p. 790.
[21] Admiral Bachmann, "Effect of the Submarine War," memorandum dated April 1, 1915, copy in the German F. O. Archives.
[22] Tirpitz, *Politische Dokumente*, II, 329.

to the fleet, one urging U-boat captains to exercise great caution before surfacing to inspect merchant ships, the other "requesting" that submarines no longer surface before attacking merchantmen.[23]

The result was not a wholesale attack against neutral commerce—for submarine commanders were still under orders to make earnest efforts to spare neutral shipping—but rather the creation of an operational twilight zone in which mistakes could be more easily made. For technical reasons the toll of ships was smaller in April than it had been the month before; but of the seventeen steamers sent to the bottom in April, six were of neutral registry.[24] It was sheer chance that none of these was American. Then during late April and early May came better weather, a significant intensification of submarine operations, and the first "mistake" involving an American ship.[25] It occurred on May 1 in the Irish Sea, when one Commander von Rosenberg of the *U30* sent a torpedo without warning into a large steamer, which he thought was being escorted by two British patrol boats. It was the American tanker *Gulflight*, 5,189 tons, from Port Arthur, Texas. During the explosion the captain died of heart failure, and two sailors were drowned when they jumped overboard.[26]

The significance of the *Gulflight* incident lay not so much in the impact that it would have upon German-American relations as in the way in which the sinking of this ship symbolized the change in the attitude of the German leaders toward the United States that had taken place since the dispatch of the "strict accountability" note to Berlin in early February. It will be recalled that the leaders of the Empire had then recoiled in fear of immediate American retaliation. Gradually during February and March that fear subsided; gradually the conviction spread,

[23] *ibid.*

[24] R. H. Gibson and M. Prendergast, *The German Submarine War, 1914-1918*, p. 37.

[25] Actually, three American ships had earlier been sunk or damaged in the war zones. Two were sunk by mines—the *Evelyn*, off Borkum Island in the North Sea on February 19, 1915, and the *Carib*, in the same area on February 22, 1915. As both ships came to grief because they had failed to travel in the safety zone marked out by the German Admiralty and there was no loss of life in either case, the incidents never became the subject either of any controversy or of much diplomatic correspondence between Germany and the United States. *New York Times*, February 22, 23, and 24, 1915; the German Ambassador to the Secretary of State, March 26, 1915, *Foreign Relations, 1915, Supplement*, pp. 669-670.

A third American ship, the *Cushing*, was bombed in the North Sea by a German airplane on April 29, 1915. Only one bomb struck the vessel, causing no loss of life and virtually no damage. New York *World*, May 2, 1915.

[26] *New York Times*, May 3 and 4, 1915; Spindler, *La Guerre Sous-Marine*, II, 100.

even among civilian leaders, that the American government had no intention of enforcing its threats. That conviction deepened in early April as a consequence of the Washington government's note to Great Britain of March 30 and its seeming reluctance to confront Japanese ambitions in China. "The United States of America," Imperial Chancellor von Bethmann Hollweg told the Committee on Foreign Affairs of the Bundesrat on April 7, "would be able to play an influential role if imaginative and strong men were at her head. That is not the case."[27] At about the same time the chief of the German General Staff commented on the "lack of farsighted, purposeful, and energetic personalities at the important posts in the American Government."[28]

In the German view, Bernstorff's messages from Washington gave proof positive that the disdain now spreading in Berlin was justified. "The policy of the American Government," he reported in a dispatch that was read by the General Staff and the Emperor, "is dominated by the one thought of not becoming involved in any complications whatever. *'We want to stay out of everything'* is the single rule. ["Then stop the ammunition!" the Emperor wrote on the side of the dispatch.] Accordingly, notes are being sent alternately to Berlin, London, Mexico, and Tokyo without any measures which would give emphasis to them." ["Peace at any price," the Emperor wrote again in derisive comment.] The Washington government, the Ambassador went on, would simply knuckle under to Great Britain, for the "Government here is continually attempting to *squirm out of* every problem without getting into severe difficulties."[29]

One development in submarine policy in mid-April gave specific evidence of the ebbing of the fear of America among the German leaders. In early April a submarine sank the Dutch steamer *Katwijk* without warning. Reaction in Holland was so violent that the Foreign Office dispatched a note of apology at once; and the Emperor, on April 18, and the Admiralty, on April 24, sent urgent new warnings to the fleet to spare neutral shipping. But on the first occasion U-boat commanders were instructed to exercise great care in dealing with Dutch ships, and on the second to avoid sinking Dutch and Italian vessels (for the Ger-

[27] E. R. May, *The World War and American Isolation*, p. 131.

[28] "Communication of General von Falkenhayn about His Conversation Today with General Conrad von Hötzendorf," memorandum dated April 5, 1915, copy in German F. O. Archives.

[29] Ambassador von Bernstorff to the Foreign Office, April 6, 1915, *ibid*. The Ambassador repeated these sentiments in a dispatch to the Foreign Office on April 19, 1915, *ibid*.

man government was then engaged in last-minute negotiations to avert Italian entry into the war on the Allied side); not a single word of caution was added about American shipping.[30] "Mistakes" involving neutral ships increased in spite of these new orders, and it was evident by the first of May that the German leaders were heading for a new showdown over the character and scope of submarine operations.

Given the fairly even balance of power that prevailed between the naval chieftains and the political leaders in Germany at this point, the outcome of their battle would depend largely upon the attitude of the neutrals. And whether the neutrals resisted to the point of threatening violent retaliation or acquiesced in an intensified submarine campaign would in large measure (especially after Italy entered the war on May 23, 1915) depend upon the reaction of the United States.

The question that the American leaders had to face in April and early May of 1915 was the basic one of determining their responses to the German submarine war in practical terms—in other words, of giving meaning to the hitherto ambiguous words "strict accountability." Would they reason that it was impossible to prevent the death grapple of the belligerents at sea and conclude that they had no choice but to acquiesce as much in the German maritime campaign as in the British? That is to say, would they forgive occasional submarine attacks against American ships so long as there was some chance that such attacks had been unavoidable in the difficult circumstances of the war at sea? Would they draw a hard line between submarine attacks that endangered American life on Allied merchantmen and on passenger ships, and accept the one and oppose the other? Or would they adopt a stern posture and hold the Germans to strict accountability in every single case involving American lives and property?

The incident that provoked the first serious discussions in Washington was one, ironically enough, that forced the American leaders to consider the submarine challenge as it endangered all American life, not merely American lives on American ships, in the war zone. It was the sinking of a small British liner, the *Falaba*, 4,806 tons, outward bound from Liverpool for West Africa, by the German *U28* in Saint George's Channel on March 28, 1915. It resulted in the death, among others, of an American citizen, Leon C. Thrasher, who was returning to his post as a mining engineer on the Gold Coast. Whether the attack was a particularly brutal one is still a subject of some debate; but there can

[30] Tirpitz, *Politische Dokumente*, II, 332; Spindler, *La Guerre Sous-Marine*, II, 110-111.

be no doubt that the commander of the *U28* fired his torpedo knowing that it would cause the death of many passengers.[31]

The leaders in Washington first read the news of the sinking and of Thrasher's death in the newspapers on the morning of March 31, 1915. Ambassador Page confirmed this report in a brief telegram on the same day, and the Consul General at London, Robert P. Skinner, added a detailed account on April 7. It would not have been possible for the President and his advisers to ignore the incident even if they had wanted to, so violent was the reaction of the American press. "Barbarism run mad," "triumph of horror," "a humiliation to all the world," "shocking bloodthirstiness," and similar expletives filled editorial pages throughout the country, although there was no apparent pressure anywhere for retaliatory action.[32]

Discussions in the inner administration circle began on April 2, when Lansing reviewed the circumstances of the case in a letter to the Secretary of State and raised the pointed question: "Ought we not to hold the German Government responsible for the death of an American through the act of their naval forces, when that act is in violation of the established rules of naval warfare?" If so, the Counselor went on, then "duty would appear to require a complaint and a demand for damages." On the other hand, to make such a complaint would compel the American government to denounce the entire German submarine campaign as it was being carried out as a violation of international law.[33]

---

[31] The commander of the *U28*, one Baron von Forstner, signaled the *Falaba* to stop. She attempted to escape, but the submarine overtook her, and von Forstner then gave the *Falaba's* captain ten minutes in which to evacuate his ship. Forstner, in fact, waited twenty-three minutes; then, seeing smokestacks approaching on the horizon, he fired his torpedo while the passengers and crew were still lowering lifeboats. This is the way that Arno Spindler, the German naval historian, has told the story after reading the log of the *U28* and talking with von Forstner. Spindler, II, 63-68.

Spindler's account, however, is apparently inaccurate in some details and omits other important ones. Eyewitnesses swore that von Forstner gave the captain of the *Falaba* only ten minutes for the evacuation of his ship. See the Consul General at London to the Secretary of State, April 7 and 9, 1915, *Foreign Relations, 1915, Supplement*, pp. 359-360, 362-363. Moreover, two British naval historians tell us that von Forstner was ruthless and savage throughout his career as a U-boat captain. Before sinking the small British liner *Aguila* on March 27, 1915, for example, he opened fire on the passengers and crew as they were taking to the boats, causing the death of eight persons. After sending a torpedo into the *Falaba* on the following day, moreover, von Forstner allegedly came up on the deck of the *U28* and jeered at the drowning passengers. See R. H. Gibson and M. Prendergast, *The German Submarine War*, pp. 35-36.

[32] See the review of press opinion in the *Literary Digest*, L (April 10, 1915), 789-791.

[33] R. Lansing to W. J. Bryan, April 2, 1915, *The Lansing Papers*, I, 365-366.

This, Lansing added in a separate memorandum, could conceivably lead to a war between the two countries that might not be disadvantageous to Germany.[34] Troubled and by no means certain where he stood, Bryan sent Lansing's letter to the White House with some questions of his own—whether the United States should not recognize the submarine campaign as proper and ask merely for monetary damages, and whether an American who voluntarily traveled on a British vessel through the war zone had the right to expect protection from his government.[35]

Wilson, apparently, shared the Secretary of State's misgivings, but his impulsive conclusion was that the submarine commander had of course violated international law, and that the American government should say that its citizens must not be endangered "by acts which have no sanction whatever in the accepted law of nations." He suggested that Lansing prepare a "brief and succinct" note to serve as a basis for discussion of the policy to be formulated.[36] Commenting two days later on Lansing's memorandum pointing up the possibility of actual conflict, the President also made it plain that he realized the dangers of testing the issue. "We must," he wrote to Bryan, "compound policy with legal right in wise proportions, no doubt."[37]

Convinced that he was dealing with an ultimate issue about which compromise was not possible,[38] Lansing set to work and completed the draft note that the President had requested on April 5. Lansing's language was, as he himself described it, "plain almost to harshness." It denounced the sinking of the *Falaba* as an outrage—a wanton and flagrant violation of "international morality"—and asserted plainly enough the right of American citizens to travel in the war zone without the peril of sudden death by torpedoes. Curiously, in view of its nearly provocative tone and language, the proposed note made no demands upon the Imperial German authorities but merely "appealed earnestly" to them to disavow the act of their submarine commander;

[34] "Memorandum by the Counselor . . . on Relations with Germany and Possibilities," dated February 15, 1915, but sent to Bryan on April 2, 1915, *ibid.*, pp. 367-368.

[35] W. J. Bryan to W.W., April 2, 1915, *ibid.*, p. 366.

[36] W.W. to W. J. Bryan, April 3, 1915, *ibid.*, p. 368.

[37] W.W. to W. J. Bryan, April 5, 1915, *ibid.*, p. 369.

[38] "I feel this: If it is decided to denounce the sinking of the *Falaba* as an act indefensible legally and morally, we will have to say so . . . ," he wrote to Bryan. "If the note is weak or uncertain, it had better not be sent. The situation does not seem to me to be one for compromise." R. Lansing to W. J. Bryan, April 5, 1915, *ibid.*, p. 369.

Doin' His Darndest to Keep Cool
Darling in the Des Moines *Register and Leader*

and it ended by expressing the American government's "sincere hope"
that this would be the outcome of the affair.[39]

Intense debate now broke out in the State Department. Chandler P.
Anderson, then serving as a special adviser, argued in a memorandum
that the sinking of the *Falaba* had not been in any way a deliberate
affront to the United States, and that since this was true the German
government's liability could not exceed a pecuniary indemnity for

[39] "Draft Instruction . . . ," *ibid.,* pp. 370-371.

Thrasher's death, provided, of course, that the Washington government could prove that the torpedoing of the *Falaba* had in fact been illegal.[40]

Bryan argued not on points of law, which he only dimly perceived, but on the high and to him familiar ground of national policy and expediency. What the administration did in the Thrasher case, he urged, must be "so obviously defensible as to appeal to the judgment of the entire country." He was confident, he continued, that it was the almost unanimous desire of the American people to avoid involvement in the war, and he could not help feeling that it would be unthinkable to permit one man to involve the entire nation. Both belligerents were waging a bitter war on the seas; both had given warning of dire peril to neutrals. What claim, therefore, could the American government rightfully make when one of its citizens lost his life by ignoring these warnings? Was the American government prepared to go the whole way and vindicate the right of its nationals to travel on belligerent ships regardless of the circumstances?[41]

Lansing in turn came back, in direct reply to Anderson and the Secretary of State, with a clear and forceful elaboration of his point of view. The American government, he said, could not debate the legality of the method employed in sinking the *Falaba*, for "debating the legality to destroy life and the legality to destroy property are very different things."[42] Moreover, the United States could not fail to adopt a clear-cut policy that could be applied to similar cases in the future. Either it had to warn Americans to keep off belligerent vessels in the war zone or else hold Germany to strict accountability for every American life lost by submarine attacks. Expediency favored the first prin-

[40] C. P. Anderson, "Memorandum on the Thrasher Case," dated April 5, 1915, Wilson Papers.

[41] The above paragraph is a composite based upon W. J. Bryan to W.W., April 7 and 8, 1915, *The Lansing Papers*, 1, 374-377. In his letter of April 7, Bryan also raised the question whether the *Falaba* had been armed and whether the United States should assert the right of its citizens to travel on armed ships. Proof soon came, however, that the *Falaba* had not been armed and that Commander Baron von Forstner had discovered this fact before attacking her. The question of the status of armed ships consequently dropped out of the discussion.

[42] R. Lansing, "Comments on Mr. Anderson's Memorandum of April 5, 1915," memorandum dated April 7, 1915, Wilson Papers. Anderson wrote at the bottom of his copy of this memorandum, now in the Anderson Papers, the following comment: "The legal questions to be determined are (1) Whether or not the law of reprisals justifies the adoption by Germany of this method of warfare in retaliation for the illegal interference by G. B. with Germany's trade with neutrals and (2) Whether or not neutrals are entitled as a matter of right to travel or work on belligerent vessels carrying contraband."

ciple; national dignity and duty appeared "to demand a policy in harmony with the second course."[43] In addition, Lansing obtained substantial confirmation of his argument from the Joint Neutrality Board. In an opinion rendered on April 8 it concluded that submarine attacks against merchant vessels without warning were "necessarily illegal" and observed that the circumstances of the destruction of the *Falaba* had been "not only illegal but revoltingly inhuman." The Board made it clear, on the other hand, that the American government was under no real obligation to concern itself with methods of warfare that did not affect its immediate interests.[44]

These were the issues that Wilson pondered as he read through all these papers. He did not give his decision quickly. The legal questions, he obviously must have concluded after reading the opinions of the experts, were neither as simple nor as clear as he had thought at the outset. Where, then, and how should the American government stand if the law provided no sure guide for policy? The answer was not easy for a man who understood so well the desperate character of the struggle on the seas and desired only to avoid entanglement. Yet the more the President thought on these things the more certain convictions must have deepened in his mind—that the fundamental issue was the protection of noncombatant life on the high seas, and that it was not possible for the Germans in the circumstances of their naval weakness to conduct a submarine campaign without resorting to grievous violence. For two weeks he said not a word to indicate the direction of his thinking. Then, on April 22, 1915, he wrote to the Secretary of State:

"Although I have been silent for a long time about the case, I have had it much in my mind, as I have no doubt you have, to work out some practicable course of action with regard to the death of Thrasher; and I have the following to suggest as the outline of a note to the German Government:

(1) State the circumstances, as we have officially received them.

(2) We take it for granted that Germany has had no idea of changing the rules (or, rather, the essential principles) of international law with regard to the safety of non-combatants and of the citizens of neutral countries at sea, however radical the present change in practical conditions

---

[43] R. Lansing to W. J. Bryan, April 7, 1915, *The Lansing Papers*, I, 373-374.
[44] Joint State and Navy Neutrality Board, memorandum dated April 8, 1915, Wilson Papers.

of warfare; and that she will, in accordance with her usual frankness in such matters, acknowledge her responsibility in the present instance.

(3) Raise in a very earnest, though of course entirely friendly, way the whole question of the use of submarines against merchant vessels, calling attention circumstantially to the impossibility of observing the safeguards and precautions so long and so clearly recognized as imperative in such matters: the duty of visit and search; the duty, if the vessel proves to belong to an enemy and cannot be put in charge of a prize crew, to secure the safety of the lives of those on board; etc.

(4) On these grounds enter a very moderately but none the less solemn and emphatic protest against the whole thing, as contrary to laws based, not on mere interest or convenience, but on humanity, fair play, and a necessary respect for the rights of neutrals.

"My idea, as you will see, is to put the whole note on very high grounds,—not on the loss of this single man's life, but on the interests of mankind which are involved and which Germany has always stood for; on the manifest impropriety of a single nation's essaying to alter the understandings of nations; and as all arising out of her mistake in employing an instrument against her enemy's commerce which it is impossible to employ in that use in accordance with any rules that the world is likely to be willing to accept."[45]

Bryan of course asked Lansing to draft a note along these lines, but his soul was greatly troubled. Such a note as the President had suggested, he wrote in a long and passionate reply, would inflame German opinion and provoke a crisis perhaps to the point of war, and simply, Bryan strongly inferred, because the Washington government was condemning German infractions of international law while condoning British violations. The fact was, he went on, that the American government had not protested against Britain's war against noncombatants or prevented British ships from using the American flag. How much better it would be, he pleaded, for the President to urge the belligerents to stop fighting than to take a position that might lead to an extension of the war![46] Sending Lansing's new draft note to the White House four days later, the Secretary of State renewed his appeal for a peace move.[47]

[45] W.W. to W. J. Bryan, April 22, 1915, *The Lansing Papers*, i, 377-378.

[46] W. J. Bryan to W.W., April 23, 1915, *ibid.*, pp. 378-380.

[47] W. J. Bryan to W.W., April 27, 1915, Wilson Papers. I have not been able to find a copy of Lansing's second draft for a Thrasher note. In the letter just cited, however, Bryan wrote that the Counselor had followed the President's outline carefully. Lansing emphasized the point that submarines could not be used properly in a war against merchant commerce.

Wilson was severely shaken. All along he had felt himself to be on uncertain ground; never, apparently, had he contemplated making any demands upon Germany that might provoke a crisis. He discussed the matter with Bryan at a Cabinet meeting on April 27 and put his doubts into writing on the following day. "As I told you yesterday at Cabinet," he wrote to the Secretary, "I am not at all confident that we are on the right track in considering such a note as I outlined for Mr. Lansing to work on. I am not sure that my outline really expressed what I would myself say in the note, for, after all, the character of a note is chiefly in the way the thing is said and the points developed. *Perhaps it is not necessary to make formal representations in the matter at all.*" What he had been thinking about most, the President added, was Bryan's suggestion of a peace move. As much as he would like to believe otherwise, Wilson went on, he was certain that such action now would do more harm than good. "I am afraid, Mr. Secretary," he concluded, "that there is much in this that will seem to you disputable; but I can only state my conviction in matter, and God knows I have searched my mind and conscience both to get the best, the nearest approach to wisdom, there is in them."[48]

Did President Wilson really mean what he clearly implied in this letter, that he had decided to make no formal protest about Thrasher's death? Probably he did. He knew, certainly, that the legal grounds for a protest were weak, and that consequently he would have to base his protest on the broad ground of outright opposition to a submarine campaign. He was under no pressure from public opinion at home to take any such forward stand. He probably assumed that the sinking of the *Falaba* had been an isolated incident, and that the German government had no intention of making ruthless war against passenger ships. And we know that he was profoundly affected by Bryan's arguments; indeed, he *probably* shared the Secretary of State's conviction that fair play and the national interest demanded that the American government respond in the same way to the challenge of the submarine as it had to the challenge of the cruiser, provided (insofar as Wilson was concerned) that the Germans made such acquiescence possible by refraining from raising the issue of national rights in an inescapable way.

Developments that immediately ensued would seem to indicate that this analysis is correct. The first was Wilson's and Bryan's decision either to let the matter of a *Falaba* note lapse for a while or not to

[48] W.W. to W. J. Bryan, April 28, 1915, *The Lansing Papers*, I, 380; italics added.

send a protest at all. More revealing was their reaction to the attacks on the *Cushing* and *Gulflight*. It will be recalled that the former was attacked by a German aircraft in the North Sea on April 29 and that the latter was torpedoed without warning by a German submarine in the Irish Sea on May 1. To Lansing the attack on the *Cushing* seemed to imply that "German naval policy is one of wanton and indiscriminate destruction of vessels regardless of nationality."[49] The torpedoing of the *Gulflight* alarmed him even more, for he thought that it was a sign that the German government meant to force a rupture with the United States.[50] Pointing to the terse language of the note to Berlin of February 10, the Counselor reminded his superiors that they would soon have to make good their earlier threats about holding the German government to "strict accountability."[51]

In contrast to Lansing's state of near panic was the calm, almost matter-of-fact, way the President and Secretary of State reacted to these first direct attacks upon American vessels in the war zone. They must have reasoned that the attack upon the *Cushing* had been an obvious mistake, for which the Berlin government would make swift and proper amends. They were, therefore, apparently not disturbed about it at all. The case of the *Gulflight* was a more serious matter. Wilson and Bryan discussed it at some length during a conference at the White House on the evening of May 3 and at a Cabinet meeting the following day.[52] We know none of the details of these conversations. There is good reason, however, for believing that the President said that some representation would have to be made, but that he intended to postpone the final settlement until the war had ended. This, in any event, was Bryan's clear understanding of Wilson's point of view.[53] In addition, the President made it plain to newspapermen

[49] R. Lansing to W. J. Bryan, May 1, 1915, *ibid.*, pp. 381-382.

[50] R. Lansing to W. J. Bryan, May 3, 1915, *ibid.*, pp. 383-384.

[51] R. Lansing to W. J. Bryan, May 5, 1915, *ibid.*, pp. 384-385. It is significant that in this letter Lansing advised keeping the Thrasher and the *Cushing* and *Gulflight* cases separate, and that he intimated that he had substantially come around to Bryan's point of view on the former. "In the Thrasher case the circumstances are different," he wrote. "There is room for argument and a discussion of the use of submarines would be appropriate since it is open to question whether the declarations [of the "strict accountability" note of February 10] apply to that particular case. I suggest, therefore, the advisability of acting in the Thrasher case before the full reports are received in the other cases, so that a more moderate and less rigid representation may be made before action is taken in the other cases."

[52] *New York Times*, May 4, 1915; New York *World*, May 5, 1915.

[53] W. J. Bryan to W.W., May 5, 1915, Wilson Papers.

that he had no intention of taking any hasty action in the *Gulflight* case.[54]

Did all this mean that the President was in fact preparing to make an expedient accommodation to the submarine campaign? We of course do not know whether he would eventually have sent a note about the Thrasher case or what kind of protest he would have made concerning the *Cushing* and *Gulflight* if the Germans had limited their war at sea to Allied merchantmen. However, it seems safe to say that at this juncture the possibilities of an American adjustment to the submarine war were by no means remote.

[54] *New York Times,* May 5, 1915.

W CHAPTER XII W

The *Lusitania* Crisis

THE darkest cloud over German-American relations in the mid-spring of 1915 was the possibility that submarine commanders would attack passenger liners in the North Atlantic. The American leaders and people might well accept the sinking of merchantmen, even of occasional American vessels, without gross alarm or the feeling that any fundamental national rights had been violated. But what would they think and do if some great catastrophe, one involving the loss of many American lives, occurred at sea? Would reason still prevail, or would emotions rule the day? And would the leaders in Washington be able to avoid confronting the Imperial government on the issue of sovereignty and national rights?

No one in Berlin appeared concerned. The failure of the American government to make any protest at all over the loss of American life on the *Falaba* lent seeming proof to the conviction that President Wilson would not interfere in the death struggle on the seas. It all depended upon the U-boat commanders themselves. They had orders to sink *all* enemy ships on sight; whether they sent their torpedoes without warning into helpless passenger ships would depend upon their judgment and consciences alone.

Nor was there much alarm in Washington. As week after week passed following the *Falaba* incident, the conviction must have deepened that another such attack was not likely to occur. Counselor Lansing was still worried, to be sure, but President Wilson and Secretary Bryan were, it seemed, growing impervious to his shrill warnings. Indeed, in all the United States, aside from Lansing, only Count von Bernstorff, Doctor Dernburg, and the men closely associated with the German Embassy rightly read the signs of danger. Convinced that the American government "underestimated the dangers of the situation," the Ambassador decided to issue a warning of his own.[1] It appeared in the American press on May 1, 1915, as follows:

[1] J. von Bernstorff, *My Three Years in America*, p. 115.

NOTICE

TRAVELERS intending to embark on the Atlantic voyage are reminded that a state of war exists between Germany and her allies and Great Britain and her allies; that the zone of war includes the waters adjacent to the British Isles; that, in accordance with formal notice given by the Imperial German Government, vessels flying the flag of Great Britain, or any of her allies, are liable to destruction in those waters and that travelers sailing in the war zone on ships of Great Britain or her allies do so at their own risk.

IMPERIAL GERMAN EMBASSY
Washington, D. C., April 22, 1915[2]

Lansing was upset, both by what he believed to be the German Embassy's "insolent proceeding" and by the fear that it was another sign that the German government was trying to force a break in relations with the United States.[3] Bryan, on the other hand, was pleased. The notice was, he thought, "evidence of a friendly desire to evade [avoid?] anything that might raise a question between Germany and the United States." Moreover, as he told the President, he could see "no more good reason why an American citizen should take the risk involved in going in one of these vessels than there is for taking the risks that are involved in going near the fighting on land."[4]

Entirely by chance it happened that Bernstorff's warning appeared in the newspapers on the same day that the *Lusitania*, 30,396 tons, of the Cunard Line, the largest ship then in service in the North Atlantic, was to sail from New York for Liverpool. As the passengers crowded at the pier for boarding on the morning of May 1, the Americans booked for passage received telegrams with signatures like "John Smith" and "George Jones" urging them not to sail. They were, moreover, accosted by strangers who repeated the warning orally. Only one passenger was impressed.[5] It was all a great hoax, several Americans told reporters as they boarded ship. Captain William T. Turner heartily agreed. "Do you think all these people would be booking passage on board the *Lusitania*," he asked the newspapermen, "if they thought she could be caught by a German submarine? Why, it's the best joke I've heard in many days, this talk of torpedoing!" Down in

[2] *New York Times*, May 1, 1915.
[3] R. Lansing to W. J. Bryan, May 1, 1915, *The Lansing Papers*, I, 381-382.
[4] W. J. Bryan to W.W., May 1, 1915, Bryan Papers, National Archives.
[5] He was the Reverend W. M. Warlow of Bennington, Vermont, who changed his booking at the last minute from the *Lusitania* to the *New York* of the American Line.

the city, officials of the Cunard Line were furious. This, declared Charles P. Sumner, general manager of the New York office, was simply another German trick to cripple the Cunard company's business. The *Lusitania*, he added, was the safest ship afloat; she could easily outrun any submarine.

The great vessel put out to sea at 12:30 with 1,257 passengers, the largest number carried by any eastbound ship in 1915, a large cargo of food, and contraband that included 4,200 cases of cartridges and 1,250 cases of empty steel shrapnel shells. She was two and a half hours late in leaving, but only because she had to take on 163 passengers from the Anchor liner *Cameronia*, which had just been commandeered by the British Admiralty.[6]

May 7 began much like any other day in the spring of 1915. In Berlin the leaders were busy trying to analyze the progress of the German army's offensive against the British at Ypres. In London Colonel House drove out to Kew with Sir Edward Grey in the morning. "We spoke," he wrote in his Diary, "of the probability of an ocean liner being sunk [by a German submarine], and I told him if this were done, a flame of indignation would sweep across America, which would in itself probably carry us into the war." A short time later House was closeted with King George at Buckingham Palace. "We fell to talking . . . ," House further wrote, "of the probability of Germany sinking a trans-Atlantic liner. . . . He said, 'Suppose they should sink the *Lusitania* with American passengers on board?'"[7]

In Washington the President met the Cabinet for a regular Friday morning session at ten o'clock. There was, apparently, no pressing business, and Secretaries Bryan, Garrison, Daniels, Lane, William B. Wilson, and Tumulty all went to the Shoreham Hotel at noon for lunch and conversation.

Meanwhile, in the Irish Sea the morning had dawned without piercing the shroud of fog that had covered the area since the night before. At five o'clock, Greenwich time, a German submarine surfaced some fifteen miles south of the peninsula on the southwestern Irish coast called the Old Head of Kinsale. It was the *U20, Kapitanleutnant* Walter Schwieger, which had sailed from Ems on April 30

[6] The foregoing two paragraphs are based upon the *New York Times*, May 2 and 9, 1915; New York *World*, May 2, 1915; A. A. Hoehling and Mary Hoehling, *The Last Voyage of the Lusitania*, pp. 37-38.

[7] House Diary, May 7, 1915.

and had been hunting in the Irish Sea since May 5. The young commander must have felt a special thrill of loneliness as he came up on deck. Beneath him he could hear the steady hum of the diesel engines as they recharged the submarine's batteries; all about was sea and fog, and a gentle breeze from the North fanned his face. For his first patrol, Schwieger must have told himself, the results—two large steamers sunk—had not been bad. He had only three torpedoes left and could do nothing, anyway, in such a fog. He waited until nine o'clock and then, when the fog still had not cleared, headed northward on the route home. An hour later the fog suddenly lifted. Seeing a patrol vessel running toward him, Schwieger submerged to a depth of eleven meters. Soon afterward he heard the hum of propellers overhead; a glance through the periscope revealed an English cruiser heading toward Queenstown. Surfacing again at 12:45 p.m. and finding clear weather but no prey, Schwieger decided to head for home. Then, at one o'clock, he sighted a large steamer and wrote in his log: "Dead ahead four smokestacks and two masts of a steamer with course vertical to us. . . . Becomes visible. The ship reveals herself to be a great passenger liner."

It was the *Lusitania* nearing the end of an uneventful voyage. Many of the passengers were still at lunch in the dining room. "It's been such a dull, dreary, stupid trip," one of them exclaimed. "I can't help hoping that we get some sort of thrill going up the channel."[8] Just about this time Captain Turner turned his ship eastward on a straight course at eighteen knots toward Queenstown. As luck would have it, the captain's change of course meant taking the *Lusitania* directly across the *U20's* line of fire, while the captain's reduced speed and failure to zig-zag, even though he had been warned of the presence of a submarine, made his ship a fairly easy mark. Schwieger followed his prey for nearly an hour; at 2:10 p.m. he had the *Lusitania* squarely in his sights and fired one torpedo. In his log he told the story of what followed:

"Clear bow shot at 700 meters. . . . Shot hits starboard bow side close behind the bridge. There follows an extraordinarily great detonation, with a very strong explosive cloud (far out from the forward smokestack). There must have come after the explosion of the torpedo still a second one (boiler or coal or powder?). The superstructure above the point of impact and the bridge are torn asunder. Fire springs

[8] A. A. and Mary Hoehling, *The Last Voyage of the Lusitania*, p. 102.

up. Smoke engulfs the high bridge. The ship stops at once and very quickly lists strongly to starboard, sinking deeper forward at the same time. It appears as though it will capsize in a short time. On the ship great confusion is evident. The boats are cleared and partially let down to the water. . . . The ship blows off. Forward the name 'Lusitania' becomes visible in gold letters. . . . Since it seemed that the vessel would be afloat only a short time, submerged to twenty meters and ran out to sea. I could not have fired a second torpedo into this throng of human beings saving themselves. [At 3:15 p.m.] went to eleven meters and took a look around. In the distance aft a number of life-boats drift about aimlessly. Nothing more is to be seen of the 'Lusi-tania.' "[9]

It was, actually, all over within eighteen minutes. Somehow 472 passengers and 289 members of the crew, incuding Captain Turner—a total of 761 souls—escaped. The victims numbered 785 passengers and 413 members of the crew, a total of 1,198 dead; among them were 270 women, 94 children, and 124 American citizens.[10]

The sinking of the *Lusitania* had a more jolting effect upon American opinion than any other single event of the World War. For most Americans, except for Southerners with long and bitter memories of Sherman's march through Georgia and the Carolinas, it was their first real introduction to total war—to war as much against civilians as against armed forces, against women and children as well as men. The German invasion and devastation of Belgium had stirred American emotions mightily, it is true; but that resentment had been tempered by the German pleas of national security and military necessity. More-over, Belgium was far away and really unknown to most Americans, and it was difficult for them to feel more than momentary anger over, say, the burning of Louvain or the bombing of Antwerp. To them the sinking of the *Lusitania* had a deeper significance. It was a crime of murder on the high seas by order of the German government, a crime with no mitigating circumstances. It confirmed (for them) what the minority of pro-Allied extremists had been saying all along—that Germany had in fact run amuck and was now an outlaw among

---

[9] From the *Kriegstagebuch* of the *U20* for the period March 18-August 31, 1915, MS. in the Kriegsarchiv der Marine, Berlin, photographic copy in the Wilson Papers.

[10] These are the casualty figures given in the report of the British Court of Inquiry, dated July 17, 1915, printed in Charles E. Lauriat, Jr., *The Lusitania's Last Voyage*, pp. 121-159.

civilized nations. To these revulsions against the useless slaughter of civilians was added the anger that stemmed from wounded national pride. This, it is fair to say, was the immediate reaction of most of the American people who had anything to say about the incident (except for the German Americans and their ardent allies), whether they were pacifists or militarists, idealists or realists. The editor of the New York *Nation* summarized these convictions well:

"Germany ought not to be left in a moment's doubt how the civilized world regards her latest display of 'frightfulness.' It is a deed for which a Hun would blush, a Turk be ashamed, and a Barbary pirate apologize. To speak of technicalities and the rules of war, in the face of such wholesale murder on the high seas, is a waste of time. The law of nations and the law of God have been alike trampled upon." The defense of a warning beforehand was outrageous, the editorial continued. "Nothing of this prevents us from regarding such miscreants as wild beasts, against whom society has to defend itself at all hazards. And so must the German Government be given to understand that no plea of military necessity will now avail it before the tribunal on which sits as judge the humane conscience of the world. As was declared by Germany's own representative at the Hague Congress, the late Marschall von Bieberstein, there are some atrocities which international law does not need to legislate, since they fall under the instant and universal condemnation of mankind."[11]

This represented an important turning point in American opinion in general. But the *Lusitania* tragedy had another, perhaps a more important, consequence: It converted some pro-Allied extremists in the United States into active interventionists, or at least into advocates of policies that they knew would probably result in war with Germany. By so doing it marked the dividing line between the time when there was no organized and vocal sentiment for American participation and the time when that sentiment existed in substantial measure. Among most of these interventionists or quasi-interventionists, the impelling motivation was anger and concern for the protection of national rights. This was true of editors like the old flamboyant southern

---

[11] New York *Nation*, c (May 13, 1915), 527. For opinions in the same vein, see also the reviews of editorial opinion in the *Literary Digest*, L (May 15, 1915), 1133-1134, and the *New York Times*, May 9, 1915. See also the New York *World*, May 8 and 9, 1915; *New York Times*, May 8, 1915; *New Republic*, III (May 15, 1915), 25; *The Independent*, LXXXII (May 17, 1915), 267; *The Congregationalist and Christian World*, c (May 20, 1915), 626; *Harper's Weekly*, LX (May 22, 1915), 481; *World's Work*, XXX (June 1915), 133-134; *Saturday Evening Post*, CLXXXVII (June 5, 1915), 24.

romantic, Colonel Henry Watterson, and Colonel George Harvey of the *North American Review*. "Must we," "Marse Henry" cried in his Louisville *Courier-Journal*, "as a people sit down like dogs and see our laws defied, our flag flouted and our protests whistled down the wind of this lordling's majestic disdain? Must we as a Nation emulate at once the impotence and the docility of China. . . ?"[12] It was true also in the main of political leaders like Senator Henry Cabot Lodge and Theodore Roosevelt. They were not oblivious to what they thought were the larger ideological issues of the war, but to them the all-important fact was that a German U-boat had killed *American* citizens on the high seas. National honor demanded retribution. "Of course I shall not be satisfied with any delay," Roosevelt wrote, for example, "in asserting in a most emphatic way all our rights—our right to send ammunitions of war to France and England, the right of American vessels to travel freely on the high seas, and the right of American citizens to travel freely on belligerent merchant ships on the high seas. It is not enough to assert these rights. We should insist on their strict observance."[13]

To other Americans (and to Roosevelt and Lodge as well) the sinking of the *Lusitania* had an even deeper meaning. For them it was full and final proof, not only of the moral degeneracy of the German government, but also of the irrepressible character of the conflict between democracy and autocracy. In such a conflict, they concluded, the great Republic of the West could not fail to take a stand. Men who reasoned thus could not be counted perhaps in the thousands, but they included leaders in all walks of life and some in positions of extraordinary importance like Colonel House, Counselor Lansing, and Senator Root. Lansing, for instance, now saw new portents of a German victory: the formation of a new Russian-Japanese-German coalition and "the overthrow of democracy in the world, the suppression of individual liberty, the setting up of evil ambitions, the subordination of the principles of right and justice to physical might directed by arbitrary will, and the turning back of the hands of human

[12] Louisville *Courier-Journal*, May 9, 1915; see also George Harvey, "The Duty of America," *North American Review*, cci (June 1915), 801-807.

[13] T. Roosevelt to J. C. O'Laughlin, May 13, 1915, Roosevelt Papers. See also Roosevelt's statement, printed in the *New York Times*, May 8, 1915; T. Roosevelt to A. B. Hart, June 1, 1915, E. E. Morison *et al.* (eds.), *The Letters of Theodore Roosevelt*, viii, 927; John A. Garraty, *Henry Cabot Lodge, A Biography*, pp. 317-318.

progress two centuries."[14] Root believed that the time had come "for the people of this country to test the value of our form of government," and that "a duty was imposed upon the American people to insist that the principles of government and humanity and civilization upon which our government was founded must be maintained."[15] "America," Colonel House advised the President, "has come to the parting of the ways, when she must determine whether she stands for civilized or uncivilized warfare. We can no longer remain neutral spectators."[16]

The significance of this sentiment lay not in the fact that it was widespread in the United States in the spring of 1915 but that it existed at all. Actually, the overwhelming majority of the American people reacted—if we may judge by editorials in newspapers and journals, the letters and petitions that poured in upon the White House, and the like—more in deep sorrow and shock than in fierce anger to the *Lusitania* tragedy. As the president of the University of Virginia put it, "The Lusitania matter has been received by the whole American people in a very remarkable way. There has been no flash of passion, no stampede of thought as marked the destruction of the Maine in '98, but rather a sort of stunned amazement that such bold savagery and ferocity could mark the public policy of any great nation."[17]

One thing can be said in all confidence about the outpouring of public sentiment following May 7—that the vast majority of the people wanted the President to voice their moral indignation without, however, incurring any great risks of involvement. As the editor of the leading Baptist weekly of the Middle West wrote: "If ever the American people stood in need of calmness and deliberation it is at this hour. While every other nation is 'seeing red,' let us do—what the German military authorities apparently have not done—count the cost, not the immediate cost, but those far-reaching values which will affect our nation decades hence. We must protect our citizens, *but we must find some other way than war.*"[18]

---

[14] Lansing Diary, July 11, 1915. See also the extract printed in Robert Lansing, *War Memoirs of Robert Lansing*, pp. 19-21.

[15] Anderson Diary, May 15, 1915. Anderson went to New York on May 15 *at Lansing's request* to ascertain Root's opinions on the present crisis.

[16] E. M. House to W.W., May 9, 1915, Wilson Papers.

[17] Edwin A. Alderman to W. H. Page, May 12, 1915, Page Papers.

[18] *The Standard* of Chicago, LXII (May 13, 1915), 1146; italics added. In the same vein, see the *Johnstown* (Pennsylvania) *Democrat*, May 10, 1915; *Athens* (Georgia) *Banner*, May 11, 1915; Dallas *Baptist Standard*, XXVII (May 13, 1915), 8-9; *The Public*,

That this was the authentic voice of the nation was confirmed over and over during these turbulent days by knowing political observers with a finger on the pulse of the American people. Among the dozens of congressmen and senators whose opinions were obtained by the newspapers, only Senators John Sharp Williams of Mississippi and Joseph L. Bristow of Kansas and Representative A. P. Gardner of Massachusetts spoke belligerently.[19] All the rest agreed that the destruction of the *Lusitania* had been a horrible crime but avowed either that it was not and should not be permitted to be a cause for war, or that Americans should not be permitted to travel on belligerent ships that carried contraband, or that the issue was safe in the President's hands.[20] The Governor of Connecticut suggested that any controversy arising from the incident be settled by arbitration. From the West came an echo from the Governor of Nebraska, who reported that 90 per cent of the people of his state favored "adjusting these differences by arbitration and by civilized and intelligent methods."[21] The British Ambassador, who had every reason to want a different reaction, gave convincing testimony of America's lack of belligerency, as follows:

"The general feeling here is that the United States Government ought to keep out of it. The detailed reports of the horrors of war

XVIII (May 14, 1915), 465-467; *The Living Church*, LIII (May 15, 1915), 81; *The Churchman*, CXI (May 15, 1915), 631-632; *Lutheran Church Work*, IV (May 27, 1915), 3-4; F. K. Hart to R. Lansing, May 11, 1915, Lansing Papers, reporting on public sentiment in northern Minnesota; Samuel Gompers, statement in the *New York Times*, June 11, 1915; and Thomas B. Love to E. M. House, June 16, 1915, House Papers, reporting on sentiment in Texas.

[19] New York *World*, May 9, 1915; *New York Times*, May 9, 1915.

[20] Senator P. J. McCumber of North Dakota, Senator B. R. Tillman of South Carolina, Representative E. E. Browne of Wisconsin, Representative T. W. Sims of Tennessee, Senator T. P. Gore of Oklahoma, Representative H. D. Flood of Virginia, Senator Hoke Smith of Georgia, Representative J. M. Evans of Montana, quoted in the New York *World*, May 9, 1915; Senator W. J. Stone of Missouri and Representative A. M. Palmer of Pennsylvania, quoted in the *New York Times*, May 9, 1915; Senator J. H. Lewis of Illinois, Senator Morris Sheppard of Texas, Senator E. D. Smith of South Carolina, Senator J. D. Works of California, Senator J. K. Vardaman of Mississippi, and Representative R. E. Difenderfer of Pennsylvania, quoted in *ibid.*, May 10, 1915; Senator R. M. La Follette of Wisconsin, quoted in *ibid.*, May 12, 1915; Senator R. L. Owen of Oklahoma to W.W., May 13, 1915, Wilson Papers; Governor Emanuel L. Philip to W. H. Taft, June 12, 1915, Taft Papers.

[21] W. H. Taft to W.W., May 10, 1915, Wilson Papers, transmitting the suggestion of Governor Simeon E. Baldwin; Governor John H. Morehead to W. J. Bryan, May 18, 1915, the Papers of William J. Bryan, Library of Congress; hereinafter cited as the Bryan Papers, Library of Congress.

and the influence of such plays as the 'War Brides' form a very strong deterrent. According to all the reports that reach me the prevailing feeling here is an intense desire to keep the peace whether in Mexico or in the Far East or in Europe and not to get mixed up in the troubles of the rest of the world. . . . The general effect is that which I remember your describing when you told me of trying to boil a potato on the top of the Andes. American sentiment at the present moment is not boiling potatoes. . . . I don't think that the American people taken as a whole have even contemplated for an instant coming to the help of the Allies or of intervening unless they were absolutely obliged to do so when their own material interests were affected. . . . The long and short of the matter is that we must count on ourselves for success or failure and that we must not expect help from this continent. I do not see why we should blame this country for acting exactly as we did in 1870."[22]

In the face of the overwhelming American convictions about the awfulness of the tragedy, German propagandists were helpless. They could not admit that the act had been wrong without indicting their own government; they could only attempt to palliate and explain. "It is deplorable, if true, that so many lives have been lost," exclaimed Captain Franz von Papen, the German Military Attaché. ". . . But it was absolutely criminal for the Cunard Company to carry—and for the British Government to allow the line to carry—neutral passengers in a ship which was transporting explosives and munitions of war." Speaking to reporters in Cleveland, Doctor Bernhard Dernburg, the best known of the German propagandists in the United States, took the offensive by contending that the German navy had the undoubted right to destroy without warning *all* ships carrying contraband, and especially the *Lusitania*, because she had been a British auxiliary cruiser.[23] At Bernstorff's suggestion,[24] the Foreign Office in Berlin sent a word of regret and of explanation to the American press and State Department on May 10. "The German Government," it read, "desires to express its deepest sympathy at the loss of lives on board the Lusitania. The responsibility rests, however, with the British Gov-

[22] C. Spring Rice to Lord Bryce, May 7, 1915, Bryce Papers; also C. Spring Rice to E. Grey, May 20, 1915, *The Letters of Sir Cecil Spring Rice*, II, 268-271.

[23] New York *World*, May 8, 1915; *New York Times*, May 9, 1915.

[24] Ambassador von Bernstorff to the Foreign Office, May 9, 1915, German F. O. Archives.

ernment, which, through its plan of starving the civilian population of Germany, has forced Germany to resort to retaliatory measures."[25] Through their press and organizations the German Americans did what they could to help.[26]

It would have been better if they had all emulated the German Ambassador's example and said nothing, because the more they talked the more they exacerbated American feeling. Resentment against Dernburg was so strong that Bernstorff hastened to send him home before the State Department could expel him.[27] The Ambassador reported these vicissitudes in a series of messages to Berlin:

"Hysteria continues. American ill-will is at the moment especially directed against Dernburg, who, in the midst of the greatest excitement, unfortunately gave the New York Monday newspapers an abrupt interview. . . . Wilson suggested to me to ask Dernburg to give no more interviews, as they only fan the excitement."[28]

"Dernburg has declared voluntarily that he is ready to leave America. The ill-will that the public bears toward him would do nothing but paralyze his usefulness in the future. . . ."[29]

"All beautifying does not help. We might as well admit openly that our propaganda here has *collapsed completely* under the impact of the Lusitania incident. For anyone who knows the character of the American people, this was to be expected. . . . In the American nature two personalities that are seemingly contradictory live side by side. The cool, calculating businessman cannot be recognized when his passions take over—here they are called 'emotions.' In such moments he can only be compared to a hysterical woman, and all talk is to no avail. . . . Our propaganda cannot begin again until this storm has abated.

"As I have already informed Your Excellency, Dernburg has decided to leave the country. . . . We both want to make clear why Mr. Dernburg sacrificed himself in this case. I believe that he has given

[25] Printed in the *New York Times*, May 11, 1915.

[26] See the *New Yorker Staats-Zeitung, New Yorker Herold*, and *The Fatherland*, quoted in the *Literary Digest*, L (May 15, 1915), 1134; Chicago *Staats-Zeitung*, May 9, 1915; *Chicagoer Presse*, May 9, 1915; Chicago *Abendpost*, May 9, 1915; statement of the Saint Louis Branch of the American Neutrality League, *New York Times*, May 10, 1915.

[27] *ibid.*, May 12, 1915; O. G. Villard, "Notes of a meeting with the German ambassador at lunch, May 15, 1915," MS. in the Wilson Papers.

[28] Ambassador von Bernstorff to the Foreign Office, May 13, 1915, German F. O. Archives.

[29] Ambassador von Bernstorff to the Foreign Office, May 15, 1915, *ibid.*

something to the Fatherland by this action, although the sacrifice was made easier by the fact that he could not continue in his present activities. . . . As long as Dernburg only wrote newspaper articles, he did excellent work which was generally recognized. When he began to give speeches at German-American meetings, however, he stepped on very dangerous ground. We are all of the opinion that any means must be tried in war, and it is simply unfortunately unavoidable when a victim falls."[30]

Let us now return to Wilson and his circle to see how they reacted. First news of the tragedy had come to Washington at about one o'clock in the afternoon of May 7 in the form of press reports that told only of the *Lusitania's* destruction and did not mention loss of life. A newspaperman handed Bryan a copy of the bulletin just as he was leaving the dining room at the Shoreham; he hurried to the State Department to await official confirmation from Ambassador Page. It arrived at 3:06 p.m. The President had finished his lunch and was about to leave for the golf course when a clerk handed him a copy of the first news bulletin. He waited at the White House for further word until late in the afternoon, when he took a motor ride. Nothing came to the White House to tell the dimensions of the tragedy until after dinner, when a report from the American Consul at Queenstown arrived at 7:55 saying that loss of life would be heavy.

The news was almost more than Wilson could bear. Before the Secret Service men knew what he was doing, he walked quietly out the main door of the White House. Crossing Pennsylvania Avenue, he started northward up Sixteenth Street. Thoughts must have whirled in confusion in his mind, pictures of horror that he could not suppress. He seemed oblivious to the light rain that was falling and to the voices of newsboys in the streets. From Sixteenth Street the President turned into Corcoran Street and then into Fifteenth and back to the White House and his study. At ten o'clock a fresh bulletin came saying that probably 1,000 souls had perished on the ship. An hour later he went to bed. He had seen and talked to no one except members of the White House Staff since receiving the first news of the disaster.[31]

For the President of the United States this was by far the severest testing that he had ever known. We cannot live all these troubled

[30] J. von Bernstorff to T. von Bethmann Hollweg, May 17, 1915, *ibid.*
[31] *New York Times*, May 8, 1915; New York *World*, May 8, 1915.

hours over again with him, but we know enough about what he thought and did to say that now as never before did his true character manifest itself in word and deed.

To begin with, he sought deliberately to set an example of calmness and detachment for his people in this time of stress. One can almost see him reading the lines of Kipling of which he was so fond:

> If you can keep your head when all about you
> Are losing theirs and blaming it on you. . . .

On the day after the sinking of the *Lusitania*, May 8, the President almost ostentatiously pursued his ordinary Saturday routine—golf in the morning and a long motor ride in the afternoon from three until six o'clock. He saw no public leader and had no communication, "directly or indirectly, by wire or wireless," as Bryan put it, with the Department of State. Then after dinner he sent the following message through Tumulty to the American people: "Of course the President feels the distress and the gravity of the situation to the utmost, and is considering very earnestly, but very calmly, the right course of action to pursue. He knows that the people of the country wish and expect him to act with deliberation as well as with firmness."[32]

He maintained his isolation from the administration circle during the two days that followed, Sunday and Monday, May 9 and 10. On Sunday morning he attended divine service, as was his habit, at the Central Presbyterian Church. Most of the afternoon he spent motoring through the Virginia countryside. There were no visitors at the White House, except for his son-in-law, McAdoo, who came for dinner. There was no sign in the entire city of Washington suggesting that the United States government was in the midst of a great international crisis.[33] When reporters and visitors crowded the Executive Offices on Monday morning, the President would see none of them, not even the chairman of the Senate foreign relations committee, who had come to confer and had to be content with talking to Secretary Tumulty.[34]

There was another reason for seclusion aside from wanting to give the appearance of entire serenity. The time was near at hand, Wilson knew, when he must make decisions that would affect the whole course of the war, perhaps the future of all mankind. He had to think, to get to basic principles once again, to see the submarine question in all its ramifications. He had to pore over the letters, telegrams,

---

[32] *New York Times*, May 9, 1915. [33] *ibid.*, May 10, 1915.
[34] *ibid.*, May 11, 1915.

and petitions that were piling upon his desk. He had to understand
the spirit of the American people so that he could exalt and instruct
that spirit and be the leader, not a "trimmer, weak to yield what
clamour claims, but the deeply human man, quick to know and to
do the things that the hour and his nation need."[35] He had to find
his moorings alone, apart from public clatter and whispered contentions.

It is not difficult to see the direction of his thoughts during these
three and a half days of meditation. Some protest, he at once concluded, had to be made; too much was at stake, and the people demanded that he speak. He had to voice the moral judgment of the
American people upon an international crime. But how? That was
the question that disturbed him. By a peremptory demand for disavowal, indemnity, and guarantees of future good behavior? By appealing on the high ground of humanity to the consciences of the
German leaders and people? In such a way that a break would come
if the Germans refused to yield? Or in a more gentle manner, so that
there need be no immediate reckoning?

On May 9 the President received his first communication from the
Secretary of State since the sinking of the *Lusitania*. Enclosing a clip-
ping from the *Washington Post* listing the contraband that the *Lusitania* had carried, Bryan suggested that ships carrying risky cargo
should not be permitted to carry passengers.[36] The following day
Bryan wrote again twice, sending three memoranda by Lansing. The
first firmly repelled Bryan's suggestion that Americans be warned
not to travel on Allied ships carrying contraband. The second took
up the possible German defenses for the sinking of the *Lusitania* and
answered them. The third, which was more important, suggested the
points that the President might want to consider in drafting a note
to Germany; they all pointed in the direction of a forceful protest.[37]

At some time between May 8 and May 10 (perhaps it was on the
morning of the latter day) Wilson tried to find the right answers
as he composed a draft note to Germany on his typewriter. As we
will soon see, his conclusions coincided more with Lansing's than
with Bryan's. At the same time, his thoughts ranged beyond the immediate note itself to its consequences. There would be no crisis, he

[35] Woodrow Wilson, *Leaders of Men*, edited by T. H. Vail Motter, p. 60.
[36] W. J. Bryan to W.W., May 9, 1915, *The Lansing Papers*, I, 386.
[37] W. J. Bryan to W.W., May 10, 1915, two letters enclosing memoranda (or letters)
by Lansing dated May 9 and May 10, 1915, *ibid.*, pp. 387-392.

thought at one time. "Strictly confidential. The situation not yet fully developed," he advised a congressman then in Hawaii who had asked whether he should return to Washington, "but need not if wisely handled involve a crisis."[38] He would not call Congress into special session, he thought again. He would see the matter through peacefully, perhaps by suggesting that the issue of the loss of American life be submitted to arbitration. On other occasions his thoughts went in a different direction. He had no alternative, it may have seemed to him, but to accept all consequences; there would be no escape from a direct clash if the Germans refused to meet him on high ground. "We defined our position at the outset," he wrote, for example, to Bryan, "and cannot alter it,—at any rate so far as it affects the past."[39]

This tug of war proceeding in the President's mind was revealed for all to see but for few to understand when he first broke silence after his withdrawal. On Monday evening, May 10, he spoke to some 4,000 newly naturalized citizens in Convention Hall in Philadelphia. Lost in his own poetic cadences while recalling the ideals of America, he exclaimed: "The example of America must be a special example. The example of America must be the example not merely of peace because it will not fight, but of peace because peace is the healing and elevating influence of the world and strife is not. There is such a thing as a man being to proud to fight. There is such a thing as a nation being so right that it does not need to convince others by force that it is right."[40]

Did he realize what he had said and mean it? The next morning a friend asked him why he had made a statement so capable of misinterpretation. "That was just one of the foolish things a man does," he replied. "I have a bad habit of thinking out loud. That thought occurred to me while I was speaking, and I let it out. I should have kept it in, or developed it further, of course."[41] A short time later he told reporters: "I was expressing a personal attitude, that was all. I did not have in mind any specific thing. I did not regard that as a proper occasion to give any intimation of policy on any special matter."[42]

Who was this man to lead a great people? A new Lincoln, as one

[38] W.W. to S. Sherley, May 9, 1915, Wilson Papers.
[39] W.W. to W. J. Bryan, May 11, 1915, *The Lansing Papers*, I, 392.
[40] *New York Times*, May 11, 1915.
[41] Frank Parker Stockbridge, undated memorandum in the Baker Collection.
[42] Transcript of press conference, May 11, 1915, Swem Papers.

Presbyterian editor suggested?[43] One in whom the spirit of Christ breathed, as a Prince of the Roman Catholic Church suggested?[44] A "man of prayer, discretion, courage, patriotism, and ability," as the bishops of the Methodist Episcopal Church, South, said?[45] Or a weakling and coward, "cordially supported," as Theodore Roosevelt put it, "by all the hyphenated Americans, by the solid flubdub and pacifist vote . . . [by] every soft creature, every coward and weakling, every man who can't look more than six inches ahead, every man whose god is money, or pleasure, or ease, and every man who has not got in him both the sterner virtues and the power of seeking after an ideal"?[46]

The President unveiled his decisions fully for the first time when he read the draft of the note that he had prepared to the Cabinet during a three-hour session in the morning of May 11, 1915. In solemn voice he began by reviewing the recent submarine incidents involving American citizens—the attacks on the *Falaba, Cushing,* and *Gulflight*—which had culminated in the sinking of the *Lusitania.* The American administration, Wilson continued, could not bring itself to believe that these acts had the sanction of a government that had always stood forthrightly for justice and humanity in international relationships. The Washington government had been apprised of the German warzone decree. It had made clear that it would hold the Imperial authorities to a strict accountability for the loss of American ships and American lives on American and *belligerent* merchant ships in the war zone. It did not understand that the German government denied American rights on the seas; indeed, it was confident that the Berlin authorities accepted the rule that the lives of noncombatants, whether neutral or belligerent, could not be put in jeopardy on *unarmed* merchantmen. Since this was true, the United States Government took the liberty of saying that the danger of the present German maritime campaign stemmed from the fact that submarines could not be used against merchantmen, as the last few weeks had shown, "without an inevitable violation of many sacred principles of justice and humanity." The American government would uphold the right of its citizens to travel upon the high seas, and no warning that "an unlawful and inhumane

[43] *The Presbyterian Banner,* CI (May 20, 1915), 7.
[44] William Henry Cardinal O'Connell to W.W., May 11, 1915, Wilson Papers.
[45] *New York Times,* May 14, 1915.
[46] T. Roosevelt to A. B. Roosevelt, May 19, 1915, Roosevelt Papers.

act" would be committed would be accepted for excuse. The Washington government was confident that the Imperial government would disavow the acts of its submarine commanders, make all possible reparation, and prevent the recurrence of any further such incidents. "The Imperial German Government," the President concluded, "will not expect the Government of the United States to omit any necessary representation or any necessary act in sustaining the rights of its citizens or in safeguarding the sacred duties of international obligation."[47]

There it was, so bold as to be almost breathtaking—no legal logic-chopping, but an appeal on the high ground of humanity to the German government to abandon its entire submarine campaign against commerce!

Wilson's conclusions and intentions were further clarified during the discussions that ensued. All the Cabinet members and the President too, presumably, agreed that the American people did not want to become involved in the war and that the administration should take no position that would make involvement likely. But, Secretary of War Garrison opined, the proposed note might lead to a rupture in diplomatic relations, and that would surely end in war. No, the President (echoing Lansing's advice) replied; in nine such cases out of ten in the past actual fighting had not occurred. There was certainly a good chance, Bryan and Postmaster General Burleson added, that the present controversy could be adjusted in a peaceful manner. Unnamed members (were they Bryan, Burleson, and Secretary of the Navy Daniels?) suggested that it might be wise to warn Americans against traveling on belligerent ships and to postpone a definitive settlement of the *Lusitania* case until after the war. Several members observed that the British had not been guiltless and suggested that a note might also be sent to London. But in the end, after three hours, all the conferees agreed that the President had said the right thing, that the proposed note should go forward without undue delay, and that a really serious crisis was not at all inevitable.[48]

Wilson sent the note to the State Department early the following morning, May 12, and Lansing and Chandler Anderson set to work to redraft it in diplomatic style. Most of their changes were merely stylistic—indeed, they improved the literary quality of the document considerably! —but some sharpened the language, and one changed its

[47] From the draft printed in *The Lansing Papers*, 1, 395-398.

[48] The above paragraph is based upon the extraordinarily full accounts of this meeting in the *New York Times*, May 12, 1915, and the New York *World*, May 12, 1915.

meaning in an important way. This was the substitution of the words "unresisting merchantman" for "unarmed merchantman."[49]

The two legal advisers completed their revision probably before noon, and Bryan forwarded it to the White House soon afterward, perhaps in the early afternoon, with his own comment. The Great Commoner had been deeply troubled ever since the Cabinet meeting of the day before. He thought that the President had stated his position clearly and forcefully; indeed, he probably agreed with much of what Wilson had said. But, as he wrote to Wilson as soon as he received the draft note, he approved the document with a heavy heart. He feared that it would encourage the jingoes, embitter the Germans, and give the appearance to the world that the American government was partial in the struggle because it had denounced German retaliatory methods without even mentioning the numerous Allied violations of the rights of man. The way to prevent irreparable damage, Bryan argued, was to issue "simultaneously a protest against the objectionable conduct of the Allies which will keep them from rejoicing and show Germany that we are defending our rights against aggression from both sides."[50]

Sending Lansing's and Anderson's draft on to Wilson, Bryan observed that in almost every case he preferred the President's milder phrases to Lansing's sharper ones. Nor did he fail to notice the change of wording about "unresisting" merchantmen. "I very much prefer your word to his," the Secretary went on. ". . . The difference is quite an important one. If the vessel is armed that, as I understand it, establishes her character and it is not necessary to wait to see whether she will resist. It is presumed that an armed vessel will resist—that is what the arms are for."[51] Even before he had received a reply from the White House, Bryan sent an urgent afterthought. He was, he wrote, so fearful that war talk in the United States would affect Germany's reply that he was venturing to suggest that the American government publish a special statement of its own when the *Lusitania* note appeared in the press, or even earlier. That statement might explain that the term "strict accountability" did not mean that the issue between the United

[49] The draft printed in *The Lansing Papers*, I, 395-398, shows the changes that Lansing and Anderson made. Anderson tells us that it was he who suggested changing "unarmed merchantman" to "unresisting merchantman." Anderson Diary, May 12, 1915.

[50] W. J. Bryan to W.W., n.d., but c. May 12, 1915, *ibid.*, pp. 392-394.

[51] W. J. Bryan to W.W., May 12, 1915, *ibid.*, pp. 399-400.

States and Germany had to be settled immediately. "In individual matters friends sometimes find it wise to postpone the settlement of disputes until such differences can be considered calmly and on their merits," Bryan's proposed announcement continued. "So it may be with nations. The United States and Germany, between whom there exists a long standing friendship, may find it advisable to postpone until peace is restored any disputes which do not yield to diplomatic treatment."[52]

Wilson replied later in the afternoon of May 12, saying that he would like to give some thought to Bryan's suggestion of a special statement and enclosing the "final form" of the *Lusitania* note, which he had just reworked. The draft revealed that in virtually every case the President had decided to adhere to his own, less caustic, wording. It revealed also that Wilson had taken Bryan's advice and used the term "unarmed merchantman" instead of "unresisting merchantman" —a decision of immense future significance because its effect was to narrow the ground of the controversy and indirectly to admit the right of submarines to attack armed merchantmen without warning. With one additional minor change, this was the version of the note that was telegraphed to Berlin on the following day, May 13, 1915.[53]

During the morning of that day, the President gave his decision on Bryan's suggestion of a special statement. He had "slept over" the suggestion, Wilson wrote, and had concluded that it would not be wise to act so directly. Bryan's purpose, he continued, would be better served if the Executive Office gave the following as a "tip" to reporters at the time the note was issued to the press:

Proposed Notice for Publication

There is a good deal of confidence in Administration circles that Germany will respond to this note in a spirit of accommodation. It is pointed out that, while Germany is not one of the many nations which have recently signed treaties of deliberation and inquiry with the United States upon all points of serious difficulty, as a means of supplementing ordinary diplomatic methods and preventing, so far as feasible, the possibility of conflict, she has assented to the principle of such a treaty; and it is believed that she will act in this instance in the spirit of that assent. A frank issue is now made, and it is expected that it will be met in good

[52] W. J. Bryan to W.W., May 12, 1915, *ibid.*, pp. 400-401.

[53] The reader may see the changes that Wilson made in Lansing's draft by comparing the latter, which is printed in *ibid.*, pp. 395-398, with the note that was sent, which is printed in *Foreign Relations, 1915, Supplement*, pp. 393-396.

temper and with a desire to reach an agreement, despite the passions of the hour, —passions in which the United States does not share,—or else submit the whole matter to such processes of discussion as will result in a permanent settlement.[54]

The meaning was clear enough—that the United States would be willing to submit the *Lusitania* case to arbitration—and Bryan was immensely pleased. The *Lusitania* note, he wrote to Wilson at eleven o'clock, would not go to Berlin until early afternoon. Thus happily there would be plenty of time to send the President's statement to Berlin so that Gerard could deliver it to the Foreign Office along with the note itself.[55] "I am sending you a statement," the Secretary of State advised Gerard as he wired a copy of the "Proposed Notice" to the Embassy in Berlin, "which will be issued from the White House at the time the note to Germany is made public, which will probably be in time for tomorrow (Friday) morning papers. This will not be published as a statement given out by the President, but will appear as a newspaper report describing the situation. It is sent to you in advance so that you can deliver it at the time you deliver the note, which will be sent you as soon as it can be transmitted."[56]

Unable to conceal his joy, Bryan showed the President's statement to Lansing, who said that he approved;[57] and a few minutes later the Secretary of State called Tumulty by telephone to tell him that the President had prepared a statement to be given to reporters. At this point the wheels of intrigue began to spin.

In spite of what he had told his superior, Lansing was actually appalled by the proposed announcement. To him, presumably, it meant drawing all the teeth from the *Lusitania* note. In great agitation he went straight to Secretary of War Garrison's office and told him what had happened.[58] Garrison informed Tumulty, who at once sought out Post-

---

[54] *"Proposed Notice for Publication,"* enclosed in W.W. to W. J. Bryan, May 13, 1915, *The Lansing Papers*, I, 402. The original copy is in the Wilson Papers.

[55] W. J. Bryan to W.W., May 13, 1915, Bryan Papers, National Archives.

[56] The Secretary of State to Ambassador Gerard, May 13, 1915, *ibid*.

[57] "Mr. Lansing approves of the statement which the newspapers are to use." W. J. Bryan to W.W., May 13, 1915, *ibid*.

[58] Lansing told Colonel House about the episode late in 1916, and the Colonel recounted the story in his Diary as Lansing had told it: "In his jubilation, Bryan mentioned the matter to several people, Lansing among the number. . . . Lansing was so disturbed that he took the story to Secretary Garrison under the seal of confidence as far as he, Lansing, was concerned, because he felt in a way it was a betrayal of Mr. Bryan. However, he felt justified because of the service he felt he was doing the President and the country." House Diary, November 3, 1916.

master General Burleson. Then Tumulty and Burleson rushed to the President's office at noon. Tumulty was nearly beside himself with excitement. Wilson, he said, could not conceivably be thinking about issuing any special statement or sending it to Berlin. It would cause the Germans to think that he did not mean what he had just said in his *Lusitania* note; they would simply ignore the protest. Wilson tried to calm his friend. Bryan, he said, was a wise politician who sensed the public feeling against war; anyway, Bryan's idea of an explanatory statement was "right." If the public ever learned of the suggestion, Tumulty shot back, they would raise a "terrible howl" and accuse the President of "double-dealing." Wilson then read the proposed statement to his callers. "It isn't so bad, Joe," Burleson said. But Tumulty persisted in language that probably was not fit for the writers of memoirs to repeat, and Wilson agreed to hold the statement for a while.[59] "White as a ghost," Tumulty then joined Garrison for lunch at the Shoreham. "I have just had the worst half hour of my life," he told the Secretary of War as he related what had occurred at the White House. "You should receive a medal of honor for this day's work," Garrison replied.[60]

Perhaps the President concluded that Tumulty was right; perhaps he simply gave in under pressure.[61] In any event, he wrote to Bryan in the early afternoon saying that he had heard something from the German Embassy, which he would rather not put into writing,[62] that had convinced him that "we would lose all chance of bringing Germany to reason if we in any way or degree indicated to them, or to our own public, that this note was merely the first word in a pro-

[59] L. M. Garrison to R. S. Baker, November 12, 1928, Baker Collection; R. S. Baker, interview with L. M. Garrison, November 30, 1928, *ibid.*; David Lawrence, *The True Story of Woodrow Wilson*, pp. 145-146, based, undoubtedly, upon information supplied by Tumulty.

[60] John M. Blum, *Joe Tumulty and the Wilson Era*, p. 97, based in part upon a letter that Garrison wrote to Tumulty on November 18, 1928, recalling the episode.

[61] During the campaign of 1916 Senator Henry Cabot Lodge made the charge, based upon an account of the episode that had allegedly come originally from the Assistant Secretary of War in 1915, Henry C. Breckinridge, that certain Cabinet members had gone to the President and threatened to resign if he did not withdraw the proposed statement, which Lodge called a "postscript" to the *Lusitania* note. J. A. Garraty, *Henry Cabot Lodge*, pp. 329-330. Breckinridge denied this part of the story, and there is no evidence to support it.

[62] At a Cabinet meeting soon afterward Wilson told Bryan that he had heard that Bernstorff was saying that the President "was going to lie down on the Lusitania incident and was not going to take any strong position thereon." L. M. Garrison to R. S. Baker, November 12, 1928, Baker Collection.

longed debate." "Please," he went on, "withdraw the message (the supplementary statement) altogether. If we say anything of the kind it must be a little later, after the note has had its first effect."[63] "I was as sorry as you can have been to withdraw the 'statement' which we had intended for the press," Wilson wrote again the following day, May 14, after Bryan had voiced his disappointment at the President's decision. "It cost me a struggle to do so. But the intimation was plain from the German Embassy (and I cannot doubt the source of my information) that we were not in earnest, would speak only in a Pickwickian sense if we seemed to speak with firmness, and I did not dare lend colour to that impression. You will notice that the hope of a pacific settlement was expressed. That, in the circumstances, was as far as I dared to go."[64]

The *Lusitania* note had already gone to Berlin in undiluted severity by the time that the President wrote these words on May 14. But defeat in this first round only strengthened Bryan's determination to find some way of making open conflict with Germany unlikely. He turned in obvious desperation to a suggestion that he had earlier made and Wilson had rejected, that American citizens be warned against traveling on British ships through the war zone, at least until negotiations with Germany had yielded some results.[65] "I believe that the issuance of such a notice," the Commoner pleaded in a letter to the White House on May 14, "would not only be likely to protect the lives of some Americans and thus lessen the chances of another calamity, but would have its effect upon the tone of the German reply and might point the way to an understanding."[66] Wilson thought no better of the proposal now than before. "It is hard to turn away from any suggestion that might seem to promise safety for our travellers, but what is suggested seems to me both weak and futile," he replied with what was for him unusual acerbity. "To show this sort of yielding to threat and danger would only make matters worse."[67] There was nothing more that Bryan could do or say.

Once the *Lusitania* note had gone to Berlin, the crucial question be-

---

[63] W.W. to W. J. Bryan, May 13, 1915, *The Lansing Papers*, I, 403.

[64] W.W. to W. J. Bryan, May 14, 1915, *ibid.*, p. 404.

[65] For the early discussions, see R. Lansing to W. J. Bryan, May 9, 1915; W. J. Bryan to W.W., May 10, 1915; W.W. to W. J. Bryan, May 11, 1915, all in *ibid.*, pp. 387-388, 392.

[66] W. J. Bryan to W.W., May 14, 1915, *ibid.*, p. 406.

[67] W.W. to W. J. Bryan, May 14, 1915, *ibid.*

fore the leaders in Washington was whether to send a parallel protest to the British government. Resentment at the Allied blockade had been mounting steadily since early April, especially among cotton producers and shippers who found their large central European market entirely barred by British cruisers. "The English are not behaving very well," Secretary of the Interior Franklin K. Lane reported to Colonel House in early May. "They are holding up our ships; they have made new international law. . . . You would be interested, I think, in hearing some of the discussion around the Cabinet table. There isn't a man in the Cabinet who has a drop of German blood in his veins, I guess. Two of us were born under the British flag. . . . Yet each day that we meet we boil over somewhat at the foolish manner in which England acts. . . . If Congress were in session we would be actively debating an embargo resolution today."[68] "A very serious change is coming over the public sentiment in this country," the President added on the same day, in a private telegram to House for delivery to Sir Edward Grey, "because of the endless delays and many wilful interferences in dealing with our neutral cargoes. The country is listening with more and more acquiescence just because of this intense irritation, to the suggestion that an embargo be placed upon the shipment of arms and war supplies, and if this grows much more before the Congress assembles in December it may be very difficult if not impossible for me to prevent action to that end. Please present to Sir Edward Grey very earnestly the wisdom and necessity of giving utmost freedom to our commerce in neutral goods to neutral ports, and the permanent settlement of all questions concerning cargoes seized or detained."[69]

What should the American government do once it found itself, only two days after these letters were written, facing a more serious crisis with Germany? To Bryan the answer was simple: The United States must either match its acquiescence in British misconduct on the seas with an acquiescence in German misconduct, or else it must condemn the one as strongly as the other—without, however, permitting hostilities to ensue in any event. How else, he asked time and again during the discussions over the *Lusitania* note, could the American government show impartiality toward the rival belligerents? Lansing strongly agreed. Recent British practice, he wrote the Secretary on May 15, had been in "flagrant violation of law and contrary to Sir Edward Grey's assurances." A note must go to London in language

[68] F. K. Lane to E. M. House, May 5, 1915, House Papers.
[69] W.W. to E. M. House, May 5, 1915, Wilson Papers.

as strong as that used in the note to Germany. And it ought to go at once: "The opportune time to send a communication of this sort seems to me to be the present, as it will evince our impartial purpose to protect American rights on the high seas, whoever is the aggressor. We have just complaints against both. We have already been too complacent with Great Britain in the enforcement of the Order in Council. For two months they have been violating the rights of neutrals."[70]

Throughout the discussions over the *Lusitania* note, Bryan seems to have taken it for granted that a similar strong protest would soon be sent to London. Indeed, he signed the former only because he believed that this was true. The President was not opposed; on the contrary, on about May 13 or 14 he asked the Secretary of State to have Lansing prepare the protest as soon as possible. Completed on May 15, it was, as the Counselor himself said, "an uncompromising presentation" that showed "its teeth"—a sweeping reassertion of American trading rights under international law accompanied by a clear warning that the United States would not fail to adopt all measures necessary to protect the rights of its citizens.[71] Bryan sent Lansing's draft to the White House on May 16 with the comment that it had been drawn along the lines suggested by Wilson.[72] "I believe it would have a splendid effect if our note to Great Britain can go at once," Bryan added the next day. "It will give Germany an excuse and I think she is looking for something that will serve as an excuse."[73]

Wilson received Bryan's letters and Lansing's draft while he was in New York City. (He had made a leisurely voyage northward aboard the presidential yacht *Mayflower* and reviewed the Atlantic Fleet in New York harbor on May 17.) On the way home he thought much about the note to Great Britain. Certainly the protest would have to be sent within the near future, he told himself; he would rework Lansing's draft as soon as he returned to the White House. But the longer he thought, the more the conviction grew that (as he explained to Bryan on May 20, after he had returned to his desk) it would not be wise to send any note to London until he had received the German reply to the *Lusitania* note. "We cannot afford," Wilson went on, "even to seem to be trying to make it easier for Germany to accede to our

---

[70] R. Lansing to W. J. Bryan, May 15, 1915, *The Lansing Papers*, I, 296-297; see also R. Lansing to W.W., May 17, 1915, *ibid.*, p. 408, for advice in a similar vein.
[71] "Draft Note to the Ambassador in Great Britain . . . ," *ibid.*, pp. 297-299.
[72] W. J. Bryan to W.W., May 16, 1915, Wilson Papers.
[73] W. J. Bryan to W.W., May 17, 1915, *The Lansing Papers*, I, 410.

demands by turning in similar fashion to England. . . . It would be so evident a case of uneasiness and hedging that I think it would weaken our whole position fatally."[74]

There was a more important reason why Wilson hesitated, one that he did not explain to Bryan at this time. Only a few days before, on May 14, Colonel House had reported from London that Sir Edward Grey had just said that he *thought* his government would be willing to lift its embargo on foodstuffs if the Germans would abandon their campaign against merchant shipping and agree to stop using asphyxiating gases and killing noncombatants.[75] It was the first ray of hope from Europe in many months; such an Anglo-German agreement would at once end all American tension with Germany and might even be the means of ending all trouble with the British. "Deeply interested in your intimation that Sir Edward Grey would be favorable to lifting embargo on food to Germany, because that would afford a solution of a situation as trying and difficult for England as it is for us," Wilson replied at once, urging House to ascertain how far Grey and the British Cabinet would go. "Almost the same thing might be accomplished by action on the part of the British Government which would assure our practically unmolested access to neutral ports with non-contraband goods, food being regarded as non-contraband goods."[76]

House had really not meant to excite the President so. It was, he knew, Bryan's old idea of a *modus vivendi*, which the British had rejected once before, and he had no idea that they would accept it now. Ambassador Page agreed; indeed, he so strongly believed that the renewal of the proposal would only embarrass the British that he refused to seek an appointment for House with Grey.[77] Thus the Colonel replied discouragingly to the President on May 18.[78] But Wilson would not give up. It was becoming more and more evident, he replied by cable on the same day, that he would soon have to address a note to Britain protesting against her "unnecessary and unwarranted" interference with "legitimate," that is, noncontraband, American trade to neutral ports. It would be a great stroke if England relieved the situation voluntarily and "so put Germany alone in the wrong." It

[74] W.W. to W. J. Bryan, May 20, 1915, *ibid.*, p. 411.
[75] E. M. House to W.W., May 14, 1915, Wilson Papers; House Diary, May 14, 1915.
[76] W.W. to E. M. House, May 16, 1915, Baker Collection.
[77] House Diary, May 19, 1915; E. M. House to W.W., May 20, 1915, Wilson Papers.
[78] E. M. House to W.W., May 18, 1915, *ibid.*

would be "a small price to pay for the cessation of submarine outrages."[79]

With no great enthusiasm for the task, House sought out Sir Edward at the Foreign Office "the first thing" on May 19. Grey listened sympathetically and then said that he would present the proposal to the Prime Minister and support it personally before the Cabinet, although he could not predict what their decision would be. The Foreign Secretary then dictated a memorandum embodying his understanding with House: Britain would permit foodstuffs to go to neutral ports without hindrance if Germany gave up her submarine campaign and the use of poisonous gases. In addition, he would take immediate steps to bring all detained American foodstuffs before the Prize Court and to clear all claims for cotton cargoes, so that the owners could be paid at once.[80]

It was assurance enough for House. Returning to the American Embassy, he now dispatched two cablegrams to Gerard in Berlin. "It is of imperative importance," the first read, "that you get the German Government to delay the answer to our note regarding the Lusitania until you receive a cable that I am sending later today." "Can you not induce the German Government," the second read, "to answer our note by proposing that if England will permit foodstuffs in the future to go to neutral ports without question that Germany will discontinue her submarine warfare on merchant vessels and will also discontinue the use of poisonous gas? Such a proposal from Germany at this time will give her great advantage and in my opinion she will make a grave mistake if she does not seize it."[81] He took this action, incidentally, entirely on his own initiative.[82]

There was much consternation at the White House in response to House's private *démarche*. The faithful Colonel had done exactly what Wilson was trying hard to avoid doing. He had given perhaps the impression that the American President was setting the British off against the Germans; and he had implicitly admitted that there *was* a connection between British and German violations of American rights insofar as the Washington government's policies were concerned.[83] Worse still, by sending his second cablegram to Gerard via

[79] W.W. to E. M. House, May 18, 1915, *ibid.*
[80] E. M. House to W.W., May 20, 1915, *ibid.*; House Diary, May 19, 1915.
[81] E. M. House to J. W. Gerard, two cablegrams dated May 19, 1915, House Papers.
[82] "I explained to Sir Edward Grey that I was willing to take this responsibility for I was certain the President would approve my action." House Diary, May 19, 1915.
[83] W.W. to E. M. House, May 20, 1915, Baker Collection.

the State Department, House had revealed the negotiations to a number of persons in the Department, including Bryan, thus raising the possibility of publicity and making it necessary for the President to explain the proceedings to Bryan and perhaps to permit him to conduct the negotiations through official channels.[84]

As it turned out, the denouement was not embarrassing in any way. On May 21 House cabled that Grey had discussed the matter with the Cabinet and was now ready to consider the proposed *modus*.[85] Sending House's message to Bryan on May 23, Wilson explained the negotiations that had already taken place and enclosed a message to be sent to Gerard for confidential presentation to the Foreign Office in Berlin.[86] It told of the British Cabinet's willingness to *consider* the compromise arrangement and voiced the hope that some such solution could be found. But the message went on to make it clear that the American government was acting only as a friend of both belligerents, and not as if it were for a moment suggesting a bargain or compromise with regard to its own rights upon the seas, "or were willing to make those rights contingent upon what England and Germany might agree upon."[87] On the same day, the President informed House of the message he had just sent Gerard. "In your conversations with Sir Edward," Wilson went on, "please make it plain that it is not foodstuff only in which we are interested, but all non contraband shipments to neutral ports, and that the purchase of our cotton illegally intercepted does not help matters because it is the principle and not the money we must insist on. We feel that the blockade recently proclaimed has not been made in fact effective and the impression prevails here that Sir Edward Grey has not been able to fulfill his assurances given us at the time of the order in council, that the order would be carried out in such a way as not to affect our essential rights."[88]

The futility of the entire undertaking was soon revealed by the replies from Berlin and London. Giving up the submarine campaign in return only for the right to import food freely would have been a poor kind of bargain for the Germans; up to this point, at least,

[84] W. J. Bryan to W.W., May 20, 1915, Wilson Papers, tells of the reception of House's second cablegram to Gerard at the Department.

[85] E. M. House to W.W., May 21, 1915, *The Lansing Papers*, I, 412-413.

[86] W.W. to W. J. Bryan, May 23, 1915, *ibid.*

[87] The Secretary of State to Ambassador Gerard, May 23, 1915, *Foreign Relations, 1915, Supplement,* pp. 406-407.

[88] W.W. to E. M. House, May 23, 1915, Baker Collection.

there was no serious shortage of food anywhere in the Empire.[89] They replied that they would be willing to consider the proposed *modus vivendi* only if it were broadened to include "cotton, copper, rubber, and such other raw material as does not directly enter into manufacture of munitions of war."[90] These conditions, House reported from London, were of course impossible.[91] It was, Wilson said, a disappointing end for an "interchange . . . that might have been the beginning of something." "It looks," he added accurately, "as if we were again in a blind alley."[92]

The necessity of doing something to ease British controls over American trade was rarely absent from Wilson's thoughts during the following weeks.[93] But he could not, he thought, make a public pro-

[89] See Paul Eltzbacher (ed.), *Die deutsche Volksernährung und der englische Aushungerungsplan* (1914); Gustav C. Roeder in the New York *World*, April 12, 1915; J. W. Gerard to W.W., June 1, 1915, Wilson Papers; and Herbert C. Hoover to W. H. Page, August 5, 1915, Page Papers, reporting: "It may be accepted as an absolute fact that the Germans have been able during the past year, to produce a sufficient food supply. . . . The forthcoming harvest in Germany will be larger in intrinsic food supply than ever before in the history of that country. . . . From the point of view of actual pressure through food supplies, the whole of the Allied programme has been an absolute failure."

[90] Ambassador Gerard to the Secretary of State, May 25, 1915, *Foreign Relations, 1915, Supplement*, p. 415; also E. M. House to W.W., May 25, 1915, House Papers, transmitting a cablegram from Ambassador Gerard, dated May 21, 1915, and saying in part, "Germany is in no need of food."

[91] E. M. House to W.W., May 25, 1915, *ibid.*

[92] W.W. to W. J. Bryan, May 27, 1915, *The Lansing Papers*, I, 416. On his own volition, Grey brought the question before the Cabinet again on June 14, 1915, suggesting that it might be well to be prepared to accept the *modus vivendi* if the American government proposed it again. The reaction in the British government was a mixed one. Lord Crewe and Eric Drummond in the Foreign Office urged favorable consideration; M. P. A. Hankey of the Imperial Defence Committee argued that the abandonment of the submarine campaign at this time would not be worth *any* concessions by the British government. This, apparently, was Grey's own opinion. He was willing to consider accepting the *modus*, if that were necessary to appease the United States and avert the adoption of retaliatory measures. But when the Washington authorities failed to apply any pressure for the adoption of the compromise during the following weeks, he was altogether content to drop the matter. E. Grey to Lord Crewe, June 14, 1915, G. M. Trevelyan, *Grey of Fallodon*, pp. 362-363; Earl of Crewe, *Memorandum by Lord Crewe, Printed for the use of the Cabinet, June 1915*, dated the Foreign Office, June 18, 1915, Asquith Papers; M. P. A. Hankey, *Notes on Lord Crewe's Memorandum, June 18, 1915*, memorandum dated June 23, 1915, copy in *ibid.*; E. Drummond to M. Bonham-Carter, June 25, 1915, *ibid.*; E. Grey, memorandum to the Cabinet, dated July 17, 1915, published in G. M. Trevelyan, *Grey of Fallodon*, p. 364.

[93] See below, pp. 596-597.

test so long as the more important controversy with Germany raged. Thus in the weeks immediately ahead he applied pressure on the London government only in a private way, as when, for example, he sent the following cablegram to House on May 26, 1915:

"Your suggestion that I also cable Page instructions about the interference of the British Government with neutral trade is wise, but there are two serious difficulties. First I hoped to influence the matter unofficially and avoid the stronger note which must otherwise be sent and second I am afraid of the constant and hopeless leaks in the State Department.

"Will you not explain to Page and ask him for me whether he will not also present to Sir Edward Grey the many arguments for respecting our rights on the high seas and avoiding the perhaps serious friction between the two governments which it is daily becoming more and more evident cannot much longer be avoided if our access to neutral ports with neutral cargoes continues to be interfered with contrary to the assurances given us in Note accompanying the Order in Council."[94]

Meanwhile, the *Lusitania* note had been published in the American press on May 14 and had evoked warmer and more overwhelming approbation than anything the President had said or done since issuing his appeal for neutrality in August 1914. In the best commentary on the reaction of the American people that was written at the time, the editors of the *New Republic* explained why this was true, as follows:

"The note is quiet, dignified, and firm. It is a model of restraint and understatement. It offers no ultimatum. It utters no threats. In presenting the American case it seeks not to wound Germany's pride or to injure Germany's legitimate interests. At the same time it declares firmly its condemnation of Germany's present submarine policy, and insists upon a change consonant with the interests of neutrals and the usages of international law. The note of Mr. Wilson possesses a still greater virtue. It reproduces with remarkable skill the mean of American opinion. It presents the picture of a nation seeking by all honorable means to avert war, but willing to go even to that extreme in defence of principles of law and humanity. It is a note satisfying alike to those anxious for immediate action and to those willing to endure even more than we have endured rather than permit a break

[94] W.W. to E. M. House, May 26, 1915, Baker Collection.

in our relations with Germany. American public opinion has coalesced about this note and the extremists on both sides have been silenced."[95]

This judgment was confirmed by the outpouring of opinion during the week following the publication of the note. Political leaders agreed that the nation stood solidly behind the President.[96] Among the English-language newspapers from one end of the country to the other apparently only two of them—the *St. Louis Times* and the *Milwaukee Free Press*—took the German side.[97] The religious editors were especially thankful for the President's appeal to conscience and for his "forbearance, dignity, courtesy and firmness."[98] Even the pro-Allied extremists and the German-American spokesmen joined in the public commendation.[99]

To Wilson it was all immensely gratifying but somewhat frightening. "Of course it goes without saying that I am deeply touched and rewarded above my desert by the extraordinary and generous support the whole country has given me in this German matter," he wrote to a close friend, "but you will understand when I say that the very completeness and generous fullness of the trust for the time reposed in me increases my sense of overwhelming responsibility,—and of a sort of inevitable loneliness; and that for a man like myself, who by no means implicitly trusts his own judgments, the burden of affairs is added to, not subtracted from, by such confidence. I know, moreover, that I may have to sacrifice it all any day, if my conscience leads one way and the popular verdict the other."[100]

For the leaders in Germany, the various aspects of the crisis were infinitely more complicated and difficult than Americans knew or even imagined, for the sinking of the *Lusitania* had forced into the open the issues of the conflict over the fundamental character of the submarine campaign that had been developing since early April 1915.

[95] *New Republic*, III (May 22, 1915), 57.

[96] For a comprehensive survey of this segment of opinion, see the *New York Times*, May 15, 1915.

[97] See the survey of newspaper opinion in the *Literary Digest*, L (May 22, 1915), 1197-1199.

[98] New York *Christian Advocate*, XC (May 20, 1915), 665-666; also Nashville *Christian Advocate*, LXXVI (May 21, 1915), 644-645; *The Standard* of Chicago, LXII (May 22, 1915), 1178; and "Voice of the Clergy on the 'Lusitania' Case," *Literary Digest*, L (May 22, 1915), 1218-1219.

[99] e.g., *The Outlook*, CX (May 19, 1915), 104-105, and the survey of the German-American press in the *New York Times*, May 15, 1915.

[100] W.W. to Mrs. Crawford Toy, May 23, 1915, Baker Collection.

The vital one, leaders on both sides agreed, went deeper than the single question of the safety of passenger vessels. It was the question whether to prosecute the submarine war in utter ruthlessness, without regard for neutrals and noncombatants, or cautiously and mildly, in such a way as to subordinate military gains to alleged political necessities.

The Imperial Chancellor raised this sharply just before the *Lusitania* incident occurred, as a consequence of the increased destruction of neutral ships that had followed when orders were changed so as to permit U-boat commanders to attack merchantmen without surfacing beforehand.[101] "During the last days . . . ," Bethmann warned Admiral Bachmann, the Admiralty chieftain, on May 6, "the submarine war has taken more and more numerous victims among neutral ships. This fact is eminently bound not only to alter our good relations with the neutral states but also to create the gravest complications and, finally, to throw those states into the enemy's camp. . . . Given the tense situation in which the total policy of the Empire finds itself at present, I cannot accept the responsibility of seeing our relations with the neutral states further worsened, to which the pursuit of the submarine war in its present form will certainly lead. I must, therefore, insist in all solemnity that the high command of the German naval forces take necessary measures to guarantee that our submarines will in all circumstances avoid attacking neutral ships, in accordance with agreements that have been made."[102] Bachmann's reply pointed up the vast gulf now separating the civilian authorities and the navy. It simply was not possible, he retorted, to give the kind of guarantee that the Chancellor had demanded. Existing limitations on the freedom of U-boat commanders were bad enough. "To impose new restrictions . . . would be equivalent to giving up the submarine war."[103]

Between this interchange of course occurred the sinking of the *Lusitania*. It jolted the German leaders almost as rudely as it did the American. There was, Admiral von Müller reported, much fright at Supreme Headquarters over "the monstrosity of the deed."[104] "I am disgusted about the torpedoing of the Lusitania, the consequences of

[101] See above, pp. 355-356.

[102] The Imperial Chancellor to the Head of the Admiralty, May 6, 1915, Spindler, *La Guerre Sous-Marine*, II, 130-131; Tirpitz, *Politische Dokumente*, II, 333.

[103] Admiral Bachmann to the Imperial Chancellor, May 10, 1915, Spindler, *La Guerre Sous-Marine*, II, 131-132.

[104] G. A. von Müller to A. von Tirpitz, May 12, 1915, Tirpitz, *Politische Dokumente*, II, 335.

which are immeasurable," wrote Colonel Karl G. von Treutler, the Foreign Office's representative at Supreme Headquarters, to Bethmann.[105]

It is conceivable, therefore, that the Chancellor might have moved at this point for a final showdown with the admirals. To be sure, the battle would have been fierce, its outcome uncertain. Tirpitz had demanded that the civilian leaders stand firm abroad and incite public opinion at home against America by playing up the munitions issue.[106] The Emperor had agreed and instructed Bethmann to inform German Embassies abroad that there would be no yielding.[107] More important still, German public opinion had been stirred to frenzy, and newspapers of almost every political complexion were demanding a sharpening of the submarine campaign. "With joyful pride we contemplate this latest deed of our Navy," the editorial spokesman of the Catholic Centre Party exulted, for example. "It will not be the last." "For the German Navy the sinking of the *Lusitania* means an extraordinary success," echoed the immensely influential *Frankfurter Zeitung.* "Its destruction demolished the last fable with which the people of England consoled themselves."[108]

An irresponsible leader might have tried to swim against the tide, but Bethmann was too wise to risk his political life uselessly. Determined to avoid war with America and the risk of war with other neutrals, he knew that the ruthless submarine campaign would have to be abandoned. But he would win his objective a step at a time and by temporizing when that was necessary, not by running the risks of a direct and immediate confrontation on the basic issues. He would force the fight first, not on the question of the *Lusitania* and passenger ships, but on the issue of respect for neutral shipping; the question of passenger ships could be disposed of easily once the first round had been won.

As a preliminary step, merely to gain a breathing space, Bethmann on May 9 persuaded the Emperor to instruct the Admiralty to avoid

---

[105] K. G. von Treutler to the Imperial Chancellor, May 9, 1915, German F. O. Archives.

[106] A. von Tirpitz to G. A. von Müller, May 9, 1915, *ibid.*

[107] T. von Bethmann Hollweg to K. G. von Treutler, May 10, 1915, *ibid.*

[108] *Kölnische Volkszeitung* and *Frankfurter Zeitung*, cited in the *Literary Digest*, L (May 22, 1915), 1206, along with the *Berliner Tageblatt, Berliner Lokal-Anzeiger*, Berlin *Kreuz-Zeitung*, Berlin *Deutsche Tageszeitung*, and Berlin *Germania*. For contemporary German comment on the legal issues of the *Lusitania* case, see Christian Meurer, *Der Lusitania-Fall, Eine Völkerrechtliche Studie*, and, by various authors, *Der Lusitania-Fall im Urteile von deutschen Gelehrten.*

the destruction of any neutral ship under any circumstances "in the near future." "The renewal of sharper action," the order added, "will remain in abeyance."[109] On the same day, the Chancellor had the Foreign Office issue a circular note to the neutral powers informing them that German naval commanders had been given "the most definite" instructions to avoid attacks on neutral vessels, and that the Berlin government would unreservedly recognize its responsibility and pay damages should neutral shipping come to harm on account of unfortunate mistakes.[110]

Safe for the moment, as he thought, from difficulties from this one source, Bethmann could now give attention to the *Lusitania* case. He moved in a leisurely way at first because the early dispatches from Washington seemed to say that no sharp German-American crisis would ensue unless new incidents suddenly occurred. "Mr. Wilson," Bernstorff wired on May 9, "treats the matter calmly."[111] "Secretary of State," the Ambassador added the following day, "is completely of the view that Germany could not act any differently against England, which wants to starve us. It is a pity that we are not as skillful as England in the art of presenting such events. He considers the indignation over the torpedoing of the Lusitania 'ridiculous' and is 'immune' against such remarks. . . . His influence, at any rate, will be exercised in favor of peace. His influence is great, since Wilson depends upon Bryan for re-election."[112] On May 13 there was a sharp warning from Bernstorff and the Austrian Ambassador in Washington, Konstantin Dumba, that war would break out if another passenger ship with Americans on board were torpedoed.[113] But as late as May 17, even after the arrival of President Wilson's *Lusitania* note in Berlin, the situation did not seem urgent, as the following message from Washington on that day indicated:

"Mr. Bryan, with whom I discussed the situation intensively, today asked me to call the attention of the Berlin cabinet to two points:

[109] G. A. von Müller to the Head of the Admiralty, May 10, 1915, Tirpitz, *Politische Dokumente*, II, 333-334.

[110] Ambassador Gerard to the Secretary of State, May 9, 1915, *Foreign Relations, 1915, Supplement*, pp. 387-388.

[111] Ambassador von Bernstorff to the Foreign Office, May 9, 1915, German F. O. Archives.

[112] Ambassador von Bernstorff to the Foreign Office, May 10, 1915, two dispatches, *ibid.*

[113] Ambassador K. Dumba to Foreign Secretary Burián, May 13, 1915, *ibid.*; Ambassador von Bernstorff to the Foreign Office, received May 16, 1915, *ibid.*

"1. The American note of protest, in view of the hysterical state of public opinion, had to be written in a much sharper form than the one sent to England on March 30. Nevertheless, it was intended in a friendly manner, and he hopes for an answer in the same friendly tone and spirit.

"2. He does not think it wise that the German Government should eventually give in on the question of the submarine war *on the condition* that the United States call the London cabinet to respect international law, especially where the import of food supplies is concerned. This would give the appearance that President Wilson had made his statements under German pressure, and it would therefore be entirely without success.

"Mr. Bryan suggests, moreover, *absolute* modification of the submarine war by the Germans, according to the spirit of his country's note. At the same time, he could, upon an official announcement by the German Government, present his case to the London cabinet. Confidentially, I learn from reliable sources that the President will take steps in London within two to three days. Therefore, it is to be recommended that Berlin wait with its answer to the American note."[114]

Bethmann did not change his pace even after the arrival of the American note in Berlin on May 15. Perhaps, he must have thought, it would be possible to prolong the negotiations; perhaps he could temporize by sending an unresponsive interim reply; best of all, perhaps it would not be necessary publicly to meet the President's challenge to the submarine campaign. Meanwhile, in good time, when a safe opportunity arose, he would deal with the admirals and make certain that no cause for further worsening of relations with America could occur.

Surveying the German scene during the next two weeks as they thought about what they should say in answer to the American President, Bethmann and Foreign Secretary von Jagow must have concluded that they had no alternative but to draft an evasive reply. It was not possible fully to satisfy the President's requests without abandoning the submarine campaign altogether, and without doing this in a public way. Bethmann might have demanded this concession if

[114] Ambassador K. Dumba, Ambassador von Bernstorff, and "Lucius" to the Foreign Office in Berlin, for Baron Burián in Vienna, May 17, 1915, *ibid.*; for a slightly different text, see *The Lansing Papers*, I, 415. W. J. Bryan to W.W., May 17, 1915, *ibid.*, pp. 408-410, also gives a summary of this conversation.

it had been absolutely necessary to avert an American declaration of war. But Bryan's tip-off to Dumba revealed that obviously it was not necessary, and Bethmann could, therefore, avoid the risks of defeat on the question of either/or and proceed to deal with the admirals in a safer fashion.

An equally important cause for caution was the excited state of public and press opinion. Public opinion was the sovereign force as much in Germany as in England or France, and more than in the United States at this time. Bethmann's power in the last analysis rested not upon the support of a timid monarch but upon the votes that he could command in the Reichstag and the confidence that he could evoke in the Empire as a whole. He might attempt to mold public opinion, but he could not defy it. The tides of public passion were running so high that the Foreign Office took the precaution of calling in the newspaper correspondents before the American note was published in Germany. The note, a spokesman for Foreign Secretary von Jagow, explained, was not an ultimatum; the government had no intention of giving up the submarine weapon; and newspapermen should take care not to excite public opinion over the issue.[115]

Perhaps this admonition did some good, but the comment that accompanied the publication of President Wilson's note in the German press on May 18, 1915, was provocative enough. "When one of our submarines again succeeds in sinking a passenger ship," the moderate *Berliner Tageblatt* declared, "we will no doubt hear another wild outburst of rage. But that our submarines will continue to sink large steamers is to be expected as a matter of course."[116] "Whoever reads this note without prejudice," the journalistic voice of the Admiralty added, "can scarcely escape the impression that the British Ambassador in Washington was not far away when it was framed. One could equally as well imagine its contents to be a speech by Premier Asquith in the House of Commons."[117] "It cannot be supposed," the leading Liberal newspaper in the Empire agreed, "that the German military authorities will depart an inch from the path which the German Government, after mature consideration, has considered necessary and followed." The American note, this editor went on, "will, we are sure, receive the answer from our government that it deserves."[118]

[115] Count Wedel to G. von Jagow, June 20, 1915, German F. O. Archives.
[116] *Berliner Tageblatt*, cited in the *New York Times*, May 19, 1915.
[117] Berlin *Deutsche Tageszeitung*, May 18, 1915.
[118] *Kölnische Zeitung*, noon edn., May 18, 1915.

Bethmann and von Jagow drafted their reply a few days later with this reaction and with a keen realization of the larger political struggle in which the Chancellor was now engaged very much in mind. About half of their note, which was delivered to Ambassador Gerard on May 28, 1915, was devoted to the *Cushing, Gulflight,* and *Falaba* cases. Regarding the first two, it declared forthrightly that the German government would make full amends if investigation showed that the ships had come to grief through acts of a German submarine commander and aviator. "The most explicit instructions," the note continued assuringly, "have been repeatedly given the German armed forces to avoid attacking such [neutral] vessels." As for the *Falaba,* the submarine commander involved had intended to give passengers and crew an opportunity to save themselves; he had not been able to do this only because the *Falaba's* captain had attempted to escape after being warned and had sent up rocket signals for help after stopping.

The German government, the note continued, had already expressed its regret over the loss of neutral lives on the *Lusitania.* Certain important points had to be cleared up now before the two governments could come to any understanding on the case. To begin with, the Imperial government had definite and reliable information that the *Lusitania,* which had been constructed in the first instance as an auxiliary cruiser for the British navy, had been armed. Secondly, British merchantmen operated under orders from the Admiralty in London to use neutral flags and to ram submarines while so disguised. Finally, the *Lusitania* on her last voyage had carried Canadian soldiers and a large cargo of munitions on board. "The German Government believes that it acts in just self-defense when it seeks to protect the lives of its soldiers by destroying ammunition destined for the enemy with the means of war at its command." The *Lusitania* had sunk rapidly, no doubt, because of the explosion of the ammunition on board. By carrying explosives and passengers on the same boat in direct contravention of American law, the Cunard Company, actually had been responsible for the death of American citizens on the liner.

These were facts sufficiently important, the note concluded, to merit a careful investigation by the American government. "The Imperial Government begs to reserve a final statement of its position with regard to the demands made in connection with the sinking of the

Lusitania until a reply is received from the American Government."[119]

That the leaders in Berlin meant their note to be regarded only as an interim reply was emphasized by Secretary von Jagow on May 30

"The German Government
believes that it was acting in justified self-defense."
Kirby in the New York *World*

in an interview for publication in the American press. "The issues involved," he explained, "are of such importance, and the view[s] in regard to the Lusitania show such variance, that the German Govern-

[119] Ambassador Gerard to the Secretary of State, May 29, 1915, *Foreign Relations, 1915, Supplement*, pp. 419-421.

ment believed it essential to attempt to establish a common basis of fact before entering into a discussion of the issues involved. . . . I hope that such a common basis of fact, once established, may serve as the groundwork for further conversation."[120]

As Bethmann well knew, the reply of May 28 settled no issue either at home or abroad; the really decisive phases of the battle lay immediately ahead. The opportunity, indeed, the necessity, for a showdown with his domestic antagonists came during the last week in May 1915, when the naval chieftains played into the Chancellor's hands. After reading the circular that the Foreign Office had sent to the neutral powers without his knowledge or consent on May 9, Admiral Bachmann lost his head and addressed an angry protest to the Foreign Secretary that seemed to say that he did not want to observe the Emperor's order of May 10 commanding respect for neutral shipping.[121] The suspicion aroused by this letter—that the navy was determined to go its own way—was seemingly confirmed on May 28, when the newspapers reported that two days earlier a submarine had attacked the American steamer *Nebraskan*, westbound from Liverpool, off the southern coast of Ireland.[122] In addition, the Foreign Office received a message from Washington on May 28 or 29 saying, in the President's own words, that "conditions now prevailing in the marine war zone are rapidly becoming intolerable."[123] Linking this to the *Nebraskan* incident, Bethmann interpreted the warning to mean that the Washington government was contemplating breaking diplomatic relations with Germany.[124]

In these new circumstances of alarm the Imperial Chancellor lost no time in proceeding to the attack. From Berlin he addressed a long and urgent message to his envoy, von Treutler, at Supreme Headquarters at Pless Castle in Silesia on May 29. It reviewed the recent troubled relations with the United States and other neutrals and

---

[120] *New York Times*, May 31, 1915.

[121] The Head of the Admiralty to the Foreign Secretary, May 26, 1915, Spindler, *La Guerre Sous-Marine*, II, 133.

[122] For details, see the *New York Times*, May 27 and 28, 1915.

[123] The Secretary of State to Ambassador Gerard, May 27, 1915, *Foreign Relations, 1915, Supplement*, p. 418.

[124] T. von Bethmann Hollweg to Envoy von Treutler, May 29, 1915, German F. O. Archives. Actually, the President had meant no such thing. He had simply tried to make clear the reason for the recent renewal of the suggestion of a *modus vivendi* between Germany and England.

warned that President Wilson had just threatened to break relations with Germany unless the submarine campaign were modified. Bethmann went on:

"If the United States goes over to our enemies, the small neutral nations will soon follow. In Holland there is great fear for the annexation of Belgium. There is, therefore, the danger that Holland, if she were invaded by our enemies, would not oppose but perhaps might even join them. I do not think that we could stand such a military attack, and I have therefore made serious reproaches to the Admiralty, which to this point have been to no avail.

"Will Your Excellency please discuss the above with General von Falkenhayn and leave it to his discretion, in case he is also worried about the threat from Holland and has the same estimate of the military situation as I do, to bring this matter before someone of importance at the right place at the right time.

"If the submarine war continues in its present form, I can no longer assume responsibility for the attitude of the neutrals."[125]

Treutler took the Chancellor's message straight to Admiral von Müller and General von Falkenhayn, and the Chief of the General Staff himself gave the warning to the Emperor.[126] In response, William signed a message to the Admiralty, which von Müller had probably drafted, reprimanding Bachmann for the "sinking" of the *Nebraskan*,[127] demanding to know what orders submarine commanders were following, and reminding the Admiralty of his order of May 10.[128] Moreover, the Emperor approved Bethmann's request for an Imperial conference to review the policies governing the conduct of the submarine war.

His Majesty, the Imperial Chancellor, Colonel von Treutler, Grand Admiral von Tirpitz, Admirals von Müller and Bachmann, and General von Falkenhayn all assembled at Pless Castle on May 31, 1915, as Bethmann had requested. Von Falkenhayn opened the discussion by saying that the army simply could not bear any additional burdens (Italy had just entered the war against Austria), and that the navy would have to carry on the submarine campaign in such a way as to avoid the risk of war with any of the neutrals. No matter how

[125] T. von Bethmann Hollweg to Envoy von Treutler, May 29, 1915, *ibid.*

[126] Envoy von Treutler to the Imperial Chancellor, May 31, 1915, transmitting a message from General E. von Falkenhayn, *ibid.*

[127] Actually, the vessel was only badly damaged and did not sink.

[128] Envoy von Treutler to the Imperial Chancellor, May 29, 1915, German F. O. Archives.

right the Germans were, the general continued, "the question of power is the decisive one . . . , and we could not withstand a war with America on the side of our enemies." He recommended, therefore, giving "an explicit order—contradicting all previous general directives —to spare the neutrals." It was not possible to do this, Tirpitz and Bachmann retorted, without abandoning the submarine campaign altogether. His Majesty would have to decide whether to continue or to end the war underseas.

The Emperor bristled at this suggestion that he take responsibility for what was bound to be an unpopular action. If the Chancellor wanted to abandon the submarine war, he said excitedly, then he would have to assume responsibility for the decision before the German people. At this point von Müller injected a calming opinion: The Imperial Chancellor did not want the submarine war to stop at all; it would certainly be possible to draft new orders that would provide for the political exigencies. Very well, the Emperor growled, let the Chancellor and the Head of the Admiralty confer and send such an order by Imperial command.[129]

Bethmann and Bachmann prepared the new order immediately following this conference. Sent to the fleet on June 1, 1915, it read:

> His Majesty the Emperor points once more to the necessity of sparing neutral ships in the conduct of submarine operations, until further orders are given. Further attacks on neutral ships would permit the danger of serious political complications, and these have to be avoided at any cost in the present circumstances. His Majesty makes it the solemn duty of submarine commanders not to attack unless they have the well-founded conviction that the ship in question is an enemy ship. In cases of doubt it is better to let an enemy freighter escape than to sink a neutral ship. You will also attempt to convey this order to U-boats now at sea.[130]

Bethmann was jubilant. "Torpedoing of neutral ships," he boasted to von Treutler, "will not happen any more except in cases of unavoidable accident. I have no objections to raise against the continuation of the submarine war in accord with these orders."[131] A short time later on the same day he had the Foreign Office address a con-

[129] The two foregoing paragraphs are based upon Spindler, *La Guerre Sous-Marine*, II, 134, which summarizes the discussions, and upon two memoranda printed in Tirpitz, *Politische Dokumente*, II, 346-347.

[130] The Head of the Admiralty to the Chief of the High Seas Fleet, June 1, 1915, copy in the German F. O. Archives.

[131] T. von Bethmann Hollweg to K. G. von Treutler, June 1, 1915, *ibid.*

ciliatory note about the *Gulflight* and *Cushing* incidents to Ambassador Gerard. The first incident had occurred, it said, because the submarine commander had thought that the *Gulflight* was an English merchantman being escorted by English patrol vessels. "The German Government expresses its regrets to the Government of the United States concerning this incident," the note went on, "and declares itself ready to furnish full recompense for the damage thereby sustained by American citizens." As for the *Cushing* incident, the German government had not yet been able to determine whether one of its aviators had actually attacked the ship, as the American government had averred; it was possible that this had been the case, and the German government would be glad to receive the evidence that the Washington authorities had gathered.[132]

For Bethmann there now remained only one urgent necessity—to obtain an order to submarine commanders to spare large passenger liners (including those of belligerent registry) before another *Lusitania* incident plunged the United States into war. He had not broached this matter at the Imperial conference on May 31, for in dealing with Tirpitz and Bachmann and the Emperor one had to avoid pressing for everything at once. Once the new order had gone to the fleet on June 1, the Chancellor lost no time in executing the strategy that he, von Müller, and von Treutler must have devised immediately after the Imperial conference broke up. First, Bethmann asked the Admiralty for a guarantee that no more enemy liners like the *Lusitania* would be sunk. When Bachmann refused, then the Chancellor signaled von Treutler and von Müller at Supreme Headquarters. With the support of General von Falkenhayn they had no difficulty in obtaining the Emperor's approval on June 5 for the dispatch of a new Imperial command to the Admiralty. "His Majesty," it read, "regrets that in the order for submarine operations of June 1 the question of large passenger ships was omitted, and he orders an immediate supplement regarding this matter."[133]

The beaten admirals did not take defeat gracefully. What a victory for deception and intrigue! What dishonor! What a shameful humiliation of the navy! "The important further limitation of submarine war which Your Majesty has today ordered means, in view of the

[132] Ambassador Gerard to the Secretary of State, June 1, 1915, *Foreign Relations, 1915, Supplement*, pp. 431-432.

[133] Imperial Order of June 5, 1915, transmitted in Envoy von Treutler to the Imperial Chancellor, June 5, 1915, German F. O. Archives.

unique nature of submarine operations, virtually a complete renunciation of the same," Tirpitz and Bachmann wrote in a direct appeal to the Supreme Warlord. "With this order, Germany loses her last weapon against England and suffers in the eyes of her enemies and the neutral powers a loss of military prestige that can never be regained. . . . The undersigned appeal most urgently to Your Majesty to withdraw your signature from this order. They themselves are not in a position to take responsibility for it."[134] The reply came swiftly from Pless Castle: "My order . . . stands. If there are political consequences, *the Imperial Chancellor carries the responsibility.*"[135]

Thus on the same day, June 6, the Admiralty sent the following order to the fleet:

His Majesty the Emperor has ordered, supplementing the order given June 1, that no *large* liner, not even an enemy one, will be sunk until further orders. His Majesty the Emperor orders you to preserve absolute secrecy on the subject of the present order and will hold the military authorities personally responsible for keeping the secret.[136]

This, then, was the situation by the end of the first week of June 1915: By firm but unwarlike diplomacy the President of the United States had won respect for American and neutral shipping and (although he did not know it) safety also for *large* passenger liners in the war zone. Peace between Germany and the United States was now at least possible. But the great objective upon which Wilson had set his heart, the entire abandonment of the submarine war, still remained to be achieved. This issue would be decided in the weeks ahead.

[134] A. von Tirpitz and Admiral Bachmann to His Majesty's Aide-de-Camp, June 5, 1915, Tirpitz, *Politische Dokumente*, II, 350.

[135] Wilhelm to the Imperial Navy Office, June 6, 1915, *ibid.*; italics added.

[136] Spindler, *La Guerre Sous-Marine*, II, 135-136; italics added. Tirpitz and Bachmann submitted their resignations at once, and the Emperor rejected them. On the margin of Bachmann's letter William wrote: "No! The gentlemen are to obey and to remain! This is nothing but a military conspiracy! Started by Tirpitz!" Tirpitz, *Politische Dokumente*, II, 351.

CHAPTER XIII

Bryan's Resignation and
the *Lusitania* Impasse

FIRST intimations of the tenor of the German note of reply came to America in the form of a press summary that was sent from Berlin on May 29, 1915, and published in the American press the following day.[1] The State Department received the official text late Sunday night, May 30,[2] and sent a copy to the White House just before noon on May 31. The President was leaving to attend brief Memorial Day exercises at Arlington Cemetery as the note arrived. Upon his return in the early afternoon he closeted himself in his study for two uninterrupted hours. He must have been, as the White House correspondents suspected, greatly disappointed by the evasiveness of the German response and by the proof that it gave that the Foreign Office in Berlin hoped to drag out the negotiations. He had an early dinner with his daughter Margaret and his cousin Helen Woodrow Bones and a short ride before dark. Then he went back to work until bed time.[3]

The next day, June 1, while editors throughout the country were still (for the most part) denouncing the German note as "the answer of an outlaw who assumes no obligation toward society,"[4] the Cabinet members met in solemn session to advise the President on what he should say now. There was some preliminary discussion about a proposed warning to the warring factions in Mexico. Then Wilson brought up the matter of the further message to the German government, adding that he wanted a full and free discussion. Garrison suggested that the next note to Berlin should "contain no discussion of details

[1] *New York Times*, May 30, 1915.

[2] *ibid.*, May 31, 1915; New York *World*, May 31, 1915. Bryan made no comment on the German note, but Lansing's opinions were sharp. See R. Lansing to W. J. Bryan, June 1, 1915, *The Lansing Papers*, I, 417.

[3] *New York Times*, June 1, 1915.

[4] As the New York *World*, June 1, 1915, put it. For a review of press opinion, see the *Literary Digest*, L (June 12, 1915), 1383-1385.

or facts. Germany should be made to say, first, whether or not she accepted the principle we stood for. If she did not, there was nothing to discuss; if she did, we could then canvass details with her." One member (was it Burleson?) asked whether a strong protest would also go to London. General hubbub ensued. Bryan, who had "seemed to be labouring under a great strain and [had] sat back in his chair most of the time with his eyes closed," now came into the discussion in an obviously excited mood. "He said," one Cabinet member wrote soon after the meeting, "that he had all along insisted on a note to England; that she was illegally preventing our exports from going where we had a right to send them; and that the Cabinet seemed to be pro-Ally." The President, this account continued, "sharply rebuked Bryan, saying that his remarks were unfair and unjust. He had no right to say that any one was pro-Ally or pro-German. Each one was merely trying to be a good American. We had lodged a protest with England and might do so again at the proper time, but this would be a singularly inappropriate time to take up such a matter with her. . . . Certainly, in any event, when we had before us a grave issue with the Germans, it would be folly to force an issue of such character with England. . . . He added that certain things were clear and that as to them his mind was made up."[5]

Another Cabinet member years later remembered Bryan saying, "You people are not neutral. You are taking sides!" and Wilson replying in a voice that was sharp and cold, "Mr. Secretary, you have no right to make that statement. We are all honestly trying to be neutral against heavy difficulties."[6]

After this the discussion dragged on a little longer, but without any further outbreaks from Bryan or protests from his friends.

It was not yet possible to know exactly where the President would stand or what he would do. Would he continue to insist that the Germans abandon the submarine campaign entirely? Or was he perhaps beginning to think that there might be times and circumstances when submarine commanders could visit and search ships before sinking them? Was he willing to accept less than the whole objective? And

[5] David F. Houston, *Eight Years with Wilson's Cabinet, 1913 to 1920*, I, 132-137. In this account, which is the only substantial one that we have of the Cabinet meeting of June 1, Houston errs in saying that the President read the draft of the note that he intended to send to Berlin. As we will see, Wilson prepared the first draft of this note on June 3 and read it to the Cabinet on the following day.

[6] R. S. Baker, interview with T. W. Gregory, March 13-15, 1927, Baker Collection.

what if Germany met his wishes? Would he then really move in a serious way against England?

Fortunately, the President revealed his thoughts and purposes in an extraordinary way on the following day, June 2, 1915, in a private interview with Ambassador von Bernstorff. If Wilson felt any personal animosity toward the German cause, he carefully concealed it on this occasion. He listened sympathetically while Bernstorff explained his government's point of view and made it clear that he, Wilson, wanted only a peaceful solution. At the same time, he revealed that he would maintain the high ground of his first *Lusitania* note while holding out the hope of great advantage for the Germans if only they would yield. But let Bernstorff tell the story of this conference:

"The seriousness of the situation over here," he reported at once to the Foreign Office in Berlin over the American diplomatic wire,[7] "has caused me to seek an audience with President Wilson. In an extraordinarily friendly conversation, in which the wish was repeatedly stressed on both sides that we might find a way out of the present difficulties, Wilson kept coming back to the point that to him only humanitarian considerations are important, and that an indemnity for the Americans who perished on the Lusitania is secondary to the humanitarian considerations. His efforts are directed at a total abolition of the submarine war. Compared with this final goal, small concessions on our side would be only a compromise. In giving up the submarine war, we should base our action on moral grounds, since only by reaching an understanding on moral grounds, and not by weapons, can the war be finally decided. If we would abandon the submarine war, he would press the English into abandoning the starvation policy. According to definite news from London, the Cabinet there would be willing to go along. With such measures Wilson hopes that a beginning for peace, which he would like to initiate as head of all the neutrals, could be made in grand style.

"The American note of reply will probably subordinate all juridical issues and stress only the humane. The latter very strongly, but, as Wilson said to me, in friendly form.

[7] During this interview Bernstorff explained that one of the greatest obstacles to a peaceful settlement of the *Lusitania* case was the extreme difficulty of confidential communication between the German Embassy in Washington and the Foreign Office in Berlin. Would the President, he asked, be willing for him to use the State Department's wire if he guaranteed to send no information that would compromise American neutrality? Wilson gladly consented, adding that Bernstorff might use the State Department's facilities until the *Lusitania* negotiations were completed.

"The President emphasized that the point on which we could unite was that Germany and the United States have always stood for the freedom of the seas."[8]

"In spite of the fact that the waves of anti-German sentiment caused by the Lusitania incident are still running strong," Bernstorff added in a kind of postscript a week later, "I can claim this good knowledge, that neither the President nor the American people want a war with Germany. Therefore, Mr. Wilson has the best chance to gain public approval for himself if he averts *conflict with us honorably, by beginning a peace movement in a grand style.* I am more than ever firmly convinced—after my recent long conference with him—that the thoughts of the President move in that direction. . . . Since I may be accused of an exaggerated optimism, I have to make the following observations: The President and the government over here are much more neutral than one would generally assume. England's influence here is tremendous because it runs through so many channels that we cannot close. In spite of this, the government in Washington has tried to maintain a neutral attitude. It is a fact perhaps astonishing to us, but a fact none the less, that prominent Americans often come here from Boston, New York and Philadelphia—general centers of English support in this country—and complain of the pro-German attitude of the government. As I have found out for certain, the government hopes even to prevent the export of arms and munitions to Europe by quickening the Mexican question."[9]

The main task now was the composition of the second *Lusitania* note. By this point Wilson had certainly made up his mind what he ought to say. But in order to heal the wound caused by his cutting words at the Cabinet meeting on the day before, he wrote to Bryan on June 2, asking the Secretary (and the Counselor, too) to prepare an outline of a note to Germany. "I feel," he added soothingly, "that I very much need all the counsel I can get, and I shall, of course, chiefly value yours."[10]

Lansing replied eagerly, not by drafting a note of reply, but by concentrating upon the legal issues and controverted facts of the case. In

[8] Ambassador von Bernstorff to the Foreign Office, June 2, 1915 (received June 6, 1915), German F. O. Archives. For astonishingly full and accurate press accounts of this interview, which must have been inspired by Bernstorff, see the *New York Times*, New York *World*, and *Providence Journal*, all dated June 3, 1915.

[9] Ambassador von Bernstorff to T. von Bethmann Hollweg, June 9, 1915, *ibid.*

[10] W.W. to W. J. Bryan, June 2, 1915, *The Lansing Papers*, I, 418-419.

one memorandum he urged the President to rectify the mistake he had made in the first *Lusitania* note when he had used the term "unarmed" instead of "unresisting" liners.[11] In another memorandum, nineteen pages long, prepared on the same day, the Counselor considered all the German allegations about the belligerent character of the *Lusitania* and answered them one by one.[12]

Like his legal adviser, Bryan did not attempt to draft a note but instead put all his effort into a last-ditch attempt to bring the President to his point of view on the fundamental issues. In a long letter on June 2 he appealed for delay ("In our peace plan we have emphasized the advantage of time for investigation and deliberation"), for agreement to submit the case to arbitration, and for willingness to discuss the facts with the German government without demanding, as Garrison had suggested, prior agreement on principles.[13] On the following morning Bryan wrote an even longer letter reviewing the German note of May 28 and saying that one way out of the crisis would be to prevent American citizens from traveling on ships carrying contraband. "A person," he added, "would have to be very much biased in favor of the Allies to insist that ammunition intended for one of the belligerents should be safe-guarded in transit by the lives of American citizens."[14] Then, during the evening of June 3, the Secretary sent a third communication to the White House. It was a relatively brief reply to Lansing's memorandum on the German allegations about the legal status of the *Lusitania*.[15]

Perhaps Wilson read Bryan's impassioned appeals,[16] but he relied upon Lansing's data and his own convictions as he set about drafting the second *Lusitania* note on June 3, 1915. All day long and far into the early morning hours of June 4 he worked, writing and rewriting, searching for the right word and phrase. Utterly fatigued, he went to bed at about two o'clock. At a little after nine o'clock in the morning Bryan came to the White House and went over the draft with his

[11] R. Lansing to W. J. Bryan, June 2, 1915, *ibid.*, p. 418. On this point, see the note in the Anderson Diary, June 1, 1915.

[12] R. Lansing, "German Allegations Regarding Lusitania," dated June 2, 1915, Wilson Papers.

[13] W. J. Bryan to W.W., June 2, 1915, *The Lansing Papers*, I, 419-421.

[14] W. J. Bryan to W.W., June 3, 1915, morning, *ibid.*, pp. 422-426.

[15] W. J. Bryan to W.W., June 3, 1915, evening, *ibid.*, pp. 427-428.

[16] He acknowledged only Bryan's letter of June 2. See W.W. to W. J. Bryan, June 2, 1915, *ibid.*, p. 421.

chief. Then the members of the Cabinet and Counselor Lansing assembled at ten to hear the President read the document.[17]

He began with a cordial acknowledgement of the recent German recognition, in connection with the *Cushing* and *Gulflight* cases, of "the principle of the freedom of the seas to all neutral ships." He was confident, he went on, that the Imperial German government would concede its responsibility "for the mistakes of its officers in those cases when it shall have acquainted itself with all the facts." Even so, he continued, recent "fatal and tragical mistakes" by U-boat commanders only pointed up the fact that the submarine campaign, even when conducted with the best intentions, posed a grave threat to the freedom of the seas. Following a paragraph on the *Falaba* case, the President came directly to the *Lusitania* affair. Reviewing the German charges that the ship had been armed and carried Canadian troops, he answered these by saying that the Imperial German government had been misinformed. He then went on to his climax, as follows:

"But the sinking of this passenger ship involves principles of humanity which throw into the background any special circumstances of detail that may have surrounded the case, principles which lift it, as the Imperial German Government will no doubt be quick to recognize and acknowledge, out of the class of ordinary subjects of diplomacy. Whatever be the other facts, the principal fact is that a great steamer, primarily and chiefly a conveyance for passengers, and carrying more than a thousand souls who had no part or lot in the conduct of the war, was sent to the bottom without so much as a challenge or a warning and that men, women, and children were sent to their death in circumstances unparalleled in modern warfare. The fact that more than one hundred Americans were among those who perished makes it the duty of the Government of the United States to speak of these things and to call the attention of the Imperial German Government to the grave responsibility which the Government of the United States conceives it to have incurred in this tragic occurence [*sic*]."

Anticlimactically, the President concluded with a statement of willingness to do what he could to help find an Anglo-German *modus vivendi* for maritime warfare, and with the following appeal:

"In the meantime, welcoming though it [the American Govern-

[17] *New York Times*, June 4 and 5, 1915.

ment] does the opportunity to clear up any question connected with the matters it has felt it its duty to present to the Imperial German Government, it confidently looks to see the justice of that great Government vindicated in cases where Americans have been drawn into what is no quarrel of theirs, and the humanity of that great Government, as well, made secure against the future, whatever in the opinion of the Imperial German Government may have been the provocation or the circumstantial justification for the past action of its commanders at sea. The Government of the United States, therefore, very earnestly renews the representations of its note of the thirteenth of May, and relies in these representations not only upon the general principles of international law hitherto recognized among nations but also upon the solemn covenants of the treaty of 1828 between the United States and [the] Kingfom [*sic*] of Prussia."[18]

Concluding, Wilson laid down his papers and turned to his advisers for their suggestions. What could they say, except that the note was excellent, or that it was firm without being provocative? The President had obviously made up his mind; any fundamental criticism would be risky now. "A confused and somewhat tiresome discussion followed. It tried the President's patience greatly and tired him perceptibly. It did not help him. . . . The meeting did not last long." The following day Wilson called Secretary Houston over the telephone and asked him what he thought the settled opinion of the Cabinet was. "He said that he had been able to get no clear notion of the view of the body at the last meeting."[19]

Bryan, apparently, said nothing at this session; he had, one might assume, already concluded that his work was done. But he had to write to the President in the afternoon to tell him about an extraordinary development that had just occurred. Two of the most powerful Democratic leaders in Congress—Thomas S. Martin of Virginia, chairman of the appropriations committee of the Senate, and Henry D. Flood of Virginia, chairman of the foreign affairs committee of the House of Representatives—had called on the Secretary and asked him to communicate a message to the President. "Senator Martin," Bryan wrote, "was the spokesman but Mr. Flood concurred in what he said. The Senator spoke with great earnestness to the effect that this country does not want war with Germany and that it expects you to find

[18] From Wilson's own typed draft, which he transcribed from his shorthand notes, in the Wilson Papers.

[19] D. F. Houston, *Eight Years with Wilson's Cabinet*, I, 139.

a way out that will not involve hostilities. He spoke of the question of passports [that is, a break in diplomatic relations] and expressed the opinion that while the demand for or giving of passports is not necessarily an act of war, that it is so near that it involved risks that ought not to be taken. He said that he had talked with three senators whom he had found in town and that they were all of the same opinion as he is and would vote against a declaration of war, if the subject were presented. Mr. Flood made the same remark in regard to the House—that he was sure that they would vote against such a declaration." "I asked them to put their views in writing, that I might be sure to submit them accurately," Bryan added, "and they said they would,[20] but as they may not have time to send me the letter this evening, I am writing you the substance of their conversation from memory."[21]

Emboldened by this unexpected support from two party stalwarts and former political foes, Bryan wrote again to the White House on the morning of June 5 in terms he had never before used in communicating with the President. Reviewing his three propositions—arbitration of the *Lusitania* dispute, action to prevent American citizens from traveling on ships carrying ammunition, and a protest to Great Britain—the Secretary went on, not without a touch of bitterness, to point out that the President had consented to the first and the third and had then changed his mind for what Bryan obviously thought were inconsequential reasons. "I beg to renew the suggestions most urgently," Bryan went on with increasing emphasis, "believing as I do, that without them the note as you outlined it at cabinet meeting would be likely to cause a rupture of diplomatic relations and this might rush us into war in spite of anything we could do. . . . This may be our last chance to speak for peace, for it will be much harder to propose investigation after some unfriendly act than *now*."[22]

Wilson received these letters after he had put the finishing touches

[20] Martin and Flood wrote their letter on the following day. "We will not go further than to say," they wrote, "that with the limited knowledge we have, we have not been able to reach the conclusion that war should result from *any* questions growing out of the destruction of the Lusitania and the incidental loss of American lives. We say this notwithstanding the fact that the reasoning of the President in his first note to Germany is exceedingly strong and we do not see how Germany can make satisfactory answer." T. S. Martin and H. D. Flood to W. J. Bryan, June 5, 1915, Bryan Papers, Library of Congress; italics added.

[21] W. J. Bryan to W.W., June 4, 1915, *The Lansing Papers*, i, 436-437.

[22] W. J. Bryan to W.W., June 5, 1915, *ibid.*, p. 437.

on the draft of his second *Lusitania* note. It was for him as much as for Bryan a time of stress. Bryan's letter conveying Martin's and Flood's warning must have affected the President deeply. The country, he knew and readily admitted, did not want war,[23] and yet the people expected him to maintain a firm position. How could he reconcile the two desires? Moreover, there was now the clear danger that the Secretary of State might resign and take the field in opposition if the President refused to meet his point of view.

All this Wilson knew, but the more he pondered, the more the conviction grew that he could not change his draft in any important way. He would stay on his high ground at least for a while longer. In this determination he had completed his revision during the evening of June 4, even though he had developed a severe headache under all the strain.[24] Sending the new draft to the State Department the following morning, *a short while after he had received Bryan's urgent letter*, Wilson conveyed his decision to the Secretary as gently as he could, as follows:

"I hope that you will realize how hard it goes with me to differ with you in judgment about such grave matters as we are now handling. You always have such weight of reason, as well as such high motives, behind what you urge that it is with deep misgiving that I turn from what you press upon me.

"I am inclined to think that we ought to take steps, as you suggest, to prevent our citizens from travelling on ships carrying munitions

---

[23] As he said in W.W. to W. J. Bryan, June 7, 1915, and W.W. to R. Lansing, June 7, 1915, both in *ibid.*, p. 439.

[24] *New York Times*, June 6, 1915; Louis Seibold in the New York *World*, June 6, 1915.

Most of Wilson's changes were stylistic in nature. His most important change was the addition of a moving new climax, as follows:

"It [the American government] conceives that it is contending for something greater than mere rights of property or privileges of commerce. It is contending for nothing less high and sacred than the rights of humanity, which every nation honours itself in respecting and which no nation can resign on behalf of those under its care and authority. No case could more vividly or thoroughly demonstrate than does this case of the *Lusitania* the overwhelming argument against the use of submarines against merchantmen where visit and search are impracticable and where the humane principles of international law are impossible of application. . . . It is upon . . . [the] principle of humanity as well as of law that the United States must stand and stand without compromise or abatement of its rights."

From Wilson's own typed draft in the Wilson Papers entitled "1st. Draft. 3rd." This is the document that the President sent to the State Deparment on the morning of June 5, 1915. It is printed in *The Lansing Papers*, I, 441-445.

of war, and I shall seek to find the legal way to do it. I fear that, whatever it may be best to do about that, it is clearly impossible to act before the new note goes to Germany.

"I am sorry to say that, study as I may the way to do it without hopelessly weakening our protest, I cannot find a way to embody in our note the principle of long discussion of a very simple state of facts; and I think that our object with England can be gained better by not sending a note in connection with this one than by sending it; and, after all, it is our object and the relief of our trade that we wish to accomplish.

"I recast the note last night. I hope you will think a little better of it.

"I would be very much obliged if you would go over it for substance, making any changes that may occur to you, and that you will ask Mr. Lansing to go over it for form and validity of statement and claim.

"With the warmest regard, and with a very solemn and by no means self-confident sense of deep responsibility."[25]

These were honeyed words but final, and for Bryan they were a sentence of political death. The President's note, he was convinced, carried the risk of war. There was no point in his making small changes; his differences with the President were too profound. He could not sign the note; he would have to resign. Ever since the Cabinet meeting of June 1 he had known that this hour might come. "More than once," his wife wrote in her diary soon afterward, "he came home with bloodshot eyes and weary steps. . . . As the days wore on his sleep became broken. He would lie awake three and four hours at a time, tossing, jotting down memoranda for next day's work, etc."[26] Now the very thought of resigning unnerved him. It was hard to give up place and power and the hope of exercising some direct influence over policy. It was hard to leave loyal friends in the Cabinet and the Department of State. It was harder still to face the consequences that he saw ahead. The nations abroad would interpret his resignation as a sign of serious division at home over foreign policy; the American people, as desertion from the helm. The consequence, Bryan knew, would be his momentary crucifixion and perhaps his political doom. Who would have been strong enough not to tremble?

What else could he do but resign when conscience spoke so clearly?

[25] W.W. to W. J. Bryan, June 5, 1915, *The Lansing Papers*, I, 438.
[26] W. J. and Mary B. Bryan, *The Memoirs of William Jennings Bryan*, pp. 420-421.

It was not so much what the President's note said as what it did not say that mattered. It was not that the President wanted war or was even being provocative. It was simply that he was not willing to do all things to avert even the possibility of war. He, Bryan, could have no part in any policy that might lead to hostilities. Having fought the good fight and lost, he must still keep the faith. The thought of threatening or blackmailing or sulking never crossed his mind. Only the conviction that he must leave in a spirit of Christian love.

Other reasons confirmed this decision. They were, he knew, not the kind that ought to matter. But how could they not? How much longer could he stand the humiliation he had recently endured? Of being always overridden and ignored, of knowing that the President really did not trust his judgment and often worked behind his back? Of knowing that Colonel House, a man of no political standing, had vastly more influence at the White House than he? Of seeing Lansing's advice accepted and his own rejected? Of seeing the President go out of his way, as he had done during the first days of the crisis, to emphasize his disassociation from the Secretary of State? Of reading the sneering comments of the newspapers and feeling the sting of his political foes? These attacks had gone on since the first week of his tenure in office, to be sure. But they had not mattered before, not so long as he had believed that his advice and influence really counted with the President. What hurt most now was the knowledge that he had become a nonentity.[27]

Reading the President's letter during the late morning of Saturday, June 5, Bryan made his final decision. Leaving his office, he went straight to McAdoo's home. "He was visibly nervous," McAdoo later wrote, "and remarked that he had not slept well. I had never before seen him so agitated." Bryan explained why he had come so unexpectedly. He had decided that he must resign, and he "wanted to see what could be done to make his resignation cause the least possible embarrassment to the Administration." For a while McAdoo pleaded for a change of mind; getting nowhere, he suggested that they go and talk to Mrs. Bryan at the Bryan home on Calumet Place. When further conversations there produced no change, McAdoo suggested that the Bryans go away for the weekend and give the matter addi-

[27] In writing the above paragraphs I have leaned heavily upon the excellent analyses by Charles Willis Thompson in the *New York Times*, May 30, 1915; by Louis Seibold in the New York *World*, June 12, 1915; and by the *New Republic*, III (June 19, 1915), 161-162.

tional thought. Agreeing, they went to the old Blair mansion, "Silver Spring," in the suburb of that name.[28] "We retired early," Mrs. Bryan writes, "were in bed eleven hours, of which Mr. Bryan slept four."[29]

McAdoo, meanwhile, after leaving the Bryan home on Saturday afternoon, had gone to the White House to break the news to the President. Wilson said that he was not surprised. "He said, however, that he would like to have Bryan remain in the Cabinet, if possible. His resignation at that critical moment might lead the German government to think that there were wide differences of opinion in the inner circles of the Administration, and he thought that would make our position more difficult." At Wilson's request, McAdoo saw the Bryans again on Monday morning, June 7, soon after their return from Silver Spring. The Secretary of the Treasury pleaded earnestly and warned that the Commoner was heading toward political perdition. "I believe you are right," Bryan replied. "I think this will destroy me; but whether it does or not, I must do my duty according to my conscience, and if I am destroyed, it is, after all, merely the sacrifice that one must not hesitate to make to serve his God and his country."[30]

The Secretary of State spent the balance of the morning of June 7 in his office going over Lansing's revision of the President's draft of the second *Lusitania* note.[31] Sending the document to the President, Bryan added a long commentary of his own that concluded with the fervent suggestion that Wilson announce that, pending negotiations with Germany, he would refuse clearance to belligerent ships carrying American passengers and to American passenger ships carrying ammunition. By such "christian forbearance" the President could "relieve the tension, deny to the jingoes foundation for their alarming statements and win the approval of our people."[32] Then "at noon . . . Bryan spent an hour with the President, passionately pleading against a course he felt certain would mean war: the President doing his best to dissuade him from resigning."[33] The more the two talked, the more distraught Bryan became. He tried to drink a glass of water but upset

[28] W. G. McAdoo, *Crowded Years*, pp. 333-334.

[29] W. J. and Mary B. Bryan, *The Memoirs of William Jennings Bryan*, pp. 423-424.

[30] W. G. McAdoo, *Crowded Years*, pp. 334-336.

[31] Lansing had taken the draft home with him over the week end of June 5-6 and had worked on it there. See R. Lansing to W. J. Bryan, June 5, 1915, *The Lansing Papers*, I, 438-439.

[32] W. J. Bryan to W.W., June 7, 1915, *ibid.*, pp. 445-449.

[33] R. S. Baker, *Woodrow Wilson: Life and Letters*, v, 356.

part of it as he raised it to his lips. With a quiver in his voice he told Wilson that his decision was final. "Colonel House," he blurted out at the end, "has been Secretary of State, not I, and I have never had your full confidence."[34]

All afternoon Bryan worked on his letter of resignation. Delivered at the White House early on Tuesday, June 8, 1915, it read:

My dear Mr. President:

It is with sincere regret that I have reached the conclusion that I should return to you the commission of Secretary of State, with which you honored me at the beginning of your Administration.

Obedient to your sense of duty and actuated by the highest motives, you have prepared for transmission to the German Government a note in which I cannot join without violating what I deem to be an obligation to my country, and the issue involved is of such moment that to remain a member of the Cabinet would be as unfair to you as it would be to the cause which is nearest my heart, namely, the prevention of war.

I, therefore, respectfully tender my resignation, to take effect when the note is sent, unless you prefer an earlier hour.

Alike desirous of reaching a peaceful solution of the problems arising out of the use of submarines against merchantmen, we find ourselves differing irreconcilably as to the methods which should be employed.

It falls to your lot to speak officially for the nation; I consider it to be none the less my duty to endeavor as a private citizen to promote the end which you have in view by means which you do not feel at liberty to use.

In severing the intimate and pleasant relations, which have existed between us during the past two years, permit me to acknowledge the profound satisfaction which it has given me to be associated with you in the important work which has come before the State Department, and to thank you for the courtesies extended.

With the heartiest good wishes for your personal welfare and for the success of your Administration, I am, my dear Mr. President,

Very truly yours,
W. J. Bryan

Sometime later in the day, perhaps in the early afternoon, Wilson sent the following reply:

My dear Mr. Bryan:

I accept your resignation only because you insist upon its acceptance;

[34] This is what the President later told Colonel House that Bryan said. House Diary, June 24, 1915.

and I accept it with much more than deep regret, with a feeling of personal sorrow.

Our two years of close association have been very delightful to me. Our judgments have accorded in practically every matter of official duty and of public policy until now; your support of the work and purposes of the Administration has been generous and loyal beyond praise; your devotion to the duties of your great office and your eagerness to take advantage of every great opportunity for service it offered have been an example to the rest of us; you have earned our affectionate admiration and friendship. Even now we are not separated in the object we seek, but only in the method by which we seek it.

It is for these reasons my feeling about your retirement from the Secretaryship of State goes so much deeper than mere regret. I sincerely deplore it.

Our objects are the same and we ought to pursue them together. I yield to your desire only because I must and wish to you Godspeed in the parting. We shall continue to work for the same causes even when we do not work in the same way.

With affectionate regard,

Sincerely yours,
Woodrow Wilson[35]

Meanwhile, Wilson had met the White House correspondents at his regular news conference at about ten o'clock on the morning of June 8. The President was obviously laboring under great strain as he faced the battery of some forty reporters. The expression of his face was grim and careworn; the lines from his eyes and mouth were deep with worry. In tones unusually brusque and severe he answered the questions put to him without any attempt to conceal his irritation. The reporters sensed that something was wrong, but none guessed the reason for Wilson's emotional turmoil.[36] A distinguished publisher who was present on this occasion wrote revealingly soon afterward:

"Things do not seem to be going well with the Cabinet, or rather with Mr. Bryan. There is no doubt that he is a thorn in the flesh both to Wilson and Tumulty, the latter confiding to me that Bryan made his task just ten times as hard as it ought to be. . . . The signs are indisputable that there is real friction and the President looked less cheerful and much more anxious than I have seen him. I had a few words with him after his session with the newspapermen. . . . He spoke of a note that I had sent him, in which I said that I believed

[35] *New York Times,* June 9, 1915.
[36] New York *World,* June 9, 1915.

that he would find his way out and accomplish his end without bringing on war, and said that he did not feel sure of this, because one
could not know what Berlin would do."[37]

Later in the morning the Cabinet met to hear a reading of the final
draft of the second *Lusitania* note before it went to Berlin. Bryan was
not present, but he called an hour later to ask if it would embarrass
anyone if he came. He arrived at the White House looking drawn
and pale.[38] "All the members stood up; there was no evidence of
embarrassment in any direction; the President greeted Bryan very
graciously and then we resumed our seats and the discussion. Bryan,
looking exhausted and appearing to be under a great emotional strain,
leaned back in his chair with his eyes closed." After it was over, the
Commoner went to the University Club for a farewell luncheon with
his friends. "I must act according to my conscience," he told them
at the end. "I go out into the dark. The President has the Prestige
and the Power on his side." Then he broke down completely but
murmured, "I have many friends who would die for me."[39]

Actually, Wilson was, as he told Colonel House a short time later,
"greatly relieved now that Mr. Bryan had gone, since he had been
a constant source of concern to him."[40] Life *would* be a lot simpler
now. But it had been a harrowing ordeal, and Wilson had suffered
from blinding headaches for several days. At his physician's command,
he went to the golf course with a cousin from Georgia in the late
afternoon. He played the first four holes badly. Then he unburdened
himself and seemed to recover his equanimity all at once: he won
the next four holes. Back at the White House for dinner and conversation, "he was perfectly delightful all the evening—Never talked more
brilliantly and never seemed better or looked better."[41]

There remained now only the final formalities and, for Bryan, the
duty of making explanations to the country. Bryan came to the White
House at 12:35 p.m. on June 9 to say good-by. It was an entirely cordial meeting. Each man congratulated the other on the purity of his
motives. Bryan said that he really felt relieved to be freed from the
burdens of office; he had, he said, slept soundly the night before for
the first time in many days. As the conversation ended both men rose

---

[37] O. G. Villard to Rollo Ogden, June 8, 1915, Villard Papers.
[38] *New York Times*, June 9, 1915.
[39] D. F. Houston, *Eight Years with Wilson's Cabinet*, I, 142-146.
[40] House Diary, June 24, 1915.
[41] Edward T. Brown to Mrs. E. T. Brown, June 8, 1915, Baker Collection.

at the same time, clasped hands, and said together, "God bless you!" Then Bryan turned and left the room with Tumulty; with their arms around each other, the two men walked to the State Department.[42]

During the following days the former Secretary of State busied himself with preparations for moving and answering a mountain of mail. In addition, he somehow found time to issue a volley of statements to the country, explaining his and the President's differences over the arbitration of the *Lusitania* question and travel by American citizens on ships carrying contraband, warning that war with Germany was possible, and announcing that he, Bryan, intended to begin a crusade for peace.[43] On June 19 he and Mrs. Bryan left Washington for a vacation in Asheville and for a future yet unknown. They left quietly, but not without the love and respect of the men with whom Bryan had worked so closely.[44] "It was hard enough to leave the Cabinet knowing it to be full of friends," the Commoner wrote from his refuge in North Carolina. "It would have been unbearable if I had been compelled to sever the ties of friendship which bind me to them."[45]

The announcement of the Secretary of State's resignation had meanwhile caused such political furor as the country had not seen since Theodore Roosevelt's entry into the Republican preconvention contest early in 1912. Indeed, the event sent a tremor through the capitals of the world,[46] for men everywhere understood its momentous meaning. They knew that hereafter the large and often silent number of Americans who wanted to avoid war for the defense of neutral rights would have a leader of unrivaled eloquence and power. They knew that whatever foreign policies the President might want to pursue, he could pursue them only at his peril if they affronted the man who would now speak as much for the people as he.

In America the upheaval reached almost incredible proportions. A few loyal friends, pacifists, church leaders, and stalwart partisans in

[42] New York *World*, June 10, 1915.

[43] There were four of these statements issued between June 9 and June 12, 1915, for which see the *New York Times*, June 10, 11, 12, and 13, 1915.

[44] For moving tributes, see R. Lansing to W. J. Bryan, June 9, 1915, Lansing Papers; J. Daniels to W. J. Bryan, June 15, 1915, Bryan Papers, Library of Congress; J. K. Vardaman to W. J. Bryan, June 9, 1915, *ibid.*

[45] W. J. Bryan to J. Daniels, June 20, 1915, Daniels Papers.

[46] See, e.g., the report on reaction in London, in the *New York Times*, June 10, 1915, and on reaction in Berlin, in *ibid.*, June 11, 1915; also the comment in the Paris newspapers, *L'Homme Enchaîné, Action Française, Liberté,* and *Le Matin,* all dated June 10, 1915.

the South and West spoke fervently if usually privately in the Commoner's defense.[47] The Hearst press and the German Americans promptly ceased flaying Bryan as an insidious friend of England and tried (quite unsuccessfully, it turned out) to entice him into their camp.[48] But these voices were only faintly heard amid the angry din.

The anti-Bryan press, which had refined the art of slander by long practice since 1896, now outdid itself. Old "Marse Henry" Watterson in Louisville cried out, for example: "Men have been shot and beheaded, even hanged, drawn and quartered, for treason less heinous. The recent Secretary of State commits not merely treason to the country at a critical moment, but treachery to his party and its official head. ... With the mind of a Barnum and the soul of a Tittlebat Titmouse he waited for the opportune moment, and when it arrived he struck, wantonly and shamelessly. Already, the summer shows pant for him. The circus tents flap for him. His treason to his country and his chief will be worth quite an hundred thousand dollars cash in hand."[49] "Was ever a high public official guilty of a more monstrous betrayal of a great trust and a great responsibility," the leading administration organ in the East exclaimed in similar words. ". . . It will go down in American history as an act of unspeakable treachery not only to the President but to the Nation in the hour of the gravest crisis since the Civil War."[50]

"Mr. Bryan's continued statements at this particular juncture make of him nothing less than a public nuisance," added the leading newspaper of the lower Southeast. "With full confidence in President Wilson's ability to handle the situation, The Constitution does not intend that his work shall be made any more difficult, or that the country shall be made to appear divided before the world by continued publications of what Mr. Bryan may have to say."[51] "Bryan as usual is

[47] e.g., Representative Joe H. Eagle to W. J. Bryan, June 10, 1915, Bryan Papers, Library of Congress; the Reverend W. E. Biederwolf, Federal Council of Churches of Christ in America, to W. J. Bryan, June 22, ibid.; The Presbyterian Banner, CII (June 17, 1915), 7; Harper's Weekly, LX (June 26, 1915), 602; James F. O'Connor to T. J. Walsh, June 10, 1915, Walsh Papers.

[48] e.g., New York American, June 9, 1915; Benedict Prieth, publisher of the Newark New Jersey Freie Zeitung, to W. J. Bryan, June 9, 1915, Bryan Papers, Library of Congress; John Hermann, president of the German American League of California, to W. J. Bryan, June 12, 1915, ibid.

[49] Louisville Courier-Journal, June 12, 1915.

[50] New York World, June 12, 1915.

[51] Atlanta Constitution, June 12, 1915.

an ass, but he is an ass with a good deal of opportunity for mischief," former President Taft privately remarked.[52]

From Europe came echoes of such opinion,[53] but none so bitter as from the American Ambassador in London. "W. J. B.—William J. B.—," Page exploded to his son, "has made a good measure of himself—his crankiness—a one-sided, crazy, fanatical mind—of his vanity and (unhappily) of his selfishness and disloyalty; and of course the old mania for the applauding multitude and for the first-page advertisement asserted itself as yearning for grog in a toper. Happy riddance. . . . Adieu William J."[54] And later: "What you write about Bryan seems good & true. Of course he's a traitor: he always had a yellow streak, the yellow streak of a sheer fool."[55]

In all the turmoil President Wilson did not face the task of naming Bryan's successor with much enthusiasm. There was of course no alternative to appointing Lansing as Acting Secretary of State once Bryan resigned, for business at the Department had to proceed while Wilson searched the field.

On June 6, as soon as he knew the Nebraskan's intentions, Wilson asked Houston and McAdoo to "think of a man for Bryan's successor, saying that he had canvassed the field and could not hit upon a satisfactory outside man." He said "that Colonel House would be a good man, but that his health would probably not permit him to take the place, and that his appointment would make Texas loom too large. He remarked that Lansing would not do, that he was not a big enough man, did not have enough imagination, and would not sufficiently vigorously combat or question his views, and that he was lacking in initiative."[56]

Briefly the President's thoughts turned to an old friend from Prince-

---

[52] W. H. Taft to C. P. Taft, June 12, 1915, Taft Papers. For other comment, some of which was not so violent, see the review of the press in the *Literary Digest*, L (June 19, 1915), 1449-1452; *New Republic*, III (June 12, 1915), 131-133; New York *Outlook*, CX (June 16, 1915), 341; *Collier's*, LV (June 26, 1915), 14.

[53] *Literary Digest*, L (June 26, 1915), 1527; London *Nation*, XVII (June 12, 1915), 344.

[54] W. H. Page to A. W. Page, June 23, 1915, Page Papers.

[55] W. H. Page to A. W. Page, August 30, 1915, *ibid.* Page's opinion of Bryan did not improve with the passing of the momentary excitement. We find the Ambassador writing in May 1916: "Bryan is the worst curse in American history. He worked against national financial credit. Now he works against national honor. He has organized ignorance into treason. . . . Bryan is the most repulsive demagogue in all history—dirty, greasy, treacherous." W. H. Page to A. W. Page, May —, 1916, *ibid.*

[56] D. F. Houston, *Eight Years with Wilson's Cabinet*, I, 141.

ton days, Thomas D. Jones, and to Secretary Houston, whom he greatly admired.[57] It does not seem likely that such thoughts went very far. He could not have forgotten the bitter fight that had broken out only a year before when he had named Jones to the Federal Reserve Board and failed to win his confirmation. Nor could he have ignored the fact that Houston knew next to nothing about the complex matters with which he would have to deal immediately as Secretary of State.

The unavailability of trained outside men and the desperate need of the moment all argued for Lansing's appointment. So did Colonel House, to whom the President turned for advice as soon as he had returned from Europe.[58] Lansing, House responded, could be used to better advantage than a stronger man, and without "half the annoyance and anxiety" that Bryan had caused. "I think," House continued, "the most important thing is to get a man with not too many ideas of his own and one that will be entirely guided by you without unnecessary argument, and this, it seems to me, you would find in Lansing. I only met him once and then for a few minutes only, and while his mentality did not impress me unduly, at the same time, I hope that you have found him able enough to answer the purpose indicated."[59]

It was undoubtedly what Wilson had himself concluded. He called Lansing to his office on June 23 and asked him to accept the assignment. After proper demurral Lansing agreed, and the President went through the ritualistic forms on the following day. It was the best decision, Wilson told Colonel House in New York later on the same day, June 24. He was, Wilson went on, practically his own Secretary of State, and "Lansing would not be troublesome by obtruding or injecting his own views."[60]

The furor over Bryan's resignation was already raging by the time the second *Lusitania* note went to Berlin. It was substantially the same

[57] So McAdoo told House in New York on June 14, 1915. House Diary, June 14, 1915.

[58] The President sent McAdoo to New York on June 14 to talk with House about the matter. House Diary, June 14, 1915.

[59] E. M. House to W.W., June 16, 1915, Wilson Papers.

[60] House Diary, June 24, 1915. Wilson further suggested that House see Lansing and tell him of his and the President's relationship. Should he tell Lansing of his "work in Europe"? House asked. "No, not fully," Wilson replied, "but enough to get him to work in harmony with us." R. Lansing, *War Memoirs*, pp. 15-17, tells the story of the episode as Lansing remembered it.

document that Wilson had originally drafted, with editorial changes by Lansing and the addition of a statement declaring that the American government relied in its representations upon "the principles of humanity, the universally recognized understandings of international law, and the ancient friendship of the German nation." Wilson himself had deleted the sentence "No case could more vividly or thoroughly demonstrate than does this case of the *Lusitania* the overwhelming argument against the use of submarines against merchantmen where visit and search are impracticable and where the humane principles of international law are impossible of application," presumably because it seemed to imply that there might be times and places where an underseas campaign would be lawful and humane. The President, obviously, was not yet ready to concede this point, not so long as there was any hope of winning his objective of entire abandonment of the submarine campaign.[61] Signed by Lansing at 12:50 in the afternoon of June 9, 1915, the note was put on the State Department wire within an hour. Gerard delivered a copy to the Foreign Office in Berlin on June 11.[62]

Published in the American press on June 10 and 11, the President's second appeal evoked almost universal commendation and considerable bewilderment over the reasons for Bryan's resignation. "The voice of the nation speaks in this note," declared the Richmond *Virginian*.

[61] This fact was clearly demonstrated by a significant exchange during the discussions over the final draft of the note. McAdoo, perhaps at Bryan's request (the records are silent on this point), sought out Lansing during the evening of June 7 with an urgent suggestion. It was to add a paragraph to the note saying that the United States had no desire to deprive Germany of the submarine weapon, provided submarine operations did not jeopardize human life or result in the *indiscriminate* destruction of neutral property, and would be willing to consider any proposals the German government might make "looking toward a modification of the existing rules of international law governing naval warfare applicable to the use of submarines." Lansing's statement of McAdoo's proposal, in R. Lansing to W. G. McAdoo, June 7, 1915, Lansing Papers.

Chandler Anderson saw Lansing later during the same evening (June 7) and made the same suggestion. Lansing replied that he personally thought well of the proposal; in the circumstances, however, he went on, he would have to leave it up to McAdoo to bring the matter before the President and Cabinet. Anderson Diary, June 7, 1915. The "circumstances" to which Lansing referred could only have been the President's obvious determination to avoid giving any sign of yielding on the fundamental issue. McAdoo, incidentally, apparently did not make his suggestion at the Cabinet meeting on June 8, when the President read the final draft of the note.

[62] For the full text, see the Secretary of State ad interim to Ambassador Gerard, June 9, 1915, *Foreign Relations, 1915, Supplement*, pp. 436-438.

That was largely true, insofar as one can judge from the comments in the press and among correspondents at the time.[63] Indeed, the only important criticism came from the nationalists who were disappointed because the President had not spoken more peremptorily. "Had it not been for the mad performance of Mr. Bryan in suddenly deciding to create a new heaven and a new earth in international affairs by his personal fiat," the New York *World* shrewdly observed, "we think the note, on the whole, would have been a disappointment to a majority of the American people. They would have expected a harder and less conciliatory answer to Germany's quibbling and unsatisfactory reply to the President's note of May 13."[64]

To that small group of pro-Allied extremists, some of whom were by now longing for an American declaration of war, the friendly tone of the note was convincing proof of what they had long suspected—that Wilson was a cowardly mollycoddle content with words and afraid of deeds. "Bryan has now split with Wilson," Theodore Roosevelt lamented, for example, to an English friend. "For a moment I thought that this meant that Wilson had waked up to the national needs, national duty. But when his note came out, I was utterly unable to see that he had changed in the least. He and Bryan apparently agree with cordiality that our policy should be one of milk and water. They only disagree as to the precise quantity of dilution in the mixture. . . . Most emphatically, if we had done what we ought to have done after the sinking of the *Lusitania*, I and my four boys would now be in an army getting ready to serve with you. . . . But our people . . . have been misled by the screaming and shrieking and bleating of the peace people until really good men and women have gotten so puzzle-headed that they advocate a course of national infamy. I have spoken out as strongly and as clearly as possible; and I do not think it has had any effect beyond making people think that I am a truculent and bloodthirsty person, endeavoring futilely to thwart able, dignified, humane Mr. Wilson in his noble plan to bring peace everywhere by excellently written letters. . . !"[65]

---

[63] See the review of press opinion in the *Literary Digest*, L (June 19, 1915), 1452-1454, from which the quotation from the Richmond *Virginian* is taken; New York *Nation*, c (June 17, 1915), 671; J. R. Lamar to W.W., June 11, 1915, Wilson Papers; C. H. Dodge to W.W., June 11, 1915, *ibid.*; New York *Christian Advocate*, xc (June 17, 1915), 806-807.

[64] New York *World*, June 11, 1915.

[65] T. Roosevelt to A. H. Lee, June 17, 1915, E. E. Morison *et al.* (eds.), *The Letters of Theodore Roosevelt*, VIII, 937. I have transposed some of the sentences in this

Few Americans shared either the disappointment of the nationalists or the malign sentiments of men who were now beginning to live upon hatred of Woodrow Wilson. The great majority approved the President's friendly appeal to the humanity of the German government at the same time that they prayed for a peaceful outcome of the negotiations. As the British Ambassador in Washington ruefully reported to London a short time later: "The prevailing sentiment is undoubtedly for peace. Not perhaps peace at any price but peace at a very considerable price."[66]

The receipt of President Wilson's second *Lusitania* note in Berlin on June 11, 1915, and its publication in the German press two days later only intensified the violence of the controversy that had long since convulsed the people and leaders of the Empire. No event since the Italian declaration of war had evoked such a spate of opinion as did the President's appeal. The pages of the newspapers on Sunday, June 13, were filled with columns of comment, and the jingoes and spokesmen for the navy were as provocative as before. "The watchword is, 'The torpedoing will go on,' " cried the *Taegliche Rundschau* of Berlin, for example.[67] "If President Wilson persists in his refusal to recognize the German declaration of a war zone," Count Ernst von Reventlow wrote in the journal that echoed the Admiralty's views, "we are not able to conceive of an agreement or even a real understanding."[68]

The world had come to expect such bitterness and inflexibility from the firebrands. It was not, however, prepared for the startling moderation of what was obviously the majority German opinion on this occasion. The assiduous work of the Chancellor and the Foreign Secretary among their editorial allies was in part responsible for this sudden turn; but it was also apparent that Wilson's appeal to German moral sentiments and friendship for America had struck a responsive chord. Everywhere throughout the Empire spokesmen agreed that the President had written in friendly terms and that some kind of understand-

---

passage. See also J. A. Garraty, *Henry Cabot Lodge*, p. 318, for an account of the Massachusetts Senator's and the British Ambassador's reactions.

[66] C. Spring Rice to E. Grey, June 23, 1915, *The Letters of Sir Cecil Spring Rice*, II, 274.

[67] Berlin *Taegliche Rundschau*, morning edn., June 13, 1915.

[68] Berlin *Deutsche Tageszeitung*, morning edn., June 13, 1915; also von Reventlow's articles in *ibid.*, morning edn., June 15, 1915, and morning edn., June 16, 1915.

ing with America had to be achieved, although not at the cost of entire abandonment of the submarine campaign. "It cannot be seen why the German Government should not be able to enter into a discussion with the American Government concerning another kind and manner of naval warfare," asserted one distinguished political analyst in the newspaper that reputedly spoke for the Imperial Chancellor,[69] while the editor of the same newspaper urged the political authorities to stand firm against the jingoes and "whip-the-world enthusiasts" at home.[70] "President Wilson," added another editor, "desires nothing more and nothing less than an understanding between Germany and England concerning the forms of maritime warfare which at the same time will insure the safety of American passengers. The task is not easy, considering the development of naval war. But it can be solved if all interests display good will."[71]

The return of reason to editorial councils was an enormous boon to Imperial Chancellor von Bethmann Hollweg and his associates as they set about to prepare a reply to the President's second note. Bethmann had apparently decided upon a policy by the time that the American note arrived at the Foreign Office. He was determined to do everything necessary to avert the break with America that Bernstorff had warned would be inevitable unless the Imperial government succeeded in calming American opinion by its next note.[72] Whether the Chancellor was moved by Wilson's suggestion, made privately to Bernstorff on June 2, that Germany and the United States join hands in a cam-

[69] Paul Michaelis in the *Berliner Tageblatt*, morning edn., June 13, 1915.

[70] Theodor Wolff in *ibid.*, morning edn., June 14, 1915.

[71] Eugen Zimmermann in the *Berliner Lokal-Anzeiger*, morning edn., June 14, 1915. This editorial, significantly, went on to argue that German indignation against the United States on account of the export of munitions to the Allies was unfair, because the American government itself was in no way involved in the traffic. "During the conversations at The Hague," the editorial further pointed out, "Germany herself brought about the defeat of the proposal to prohibit the delivery of war materials by neutral states to belligerents."

This first admission by a responsible German spokesman that there were two sides to the munitions question stirred a noisy controversy in the German press. It was, Count von Reventlow thundered, one of the most incredible things that had occurred since the beginning of the war. E. von Reventlow, "German Propaganda for Deliveries of Weapons to Germany's Enemies," Berlin *Deutsche Tageszeitung*, morning edn., June 16, 1915. In the same vein, see the Berlin *Kreuz-Zeitung*, June 16 and 19, 1915. For opinions supporting the editor of the *Lokal-Anzeiger*, see the Berlin *Vorwärts*, June 15 and 16, 1915, and the Berlin *Boersen Zeitung*, June 16, 1915.

[72] Ambassador von Bernstorff to the Foreign Office, June 2, 1915, German F. O. Archives.

paign to restore the freedom of the seas, we do not know. It did not matter, anyway. Bethmann knew that he could not respond affirmatively to Wilson's appeal: the risks at home of a public abandonment of the submarine campaign were still too great. However, he could and would insist upon enough to preserve the precarious peace.

Before beginning conversations about a reply to the second American note, Bethmann waited for the arrival of a special emissary from Washington. He was Doctor Anton Meyer Gerhard, a former adviser in the Colonial Office who had served as the representative of the German Red Cross in New York since the beginning of the war, and whom Bernstorff had sent to Berlin on June 3 to explain the American point of view and what would be necessary to avert a rupture in diplomatic relations.[73] Arriving in the German capital on June 16, Meyer Gerhard had his first conferences at the Foreign Office two days later.[74] He merely repeated what Bernstorff had already made clear in his long dispatch of June 2, that the least the German government could do was to promise to respect all neutral shipping and all enemy passenger ships that were unarmed and carried no contraband.[75]

The Imperial Chancellor and Foreign Secretary opened the discussions about a note of reply during the last days of June 1915 with their determination strengthened by the advice of Bernstorff's emissary. As a warning to the firebrands and the Admiralty as well, the Foreign Office suppressed the powerful *Deutsche Tageszeitung* on June 21 for printing Count von Reventlow's tirades against America, and it gave public notice that it would not tolerate any propaganda aimed at thwarting a peaceful settlement with America.[76] Then, on the day after the punishment of the *Deutsche Tageszeitung*, Bethmann and von Jagow, in company with Meyer Gerhard, cornered the Admiralty chieftain, Bachmann, to discuss "over beer and cigars" the draft of a note of reply that Meyer Gerhard had prepared, one that promised safety for American citizens on enemy ships in the war

[73] This was done with the enthusiastic approval of President Wilson, who had the State Department make the necessary arrangements for obtaining safe passage for Meyer Gerhard. See Ambassador von Bernstorff to the Foreign Office, June 2, 6, and 12, 1915, *ibid.*; *New York Times*, June 4 and 5.

[74] *ibid.*, June 18, 1915; New York *World*, June 19, 1915.

[75] Meyer Gerhard's advice is summarized in the draft of the note that he prepared for the Foreign Office, printed in part in Tirpitz, *Politische Dokumente*, II, 363.

[76] Berlin *Deutsche Tageszeitung*, June 21, 1915; Berlin *Norddeutschen Allgemeinen Zeitung*, June 22, 1915. The former reappeared on June 24, 1915, with an article covertly attacking President Wilson.

zone under certain conditions. He would never consent to any such guarantee, Bachmann replied; it would be tantamount to a public apology for the sinking of the *Lusitania*, and Germany had nothing to apologize for. Bethmann in rebuttal was not gentle. Bachmann's position, he said, was unheard of. Germany had to make concessions to avoid a break with America.[77] It was a question of power. Moreover, the United States had a right to demand certain guarantees for its citizens.[78] He would, the Imperial Chancellor went on, have to go to Pless and report the admiral's point of view to the Emperor. After this conference, Bethmann stopped Bachmann alone in an anteroom and pleaded in a more conciliatory vein. He did not want an open break with the navy, the Chancellor said, but if a test of strength did occur he would have General von Falkenhayn's support, and he would win.[79]

After this initial confrontation, rather frenzied discussions over the crucial issue of the safety of passenger vessels proceeded on the high level during the last week in June and the early days of July 1915. It was not easy to find the right formula, one that would yield enough to guarantee peace without giving up more than was necessary. But throughout the struggle Bethmann had the upper hand. He went to Supreme Headquarters soon after his conference with Bachmann; there, on June 24, he sat down with Admiral von Müller, Chief of the Naval

[77] "In order to prevent this," Bachmann reported Meyer Gerhard as saying, "it was necessary to send a reply to the Lusitania note which was calculated to win public opinion in the United States to our side. This could be done only with such a note as he had composed. This was not only his firm conviction but also that of the Ambassador in Washington and of the Naval Attaché, Boy-Ed."

[78] "If the United States had no right to make such demands," Bachmann reported von Jagow as adding, "it at least had a strong justification. I would like to know, he said, what we would say if in a war between other powers a ship with 1,500 innocent German passengers were sunk."

[79] "Memorandum by the Chief of the Admiralty of a Conference with the Imperial Chancellor, 22 June 1915," Tirpitz, *Politische Dokumente*, II, 364-366. The passages quoted in the two preceding footnotes are taken from this memorandum.

What Bethmann told Bachmann about von Falkenhayn's position was correct. As recently as June 17, 1915, the Chief of the General Staff had warned Bachmann that he could not take responsibility for the continuation of the war if the United States were driven into the enemy camp because of the submarine war. "Not the armed might of the United States," von Falkenhayn went on, "but rather the moral weight which it as an enemy power would have on the neutrals against us, above all on Rumania, Bulgaria, and Holland, would be fatal for us." "Memorandum by the Chief of the Admiralty of a Conference with the Chief of the General Staff, General v. Falkenhayn, on 17 June 1915," *ibid.*, pp. 359-360.

Cabinet, and reworked that part (it was called Part Four) of Meyer Gerhard's draft note which offered safety for American passengers on enemy ships under certain conditions. The new version promised that submarine commanders would make extraordinary efforts to save the lives of passengers and crews but warned that it would not be possible "in every single case" to warn enemy ships before sinking them. "It should and will be done always," Bethmann's and von Müller's draft went on, "if it is possible without losing the chance of sinking the ship and without endangering our own submarines."[80]

This was the juncture at which the naval spokesmen made their hardest fight. On June 23 Bachmann and Tirpitz submitted to Bethmann their own draft of a proposed note to the United States; it revealed their determination to offer no important concessions.[81] The two admirals came back a few days later with a long memorandum of their own and with one that had been prepared by three submarine commanders. Both elaborated the same arguments—that it was technically impossible and totally unsafe for submarines to visit and search most enemy merchantmen, even passenger ships, before sinking them—and pointed to the same conclusion—that any yielding to America on the issue of the safety of passenger ships would fatally weaken the entire U-boat campaign. Indeed, the three submarine commanders asserted, it was not possible to conduct an effective underseas campaign under present orders requiring U-boats to respect neutral shipping.[82] Finally, on June 28, Bachmann appealed directly to the Emperor, requesting an Imperial conference and permission to bring the head of the High Seas Fleet and the three submarine commanders to Supreme Headquarters for a hearing.[83]

It was obviously impossible for Bethmann and von Jagow, who had managed the discussions in Berlin and at Pless during the last days

[80] Printed in *ibid.*, p. 374.

[81] The key sentence in this draft follows: "However, the German Government, to its greatest regret, is not in a position to abandon its position . . . that it cannot take responsibility for sparing enemy ships in the war zone because their destruction might perhaps endanger the lives of American citizens who, in spite of all warnings, happen to be traveling on them." Admiral Bachmann to T. von Bethmann Hollweg, June 23, 1915, German F. O. Archives.

[82] "Position of the Admiralty. Reasons Against Number 4 of the Stipulation of the Imperial Chancellor," memorandum dated June 27, 1915; "Position of the U-Boat Officers Bauer, Bartenbach, and Hansen Regarding the Practical Part of the Reply Note to America," memorandum dated June 28, 1915, both printed in Tirpitz, *Politische Dokumente*, II, 367-372.

[83] Admiral Bachmann to the Emperor, June 28, 1915, *ibid.*, p. 367.

of June while the Chancellor was in Vienna, to ignore these representations, especially when they were supported, probably at Tirpitz's instigation, by the leaders of some of the most powerful organizations in the Empire.[84] Unwilling to stretch his luck too far, Bethmann at first decided not to go beyond the vague assurances embodied in his and von Müller's draft of June 24. However, under strong pressure from von Jagow, Meyer Gerhard, and Doctor Dernburg,[85] all of whom warned that the German government would have to offer some specific provision for the safety of American passengers traveling in the war zone, Bethmann and von Müller now began to consider various alternatives. One was to put it to the Washington authorities to suggest proposals of their own for easing the naval war; another, to offer free passage for a limited number of English passenger ships; another, to suggest the use of the German liners lying in American harbors as carriers under the American flag.[86]

In this moment of indecision in Berlin, Ambassador Gerard volunteered his services as consultant to the Foreign Office. In a conference with von Jagow on July 2 he helped to draft a version of Part Four which, he said, included the minimum concessions that the Washington government would probably accept. They were, first, a guarantee of absolute safety for all American ships in the war zone, provided they carried no contraband, and, second, a pledge that German submarines would not sink a specified number of enemy passenger ships without warning, provided the American government guaranteed that they did not carry munitions, were unarmed, and would not attempt to ram submarines when the latter undertook to exercise the right of visit and search.[87]

[84] Representatives of the Estate Owners' League, the German Peasants' League, the German Christian Peasants' League, the Westphalian Peasant League, the Central League of German Industrialists, the League of Industrialists, and the German Middle Class League to the Imperial Chancellor, June 28, 1915, German F. O. Archives. This memorial reads suspiciously like the memorandum that Bachmann sent to the Chancellor on June 28, 1915.

[85] Dernburg had recently arrived in Berlin.

[86] Tirpitz, *Politische Dokumente*, II, 374-375.

[87] G. von Jagow, memorandum dated July 2, 1915, and a memorandum dated July 8, 1915, attached to four handwritten drafts by Gerard, both in the German F. O. Archives; draft of Part Four, which Gerard approved, printed in Tirpitz, *Politische Dokumente*, II, 375-376.

Gerard's procedure was, to say the least, somewhat unorthodox in view of the fact that he was acting without instructions from his superiors. He was, however, only trying to be helpful. He had unconcealed detestation for the German military lead-

To Bethmann and von Jagow (although not entirely to von Müller), Gerard's advice was conclusive. Bachmann and Tirpitz fought a rearguard action between July 3 and 7;[88] but the Emperor had refused to convoke an Imperial conference,[89] and they had almost no hand in the preparation of the final draft. Completed on July 8 and given to Gerard late in the same day, it began with what Tirpitz later called its "ornamental" part—an affirmation that the Imperial govern-

---

ers and no great love for any of the civilian officials. At the same time, he wanted to do what he could to avert an open German-American rupture. As he wrote to Colonel House, "Of course in any event it seems rather ridiculous to enter this awful war to enforce a right which is of no practical use. Americans can just as well travel on American, Danish or Norwegian ships and keep us out of complications." J. W. Gerard to E. M. House, July 13, 1915, House Papers.

Gerard kept the State Department informed about the progress of the discussions in Berlin, although he did not disclose the role that he played in helping to prepare the draft of the German reply. In a telegram of July 3 he advised his superiors that he had just read a draft of the German note, transmitted a summary of it, and requested instructions. Two days later the Ambassador dispatched a second telegram summarizing the contents of another draft of the German note that he said he had just seen. "I am sending you above sketch of note with the knowledge of friends in the Foreign Office and the note will not be delivered until I hear from you," the telegram continued. "I hope you will cable that this plan is acceptable. . . . On all propositions made I of course stated that I had no idea whether the proposition would be acceptable to America or not." Ambassador Gerard to the Secretary of State, July 3 and 5, 1915, *Foreign Relations, 1915, Supplement*, pp. 459-462.

Lansing answered Gerard's first telegram on July 6 with the curt statement that the American government did not think it advisable to engage in any negotiations with Berlin at this point. The Secretary of State to Ambassador Gerard, July 6, 1915, *ibid.*, p. 462. However, when Lansing informed the President, who was then in Cornish, New Hampshire, of his reply, Wilson suggested that Lansing tell Gerard that although the American government was determined to yield none of its rights, it would be heartily willing to exercise its good offices "with regard to effecting any arrangements which will open the sea to common use with as little danger as possible to non-belligerents." R. Lansing to W.W., July 7, 1915; W.W. to R. Lansing, July 7, 1915, *The Lansing Papers*, I, 453-454. Lansing sent a telegram in this vein to Gerard at 4 p.m. on July 8, 1915 (*Foreign Relations, 1915, Supplement*, p. 462), but it is not likely that it reached Berlin and was translated and delivered to the Foreign Office before von Jagow handed his second *Lusitania* note to Gerard.

[88] Tirpitz, *Politische Dokumente*, II, 376; Chief of the Admiralty to the Foreign Secretary, July 7, 1915, German F. O. Archives.

[89] Commenting on Bachmann's request for an Imperial conference and further negotiations, the Emperor wrote: "They just won't take place at all. Only the answering of the Note will take place, and this is none of his concern." Commenting on the admirals' request for permission to bring the Chief of the High Seas Fleet and the three U-boat commanders to the Imperial conference, William wrote: "Totally superfluous, since my viewpoint has already been clearly expressed. I do not desire an Imperial council of war!" K. G. von Treutler to the Foreign Office, June 28, 1915, *ibid.*

ment shared the Washington authorities' concern for the principles of humanity—and an invocation of the long and unbroken traditions of friendship and cooperation between Germany and "the Republic of the West." Then followed a review of alleged British violations of international law, a reiteration of the plea that the submarine campaign had been launched only in self-defense and reprisal against enemies who would stop at nothing to destroy the German nation, and a paragraph throwing the blame for the destruction of the *Lusitania* upon the British. Finally came the paragraphs embodying the concessions, almost exactly as Gerard had written them. The Imperial government, the note said, would do everything within its power to prevent the jeopardizing of the lives of American citizens. Its submarines would respect all legitimate American shipping and safeguard American lives on all other neutral vessels. It could not see why Americans had to travel on enemy passenger ships; however, if not enough American and neutral passenger liners were available for the North Atlantic traffic, then the Imperial government would not object if four enemy liners[90] ran up the American flag; indeed, it would guarantee safe passage for them. Abruptly the note concluded with a brief paragraph saying that the Imperial German Government hoped that the American President's efforts in the present negotiations would lead to an understanding.[91]

Gerard sent the note in five separate sections by way of Copenhagen on July 9, and it was not until the morning of July 11 that all of them had arrived at the State Department. The American press published a summary that had been given to correspondents in Berlin on July 10 and the full text of the note on the same day that Gerard's final section reached the Department.

Editors throughout the United States lost no time in denouncing the German reply as totally unresponsive and unacceptable. It was, one of them declared, an "astounding document . . . [that] sweeps aside as by a wave of the hand every principle of international law and every custom of civilized nations that interferes with the selfish

[90] The addition of this specific number was the only important change that Bethmann and von Jagow made in the draft of Part Four that Gerard had prepared. Tirpitz, *Politische Dokumente*, II, 376-377.

[91] Ambassador Gerard to the Secretary of State, July 8, 1915, *Foreign Relations, 1915, Supplement*, pp. 463-466.

purpose of a single combatant power."[92] "Not one of our moderate demands is accorded even the courtesy of frank recognition," Colonel George Harvey added bitterly; "all are in effect denied; each and every one is either tacitly spurned or impudently ignored."[93]

Such expressions of anger abounded in the editorial columns of the metropolitan press, particularly in the East, but careful observers could see the signs of an important upheaval in American opinion that was now occurring under the surface of the editorial condemnation of the German note.

One of these was the obvious fact that antiwar sentiment had increased sharply among the rank and file of the people in the face of the crisis with Germany and was now at such a high pitch that the leaders in Washington could not safely ignore it. From all sides were coming appeals against permitting the *Lusitania* negotiations to lead to a break in relations. "Since the sinking of the Lusitania," an Indiana Democratic congressman reported at this time, "I have been all over my district and talked with men of all parties, nationalities, creeds and denominations and it is almost an unanimous voice to keep out of this war and the people are very much afraid that the administration is going to pursue Germany until we become involved with her or at least until there is a severance of diplomatic relations which is tantamount to a declaration of war. I cannot but believe that my district is but a sample of all the districts in the state of Indiana.[94] "We evidently cannot compel Germany without war," an Ohio congressman warned, "and under no circumstance now in sight will Congress vote for war."[95] Even the strongly nationalistic editors admitted that a majority of the American people preferred a deadlock rather than a pressing of American demands to the point of risking a rupture in relations with Germany.[96]

The German reply tremendously heartened the German Americans,

[92] *The Independent*, LXXXIII (July 19, 1915), 71.

[93] G. Harvey, " 'America First!' " *North American Review*, CCII (August 1915), 167. See also the editorials cited in "Trying to Solve the Deadlock with Germany," *Literary Digest*, LI (July 24, 1915), 141-143.

[94] W. E. Cox, from Jasper, Indiana, to A. S. Burleson, July 20, 1915, the Papers of Albert Sidney Burleson, Library of Congress; hereinafter cited as the Burleson Papers.

[95] E. R. Bathrick to R. Lansing, July 13, 1915, Lansing Papers.

[96] See especially "American Feeling About the German Note," New York *Nation*, CI (July 15, 1915), 83; and the survey of press opinion in the *Literary Digest*, LI (July 24, 1915), 141-143.

virtually all of whom had been downcast and silent since the sinking of the *Lusitania*. Now they were reviving hopefully, and German-American editors to a man were asserting that the Imperial government had met the American demands halfway and removed any barriers to understanding;[97] the National German-American Alliance was voicing its hopes for a German victory once again;[98] and various German- and Irish-American spokesmen were at work renewing the movement for an arms embargo.[99]

The third and perhaps the most important development of all in public opinion was the obvious way in which the conviction that the American government should come to some reasonable terms with Germany was beginning to spread. Bryan was now the most active and influential champion of this point of view,[100] but it was by no means confined to a single individual or faction. "The people do not want war with Germany," one congressman warned the Postmaster General. ". . . Nothing short of war. They are arguing and doing it openly. 'To thunder with the free seas. Stay out of the war zone then there will be no Americans sent to the bottom of the ocean.' "[101] The American government, the most powerful editorial voice in the Middle West declared, should come to terms with the German government in the same way that it had come to a wise understanding with authorities in London. "An agreement can be reached with Germany which will give Americans safe conduct," this editor continued, "and it need not be a part of the agreement that we recognize the principles of German submarine warfare. We do not need to mortgage the future for present security. All we have to do is to accept present conditions, keep whatever opinion we wish to hold regarding the violations of law and

[97] e.g., the *New Yorker Staats-Zeitung, New Yorker Herold*, Chicago *Illinois Staats-Zeitung*, Chicago *Abendpost*, Milwaukee *Germania Herold*, Detroit *Abendpost*, Denver *Colorado Herold*, Cincinnati *Freie Presse*, Cincinnati *Volksblatt*, all dated July 10, 1915.

[98] New York *World*, August 3, 1915, reporting an address by C. J. Hexamer, president, before the eighth biennial convention of the National German-American Alliance in San Francisco on August 2, 1915.

[99] George W. Mead, secretary, the American Truth Society, form letter dated July 29, 1915, Walsh Papers; Charles F. Aked and Walter Rauschenbusch, "Private Profit and the Nation's Honor: A Protest and a Plea," *The Standard*, LXII (July 31, 1915), 1486-1487; Boston *American*, August 11, 1915, demanding the enactment of an arms embargo.

[100] See the account of Bryan's speech in Los Angeles on July 16, 1915, in the *New York Times*, July 17, 1915; and W. J. Bryan, "WRITE AND WRITE *NOW*" and "Neutrality Toward Both," *The Commoner*, xv (August 1915), 1, 3.

[101] W. E. Cox to A. S. Burleson, July 20, 1915, Burleson Papers.

humanity, and preserve not all our rights but a practical working application of them."[102]

President Wilson heard these reverberations clearly enough, even though he was enjoying a brief respite from the oppressive heat and clamor of Washington with his family and intimates at his summer home, "Harlakenden," at Cornish, New Hampshire. He received the text of the German note by wire from the State Department on the afternoon of July 12, 1915. Giving up his daily automobile ride, he studied the note for several hours until the late afternoon, when he went out for a game of golf.[103]

In his study that evening he pondered what he should say in reply, or, more accurately, how he should say it, as he had apparently already made up his mind about the points to be included in a third *Lusitania* note.[104] The extent of antiwar sentiment had obviously impressed him profoundly and confirmed his conviction that he would have to try to find some settlement.[105] He was, consequently, not inclined to *demand* immediate apology and settlement for the loss of American life. More important, he was now prepared to effect a momentous change in policy—to abandon the high ground of opposition to the submarine campaign that he had occupied since the beginning of the *Lusitania* negotiations and to explore the possibility of a new approach, one involving American acquiescence in the submarine campaign if the Germans would only meet him halfway by agreeing to follow the rules of cruiser warfare in attacking passenger ships.[106] This, Wilson must

[102] *Chicago Tribune*, July 12, 1915. The *Literary Digest*, LI (July 24, 1915), 142, noted that "scores of papers," among them the Cleveland *Leader*, Cleveland *Plain Dealer*, Detroit *News*, Des Moines *Capital*, Omaha *Bee*, Omaha *World-Herald*, Kansas City *Journal*, San Francisco *Chronicle*, and Seattle *Post-Intelligencer*, expressed much the same point of view as the *Chicago Tribune*.

[103] *New York Times*, July 13, 1915.

[104] As he intimated in W.W. to R. Lansing, July 9, 1915, *The Lansing Papers*, I, 454.

[105] Sending to Colonel House a letter from Representative Warren Worth Bailey of Pennsylvania, which told how the people of his district and the entire American nation wanted peace and not war, Wilson wrote: "I know you will read the letter enclosed with interest. I send it to you because it is a sample of, I might almost say, all the letters I am receiving nowadays, and I am receiving them, of course, from many quarters and from many different kinds of persons." W.W. to E. M. House, July 14, 1915, Wilson Papers, enclosing W. W. Bailey to W.W., July 12, 1915, original in *ibid*.

[106] As we have seen, McAdoo, Lansing, Chandler Anderson, and perhaps others in the administration had been eager to follow this line in the second *Lusitania* note. See above, p. 429.

have reasoned, would reduce the issues of the controversy to the single uncompromisable one of the safety of American life. It would enable the Germans to yield little and retain much. As an added inducement, he would hold out the promise of a real American effort to win the freedom of the seas, that is, a loosening of the British maritime system, if the Germans would yield the right of Americans to travel in the war zone without fear of sudden death.

On the other hand, the President was also obviously determined to have an end to the transatlantic dialogue and to tell the Berlin authorities that their preferred concessions were not enough, and that any further incidents might well lead to war. Combining large concessions of his own with the demand for the protection of American travelers was the only way, he must have thought, that he could satisfy demands at home that he avert a break even while he stood immovable on the fundamental issue. "Perhaps it might be just as well for you to see Bernstorff," he wrote, for example, to Colonel House, who had recently returned to America, "if only to make him feel not only that some way out *should* be found but some way out *must* be found and that his Government owe it to themselves and to the rest of the world to help find it. . . . Apparently the Germans *are* modifying their methods; they must be made to feel that they must continue in their new way unless they deliberately wish to prove to us that they are unfriendly and wish war."[107]

On the morning of July 13, only a day after he had received the text of the German note, the President put his thoughts about a reply on paper ("I am not selecting words; I am merely trying to outline an argument") in a long letter to Secretary of State Lansing. He began by listing the major points that he wanted to make, as follows:

1. We cannot discuss special arrangements whereby a few vessels may enjoy the rights all are entitled to, nor admit that such arrangements would be in any way adequate to meet the contentions of this Government.

2. We are not merely contending for the rights of Americans to cross the seas as they will without fear of deliberate breaches of international law, but conceive ourselves as speaking for the rights of neutrals everywhere, rights in which the whole world is interested and which every nation must wish to see kept inviolable.

3. These rights the Imperial German Government itself recognizes in theory, professes itself anxious to see safeguarded, and is surely ready

[107] W.W. to E. M. House, July 14, 1915, Baker Collection.

to admit as quite as vital to itself, both now and in the years to come, as any other nation.

4. Violations of neutral rights and of the general obligations of international law by the Government of Great Britain we of course cannot discuss with the German Government; but will discuss with the British Government, so far as they affect the rights of Americans. . . .

5. We note with interest the fact that in the more recent operations of German submarines it has been feasible to keep within the limits and restrictions of international practice and to act upon the general principles upon which we have insisted.[108] We can see no reason, therefore, why there is not opened a way of immediate agreement between the two governments and of such action as will sufficiently safeguard all legitimate interests and enable the German Admiralty to return to the practice long established and fully recognized in their own instructions already more than once referred to.

How, Wilson went on in this same letter, did Lansing think the final passage of the note should read? How could they bring the correspondence to a definite issue? "Two things are plain to me, in themselves inconsistent," he concluded, "viz. that our people want this thing handled in a way that will bring about a definite settlement without endless correspondence, and that they will also expect us not to hasten an issue or so conduct the correspondence as to make an unfriendly issue inevitable."[109]

Wilson then called Lansing by telephone to tell him the gist of the letter that was on its way to Washington, and to urge him to send his own thoughts and suggestions on to Cornish as quickly as possible. Next he wrote out the following statement for the press, which he sent by wire to Tumulty:

Please say that from the moment of the arrival of the official text of the German note I have given the matter the closest attention, keeping constantly in touch with the Secretary of State and with every source that would throw light on the situation; that as soon as the Secretary of State and I have both maturely considered the situation I shall go to Washington to get into personal conference with him and with the

---

[108] The President was here referring to an incident that had occurred only a few days before. On June 30 a German submarine had stopped and warned the British mule ship *Armenian* before sinking her off the coast of Cornwall. The incident had caused the newspapers to speculate whether it signified that the Germans had changed their methods of conducting the submarine campaign. *New York Times*, July 1, 2, and 3, 1915; New York *World*, July 2, 1915.

[109] W.W. to R. Lansing, July 13, 1915, *The Lansing Papers*, I, 455-456.

Cabinet; and that there will be as prompt an announcement as possible of the purposes of the Government.[110]

By early afternoon there was nothing more that Wilson could do; he spent the balance of the daylight hours in his automobile and on the golf course.

Life went on leisurely at "Harlarkenden" until the morning of July 16. Then a letter from Lansing arrived, accompanied by a bundle of memoranda, thirteen in number, which the Secretary had sent in response to the President's request made over the telephone three days before. They were, as Lansing said, undigested notes but they covered all the major points in dispute.[111] In addition, Lansing sent along a closely reasoned analysis, eight and a half pages long, by Chandler P. Anderson, which argued that the Germans were maneuvering to induce the United States to retaliate against the British as a means of avoiding difficulty with Germany, and that they would quit temporizing and yield to the President's demands only out of fear of actual war with the United States.[112] On the following morning, July 17, another letter from Lansing arrived at Cornish. It conveyed the Secretary's enthusiastic approval of the President's outline of a third *Lusitania* note, as well as Lansing's reluctance to venture suggesting a way out of the dilemma posed by the alleged desire of the American people to avoid both war with Germany and surrender of any national rights. As Lansing wrote:

"This brings up the question, which you ask, as to 'the concluding terms of demand.' Frankly I am not prepared yet to answer that question. I would prefer to wait until the note is drafted in a tentative form and see what demands would be consistent and appropriate. Of course the demands we make will be the most difficult part of the note. Is it possible to be firm and at the same time to compromise?

"I think that in formulating the demands the possible consequences must be considered with the greatest care. In case of a flat refusal what will happen? In case of counter proposals what then? Should the demands be so worded as to admit of only 'Yes' or 'No' as an answer,

---

[110] *New York Times*, July 14, 1915.

[111] R. Lansing, memoranda dated July 11, 13, and 14, 1915, Wilson Papers; R. Lansing to W.W., July 14, 1915, *The Lansing Papers*, I, 457-458.

[112] C. P. Anderson, "Memorandum on questions presented by the correspondence between the United States and Germany on the subject of the violation of the American rights by the German submarine methods of warfare," dated July 13, 1915, Wilson Papers.

or should a loophole be given for counter proposals? Can we take a course which will permit further correspondence? These are the questions which are running through my mind and I have not as yet been able to answer them. I wish more time to consider them."[113]

The President, meanwhile, had begun to sketch out a draft of a third *Lusitania* note on July 16. He finished it perhaps the following day; then on the afternoon of July 18 he boarded his railroad car for the return to Washington. Excited throngs greeted the train at all its stops from Cornish to New Haven, for the newspapers had just told of an incident that seemed to presage a break with Germany. It was the unsuccessful torpedoing of the Cunard liner *Orduna*, 15,499 tons, westbound to New York from Liverpool with twenty-one Americans among her 227 passengers, thirty-seven miles south of Queenstown on July 9, 1915.[114] The excitement of the crowds mounted as the President's train neared New York. Was he bringing a message of peace or of war to the capital?[115]

Events of the next few days revealed that the President had determined not to permit the *Orduna* incident—in which, after all, no American lives had been lost—to disturb the final phases of the negotiations over the *Lusitania*. Arriving in Washington early on July 19, he talked with Lansing at the White House for more than an hour later in the morning about the draft of the note that he had prepared.[116] Lansing took the document with him to the State Department and quickly worked it into shape.[117] After Wilson had gone over it for a

[113] R. Lansing to W.W., July 15, 1915, *The Lansing Papers*, I, 459.

[114] *New York Times*, July 18, 1915. The attack was made without warning by the *U20* and by the same commander, Schwieger, who had sunk the *Lusitania*. Evidently mistaking the *Orduna* for a large merchantman, because it carried only one smokestack, Schwieger fired one torpedo which missed the stern of the boat by only ten feet. Schwieger then surfaced and tried unsuccessfully to halt the *Orduna* by gunfire. Spindler, *La Guerre Sous-Marine*, II, 152.

[115] *New York Times*, July 19, 1915.

[116] *ibid.*, July 20, 1915.

[117] He transposed one paragraph, made a number of editorial changes, and composed two new paragraphs. One of them said that the American government could not believe that the German authorities would longer refrain from disavowing "the wanton act" of their naval commander in sinking the *Lusitania*, "or from offering reparation for the American lives lost, so far as reparation can be made for a needless destruction of human life by an illegal act." The other was a new final paragraph, which read as follows: "In the event that this situation should unhappily arise the heavy responsibility would rest upon the Imperial Government for the inevitable consequences. The people and Government of the United States are determined to maintain their just rights and will adopt the steps necessary to insure their respect by all

final editing,[118] it was hurriedly put on the State Department wire late in the evening of July 21, 1915, in order, as Lansing said, "to put an end to newspaper speculations."

Deliberately brief and to the point, the note began with the frank statement that the American government had found the German communication of July 8 "very unsatisfactory."[119] Then followed a vigorous defense of neutral rights on the seas and an assertion of the duty of belligerents to respect these rights even when acting in reprisal against the enemy, reaching its climax in the following peroration entirely in Wilson's words:

"The Government of the United States is not unmindful of the extraordinary conditions created by this war or of the radical alterations of circumstance and method of attack produced by the use of instrumentalities of naval warfare which the nations of the world can not have had in view when the existing rules of international law were formulated, and it is ready to make every reasonable allowance for these novel and unexpected aspects of war at sea; but it can not consent to abate any essential or fundamental right of its people because of a mere alteration of circumstance. The rights of neutrals in time of war are based upon principle, not upon expediency, and the principles are immutable. It is the duty and obligation of belligerents to find a way to adapt the new circumstances to them."

Actually, the note continued, events of the past two months had clearly demonstrated that it was possible to conduct a submarine campaign against merchant shipping in "substantial accord"[120] with the rules of cruiser warfare. "The whole world has looked with interest and increasing satisfaction at the demonstration of that possibility by

---

nations." R. Lansing to W.W., July 21, 1915, *The Lansing Papers*, 1, 463; draft of the note, dated July 19, 1915, showing Lansing's changes imposed upon Wilson's text, in the State Department Papers.

[118] Wilson accepted most of the Secretary's changes but did not like and deleted the new final paragraph. "It has," he wrote to Lansing on July 21 when he returned the final draft to the State Department, "the tone of an ultimatum, and does not seem to me in fact to add to the meaning of the document as a whole, —the manifest meaning of it. I do not think that we need add a *sting*." W.W. to R. Lansing, July 21, 1915, *The Lansing Papers*, 1, 464. In addition, the President added a new paragraph of his own, the one quoted below beginning "The Government of the United States is not unmindful of the extraordinary conditions. . . ."

[119] These were Lansing's words. Wilson had originally written "very disappointing."

[120] In his original draft Wilson had written "in entire accord." Lansing changed this to read "in general accord." In his final editing Wilson struck out "general" and wrote "substantial."

German naval commanders. It is manifestly possible, therefore, to lift the whole practice of submarine attack above the criticism which it has aroused and remove the chief causes of offense." The immediate issue of the *Lusitania,* the note went on, of course still remained unsolved. The American government could not believe that the German authorities would any longer refrain from disavowing the sinking of this liner or from offering reparation for the needless destruction of American lives. The American government could not accept the German proposal for the free passage of certain designated vessels, for such an agreement would in effect subject all other vessels to illegal attack. Then came the moving final paragraphs, full of promise and warning:

"The Government of the United States and the Imperial German Government are contending for the same great object, have long stood together in urging the very principles upon which the Government of the United States now so solemnly insists. They are both contending for the freedom of the seas. The Government of the United States will continue to contend for that freedom, from whatever quarter violated, without compromise and at any cost. It invites the practical cooperation of the Imperial German Government at this time when cooperation may accomplish most and this great common object be most strikingly and effectively achieved.

"The Imperial German Government expresses the hope that this object may be in some measure accomplished even before the present war ends. It can be. The Government of the United States not only feels obliged to insist upon it, by whomsoever violated or ignored, in the protection of its own citizens, but is also deeply interested in seeing it made practicable between the belligerents themselves, and holds itself ready at any time to act as the common friend who may be privileged to suggest a way.

"In the meantime the very value which this Government sets upon the long and unbroken friendship between the people and Government of the United States and the people and Government of the German nation impels it to press very solemnly upon the Imperial German Government the necessity for a scrupulous observance of neutral rights in this critical matter. Friendship itself prompts it to say to the Imperial Government that repetition by the commanders of German naval vessels of acts in contravention of those rights must be regarded by the Government of the United States, when they affect American citizens, as deliberately unfriendly."[121]

As if to emphasize that he expected no crisis, either on account of the note or of the attack on the *Orduna*, the President left Washington again on July 23 for Cornish, arriving at "Harlarkenden" on the following day, at the very time when the text of the document was being published in the American press and the approbation of editors and leaders was reverberating through the nation.[122]

He hurried back to "Harlarkenden" for another reason, a deeply personal one. He had recently fallen in love with Mrs. Edith Bolling Galt, a young and charming widow of Washington, whom he had met in March 1915 through his cousin and White House hostess Helen Woodrow Bones. And Mrs. Galt was spending the month with the intimate family group at "Harlarkenden."

The President's "last word" on the *Lusitania*, as the newspapers immediately called his note of July 21, 1915, stirred a violent storm in Germany as soon as Gerard delivered it at the Foreign Office in Berlin on July 23. The effusive language of the American note of June 9 and Gerard's collaboration in the preparation of the Foreign Office's reply had caused the German leaders to think that there was a good chance the President might accept their proposals for a *modus vivendi*. The President's message of July 21 not only blasted these hopes but also made a direct threat of war, or at least of a rupture in diplomatic relations, if any new incidents occurred. The reaction of the Emperor was by no means untypical of sentiments that surged through the German people. Reading a copy of the note that had been forwarded to Supreme Headquarters, he penciled the following comments on

---

[121] The Secretary of State to Ambassador Gerard, July 21, 1915, *Foreign Relations, 1915, Supplement*, pp. 480-482.

[122] Editors and spokesmen, including even most of those who had earlier advocated coming to some agreement with Germany, were virtually unanimous in their approval. See the review of press opinion in the *Literary Digest*, LI (August 7, 1915), 234-236; the New York *World*, July 24, 1915; New York *Nation*, CI (July 29, 1915), 135; and Chicago *Public*, XVIII (July 30, 1915), 729. The only dissenters of any consequence were the German-American spokesmen, the Hearst press, and Senator Hoke Smith of Georgia. For a summary of German-American opinion, see the survey in the *Literary Digest*, just cited, and the resolution adopted by the German-American Alliance of New York State on July 25, printed in the *New York Times*, July 26, 1915. For a sample of the editorial comment of the Hearst press, see the New York *American*, July 25 and 26, 1915. Hoke Smith's statement was printed in the *New York Times*, July 25, 1915.

the margin: "Immeasurably impertinent!" "You don't say so!" "There you are!" "Commands!" "Unheard of!" "i.e., war" And at the bottom of the note: "In tone and bearing this is about the most impudent note which I have ever read since the Japanese note of August last! It ends with a direct threat! W."[123]

The Foreign Office withheld the text from the public as long as it could. However, there was no way to restrain the German press once the note had appeared in American newspapers on July 24, and so the authorities released it for publication in the morning newspapers on the following day. Without exception editors and analysts, moderates and jingoes alike, echoed the Emperor's bitter words. Theodor Wolff of the *Berliner Tageblatt*, who had heretofore supported the Chancellor's efforts to maintain good relations with America, epitomized the anger that most Germans felt, as follows:

"But Mr. Wilson's standpoint is under all circumstances . . . the diametrical opposite of common sense and right. We here are by no means so slavishly unfree in our thinking as the American reader is told. But we believe that Mr. Wilson is at heart unfree and understands instinctively how to fit his ideas of humanity and neutrality to the business interests of his major electors. . . . We appreciate that the neutral state, the little as much as the great, seeks to guard its neutrality and the personal rights of its citizens. But it appears to us that one cannot say to one belligerent party: 'The war does not matter to us,' when one tries to profit as much as possible from the war by an eager munitions trade with the other belligerent power."[124]

Perhaps the Imperial Chancellor and Foreign Secretary initially shared these same sentiments. Perhaps they also feared at first that they would have to make some direct reply to the President, for Bernstorff wrote gloomily on July 22, saying that a break in relations and war had been narrowly averted and warning that the American au-

[123] This document is in the German F. O. Archives.

[124] *Berliner Tageblatt*, morning edn., July 26, 1915; also "Captain Persius" in *ibid.*, morning edn., July 25, 1915; Eugen Zimmermann in the *Berliner Lokal-Anzeiger*, morning edn., July 26, 1915; Berlin *Vossische Zeitung*, morning edn., July 25, 1915; Count E. von Reventlow in the *Deutsche Tageszeitung*, morning edn., July 25, 1915; Berlin *Taegliche Rundschau*, morning edn., July 25, 1915; Berlin *Kreuz-Zeitung*, *Boersen Zeitung*, and *Morgen Post*, all quoted in the New York *World*, July 26, 1915; and the reviews of German editorial opinion in the *New York Times*, July 26 and 27, 1915, the New York *World*, July 27, 1915, and the *Literary Digest*, LI (August 7, 1915), 239.

thorities expected a favorable reply to their third *Lusitania* note.[125] If these were Bethmann's and von Jagow's feelings and fears, however, they did not long survive a sober second thought and the encouraging reports that soon came from Washington.

In the first place, a careful reading of the President's note of July 21 soon revealed that the area of disagreement between the two governments over the submarine issue had been progressively narrowed since the first American note on the *Lusitania* was penned. Wilson had opened the negotiations by asking for nothing less than the entire abandonment of submarine attacks against merchantmen on the ground, it will be remembered, that submarines could never fulfill certain obligations to humanity under international law. He had ended the correspondence by not only withdrawing this demand, if such it may be called, but by also giving public approval to a submarine campaign conducted as best it might be according to the rules of cruiser warfare. As a consequence, the only critical issues that remained in dispute were those of disavowal of the *Lusitania* incident, and safety for American travelers on belligerent passenger ships. (The issue of security for all belligerent merchantmen actually had not become a matter of controversy, although Wilson had raised it generally in the correspondence.) Remembering the Imperial order of June 6 forbidding submarines to attack large passenger liners without warning, Bethmann must have told himself that any new dire threat to the German-American peace could be averted by a simple disavowal if accidental attacks against such liners did occur.

Even more encouraging than these signs of accord between the two governments were the numerous evidences that came to the Imperial Chancellor and the Foreign Office that the American leaders really did not intend to press hard for an apology and reparation for the loss of American lives on the *Lusitania*—indeed, that the Washington government might be willing to accept an impasse. The first indication that this might be true came on July 24, when Ambassador Gerard talked in a "personal" way to Count Max Montgelas, the head of the American section of the Foreign Office. It might be best, Gerard observed, for the German government to send no reply at all to the third American note; the question of indemnity might be worked out by informal negotiations. This, the Ambassador quickly added,

[125] Ambassador von Bernstorff to T. von Bethmann Hollweg, July 22, 1915, German F. O. Archives. Here Bernstorff must have been reporting his conversation with Lansing, which Lansing (*War Memoirs*, p. 40) dates July 23, 1915.

was only his personal opinion; Washington, Gerard went on with some bitterness, had never paid any attention to his suggestions, and his superiors might have an entirely different point of view.[126]

More impressive, certainly, were the advices from Bernstorff. He saw the Secretary of State frequently during the week or ten days following the dispatch of the third American note and was able to report a substantial moderation of official sentiment in Washington and, even more hopefully, that there were signs that President Wilson intended to move against the British government soon.

"I hear confidentially," Bernstorff wired on July 27, 1915, "that the American Government believes that it would be better for relations between both governments and peoples not to answer the American note at all if our reply cannot be favorable."[127]

"Secretary of State," he added a day later, "says that the American note is 'rubber-like.' He does not desire a conflict, and he has dragged out the negotiations with England here on purpose in order to see how this matter goes. Secretary of State seemed to me completely calm."[128]

On the same day, July 28, the Ambassador wrote an extraordinarily revealing report to the Imperial Chancellor. It is a long document, but it sheds so much light on the thoughts and purposes of the President and Secretary of State at this time that its most important passages are reproduced here:

"Through other channels I have respectfully asked that Your Excellency wait for this report before making any decision if and how the last American *Lusitania* note should be answered. Since neither the Government here nor public opinion thinks an answer absolutely necessary, and since, therefore, no danger is involved, I would like to suggest respectfully that, in view of all the circumstances, you conduct further negotiations here orally and confidentially, even if instructions have to be sent by mail. It is my experience that we can negotiate successfully with the American Government only in Washington. President Wilson as well as Secretary of State Lansing is now ready to give this method a try to achieve agreement. This situation

[126] Count Montgelas, memorandum dated July 25, 1915, German F. O. Archives. Jagow wrote on the margin of this document: "The well-known pro-German journalist [Karl H.] von Wiegand expressed himself in exactly the same sense yesterday to me. He stressed that he has come to this viewpoint on the basis of an exchange of opinion with the Ambassador."

[127] Ambassador von Bernstorff to the Foreign Office, July 27, 1915, *ibid.*

[128] Ambassador von Bernstorff to the Foreign Office, July 28, 1915, *ibid.*

is perhaps not recognized in Germany, since the language of the American note must seem unnecessarily sharp there.

"The sharpness can be explained because Mr. Wilson was carried away by his emotions about the sinking of the Lusitania. Stimulated by this emotion, he has taken such an inflexible position that he cannot retreat without making himself impossible in the eyes of public opinion here. Moreover, he believes that because of Mr. Bryan's resignation and the now-famous Dumba telegram[129] . . . that we do not take his notes seriously. Finally, he desires that the exchange of notes with us should be brought to an end, since he now wants to move against England; and in his well-known stubbornness he believes that negotiations have to be finished with us first before he can take up the English question. However, it must be stressed that Mr. Wilson does not want to wage war against us or to become a partisan of England. About this matter one should not be fooled by the eastern press in the United States. These as well as other powerful spokesmen take up for England and would gladly welcome a war with Germany. But for Mr. Wilson and the overwhelming majority of the American people, this is *not* the case.[130]

"The great danger of the situation is that the above-mentioned press could push us into war, just as a new Lusitania incident would do. What Mr. Wilson wants is the following: He wants to satisfy public opinion here by the sharp language of the note which he addressed to us. Then if he could gain concessions from us he would like to press mediation of the German and English points of view—in other words, his pet project, 'freedom of the seas.' In his note, the President has definitely come close to our position, for he now considers the submarine war as legitimate, while he earlier thought that it could not be executed at all according to international law.

"It is not my duty to decide, and from here I am not able to see the whole situation and to judge if from our viewpoint it is better to answer the American note or not. . . . If, however, the submarine war is a means toward an end—the cessation or loosening of the British blockade—it would, according to my humble opinion, be wise to gain this purpose with the help of President Wilson, by granting him the concessions. He has said to one of my trusted men: 'If I receive

---

[129] See above, pp. 400-401.

[130] It is interesting that the British Ambassador, in his reports to Sir Edward Grey, agreed emphatically with Bernstorff on this point. See C. Spring Rice to E. Grey, May 20, June 10 and 23, 1915, *The Letters of Sir Cecil Spring Rice*, II, 268-271, 272, 274.

a favorable answer from Germany I will see this thing through with England to the end.' . . . I believe a satisfactory basis has been created for using Wilson as a battering ram against England. If we help him out of his present difficult situation, I am convinced that he will execute energetically his plans against England for the re-establishment of international law even while the war continues. The flexible phrase 'it can be' the President has inserted in the note himself. These three words express Wilson's firm conviction that he can force England to give in.[131]

"As I have already reported through other channels,[132] our answer would concern the following three points, and I urgently hope that it will be possible to give them:

"1. Conclude the Lusitania incident by saying that we were justified under the law of reprisal in attacking it, but that we are sorry we killed Americans and regret the chain reaction that it set off. Offer indemnity to suffering victims.

"2. We intend to maintain our present methods of submarine warfare. This means we do not sink passenger ships without warning.

"3. We would be willing to join with President Wilson in re-establishing international law during the war, and we leave it to his discretion to begin negotiations with the English Government about this. As a basis, we suggest using the Declaration of London, as the American Government itself formerly proposed.

"At the worst, the negotiations with England might fail. But then the question of guilt would be obvious to the entire world, and we would have won Mr. Wilson to our side. Knowing the character of the President, I have not the slightest doubt about this."[133]

Was this the way out for Germany? the Imperial Chancellor must have asked himself.[134] It would be extraordinarily difficult to do what Bernstorff had suggested, especially to avow publicly what had thus

---

[131] Bernstorff was here referring to the sentences in the next-to-the-last paragraph in Wilson's note of July 21, which read as follows: "The Imperial German Government expresses the hope that this object [the freedom of the seas] may be in some measure accomplished even before the present war ends. It can be."

[132] Ambassador von Bernstorff to the Foreign Office, July 27, 1915, German F. O. Archives.

[133] J. von Bernstorff to T. von Bethmann Hollweg, July 28, 1915, *ibid*.

[134] Although Bernstorff's long report of July 28, 1915, printed above, was sent by mail or courier and did not reach Berlin until about August 12, the Ambassador's wireless summary of July 27, 1915, cited above, was in the Chancellor's hands as he contemplated future policy toward the United States at the end of July.

far been kept a close secret—that the Imperial government had already yielded on the question of the inviolability of large liners. Would the President really carry through against England and contend for the freedom of the seas, as he had said in his last note, "from whatever quarter violated, without compromise and at any cost"? And was it worth surrendering the effective submarine weapon even if he should succeed in forcing the British to loosen their grip on seaborne commerce?

Bethmann gave no definitive answers at this time, but he took two steps that gave some indication of the direction in which his thoughts were running. First, on July 29 he intimated to Gerard that the Foreign Office would not answer the last American note but would rather offer informally to submit the question of damages to the Hague Court for arbitration.[135] Second, on July 30 the Chancellor had the Foreign Office send a further reply to a series of American representations about the sinking of the American merchantman *William P. Frye* by a German auxiliary cruiser on January 28, 1915. This particular case had never been a subject of serious controversy, but what the Foreign Office said in its note of July 30 had far-reaching implications for German-American relations. It was that the German government admitted its obligations under the Prussian-American treaties of 1785 and 1799 to pay full damages for the destruction of American ships and cargoes *according to the rules of cruiser warfare*, even when such destruction was justified under international law because the ships were carrying contraband to the enemy.[136] The Foreign Office could not have gone much further than this in acknowledging American neutral trading rights at sea.

The official American reaction to these developments gave convincing proof that the President and his colleagues thought that the really critical phase of the controversy with Germany had passed. Lansing and his adviser, Chandler P. Anderson, were immensely pleased by the *Frye* note and by the report, which Bernstorff must have relayed to them, that Germany might be willing to submit the question of indemnity for the loss of American life on the *Lusitania* to arbitration.

---

[135] Ambassador Gerard to the Secretary of State, July 29, 1915, *Foreign Relations, 1915, Supplement*, p. 491; see also the Foreign Office to Ambassador von Bernstorff, August 3, 1915, German F. O. Archives.

[136] Ambassador Gerard to the Secretary of State, July 30, 1915, *Foreign Relations, 1915, Supplement*, pp. 493-495.

It was, Anderson wrote in his diary, all that the American leaders had a right to ask and more than they had expected, especially if the Germans should continue to give safe passage to liners.[137] The President, who was still at Cornish, indicated that he preferred to let the *Lusitania* negotiations rest for a time, as he did not think that American public opinion would permit arbitration "at present."[138] On the other hand, he, too, was obviously pleased by the apparent progress toward substantial agreement with Berlin.

There were, moreover, some signs that it would not be long before the President would have to honor the promises that he had made to Bernstorff on June 2 and in his note to Germany of July 21, to stand forthrightly for the freedom of the seas as much against Britain as against Germany, and that he might have to do this in the absence of a full settlement with Germany because of unbearable pressure from American public opinion.[139]

Was it possible that relative accord with Germany and a really serious controversy with Great Britain now impended? Would the final result of the *Lusitania* case be to clear the air in German-American relations and to sharpen old hostilities with England? So it seemed in that mid-summer of 1915. So Wilson and many of his advisers believed. It would all depend upon events of the next few weeks. They would show whether the submarine crisis was actually ended and the President could strive in all earnestness for freedom of the seas, or whether the future would contain renewed tension and perhaps war between Germany and the United States.

[137] Anderson Diary, July 30, 1915; C. P. Anderson, memorandum on the *Frye* case, dated August 5, 1915, *The Lansing Papers*, I, 465-466.

[138] W.W. to R. Lansing, August 9, 1915, *ibid.*, p. 466.

[139] See below, pp. 594-597.

CHAPTER XIV

Mexico: Confusions and Intrigues

AT NO time between the beginning of the submarine campaign and the *Lusitania* crisis had developments in Mexico ceased to be a source of perplexity to the harried leaders in Washington. It will be recalled that the revolutionary movement in Mexico had ruptured soon after its triumph over Huerta; that the American government had given a certain encouragement to the faction dominated by Pancho Villa but had carefully avoided any risk of direct involvement; and that Villa, after suffering his first defeat at the hands of his rival, Venustiano Carranza, had retreated in haste northward from Mexico City in late January of 1915.

Events of the ensuing weeks and months put an almost unbearable strain upon President Wilson's always strong determination to avoid entanglement in the Mexican civil war. Difficulties began early in 1915, in the first instance because the leaders in Washington had not expected and were obviously not prepared for the turn in the military tide in Mexico that began after the battle of Puebla on January 7, 1915. The State Department had, in fact, broken *de facto* relations with the Carranza government after it withdrew from Mexico City to Veracruz in November 1914. Although the break had not been an open one, it had been accomplished in a way that must have been particularly humiliating to the proud First Chief. The Department's policy during December 1914 and January 1915 had been simply to ignore the existence of the government in Veracruz and at the same time to carry on *de facto* relations with the Conventionist "government" through the very men—Vice Consul John R. Silliman and the Brazilian Minister in Mexico City, J. M. Cardoso de Oliveira[1]—through whom it had formerly done business with Carranza. In view of Obregón's occupation of the capital in late January and the further decline in Villa's

---

[1] The Brazilian Minister had assumed responsibility for protecting American interests in Mexico when Huerta broke diplomatic relations with the United States at the time of the Veracruz affair. The State Department had continued to use the Brazilian Minister as its formal representative in Mexico City.

military power soon afterward, it was now no longer possible to ignore the First Chief. The State Department, consequently, resumed informal *de facto* relations in February 1915 by sending Silliman to Veracruz as its Special Agent "near" Carranza and by dealing with Obregón in Mexico City through the Brazilian Minister. This act of informal recognition did not, however, mark the beginning of a period of friendly relations between the United States and the Constitutionalist regime. On the contrary, it came at the very time that new problems were arising to create extraordinarily dangerous tensions between the two governments.

To begin with, there was the difficulty of dealing with Carranza on any workable basis at all. Feeling not without reason that he had been ignored and insulted by the American and other governments with diplomatic representatives in Mexico, the First Chief lost no opportunity to reply in kind. On February 3, 1915, for instance, he formally transferred the capital of Mexico to Veracruz, reduced Mexico City to the status of the capital of the new State of Valle de México, and studiously refused to have any communication with the diplomatic corps in Mexico City.[2] A short time later, Carranza closed the port of Progreso in Yucatan to prevent the export of a large quantity of sisal hemp that American manufacturers of binder twine for reapers desperately needed, in order, it seemed, merely to spite the United States government.[3]

The source of the gravest danger of conflict between Washington and Veracruz during the first weeks after the resumption of diplomatic relations, however, was Mexico City and its fate under Constitutionalist military rule. Carranza and Obregón were bent upon humbling the imperial city, so long the seat of the rich and mighty Mexican exploiters and of the proud foreigners who owned so much of Mexico's resources. From early February until near the middle of March 1915, when they nonchalantly abandoned the former capital to the *Zapatistas*, the Constitutionalist leaders seemed determined to compound its agony, indeed, to hasten its death. When *Zapatista* soldiers destroyed the water supply station in the southern suburbs, for example, Obregón made no effort to repair the damage and calmly announced that Mexico City was of no value to anyone anyway.[4] When

---

[2] The Brazilian Minister to Mexico to the Secretary of State, February 3, 1915, *Foreign Relations, 1915*, pp. 649-650.

[3] For documents relating to this episode, see *ibid.*, pp. 821-824.

[4] J. R. Silliman to the Secretary of State, February 12, 1915, State Department Papers.

the city seemed on the verge of starvation and anarchy, Carranza and Obregón refused to permit trains to be used to bring in supplies, while Obregón personally harassed local merchants, priests, and foreigners who tried to obtain help and virtually invited the hungry mobs to plunder stores and warehouses. The distraught Brazilian Minister described the situation in one of his many appeals to Washington, as follows:

"As far as can be judged from the facts, the present distressed condition of the city has been purposely brought about by the constitutionalists by closing all government offices and public works, by cutting the railway traffic in all directions in order to prevent the incoming of supplies for the factories which had to let out all their men, and by not letting staple articles find their way into the city; and finally by transporting to Vera Cruz whatever there was in the city—all with the avowed purpose of forcing the people to go into his [Obregón's] army or starve with the possible alternative of, through his systematic incendiary declarations in the press, rousing them against foreigners and well-to-do Mexicans so as to create a truly chaotic state of things in the Capital."[5]

Such reports had a jolting impact upon President Wilson and Secretary Bryan. Earlier, during the heyday of Villa's brief reign in Mexico City, Wilson had replied to his critics at home[6] by defiantly proclaiming that he would permit no one to impede the struggle of the Mexican people for liberty and the self-determination of their internal affairs. "Now there is one thing I have got a great enthusiasm

[5] J. M. Cardoso de Oliveira to the Secretary of State, March 2, 1915, *ibid.*; punctuation added and slightly altered; also J. R. Silliman to the Secretary of State, February 8, 1915, *ibid.*; J. M. Cardoso de Oliveira to the Secretary of State, March 2, 1915, transmitting a message from the International Relief Committee, *Foreign Relations, 1915*, p. 654.

[6] Criticism and charges that Wilson's Mexican policy had failed and that he was in large measure personally responsible for the chaotic conditions in Mexico did not begin in a significant way until the announcement that American forces would be withdrawn from Veracruz, but they soon attained sizable proportions after this date, especially when Theodore Roosevelt joined the President's critics with a violent blast in the press in December 1914. The rising tide of criticism can be seen in the following editorials and articles: Louisville *Courier-Journal*, November 19, 1914; *New Republic*, 1 (November 21, 1914), 3-4; New York *World*, November 24, 1914; "Unhappy Mexico: America's Responsibility," New York *Outlook*, cviii (December 2, 1914), 752-753; *Collier's*, liv (December 5, 1914), 12; T. Roosevelt, "Our Responsibility in Mexico," *New York Times*, December 6, 1914; *Chicago Daily Tribune*, December 7, 1914; and the critical newspaper comment cited in "Our Evacuation of Vera Cruz," *Literary Digest*, xlix (December 5, 1914), 1104-1105.

about, I might almost say a reckless enthusiasm, and that is human liberty," he had declared in a Jackson Day address at Indianapolis on January 8, 1915. ". . . I hold it as a fundamental principle, and so do you, that every people has the right to determine its own form of government, and until this recent revolution in Mexico, until the end of the Diaz regime, 80 per cent. of the people of Mexico never had a 'look-in' in determining who should be their Governors, or what their Government should be. Now, I am for the 80 per cent. It is none of my business, and it is none of your business how long they take in determining it. It is none of my business and it is none of your business how they go about the business. The country is theirs. The Government is theirs. The liberty, if they can get it, and God speed them in getting it, is theirs. And so far as my influence goes, while I am President nobody shall interfere with them."[7]

It was a political doctrine sincerely meant when Wilson uttered it, but it was somewhat less than easy to follow when the President had to confront the necessity of dealing with Carranza about the difficulties that arose soon afterward. What followed in consequence of the confrontation was an end to the hopeful complacency of the Washington administration and the beginning of a policy of interference that would become increasingly active and, to Mexicans, menacing.

Baffled by the dizzy pace of change in Mexico in January 1915, Wilson's and Bryan's thoughts inevitably turned to the necessity of sending a new Confidential Agent to investigate and report. Agreeing that Paul Fuller, Senior, should be, as Wilson put it, reserved for "larger and more lasting functions,"[8] they selected Duval West of San Antonio, a former federal district attorney and a student of Mexican affairs, whom Fuller had probably recommended. The President's letter of instructions to West revealed that he was contemplating assuming a more active role in the direction of events. It follows:

"I do not believe that it is necessary for me to give you detailed suggestions as to your mission in my behalf in Mexico, for I know you have talked the matter over, I hope quite fully, with the Secretary of State.

"My wish in general is this: To have you meet and, as far as possible, assess the character and purposes of the principle [*sic*] men down there of the several groups and factions, in the hope that you may be able to form a definite idea not only as to their relative strength

[7] *New York Times*, January 9, 1915.
[8] W.W. to W. J. Bryan, January 14, 1915, Wilson Papers.

and their relative prospects of success, but also as to their real purposes.

"Above all, I want to find out just what prospects of a settlement there are and what sort of settlement it would be likely to be. If the settlement contemplated is not seriously intended for the benefit of the common people of the country, if the plans and ambitions of the leaders center upon themselves and not upon the people they are trying to represent, of course it will not be a permanent settlement but will simply lead to further distress and disorder. I am very anxious to know just what the *moral* situation is, therefore, and just what it *behooves us to do to check what is futile and promote what promises genuine reform and settled peace.*"[9]

Entering Mexico on February 19, 1915, West visited Villa, Carranza, and Zapata; and his reports on the rival chieftains and conditions in the territories under their control would later have a profound effect upon the formation of American policies. Meanwhile, the two problems of Mexico City and Carranza's blockade of Progreso seemed to demand some immediate solution.

Conditions in the former capital had been disquieting enough during February, but developments in early March seemed to threaten nothing but unalloyed catastrophe to the 2,500 Americans and the more than 23,000 other foreigners trapped in the city. Something had to be done. The American government could not stand by and see its own citizens being starved and possibly slaughtered; and every day envoys of the European powers were calling at the State Department to plead for protection for their own nationals. Having failed to obtain any relief by polite suggestions, Bryan addressed a sharp warning to Carranza on March 5.[10] Immediately afterward two really frightening dispatches from the Brazilian Minister in Mexico City arrived at the State Department.[11] "I am wondering," the Secretary of State wrote at once to the White House, "whether it may not be necessary to speak more emphatically than we have done. I have used all the adjectives that properly go with persuasion but things seem to grow worse instead of better and the representatives of other nations are very much concerned. Mr. Lansing has suggested it might be worth while to notify Carranza and Obregon that in view of the

[9] W.W. to Duval West, February 5, 1915, *ibid.*; italics added.

[10] W. J. Bryan to J. R. Silliman, March 5, 1915, State Department Papers.

[11] They were J. M. Cardoso de Oliveira to the Secretary of State, March 4, 1915, 5 p.m., and March 4, 1915, 11 p.m., *Foreign Relations, 1915*, pp. 656-658.

language which is being employed by Obregon to excite hatred of foreigners, thus greatly increasing the risks, and in view of the interruption of traffic and communication by Carranza, thus further increasing the risks, that we would hold Carranza and Obregon personally responsible for injury that resulted from the methods which they are employing."[12]

"I had seen these despatches," Wilson replied, "and they had given me deep anxiety and perplexity, as they have given you. Nothing better than what Mr. Lansing suggests occurs to me, and I hope that you will act at once on his suggestion. In addition, I hope that you will say to Carranza that the extraordinary and unpardonable course pursued by General Obregon, under his command, has renewed the talk of joint action by several of the chief governments of the world to protect their embassies and their nationals at Mexico City, and that he is running a very serious risk. Will you not be kind enough to ask [Secretary of the Navy] Daniels if he has ships with long range guns (not necessarily battle ships) which he could order at once to Vera Cruz, and, if so, to let me know?"[13]

Events now moved rapidly toward a sharp crisis. At nine o'clock in the evening of March 6 the State Department sent an identic ultimatum to Obregón in Mexico City and Carranza in Veracruz. Drafted by Lansing in strong and insulting language, it accused the Constitutionalists of deliberately seeking to punish and starve the inhabitants of the former capital and to incite them to riot. "When a *factional* leader," it went on, "preys on a starving city to compel obedience to his decrees by inciting outlawry and at the same time uses means to prevent the city from being supplied with food, a situation is created which it is impossible for the United States to contemplate longer with patience. Conditions have become intolerable and can no longer be endured. The Government of the United States therefore desires General Obregon and General Carranza to know that it has, after mature consideration, determined that if, as a result of the situation for which they are responsible, Americans suffer by reason of the conduct of the Constitutionalist forces in the City of Mexico or because they fail to provide means of protection to life and property, the Government of the United States will hold General Obregon and General Carranza *personally* responsible therefor. Having reached this determination with the greatest reluctance, the Government of the

[12] W. J. Bryan to W.W., March 5, 1915, State Department Papers.
[13] W.W. to W. J. Bryan, March 6, 1915, *ibid.*

United States will take such measures as are expedient to bring to account those who are personally responsible for what may occur."[14]

Precisely what kind of retaliation Wilson had in mind is not clear. He knew, certainly, that he might have to send an expeditionary force to Mexico City to rescue the foreign colony if conditions there grew much worse; but the ultimatum of March 6 committed him far beyond even this drastic action—to a war to the finish against the entire *Carrancista* regime if American citizens in the former capital were harmed. The President, obviously, expected his warning and a show of force to suffice. He made provision for the latter after a conference with Secretary of the Navy Josephus Daniels on March 8, by sending the battleship *Georgia* and the armored cruiser *Washington* from Guantánamo, Cuba, to join the small American naval force already stationed off Veracruz.[15]

It was during this period of alarm that the less dramatic crisis over Progreso also came to a head. Since late February Carranza had rejected all American pleas that he permit the export of some 200,000 bales of sisal hemp, without which, American manufacturers said, there would be so little binder twine that much of the American wheat crop could not be harvested in 1915.[16] By March 12, 1915, when the Cabinet discussed the matter, President Wilson was plainly tired of the futile parleying. "I think," he wrote to Bryan soon afterward, "that we are justified, in all the circumstances, in saying to Carranza that we cannot recognize his right to blockade the port to the exclusion of our commerce; that we must beg him to recall his orders to that effect; and that we shall feel constrained, in case he feels he cannot do so, to instruct our naval officers there to prevent any interference with our commerce to and from the port. He should be told, at the same time, that we are doing this in the interest of peace and amity between the two countries and with no wish or intention to interfere with her internal affairs, from which we shall carefully keep our hands off."[17] Bryan sent Wilson's message to Silliman on the fol-

[14] The Secretary of State to the Brazilian Minister to Mexico and to Special Agent Silliman, March 6, 1915, *Foreign Relations, 1915*, pp. 659-661; italics added.

[15] It consisted of the battleship *Delaware*, the cruisers *Des Moines* and *Tacoma*, and the gunboats *Sacramento* and *Petrel*. *New York Times*, March 9 and 10, 1915.

[16] G. A. Ranney (?), secretary, International Harvester Company, to W. J. Bryan, February 22, 1915, Bryan Papers, Library of Congress.

[17] W.W. to W. J. Bryan, March 12, 1915, Bryan Papers, National Archives.

lowing day;[18] but Carranza had lifted the blockade by the time the dispatch arrived, and the Special Agent in Veracruz consequently did not need to deliver the President's second ultimatum within a week to the First Chief.[19]

Meanwhile, the threat of hostilities between the American government and the *Carrancista* regime over Mexico City had also passed, at least momentarily. Silliman delivered the President's ultimatum to the First Chief on March 8, 1915. Carranza was so angry that he told the Special Agent on the following day that the Secretary of State would sooner or later have to answer to him for the note.[20] Refusing to answer Bryan, Carranza addressed a long personal reply to President Wilson. Temperate and altogether friendly in tone, it categorically denied all the American charges, asserted that there had been no "mobs, assassinations, [or] looting" since Obregón's occupation of Mexico City, and conveyed Carranza's promise to afford all possible protection to Americans and other foreigners.[21] Moreover, at the very time that he was sending this message to Washington, the First Chief was disengaging himself by effecting a withdrawal of his forces from Mexico City.[22] Obregón completed the evacuation in an orderly fashion during the evening of March 10; it was "certainly due," the Brazilian Minister in the city wrote to the Secretary of State on the following day, "to your opportune note which frustrated all plans."[23]

One phase of the Mexican policy of the United States came to an end and the foundations of another were laid during the interval between Obregón's entry into Mexico City on January 28 and his withdrawal on March 10, 1915. During the first phase the President and his advisers had studiously avoided any direct interference in Mexican affairs, aside from encouraging plans for unification of the Constitutionalist forces under Villa's leadership. The second phase, only the beginnings of which we have thus far seen, witnessed the sudden

[18] W. J. Bryan to W.W., March 13, 1915, *ibid.*; the Secretary of State to Special Agent Silliman, March 13, 1915, *Foreign Relations, 1915*, p. 824.

[19] Special Agent Silliman to the Secretary of State, March 15, 1915, *ibid.*; *New York Times*, March 16, 1915.

[20] J. R. Silliman to the Secretary of State, March 10, 1915, 10 a.m., State Department Papers.

[21] General Carranza to the President, March 9, 1915, transmitted in Special Agent Silliman to the Secretary of State, March 10, 1915, *Foreign Relations, 1915*, pp. 666-668.

[22] *New York Times*, March 10, 1915.

[23] The Brazilian Minister to Mexico to the Secretary of State, March 11, 1915, *Foreign Relations, 1915*, p. 668.

decline in Villa's fortunes in Mexico and a transition in Washington from policies of nonintervention to new programs for involvement shaped, in part, by a growing aversion to Carranza and his regime.

That such a change was gradually taking place was revealed by the President himself in mid-March of 1915, near the end of the transition from nonintervention to involvement. One revelation came in the comment that Wilson made on a memorandum that Lansing had submitted, suggesting that perhaps the American government ought to begin to prepare for the necessity of a full-scale military intervention in Mexico by exploring the possibilities of cooperation by the so-called ABC powers of South America.[24] "This is an important memorandum," Wilson wrote in comment, "and supplies much to think about. I do not yet allow myself to think of intervention as more than a remote *possibility*; but I suppose I must admit that it is at least a possibility, and, if it is, the possibility is worth preparing for."[25] The President certainly would not have written in this fashion in early January, when he announced his doctrine of absolute nonintervention in his Jackson Day Address.

The second revelation of Wilson's growing determination to play a more active role came in the reply that he sent to Carranza's personal message of March 9. After thanking the First Chief graciously for his assurances, Wilson proceeded to issue a clear and even dire warning, as follows:

"We seek always to act as the friends of the Mexican people, and as their friends it is our duty to speak very plainly about the grave dangers which threaten her from without whenever anything happens within her borders which is calculated to arouse the hostile sentiment of the whole world.

"Nothing will stir that sentiment more promptly or create greater dangers for Mexico than any, even temporary disregard for the lives, the safety or the rights of the citizens of other countries, resident within her territory, or any apparent contempt for the rights and safety of those who represent religion; and no attempt to justify or explain these things will in the least alter the sentiment or lessen the dangers that arise from them.

"To warn you concerning such matters is an act of friendship, not of hostility, and we cannot make the warning too earnest. To speak

[24] The Counselor to the Secretary of State, March 8, 1915, *The Lansing Papers*, II, 529-531.

[25] President Wilson to the Secretary of State, March 18, 1915, *ibid.*, p. 532.

less plainly or with less earnestness would be to conceal from you a terrible risk which no lover of Mexico should wish to run."[26]

Carranza could not have failed to understand that what the President called "a terrible risk" was nothing other than the military occupation of Mexico by the United States.[27]

Tension between Washington and Veracruz eased hardly at all following Obregón's withdrawal from Mexico City, the lifting of the blockade of Progreso, and the exchange of notes between the First Chief and the President. This was true, in the first place, because the plight of Mexico City grew worse instead of better, and because Carranza stubbornly refused to permit food supplies to enter the former capital from Veracruz or to accept the suggestions offered by Secretary Bryan for the neutralization of the railway line between Mexico City and Veracruz and of the former capital itself.[28] It was true, secondly, because of the persistence of the belief in Washington that Carranza could never bring an end to the conflict in his country. This conviction was strengthened at this time by the first report from Duval West, the President's newest Confidential Agent. West visited Villa's provisional capital at Chihuahua City in late February and then went on to interview Villa at Guadalajara in early March 1915. Writing to the Secretary of State on about March 15, he fairly exuded praise of Pancho and his regime in northern Mexico and confidence in Villa's ultimate triumph. Although he did not say so openly, West implied that Pancho, and not the First Chief, was still the best hope for peace in Mexico.[29]

Not long after the Confidential Agent voiced these expectations occurred the decisive turning point in the struggle for control of Mexico. During the first days of April 1915 Villa massed virtually his entire fighting force, some 30,000 men strong, together with a large num-

[26] The President to General Carranza, March 11, 1915, *Foreign Relations, 1915,* pp. 668-669. This message, like most of the dispatches that Wilson sent to Mexico, was written by the President on his own typewriter.

[27] As the New York *World's* correspondent in Veracruz reported. New York *World,* March 15, 1915.

[28] The Secretary of State to Special Agent Silliman, March 23, 29, and 31, 1915; Special Agent Silliman to the Secretary of State, March 30 and April 5 and 9, 1915, *Foreign Relations, 1915,* pp. 676, 683, 684-688.

[29] "Preliminary Report to the Honorable Secretary of State of the Conditions in Mexico by Duval West, Acting Under Authority Conferred by the President, Dated February 10, 1915, Requesting Him to Investigate Same," undated memorandum in the State Department Papers.

ber of cannon, at Irapuato, northwest of Mexico City, for a showdown
with Obregón's division entrenched at Celaya, about thirty-seven miles
to the southeast. Villa's purpose, as he told the Special Agent attached
to his headquarters, George C. Carothers, was to wipe out Obregón's
force, open the road to Mexico City, and then begin a systematic campaign to destroy the remaining *Carrancista* garrisons at Matamoros,
Veracruz, and Tampico.[30] Villa hit Celaya on April 6 with part of
his division but drew back after thirty hours of bloody and indecisive
fighting.[31] He then returned on April 13 with his regrouped force
and charged head-on in reckless fashion, over and over, into Obregón's
lines. After two days of violent fighting, Obregón succeeded in effecting
the classic maneuver of drawing the enemy into the center and then
mauling him from the right and left flanks with his reserves. The
result was the near-destruction of the once-proud Division of the North
and the withdrawal of Villa and the remnants of his army to Aguascalientes. "We have picked up from the field," Obregón reported to
Carranza at the end of the battle on April 15, "over thirty cannons
in perfect condition, with all their ammunition and beasts of burden;
over five thousand Mauser rifles; more than eight thousand prisoners;
large numbers of horses, saddles and other war material. . . . At this
time I calculate that the enemy's losses exceed fourteen thousand men,
between dead, wounded and dispersed. Our losses do not exceed two
hundred men between dead and wounded."[32]

While Villa and his men were reeling in confusion northward,
Carranza's generals pressed forward in a broad campaign to clear all
of central Mexico and envelop *Villista* garrisons in the North. Constitutionalists occupied Guadalajara, a city far to the west of Mexico
City, on April 18. On May 21 *Villista* garrisons at Monterrey and
Saltillo in northeastern Mexico withdrew in the face of strong Constitutionalist forces. At about the same time Obregón began moving
his veterans northward from Celaya toward Aguascalientes. He climaxed his advance with an important victory over the combined forces
of Villa and his chief lieutenant, General Felipe Angeles, at Léon,

---

[30] G. C. Carothers to the Secretary of State, April 5, 1915, *ibid.*

[31] J. R. Silliman to the Secretary of State, April 7, 1915, *ibid.; New York Times,*
April 9, 1915.

[32] V. Carranza to E. Arredondo, April 15, 1915, quoting the report just received
from General Obregón, enclosed in E. Arredondo to W. J. Bryan, April 16, 1915, State
Department Papers. For Villa's own estimate of his losses, see G. C. Carothers to the
Secretary of State, April 20, 1915, *ibid.*

some eighty-one miles south of Aguascalientes, on June 7, and with the capture of Aguascalientes itself on July 10, 1915.

This plummeting of Villa's military fortunes came as a rude shock to President Wilson and his advisers in Washington. "If it should prove to be true that the Carranza forces have defeated Villa," Bryan wrote on April 18, "there is much to meditate upon."[33] Once they knew the full dimensions of the debacle at Celaya, they confessed readily enough to newspapermen that the man upon whom they had pinned their hopes for the pacification of Mexico could no longer be counted a decisive factor in the revolutionary movement.[34] And for a brief moment it seemed that they might even give serious thought to the possibility of recognizing Carranza's government. John Lind, Wilson's former Confidential Agent in Mexico, first broached the subject in a long letter to Bryan on April 16, 1915, which was filled with glowing praise of the First Chief and his regime, and in a more urgent appeal a few days later.[35] Then on April 23 a personal message from Carranza himself arrived at the State Department to bolster Lind's appeal. It was a statement promising the speedy inauguration of a civilian government in Mexico and the adoption of the kind of program that the First Chief knew would please the Washington authorities.[36]

Wilson and Bryan did not, however, heed these appeals or follow the logic of events in Mexico to its seemingly inexorable conclusion

[33] W. J. Bryan to J. Lind, April 18, 1915, Bryan Papers, National Archives.

[34] This is what "administration officials" told reporters on April 19, 1915, *New York Times*, April 20, 1915.

[35] J. Lind to W. J. Bryan, April 16, 1915, Bryan Papers, National Archives; J. Lind to W. J. Bryan, April 21, 1915, enclosing "Memorandum Submitted by John Lind," dated April 20, 1915, Wilson Papers.

[36] It included, among other things, (1) the definite guarantee that all foreigners would be given ample protection in life and property in accordance with Mexico's treaty obligations and be compensated for the losses they had suffered during the civil war; (2) the promise of a general amnesty for Mexicans and foreigners who had taken part in the troubles since early 1913; (3) separation of church and state and freedom of religion and worship under the provisions of the Reform Laws, but "clergymen who take or may have taken part in the internal strife shall not invoke their clerical investiture to evade responsibilities"; (4) settlement of the agrarian problem without resort to confiscations; (5) development of public education; and (6) specific provisions for ending military rule and inaugurating civil government. "The above articles," Carranza wrote in conclusion, "are a part of the program of the Revolution and constitute a pledge to the country, which the Constitutionalist Government will not fail to observe." V. Carranza to E. Arredondo, April 23, 1915, Bryan Papers, National Archives. Carranza later issued this statement in the form of a manifesto to the Mexican people. See below, p. 478.

during the following weeks by preparing the way for the recognition and outright support of the *Carrancista* regime. On the contrary, the stronger Carranza grew the stronger seemed to become the determination of the President and his advisers not to recognize the First Chief, and the more they began to mature plans of their own for the pacification of Mexico.

A number of forces and events combined during late April and May of 1915 to cause this hardening of attitude in Washington. One force was the heavy weight of organized Roman Catholic opinion in the United States. Ever since the triumph of the Constitutionalists over Huerta, Roman Catholic spokesmen had maintained a steady fire against the Wilson administration, accusing it of supporting a government that desecrated churches and murdered priests, nuns, and bishops.[37] The uproar became so great that the President himself, in March 1915, tried to quiet it by drafting a public letter affirming the administration's support of religious liberty in Mexico.[38] The one significant result of the publication of this letter on April 22 was to provoke the American bishops to remind Wilson that they were all still firmly opposed to any recognition of Carranza.[39] Neither at this time nor later was the President willing to concede that the Roman Catholic hierarchy had the right to dictate his Mexican policy.[40] None the less, they could not easily be ignored; and their attitude was a significant limiting factor in the formation of policy.

The decisive factor in the administration's refusal to think in terms

[37] See, e.g., the speech of Bishop Joseph Schrembs of Toledo at Baltimore on September 27, 1914, which James Cardinal Gibbons said he approved, in the New York *World*, September 28, 1914; speech of William Henry Cardinal O'Connell at Boston on November 15, 1914, *ibid.*, November 16, 1914; Archbishop John Ireland to Theodore Roosevelt, December 7, 1914, Roosevelt Papers; *America*, xi (July 18, September 5, October 3 and 10, 1914), 328, 502, 606, 630; *ibid.*, xii (November 7, December 12, 1914), 94-95, 222-223.

[38] It was W. J. Bryan to the Reverend Francis C. Kelley, president of the Catholic Church Extension Society, n.d., printed in the *New York Times*, April 22, 1915. For Wilson's draft, which he composed on his own typewriter, see W.W. to W. J. Bryan, March 17, 1915, enclosing "DRAFT OF LETTER," Bryan Papers, National Archives.

[39] As Dudley Field Malone implied in a letter to Wilson on April 22, 1915, Wilson Papers.

[40] Actually, President Wilson's sympathies in this whole question evidently lay more with the Constitutionalists than with the Roman Catholic spokesmen. Commenting upon the statement that Carranza had made in his message of April 23, 1915, cited above, Wilson wrote: "The position taken about the Church seems to me entirely justified in view of the history of that matter in Mexico." W.W. to W. J. Bryan, April 27, 1915, Bryan Papers, National Archives.

of recognizing Carranza was a deepening of conviction that the First Chief could never pacify Mexico, and that American support of his regime would only compound Mexico's misery and the plight of Americans in that country. For men far removed from the Mexican scene, this was not a wholly irrational conclusion. Villa still controlled vast stretches of territory in central and northern Mexico in the mid-spring of 1915, and these were the very areas where the bulk of American investments in Mexico were concentrated. American recognition of Carranza at this time might well have incited Villa to a campaign of depredation and might thus have necessitated the very thing that Wilson sought to avoid, that is, military intervention. Then there were other evidences of Carranza's inherent weakness—his apparent inability to capture or to hold Mexico City, his lack of any military power of his own, and what seemed to be his obvious inability to organize and govern the territories under his nominal control.

This view of Carranza was confirmed in a decisive way by Duval West at the very time that Obregón was pressing his campaign in central Mexico. The Confidential Agent went to Veracruz on March 24, 1915, and visited with the First Chief and his advisers until about April 5. West was much impressed by Carranza's character and patriotism, but equally so by what seemed to him overwhelming evidences of the First Chief's utter incapacity. The report that he sent in, telling of starvation, insubordination, near anarchy, and abuse of foreigners and their property in territories under Carranza's control, was, therefore, a gloomy one. Nor was he any more hopeful about the future:

"The Constitutionalist Government, under its present leaders, cannot establish peace in Mexico, because of the failure of its military leaders to obey the orders and decrees of the First Chief. Law and order must be first physically established by the exercise of force. General Carranza, personally, has not the qualifications for military leadership and, even if the movement were successful, the military leaders themselves would, undoubtedly, set General Carranza aside and bring about further differences. . . . The main factor in the revolutionary game is purely selfish. The common people are bearing the burden; they are paying the price and their interests *are not* being advanced by the revolution."[41]

West's report arrived in Washington in late April, well after the

[41] Duval West to the Secretary of State, from Veracruz, April 5, 1915, State Department Papers.

battle of Celaya and Carranza's occupation of Guadalajara. But since
the Confidential Agent confirmed what President Wilson and his advisers already believed was true, they accepted West's conclusions and
rather casually ignored the recent events on the battlefields of Mexico.
"I think we sent the right man," the President wrote to Secretary
Bryan on April 26, after reading West's report from Veracruz. "This
report carries conviction. It is disappointing, of course, but what we
wanted was the truth. I hope that West is to be here soon."[42]

The impact of West's report can be seen even more directly in a letter that Wilson wrote on the following day. Bryan had just sent him
a copy of Carranza's message of April 23 specifying the objectives of
the Constitutionalist movement. "This is a very sensible document
and I hope is sincerely meant," Wilson replied to the Secretary of
State, "though West's report, which you sent me the other day, does
not seem to afford much prospect of real control by Carranza."[43]
"There is nothing that we have at this time," Bryan thus told reporters
a few days later, "that we can regard as sufficient to raise a discussion
of the question of recognition of any government in Mexico."[44]

If not support of Carranza, then what? That was the question that
demanded some kind of an answer in Washington during May and
early June of 1915. Reports from Mexico City told of its agony not
only enduring but also increasing—of outright starvation among the
populace, of looting and murder of foreigners by hungry mobs, and
even of attacks upon members of the diplomatic corps.[45] Reports from
American consuls in various districts were equally gloomy; they described a Mexico in "the throes of anarchy, . . . prostrate in misery,
[with] famine . . . increasing and absolutely no hope . . . left."[46]

What could the American leaders possibly do? This was the period
of sharpest tension with Germany over the sinking of the *Lusitania*.

[42] W.W. to W. J. Bryan, April 26, 1915, Bryan Papers, National Archives.
[43] W.W. to W. J. Bryan, April 27, 1915, *ibid*.
[44] *New York Times*, April 30, 1915.
[45] The Brazilian Minister to Mexico to the Secretary of State, May 7, 1915, transmitting a message from the American Society of Mexico and the International Committee, *Foreign Relations, 1915*, pp. 689-690; the Swedish Legation at Mexico City to
the Swedish Minister in Washington, May 20, 1915, copy in the State Department
Papers.
[46] L. J. Canova to the Secretary of State, May 24, 1915, summarizing various dispatches and telegrams from Mexico, Wilson Papers. See also the long report on famine
conditions in Mexico issued by the American Red Cross and printed in the *New York
Times*, May 31, 1915.

It was difficult for President Wilson and Secretary Bryan to find any time at all during May 1915 to think about Mexico. And when they were able to turn aside from the more urgent business of state, their thoughts certainly did not stray toward military involvement south of the border. But while Wilson and Bryan were seeking ways to preserve the peace with Germany, other men were hard if quietly at work to lure them into deep entanglement in Mexico. Herein lies a story the full details of which still elude us, of how Leon J. Canova and other men in the administration almost succeeded in leading the President into intervention in behalf of a Mexican general in exile, Eduardo Iturbide, the former Governor of the Federal District of Mexico.

It began, perhaps, in December 1914, when Canova, who had gone with Villa to Mexico City following the Aguascalientes convention, spirited Iturbide out of the capital and helped him to escape from certain death before a *Villista* firing squad. Fleeing to the United States, Iturbide lost no time in rallying all the important refugee Mexican politicians, former *Huertista* generals, some disillusioned *Maderistas*, and Roman Catholic bishops, and in winning their support for a new counterrevolution, which he himself volunteered to lead. This movement he launched with the aid of certain American Catholic leaders at a so-called "Pacification" conference at San Antonio, Texas, on February 6, 1915.[47] Establishing his headquarters in New York soon afterward, Iturbide went to work to gather money and to win the one thing without which his project could never succeed—the support of the American government.

Whether Canova, who returned to the State Department to become assistant chief of the Latin American Affairs Division on April 16, 1915, and chief of the Mexican Affairs Division later in July, had any hand in the first stage of the Iturbide intrigue is not known, although it is certainly possible that he did. Moreover, Canova's exact connection with Iturbide from April on cannot be definitely determined.[48] But it seems altogether likely that Canova was working behind the scenes to open official doors to the counterrevolutionist and his co-conspirators.

In any event, they began by going as near to the supreme power

[47] Anderson Diary, February 2, 1915; *Washington Post*, February 6, 1915; the Reverend Francis C. Kelley to W.W., January 26, 1915, Wilson Papers.

[48] For evidence indicating a close understanding, see William Teitlebaum to H. J. Wright, August 17, 1915, State Department Papers.

as they could. On April 23, 1915, Manuel Calero, former Mexican Ambassador to the United States, had a long conference with Chandler P. Anderson, Lansing's assistant in the State Department, and told him some of Iturbide's plans.[49] Anderson was so impressed that he visited Iturbide in New York and returned to Washington to arrange a meeting between Iturbide and Bryan and Lansing.[50] It took place in Lansing's office, apparently, on May 19. Iturbide was optimistic and becomingly modest as he outlined his intentions. He had at least 20,000 armed men in Mexico who would rally at once to his standard, he said; indeed, the entire Mexican people would rise in support of his movement, for it was the only hope of constitutional government and permanent peace. The decisive factor, Iturbide went on to say, would be the moral support of the American government. With such assistance he could raise the money that he needed; without it, he would fail. He would not insist upon his own plans but would follow any leader who promised to bring peace to his country.

Bryan was not much impressed. Actually, he knew more about Iturbide's intrigue than the general suspected. He knew, for example, that the Roman Catholic leaders associated with Iturbide hoped to use the counterrevolutionist (and the State Department as well) to win repeal of the Reform laws of the Juárez era that provided for the disestablishment of the Church in Mexico.[51] The Secretary of State knew also that a number of former *Huertista* generals were already secretly recruiting men and gathering ammunition in El Paso, and that certain unnamed American and British investors were prepared to furnish money for the enterprise if it could win the endorsement of the Washington authorities.[52] To Bryan the whole business smelled of conspiracy

[49] Anderson Diary, April 23, 1915.

[50] *ibid.*, May 14, 1915. It should perhaps be added that Anderson had known about the Iturbide intrigue as early as February 2, 1915, when Iturbide's legal adviser in the United States had tried to persuade him to join forces with the counterrevolutionist. *ibid.*, February 2, 1915.

[51] Monsignor Francis C. Kelley of the Catholic Church Extension Society, who was the liaison between the Mexican and American bishops, had been interested in the Iturbide intrigue from its inception and had early tried to win Wilson's and Bryan's support for it. The two leaders learned from Father Kelley in mid-April 1915 that the hierarchy hoped to obtain the repeal of the Reform laws. See the Reverend F. C. Kelley to W.W., January 26, 1915, Wilson Papers, and W. J. Bryan to W.W., April 19, 1915, Bryan Papers, National Archives, summarizing F. C. Kelley to W. J. Bryan, c. April 17, 1915, a copy of which cannot be found.

[52] Z. L. Cobb to the Secretary of State, May 11 and 12, 1915, State Department Papers.

and reaction.[53] He was friendly enough in reply, but he made it plain to Iturbide that he would actively oppose his movement, and he warned that it was "not permissible" for any member of the administration to encourage it in any way. "The impression made upon me," wrote Chandler P. Anderson, who was present at the meeting, "was that the Secretary failed to see what practical advantages there were in Iturbide's movement, and had some undisclosed reason for discouraging it."[54]

With one avenue to the President thus barred, Iturbide tried another. Perhaps at Anderson's or Canova's suggestion (for Canova probably had some hand in these negotiations), he next appealed to the voluble Secretary of the Interior, Franklin K. Lane, who thought of himself as something of an expert on Mexico. Completely enchanted, Lane wrote at once to the President to tell him about Iturbide's plans and to give them his strong endorsement.[55]

Following this opening, Canova now came forward with the first of his several schemes to commit American power to the Iturbide movement and the destruction of the *Carrancista* regime. The President and Secretary of State had both been deeply moved by reports of starvation in Mexico and eager to find some way to use the American Red Cross for relief purposes.[56] Canova was encouraging. "I feel," he wrote to Bryan, "that this country has a great work before it, and that THE ADMINISTRATION IS ON THE THRESHOLD OF ITS OPPORTUNITY."[57] But how could such healing work be done? As it happened, Canova had a plan. Let the President put an embargo on the

---

[53] Two weeks later Bryan told C. P. Anderson that he mistrusted the Mexican exiles, as they had all supported Huerta. When Anderson replied that they were the conservative and intelligent class in Mexico and had learned their lesson, Bryan retorted that he feared "that the [same] people of this country had not learned their lesson; that the corresponding class in this country . . . were still reactionaries." Anderson Diary, June 1, 1915.

[54] *ibid.*, May 19, 1915.

[55] Apparently Iturbide talked much more fully to Lane than he had to Bryan. He told Lane that he planned to establish a new constitutional government under Manuel Bonilla of Chihuahua, who was the surviving member of the Madero Cabinet who could claim the succession to the presidency under the Mexican constitution; that he had 28,000 men at his disposal; and that there would be no lack of popular support if he could enter Mexico with food for the starving people. F. K. Lane to W.W., c. May 26, 1915, enclosing a memorandum of his conversation with Iturbide dated May 25, 1915, Wilson Papers.

[56] W. J. Bryan to W.W., May 22, 1915; W.W. to W. J. Bryan, May 23, 1915, both in the Bryan Papers, National Archives.

[57] L. J. Canova to the Secretary of State, May 24, 1915, Wilson Papers.

shipment of arms to Mexico and then issue a statement warning the Mexican factions that the American government was determined to save the people of Mexico from starvation. "And, while engaged in relieving the corporal needs of the people," the statement might continue, "attention will be given to the political requirements of your country, the communal interests of your people being studiously guarded until a new government, of the Mexican people and for the Mexican people, can be established, and then our duty to humanity and to the world at large will have been done. Religious liberty will be re-established, and the clergy of all denominations will be entitled to exercise their offices. All church, or other real property, confiscated by revolutionary bands, or others, without proper or due process of law, since February 1913 shall be re-occupied by their legal owners."[58]

Canova talked with Chandler Anderson about his plan on May 28, 1915; perhaps he also talked with Iturbide at the same time. "It would seem to be an easy matter," Anderson agreed, "to bring about an universal appeal from the Mexican people to this Government, or to the people of the United States, to save them from starvation; in other words, to open the way for peaceable intervention."[59] Better still, here was the perfect opportunity for the Iturbide movement. It was, Anderson suggested to the Secretary of State on June 1, to ask the Iturbide people to distribute the food throughout Mexico under the aegis of American consuls and the American army.[60]

Bryan's heart warmed at the thought of doing so much good, but he promptly vetoed the suggestion that the Mexican exiles in the United States be used as the instruments of any salvation.[61]

The conspirators in the State Department were, however, not discouraged. They and Iturbide now had direct access to the President and the Cabinet through Secretary Lane. More important, the President himself was deeply concerned and beginning to take a direct hand. Three developments precipitated the sudden revival of Wilson's interest. First, Duval West came to the White House on May 24 to supplement his written dispatches with an oral report. Since writing in early April from Veracruz, West had gone to Zapata's headquarters at Tlaltizapan, south of Mexico City.[62] To the President he confirmed what

---

[58] Copy of Canova's draft statement, received June 1, 1915, in the Papers of Chandler P. Anderson, Library of Congress.

[59] Anderson Diary, May 28, 1915.   [60] *ibid.*, June 1, 1915.

[61] *ibid.*

[62] For his report, see his memorandum, "Mexico City to Tlaltizapan," dated April 16, 1915, State Department Papers.

his last two reports had affirmed, namely, that conditions in Mexico were indescribably bad and that none of the three revolutionary factions had the ability to dominate and pacify the country.[63] Second, about two days after West's visit Wilson received a long letter from the correspondent David Lawrence, who was on intimate terms with the *Carrancista* representatives in Washington and whose judgment Wilson deeply respected. Confirming all that West had said, Lawrence went on to warn that it would be difficult to avoid wholesale intervention if conditions grew much worse. To avoid this dire consequence, Lawrence suggested that the President open negotiations with all the Mexican leaders, the subordinate generals as well as Carranza, Villa, and Zapata, and demand that they resolve their differences and form a provisional government that the United States could recognize. Carranza would probably object, Lawrence added, but Obregón might cooperate, and Villa would certainly do so.[64] The third precipitating factor was the arrival in Washington on about May 27 of a report that Carranza's forces had seized six hundred tons of corn purchased by the International Relief Committee of Mexico City while it was en route to the former capital.[65]

It took Wilson little time to conclude that the policy of watchful waiting, which he and Bryan had followed substantially since the late summer of 1914, must soon come to an end. He gave no indication at this time of what he thought of the Iturbide intrigue; perhaps he was not much impressed and shared Bryan's suspicions of the exiles. In any event, he decided to avoid any commitment for the time being and to try Lawrence's suggestion first. Thus on May 27 and 28, while he was preparing and issuing an appeal for American contributions for Mexican relief,[66] he also drafted a warning to be sent to the Mexican leaders and told reporters that he would issue an important statement within a few days.[67] Then followed a heated Cabinet discussion of the President's draft on June 1. Lane pressed Iturbide's claims with undisguised partisanship, while Bryan "thought the way ought to be left open to recognize one of the men, Carranza, who had been fighting so long for liberty, and not take up a man who would probably play in with the reactionaries."[68] He was no champion of any faction,

[63] *New York Times*, May 26, 1915; New York *World*, June 1 and 2, 1915.
[64] D. Lawrence to W.W., May 27, 1915, Wilson Papers.
[65] *New York Times*, May 29, 1915.
[66] For which, see the New York *World*, May 29, 1915.
[67] *ibid.; New York Times*, May 29, 1915.
[68] D. F. Houston, *Eight Years with Wilson's Cabinet*, I, 133.

the Secretary of State went on, but the President ought to make certain that he did not exclude the possibility of recognizing one of the warring factions in Mexico if it came out on top in the near future.[69]

Wilson did not take sides at the Cabinet meeting on June 1, but on the following day, in an exchange with Bryan about the final wording of the warning to the Mexican leaders, he indicated clearly enough that he agreed with the Secretary of State and had no intention of making a commitment to any Mexican individual or faction. "I am entirely open to anything that events may open to us," he wrote to Bryan on June 2, "even the recognition of Carranza if he should develop the necessary influence and begin to bring real order out of chaos. But I think our statement ought to precipitate things (in the chemical sense) and open up either this or some other channel of action."[70]

The President revised his draft after the Cabinet meeting in response to Bryan's criticism and sent the new version to the State Department on June 2. Bryan and Counselor Lansing made a few hurried changes and then put it on all the wires to Mexico.[71] Written in the form of a personal statement by the President of the United States, it began with a recital of recent events in Mexico and a description of that country's tragic plight. The American people and government, the statement went on, did not claim the right to settle Mexican affairs, but they could not stand by indifferently while their neighbors starved and were denied the blessings of constitutional government. In words increasingly ominous the President spelled out his warning:

"It is time, therefore, that the Government of the United States should frankly state the policy which, in these extraordinary circumstances, it becomes its duty to adopt. It must presently do what it has not hitherto done or felt at liberty to do, lend its active moral support to some man or group of men, if such may be found, who can rally the suffering people of Mexico to their support in an effort to ignore, if they cannot unite, the warring factions of the country, return to the Constitution of the republic so long in abeyance, and set up a Government at Mexico City which the great powers of the world can recognize and deal with—a government with whom the program of the revolution will be a business and not merely a platform.

[69] W. J. Bryan to W.W., June 2, 1915, *The Lansing Papers*, II, 533, recapitulating Bryan's arguments of the day before.

[70] W.W. to W.J. Bryan, June 2, 1915, *ibid.*, p. 534.

[71] For the discussions over the editing of the revised version, see the letters printed in *ibid.*, pp. 532-535.

"I, therefore, publicly and very solemnly, call upon the leaders of factions in Mexico to act, to act together, and to act promptly for the relief and redemption of their prostrate country.

"I feel it to be my duty to tell them that, if they cannot accommo-

The Class in Reading and Writing
Kirby in the New York *World*

date their differences and unite for this great purpose within a very short time, this Government will be constrained to decide what means should be employed by the United States in order to help Mexico to save herself and serve her people."[72]

[72] *New York Times*, June 3, 1915.

What did it all mean? Did it signify, as some Washington correspondents believed, that the President intended to recognize Carranza if he could occupy Mexico City and give some proof of capacity to control the *Villistas*?[73] Did it mean, as the German Ambassador was told, that the administration planned to use General Iturbide to establish order in Mexico?[74] Or did it mean that the President had in mind establishing his own regime? No one, not even President Wilson himself, knew the answers in the early days of June 1915.

Virtually all reports from Mexico during the two weeks following the issuance of President Wilson's warning seemed to bring good news. To allay the President's fears for Mexico City, Carranza had announced on June 1 that he would permit foodstuffs to go to the former capital.[75] Even more encouraging was the fact that Constitutionalist spokesmen in Veracruz intimated to American reporters that Carranza would welcome Wilson's mediation, while the First Chief told Special Agent John R. Silliman on June 7 that "he would disappoint any enemies of Mexico and the United States who expected defiance from him."[76] On June 11 Carranza issued a manifesto to the Mexican nation announcing the near-triumph of his armies, calling upon his rivals to submit to his authority, and promising the speedy inauguration of a full-fledged constitutional government through national elections.[77] Finally, on about June 14 a Constitutionalist army under General Pablo Gonzáles opened a campaign to capture Mexico City. Its success, which seemed beyond doubt, would mean the final destruction of the now-farcical Conventionist "government," which had answered Wilson's warning of June 2 defiantly, and the withdrawal of the *Zapatistas* to the State of Morelos—good results from Wilson's point of view. At about the same time, General Villa addressed a concilatory overture to Carranza[78] and a reply to the President of the United States. It affirmed that the *Villistas* stood ready to "invite again to concord all the

[73] *ibid.*, June 5, 1915.
[74] Ambassador von Bernstorff to T. von Bethmann Hollweg, June 9, 1915, German F. O. Archives.
[75] E. Arredondo to W.W., June 2, 1915, Wilson Papers.
[76] New York *World*, June 7, 1915; J. R. Silliman to the Secretary of State, June 7, 1915, State Department Papers.
[77] V. Carranza, "Manifesto to the Nation," *Foreign Relations, 1915*, pp. 705-707; *New York Times*, June 13, 1915.
[78] F. Villa to V. Carranza, June 10, 1915, printed in the *New York Times*, June 15, 1915.

Mexican people so that we may united work for the establishment of the revolutionary principles, and especially for the solution of the agrarian question and for the dissemination of education among the masses."[79]

To Wilson it was all enormously encouraging, particularly the unexpected display of seeming good will in Veracruz. Perhaps Mexico was nearing the end of her troubles; perhaps Carranza would accept American help. What seemed to be an almost certain indication came to the President on June 16 in a letter from his new adviser David Lawrence. He reported that Charles A. Douglas, Carranza's legal agent in Washington, had just said that the First Chief knew that no Mexican government could long survive without American support, and that Carranza would accept American "interference" at this time even though he might resent it.[80] "I have been feeling, the past twenty-four hours or so," Wilson wrote to Lansing after reading Lawrence's letter, "that it was possible we were not using all the influences we might use in Mexico to guide what is taking place there. Would it be possible to find some direct but unofficial channel through which we could convey to General Carranza this impression: That it was within the possibilities that we might recognize him, as things are now apparently shaping themselves, —at any rate that that possibility was not excluded by anything we had yet determined upon, —but that he need not expect us to consider that course seriously unless he went the full length of conciliation and conference with all factions with a view to the accommodation upon which the opinion of the whole world now insists. He cannot in our view afford to insist upon establishing his own dominion unless he first makes a genuine effort to unite all groups and parties."[81]

Lansing, who had succeeded Bryan as Acting Secretary of State only a few days before, quickly drafted the message and sent it to Silliman on June 18. It contained both a threat and a promise. The former consisted of a warning that the American government was determined to adopt such measures as might "be expedient to preserve Mexico for herself and the world." The promise was a large one—that the United States *might* recognize Carranza if only he would go "the full length of conciliation and conference with all the principal factions,

[79] F. Villa, proclamation dated June 10, 1915, *Foreign Relations, 1915*, pp. 701-703. This message was brought to Washington by Villa's personal envoy, Manuel Bonilla.
[80] D. Lawrence to W.W., June 16, 1915, Wilson Papers.
[81] W.W. to R. Lansing, June 17, 1915, *The Lansing Papers*, II, 535.

with the aim of adjusting differences and restoring peaceful conditions."[82]

It was, Wilson knew, the most important note that he had sent to Mexico since the fall of Huerta, and he wondered whether Silliman alone could make the right kind of impression upon the First Chief. "I fear," the President wrote to Lansing on June 18, "he rather bores and irritates Carranza, from what I have learned." As it turned out, Charles A. Douglas was about to leave for Veracruz. "Would it not be well," Wilson continued, "to have a talk with him (not at your office, but at your house and as privately, as much away from the newspapers, as possible) and let him go down with a full understanding of our position, namely that Carranza must meet every honest advance half way if he expects to win our confidence, and that he must win our confidence, at least in some degree, if he hopes for ultimate recognition."[83]

Wilson's hopes for an early peaceful settlement did not long survive once Carranza understood the full import of the President's message. Silliman saw the First Chief on June 21 and urged him to take some initiative in calling an all-Mexican peace conference. Under no circumstances would he deal with Villa, Carranza retorted. Villa and his cohorts must either submit to military trial or else leave the country. "He appeared somewhat perplexed," Silliman continued in his report, "that the Government of the United States should be concerned for adjustment [upon a basis of] conciliation . . . since any revolutionary Government established upon such theories would inevitably and necessarily soon be found to be disappointing, ineffective and fruitless. The intimation of possible recognition did not in the least affect his impassive face. He did not want recognition conditioned on conciliation. The determination of the United States to adopt any other measures than the recognition and support of the Constitutionalist cause would be a regrettable injustice and great calamity for two friendly nations. If the Government of the United States will maintain neutral attitude the Constitutionalist cause will subdue the opposition and win recognition."[84] In other words, the war in Mexico must proceed in its bloody gyrations.

[82] The Secretary of State ad interim to Special Agent Silliman, June 18, 1915, *Foreign Relations, 1915*, pp. 715-716.

[83] W.W. to R. Lansing, June 18, 1915, State Department Papers.

[84] Special Agent Silliman to the Secretary of State ad interim, June 22, 1915, *Foreign Relations, 1915*, pp. 718-719.

To this news from Veracruz Wilson reacted with disgust and anger generated as much by the memory of old frustrations in dealing with the First Chief as by Carranza's immediate refusal of cooperation. "I think I have never known of a man more impossible to deal with on human principles than this man Carranza," the President wrote, for example, on July 2, 1915.[85]

Now what? The American government had pledged its solemn word to the world and given explicit warning to the First Chief that it would impose its own solution if the factional leaders could not find one. Inaction no longer seemed possible, and Wilson's thoughts turned to a solution that Lansing had first proposed in March 1915 and Canova had revived only a few days before Carranza refused to deal with Villa.[86] It was the suggestion of Pan-American cooperation in some kind of intervention, such as would allay Latin American fears of *Yanqui* imperialism and give a kind of legitimacy to what would actually have to be unilateral action by the United States. Wilson and Lansing had discussed the possibility before Carranza's reply of June 22 arrived in Washington; now they acted quickly to sound out the Ambassadors of Argentina, Brazil, and Chile, and the Ministers of three small Central and South American republics.[87]

This would be the administration's policy for Mexico, but how could it be carried out, and to what end? In a long letter to the President, now at his summer home at Cornish, New Hampshire, Lansing offered an answer on July 5, 1915. It was plain, he wrote, that responsible government in Mexico could come only through the "revolutionary element now composed of hostile factions," and not through the old aristocratic party. The main problem, therefore, was to harmonize the factions representing the Revolution. The ideal solution would be a conference of the revolutionary leaders such as Wilson had already suggested. But it was obvious, Lansing went on, that Carranza would never cooperate. Since this was true, the Secretary of State further explained, the "attitude" of the American government should be "embodied in the following propositions":

[85] W.W. to R. Lansing, July 2, 1915, State Department Papers.

[86] For Lansing's early proposal, see above, p. 464; for Canova's suggestion, see R. Lansing to W.W., June 16, 1915, *ibid.*

[87] W.W. to R. Lansing, June 22, 1915, *The Lansing Papers*, II, 536; R. Lansing to W.W., June 25, 1915, *ibid.*, p. 537; W.W. to R. Lansing, June 26, 1915, State Department Papers; W.W. to R. Lansing, July 2, 1915, *The Lansing Papers*, II, 537.

1. It is manifest that, in view of the personal animosities, jealousies and ambitions of the factional leaders nothing can be accomplished through them to restore peace and stable government.

2. Carranza, Villa and other factional leaders must retire and not seek dominant leadership.

3. This Government will not recognize as legal any government headed or controlled by any one of these leaders and will exert its moral influence to prevent the establishment of such a government in any part of Mexico.

4. The determination of this Government to eliminate the present factional leaders by withdrawal of moral support should be notified in plain terms to the various factions.

5. An invitation should be issued to the factions by the American Government, agreeing to identical action, to meet in conference through their lesser chiefs for the purpose of organizing a coalition provisional government with the understanding that, provided such government is unquestionably representative of the bulk of the revolutionary element, this Government and the other [Latin American] governments cooperating with it, will recognize it and renew diplomatic relations with Mexico.

6. This Government will aid so far as possible such coalition government by preventing arms and ammunition from reaching parties hostile to it and by employing such other means as it may properly employ to insure the stability and permanency of such government until constitutional government can be restored.[88]

It was, obviously, a plan not without certain fateful possibilities—the possibility, for example, of armed conflict if Carranza refused to retire and the American government then had to compel his withdrawal. As events would soon demonstrate, moreover, it was also a somewhat naïve solution because it was grounded upon the assumption that Carranza's subalterns in the field would gladly dispose of him and accept American mediation of the civil war. None the less, Wilson eagerly endorsed the policy that Lansing had outlined. "The suggestions contained in your letter of the fifth," he replied at once to the Secretary of State, "furnish an excellent foundation, it seems to me, for planning something definite and final in the Mexican matter, and run very nearly along the lines of my own thought." What, Wilson went on, expressing his random thoughts, did Manuel Bonilla and General Felipe Angeles, two *Villistas* who were then in Washington, have in mind? Did Iturbide represent anything substantial, or was

[88] R. Lansing to W.W., July 5, 1915, *ibid.*, pp. 538-539.

he working with "the scoundrel, Huerta"?[89] In the event that Carranza refused to cooperate, should not the ABC diplomats preside at the conference of Mexican revolutionary leaders? It would be well, the President added, to avoid wounding Mexican sensibilities; the revolutionary leaders could be used and controlled, provided one knew how to "play these men as they are."[90]

The outcome of this interchange was Wilson's suggestion or approval of two initial moves. First, Lansing should press ahead to obtain an early meeting with the Pan-American diplomats. Second, the Secretary of State should call Wilson's former Confidential Agent, Paul Fuller, Senior, to Washington and ask him to establish close liaison with the representatives of the various Mexican factions who were then in Washington. As it turned out, Lansing was not able to arrange a meeting with the Latin American envoys until early August, but Fuller came to Washington and set to work at once.

Other men, eager to make the most of the new opportunities afforded by the administration's decision for intervention, were also hard at work at the same time. For Canova it was a time of vindication and seeming fulfillment. Having sought for months by devious means to commit his government to the destruction of Carranza's regime, he now came forward on July 17 in open championship of the counter-revolutionary elements clustered around General Iturbide. The time was ripe for action, he explained in a long letter to the Secretary of State. He had been, Canova continued, in close communication with Iturbide and all the spokesmen of the various Mexican leaders and parties, including Federico Gamboa of the Catholic Party. All of them had promised to "unite under the standard of any man or group of men who would be countenanced by President Wilson." If Lansing approved, Canova went on, he could submit the names of leaders who

[89] General Victoriano Huerta, the deposed dictator of Mexico, had come to the United States from his exile in Spain in April 1915, and once on American soil he had begun to organize a counterrevolution among ex-Federal soldiers in El Paso and Juárez. Just a few days before Wilson wrote this letter to Lansing, the old warrior had set out for El Paso and had been arrested and removed from his train at Newman, New Mexico, by a United States deputy marshal on a warrant charging Huerta with conspiring to violate American neutrality laws. *New York Times*, June 27, 1915. Taken to El Paso, Huerta was released on bond but was rearrested and imprisoned again on July 3, 1915. Failing to produce bond, he remained in jail until later in the year, when he developed severe intestinal troubles and was removed to a private home in El Paso under guard. He died there on January 13, 1916, after receiving the last rites of the Roman Catholic Church, at the age of sixty-one. *ibid.*, July 4, 1915, January 14, 1916.

[90] W.W. to R. Lansing, July 8, 1915, State Department Papers.

could unite all the factions except the inner group around Carranza. This *junta* would control most of northern Mexico from the outset; it would soon sweep southward with the support of most of the *Carrancistas*; more important, its objective was peace and order "under conditions which will be laid down to its leaders by President Wilson." It was, Canova urged, obvious that the criminals and anarchists around Carranza could never re-establish constitutional government. Support of the better elements who wanted to do the job with American help was "the quickest and best solution with the least responsibility for the United States and the greatest guarantees for the welfare of Mexico."[91]

Between the middle and the end of July 1915 leaders in the State Department concerned with Mexico—Lansing, Fuller, Boaz W. Long, head of the Latin American Affairs Division, and Chandler P. Anderson—matured a comprehensive plan for intervention to present to the Pan-American diplomats. The convictions of all these officials were substantially the same as those that Canova held.[92] Their plan, which was completed on about July 30, was also like Canova's—indeed, was modeled on it. It envisaged the establishment of a new provisional Mexican government under a leader, perhaps a member of Madero's Cabinet, whom most of the factions would support; the retirement of Carranza, Villa, and Zapata; and American and Pan-American recognition and financial support of the new regime.[93]

Precisely who the new Provisional President would be, the leaders in the State Department were not yet ready to say, except that he could not be Carranza or any leader prominently associated with his government. Perhaps he would be one of the men around Villa, like Vasquez Tagle, General Angeles, or Manuel Bonilla. Fuller was intimate with this group and seemed to favor them. Perhaps he would be Iturbide or another of the exiles. Iturbide was still willing; indeed, at this time he was busier than ever lobbying among administration leaders and personal friends of President Wilson. As volunteers abounded, the question of leadership did not seem acute. The larger task ahead was to win the blessing of the Pan-American diplomats and their governments for the plan. Once this was done, the job of reconstructing Mexico could begin.

[91] L. J. Canova to R. Lansing, July 17, 1915, *ibid.*

[92] e.g., see B. W. Long's comments on a series of documents that Lansing sent to Fuller on July 30, 1915. R. Lansing to P. Fuller, Sr., with enclosures, July 30, 1915, *ibid.*

[93] *ibid.; New York Times*, July 31, August 3 and 5, 1915.

Sharp new dangers that threatened to provoke unilateral military action by the United States arose even before the Pan-American conference could assemble.

The first was the possibility that the plight of Mexico City would become so horrible that the American Government could no longer avoid going to its rescue. During the last two weeks in June, General Gonzáles and his Constitutionalist army slowly closed like a vise upon the beleaguered city now cut off from all sources of supply and communication with the outside world. While armies fought in the outskirts, the hungry mobs rioted and looted for food within. "The very much feared bread riots began this morning when the mobs sacked all the markets and grocery stores," the Brazilian Minister reported on June 25.[94] Neither the Minister nor the newspaper correspondents could get any messages through to Washington for the next two weeks. When a report from Silliman in Veracruz did arrive at the State Department on about July 10, it told of continued anarchy and wholesale threats by the *Zapatistas* in Mexico City to kill all Americans before they evacuated the city.[95] Actually, no such catastrophe occurred when Gonzáles finally entered the former capital on July 10, 1915.

He brought food and order with him, but a worse crisis than before ensued when he left the city in pursuit of the *Zapatistas* on July 18. For a brief time the local authorities tried to exert some control, but the city was in a state of anarchy and starvation by July 26.[96] "As to food, we have nothing," the Brazilian Minister reported three days later. ". . . It is really an unbearable situation for all."[97] "Conditions desperate. Getting worse daily," the American Red Cross representative in Mexico City added in a dispatch on July 31. ". . . Practically no grain for sale. Authentic cases of death and collapse from starvation. Some people eating weeds, grass, leaves, dead horses, and mules."[98]

Officials in Washington had followed these developments with growing alarm but had postponed action in the hope that the crisis would soon pass. After receiving the reports from Silliman and Consul Wil-

[94] J. M. Cardoso de Oliveira to the Secretary of State, June 25, 1915, sent to Veracruz by courier and transmitted from there on June 30, 1915, State Department Papers. For a report on how this message was transmitted, see the *New York Times*, July 1, 1915.

[95] J. R. Silliman to the Secretary of State, July 10, 1915, State Department Papers.

[96] J. R. Silliman to the Secretary of State, two telegrams, July 28, 1915, *ibid.*; Consul W. W. Canada (Veracruz) to the Secretary of State, July 28, 1915, *ibid.*

[97] J. M. Cardoso de Oliveira to the Secretary of State, July 29, 1915, *Foreign Relations, 1915*, pp. 731-732.

[98] Dispatch of Charles J. O'Connor, printed in the *New York Times*, August 3, 1915.

liam W. Canada in Veracruz on July 29,[99] however, Lansing could delay no longer. "Say to . . . [Carranza]," he instructed Special Agent Silliman, "that this Government looks to him to open quickly the railway to Mexico City and to use every effort at his command to keep it open in order that this horrible situation which has existed for months with growing intensity may be relieved immediately."[100] The First Chief must have acted quickly in response, for González occupied Mexico City again on August 3, brought in food and supplies, and reopened railway communication with Veracruz soon afterward. The long ordeal of the once splendid city was finally over.

While the situation in Mexico City was at its worst, a second crisis was coming to a head in Veracruz. It had been set off on June 18, 1915, when William W. Canada, the American Consul in the city and a violent foe of the *Carrancista* regime, had reported that the Governor of the State of Veracruz, General Cándido Aguilar, was inciting Mexicans to attack foreigners.[101] Lansing sent a sharp note to Carranza on June 22 demanding Aguilar's removal; and when no reply came promptly, he repeated the demand on July 3 in words that threatened war. "Say to Carranza," the Secretary's instructions to Silliman read, "[that] retention this official in position where rights [of] foreigners [are] concerned would be indication [of] lack of regard for foreign interests and unfriendly act toward Government of United States."[102] Appalled by the severity of the ultimatum, Silliman obtained permission to soften the note that he presented to the First Chief on about July 12, 1915.[103] Carranza refused to acknowledge, much less to heed, the demand and Lansing struck back on August 10 by asking Secretary of the Navy Daniels to send the battleships *Louisiana* and *New Hampshire* and other lesser craft to Veracruz.[104] The crisis passed quickly, however, when Silliman reported on August 11 that all threats against foreigners in Veracruz had ceased, and that General Aguilar had issued a public statement expressing his regret that any had ever been made.[105]

[99] For these, see above, fn. 96.

[100] R. Lansing to Special Agent Silliman, July 29, 1915, State Department Papers.

[101] W. W. Canada to the Secretary of State, June 18, 1915, *ibid*.

[102] R. Lansing to Special Agent Silliman, July 3, 1915, *ibid*.

[103] J. R. Silliman to the Secretary of State, July 7, 8, and 12, 1915; R. Lansing to J. R. Silliman, July 9 and 10, 1915, all in *ibid*.

[104] R. Lansing to the Secretary of the Navy, August 10, 1915; R. Lansing to W.W., August 10, 1915, both in *ibid*.; *New York Times*, August 11, 1915.

[105] *ibid*., August 12, 1915. In response Lansing arranged to cancel the sailing of the warships to Mexican waters.

Finally, there was the danger that Villa, whose power and resources were waning by the day,[106] would launch a desperate campaign of depredation against foreigners in northern Mexico and thus provoke American military intervention before the President's and Secretary of State's plans could be fairly launched. In dire need of funds, Villa seized the stock of foreign merchants in Chihuahua and gave signs of preparing a wholesale campaign of loot in late July and early August;[107] shortly afterward, he threatened to impose a confiscatory tax on foreign mining companies in the territory under his control. Conflict with Villa was far from Lansing's plans at this time, for American action against Pancho might disrupt the Pan-American discussions, now in their early stages, and end by destroying the strongest counterbalance to Carranza's power.[108] The Secretary of State, therefore, made arrangements with Secretary of Agriculture David F. Houston to permit the inspection and importation of Mexican cattle at El Paso, so that Villa could obtain funds by the sale of beef in the United States. At the same time, Lansing sent General Hugh L. Scott to the border to tell his old friend Villa about the new arrangement and to persuade him to withdraw his threat to levy heavy new taxes on foreign mining interests.[109] The Secretary of State apparently also instructed Scott to inform Villa that the United States would never recognize Carranza.[110]

By thus threatening Carranza and cajoling Villa, Lansing averted any open conflict on the eve of the Pan-American conference on Mexico. That conference, Lansing believed, could now proceed to plan definitively for the future of the Mexican people.

Envoys from six Latin American nations[111] met the Secretary of State and Paul Fuller, Senior, for the opening discussions in Lansing's

[106] e.g., Z. L. Cobb to the Secretary of State, July 14, 1915, State Department Papers.

[107] Z. L. Cobb to the Secretary of State, July 19, August 1, 1915; G. C. Carothers to the Secretary of State, July 19, August 3 and 5, 1915, all in *ibid.*

[108] As Lansing explained in a letter to the President on August 9, 1915, *The Lansing Papers*, II, 547-548.

[109] H. L. Scott to the Secretary of State, August 10, 1915, State Department Papers.

[110] "You remember I told you that Mr. Lansing told me to say to Villa that under no circumstances would we recognize Carranza. I had a lucid interval down there while talking to Villa, and did not tell him what Secretary Lansing told me to tell him, as I believe that matters of that kind should be held back when dealing with primitive people." H. L. Scott to J. R. Garfield, October 14, 1915, Scott Papers.

[111] They were Ambassador Domicio da Gama of Brazil, Ambassador Eduardo Súarez-Mujica of Chile, Ambassador Romulo S. Naón of Argentina, Minister Ignacio Calderón of Bolivia, Minister Carlos Maria de Pena of Uruguay, and Minister Joaquín Méndez of Guatemala.

private office during the late afternoons of August 5 and 6, 1915. From the outset Lansing dominated the conversations and revealed his obvious purpose, which was to lead his colleagues to approval of the Washington government's plan by gradual stages. His argument, phrased so as to appeal to the Latin American mind, ran something like this: The American government has no desire to interfere in the internal affairs of its southern neighbor; it wants only to help the Mexican people restore peace and constitutional government. Villa, Zapata, and Carranza have all demonstrated their inability to do the job, but the task cannot be accomplished by outsiders, for the sovereignty of Mexico now resides in the various revolutionary factions. The solution lies, therefore, in finding some factional leader, perhaps the constitutional successor to Madero, behind whom the vast majority of the revolutionary element can and will unite.

The Latin American diplomats, all of whom represented conservative regimes but were also somewhat fearful of the threat of American military intervention, responded exactly as Lansing had hoped they would. "In the discussions," the Secretary reported to the President after the second session on August 6, "I found that there was unanimous agreement that Carranza was impossible, that even if he triumphed it would mean continued disorder. The disposition was to eliminate from consideration as the head of a government to be recognized all the present heads of factions and to seek a man who would draw the secondary chiefs to him. It was felt too that the man to establish the government must be named to us by Mexicans and, if possible, should be one with a measure of constitutional right."[112]

The upshot of these exploratory talks was agreement on two procedures. The first was that the appeal to the Mexican leaders, which the Chilean Ambassador had prepared earlier at Lansing's request, should be dispatched within a few days. Lansing was frankly doubtful that this move would yield any results, but he concurred, mainly in order to avoid controversy and because he thought the step would do no harm. The second was agreement that the conferees should proceed as soon as possible to work out plans for establishing a Mexican regime that their own governments should recognize and support if, as Lansing was confident would happen, the revolutionary leaders failed to unite on their own in a new all-Mexican revolutionary regime. In this step, the Secretary advised the President, "lies our hope." "For a con-

---

[112] R. Lansing to W.W., August 6, 1915, State Department Papers, printed in part in *The Lansing Papers*, II, 543-544.

ference composed largely of Latin-Americans," he added, "we made rapid progress."[113]

To President Wilson, the question was whether the conferees in Washington had not made too rapid progress in the wrong direction. During these days he was at "Harlarkenden" in New Hampshire, far removed from the heat and excitement of the capital. From there he followed the proceedings of the Pan-American conference with a watchful eye; and all the while convictions were forming in his mind that were capable of compelling a sudden turn in American policy toward Mexico.

As late as July 8, 1915, it will be recalled, the President had strongly endorsed Lansing's plan for the removal of Villa, Zapata, and Carranza and the establishment of a new provisional Mexican government under Pan-American auspices. Lansing and his advisers in the State Department had then proceeded with these plans on the assumption that the President still approved. At some time during the following month, however, Wilson must have given a searching second thought to all aspects of the Mexican problem. We do not know precisely *when*, nor can we say with any great confidence *why*, this re-evaluation occurred. He was, certainly, impressed by the steady growth of Carranza's military power during July and early August, and he believed, as he wrote to Lansing, that Villa was "on the verge of collapse."[114] He had, apparently, never believed that Iturbide or any of the other leaders in exile offered hope for the reconstruction of their country. On the contrary, he seems to have had a growing suspicion that there was a sinister connection between the counterrevolutionary *juntas* and the monied interests in the United States who were (as he thought) scheming to regain control in Mexico.[115] Finally, for reasons that we do not know, his faith in the Mexican Revolution seemed to grow during the summer of 1915, in spite of his intermittent irritation with that Revolution's leaders. What was happening, he obviously still believed, was a bright chapter in the history of mankind's struggle for freedom and democracy. He voiced these sentiments in a moving

[113] *ibid.* See also the two transcripts of the stenographic record of these discussions entitled "Conference Held at the Office of the Secretary of State . . . August 5, 1915," and "Continuation of Mexican Conference, August 6, 1915," MSS. in the State Department Papers; *New York Times*, August 6 and 7, 1915; and New York *World*, August 6, 1915.

[114] W.W. to R. Lansing, August 7, 1915, *The Lansing Papers*, II, 546.

[115] e.g., W.W. to E. M. House, telegram and letter, July 3, 1915, Baker Collection and Wilson Papers.

way in an address at Independence Hall in Philadelphia on July 4, 1915, as follows:

"You know what a big question there is in Mexico. Eighty-five per cent. of the Mexican people have never been allowed to have a look-in in regard to their Government and the rights which have been exercised by the other 15 per cent. Do you suppose that circumstance is not sometimes in my thought? I know the American people have a heart that will beat just as strong for those millions in Mexico as it will beat for any other millions anywhere else in the world, and when they once know what is at stake in Mexico they will know what ought to be done in Mexico.

"You hear a great deal stated about the property loss in Mexico, and I deplore it with all my heart. . . . Man's individual rights have met with many deplorable circumstances, but back of it all is the struggle of the people, and while we think of the one in the foreground, let us not forget the other in the background."[116]

Even though he must have been growing extremely dubious about Lansing's plans for intervention, Wilson said nothing to indicate this change of mind until the Secretary of State sent him a copy of the appeal to the Mexican revolutionary leaders that the Chilean Ambassador had drafted. This appeal included a plea for general elections and the speedy establishment of a constitutional government. "Approve communication drawn by conference and plan for session in New York on Wednesday to consider second step [that is, that the conference proceed to consider plans to establish a new provisional Mexican government if the revolutionary chieftains failed to come together]," Wilson informed Lansing at once by telegram on August 8. "Would suggest, however, that this point be dwelt upon: the first and most essential step in settling affairs of Mexico is not to call general elections. It seems to me necessary that a provisional government essentially revolutionary in character should take action to institute reforms by decree before the full forms of the constitution are resumed. This was the original program of the revolution and seems to me probably an essential part of it."[117]

It was a message vastly more meaningful than is apparent at first glance. To be sure, Wilson apparently still approved Lansing's plan to proceed to the "second step" beyond the issuance of the appeal to the revolutionary leaders. On the other hand, his insistence that the

[116] *New York Times*, July 5, 1915.
[117] W.W. to R. Lansing, August 8, 1915, *The Lansing Papers*, II, 547.

Mexican leaders be permitted to impose a revolutionary instead of a "constitutional" solution signified that a decisive change in Wilson's thinking about the Revolution had occurred. Heretofore he had bent all his energies and aimed all his policies at forcing the Revolution into "constitutional" channels. Now, obviously, he was finally willing to accept the Revolution on its own terms.

Even more important, at least from the short range, was the change of mind that the President made known after reading a copy of the stenographic report of the first two sessions of the Pan-American conference, which Lansing had sent to Cornish on August 10. Noting the conversations about the elimination of Carranza and the establishment of a new provisional government under foreign auspices, Wilson must have asked himself whether they really made sense any longer. The answer came perhaps in a flash of insight; in any event, he expressed his new conviction in a telegram to the Secretary of State on the morning of August 11, only a few minutes after he had received the stenographic report from Washington. "I think," he wrote, "it would be unwise for the conference to take for granted or insist upon the elimination of Carranza. It would be to ignore some very big facts. It seems to me very important that the plan now formed should leave the way of action open in any direction and not assume a beginning over again with a clean sheet of paper to write on. Carranza will somehow have to be digested into the scheme and, above all, the object of the revolution will have to be in any event conserved."[118]

This was nothing less than startling in its implications. It meant, actually, the virtual repudiation of all plans for intervention through support of any newly constituted provisional government or some *junta* of exiles. Read in conjunction with Wilson's telegram of August 8, it signified the adoption of Mexican policies that were in large measure new—insistence upon the right of the Revolution to impose its own solution in its own way, and possible acceptance of the *Carrancista* regime as the rightful spokesman of the Mexican people.

Lansing received the President's second telegram certainly not more than a few hours before the third session of the Pan-American parley opened at the Hotel Biltmore in New York City on August 11, 1915, too late to explain the change in policy to his colleague, Paul Fuller, Senior. The telegram arrived none too soon, for this was the session at which the envoys were to discuss the constitution of a new provi-

[118] W.W. to R. Lansing, August 11, 1915, *ibid.*, p. 549.

sional regime to be recognized in the event that the revolutionary leaders failed to unite voluntarily. If the Secretary of State was shaken by Wilson's change of policy he gave no indication of the fact in the discussions that ensued. He led off boldly by declaring that it might as well be admitted that the *Carrancistas* were the dominant element in the Revolution, and that it would be foolish at this time to talk about establishing any other provisional government in Mexico. If the *Carrancistas* "should stand together firmly," Lansing went on, "we have a new problem to face and we cannot decide it at this conference." The Pan-American conferees, he added, would not be able to decide the question of recognition until they had received responses to their appeal to the revolutionary leaders.

Fuller's mind was in some confusion at this point over Lansing's sudden ardent espousal of Carranza's cause. Where, Fuller asked, did all this leave the large body of Mexicans who had taken no part in the Revolution? The conferees could not agree to support a provisional government that excluded them. "I am afraid I cannot agree with Mr. Fuller," the Secretary of State replied in eloquent enunciation of the President's own views. "I am convinced that you must have a provisional government founded on the revolution; that after that it is a matter of internal policy on the part of the new government as to how far they should go in restoring rights of citizenship to others. We cannot compel them, we cannot demand of them—that is a matter for Mexico to decide. . . . The Mexicans who resisted the revolution led by Madero, the Mexicans who supported the Huerta revolt against constitutional government, and the Mexicans who oppose the principle of reform of the revolution, are not entitled to participate in the initial reestablishment of government in Mexico." The United States, he went on, would support no reactionaries, no counterrevolutionary movement; it would support only a government that sprang from the Revolution itself. "We never will accomplish anything," he concluded in a grand flourish, "unless we recognize that the revolution is triumphant and that the body of the Mexican people, composing the revolution, are the ones who for the present possess the right of sovereignty and the right to establish a provisional government."

Fuller came back, arguing that Carranza's hold was weak. But Lansing's eloquence, and above all his insistence upon the right of the Mexican people to solve their own problems without any outside dictation, easily carried the day with the Latin American diplomats. Without further ado they agreed to send their appeal to the Mexican chieftains and to postpone all discussion of recognition of any faction until the replies were in.[119]

Entitled "A communication, made severally and independently, to all prominent civil and military authorities in Mexico, from the Secretary of State and the diplomatic representatives at Washington of Brazil, Chile, Argentina, Bolivia, Uruguay, and Guatemala," the appeal was put on the wires to Mexico on August 13, 1915. Phrased in the polite language of Latin American diplomatic discourse, it informed all civil and military leaders of all factions that the signers were inspired by "the most sincere spirit of American fraternity" to offer their help to a sister republic. Then came a description of Mexico's sad plight, and the important part of the appeal, as follows:

"We, the undersigned, believe that if the men directing the armed movements in Mexico—whether political or military chiefs—should agree to meet, either in person or by delegates, far from the sound of cannon, and with no other inspiration save the thought of their afflicted land, there to exchange ideas and to determine the fate of the country—from such action would undoubtedly result the strong and unyielding agreement requisite to the creation of a provisional government, which should adopt the first steps necessary to the constitutional reconstruction of the country—and to issue the first and most essential of them all, the immediate call to general elections.

"An adequate place within the Mexican frontiers, which for the purpose might be neutralized, should serve as the seat of the conference; and in order to bring about a conference of this nature the undersigned, or any of them, will willingly, upon invitation, act as intermediaries to arrange the time, place, and other details of such conference, if this action can in any way aid the Mexican people.

"The undersigned expect a reply to this communication within a reasonable time; and consider that such a time would be ten days after the communication is delivered, subject to prorogation for cause."[120]

Precisely what it all meant, no one in Washington was prepared to say, no one, that is, except newspapermen who mistakenly believed that the American government was still committed to a program of direct intervention and who believed that the appeal to the Mexican chieftains was the prelude to the execution of these plans. Wilson and

[119] "Continuation of the Conference on Mexican Affairs, Biltmore Hotel, New York City, August 11, 1915," transcript of the stenographic report, State Department Papers.
[120] As printed in *Foreign Relations, 1915*, pp. 735-736.

Lansing did not regard the appeal seriously. Having abandoned the objective for which they had originally convened the Pan-American conference, they had consented to the sending of the message (even though it still included a suggestion for the holding of immediate elections) only because they now hoped that the replies might show the true strength of Carranza's regime, not because they expected the First Chief to accept an authentic Pan-American mediation of the Mexican civil war.

No one could predict what the weeks ahead would bring, whether unexpected new conflicts with Carranza, a sharp turn in the war in Mexico, or the culmination of the new American policy in the recognition of the *Carrancista* government. Only this much was clear by mid-August 1915: The American government was further from military intervention and nearer to what events had already proved would be a realistic solution of the Mexican dilemma than it had been at any time since the evacuation of Veracruz.

For this fact, the historian feels constrained to add, the American and Mexican peoples had mainly Woodrow Wilson to thank. During the long period of confusion he almost alone had had the patience to await the outcome on the fields of battle, although, to be sure, his patience at times had worn dangerously thin. During the weeks when most of his advisers were becoming entangled in intrigue and personally committed to the support of one hopeless faction or another, he almost alone in Washington kept himself free. And finally, when it seemed that his administration, including even his Secretary of State, had become committed beyond recall to a policy that could have ended only in military involvement, he took hold singlehandedly and set American policy upon a different course. The road ahead in Mexican-American relations would still be difficult and perilous. At least it would not *necessarily* lead to futile and ruinous war between two great peoples.

CHAPTER XV

The Caribbean: Involvement and Intervention

AT the very moment when President Wilson was veering toward dis-entanglement in Mexico, a political explosion in the Negro republic of Haiti rocked the Caribbean and impelled the Washington government into the kind of military and political intervention that Wilson had thus far managed to avoid in Mexico. Not long afterward, in 1916, American military forces occupied the Dominican Republic, Haiti's eastern neighbor on the island of Hispaniola. And before the end of Wilson's first term in the White House, diplomatic and naval officers subject to his personal command were hard at work governing alien peoples.

A certain strain of irony runs through this story. An idealistic Pres-ident who talked movingly of Pan-American brotherhood and of the equality of nations great and small, and who worked hard in many ways to give reality to these ideals, became in fact the most extraor-dinary interventionist in Latin America in the history of the United States. The man who usually abhorred the very thought of employing force in international relations became the first President in American history to use violent means to impose the will of the United States (by occupation and control) upon nations that were at least technically free and sovereign.

We have already described the ideals and aspirations that provided the compulsive motivation for the President's Latin American policies. We have also seen how tensions between what Wilson and Bryan wanted to do in Latin America and what they felt compelled to do racked the administration from the beginning when it set out to find realistic solutions for realistic problems in Nicaragua and the rest of Central America.[1] It will suffice at this point, therefore, to say that the policies that culminated in the occupation of Haiti and the Do-minican Republic evolved at the same time and in response to the same impulses and pressures that led the Washington authorities into a milder intervention in Central America. In all these episodes the

[1] A. S. Link, *Wilson*, II, 319-346.

story is remarkably the same in its larger outlines and meaning. It is one of men with noble motives being lured on by their own good intentions and sometimes by foolish or interested advisers, being influenced by subtle pressures and subconscious motivations that they did not recognize, and finally being trapped by events that they could not control. In short, it is a tale of what happened when evangels of democracy set out to teach other peoples how to elect good leaders and govern themselves well.

To gain proper perspective we have to digress for a moment and begin at the beginning of the story, which started, actually, in the Dominican Republic and not in Haiti. American relations with the former country had been intimate ever since 1905, when President Theodore Roosevelt responded to appeals from various Dominican leaders and averted national bankruptcy and probable European intervention by establishing an American receivership of the Dominican customs. During the next four years American experts refinanced the Dominican foreign and domestic debts, and the Receiver-General did his job so well that the national treasury literally overflowed. During this period Dominicans enjoyed another unaccustomed blessing—a stable and responsible government under the presidency of an apparently authentic patriot, General Ramón Cáceres.

Chaos came again, and a new epoch in Dominican history began when President Cácares fell victim to an assassin's bullet on November 19, 1911. He was succeeded by Don Eladio Victoria, a member of the majority political faction known as the *Horacistas*, who derived their name from their leader, General Horacio Vásquez. Victoria, unhappily, failed either to please his friends or to reconcile his enemies among the several opposing factions. Civil war and near anarchy broke out; and in the ensuing melee in the autumn of 1912 the American State Department, now under the direction of President Taft's usually inept Secretary of State, Philander C. Knox, forced the installation of a nonpartisan government under the presidency of the reluctant statesman, *Monseñor* Adolfo A. Nouel, Archbishop of Santo Domingo. Devoid of political ambition or ability and weakened by ill health, the poor Archbishop was never more than an inefficient caretaker. He finally resigned on March 31, 1913, in spite of renewed importunities from Washington, and was succeeded by a *Horacista*,

José Bordas Valdés, elected to the presidency by the Dominican Congress some two weeks later.[2]

This, then, was the political situation in the Dominican Republic when Woodrow Wilson and William Jennings Bryan assumed direction of American foreign policy in March 1913. As we can now see, the months ahead would be a decisive period in Dominican history: a time when the more responsible leaders of the country might succeed in ending the chaos of their national life that had begun with the assassination of Cáceres two years before. And the outcome would depend in large measure upon the policies of the Washington government toward its island dependency.

Neither knowledge of Caribbean affairs nor wisdom in dealing with small quasi-protectorates was common anywhere in the Wilson administration, least of all in the Department of State, during the early months of the New Freedom. To begin with, the President was almost totally ignorant in such matters and too engrossed in other concerns to have any time to learn. To be sure, he did have certain strong convictions about the general political development of mankind and the responsibilities that great powers had for less advanced neighbors; and he was not at all averse to applying them to the peoples of the Caribbean and Central American regions. He believed that democracy was the highest form of political life and that peoples could rise to its mature level only through generations of experience or tutelage. He did not believe that the peoples of northern Latin America were much beyond the stage of political infancy; and he assumed that it was his responsibility as well as his privilege to teach his unenlightened neighbors how to write good constitutions and elect wise leaders, even though the effort might require a partial or total denial of the sovereignty of the recipients of such assistance. One of the President's first important acts after his inauguration was to announce, as we have noted in the preceding volume in this series, that his administration could have no sympathy with would-be revolutionists in Latin America who sought "to seize the power of government to advance their own personal interests or ambition."[3] It was easy to go on from there to say, as Wilson later did, that the American government would not permit revolutions in certain countries, and, finally, that it would assume the tasks of government if native peoples proved incapable of

[2] In writing the above summary I have leaned heavily upon Sumner Welles' *Naboth's Vineyard, The Dominican Republic, 1844-1924,* ii, 601-709.

[3] A. S. Link, *Wilson,* ii, 319-320.

solving their problems by constitutional procedures. The President remained by and large content with these generalizations; either because of lack of interest[4] or of energy, he attempted to master fast-moving events in the Dominican Republic or in Haiti only at times of crisis. On these occasions he did not hesitate to make vital decisions; but he usually acted without benefit of the wisdom that would have come from firsthand knowledge of day-to-day developments.

Nor was Secretary Bryan any more likely to provide wise leadership in the formulation of Caribbean policies. He shared the President's initial ignorance, his belief in the beneficence and general adequacy of constitutional remedies, his convictions about the mission of the United States in the New World, and his unconcern about the sovereignty of the peoples of the small republics of northern Latin America. Unlike the President, the Secretary of State could not confine himself to ideals and generalities; as the official primarily responsible for policy in the Caribbean area, he had to be concerned with mundane details. But since he knew so little about the subject himself, he had no choice but to rely upon his advisers in the Department and upon the diplomatic officers in the field for information and guidance.

Here was where Bryan's wrecking of the departmental staff and the Foreign Service, of which we have written in the preceding volume, had the most baneful consequences. Once in office, the Commoner had dismissed not only the high-ranking Assistant Secretaries but the Chief of the Latin American Affairs Division as well. The new Chief of this division, upon whom Bryan would have to depend directly for guidance in dealing with the Caribbean republics, was Boaz W. Long, a "deserving Democrat" like Bryan's other appointees. Long was a businessman, the proprietor of a large commission house. He was not without considerable intelligence, but his reputation as an expert on Latin America rested solely upon the fact (which he carefully noted

---

[4] One significant example of Wilson's lack of any keen interest occurred in March 1913. Professor Jacob H. Hollander of The Johns Hopkins University, who had been primarily responsible for the refinancing of the Dominican debt during the administration of Theodore Roosevelt, wrote to the President on March 22, 1913, suggesting that he come to the White House to bring the President up to date on developments in the Dominican Republic. Wilson suggested instead that Hollander prepare a memorandum on the subject. He apparently read the memorandum that Hollander submitted, but he made no attempt to follow through by obtaining any additional expert advice during the following months. See J. H. Hollander to W.W., March 22, 1913; W.W. to J. H. Hollander, March 24, 1913; and W.W. to W. J. Bryan, April 8, 1913, all in the Wilson Papers. The Hollander memorandum is undated and may be found in the State Department Papers.

in his biographical sketch in the State Department *Register*) that his company had a branch office in Mexico City. Without diplomatic experience of any kind when he took up his post in the Department on May 14, 1913, Long knew no more about Caribbean affairs than his superiors did. Nor could he turn to anyone for advice, for Bryan had earlier dismissed the professional assistant in the Division.[5]

In Caribbean policy, therefore, it was a case of the blind leading the blind. So far as relations with the Dominican Republic were specifically concerned, much in these circumstances would depend upon the Minister accredited to Santo Domingo. During the first days of his tenure Bryan had dismissed the experienced envoy in that city, William W. Russell, along with most other heads of Legation. Able and informed consuls and a Chargé remained in the principal Dominican cities and capital, it is true, but they would not normally presume to advise the Secretary of State upon matters of policy once the new Minister had taken up his post.

With civil war impending in the Dominican Republic, the situation obviously demanded a man of infinite tact and wisdom, as well as one with some training in diplomacy and knowledge of Caribbean affairs. Bryan met the need by appointing James M. Sullivan, a New York lawyer of dubious character and a former prize fight promoter with connections in the underworld. It is hardly necessary to say that he was not an authority on Dominican affairs. Worse still, he was closely allied with a group of New York financiers, the owners of the *Banco Nacional de Santo Domingo*, who were scheming at this time to win custody of the deposits of the American Receiver-General. It was this group who were primarily responsible for Sullivan's appointment. We have already told how Bryan was victimized by this intrigue and described the scandal that broke over the administration when the New York *World* exposed the truth of the affair in late 1914.[6] What now remains is to tell the more important story of Sullivan's short-lived career in Santo Domingo.

Portents of a political explosion in the Dominican Republic were evident on all sides by the time that Sullivan received his appointment on August 12, 1913. The chief cause of the trouble was the unexpected

[5] Long finally obtained an assistant in September 1913, the young career diplomat, Jordan H. Stabler; but Stabler came from the Legation in Stockholm and was no great expert on Latin American affairs even though he had earlier served briefly at Quito and Guatemala.

[6] A. S. Link, *Wilson*, II, 107-110.

behavior of José Bordas Valdés. Elected as a *Horacista*, he had been inaugurated Provisional President on April 14, 1913, for a term not to exceed one year. Once in power, Bordas had turned against his friends in the majority party and formed new alliances with his erstwhile enemies, the chief among whom was the demagogue and free-wheeling smuggler General Desiderio Arias. To the *Horacistas* it was bad enough when Bordas packed the government with some of the worst characters in political life, reneged on his promise to call a constitutional convention to undertake electoral reform, and gave every sign of seeking to prolong his occupancy of the presidential mansion. However, it was more than the *Horacistas* could abide when the Provisional President removed certain leaders of their party as managers of the Central Dominican Railroad and gave control of this rich source of patronage to henchmen of Arias. In retaliation, the *Horacista* Governor of the Province of Puerto Plata, General Jesús Maria Céspedes, declared himself Provisional President of the republic on September 1, 1913; and leaders throughout the length of the northeastern section of the country—in Samaná, Sánchez, Moca, San Francisco de Macorís, and Santiago—at once unfurled the standards of revolt against the Bordas regime.[7]

This occurred at the very moment that Boaz W. Long was preparing instructions in the State Department in Washington for Minister Sullivan. The *Horacista* revolt, Long rather blithely concluded, was simply outrageous. General Horacio Vásquez, the leader of the party, he informed the Secretary of State, was "reported to be" one of the most unruly agitators in the Dominican Republic. The American government should make it absolutely clear that it would not countenance such treason against the constitutional authorities.[8] Concurring enthusiastically, Bryan seized the opportunity to nip a bad revolution in the bud, to teach Dominicans a lesson in democracy, and to announce the administration's policy toward the Caribbean republics at one and the same time. This he did with unfeigned zeal in the instructions that he prepared on the eve of Sullivan's departure:

> The President directs me to say for your instruction that the influence of this Government will be exerted for the support of lawful authorities

[7] Chargé Charles B. Curtis, from Santo Domingo, to the Secretary of State, September 3, 1913, State Department Papers; also Consul Charles M. Hathaway, Jr., from Puerto Plata, to the Secretary of State, October 6, 1913, *ibid.*, for a penetrating analysis of the causes of this revolution.

[8] B. W. Long to W. J. Bryan, September 4 and 11, 1913, *ibid.*

in Santo Domingo, and for the discouragement of any and all insurrectionary methods. You will carry with you a copy of the President's statement of last March which sets forth fully, and in such a way as to leave no doubt, his position on two important points, namely: First, that we can have no sympathy with those who seek to seize the power of government to advance their own personal interests or ambition; and, second, that the test of a republican form of government is to be found in its responsiveness to the will of the people, its just powers being derived from the consent of the governed.

It is not to be expected that those in power will be able to avoid mistakes but mistakes should be corrected by constitutional means. Neither is it to be supposed that reforms will in all cases be brought about as soon as they ought to be, but the remedy for this is agitation—not insurrection.

Say to any who may feel aggrieved or who may be disposed to resort to violence that the good offices of this Government can be counted upon at all times to assist in the establishment of justice, in the remedying of abuses, and in the promotion of the welfare of the people. We must depend, therefore, upon all the people of Santo Domingo, of whatever party or faction, to join in securing justice through law and in the election by free and fair ballot of officials whom the people desire. You will make it known to those now in insurrection that this Government will employ every legitimate means to assist in the restoration of order and in the prevention of further insurrections, holding itself open at all times to advise with the government in behalf of those who feel that they have a grievance.

I am sure that when the disinterestedness of our Government is fully understood, its friendship will be appreciated and its advice sought.[9]

Thus armed with the first lesson, Sullivan set out for his new station aboard a naval transport. Stopping briefly at Santiago de Cuba, he found supplementary instructions from Washington awaiting him. They directed him to confer with Vásquez and Céspedes at Puerto Plata and to convey to them the blunt warning that the American government would not recognize their regime even if they succeeded and would "consequently withhold the portion of the customs collections belonging to Santo Domingo as long as an unrecognized de facto government should exist."[10]

Sullivan performed his duty with all the zeal of a man determined to make good. Confronting Vásquez and Céspedes at Puerto Plata on

[9] The Secretary of State to Minister Sullivan, September 9, 1913, *Papers Relating to the Foreign Relations of the United States, 1913*, pp. 425-426; hereinafter cited as *Foreign Relations, 1913*.

[10] The Secretary of State to the American Consul at Santiago de Cuba, September 12, 1913, *ibid.*, p. 427.

September 17, 1913, the Minister read his instructions to the revolutionary leaders and added an even sterner warning of his own, that the American government would use all its power to maintain the constitutional (that is, the Bordas) government and would advise the authorities in Santo Domingo to deal with the revolutionists as outlaws, "not [as] leaders of armies but [as] mere breakers of law who will answer with their persons for the loss of life and property they may occasion." On the other hand, Sullivan added, the American government would gladly support all demands for an "honest ballot cast at a properly regulated election" if the revolutionists would only abandon their employment of violence.[11] Since Vásquez and Cépedes were reluctant rebels and reasonable men, they replied that they would gladly give up their arms provided Bordas took no reprisals and permitted Céspedes to remain as Governor of Puerto Plata, and Sullivan guaranteed "an honest ballot at a fair election in the near future."[12]

Proceeding thence to Santo Domingo, Sullivan found Bordas emboldened by the promise of American assistance but also somewhat cautious. He would meet the rebels halfway, the Provisional President declared; Céspedes would have to retire as Governor of Puerto Plata, but he might name his own successor. On the other hand, Bordas continued, he would insist upon maintaining his blockade of the ports of Sánchez, Samaná, and Puerto Plata until the revolutionists laid down their arms.[13] The Washington authorities were delighted by this display of backbone. The Dominican government, Bryan replied at once on September 25, 1913, should not only maintain the blockade of the northeastern coast and demand Céspedes' withdrawal; it should also proceed at once to dismiss all *Horacista* governors in all rebellious provinces and to appoint men whom it could trust.[14] As an earnest of his intention, Bryan on the following day asked the Secretary of the Navy to send warships to Puerto Plata and Samaná Bay to do what they could to help maintain the blockade.[15]

Facing such awesome prospects, Vásquez and his friends saw no alternative but to sign the so-called peace agreement that Bordas offered.

[11] From a copy of one of the several statements that Sullivan handed to Vásquez and Céspedes, enclosed in J. M. Sullivan to the Secretary of State, September 24, 1913, State Department Papers.

[12] Minister Sullivan to the Secretary of State, September 19, 1913, *Foreign Relations, 1913*, p. 428.

[13] Minister Sullivan to the Secretary of State, September 22, 1913, *ibid.*, p. 430.

[14] The Secretary of State to Minister Sullivan, September 25, 1913, *ibid.*

[15] The Secretary of State to the Dominican Minister, September 26, 1913, *ibid.*, p. 431.

It stipulated that a partisan of Arias should be Governor of Puerto Plata, vested full control of all rebellious provinces in the hands of the authorities in Santo Domingo, and promised the holding of early presidential elections. As Vásquez made clear to the American Consul at Puerto Plata, responsibility for the safety of the *Horacistas* and the future peace of the republic now rested with the Washington government.[16] As Sullivan explained a short time later:

"If the result desired is to be obtained, there can be no evasion of our responsibility in the premises. . . . I promised solemnly and repeatedly renewed the promise that, in good faith, President Wilson would use the influence of the United States, within legitimate lines, to the end that a reasonably fair constitutional remedy would be at the disposal of the people in the way of a decent election. This promise held in it the alternative for the rifle, and the revolutionists, though reluctantly, did finally accept the bargain the American Government offered. The terms of the bargain are known to all the people. . . . The question now being asked at every corner is—'Will the Americans keep their word?' If we do not, I respectfully venture to suggest that there is no moral force behind any further demand that men shall not fight for their rights here."[17]

The first test of the State Department's good faith came soon after Minister Sullivan penned the above warning, during a turbulent campaign for the election of members of municipal councils and of a constitutional convention that was scheduled for December 15, 1913. From the outset it was clear that Bordas intended to control the voting in customary dictatorial fashion and to stay on in the presidential palace after his term expired in April 1914. Bryan sent a lengthy discourse on elementary democratic electoral procedures to the Provisional President on November 24.[18] Bordas returned profuse thanks and then proceeded to imprison the *Horacista* leaders and to disperse their meetings with gunfire.[19]

What could the men in the State Department do now? They had

[16] Minister Sullivan to the Secretary of State, October 10, 1913, *ibid.*, pp. 433-434; Consul Hathaway to the Secretary of State, October 16 and 31, 1913, State Department Papers.

[17] Minister Sullivan to the Secretary of State, November 21, 1913, *ibid.*

[18] The Secretary of State to Minister Sullivan, November 24, 1913, *Foreign Relations, 1913*, p. 436.

[19] Minister Sullivan to the Secretary of State, December 2 and 3, 1913, State Department Papers.

promised free and fair elections, and the *Horacistas* had published these promises on placards posted about the country. Earlier, while the campaign was getting under way, Sullivan had suggested "a non-interfering scrutiny by open agents appointed by the Department at the principal towns and polling-places," to be accompanied by the warning that the American government would take full control of the presidential election that was to follow unless the election on December 15 were free.[20] Alarmed by the reports of Bordas' repression of the opposition, the State Department was disposed to go even further than Sullivan had advised, by sending an American commission to take actual if not legal control of the ballot boxes.[21] But the authorities in Santo Domingo protested so violently that Bryan and Long hesitated; as Long confessed, it would be virtually impossible to obtain free elections in such circumstances anyway.[22]

Explaining that the American government bore some responsibility for the coming election, Bryan laid the issue before President Wilson on December 6. Although he could not have given more than casual attention to Dominican affairs to this point, the President made his decision quickly. As he explained in a message that he drafted for transmission to Minister Sullivan:

"Say to President Bordas that the President of the United States has planned to send a number of Americans to visit the principal polling-places on election day, not as a 'commission' for which this Government asks any official recognition but only as individuals, to lend by their presence moral support of the efforts that President Bordas has so freely pledged himself to make to keep the election free and un-influenced in all respects, and in order that, if any question should arise as to the good faith of anyone concerned, undeniably impartial witnesses may be available.

"The President of the United States trusts that this communication may be given full publicity in order that the intentions and attitude of this Government may not possibly be misconceived. It merely asks

[20] Minister Sullivan to the Secretary of State, November 22, 1913, *Foreign Relations, 1913*, pp. 435-436.

[21] The Secretary of State to Minister Sullivan, December 2 and 4, 1913, *ibid.*, pp. 438, 439-440.

[22] Minister Sullivan to the Secretary of State, December 5, 1913, *ibid.*, pp. 440-441; the Dominican Minister to the Secretary of State, December 6, 1913, *ibid.*, pp. 441-443; B. W. Long to W. J. Bryan, December 4, 1913, State Department Papers.

the privileges of friends for those *who have been requested to be present.*"[23]

Consequently, three representatives from the State Department and thirty agents from the Governor's office in Puerto Rico arrived in Santo Domingo City on December 11 and 12 and scattered throughout the country. Whether their presence had any really decisive influence on the election that came off on December 15 and 16, it was impossible to say. Government troops imprisoned the opposition leaders in the capital, but the balloting was apparently reasonably free in the interior towns. And the total results seemed to indicate a decisive victory for the *Horacistas* and the other factions arrayed against Bordas.[24]

Events of the ensuing months revealed clearly enough the dangers of the kind of interference that the American government had practiced in Dominican affairs since the arrival of Minister Sullivan in Santo Domingo. There was a momentary lull in the political excitement following the election in mid-December, but the situation was still dangerously unstable. Bordas and his henchmen continued to control the army and the executive branch, but only because the State Department had prevented the majority factions from driving them from power, and because their principal ally, General Arias, still thought it was more profitable to cooperate than to revolt. Worse still, the government was nearing bankruptcy without any means of obtaining relief constitutionally, as the lower house of the Congress was in the hands of its opponents and would not approve the floating of any loans. And ahead lay the turmoil of a presidential election scheduled to take place in April 1914.

In these circumstances, the leaders in Washington and Minister Sullivan in Santo Domingo continued their day-to-day interference without, however, attempting to work out, much less to apply, any long-range constructive policies. They gave abundant advice on the proper treatment of political prisoners and the blessings of certain democratic institutions.[25] They contributed, besides, frequent homilies on the need

[23] The Secretary of State to Minister Sullivan, December 7, 1913, *ibid.*; italics added. Wilson wrote this message—his first concerning Dominican affairs—on his own typewriter. The italicized phrase is somewhat curious, as no Dominican official had "requested" the presence of American commissioners or observers.

[24] "Report to the Secretary of State made by the representatives of the Department of State . . . ," dated December 20, 1913, *Foreign Relations, 1913*, pp. 449-453; Minister Sullivan to the Secretary of State, December 23, 1913, *ibid.*, pp. 453-454.

[25] Minister Sullivan to the Secretary of State, January 9, 1914, *Foreign Relations, 1914*, p. 195; the Secretary of State to Minister Sullivan, January 18, 1914, *ibid.*, p. 198.

for economy and honest administration, and periodic small advances from the funds of the Receiver-General in order to keep the Santo Domingo government solvent. Finally, with President Wilson's approval, they obtained Bordas' consent to the appointment of an American financial adviser to supervise the daily expenditures of the central government.[26] But these halfway measures only weakened the Provisional President's standing at home without establishing any effective control. By February 1914 he presented the pitiful spectacle of a head of a minority and bankrupt regime living from hand to mouth by sufferance of the State Department.

The Dominican cauldron began to boil furiously again in February when the most accomplished thieves, Bordas and Arias, at last fell out over the spoils. Bordas enjoyed the rewards and privileges of power too much to want to give them up; being President under humiliating circumstances was, after all, better than a guerrilla existence in the jungle or death before a firing squad, or even lonely exile. He controlled a majority of the provincial governments and hence the electoral machinery; he could arrange his own election; and with American support he might conceivably survive. Thus in mid-February he launched his candidacy in the forthcoming presidential canvass. Arias,

---

[26] For the discussions between Bryan and Wilson on this matter, see W. J. Bryan to W.W., January 27 and February 5, 1914; W.W. to W. J. Bryan, February 9, 1914, all in the Wilson Papers.

The negotiations over the appointment of an American financial adviser were protracted and, to the American leaders, exasperating. Bordas quite naturally wanted to yield as little control as possible, but he desperately needed the assistance of the State Department in obtaining the short-term advances from banks and commercial houses upon which his government was operating, and he had no alternative in the end but to yield to the demand from Washington. For the negotiations on this point, see Minister Sullivan to the Secretary of State, January 12, 1914, *Foreign Relations, 1914*, p. 197; the Acting Secretary of State to Minister Sullivan, January 26, 1914, *ibid.*, pp. 199-200; Minister Sullivan to the Secretary of State, January 28, 1914, *ibid.*, pp. 201-202; the Secretary of State to Minister Sullivan, January 30 and February 3 and 12, 1914, *ibid.*, pp. 203, 204-205, 207-208; Eliseo Grullón to J. M. Sullivan, March 20, 1914, State Department Papers; W. J. Bryan to J. M. Sullivan, May 4 and 14, 1914, *ibid.*; Minister Sullivan to the Secretary of State, May 10, 1914, *ibid.*; Minister Sullivan to the Secretary of State, May 16, 1914, *ibid.*; the Dominican Chargé to the Secretary of State, May 26, 1914, *Foreign Relations, 1914*, pp. 233-234; the Secretary of State to the Dominican Chargé, June 1, 1914, *ibid.*, pp. 235-236.

On June 1, 1914, after the above negotiations had yielded firm agreement with the Bordas regime, Secretary Bryan appointed Charles M. Johnston to the new post with the title of Financial Expert to the Dominican Republic. See the Secretary of State to C. M. Johnston, June 1, 1914, *ibid.*, pp. 236-237; and the Secretary of State to the Dominican Chargé, June 1, 1914, *ibid.*, pp. 235-236.

unhappily, was not inclined at this point to be self-effacing. He wanted to be either President or the dominant power behind the throne, and he thought his turn had come.[27] Gathering around him the leading Dominican cutthroats, Arias made it known that he would revolt should Bordas attempt to thwart his bid for power.[28]

The State Department, assuredly, was not without some responsibility for the situation. It had maintained the Bordas regime against the *Horacistas*, and it had approved the removal of *Horacista* officials and the appointment of Arias and his friends in their stead in the northern section known as the Cibao. To Minister Sullivan there was no choice but to support Bordas: given sufficient money to pay his troops, the Minister promised, the Provisional President could make short work of his rival.[29] The professional assistant in the Latin American Affairs Division agreed; Arias, he advised the Secretary of State, was nothing but a "smuggler, brigand and professional revolutionist."[30] Bryan, however, was not quite so certain. "It presents a serious situation upon which I would like to have your advice before answering [Sullivan]," he wrote to the President on February 26. "My impression is that before deciding that Arias must be dealt with as an *outlaw* it would be worth while to have Sullivan confer with him personally and get his point of view as well as to find out his grievance. It is possible that by emphasizing that the day of revolutions has passed and that our Government will use whatever influence it has to secure a stable and constitutional government, Mr. Sullivan might be able to bring Arias into line. It might be that some concession could be made to Arias, or he might be employed in some important business while the constitution is being reformed. A revolution once commenced is not easily terminated, not to speak of the cost of money and lives."[31]

[27] On November 7, 1913, Arias had told the American Consul at Puerto Plata that he, Arias, could gain control of the republic and save the United States the trouble and expense of intervention, if only the American government would support his movement. E. M. Hathaway, Jr., to the Secretary of State, November 13, 1913, State Department Papers.

[28] Minister Sullivan to the Secretary of State, February 12, 1914, *Foreign Relations, 1914*, pp. 206-207; Frank A. Henry, Consul at Puerto Plata, to the Secretary of State, February 24, 1914, State Department Papers.

[29] Minister Sullivan to the Secretary of State, February 21 and 25, 1914, *Foreign Relations, 1914*, pp. 210-211, 211-212.

[30] J. H. Stabler, "Political Conditions in the Dominican Republic . . . ," memorandum dated February 18, 1914, State Department Papers.

[31] W. J. Bryan to W.W., February 26, 1914, Wilson Papers.

The President apparently agreed, and the hopeful Secretary of State proceeded to the task of taming the rapacious bandit of the North. At the State Department's instruction Sullivan conveyed the warning that the United States would not permit a revolution to succeed and the demand that Arias come in person to Santo Domingo or else suffer the consequences of American displeasure.[32] Arias refused, saying that he was "a citizen of a free country, a high officer of a Sovereign State, . . . not subordinate in any shape or manner to any Foreign Official,"[33] and published the correspondence in the Dominican press.[34] Meanwhile, the American Minister had also persuaded Bordas to meet Arias in his lair in the Cibao; and Secretary Bryan had contributed a new discourse on democracy for delivery to the bandit chieftain by the Provisional President.[35] The conference took place as Sullivan planned; but it was totally fruitless, and Bordas returned to the capital and forthwith removed the Governors of Monte Christi, Puerto Plata, Santiago, and the Seybo—all followers of Arias.[36] It was tantamount to a declaration of war just as the factions were beginning the presidential campaign.

By this time Bryan was almost totally confused. He had held out the hope of financial assistance to the Bordas government; but, as he wrote to the Legation in Santo Domingo, should he put money into Bordas' hands "so same may be used just prior to or during elections?"[37] That, replied Minister Sullivan, was precisely what the Washington government should do, as the alternative to Bordas' re-election was the triumph of Arias.[38] Still the Secretary of State hesitated. He could not permit his government to become so deeply committed as to furnish money, in opposition to the expressed will of the Dominican Congress, to enable Bordas to buy his own re-election.[39] "In your utterances," Bryan further advised Sullivan, "you will use caution when speaking

[32] The Secretary of State to Minister Sullivan, February 27, March 1, 1914, *Foreign Relations, 1914*, pp. 212-213.

[33] D. Arias to Commander B. B. Bierer, U.S.S. *Wheeling*, March 15, 1914, State Department Papers.

[34] Santo Domingo *El Radical*, March 20, 1914.

[35] It was transmitted in the Secretary of State to Minister Sullivan, March 5, 1914, *Foreign Relations, 1914*, p. 215.

[36] Minister Sullivan to the Secretary of State, March 20, 1914, *ibid.*, p. 218.

[37] The Secretary of State to Minister Sullivan, March 23, 1914, *ibid.*, p. 220. Wilson read and approved this message before it went to Santo Domingo.

[38] Minister Sullivan to the Secretary of State, March 26, 1914, *ibid.*, p. 221.

[39] The Secretary of State to Minister Sullivan, March 30, 1914, State Department Papers.

of the coming election and the candidates. The United States *has no interest except to aid in the election of a candidate desired by the voters through the medium of free and fair means.*"[40]

Perhaps the best that Bryan (with Wilson's approval) could do was to keep on talking as if the Dominican Republic were Nebraska or New Jersey. The irrelevance of such advice finally became obvious even to the Secretary of State in early April, when Arias broke out in open rebellion at Puerto Plata, and Bordas set out from the capital with 1,500 troops to subdue him. There was nothing left, Bryan concluded, but to take sides. "I think from what you have said," he wrote to President Wilson on April 4, "you will favor giving immediate financial assistance to Bordas and in this I heartily concur. If there must be violence before peace the more quickly and decisively the government acts the better."[41] Wilson agreed, and Bryan at once informed the Santo Domingo authorities that he was increasing their daily allowance from the funds of the Receiver-General from $5,000 to $7,000, but only for one month.[42]

For a brief time it seemed that Bordas might actually succeed. Sweeping through the Cibao with his little army, he drove Arias into his stronghold of Monte Christi near the Haitian border and laid siege to Puerto Plata. Meanwhile, after conducting carefully rigged elections in certain towns on April 1 and 2, he had announced his intention to serve out the balance of the term of President Cácares, which expired on June 30, 1914, and to hold presidential elections again in early June. The *Horacistas* and the two other major factions, the *Jiménistas* and the *Veláquistas*,[43] seemed inclined to accept this solution. The situation, Sullivan could report in mid-April, was virtually serene. "With the present spirit continuing to grow," he wrote in one dispatch, "and with the lesson being learned that revolution does not point out the way to profit and power, there is hope for tranquility here, and I believe that

[40] The Secretary of State to Minister Sullivan, April 2, 1914, *Foreign Relations, 1914,* p. 222; italics added.

[41] W. J. Bryan to W.W., April 4, 1914, Wilson Papers.

[42] W. J. Bryan to W.W., April 7, 1914; the Secretary of State to Minister Sullivan, April 9, 1914 (sent with Wilson's approval), both in *ibid*. When Bordas protested that the sum offered would not suffice, Bryan agreed to increase the daily allowance by $3,500, but only for a period of fifteen days. The Secretary of State to Minister Sullivan, April 14, 1914, *Foreign Relations, 1914,* p. 225.

[43] Adherents of Juan Isidro Jiménez and Federico Velásquez, two of the most active Dominican politicians who worked usually in opposition to General Vásquez and his *Horacista* party.

in a year the professional revolutionist will have neither a home nor a habitation in the land."[44]

Never did a prophet miss the mark more widely. Not long afterward General Horacio Vásquez eluded Bordas' agents in Puerto Rico, where he had been living in exile, and landed on the northern coast of his home land. Gathering followers as he went, he made his way to Puerto Plata and there raised a new rebellion that united *Horacistas, Jiménistas, Velásquistas*, and even the supporters of Arias in a coalition known as the *Legalistas* against the alleged usurper Bordas. By the beginning of May 1914 the entire Cibao was in revolt; by the end of the month near anarchy existed throughout large sections of the country, as the Provisional President was totally powerless to cope with the uprising. "The present situation," warned the American Consul at Puerto Plata on May 22, "is daily becoming intolerable. There is nothing in sight to end it. In the meantime the country is being impoverished, the customs revenues of the port have ceased, agriculture has been abandoned, and property destroyed."[45]

By this time the Secretary of State and his advisers in Washington were lost in bewilderment and ready to adopt any expedient that offered some hope of solution. When Bordas declared a blockade of Puerto Plata, the principal port on the northern coast, the State Department approved.[46] When this proved unavailing and the Santo Domingo authorities, confessing their helplessness, called upon the American government to suppress the insurrection in the northern port towns,[47] Bryan next tried conciliation, by urging all the rival leaders to declare an armistice and give their allegiance to "an honest and upright citizen of Santo Domingo who has no connection with politics or with the present situation and one who should be able to give to the country civil and legislative reforms which are necessary."[48] A series of conferences between Bordas and his enemies, held aboard the American warships *Washington* and *South Carolina* in the harbor of Puerto Plata, did take place at Bryan's insistence, but all efforts at

[44] Minister Sullivan to the Secretary of State, April 17, 1914, *Foreign Relations, 1914,* pp. 225-227; also Minister Sullivan to the Secretary of State, April 11 and 15, 1914, State Department Papers.

[45] F. A. Henry to the Secretary of State, May 22, 1914, *ibid.*

[46] The Secretary of State to the American Legation, May 9, 1914, *ibid.*

[47] Minister Sullivan to the Secretary of State, May 25, 1914, *Foreign Relations, 1914,* pp. 232-233.

[48] The Secretary of State to Minister Sullivan, May 28, 1914, *ibid.*, p. 234.

mediation failed because Bordas would not agree to retire.[49] On the contrary, a short time later, on June 7 and 8, the former Provisional President held private elections in eight of the twelve Dominican provinces; unopposed, he was unanimously elected constitutional President of the republic.[50] All the while the revolution continued, and the country sank deeper into the morass. "Business situation universally bad," the American financial expert who had recently arrived in Santo Domingo reported in mid-July, "labor unemployed, contracts repudiated, mail and telegraphic communication suspended, foreign commerce paralyzed."[51]

Viewing the Dominican scene in the mid-summer of 1914, leaders in the Washington government were compelled to confess to themselves, if not to each other or to the American people, that their Dominican policy, if such it could be called, was bankrupt. Everything they had done had somehow gone wrong. In the hope of establishing a new political order in the Caribbean republic they had prevented the most responsible faction from driving Bordas from office. Then they had given the Bordas regime enough support to cause all the rival factions to turn against it, but not enough to enable it to maintain itself in power. That regime was now not only totally discredited but also so helpless that only a full-fledged American military occupation could have saved it from speedy extinction. This was the impasse to which ignorance in Washington and foolish advice from the Legation in Santo Domingo had brought the American government

At this point the man upon whom the State Department had mainly relied for advice, James M. Sullivan, became wholly irrational, or corrupt. All along he had played the fool in his personal relations with the Dominican leaders. Perhaps he had played a role even worse—as a friend of corrupt concessionaires, including his cousin Timothy J. Sullivan, in the Dominican Department of Public Works and in the *Banco Nacional de Santo Domingo*. The New York *World* later published much damaging evidence that seemed to indicate that the Minister had personally profited from a number of deals between

[49] E. W. Eberle to the Secretary of the Navy, n.d., copy in State Department Papers; F. A. Henry to the Secretary of State, May 30 and June 6, 1914, *ibid.*; Minister Sullivan to the Secretary of State, June 6, 1914, *ibid.*

[50] Minister Sullivan to the Secretary of State, June 9 and 13, 1914, *ibid.*

[51] F. A. Henry to the Secretary of State, July 17, 1914, transmitting report of C. M. Johnston, *ibid.*

businessmen and the Bordas regime.[52] It is certainly not impossible that Sullivan was so deeply involved by the summer of 1914 that he had no choice but to work as hard as he could for his Dominican friends. Whatever the reason, Sullivan sent in a series of reports during June and early July that completely falsified the Dominican picture in order to persuade his superiors in Washington to embark upon a policy of all-out support of Bordas in his extremity.[53]

Ignoring Sullivan's advice and leaning upon other observers for information,[54] the leaders in the State Department somewhat ruefully set to the task of devising their own solution. Bordas, they agreed, would have to go. That much was obvious.[55] But then what? A policy of complete noninterference, which would result in the triumph of the *Horacistas* and *Jiménistas*? That was impossible because it would mean a prolongation of the civil war, the utter impoverishment of the republic, and an open confession of the failure of American policy heretofore. The only solution, Bryan and President Wilson agreed— they must have conferred about the Dominican situation several times during the last two weeks of July 1914, although the written record is silent about their deliberations—was American intervention to end the fighting and to establish a new provisional government that a majority of the factions would support. This would be done peacefully if the Dominican leaders cooperated, by force if they resisted. But it would be done.

Working from a memorandum submitted by the professional assistant in the Latin American Affairs Division,[56] President Wilson himself prepared the final statement of American intentions, subsequently called the Wilson Plan. It is somewhat long, but it so clearly reveals Wilson's thinking at this time that it is reproduced in full, as follows:

> The Government of the United States desires nothing for itself from the Dominican Republic and no concessions or advantages for its citizens which are not accorded citizens of other countries. It desires only to prove its sincere and disinterested friendship for the republic and its

[52] New York *World*, December 7, 10, 11, and 13, 1914.

[53] e.g., Minister Sullivan to the Secretary of State, June 13, 1914, State Department Papers.

[54] Particularly John T. Vance of the Receiver-General's office and C. M. Johnston. See J. T. Vance to W. J. Bryan, June 9, 1914, State Department Papers, and F. A. Henry to the Secretary of State, July 17, 1914, transmitting a long report by C. M. Johnston, *ibid*.

[55] J. H. Stabler to W. J. Bryan, July 9 and 17, 1914, *ibid*.

[56] J. H. Stabler to W. J. Bryan, July 17, 1914, *ibid*.

people and to fulfill its responsibilities as the friend to whom in such crises as the present all the world looks to guide Santo Domingo out of its difficulties.

It, therefore, makes the following earnest representations not only to the existing de facto Government of the Dominican Republic, but also to all who are in any way responsible for the present posture of affairs there:

I. It warns everyone concerned that it is absolutely imperative that the present hostilities should cease and that all who are concerned in them should disperse to their several homes, disbanding the existing armed forces and returning to the peaceful occupations upon which the welfare of the people of the republic depends. This is necessary, and necessary at once. Nothing can be successfully accomplished until this is done.

II. It is also necessary that there should be an immediate reconstitution of political authority in the republic. To this end the Government of the United States very solemnly advises all concerned with the public affairs of the republic to adopt the following plan:

(1) Let all those who have any pretensions to be chosen President of the Republic and who can make any sufficient show of exercising a recognized leadership and having an acknowledged following agree upon some responsible and representative man to act as Provisional President of the Republic, it being understood that Mr. Bordas will relinquish his present position and authority. If these candidates can agree in this matter, the Government of the United States will recognize and support the man of their choice as Provisional President. If they cannot agree, the Government of the United States will itself name a Provisional President, sustain him in the assumption of office, and support him in the exercise of his temporary authority. The Provisional President will not be a candidate for President.

(2) At the earliest feasible date after the establishment and recognition of the Provisional Government thus established let elections for a regular President and Congress be held under the authority and direction of the Provisional President, who will, it must of course be understood, exercise during his tenure of office the full powers of President of the Republic; but let it be understood that the Government of the United States will send representatives of its own choosing to observe the election throughout the republic and that it will expect those observers not only to be accorded a courteous welcome but also to be accorded the freest opportunities to observe the circumstances and processes of the election.

(3) Let it be understood that if the United States Government is satisfied that these elections have been free and fair and carried out under conditions which enable the people of the republic to express their real choice, it will recognize the President and Congress thus chosen as the

legitimate and constitutional Government of the Republic and will support them in the exercise of their functions and authority in every way it can. If it should not be satisfied that elections of the right kind have been held, let it be understood that another election will be held at which the mistakes observed will be corrected.

III. A regular and constitutional government having thus been set up, the Government of the United States would feel at liberty thereafter to insist that revolutionary movements cease and that all subsequent changes in the Government of the Republic be effected by the peaceful processes provided in the Dominican Constitution. By no other course can the Government of the United States fulfill its treaty obligations with Santo Domingo or its tacitly conceded obligations as the nearest friend of Santo Domingo in her relations with the rest of the world.[57]

Completing this statement during the last week in July 1914, President Wilson at once informed the Dominicans that he would shortly propose a plan for the restoration of peace.[58] At the same time he demanded and obtained an armistice just when the *Legalistas* were preparing a final offensive against the weakened Bordas forces around Puerto Plata.[59] He then called his friend, John Franklin Fort, a former Governor of New Jersey, and Charles Cogswell Smith, an attorney from New Hampshire, and asked them to go with Minister Sullivan[60] as his personal envoys to Santo Domingo to put the Wilson Plan into effect. "You will say to the various leaders," Bryan instructed Fort, chairman of the commission, as he handed him a copy of the President's statement on August 10, "that the United States will thereafter [after the installation of a new Provisional President] employ such force as is necessary to maintain constitutional government and put down insurrections. . . . . The President feels that the step which he is taking is not only one to which he is compelled by the obligations which the country has assumed, but that this Government will be performing a neighborly act, entirely consistent with the feeling of sincere friendship entertained by the people of the United States for the people of Santo Domingo."[61] "No opportunity for argument should be given to any person or faction," the Secretary of State further advised the

[57] "Plan of President Wilson . . . ," *Foreign Relations, 1914*, pp. 247-248. The copy of this document in the Wilson Papers is dated July 27, 1914.

[58] The Secretary of State to Chargé White, July 29, 1914, *ibid.*, pp. 246-247.

[59] S. Welles, *Naboth's Vineyard*, II, 734-735; Consul Henry to the Secretary of State, August 6, 1914, *Foreign Relations, 1914*, p. 247.

[60] Sullivan had meanwhile been recalled to Washington for consultation.

[61] W. J. Bryan to J. F. Fort, August 10, 1914, Wilson Papers.

commissioners as they were en route to the Dominican capital. "It is desired that you present plan and see that it is complied with."[62]

Arriving first at Puerto Plata on about August 15, 1914, where they presented the Wilson Plan to all the factional leaders, the American commissioners then proceeded to Santo Domingo for the final conferences at which the rival chieftains were to meet and nominate a new Provisional President. On the day appointed for this meeting Bordas refused to appear; he was the *de jure* President of the Republic, he announced through his envoys, and he could not resign. The commissioners replied in a not very neighborly manner—by ordering Bordas to resign forthwith and to appear personally before them to hear his fate. If he refused, the commissioners advised the State Department, there would be no alternative but to withdraw recognition from the Bordas regime and to land troops to install the new provisional government. What, they asked in some haste, should they do?[63]

Bryan sent their message to the White House late in the afternoon of August 23. The President went to his study after dinner and typed out his "Points of Answer," as follows:

"1. Yield nothing; insist upon full and literal compliance with plan.

"2. Time limit [for Bordas' resignation] left to judgment of commission, but should be short.

"3. Bordas should be given distinctly to understand that the U.S. means business. This government will not brook refusal, changes of purpose, or unreasonable delay."[64]

A message in these words went that very night to Santo Domingo.[65] It sufficed. Bordas resigned on August 26, and after some haggling the Dominican leaders agreed upon Doctor Ramón Báez, a leading physician and professor at the University of Santo Domingo, as the interim Provisional President. He was inaugurated on August 27 and accorded immediate diplomatic recognition by the Washington government.

The months that followed were blessed by the speedy return of peace and order to the troubled land. Under the daily scrutiny and tutelage of the American commissioners, the new Provisional President

[62] The Secretary of State to Minister Gonzales, August 13, 1914, *Foreign Relations, 1914,* p. 247.

[63] The Commissioners to W. J. Bryan, August 23, 1914, Wilson Papers.

[64] W.W., "Points of Answer," MS. received from the President, 8:30 p.m., August 23, 1914, State Department Papers.

[65] W. J. Bryan to the American Commissioners, August 23, 1914, Wilson Papers.

rebuilt the structure of civil government and held presidential elections on October 25, 26, and 27, 1914. The results were a bare majority for General Juan Isidro Jiménez for President, in part because Jiménez won Arias' support by promising him a cabinet appointment and patronage for his followers.[66] Whether the election was genuinely free is still a matter of some dispute. The *Horacistas* charged that Báez favored Jiménez and that election officials perpetrated huge frauds at the polls, despite the presence everywhere of American observers. The American commissioners, on the other hand, reported differently. "The result of the election," Governor Fort wrote, "was fine; about 80,000 votes were polled. It was absolutely free. . . . Don Juan Jimenez was selected as President. . . . I believe him to be fairly in sympathy with the United States, and to be a man who, if necessary, will ask us to protect the Dominican Government."[67]

There followed a brief tense period in late November and early December, when it seemed that *Horacista* and other opposition members of the Dominican Congress might refuse to attend the sessions of the legislature in order to prevent the quorum necessary for Jiménez' inauguration. Secretary Bryan was prepared to recognize the new President and to do business with him even if he could not take office according to proper constitutional forms.[68] This, as it turned out, was not required, as a majority of the members of a joint session of the Dominican Congress proclaimed Jiménez President on December 4, and he took the oath of office on the following day.

In the meantime, President Wilson and his advisers had grown increasingly alarmed about what seemed to be the endemic political and economic instability of the Dominican Republic's western neighbor, Haiti. By the closing months of 1914 the men at the helm in Washington had concluded that they would be compelled sooner or later to assume burdens in Haiti such as they were now carrying in the Dominican Republic. But the policies toward the two Caribbean republics, although they now seemed to be heading fast in the same general direction, had begun in an altogether different way.

When Wilson came into power, relations between Haiti and the

[66] Chargé White to the Secretary of State, November 18, 1914, *Foreign Relations, 1914*, p. 256; S. Welles, *Naboth's Vineyard*, II, 744-746.

[67] J. F. Fort to J. P. Tumulty, November 16, 1914, Wilson Papers.

[68] The Secretary of State to Chargé White, December 4, 1914, *Foreign Relations, 1914*, pp. 257-258.

United States were not particularly intimate. American bankers owned one fourth of the capital stock of the National Bank of Haiti, while the Grace Syndicate had acquired a concession to build a railroad from the Haitian capital, Port-au-Prince, to Cap Haïtien on the northern coast.[69] But other American investments were inconsequential and altogether could not have totaled more than $15,000,000.[70] Nor had American political relations ever been very close. The United States had not recognized the Republic of Haiti until 1864; only sporadically since that date had the State Department evinced anything more than a casual interest in domestic developments in the little country.

No one in Washington seemed concerned about Haiti in the spring of 1913, even though frightful conditions existed and national bankruptcy threatened as a consequence of a series of revolutions since 1903. One of these periodic changes of so-called government occurred soon after President Wilson was inaugurated, when the President of Haiti, Tancrède Auguste, died presumably of poisoning on May 2 and a successor, Michel Oreste, was elected by the customary methods.[71] The State Department extended recognition to the new government as a matter of course.[72] There was a slight flurry of concern among the leaders of the Washington administration during the early summer of 1913 when Wilson and Bryan became interested in acquiring a naval base at the Môle St. Nicholas, a harbor on the end of the northwestern peninsula of Haiti.[73] Indeed, Bryan sent his Assistant Secretary of State, former Governor John E. Osborne of Wyoming, on a highly secret mission to Port-au-Prince to undertake negotiations with the Haitian authorities. But there was no feeling of urgency anywhere about the project, even when President Oreste refused to consider a treaty of cession; and Bryan rather gladly abandoned the negotiations when Oreste promised that his government would never alienate the Môle to any foreign power.[74]

[69] Raymond L. Buell, "The American Occupation of Haiti," *Foreign Policy Association Information Service*, v (November 27-December 12, 1929), 334-335.

[70] Arthur C. Millspaugh, *Haiti Under American Control, 1915-1930*, p. 22. The estimate is my own.

[71] Minister H. W. Furniss to the Secretary of State, May 10, 1913, State Department Papers.

[72] The Secretary of State to Minister Furniss, May 12, 1913, *Foreign Relations, 1913*, p. 574.

[73] W. J. Bryan to W.W., June 14, 1913, Wilson Papers; W. J. Bryan to W.W., June 20, 1913, Bryan Papers, National Archives; W.W. to W. J. Bryan, June 17 and 23, 1913, Wilson Papers.

[74] This commitment, which was made informally, was explained in B. W. Long to

American relations with the Negro republic would probably have continued in this casual way had conditions in the country remained in no more than their usual state of instability. However, Oreste soon proved to be an extraordinarily inefficient President, even by Haitian standards.[75] He crowned a series of blunders by cutting off the ordinary governmental subsidies to the *cacos*, professional revolutionists in the North, who sold their services to aspirants to the presidency.[76] The inevitable revolution broke out in La Plaine du Cul de Sac, the area immediately east of the capital, on January 1, 1914, and soon spread to Cap Haïtien and the northeastern sector near the Dominican border.[77]

Haitians, actually, were only engaging in their favorite national activity and effecting a change of government in the usual way. But circumstances were propitious, and a small group of men in the United States used the opportunity afforded by the new outbreak to press for their objective of establishing an American receivership of the Haitian customs like the one that had so long existed in the Dominican Republic. The leader of what might be called this cabal was Roger L. Farnham, an officer of the National City Bank of New York, vice president of the National Bank of Haiti, and president of the American-owned *Compagnie Nationale des Chemins de Fer d'Haïti*. A friend of Boaz W. Long of the Latin American Affairs Division, Farnham visited the State Department on January 22, 1914. During the course of a long conversation with the Secretary of State, he described the revolutionary activities that had heretofore prevented the development of Haitian resources; more important, he gently hinted that the administration might well consider the duty that it owed the Haitian people to establish and maintain a stable government.[78] Long

W. J. Bryan, February 3, 1914, Wilson Papers; and in the Secretary of State to Minister Madison R. Smith, February 26, 1914, *Foreign Relations, 1914*, p. 340.

[75] This, at any rate, was the opinion of the American Minister in Port-au-Prince. See Minister Furniss to the Secretary of State, June 28, 1913, State Department Papers. On the other hand, one Haitian historian writes that much of Oreste's difficulty stemmed from the fact that he did honestly try to achieve certain long-needed administrative reforms, thereby provoking the opposition of various groups and interests. See Dantès Bellegarde, *La Nation Haïtienne*, pp. 151-153.

[76] *ibid.*; A. C. Millspaugh, *Haiti Under American Control*, p. 13.

[77] Minister Smith to the Secretary of State, January 7 and 21, 1914, State Department Papers; Consul Lemuel W. Livingston from Cap Haïtien to the Secretary of State, received January 21, 1914, *ibid.*

[78] R. L. Farnham to W. J. Bryan, January 22, 1914, *ibid.*, recapitulating what Farnham had told the Secretary of State on the same day.

added his endorsement on the following day. "The political system which obtains throughout the country," he wrote in a memorandum for the Secretary of State, "constitutes a certain form of slavery for the masses, and no helping hand has been stretched out to the common people in an effort to improve their condition." The solution, Long went on, was American control of the customhouses; this might be achieved at once if the Secretary would send a special commissioner to Haiti to negotiate with the man who emerged on top of the present revolution.[79]

Bryan was much impressed by Farnham, even though he was a Wall Street banker with certain obvious interests at stake in Haiti. Furthermore, the Secretary was strongly tempted by this new opportunity to strike a blow for the common man. He forwarded Long's memorandum to the White House and conferred with the President and then with Long about the Haitian situation soon afterward.[80] But there was no way the Secretary could undertake any important new policy until a measure of quietude prevailed in Haiti. To be sure, he did offer a word of good advice to the revolutionists at Cap Haïtien, urging them to read President Wilson's statement of March 12, 1913, and insisting that they use only "constitutional methods for reform of any abuses."[81] When President Oreste abdicated on January 27 and fighting broke out near Port-au-Prince between two rival revolutionary factions, Bryan had the Navy Department send small American forces ashore at the capital to join German, British, and French contingents in the protection of foreigners and their property.[82] Beyond such action, however, it was not possible to go.

Conditions returned to normal within a few days after the landing of the American troops. Oreste Zamor, the leader, along with his brother Charles, of one of the revolutionary factions, defeated Senator Davilmar Théodore, the chief of the other, in a decisive battle at Gonaïves in the North on February 1, 1914. Oreste Zamor then marched his army to Port-au-Prince, where he took possession of the government and was duly elected to the presidency by the National Assembly a week later. He next routed the remainder of Théodore's

[79] B. W. Long to W. J. Bryan, January 23, 1914, Wilson Papers.

[80] *New York Times*, January 25, 1914.

[81] The Secretary of State to Minister Smith, January 25, 1914, *Foreign Relations, 1914*, p. 336.

[82] *New York Times*, January 25 and 28, 1914; Minister Smith to the Secretary of State, January 27 and 30, 1914, *Foreign Relations, 1914*, p. 336.

forces, occupied the northern port town of Cap Haïtien, and appealed to Washington for recognition.[83]

Undecided whether to strike now for American control of the Haitian customhouses, Bryan hesitated, even though the American Minister in Port-au-Prince, Madison R. Smith, had reported that Zamor was regarded as being pro-American and that a number of German merchants in Haiti were already scheming against the new regime.[84] After much discussion with the President,[85] the Secretary of State apparently decided that this was no time to intervene decisively. On February 26 he instructed Minister Smith to tell the Haitian Foreign Minister, J. N. Léger, that the State Department was considering recognizing the Zamor government; that the American authorities, eager to extend their disinterested help to the people of Haiti, would be "well disposed" to assist in the collection of the customs; and that the Washington government hoped that the new Haitian leaders would ratify former President Oreste's assurances about the nonalienation of the Môle St. Nicholas.[86] It was all done quite gently; and when Léger replied that he could give no definite answers until relations between the two governments were on a regular basis, Bryan extended formal recognition almost at once, on March 1, 1914.[87]

A brief period of quiescence in Haitian-American relations followed the inauguration of President Zamor, and the project for an American receivership dropped momentarily out of sight. Obviously, neither Wilson nor Bryan was eager to go very deep into the jungle of Haitian politics, especially since their energies were being daily diverted by the *Legalista* rebellion against the Bordas regime in the Dominican Republic, to say nothing of the Mexican problem. However, two developments during the early spring of 1914 drew the attention of leaders in Washington, almost against their will, to plans for intimate participation in Haitian affairs.

[83] Minister Smith to the Secretary of State, February 3, 7, 8, 10, and 21, 1914, *ibid.*, pp. 337-339; Minister Smith to the Secretary of State, February 16, 1914, State Department Papers.

[84] Minister Smith to the Secretary of State, February 20 and 21, 1914, *ibid.*

[85] e.g., W. J. Bryan to W.W., February 11 and 21, 1914, Wilson Papers.

[86] The Secretary of State to Minister Smith, February 26, 1914, *Foreign Relations, 1914*, pp. 339-340.

[87] Minister Smith to the Secretary of State, February 28, 1914; the Secretary of State to Minister Smith, March 1, 1914, *ibid.*, pp. 340-341.

The first was an announcement by the French and German governments that, in view of the large economic interests of their nationals in Haiti, they would insist upon sharing control of any receivership of the republic's customs that might be established.[88] In addition, there were rumors, which were apparently quite untrue, that the German government had offered substantial financial assistance to President Zamor in return for a coaling station in Haiti.[89] Although neither the Paris nor the Berlin Foreign Office had given any sign that it meant to take the initiative in establishing a joint receivership, Wilson and Bryan were plainly disturbed by this European claim to participation if the American government imposed any such arrangement.[90] It was, the President and Secretary of State must have concluded, reason enough for going forward on their own as rapidly as possible.

More important in reviving the Washington administration's concern was the beginning of a new insurrection against the Zamor regime, one organized among the *cacos* of the North by the recently unsuccessful revolutionist, Davilmar Théodore, only six weeks after the inauguration of President Zamor.[91] With any kind of financial support, Zamor might easily have suppressed the new uprising. But the national treasury was empty, the authorities in Port-au-Prince were living from hand to mouth on advances from the National Bank of Haiti, and the Bank was threatening to cut off these advances. When intimations came to Washington that Théodore and Zamor would both welcome American mediation, Bryan sent an emissary to Théodore's camp, only to discover that this chieftain and his followers would accept nothing less than Zamor's retirement.[92]

The rhythm of revolution in Haiti was obviously quickening. Théodore would undoubtedly succeed and then just as surely fall victim to some new rival. How long could this go on before total anarchy ensued? The only remedy, Boaz W. Long declared in a memorandum that surveyed political conditions in northern Latin America, was for the United States to assume financial responsibility for all the revolution-ridden countries. The customhouses were the great lure; only when

[88] W. J. Bryan to W.W., March 24, 1914, Wilson Papers.
[89] *New York Times*, May 14, 1914.
[90] The Franco-German suggestion, Wilson said, was simply out of the question. W.W. to W. J. Bryan, March 26, 1914, Wilson Papers.
[91] Minister Smith to the Secretary of State, March 14, 1914, *ibid*.
[92] Consul Livingston to the Secretary of State, May 26, 1914; Minister Smith to the Secretary of State, June 9, 1914, *Foreign Relations, 1914*, pp. 344-346.

they were safely beyond the grasp of venal politicians would revolutions cease.[93]

In response the Washington authorities agreed that they must go forward with the project for control of the Haitian customs. The records do not reveal whether it was Wilson or Bryan who took the initiative in making this decision. The two men discussed the matter at some time during the third week of June, and Bryan sent a copy of the convention establishing the American receivership of the Dominican customs to the White House for the President's perusal. Returning the document to the Secretary on June 25, Wilson gave his approval to the Haitian project, as follows: "The general administrative arrangement is no doubt such as we could enter into with Haiti. I suggest that with the aid of memoranda from our representatives in Haiti we attempt a similar statement of the circumstances and have a convention tentatively drawn up along the same lines."[94] It was quickly done, and the draft treaty, which provided not only for American collection of the Haitian customs but also for the appointment of an American financial adviser with broad powers over expenditures, received the President's approval on July 1, 1914.[95]

Bryan forwarded a copy of the proposed convention to the new American Minister in Port-au-Prince, Arthur Bailly-Blanchard, on the following day, together with instructions that made it clear that the Secretary was acting only out of disinterested friendship and had no intention of imposing the arrangement upon the Haitians against their will.[96] At the same time, Bryan asked Roger L. Farnham, who was then in northern Haiti, to do what he could to persuade President Zamor and his brother Charles to accept the proffered helping hand.[97]

It seemed at first that the hard-pressed brothers would clutch at the straw of American intervention. Farnham, Blanchard, and the American Consul at Cap Haïtien, Lemuel W. Livingston, were unable to find President Oreste Zamor, for he was somewhere in the jungle at the head of his little army. The American agents did, however, have several conferences with General Charles Zamor at Cap Haïtien. He

[93] B. W. Long, "The Professional Revolutionist," MS. dated June 12, 1914, State Department Papers.

[94] W.W. to W. J. Bryan, June 25, 1914, Wilson Papers.

[95] W.W. to W. J. Bryan, July 1, 1914, *ibid*. The draft treaty is printed in *Foreign Relations, 1914*, pp. 349-350.

[96] The Secretary of State to Minister Blanchard, July 2, 1914, *ibid*., pp. 347-350.

[97] The Secretary of State to the American Consul, Cap Haïtien, July 10, 1914, State Department Papers.

and his brother, Charles Zamor declared, were now prepared to acquiesce in the Farnham Plan, as the proposal for an American receivership was by this time known. However, Zamor went on, it would not be easy to persuade the other Haitian leaders to agree. In these circumstances, he suggested, the best arrangement would be one by which American forces would occupy Port-au-Prince upon the outbreak of disorder in the capital, and the Zamor government would accept the Farnham Plan at the demand of the State Department.[98]

Implied in Zamor's offer was the further condition that the United States would also protect and maintain his brother's government once it had yielded to the American demand for financial control. Bryan, surely, realized this fact, but he approved the proposed procedure none the less and moved at once to have a warship dispatched to Port-au-Prince and some seven hundred marines sent to the American base at Guantánamo, Cuba, for use at the Haitian capital when the time was ripe.[99]

That moment came quickly, when sharp fighting broke out in Port-au-Prince on July 20, 1914. Bryan was eager to move, but he could not act until President Oreste Zamor had given the signal.[100] Farnham and Minister Blanchard, therefore, set out from Port-au-Prince on July 23 in search of the fugitive leader. They never found him; but they did run down Charles Zamor at Cap Haïtien, who told them that the President was no longer interested in any plans for American intervention and control. This sudden change of mind, Blanchard explained after he and Farnham had returned to the capital, had occurred because the bankrupt Zamor government had just borrowed a small sum from German merchants in Cap Haïtien and hoped soon to obtain a large loan from private American sources.[101]

It was the end of all such negotiations with the Zamor brothers until the mid-autumn of 1914. Then, on October 22, after their power had collapsed in the North and the entry of the revolutionary forces under Théodore into Port-au-Prince impended, they sent a desperate call for

[98] J. F. Cleary, transmitting a message from R. L. Farnham, to the Secretary of State, July 10, 1914, *ibid.*; Consul Livingston to the Secretary of State, July 12, 18, and 23, 1914, *ibid.*

[99] W. J. Bryan to W.W., c. July 18, 1914, Wilson Papers; *New York Times*, July 22, 1914.

[100] The Secretary of State to Minister Blanchard, July 22, 1914, State Department Papers.

[101] Minister Blanchard to the Secretary of State, July 23 and 31, 1914, *ibid.*; also Minister Blanchard to the Secretary of State, August 10, 1914, *ibid.*

help to Minister Blanchard. Blanchard replied coldly, saying that the Zamors knew well enough what they would have to do in order to renew the negotiations that they had broken off so abruptly in July. An envoy returned to the American Legation on October 24 bearing a letter from Charles Zamor, and an offer, as follows: "That the United States lend an effective assistance to the Haitian Government to triumph over the revolution and in return he, Charles Zamor, would guarantee (se fait fort) to have adopted the views of the United States Government."[102]

Bryan was absent from Washington when this news came to the State Department, but President Wilson and Acting Secretary of State Robert Lansing lost no time in proceeding to what they hoped would be the final solution.[103] On October 29 they dispatched the transport *Hancock* with 800 marines from Guantánamo and the battleship *Kansas* from Mexican waters to Port-au-Prince. "Department is contemplating convention along the lines of its instruction of July 2," Lansing cabled Blanchard on the same day. ". . . Upon arrival of the *Hancock* you will at your discretion request commanding officer to take charge of Port au Prince and will restore Charles Zamor to his Cabinet functions."[104]

It was too late. President Oreste Zamor had already resigned, released his troops, and boarded a Dutch steamer at Gonaïves by the time Lansing's message reached Port-au-Prince, and Charles Zamor had fled to the French Legation in the capital. "I had an interview with Charles Zamor . . . at the French Legation," Blanchard reported on October 30. "After a consultation with his supporters he stated that as far as he was concerned it was too late; conditions were entirely changed. Abandoning hope of aid from the Government of the United States in the present revolution the President had resigned . . . ; troops were disbanded and had possibly joined the revolution. He thought that armed intervention alone from the Government of the United States could save the country from anarchy."[105]

The excuse as well as the opportunity for the American occupation of Port-au-Prince soon passed. The *Hancock* arrived at the capital on

[102] Minister Blanchard to the Secretary of State, October 25, 1914, *ibid.*

[103] R. Lansing to W.W., October 26, 1914, *ibid.*; R. Lansing to W.W., October 28 and 29, 1914, Wilson Papers.

[104] *New York Times,* October 30, 1914; the Acting Secretary of State to Minister Blanchard, October 29, 1914, *Foreign Relations, 1914,* p. 355.

[105] Minister Blanchard to the Secretary of State, October 30, 1914, *ibid.*, p. 356.

October 31, but the fighting in the city was over by this time. Théo-dore's troops entered in force on November 3, followed by their leader on November 6. Meeting in special session on the following day, the National Assembly elected Davilmar Théodore to the presidency of the republic for a full seven-year term. He took the oath of office on November 10, 1914.[106]

For a brief moment before Théodore reached Port-au-Prince, Wilson and Lansing had contemplated attempting to impose the Wilson Plan, which had already been carried out in the Dominican Republic,[107] upon Haiti.[108] They soon abandoned such intentions and decided in-stead to negotiate in a more conventional way with the new Théodore government. Consequently, after returning to his desk, Bryan instructed Blanchard to tell the Haitian authorities that the American government would recognize their regime if they would send three commissioners to Washington empowered to sign a treaty providing for an American receivership of the Haitian customs, the appointment of an American financial adviser in Port-au-Prince, and the settlement of certain other issues, including the permanent nonalienation of the Môle St. Nich-olas.[109] Théodore and his Foreign Minister, Joseph Justin, were not altogether hostile to the proposition. Unfortunately, news about it soon spread rapidly through the city, and violence broke out when a senator interpellated Justin in the upper house on December 3, 1914. The For-eign Minister made the error of seeming to admit the necessity for foreign assistance. "With cries of 'Vive la Liberté' the audience with one accord, armed with canes, knives, and even revolvers, surged towards the speaker. In the mêlée Mr. Justin received several blows and, except for the protection afforded him by the other Cabinet mem-bers and Senators, would have been assassinated. . . . The fury of the audience was calmed by a speech of Dr. Bobo, Minister of the Interior, who concluded with the words—'The Government will shroud itself in the folds of the National Flag rather than ever to consent to the least attaint to the Haitian autonomy.'"[110]

[106] Minister Blanchard to the Secretary of State, November 10, 1914, State Depart-ment Papers.

[107] See above, pp. 512-515.

[108] The Acting Secretary of State to Minister Blanchard, November 4, 1914, *Foreign Relations, 1914*, pp. 357-358.

[109] The Secretary of State to Minister Blanchard, November 12, 1914, *ibid.*, p. 359.

[110] Minister Blanchard to the Secretary of State, December 16, 1914, State Depart-ment Papers.

Still eager to obtain American recognition and coin for the bankrupt national treasury, President Théodore and his Cabinet (without Foreign Minister Justin, who had just resigned) met Blanchard on December 10 in an extraordinarily frank confrontation. An American receivership, the Haitian leaders explained, was simply out of the question, as no government that approved it could long survive the popular wrath. They had a counterproposition of their own to offer. Let the State Department help the Haitian government obtain a large loan and reform its monetary system; in return they would be willing to grant extensive mining concessions and commercial and industrial privileges to American citizens.[111] Only by some such arrangement, actually, could the Théodore government hope to remain alive, for the National Bank of Haiti had cut off all allowances to the government, which was at this very time resorting to the expedient of paper money in violation of its contract with the Bank. The new Minister for Foreign Affairs, Louis Borno, moreover, came back to the Legation on December 14 to offer a new counterproject, one providing merely for settlement of all Haitian-American differences and the State Department's recognition of the Théodore government.[112]

Bryan was deeply offended by the first Haitian offer. It was, he thought, an outright attempt at bribery. Upon receiving Blanchard's message conveying its terms, he rushed to the White House and there composed with the President a reply which went to Port-au-Prince an hour later: "Please say to the Government that this nation has no desire to assume responsibilities in regard to Haiti's fiscal system except in accordance with the wishes of the Government. In expressing a willingness to do in Haiti what we are doing in Santo Domingo, this Government was actuated wholly by a disinterested desire to render assistance."[113] And when Blanchard's telegram of December 15 telling of Borno's second counterproject arrived, Bryan ignored it and replied with an eloquent statement of American policy:

"While we desire to encourage in every proper way American in-

[111] Minister Blanchard to the Secretary of State, December 12, 1914, received at 4 p.m., State Department Papers. The copy of this telegram printed in *Foreign Relations, 1914*, pp. 367-368, is misdated December 12, 1914, 11 p.m., and is printed out of order.

[112] Minister Blanchard to the Secretary of State, December 15, 1914, Wilson Papers; Minister Blanchard to the Secretary of State, December 21, 1914, State Department Papers, enclosing a copy of the counterproposition.

[113] The Secretary of State to Minister Blanchard, December 12, 1914, 5 p.m., *Foreign Relations, 1914*, p. 367.

vestments in Haiti, we believe that this can better be done by contributing to stability and order than by favoring special concessions to Americans. . . . If the United States can, as a neighbor and friend, assist the Government and people of Haiti as it has assisted the Government and people of Santo Domingo, it will gladly do so provided that assistance is desired; but . . . this Government does not care to assume these responsibilities except on request of the Haitian Government. The Government of the United States does not deem it proper to enter into such arrangements as those outlined in the proposition just submitted. . . . Our obligation to the American people requires that we shall give all legitimate assistance to American investors in Haiti, but we are under obligations just as binding to protect Haiti, as far as our influence goes, from injustice or exploitation at the hands of Americans."[114]

The counterproject, Bryan commented somewhat bitterly as he sent a copy of the above dispatch to the White House, "is so evidently an attempt to negotiate for concessions that I think it is well for us to let them distinctly understand that this Government is not disposed to make a bargain of that kind."[115] The Secretary of State undoubtedly meant what he said, but the truth also was that neither he nor the President was disposed to do anything at all to help the Théodore government if they could not have their way about the receivership. They did not openly attack the new regime, but they refused to grant it diplomatic recognition, and indirectly they harried the new authorities in Port-au-Prince.[116] The result, inevitably, was to hasten the end of a bankrupt and helpless regime. It came with startling speed after one of Théodore's former comrades in arms, Vilbrun Guillaume Sam,

[114] The Secretary of State to Minister Blanchard, December 19, 1914, *ibid.*, pp. 370-371.

[115] W. J. Bryan to W.W., December 18, 1914, Wilson Papers.

[116] For one thing, Bryan used marines from the transport *Hancock* to seize $500,000 in gold belonging to the Republic of Haiti on December 17, 1914, and transferred it to the National City Bank of New York on board the gunboat *Machias*, after the long-standing dispute between the Port-au-Prince authorities and the National Bank of Haiti had come to a head and the latter had asked the American government to seize the funds. (For the documents relating to this affair, see *Foreign Relations, 1914*, pp. 365-366, 369, 371-375, 377-382.) Then, when the Haitian Congress proceeded with the issuance of paper money and gave signs of intending to punish the Bank, Bryan warned that the American government would refuse to recognize the legality of the issue and would not tolerate any interference with the institution, "in view of the fact that it is owned and operated by Americans and other foreigners." (The Secretary of State to Minister Blanchard, December 31, 1914, *ibid.*, p. 382.)

rallied the *cacos* in early 1915 and captured Cap Haïtien on January 18. With the support of most of the army, Sam swept down from the North and took possession of the capital on February 25 and the presidency on March 4, 1915.

It was all terribly discouraging to the usually hopeful head of the State Department. "The situation in Hayti," he wrote in a long letter to the President reviewing the situation soon after the beginning of Sam's revolt, "is still embarrassing and we have apparently made no progress." Théodore's tenure obviously would be brief; Haitian finances were in chaos; and there was the problem of protecting the National Bank of Haiti. What, Bryan went on, could the American government do? He did not like the idea of using force to intervene; perhaps the best solution lay in sending a commission to put the Wilson Plan in effect and to institute an American receivership. "The success of this Government's efforts in Santo Domingo [*sic!*] would, it seems to me, suggest the application of the same methods to Hayti whenever the time is ripe."[117]

Wilson even more than Bryan was ready to move vigorously, without waiting for any invitation from Port-au-Prince. "The more I think about that situation," he replied, "the more I am convinced that it is our duty to take immediate action there such as we took in San Domingo. I mean to send commissioners there who will seek and obtain an interview with the leaders of the various contending factions of the republic and say to them as firmly and definitely as is consistent with courtesy and kindness that the United States cannot consent to stand by and permit revolutionary conditions constantly to exist there. They ought, as in San Domingo, to insist upon an agreement for a popular election under our supervision and to be told that the result of the election would be upheld by the United States to the utmost."[118]

There were, as subsequent investigation revealed, certain technical difficulties in trying to apply the Wilson Plan in Haiti: Elections for a new Haitian Congress could not be held constitutionally until 1916; the President would have to be chosen by the two houses in joint

[117] W. J. Bryan to W.W., January 7, 1915, Wilson Papers.
[118] W.W. to W. J. Bryan, January 13, 1915, *ibid.* See also W. J. Bryan to W.W., January 15, 1915, and W.W. to W. J. Bryan, January 16, 1915, State Department Papers, in which the two leaders agreed to ask John Franklin Fort and Charles Cogswell Smith, who had earlier served as commissioners to the Dominican Republic, to go on a special mission to Haiti.

session, not by popular vote; there was little likelihood that any Haitian government would accept a treaty providing for an American receivership. Finally, there was the fact that the new Sam regime would soon be coming to power. In these circumstances, Bryan wrote to President Wilson near the end of February 1915, what could the American government do but go ahead and send a commission and support the Haitian President in office if he seemed at all capable of governing, without insisting upon approval of a treaty as a condition of recognition?[119] "I do not see," the President agreed, "what other course we can follow."[120]

Bryan called the two former commissioners to the Dominican Republic, John Franklin Fort and Charles Cogswell Smith, who had earlier agreed to serve again, to Washington on February 27, 1915, and sent them on their way with a special letter of instructions. It directed them to ascertain whether President Sam had enough popular support to survive with American assistance, and to inquire about the methods the American government might use to render disinterested service to Haiti in her present plight.[121] Arriving at Port-au-Prince on March 5, the two envoys joined the third member of the commission, Minister Blanchard, and finally obtained an interview with the newest occupant of the presidential palace on March 11. Governor Fort began by saying that the American government wanted only to assist the Haitian people in some honorable and acceptable way. He was very grateful, General Sam replied, and he would listen to anything that his visitors had to say. But, he added, he could not discuss any matter in his official capacity until the United States had recognized his government and had formally accredited the commissioners.[122] As further conversations were obviously useless, the commission withdrew, and Fort and Smith returned to Washington on March 15, 1915.

Accepting the rebuff calmly, the Washington authorities decided simply to withhold recognition and to wait a while longer, in the hope that the new Haitian leaders would conclude that American intervention was better than bankruptcy and continued domestic strife. However, a sudden turn of events soon jolted the President and Sec-

[119] W. J. Bryan to W.W., February 25, 1915, Bryan Papers, National Archives.
[120] W.W. to W. J. Bryan, February 26, 1915, *ibid.*
[121] W. J. Bryan to J. F. Fort, February 27, 1915, State Department Papers.
[122] J. F. Fort, A. Bailly-Blanchard, and C. C. Smith to W. J. Bryan, March 13, 1915, Wilson Papers.

retary of State. On March 25 word came to the State Department that the Italian, German, and French governments had recognized the Sam government; it was accompanied by a report from Roger L. Farnham that a private French firm had just lent the government one million dollars.[123] Two days later Farnham brought in person the even more discouraging news that French interests in the National Bank of Haiti had recently taken control of that institution, and that the French and Germans (then at war in Europe!) were cooperating to drive American investors out of Haiti and to gain control of the Môle St. Nicholas. The bank's American stockholders, Farnham further reported, had concluded that they would have to "retire from the field" unless the American government intervened to protect their position and to end "the intolerable conditions which have prevailed in Haiti for the past four years."[124] "The American interests," Bryan added a few days later, recalling his conversation with Farnham, "are willing to remain there, with a view of purchasing a controlling interest and making the Bank a branch of the American [i.e., the National City] bank—they are willing to do this provided this Government takes the steps necessary to protect them and their idea seems to be that no protection will be sufficient that does not include a control of the Custom House."[125]

Farnham's story about a Franco-German intrigue was an unlikely one indeed,[126] but Bryan and Wilson did not bother to inquire whether it was true, or to ask themselves whether the New York banker was trying to serve interests of his own. They simply swallowed the bait, if, indeed, it was that. "This whole matter has a most sinister appearance," the President responded in obvious alarm after reading Bryan's account of his conversation with Farnham and a memorandum that the banker had dictated at the State Department. "The more we get into it the more unpleasant and unpropitious it looks. I think that the American interests should stay in and that we should sustain and assist them in every legitimate way. I think, too, that it is evident

[123] Minister Blanchard to the Secretary of State, two telegrams, March 25, 1915, *Foreign Relations, 1915*, p. 469; W. J. Bryan to W.W., March 25, 1915, Bryan Papers, National Archives. For Wilson's comment, see W.W. to W. J. Bryan, March 25, 1915, *ibid*.

[124] W. J. Bryan to W.W., March 27, 1915, *ibid*.; R. L. Farnham, "Confidential Memorandum in Respect to American Interests in the National Bank of Haiti, Dictated March 27, 1915," MS. in *ibid*.

[125] W. J. Bryan to W.W., April 3, 1915, *ibid*.

[126] As the spokesman for the American group with a large interest in the National Bank of Haiti, Farnham was, needless to say, not an unbiased witness. No official American representative in Haiti substantiated his report.

we shall have to take a very decided stand with the government of Haiti, and demand certain things as a condition precedent of recognition. You know much more of the detail than I do. Will you not be kind enough to think out a plan of controlling action which we can take, and take before the tangle gets any greater,—while the threads can be pulled together rather than cut?"[127]

It was not easy, however, to pull the threads together without being prepared to use force upon the Haitians. *That*, Bryan wrote to Wilson, was what had disturbed him most. But, he went on, the United States could not permit a foreign government to control an American state through its financiers; and revolutionary leaders in Haiti often assisted troublemakers in the Dominican Republic. Something, therefore, had to be done quickly; however, the Secretary went on, it might be better to begin slowly, by requiring the Haitians to accept an American resident adviser. "That might not be so offensive as to have foreign officials actually collecting the customs, as in Santo Domingo."[128] The President's patience, in contrast to Bryan's, had worn dangerously thin by this time. Bryan's proposal, he replied, was good as far as it went, but it did not go far enough. "I think," he added, "that the sooner we get our plans going in Haiti for a stable arrangement that will preclude anxieties such as we have recently felt the better."[129]

In the end, however, Wilson decided to let Bryan try again in his own way. In late April 1915, consequently, the Secretary of State asked Paul Fuller, Junior, a son of the President's Confidential Agent in Mexico, to convey a new proposal to President Sam in Port-au-Prince. As Bryan's letter of instruction, drafted on May 6, made clear, the American government was prepared to recognize the Sam government and to lend it effective support "by the employment of such force as may be necessary to prevent insurrection and insure stability." In return the United States asked nothing for itself and no special privileges for its citizens, only that the President of Haiti agree to follow the advice of the American Legation at Port-au-Prince in matters concerning the honest and efficient administration of the government, and that the informal understanding about the nonalienation of the Môle St. Nicholas be continued, unless the Haitians wished to lease the Môle to the United States.[130]

[127] W.W. to W. J. Bryan, March 31, 1915, *ibid.*
[128] W. J. Bryan to W.W., April 3, 1915, *ibid.*
[129] W.W. to W. J. Bryan, April 6, 1915, *ibid.*
[130] W. J. Bryan to Paul Fuller, Jr., May 6, 1915, State Department Papers; also W. J. Bryan to W.W., May 6, 1915, Bryan Papers, National Archives.

Fuller arrived at the Haitian capital on May 14, 1915, just at the time when a new revolution, one headed by a former Minister of the Interior, Doctor Rosalvo Bobo, was breaking out in northern Haiti around Cap Haïtien.[131] The negotiations went forward rapidly between May 17 and June 5 in the knowledge that their failure meant the probable triumph of the new rebellion. To President Sam, Foreign Minister Ulrick Duvivier, and numerous other Haitian leaders with whom he talked, Fuller made it clear that the American government did not desire to control the Haitian customs or to impair the autonomy of the republic in any way. As an earnest of good faith, he offered a treaty providing only for a close understanding between the Haitian government and the American Minister in the capital, and for American recognition and support of the government "by the employment of the United States Army and Navy to the extent needed." As the forces under Doctor Bobo were now gaining ground daily, Sam was not disposed to sneer at the offer; he simply had to avoid seeming to give the appearance of bargaining away his country's independence. Consequently, without rejecting the proffered American treaty outright, he came back with one of his own, providing for American protection against external aggression, assistance (but only at the request of the President of Haiti) in the maintenance of internal order and the reorganization of the Haitian fiscal system, and the permanent nonalienation of the Môle St. Nicholas. Fuller, however, did not feel like bargaining. He returned to Washington on June 6 convinced that most "honest" Haitians actually desired thoroughgoing American control of their domestic affairs, and that the Sam government would soon be in such dire straits that it would eagerly accept the treaty that he, Fuller, had offered.[132]

While President Wilson and officials in the State Department pondered Sam's proposal and Fuller's recommendations,[133] the situation in Haiti gradually deteriorated. For a time it seemed that a government in Port-au-Prince was at last strong enough to cope with a revolution. With a treasury full of the paper money authorized by the Théodore government, General Sam was able to reinforce his army and begin a surprise offensive that culminated in the recapture of Cap

---

[131] Consul Livingston to the Secretary of State, May 1 and 10, 1915, State Department Papers.

[132] Paul Fuller, Jr., to the Secretary of State, June 14, 1915, *ibid.*

[133] e.g., W.W. to R. Lansing, July 2, 1915; L. H. W., "Mr. Paul Fuller's Report on Haiti," undated MS., both in *ibid.*

Haïtien on June 19, 1915. There was not much change in the situation during the following five weeks. On July 27, however, an insurrectionary group overpowered the President's guard and besieged the presidential palace, and the Governor of Port-au-Prince, General Oscar Etienne, immediately ordered the execution of nearly two hundred political prisoners, including former President Oreste Zamor, who had meanwhile returned from exile and had fallen into the government's hands. The prisoners were tortured and then killed in brutal fashion, mainly by the machete. News of the massacre spread rapidly through the city and set off a wave of hysteria. A frenzied mob seized General Oscar as he left the prison and shot him in the streets. It would have dealt in similar fashion with Sam except for the fact that he had escaped to the French Legation. Larger mobs formed, until by nightfall they roamed in aimless anarchy and undisputed control. The following day, July 28, the mob attacked the French Legation. Overcoming the guard, the leaders of the mob dragged the President from a hiding place off the French Minister's bedroom, hacked his body to pieces, and threw the parts to the ecstatic crowd outside. But let an eyewitness, the American Chargé in the Haitian capital, describe the scene:

"Before I reached the [French] Legation there was one terrific howl of fury from that direction. Turning into the street which runs behind the French Legation, I found my way completely blocked by a mob which filled the street from wall to wall. . . . I could see that something or somebody was on the ground in the center of the crowd, just before the gates, and when a man disentangled himself . . . and rushed howling by me, with a severed hand from which the blood was dripping, the thumb of which he had stuck in his mouth, I knew that the threatened assassination of the President was accomplished. Behind him came other men with the feet, the other hand, the head, and other parts of the body displayed on poles, each one followed by a mob of screaming men and women. The portion of the body that remained was dragged through the streets by the crowd."[134]

The storm had broken so suddenly that officials in Washington were unprepared immediately to cope with its violence. There were no American naval forces in the harbor of Port-au-Prince on the morning of

---

[134] The foregoing account of the disturbances in Port-au-Prince and the quoted passage are based upon and taken from the long report by Chargé Robert B. Davis, Jr., undated but sent to the Secretary of State on January 12, 1916, *ibid.*, and the *New York Times*, July 28 and 29, 1915.

July 27, 1915, when it all began, but the armored cruiser *Washington*, under the command of Rear Admiral William B. Caperton, had recently arrived at Cap Haïtien from Mexican waters. Steaming under forced draft, Caperton arrived at Port-au-Prince at eleven o'clock in the morning of July 28 and landed some four hundred marines and sailors later in the day—in time, it turned out, to obviate the necessity for the landing of any large number of men from the British and French cruisers lying in the harbor. There was only sporadic resistance from the 1,500 *cacos* in the capital (two Americans were killed by snipers during the night of July 29); and with the help of a local committee of safety, which disarmed the citizenry, Caperton had restored a measure of order by August 1. Meanwhile, an additional company of marines from Guantánamo had arrived at the Haitian capital aboard the U.S.S. *Jason*; and the U.S.S. *Connecticut*, with two battalions of the Second Marine Regiment aboard, had sailed from Philadelphia on July 31.[135]

All this, of course, was a rather commonplace police action, such as great powers often undertook in small countries to end anarchy and protect foreign lives and property. The question now confronting the leaders in Washington was not whether their forces would occupy Port-au-Prince, but how long they would stay and to what purpose. We cannot know what Bryan would have done or advised doing in these circumstances. Certainly his policies had long been heading toward intervention and toward some kind of comprehensive American control of Haitian affairs, although all along he had been reluctant to use force to achieve this end. But a new Secretary of State, Robert Lansing, now sat in Bryan's chair, and Lansing was of a harder, more "realistic" turn of mind than his predecessor. He had probably already concluded that American interests in the Caribbean were so vital and the threat of European penetration of the region was so dangerous that the United States had no choice but to discipline and control the revolution-ridden republics when they failed to govern themselves responsibly.[136]

[135] *ibid.*, July 29, 30, 31, August 1, 1915; various documents printed in *Foreign Relations, 1914*, pp. 475-477; R. Lansing to the Secretary of the Navy, July 30, 1915, State Department Papers; J. Daniels to W.W., July 30, 1915, Daniels Papers; W.W. to J. Daniels, July 31, 1915, Wilson Papers. One of the Americans killed by snipers on July 28 was William Gompers of Brooklyn, nephew of Samuel Gompers, president of the American Federation of Labor.

[136] He set forth this view later in R. Lansing to W.W., November 24, 1915, and in R. Lansing, "PRESENT NATURE AND EXTENT OF THE MONROE DOC-

In any event, this was Lansing's conclusion about Haiti as he discussed the necessity of working out a long-range policy with the President in early August of 1915. He had conferred with Farnham, with Paul Fuller, Junior, and with one Casenave, a French agent in the National Bank of Haiti, the Secretary of State wrote to President Wilson, then at Cornish, New Hampshire, on August 3. There seemed to be no way out, Lansing continued, but to stay in Haiti until a responsible government and American control of Haitian finances had been established. The main difficulty was that the American government could justify such action only upon humane grounds and not upon treaty rights or international law.[137]

At Cornish Wilson had followed the reports from Haiti with close attention. He had been visibly depressed by the news of the death of the first two Americans who lost their lives as a consequence of the occupation of Port-au-Prince. He, like Lansing, was not moved by any threat of *military* intervention by the European powers if the United States refused to act.[138] He had long since made up his mind what had to be done in Haiti, and he was tired of temporizing and

TRINE," memorandum dated November 24, 1915, both in *The Lansing Papers*, II, 466-470.

[137] R. Lansing to W.W., August 3, 1915, State Department Papers.

[138] This is a point about which there has been considerable misunderstanding, caused in large measure by Lansing's declaration, made in 1922 in a letter to a senatorial committee of investigation, that fear of European and particularly German attempts to gain a foothold in Haiti had been a prime motive for the American occupation. There was, Lansing informed the senators, "good reason to believe that in the years 1913-14 Germany was ready to go to great lengths to secure the exclusive customs control of Haiti, and also to secure a coaling station at Mole St. Nicholas." The United States occupied Haiti, Lansing went on, because it desired to "forestall any attempt by a foreign power to obtain a foothold on the territory of an American nation which, if a seizure of customs control by such power had occurred, or if a grant of a coaling station or naval base had been obtained, would have most certainly been a menace to the peace of the Western Hemisphere, and in flagrant defiance of the Monroe Doctrine." R. Lansing to M. McCormick, May 4, 1922, *Senate Report No. 794*, 67th Cong., 2d sess., pp. 32, 37.

The historian can only observe that Lansing was either using the bogey of European intervention to answer his critics, or else relying entirely upon a bad memory. His statement about alleged German intrigues in Haiti was considerably overdrawn; and his more general statement about the fear of European intervention if the United States did not act was grossly exaggerated if not altogether false. At any rate, the historian can find no evidence in the voluminous correspondence of the time to support these statements. Such fears did not exist for the obvious reason that France and Germany, the only two European powers with any important interests in Haiti, were not in any position in 1915 to send a military expedition to the New World even had they been prepared thus to antagonize the American government and people.

determined to avoid any further futile negotiations. He would, he quickly decided, take control of Haiti and establish constitutional government there. He explained all this in a letter to Lansing on August 4, as follows:

"These are serious matters, and my own judgment is as much perplexed as yours.

"I fear we have not the legal authority to do what we apparently ought to do; and that if we did do what is necessary it would constitute a case very much like that of Mr. Roosevelt's action in Santo Domingo, and have very much the same issue.

"I suppose there is nothing for it but to take the bull by the horns and restore order. A long programme . . . involves legislation and the cooperation of the Senate in treaty-making, and must therefore await the session of our Congress.

"In the meantime this is plain to me:

"**1. We must send to Port au Prince a force sufficient to absolutely control the city not only but also the country immediately about it from which it draws its food. I would be obliged if you would ascertain from the Secretary of the Navy whether he has such a force available that can reach there soon.

"2. We must let the present [Haitian] Congress know that we will protect it but that we will not recognize any action on its part which does not put men in charge of affairs whom we can trust to handle and put an end to revolution.

"3. We must give all who now have authority there or desire to have it or who think they have it or about to have it to understand that we shall take steps to prevent the payment of debts contracted to finance revolution: in other words, that we consider it our duty to insist on constitutional government there and will, if necessary (that is, if they force us to it as the only way) take charge of elections and see that a real government is erected which we can support. . . .

"**This will probably involve making the city authorities virtually subordinate to our commanders. They may hand the city government over to us voluntarily."[139]

The President had made the decision, and Lansing, through Admiral Caperton and American diplomatic officers in Haiti, proceeded to execute it during the next few months.

[139] W.W. to R. Lansing, August 4, 1915, State Department Papers.

Caperton set immediately to the first task, that of pacification, with a grim thoroughness. Reinforced with additional ships and men by the request of the Secretary of State, the admiral occupied Cap Haïtien and the other port towns and quickly established control throughout the interior in southern and central Haiti. Then in late September 1915, after bands of *cacos* began to harry his lines, the American commander pressed a sharp campaign in the North that drove the guerrillas into the mountains. There were sporadic outbreaks afterward but no major resistance until 1918; late in that year the *cacos* rebelled, and American marines and Haitian *gendarmes* had to fight a two-year campaign and kill some two thousand Haitians before peace was finally restored.[140]

Meanwhile, Caperton had been at work with equal determination to find what his superiors in Washington demanded, a puppet Haitian government through which they could begin to establish the new "constitutional" order. By August 9, 1915, the admiral had taken complete control of the Haitian government's offices, military installations and equipment (including its gunboat, *Pacifique*), and customhouses throughout the republic. Acting under explicit orders from President Wilson and Secretary Lansing,[141] Caperton on August 11 and 12 permitted the Haitian National Assembly to elect to the presidency Senator Sudre Dartiguenave, who had given assurances that he would cooperate.[142] Next came the laborious and, as it turned out, unpleasant task of forcing the so-called Haitian government to sign a treaty regularizing the republic's new status as a semi-protectorate. The treaty made provision for everything that the American government had heretofore demanded and a good deal more, including the establishment of a native constabulary under American officers and the virtual control of Haiti's foreign relations by the State Department.[143] Even at this late date the Haitian leaders balked and tried desperately to

---

[140] Ludwell L. Montague, *Haiti and the United States, 1714-1938*, pp. 232-234; James H. McCrocklin, *Garde d'Haiti, Twenty Years of Organization and Training by the United States Marine Corps*, pp. 24-35, 103-125; Dantès Bellegarde, *La Résistance Haïtienne (L'Occupation américaine d'Haïti)*, pp. 55-71; R. L. Buell, "The American Occupation of Haiti," *loc. cit.*, pp. 350-352.

[141] See W.W. to R. Lansing, August 9, 1915, State Department Papers; R. Lansing to W.W., August 10, 1915, *ibid.*, the Secretary of State to Chargé Davis, August 10, 1915, *Foreign Relations, 1915*, pp. 479-480.

[142] W. B. Caperton to the Secretary of the Navy, August 11, 1915, State Department Papers; Chargé Davis to the Secretary of State, August 12, 1915, *ibid.; New York Times*, August 12 and 13, 1915.

[143] *Foreign Relations, 1915*, pp. 449-451, prints the text of this treaty.

preserve some degree of sovereignty;[144] they signed on September 16 after Caperton had made it plain that he would establish a military government if they refused. The treaty was approved by the Haitian Senate on November 16, 1915, and by the United States Senate on February 28, 1916.

This ends our account of the tortured progress of the Wilson administration along the road that led to the occupation (invasion, Haitians called it) and administration of the hitherto fiercely independent Republic of Haiti. Ahead lay the political and economic reconstruction of the revolution-torn country; but this is a story beyond the scope of this biography, as Wilson gave only casual attention to the task in Haiti after 1916.

There now remains one final question, whether what happened in Haiti was the inevitable result of policies of helpfulness, of the effort of good men to be good neighbors. An account of the working out of these policies in the Dominican Republic may help to yield some answers.

The reader will perhaps recall the point at which we left the story of events in the Dominican Republic earlier in this chapter. The *Legalista* rebellion against the government of José Bordas Valdés and the impending collapse of order throughout the country in the summer of 1914 had prompted President Wilson and Secretary Bryan to send the Fort commission to impose the Wilson Plan for an end to revolutionary activity and the election of a new constitutional government under American auspices. The result had been the election and installation of a new President, Don Juan Isidro Jiménez, in November and December 1914 and the beginning of what seemed to be an era of peace in the island republic.

As events would later prove, it was the last chance at self-government for the Dominican people, at least for many years. Unfortunately, Jiménez was old and tired and possessed few qualities of leadership. Worse still, he was under such heavy obligations for his election and for majority support in the Dominican Congress to that incurable freebooter, General Desiderio Arias, that he was compelled to appoint

---

[144] "These poor chaps," Wilson observed rather feelingly, "are between the devil and the deep sea. They dare not offend us, and yet if they yielded to us their enemies would make a great case against them in any subsequent elections. But we must insist. Control of the customs is the essence of the whole matter." Note to Edith B. Galt, written on Chargé Davis to the Secretary of State, August 23, 1915, Wilson Papers.

Arias Minister of War and Arias' chief lieutenant to the post of Minister of the Interior. This boded no good for Jiménez's administration, as Arias was now more than ever determined to gain presidential power.[145]

Trouble began almost at once, when Arias resigned as Minister of War and threatened to revolt because Jiménez refused to give him a free hand in running the government, and when the *Horacistas* showed signs of raising a new rebellion of their own.[146] In Washington the leaders were not inclined to view such insubordination lightly. Bryan reported the news to the President at Cabinet meeting on January 12, 1915, and the two men decided then and there to make their determination unmistakably clear. Returning to the Department, Bryan called in the Dominican Minister and advised him to tell Jiménez "that he ought to accept the resignation of Arias whenever it was tendered and then notify him that if he made any trouble he would be put out of the country immediately."[147] In addition, the Secretary dispatched the following warning directly to Santo Domingo: "You may say to President Jiménes that this Government will support him to the fullest extent in the suppression of any insurrection against his Government. The election having been held and a Government chosen by the people having been established, *no more revolutions will be permitted*. You may notify both Horacio Vásquez and Arias that they will be held personally responsible if they attempt to embarrass the Government."[148]

These heavy-handed tactics worked at least momentarily. Arias withdrew his resignation at once. And when a small outbreak occurred at Puerto Plata two weeks later, Bryan rushed a gunboat with a contingent of marines to the scene of danger. Prepared for action, they stood by while the rebels surrendered to the government's forces. This, Bryan explained, was the method that would be used whenever disturbances erupted. "The sooner this is understood by everybody in Santo Domingo," he advised Minister Sullivan, "the better."[149]

There was more than met the eye in Bryan's method. At the very

---

[145] S. Welles, *Naboth's Vineyard*, ii, 747-748.

[146] Minister Sullivan to the Secretary of State, January 9, 1915, *Foreign Relations, 1915*, p. 279.

[147] W. J. Bryan to W.W., January 15, 1915, Bryan Papers, National Archives.

[148] The Secretary of State to Minister Sullivan, January 12, 1915, *Foreign Relations, 1915*, p. 279; italics added.

[149] The Secretary of State to Minister Sullivan, February 13, 1915, State Department Papers.

moment that he was personally chastising Dominican troublemakers, he was putting increasing pressure upon President Jiménez to accord official status as Comptroller of the Finances of the Dominican Republic to Charles M. Johnston, the financial expert who had earlier been accredited to the Bordas government. Bryan was demanding, besides, that Jiménez agree to place the collection of the country's *internal* revenues in the hands of the American Receiver-General and to give the State Department wider control than it already possessed over the Dominican Department of Public Works.[150]

Jiménez was willing; indeed, before his election he had promised the State Department that he would undertake to retain Johnston as Financial Adviser.[151] But the President raised a storm of opposition when he attempted to put a resolution authorizing Johnston's appointment through the Dominican Congress. The proposal was at least ostensibly the cause of the threatened outbreak of Arias and the *Horacistas*, which Bryan suppressed so sternly. No open revolt occurred consequently, to be sure, but in April 1915 the leaders of all the parties in the Congress except the *Jimenistas* moved to impeach Jiménez on the ground that he had failed to heed a congressional resolution demanding Johnston's removal as Financial Adviser. Bryan blocked this coup by dispatching a warning that he would not permit any attacks upon the President and would lend all assistance necessary "to compel respect for his administration."[152] What he meant, the Secretary explained a short time later, was that the American government was prepared to use its own troops to suppress insurrections and punish troublemakers (thereby saving the Jiménez government "needless expense"), and would do so upon the slightest provocation.[153]

Caught in the crossfire of the State Department and the opposition at home, Jiménez escaped momentarily by sending a commission to Washington to work out a new arrangement, and by agreeing in the end that Johnston should exercise wide controls over Dominican expenditures as an agent of the Receiver-General's office and not the

[150] The Secretary of State to Minister Sullivan, January 9, 1915, enclosing a memorandum embodying the terms of the proposed arrangement, *Foreign Relations, 1915,* pp. 297-299.

[151] Chargé White to the Secretary of State, November 14 and 18, 1914, *Foreign Relations, 1914,* pp. 255-256.

[152] Minister Sullivan to the Secretary of State, April 8, 1915; the Secretary of State to Minister Sullivan, April 9, 1915, *Foreign Relations, 1915,* pp. 283-284.

[153] The Secretary of State to Minister Sullivan, April 20, 1915, *ibid.,* pp. 284-285.

Dominican government.[154] But this did not solve Jiménez's problems at home. In the eyes of virtually all Dominicans he had become the puppet of a State Department that was moving inexorably to extinguish the remnants of their independence. What was more galling, the President knew that this was largely true, and that he continued to hold power only because the armed might of the United States stood between him and the vast majority of his fellow-countrymen. "So charged had the political atmosphere in the Republic become by midsummer of 1915," one authority writes, "that President Jiménez, upon whom the constant burdens which he had been called to assume had weighed heavily, suffered a physical and mental breakdown."[155] He was "old and fatigued," the Chargé at the American Legation in Santo Domingo reported, "and recent cares of state are telling upon him."[156]

So numerous were the signs of danger by the late summer that the leaders in the State Department could no longer deny that the entire situation in the Dominican Republic stood on the verge of collapse or of explosion. President Jiménez had given up trying to govern; the financial affairs of the republic were in utter chaos; and political discontent had failed to lead to a general uprising only because the Dominican leaders knew not what to do and General Horacio Vásquez was opposed to any resort to violence.

This, then, was the sad working out of the Wilson Plan. To American officials in Washington and Santo Domingo, it was obvious that it had failed. But they could not, or would not, see that the cause was their own increasing domination and policy of threatening, which had thoroughly alienated Dominican public opinion and fatally weakened President Jiménez. The cause, they concluded, was simply the venality of Dominican politicians and the nearly inherent inability of the Dominican people to govern themselves.[157] Therefore, the solution lay, not in giving up, but in trying harder—in fastening American control more securely.

Under the guidance of the new Secretary of State, Robert Lansing, the Latin American Affairs Division proceeded to work out a remedy. Embodied first in the instructions handed to the new Minister to the Dominican Republic, William W. Russell,[158] on September 17, 1915,

---

[154] S. Welles, *Naboth's Vineyard*, II, 751-755.

[155] *ibid.*, p. 757.

[156] Chargé Stewart Johnson to the Secretary of State, August 12, 1915, State Department Papers.

[157] C. M. Johnston to B. W. Long, September 9 and 27, 1915, *ibid.*

[158] Minister James M. Sullivan had been permitted to resign on July 8, 1915, after

and formally presented to the Jiménez government on November 19, the Department's plan spelled the momentary doom of Dominican independence. It provided for the appointment of an American financial adviser with full control over the treasury's disbursements, and for the creation of a native constabulary charged with responsibility for preserving the peace and order of the republic under the command of an American officer nominated by the President of the United States.[159] The most startling aspect of this business was not the plan itself but the way in which it was presented. Knowing well that the Dominican Congress would never approve a treaty that made the republic in effect a protectorate of the United States, the leaders in the State Department had hit upon a clever way of circumventing Dominican constitutional procedures. It was to present the plan, not in the form of a treaty or even a diplomatic proposal that would be subject to negotiation, but as a statement of what the American government believed that it had a *right* to do under the terms of the Dominican-American Convention of 1907. The fact that this was a somewhat exaggerated interpretation did not seem at all to bother the men who advanced it.

A wave of hysteria swept across the island republic in the wake of the publication of the American demands. "We are passing through one of those dark hours which occur in the life of peoples when it seems as if everything has been lost," General Vásquez declared in a public letter to President Jiménez.[160] There were threats of armed resistance throughout the country and rumors that Jiménez would resign and that Arias would be chosen to defend the national sovereignty.[161] Even the puppet had to echo the public sentiment. To reestablish the office of Financial Adviser, he protested in a formal reply to the American Minister, "would be the cause for stirring up an ab-

---

a special presidential commission appointed to investigate charges of misconduct against him had reported that he was unfit to hold office and should be dismissed. In order to avoid the risk of any new scandal, Lansing had recommended that the President appoint Russell, who had been removed from his post at Santo Domingo in 1913, as Sullivan's successor. Agreeing, the President had named Russell on August 16, 1913. R. Lansing to W.W., July 29, 1915; W.W. to R. Lansing, July 31, 1915, both in the Baker Collection.

[159] The Acting Secretary of State to Minister Russell, September 17, 1915; W. W. Russell to the Dominican Minister for Foreign Affairs, November 19, 1915, *Foreign Relations, 1915*, pp. 321-325, 333-337.

[160] S. Welles, *Naboth's Vineyard*, II, 763.

[161] Minister Russell to the Secretary of State, November 20, 1915, *Foreign Relations, 1915*, p. 331.

solutely dangerous public sentiment," while any attempt to create an American-officered constabulary would be "an inextinguishable germ of trouble, of protest, and of violent attacks."[162]

In these circumstances the authorities in Washington decided simply to temporize. They could not impose their demands at this point without occupying the republic, and such action would assuredly provoke fierce resistance from most Dominicans. But if they waited they might have their way more easily. President Jiménez might yield, or the threatened revolution might break out to give American leaders the pretext and opportunity for full-scale military intervention.[163] Preferring the easier method, the State Department bent all its efforts in Santo Domingo toward maintaining Jiménez in power in the face of a rising opposition.[164]

An explosion was, however, inevitable. It occurred in late April and early May of 1916, when Arias, still Minister of War, took military control of the capital with his own troops and the Dominican Congress adopted a resolution impeaching the President "for violations of the Constitution and laws." With unexpected bravado Jiménez denounced the impeachment as illegal, gathered a few loyal troops, and demanded the surrender of the city. It all happened quickly, but the American authorities, both in Washington and Santo Domingo, were not unprepared. The U.S.S. *Castine* was already in the harbor with a contingent of marines; it was joined by the U.S.S. *Prairie*, Commander W. S. Crosley, with a larger force of marines aboard, on May 2, 1916. When fighting broke out three days later, Crosley landed his troops to assist the President. But at this point Jiménez lost his nerve and resigned in a grand farewell to the nation: "I descend the steps of the Capitol, and with my conscience serene with the conviction of duty accomplished, feeling in the twilight that the sun shines upon my gray hairs, I withdraw to the serenity of a tranquil home."[165]

[162] B. Pichardo to Minister Russell, December 8, 1915, *ibid.*, p. 338.

[163] Minister Russell to the Secretary of State, January 19, 1916; J. B. Wright of the Latin American Affairs Division to the Secretary of State, January 24, 1916, both in State Department Papers.

[164] The Secretary of State to Minister Russell, January 24, 1916, *ibid.* The extract of this telegram printed in *Papers Relating to the Foreign Relations of the United States, 1916*, p. 220 (hereinafter cited as *Foreign Relations, 1916*), is quite incomplete.

[165] S. Welles, *Naboth's Vineyard*, II, 770. The foregoing account of events in Santo Domingo in late April and early May of 1916 is based upon *ibid.*, pp. 766-770; various reports from Minister Russell to the Secretary of State between April 15 and May 7, 1916, *Foreign Relations, 1916*, pp. 221-224; W. S. Crosley to the Secretary of the Navy, May 6, 1916, State Department Papers; W. B. Caperton to the Secretary of the Navy,

There then ensued a period of high tension and confusion in Santo Domingo. The small American marine detachments encamped at the American and Haitian Legations numbered probably not more than 150 men and were no match for Arias and his troops who controlled the city. Political affairs were nearly chaotic. A Council of Ministers composed of Cabinet members who had remained loyal to Jiménez exercised the executive power with the support of Minister Russell. But the Dominican Congress was hostile and would have elected Arias to the presidency except for the fact that the *Horacista* members had boycotted the sessions in order to prevent a quorum and the naming of their foe.

To the Secretary of State and his advisers it was obvious that the opportunity for full-scale intervention and a final solution of the Dominican problem was at last at hand. Lansing certainly must have consulted the President and obtained his approval of the plans about to be put into execution, but Wilson was in no way intimately involved. The fate of the Dominican Republic was in Lansing's hands, and Lansing did not hesitate. He had destroyers dispatched to the Dominican ports of Puerto Plata, Macorís, and Sanchez on May 6. Then, after Jiménez resigned, the Secretary of State sent Admiral Caperton, that veteran tamer of revolutionists, from Port-au-Prince with additional marines and orders to deal with Arias and occupy the capital.

Arriving at Santo Domingo aboard the U.S.S. *Dolphin* on May 13, Caperton joined Minister Russell and proceeded forthwith to order Arias either to disarm his forces or to get them out of the city within two days. Choosing the less humiliating alternative, Arias withdrew at the head of his troops during the night of May 13. Then at daybreak on May 15 Caperton sent some six hundred marines and sailors ashore and took complete control of the capital city. It was, of course, only the first step in the full-scale military occupation of the Dominican Republic, which proceeded systematically under Caperton's direction as fast as reinforcements arrived. By mid-July of 1916 the Admiral, with nearly two thousand marines and bluejackets in the field, had seized all the strategic centers of the country; Arias had surrendered to the Governor of Santiago; and the "pacification" was fairly complete. It had been accomplished with little bloodshed because the disorganized Dominican forces had rarely attempted to resist.[166]

May 7, 1916, transmitting a message from Commander Crosley, *ibid.; New York Times*, May 3, 5, and 6, 1916.

[166] The foregoing is based upon various reports sent by Admiral Caperton and

In the meantime, however, Caperton and Russell had made little progress toward a *modus operandi* with the political leaders of the republic. Fearing that the Dominican Congress would elect Arias or one of his friends to the presidency, the American proconsuls demanded that the election be postponed until the pacification of the country had been completed.[167] And when the Dominicans defiantly set in motion the constitutional machinery for the election of Doctor Federico Henríquez y Carvajal, president of the Supreme Court and a friend of Arias, the American authorities (acting through the Council of Ministers, which still exercised the executive power) arrested seven senators and one deputy on June 4 in order to prevent the presence of a quorum in the joint session of the Congress.[168] This, the men in Washington agreed, was going too far.[169] "Senators," the Acting Secretary of State advised the American Minister in Santo Domingo, "should not be arrested." The United States, however, would not "countenance the election of Arias or any of his friends or even Henriquez"; if the Dominican Congress was determined to name a President, then let it elect one who was acceptable to the American government. "If this should prove impracticable," these instructions concluded, "would it not be possible to assure the Council of Ministers now exercising the executive power, that they would have our support should they undertake to carry out our policy *even if it were necessary for them to dissolve Congress . . . and proceed to the election of a new Congress?*"[170]

The crisis passed—the congressmen were released from prison on June 6 and Henríquez withdrew his candidacy[171]—but the problem of finding a native leadership acceptable to the Dominican people as well as to the State Department remained unresolved. Taking matters into its own hands before it had to adjourn by constitutional limitation near the end of July 1916, the Dominican Congress elected Doctor Francisco

---

Minister Russell between May 13 and July 7, 1916, printed in *Foreign Relations, 1916*, pp. 226-232; W. B. Caperton to the Secretary of the Navy, May 15, 1916, 10:57 p.m., and June 3, 1916, State Department Papers; Minister Russell to the Secretary of State, June 3, 1916, *ibid.*; *New York Times*, May 16, June 22, and July 6, 1916.

[167] Minister Russell to the Secretary of State, May 15, 1916, *Foreign Relations, 1916*, pp. 227-228.

[168] Minister Russell to the Secretary of State, June 5, 1916, State Department Papers.

[169] Acting Secretary of State Frank L. Polk to W.W., June 3, 1916, Wilson Papers.

[170] The Acting Secretary of State to Minister Russell, June 3, 1916, State Department Papers; italics added.

[171] Minister Russell to the Secretary of State, June 6, 1916, *ibid.*; Minister Russell to the Secretary of State, June 14, 1916, *Foreign Relations, 1916*, p. 231.

Henríquez y Carvajal, a brother of Federico Henríquez, as Provisional President for a five-month term.[172]

It was, Dominicans well knew, their last hope for even a modicum of self-government, and the Provisional President, trying desperately to save the republic, assembled an administration of the ablest men in Dominican public life. Next he went to Minister Russell to beg for help and understanding, and to make it clear that he would accept a large measure of American control if the United States would grant him recognition and support without compelling him to sign the treaty sealing the republic's fate as a protectorate.[173] Everything now depended upon the response of officials in the State Department. They (including Minister Russell) were not unmindful of the problems that Henríquez faced, but they were determined to have their way without any negotiation. The American government, the State Department therefore replied, would recognize the provisional government only if it accepted the treaty for comprehensive American control. If the Santo Domingo authorities refused, the Washington government added ominously, then they would receive not a penny of the Dominican revenues, all of which were now being collected by the Receiver-General and the American military authorities.[174]

Throughout the late summer of 1916 the Provisional President worked to avoid a total impasse, offering to put the American demands into effect by informal agreement and to *consider* a treaty regularizing the arrangement if the State Department would yield the recognition and the money without which his entire government would soon collapse.[175] The leaders in Washington, however, refused even to hear Henríquez's offers; the Provisional President, they insisted sternly, must first formally accept the American demands before any discussions could begin.[176] This, Henríquez finally replied, he could not do without violating the Dominican constitution.

By mid-autumn the deadlock was complete, and the leaders in Washington had to accept the consequences of their hard policy. Civil authority had virtually broken down throughout the Dominican Republic; the life of the provisional government was about to expire by con-

[172] Minister Russell to the Secretary of State, July 25, 1916, *ibid.*, p. 233.

[173] Minister Russell to the Secretary of State, August 10, 25, and 26, 1916, *ibid.*, pp. 234-235.

[174] The Secretary of State to Minister Russell, August 26 and 29, 1916, *ibid.*, p. 235.

[175] e.g., Minister Russell to the Secretary of State, September 5 and 14, 1916, *ibid.*, pp. 236-237.

[176] The Secretary of State to Minister Russell, September 8, 1916, *ibid.*, pp. 236-237.

stitutional stipulation; and unrest and bitterness were finding outlets in attacks against isolated American military personnel. On October 31 all the men in the administration immediately responsible for Dominican policy[177] met at the State Department to consider "the present situation in the Dominican Republic and . . . to find a practical solution of the many difficulties presented." The deadlock, the conferees agreed, could "not be broken by diplomatic methods." The only way out was to declare martial law and to institute a full-fledged American military government.[178]

All that remained was to wait for the proper moment to ask for the approval of the President and the Secretary of State. It came late in November, when the expiring provisional government in Santo Domingo issued a call for the election of a new Dominican Congress. "It is apparent," wrote Jordan H. Stabler, Chief of the Latin American Affairs Division, to the Secretary of State, "that the majority of the senators and deputies will be from the Arias faction, hence giving Arias, who has been the disturbing element in Santo Domingo for many years, complete governmental control." There was no other solution at hand, Stabler urged, but "the declaration of martial law and placing of Santo Domingo under military occupation."[179] Approving the recommendation, Lansing wrote at once to the President, enclosing a copy of Stabler's letter and of a proclamation of martial law for the Dominican Republic that Captain Knapp had prepared at the conference on October 31.[180]

What else could President Wilson do but approve when all his advisers agreed? "It is with the deepest reluctance that I approve and authorize the course here proposed," he replied to Lansing on November 26, "but I am convinced that it is the least of the evils in sight in this very perplexing situation. I therefore authorize you to issue the necessary instructions in the premises. I have stricken out the sentences in the proposed proclamation which authorizes [*sic*] the com-

[177] Counselor Frank L. Polk; Jordan H. Stabler, Chief of the Latin American Affairs Division; Minister Russell; Captain Harry S. Knapp, commander of the naval forces in Dominican waters; and Rear Admiral William S. Benson, Chief of Naval Operations.
[178] J. H. Stabler, "*RE DOMINICAN SITUATION*, Conference with Mr. Polk," memorandum dated October 31, 1916, State Department Papers.
[179] J. H. Stabler to the Secretary of State, November 21, 1916, *Foreign Relations, 1916*, p. 241.
[180] R. Lansing to W.W., November 22, 1916, *ibid.*, pp. 240-241.

manding officer to remove judges and others in certain circumstances.[181] It may be necessary to resort to such extreme measures, but I do not deem it wise to put so arbitrary an announcement in the proclamation itself."[182]

It was swiftly done. Lansing notified Secretary of the Navy Josephus Daniels of the President's decision on November 27; Daniels passed the word to Captain Knapp, who had meanwhile returned to Santo Domingo aboard his flagship, the U.S.S. *Olympia*; and Knapp issued the proclamation in his own name on November 29, 1916. It put the "Republic of Santo Domingo" in a "state of Military Occupation," subject to "the exercise of military law applicable to such occupation"; declared that the laws of the republic remained in force unless they conflicted with military law; and continued Dominican civil officials and judges in office subject to the control of the military governor.[183]

Thus ended the Wilson administration's long attempt to teach the fundamentals of constitutional democracy to the Dominican people; thus began a new, severer schooling that lasted until the marines were withdrawn in 1924.

As the story of the subsequent political and economic reconstruction of the two Caribbean countries lies beyond the scope of this biography, only a few retrospective words need be added.

The first point can perhaps best be put in the form of a question: How did it happen that idealists such as Wilson and Bryan, if not Lansing, should have come to eminently "realistic" ends in their Caribbean policies? We cannot see the whole or even the most important part of the answer if we search for "realistic" explanations for what looked suspiciously like "realistic" policies. Concern for national security, for example, played no immediate part in the working out of policies toward the Dominican Republic, for there were never any threats to American supremacy in that country during the Wilson era. Wilson and Bryan were eager to diminish foreign economic influences in Haiti, it is true, but only because they believed they contributed to the political instability of the country; and the fear of European military intervention grew increasingly remote after the sum-

[181] "For malfeasance in office, or for other proper and sufficient cause, the military government will remove any Dominican judge or other court official and will appoint his successor in office."

[182] W.W. to R. Lansing, November 26, 1916, *ibid.*, p. 242.

[183] The proclamation is printed in *ibid.*, pp. 246-247.

mer of 1914.[184] A second conventional "realistic" explanation—financial and commercial imperialism—contributes even less to an understanding of the Caribbean policies of the Wilson administration. The desire for markets and raw materials and outlets for capital investment was never an impelling motive.

The answer to our question, obviously, lies elsewhere—in motives and assumptions that seem scarcely credible to the mind of the mid-twentieth century. Wilson and Bryan (and Lansing to a certain extent) had a genuine compassion for the victims of the unending instability of the Caribbean republics. The trouble, they believed, lay in defective political institutions and evil men; the solution, in the establishment of constitutional democracy. Being moral and political activists, they inevitably wanted to help; indeed, they could not avoid trying to help, any more than they could avoid trying to right political and economic wrongs at home. Thus they became involved, from the beginning in the Dominican Republic, because of the already intimate relations between that country and the United States, and gradually in Haiti, as the need for American aid seemed to the leaders in Washington to become more compelling.

There was a certain self-perpetuation about the working out of policies of helpfulness in the Caribbean. Indeed, it might be that the objectives and peculiar motivation of these policies made their violent end inevitable. Their objective was the establishment of constitutional democratic government in so-called backward areas through American guidance. Experience soon revealed that policies of helpfulness were, to say the least, inadequate to achieve the objective. Wilson's and Bryan's sermonizing, their interdictions of revolutionary activity, and even their attempts to hold "fair" elections had little meaning in countries where democracy had never existed and revolution was the ordinary vehicle of political change. Policies of helpfulness failed in their first mild stage, therefore, because they bore so little relation to the political traditions and experiences of the Caribbean peoples. But the

[184] This is not to argue that Wilson and his Secretaries of State would not have acted vigorously to defend American interests had there been any actual threat to national security in the Caribbean at this time. Wilson and Bryan showed in their Nicaraguan policy how sensitive they were to strategic necessities like the defense of the Panama Canal. (A. S. Link, *Wilson*, II, 328, 349.) It is not to argue, either, that Lansing did not give weight to long-range considerations when he tried to work out the principles to guide the administration in Caribbean policy. (See above, pp. 534-535.) It is simply to say that strategic factors played no immediate and vital role in the decisions to occupy Haiti and the Dominican Republic.

objective and the desire to achieve it remained; indeed, that desire was stronger after failure than before. It soon grew into the conviction that the United States had no choice but to impose its own solutions, even if this meant using force against hitherto sovereign peoples and governments. It goes without saying that such conclusions were possible because Wilson, Bryan, and Lansing assumed that the ordinary rules of international comity did not apply when small republics had demonstrated their incapacity to govern themselves.

All the while the movement toward the violent conclusion was speeded by certain other factors. Helpfulness via total control was invitingly easy to execute, vastly easier than trying to work through incompetent and often corrupt native leaders. Nothing stood in the way at home or abroad. The American people were almost totally uninterested. The peoples of the Caribbean republics were powerless to resist. The European powers were encouraging. Finally, there was the subtle but impelling force of the corruption which, as Lord Acton once observed, inevitably accompanies power, even when power is wielded by good men. In their dealings with Haiti and the Dominican Republic the American leaders exercised an almost absolute power. It was not a situation conducive to restraint or moderation, or to a willingness to accept solutions not of their own devising.

CHAPTER XVI

Renewal of Tension with Germany:
The First *Arabic* Crisis

DURING the midsummer of 1915 the American people paid scant attention to the turmoil in the Caribbean that led to the occupation of Haiti by United States marines, nor were the leaders in Washington much more engrossed. There was still but one overriding concern—whether the future would bring war or peace with Germany over the issue of submarine warfare. At the beginning of August, following the exchange of the *Lusitania* notes, the answer was neither obvious nor foreordained. President Wilson, after taking the high ground of complete opposition to submarine attacks against merchant shipping, had then beaten a slow retreat toward acceptance of a "legal" underseas campaign and a narrowing of the issue with Germany to the safety of Americans on belligerent passenger ships. He had made it clear, too, that he would not insist upon immediate German apology and reparation for the loss of American lives on the *Lusitania*, and he had even indicated that he might be willing to accept arbitration of this case at some future date. Finally, he had accompanied his stern warning against a renewal of unlimited underseas attacks on passenger ships with an earnest invitation to the German authorities to join him in a campaign for the freedom of the seas as long as the present war should last. Whether this invitation would lead to collaboration depended now upon the response of the leaders in Berlin.

The subject was first seriously raised in that city, not by Imperial Chancellor von Bethmann Hollweg, but by the Imperial Secretary of the Treasury, Karl Helfferich, a learned economist who wielded considerable influence in official circles. In a long memorandum for the Chancellor dated August 5, 1915, one that ranged over all aspects of America's relation to the war in Europe, Helfferich argued openly and persuasively for a positive reply to Washington.

Germany, he bluntly warned at the outset, simply could not survive if the United States joined her enemies, for American belligerency would mean the unlimited and unending economic reinforcement of the Allies, the shutting off of cotton imports without which the German people could not maintain their war effort, and the almost certain turning of other neutrals against the Central Powers. War with America, Helfferich went on, had to be avoided in any event during the next few weeks, so long as the fate of Germany's campaigns in Russia and the Balkans was in doubt. It might, therefore, be necessary to make an open surrender on the submarine issue; and it might be possible to make a virtue out of necessity. The trump card of the submarine war had already been played, and not without some success. Germany's hope now lay in decisive American action against the British to assure the free flow of food and raw materials to Central Europe. What, Helfferich went on with mounting urgency, could be lost by testing the President's sincerity by a positive reply, that is, by open concession of the American demands for submarine operations according to the rules of cruiser warfare? Much, indeed everything, might be gained—the safeguarding of the American rear, the gaining of much good will in the United States, and perhaps the loosening of the British blockade. Nothing, at any rate, would be lost. Having protected its freedom of action for the future, the German government could still resume unlimited submarine operations if the American President did not succeed in his campaign for the freedom of the seas. "Only in the event," Helfferich concluded, "that a strong possibility of gaining a decisive victory against England during the next few weeks by an all-out continuation of the U-boat war were to exist would the temporary relaxation of the submarine campaign mean a disadvantage that could outweigh the great decisive advantages of the suggestions elucidated above."[1]

It was the most courageous appraisal of the present realities and future possibilities of the German-American situation made by any German statesman during the war, and it set off a round of discussion and some furor. Receiving the document from Helfferich during the evening of August 5, Bethmann at once dispatched copies to the members of the Emperor's entourage and then started out for Supreme Headquarters at Pless Castle in order to discuss the memorandum with them personally. Admiral von Müller, the Chief of the Naval Cabinet,

---

[1] K. Helfferich to T. von Bethmann Hollweg, August 5, 1915, German F. O. Archives. Helfferich composed a second memorandum a month later reiterating what he had said in the first. See K. Helfferich, memorandum dated September 4, 1915, copy in *ibid*.

was in entire agreement with the head of the Treasury; General von Falkenhayn, the Chief of the General Staff, apparently also concurred. The inevitable explosion occurred when the Imperial Chancellor discussed the matter with the naval secretary, Grand Admiral von Tirpitz, on August 7. Suspecting that the Helfferich memorandum was, as he termed it, a "put-up job" engineered by Foreign Secretary von Jagow[2] and that Bethmann was using it as the instrument to achieve the entire abandonment of the submarine campaign, the old sea dog struck back furiously in sublime irrationality. America, he declared, was already firmly committed to the Allies economically and politically, and nothing that Germany could do would weaken that connection. It did not matter anyway. American businessmen would lend money to the Allies only if they could profit by doing so. It made no difference if American cotton no longer came to Germany. The Fatherland was secure against starvation. Let Germany persevere in strength, trusting only in its own resources and in the submarine as the best hope of winning freedom of the seas. As for himself, he added, he would resign if Bethmann made the kind of surrender that Helfferich had proposed.[3]

These were fiery words and dire threats, but Bethmann might have succeeded if he had pressed hard at this point for agreement with the United States on the basic issues of the maritime war. But, characteristically, he chose to temporize rather than to act boldly. Understandably, he shrank from the consequences of an open battle, even one that he might win; for he might triumph over von Tirpitz only to lose the confidence of the Reichstag and the German press and public opinion. As we have seen, feeling was at a high pitch of indignation against President Wilson's third *Lusitania* note. Equally important, Bethmann certainly had grave doubt that such a *démarche* as Helfferich was proposing could succeed. The United States, the Chancellor himself was beginning to think, *was* already inextricably bound to the Allies; President Wilson would not dare to move seriously against the British blockade because American public opinion would not tolerate any disturbance of commercial relations with the *Entente*.[4] He was not, how-

[2] Neither Bethmann's nor Helfferich's memoirs sheds any light on this point.

[3] The above account of these discussions at Supreme Headquarters is based upon Tirpitz, *Politische Dokumente*, II, 384-396, wherein Tirpitz prints the Imperial Chancellor to A. von Tirpitz, August 6, 1915; his own recollections and observations; and the notes that he made of his conversation with Bethmann on August 7, 1915; and upon Spindler, *La Guerre Sous-Marine*, II, 248-254.

[4] These, at any rate, are the conclusions that Bethmann later said he came to as he

ever, dogmatic in these views; and he announced at the end of the discussions at Supreme Headquarters that he would defer his final decision until a report from Ambassador von Bernstorff had arrived. Meanwhile, he would simply let the present German-American diplomatic impasse continue undisturbed.[5]

An evil star seemed to hover over German-American relations during the summer of 1915. Bernstorff's report, which had been written on July 28 and sent by mail or courier to Berlin,[6] might have caused the Chancellor to take up the cudgels at once. As events soon proved, his decision to defer the final discussions was almost fatal to the German-American peace. By the time that Bernstorff's report arrived in the German capital, the situation in America had changed too much to permit any seemingly free response to the President's invitation to the Imperial authorities. By now American opinion, which had been quieting down since the first days of the *Lusitania* crisis, was in a new state of anti-German agitation.

The incident that set off this new outbreak was the publication by the New York *World* of a collection of documents that exposed the operation of certain German agents in the United States. How this feat was accomplished can be briefly told.

Ever since the middle of May 1915 the United States Secret Service, a branch of the Treasury Department, had been hard at work shadowing various Germans suspected of violations of American neutrality. In New York City on Saturday afternoon, July 23, an operative named Frank Burke followed *Geheimrat* (Privy Councillor) Doctor Heinrich F. Albert, Commercial Attaché in the German Embassy, as he left the offices of the Hamburg-American Steamship Company on lower Broadway. Boarding a Sixth Avenue elevated train at Rector Street, Albert rode to Fiftieth Street, where he got off in such a hurry that he left a large brief case behind. Burke snatched up the satchel; Albert rushed back into the car to recover it; and Burke escaped with the *Geheimrat* in hot but futile pursuit. Burke went straight to William J. Flynn, chief of the Secret Service. Flynn looked through the contents of the

---

contemplated the possibilities inherent in President Wilson's invitation to the German government to cooperate in a campaign to establish freedom of the seas. T. von Bethmann Hollweg, *Considérations sur la Guerre Mondiale*, II, 236-238.

[5] As he told von Tirpitz on August 8, 1915. Tirpitz, *Politische Dokumente*, II, 398-399.

[6] For which, see above, pp. 451-453.

brief case, telephoned the vacationing Secretary of the Treasury Mc-Adoo at North Haven, Maine, and then took the first train for North Haven, where he, Flynn, delivered the bag to the Secretary on the following day, July 24.[7]

McAdoo's eyes must have bulged in astonishment as he looked through the contents, for they were documents revealing that the *Geheimrat* was the head of an important part of the German propaganda and undercover efforts in the United States. More important, the documents exposed many of these activities in all their intimate details—for example, how Albert and his colleagues had spent money to furnish "news" materials to American newspapers, subsidize the leading German-American organ, George Sylvester Viereck's *The Fatherland*, and a number of German- and Irish-American organizations, and encourage American correspondents in Germany and Austria who were friendly to the Central Powers; how these agents had bought a large munitions plant in Bridgeport, Connecticut, to prevent its output from going to the Allies and had attempted to corner the products of certain chemical works; and how they had tried to stimulate resentment in Texas against the suppression of cotton exports to Germany.

In great excitement McAdoo, some time near the end of July, took the evidence to the President, who had returned to his summer home at Cornish after dispatching the third *Lusitania* note. Wilson asked McAdoo to confer with Secretary of State Lansing and then with Colonel House. The three of them, the President presumably added, could decide what to do with the documents. McAdoo saw Lansing in New York on about August 7 and House at his summer home in Manchester, Massachusetts, on August 10. The upshot was a decision to give the materials to the New York *World* for publication upon only one condition, that the *World's* editor, Frank Cobb, should never divulge the source.[8] "It may, in my opinion," House wrote to Wilson just after his talk with McAdoo, "even lead us into war, but I think the publication should go ahead. It will strengthen your hands enormously, and will weaken such agitators as Mr. Bryan and Hoke Smith. The people will see things as those of us that know the true conditions have long seen them, and it will make it nearly impossible to continue the propaganda."[9]

[7] W. G. McAdoo, *Crowded Years*, pp. 323-327.

[8] W. G. McAdoo to E. M. House, August 4, 6, and 13, 1915, House Papers; House Diary, August 10, 1915.

[9] E. M. House to W.W., August 10, 1915, Wilson Papers.

Published with great fanfare in the New York *World* from August 15 through August 23 and reprinted at once by newspapers throughout the country, the Albert documents provoked an enormous anti-German outpouring. Commentators and federal officials were quick to admit what was true, that the evidence revealed no indictable violations of American neutrality by German agents.[10] But that, the commentators said, was beside the point. The German government now stood convicted of a vast undercover campaign to suborn American opinion and influence American foreign policy. "The German propaganda," Frank Cobb wrote in a typical editorial, "is carried on from Berlin, and its sole purpose is to destroy American neutrality, sacrifice American interests and annihilate American rights for the advancement of German arms. . . . The German propaganda is not only deliberately but continuously unfriendly. . . . There can be no more unfriendly act on the part of one Government toward another with which it is nominally at peace than that of inciting sedition and subsidizing disloyalty."[11] "The work of the secret agents and the subsidized emissaries," agreed the editor of the New York *Evening Sun*, "has all the meanness and treachery of the spy system plus the offensiveness of actual hostile activity. It belongs morally in the same classification with political assassination."[12] Authorities in Washington, editors by the score asserted, should reply sternly and quickly, by cleaning out the entire nest of conspirators, including Bernstorff and most of the German Embassy in Washington and the German Military and Naval Attachés as well.[13]

The Albert affair not only thus exacerbated American opinion against Germany at a critical period; it also dealt a crippling blow to all organized efforts, even perfectly legitimate ones, to present the German point of view to the American public. Henceforward it would be as one New York editor warned: "Woe to the American politician whose name appears on German-American platforms hereafter! The taint of Cobden Club gold will be as nothing henceforth. And woe to the newspaper or lecturer that takes the German side. 'How much are you being paid by the Germans?' will be an inevitable question."[14]

[10] As Doctor Albert himself pointed out in a long statement printed in the New York *World*, August 20, 1915.

[11] *ibid.*, August 16, 1915.

[12] New York *Evening Sun*, as cited in *ibid.*, August 17, 1915.

[13] See "Light on German Propaganda," *Literary Digest*, LI (August 28, 1915), 388, and the editorials printed in the New York *World*, August 17, 1915.

[14] "The German Exposures," New York *Nation*, CI (August 19, 1915), 219.

Feeding the Animal
Kirby in the New York *World*

By itself the Albert Affair would probably not have had any profoundly damaging impact upon the attitude toward the German government of the men directly at the helm in Washington. They were
appalled, to be sure, by the revelations of what Colonel House called
this "dastardly proceeding";[15] however, except for the excitable Mc-
Adoo, who wanted to denounce Bernstorff publicly and to send all
German "secret and commercial agents" in the United States home

[15] House Diary, August 10, 1915.

by the first boat,[16] most members of the administration were not inclined to read any really sinister meaning into the Albert documents. The matter, the President wrote privately, for example, was not as simple as McAdoo thought;[17] Lansing gave no evidence of undue agitation; and Attorney General Thomas W. Gregory undoubtedly echoed the President's and Secretary of State's views when he told reporters that the evidence offered no ground for any formal action by the federal government.[18]

What was more jolting to the leaders in Washington, and what also gave a new and more baneful dimension to the Albert affair itself, was the exposure to official if not yet fully to public view of certain German intrigues against the domestic tranquility, neutrality, and peaceful foreign relations of the United States. Occurring on the eve of the sharpest crisis in German-American relations to this point, this was an event of immense importance. One of its most vital consequences was the severe shaking of official American confidence in German good faith at precisely the time when mutual trust was most desperately needed for the maintenance of peace. Before we discuss this episode, however, we must digress for a moment to relate something of its background, that is, the earlier intrigues by German agents and the way that American leaders had dealt with them.

Commencing immediately after the outbreak of war, German infractions of American neutrality statutes had proceeded with annoying persistence during the following months. Ambassador von Bernstorff, the Imperial Military and Naval Attachés with offices in New York City, and various other German nationals had worked assiduously and often successfully to supply German cruisers at sea with coal and provisions and, above all, to furnish bogus passports to German reservists returning to the Fatherland by way of neutral European ports.[19]

Evidence of the wholesale forging of American passports came initially to the President and the Attorney General in December 1914 and January 1915.[20] Setting the Justice Department's Bureau of Investi-

---

[16] W. G. McAdoo to W.W., August 16, 1915, Wilson Papers.

[17] W.W. to W. G. McAdoo, August 21, 1915, Baker Collection.

[18] Gregory expressed this opinion to reporters following a conference with the President on August 19. *New York Times*, August 20, 1915.

[19] See J. H. von Bernstorff, *My Three Years in America*, pp. 85-88, and R. Lansing, *War Memoirs*, pp. 67-71, 73-75, for excellent summaries of the German efforts to supply cruisers at sea and of the German so-called passport frauds.

[20] W.W. to T. W. Gregory, December 16, 1914, the Papers of Thomas Watt Gregory,

gation upon the trail, they soon brought some of the ringleaders to trial and imprisonment.[21] Proof of the first large-scale violations of American neutrality that had occurred—the supplying of German cruisers from American ports during the first months of the war— was not obtained until late in 1915, long after these activities had ended. It led to the conviction of several officials of the Hamburg-American Company in New York City.[22]

At no time during the early months of the war did President Wilson and his advisers seem unduly disturbed, even when the evidence directly implicated von Bernstorff and Captain Franz von Papen, the Military Attaché. The Washington authorities were perhaps annoyed, but they certainly understood the natural desire of German soldiers to return home, and they were not inclined to blame German envoys for trying to make this possible. Wilson indicated as much when he sent the first evidence of the passport frauds to the Attorney General in December 1914. "As the Secretary of State requests," the President wrote, "I am handing you the enclosed papers. The subject-matter is evidently of the most sensational kind [for it directly implicated the German Ambassador]. I hope that you will have it looked into thoroughly, but that, at the same time, you will have all possible precaution taken that no hint of it may become public unless and until it materializes into something upon which we *have no choice but to act*."[23] And when action did become necessary, the President and his subordinates were apparently happy to settle for the conviction of a few underlings in return for Bernstorff's implied promise that the forging of passports would cease. This, at any rate, is one conclusion that can be drawn from the two following dispatches from the Ambassador to the Foreign Office in Berlin:

"Owing to private letters addressed to me from the Foreign Office and the official instructions to Mr. von Papen to send home as many German officers as possible, it has been necessary to give the latter false passports about which, under the present circumstances, I have no qualms. Individual cases have, unfortunately, been made known to the public, and the American government has begun an investigation in which the compromising of the Embassy is not to be feared. The

---

the Library of Congress, hereinafter cited as the Gregory Papers; Hans Adam von Wedell to Ambassador von Bernstorff, January 4, 1915, copy in the Wilson Papers.

[21] *New York Times*, February 26 and 27, 1915.

[22] *ibid.*, November 21, December 3, 1915.

[23] W.W. to T. W. Gregory, December 16, 1914, Gregory Papers; italics added.

State Department informs me definitely that the administration here does not pay any intention to the rumor that the Embassy is participating."[24]

"Between the Military Attaché, Captain von Papen, and the former employee of the North German Lloyd, [Carl] Ruroede, New York, who has helped numerous German military personnel to obtain American passports so they could return to the home country, and now for this reason stands trial, the following agreement has been made:

"Ruroede will plead guilty . . . so that further discussions and cross-examinations are impossible. For this Ruroede receives $10,000 for the support of his family (regardless of the length of his prison term, from one to five years) and, after he is discharged from prison, $5,000 for a new start.

"I believe that the arrangement is the most favorable that could be reached . . . because it fulfills our moral obligation to Ruroede, excludes a very disagreeable public discussion,[25] and, finally, saves a great deal in lawyers' fees. I have therefore approved this agreement and have given him the money for a settlement."[26]

Bernstorff and his colleagues in Washington and New York apparently decided to refrain from further illegal activity on a large scale after their escape from official implication in the passports frauds. As late as May 15, 1915, the Ambassador could declare with seeming sincerity to a highly placed American friend that he had no knowledge of any illegal activities by German nationals or German Americans.[27] He could also undoubtedly congratulate himself upon the obvious fact that no real damage had been done. The Embassy's and Doctor Albert's undercover work of propaganda and efforts to stop the flow of munitions to the Allies was of course proceeding apace, but exposure of this activity could not, Bernstorff knew, do any great harm to relations with the American government.

[24] Ambassador von Bernstorff to the Foreign Office, January 7, 1915, German F. O. Archives.

[25] Of the type that occurred, Bernstorff undoubtedly meant, when another German accused of forging passports, one Richard Peter Stengler, turned state's evidence before his trial in New York and accused Captain Karl Boy-Ed, the German Naval Attaché, of participation in the passport ring. *New York Times*, February 26 and 27, 1915.

[26] Ambassador von Bernstorff to T. von Bethmann Hollweg, March 6, 1915, German F. O. Archives. Von Papen informed the Foreign Office on the following day that Ruroede's trial had ended on March 6 and that he had received a sentence of three years' imprisonment.

[27] Oswald G. Villard, "Notes of a meeting with the German ambassador at lunch, May 15, 1915, at the Embassy," MS. in the Wilson Papers.

This, then, was the generally quiescent state of affairs in this particular aspect of German-American relations in the spring of 1915. And this was the time when certain officials in Berlin conceived plans for a new campaign of intrigue and sabotage in America which, when they were exposed to official view in Washington, shook the very foundations of the German-American peace.

The origins of this affair are still so obscure that they can be only imperfectly related. At some time during the late winter of 1915 intelligence officers in the German General Staff and Admiralty became alarmed by the increasing export of American munitions and set to work on plans to impede that flow. They hit upon the scheme of sending an agent to the United States who should have considerable initiative and apparently enormous sums with which to execute whatever steps might seem feasible—a sort of superagent to act perhaps in collaboration with the Ambassador and the Military Attachés, but on his own authority, so as not to compromise the standing of these officials. Precisely who the authors of this plan were, and whether they included the Imperial Chancellor and Foreign Secretary, one cannot say. For the task the German leaders involved chose a young and apparently quite dashing officer on the Admiralty's intelligence staff, Commander Franz Rintelen von Kleist, who spoke English fluently and had moved in high Anglo-German-American social circles before the war.[28]

Traveling on a forged Swiss passport under the name of Emil V. Gaché, Rintelen arrived in America in early April 1915 and set immediately to work at headquarters that he opened in New York City. He remained in the country only a short time, but his accomplishments were truly prodigious. The following is a summary of the ones that can be fairly well authenticated:

1. He organized an unsuccessful conspiracy to destroy the Welland Canal in Canada and thus to cut the important Great Lakes-St. Lawrence waterway.

2. Gathering willing helpers from among the employees of the German steamship companies and the underworld, he established facilities for the manufacture of various types of time bombs for the destruction of munitions piers and ships in New York Harbor and of ships at sea.[29]

3. Through paid American agents he formed a bogus labor union, Labor's National Peace Council, among longshoremen in all major

[28] Captain von Rintelen (Franz Rintelen von Kleist), *The Dark Invader, Wartime Reminiscences of a German Naval Intelligence Officer*, pp. 60-74.

[29] For particulars, see the New York *World*, September 13 and December 8, 1915.

port cities and engineered a short-lived strike aimed at preventing the loading of munitions ships.

4. With the special sanction of his superiors at the Admiralty in Berlin, he spent some $12,000,000 (officials of the Justice Department later reported) in financing the counterrevolution against the Mexican leader, Carranza, then being set on foot in the United States by the deposed dictator, Victoriano Huerta, and others. The object of this most ambitious and costly of Rintelen's undertakings was to encourage hostilities between Mexico and the United States in order to divert the flow of American munitions southward.[30]

Having begun so auspiciously, Rintelen's career as superspy came to an unexpected and, as it turned out, somewhat inglorious end. In late June 1915 he received a cryptic but urgently worded message written in the most secret German code ordering him to report to his superiors in Berlin at once. Sailing aboard the first Dutch boat bound for Europe, he was arrested by British security officers off Dover on August 13 and taken to London, where to his horror he learned, at least according to his own account, that the message ordering his return had been sent by the British naval intelligence department, which had earlier come into possession of the German code. Held for a year and a half as a prisoner of war in England, he was transported to the United States in April 1917, there to be convicted of violations of the American neutrality laws, as a result of which he spent nearly four years in an assortment of state and federal prisons.[31]

Rintelen would probably have seen the inside of a federal prison long before 1917 had he not left the United States when he did, for by the time of his departure officials in Washington were already close on his trail. His discovery occurred in a most unlikely way. During late June or early July the German agent spent a vacation at a fashionable hotel in Kennebunkport, Maine. There he met a charming young American lady named Anne L. Seward who won his confidence as well, apparently, as his heart. During a moment of extravagant intimacy, he told Miss Seward that he was a secret German agent, and

[30] Rintelen amplifies the above summary in some detail in *The Dark Invader*, pp. 91-182. His own account is substantiated by the reports that agents of the Department of Justice made in late 1915. They were summarized with astounding accuracy in the *New York Times*, November 22 and December 5, 8, and 18, 1915, and in the New York *World*, December 8, 1915. The Justice Department later produced much of this same evidence when it brought Rintelen and other German conspirators to trial in New York City in April 1917.

[31] Captain von Rintelen, *The Dark Invader*, pp. 184 ff.

that he had planned the destruction of the *Lusitania*. Miss Seward at once wrote to Secretary Lansing, whom she knew, saying that she had information of vital importance to the country, which she could disclose only in person. Without hesitating Lansing sent his assistant, Chandler P. Anderson, to Kennebunkport; there Miss Seward related the fantastic story.[32]

The wheels turned rapidly as soon as Anderson returned to Washington on July 10, 1915. The Assistant Attorney General, Charles Warren, took personal charge of the matter and set several agents of the Bureau of Investigation[33] on the trail. They reported on about July 21 that Rintelen was none other than the actual head of a powerful and widespread underground organization that was engaged in fomenting strikes, hindering the export of munitions in various other ways, and provoking hostilities between the United States and Mexico. Further, the report continued, Rintelen had told one of the federal agents that he had personally sent the order for the sinking of the *Lusitania*.[34] More investigation soon added additional details about Rintelen's negotiations with Huerta and other Mexican counterrevolutionaries.[35]

These disclosures struck like a bolt of lightning among officials in Washington. We do not know precisely when Lansing informed the President; it must have been soon after the Secretary learned the facts himself, for we find Wilson writing in some anger and alarm on August 4, "I am sure that the country is honeycombed with German intrigue and infested with German spies. The evidence of these things are [*sic*] multiplying every day."[36] Lansing reacted in much the same way, although he was more worldly-wise in such affairs than his chief. Like Wilson, the Secretary of State at once suspected that Bernstorff was deeply involved. The following entry in Lansing's diary was written nine months later, but it undoubtedly reflected the opinions that he formed in the wake of the Rintelen exposure:

"From numberless circumstances, which came to my knowledge, I have not the slightest doubt but that Bernstorff, during the early part of the war, not only was cognizant of all that was going on but prob-

[32] Anderson Diary, July 9, 1915.

[33] Among whom was almost certainly A. Bruce Bielaski, chief of the Bureau of Investigation.

[34] Anderson Diary, July 22, 1915, recording the proceedings of a conference at the State Department at which Warren read the report by the federal agents to Lansing and to Anderson.

[35] C. Warren to R. Lansing, September 15, 1915, Lansing Papers.

[36] W.W. to E. M. House, August 4, 1915, Baker Collection.

ably directed the activities of his country's agents which had as their object the sending of supplies to German cruisers and the smuggling of war materials through the fleets of the Allies. Four fifths of his time in those days he spent at the Ritz-Carlton in New York. How far he was directly involved in the passport frauds I do not know but I strongly suspect that he furnished the funds. I had suspicions also that he was not entirely innocent of the conspiracies to blow up munitions factories and to cause strikes among the employees. . . . I felt that he was sly and unscrupulous, that he would go to any lengths to gain his end, and that he was, therefore, untrustworthy in every way. He had large sums of money at his disposal and I had no doubt that he would expend them lavishly to cause trouble for the United States with Mexico or Japan, or to organize the German vote against the President if it seemed to be for his interest to do so. I had every reason to believe and some evidence to prove that he was indirectly employing a large number of spies and many agents in this country. Take it all together Count Bernstorff was a dangerous man and required constant watching."[37]

Wilson and Lansing were irritated and alarmed but not panicstricken. Eager to avoid new public agitation and any further straining of official relations with Germany at this juncture, they did not tell their secret to other Cabinet members or even to Colonel House, and certainly not to reporters. On the other hand, they did convey a warning in the newspapers to Bernstorff and his colleagues, one that only the latter could fully understand. It was in the form of an inspired report from Washington on August 15 to the effect that the Washington authorities were about to launch a thorough investigation into various German intrigues; that the government had already accumulated considerable evidence on this subject in "New England"; and that the leaders in Washington hoped that German officials were not involved, as German-American relations were already in a delicate condition and the administration had no desire to strain them further.[38]

Doctor Albert could not have chosen a worse time to leave his brief case in an elevated train or Rintelen to engage in foolish indiscretions. The consequences would have been serious enough in any event, but they occurred on the eve of an incident—and it, too, was ironically an accidental one—that would strain German-American relations nearly

[37] "Count von Bernstorff," entry in the Lansing Diary dated "May 1916."
[38] *New York Times*, August 16 and 17, 1915.

to the breaking point. This was the sinking by a German submarine
of the passenger liner *Arabic* with the loss of American life, which
happened as follows:

The weather was clear and bright off the southern Irish coast on
the morning of August 19, 1915, as Commander Schneider brought
his submarine, the *U24*, to the surface. Sighting an English steamer,
the *Dunsley*, Schneider gave pursuit and, when the *Dunsley* tried to
escape, sank her by cannon fire after the crew had evacuated the ship.
"At 7 hours 45 [7:45 a.m.]," Schneider wrote soon afterward in his
log, "abandoned the steamer *Dunsley* while sinking on account of the
approach of a large steamer with one smokestack and four masts. As
I had been cannonaded on the fourteenth [of August] by a large ship,
I decided to attack this one submerged. . . . The steamer headed toward
the straits where the *Dunsley* was sinking. I went down to fire by
the forward tube and fired, at 11 hours 30,[39] by tube number 2. Forty
seconds later the torpedo struck the ship in the rear. . . . I could not
see the name of the boat. It carried no flag and appeared to be a mixed
[cargo and passenger] ship of about 5,000 tons."[40]

The ship that Schneider had sent to the bottom so nonchalantly
was no medium-sized freighter but the *Arabic*, 15,801 tons, pride of
the White Star Line and the heaviest carrier of contraband in the North
Atlantic run.[41] On this, her last, voyage she was outward bound from
Liverpool with a cargo consisting mostly of mail and with 423 passengers and crew. There were forty-four casualties, mainly from the torpedo's blast, among whom were two American citizens.

President Wilson had recently returned from New Hampshire and
was at the White House when press dispatches brought the first news
of the torpedoing just before two o'clock in the afternoon of August 19.
Official confirmation from the American Vice Consul at Queenstown
followed an hour later. Canceling his afternoon's golf engagement,
Wilson at once called Secretary Lansing by telephone. Afterward he,
or one of his secretaries, met reporters who had crowded into the
presidential mansion and told them that the American government
would take no action until it had learned all the facts.[42] Giving em-

---

[39] All other eye-witness accounts placed the time of the firing of the torpedo at
about 9:30 a.m.

[40] Spindler, *La Guerre Sous-Marine*, II, 335.

[41] See the New York *World*, August 20, 1915, for a list of her cargo on her last three
eastbound voyages.

[42] *New York Times*, August 20, 1915.

phatic confirmation of the absence of any kind of panic in the administration, the President set out early the next morning by automobile for Philadelphia, to keep an appointment with an oculist in that city. While he was gone, the Secretary of State displayed a studied calm as he told reporters that there would be no final decisions until after a report on the *Arabic's* destruction had come from the American Consul at Queenstown.[43]

During all the following week, while the affair moved toward the inevitable crisis, Wilson maintained this public posture of implacable calm, refusing to do anything that might further exacerbate public opinion and thus endanger a peaceful solution. When Secretary Lansing, on August 20, suggested that the President hold a special meeting of the Cabinet in order to emphasize the gravity of the situation,[44] for example, Wilson refused. "I do not think," he replied, "that an immediate summons of the Cabinet would be wise. We should first know all the facts. . . . Haste in the matter would be likely to give the country the wrong impression, I fear with regard to our frame of mind."[45] When the Baltimore *Sun,* on August 24, published an article saying that the Army War College was making elaborate plans for war with Germany, the President ordered an immediate investigation to determine if any army officer had been responsible for the sensational report; and an official denial ensued.[46]

These outward signs gave no hint of the deep emotional turmoil through which Wilson was going while he faced the crisis in almost total isolation from his family and dearest friends. He knew clearly enough what he might have to do if investigation confirmed the first reports that the *Arabic* had been sunk without provocation or warning, and if the German government refused to make prompt amends. He knew that the unequivocal language of the third *Lusitania* note left no choice in these circumstances but to break diplomatic relations with Berlin. Perhaps he *would* do this if there were no honorable alternative. But it was an almost unnerving thing to contemplate, for the great majority of Americans shuddered, he was sure, at the thought of war, which might easily come once relations with Germany were severed. There

[43] *ibid.,* August 21, 1915.
[44] R. Lansing to W.W., August 20, 1915, *The Lansing Papers,* I, 467-468.
[45] W.W. to R. Lansing, August 21, 1915, *ibid.*
[46] W.W. to the Assistant Secretary of War, August 24, 1915, Wilson Papers; the Assistant Secretary of War to W.W., August 25, 1915, enclosing W. W. Macomb, Chief of the War College Division, memorandum for the Chief of Staff, dated August 24, 1915, *ibid.*

was also the knowledge that, except for a few extremists,[47] the American people trusted him so completely and would follow where he led;[48] and that so much depended upon his success in managing the negotiations so as to strengthen the Imperial German Chancellor in his struggle with the navy, about which Wilson already knew a good deal from press dispatches, Gerard's reports, and other sources.

In a moment of obvious emotional distress on August 21, Wilson turned to Colonel House for support. "I greatly need your advice what to *do* in view of the sinking of the *Arabic*, if it turns out to be the simple case it seems," the President wrote on his own typewriter. "I know that Lansing will be as desirous as I am to learn what you are thinking. Two things are plain to me: 1. The people of this country count on me to keep them out of the war;[49] 2. It would be a calamity to the world at large if we should be drawn actively into the conflict and so deprived of all disinterested influence over the settlement." "We must," he added, trying to think of other alternatives, "write to England, and in very definite terms. Do you think that there is any chance of our getting them to rescind the Order in Council and depend altogether upon the contraband list to carry out their policy of keeping from Germany what she can use against the Allies?"[50]

Shocked by his friend's seeming indecision,[51] House replied in two

[47] Like Theodore Roosevelt and William J. Bryan, whose statements may be found in the *New York Times*, August 22 and 23, 1915.

[48] This, clearly, was the tenor of the great majority of newspaper editorials at the outset of the crisis. For surveys of press opinion, see *ibid.*, August 20 and 21, 1915, and "The Attack on the Arabic," *Literary Digest*, LI (August 28, 1915), 387-388.

[49] The British Ambassador made the following comment on this point: "The situation in Europe and in Mexico is such that many people say the Government ought to take a firm stand. But there can be little doubt that public opinion desires, on the whole, that the Government should take no action which could possibly lead to a breach of the peace. That is the only policy upon which the majority of the people have made up their mind. It does not, of course, follow that this determination will remain unaltered. But if the policy of the Government alters in advance of public opinion the Government will lose touch with the country and would lose its control." "Notes by Sir C. Spring-Rice on the Situation in the United States," memorandum dated the British Embassy, Washington, August 19, 1915, *Printed for the use of the Cabinet. September 1915*, copy in the Asquith Papers.

[50] W.W. to E. M. House, August 21, 1915, Baker Collection.

[51] "The President," House wrote in his Diary on August 22, 1915, "has clearly put it up to me and I have not flinched in my advice. I am surprised at the attitude he takes. He evidently will go to great lengths to avoid war. He should have determined his policy when he wrote his notes of February, May, June and July. No citizen of the United States realizes better than I the horrors of this war, and no one would go

letters on the following day. In the first he urged the President to settle the *Arabic* case before taking up the cudgels again in the old dispute with England; he also enclosed a copy of an insulting letter from Bernstorff accusing the United States of outright unneutrality and intimating that his government was in no mood to make any new concessions.[52] In his second letter, House spoke even more bluntly:

"Our people do not want war, but even less do they want you to recede from the position you have taken. Neither do they want to shirk the responsibility which should be ours. Your first note to Germany after the sinking of the Lusitania made you not only the first citizen of America, but the first citizen of the world. If by any word or act you should hurt our pride of nationality you would lose your commanding position over night. Further notes would disappoint our own people and would cause something of derision abroad. In view of what has been said, and in view of what has been done, it is clearly up to this Government to act. The question is, when and how?"[53]

Wilson's reaction as he read these letters was particularly revealing of his distraught and, one is tempted to add, increasingly indecisive state of mind. It was as if he thought that House was right but resented being thus reminded. "Of course I shall deal with Germany first. What an Impertinent Prussian Bernstorff is!" he wrote on House's first letter as he sent it on to Mrs. Galt to read. "All this is true,—only too true!" he wrote on the second letter. "I wish he had not put in the sentence I have marked in the margin.[54] It is not of how *I* will stand that I am thinking, but of what it is right to do. You see he does not advise: he puts it up to me!"[55]

The President reacted much the same way two days later when he received a message marked "Confidential for the Secretary and the President" from Ambassador Page in London. Any American delay in pressing for satisfaction for the destruction of the *Arabic*, Page warned, would "deepen the impression throughout Europe that the United States is seeking to maintain peace at the price of humiliation

---

further to avoid it, but there is a limit to all things, and, in the long run, I feel the nation would suffer more in being supine than in taking a decided stand."

[52] E. M. House to W.W., August 22, 1915, Wilson Papers, enclosing a copy of J. von Bernstorff to E. M. House, August 21, 1915. The original of Bernstorff's letter is in the House Papers.

[53] E. M. House to W.W., August 22, 1915, Wilson Papers.

[54] "If by any word or act you should hurt our pride of nationality you would lose your commanding position over night."

[55] House's letters, with Wilson's marginal comments, are now in the Wilson Papers.

in the face of repeated offences."[56] "It is a little provoking to have Page do this kind of thing," Wilson wrote on the flimsy of the message that he sent to Mrs. Galt. "*Of course* that is the view over there; but we know how crazy they are to have us follow them. This makes one wish to order P. to visit his native land!"

It was no use, however, kicking against the pricks. Something, Wilson knew well enough, had to be done to make the Germans realize the gravity of the affair. But what? As early as August 21 he agreed with Lansing that the crisis was "of a most serious nature," and that the American government could not temporize if investigation proved that the attack on the *Arabic* had been wanton.[57] Wilson gave his answer to the world on the following day, August 22, in the form of an inspired White House news report. "There is much speculation in Government circles," it read, "as to what the President will do in case the final reports on the sinking of the Arabic make the act of the German submarine 'deliberately unfriendly.' Here is what most likely will happen if the facts are against Germany: The President will recall Ambassador Gerard and all the American Consuls from Germany, and give to Ambassador Bernstorff and all of his assistants their passports. That would sever all relations between the two Governments. . . . It was stated on the highest authority to-day that the President will act quickly and firmly if the testimony shows that the German *Government* wantonly disregarded his solemn warning in the last note on the Lusitania tragedy."[58]

There it was for all to read, a clear-cut statement of the President's resolution: no bluster or threat of war, only a quiet invitation to negotiation and an implied assurance that a peaceful solution was possible. The outcome, as this dispatch itself said, all depended now upon the German government. By defending the sinking of the *Arabic* and refusing to make proper amends, it would make a rupture inevitable; by disavowing the act and conceding the minimum American demands for the safety of passenger ships, it could not only prevent a break but also perhaps pave the way for a general settlement.

So eager were the leaders in Washington for a peaceful solution that they did not wait for the authorities in Berlin to open negotiations but

[56] Ambassador Page to the Secretary of State, August 24, 1915, Wilson Papers, also printed in *Foreign Relations, 1915, Supplement*, pp. 524-525.

[57] R. Lansing to W.W., August 20, 1915; W.W. to R. Lansing, August 21, 1915, *The Lansing Papers*, I, 467-468.

[58] New York *World*, August 23, 1915, italics added; also the *New York Times*, August 23, 1915.

took the initiative themselves in what was, given the circumstances, a rather extraordinary overture.

Three days after the destruction of the *Arabic*, Chandler P. Anderson and Secretary Lansing discussed the crisis by telephone. The American government, Anderson argued, was not, legally speaking, in a strong position at this point in its controversy with Germany, because it had virtually recognized the German claim that the submarine campaign was a legitimate reprisal against the British blockade of neutral commerce. If this were true, Anderson went on, then the United States had no right to make an issue of the safety of American citizens on *belligerent* ships. How, then, could the Washington authorities extricate themselves from the "unfortunate position" that the President had taken by insisting upon a guarantee of safe passage for Americans on belligerent merchantmen? The chief hope, he continued, lay in persuading the Germans to abandon their submarine campaign in order to throw all onus for the denial of neutral trading rights upon Great Britain. Would Lansing like him to see Bernstorff and make this suggestion to him informally and personally? Anderson asked. The Secretary of State "heartily" approved, and Anderson arranged to meet the German Ambassador at the Ritz-Carlton Hotel in New York on the following day.[59]

Anderson pressed his arguments upon Bernstorff with great vigor at this secret rendezvous. The Ambassador, who had apparently been in deep gloom, took heart. "He saw at once," Anderson reported to Lansing, "that they could throw the entire responsibility for illegal interference with American rights upon G. B. by adopting this course and if G. B. did not adopt the same course our relations to the situation would be on a different basis.[60] He is turning the matter over in his mind and is going to prepare a cable to his Government which he will show to you as soon as he comes to Washington as he intends to do as soon as he gets authority to deal with the situation which he has cabled for."[61]

Meanwhile, "all hell had broken loose once again" in Berlin.[62] News

[59] Anderson Diary, August 22, 1915.

[60] This was a point that Anderson made in presenting his views to Bernstorff.

[61] C. P. Anderson to R. Lansing, August 23, 1915, *The Lansing Papers*, I, 469-470; also the account of the meeting in the Anderson Diary, incorrectly dated August 22, 1915.

[62] As Count Kuno von Westarp, the leader of the Conservative Party, put it in a

of the sinking of the *Arabic* and of the ensuing excitement in America first came to the German capital in news dispatches on August 21. "In case Reuter news that four Americans were drowned is correct," the Imperial Chancellor wired almost in panic to the Foreign Office's envoy at Supreme Headquarters, "the danger of a break with America would again become acute. Admiralty without information. Please wire if Imperial order for the sparing of large passenger ships has recently been suspended."[63] No one seemed to know what had happened. "About Arabic still no further news. Imperial order still in force," came the reply from Pless on August 22.[64]

The suspense in Berlin became almost unbearable as days passed without any official report from the Admiralty or a single word from Bernstorff.[65] The more leaders at the Foreign Office contemplated the dire possibilities ahead, the more they all agreed that they had reached the end of the line in their struggle with the navy. "The attacks on the Orduna and the Arabic prove that new incidents with America are possible at any time," the head of the American section, Count Max Montgelas, warned his superiors on August 24. ". . . Both ships were torpedoed without previous warning while sailing *to* America. That the torpedo fired at the Orduna missed is only an accident." It was obvious, Montgelas went on, that any submarine captain could cause a break between America and Germany at any time. This was an impossible state of affairs. A rupture could be averted only by making the concessions that Count von Bernstorff had suggested earlier; "the submarine war against enemy *passenger* ships *has* to be conducted according to the rules of cruiser warfare."[66] Bethmann agreed emphatically. In a message for the Chief of the Naval Cabinet, Admiral von Müller, on the following day, the Chancellor paraphrased Montgelas' memorandum in angry words and made his own determination clear, as follows:

". . . Unhappily, it depends upon the attitude of a single submarine commander whether America will or will not declare war. It is

---

letter that he wrote from Berlin on September 1, 1915. Count Kuno F. V. von Westarp, *Konservative Politik im Letzten Jahrzehnt des Kaiserreiches,* II, 112.

[63] The Imperial Chancellor to Envoy K. G. von Treutler, August 21, 1915, German F. O. Archives.

[64] K. G. von Treutler to the Foreign Office, August 22, 1915, *ibid.*

[65] Bernstorff sent his first message on the *Arabic* on August 20, 1915. It was unaccountably delayed in transmission and, as we will see, did not arrive in Berlin until August 26.

[66] Count Montgelas, memorandum dated August 24, 1915, German F. O. Archives.

impossible to curtail American hysteria if we do not receive a quick report from the submarine commander in question, and the danger increases the longer we wait. Whether we can succeed in settling the Arabic case remains to be seen.

"For my part, I now see no other solution but to change the Imperial order to the effect that enemy passenger ships are not permitted to be sunk without warning and until passengers and crews have been given sufficient time for rescue. In other words, the submarine war against passenger ships must be conducted like cruiser warfare. This order should be communicated to Washington. Moreover, Count Bernstorff should be empowered to negotiate about an indemnity for the victims of the Lusitania and eventually of the Arabic, and to ask the American Government to begin negotiations with the English Government looking toward placing the conduct of the war at sea on a basis of the Declaration of London."[67]

Bethmann also decided that he would see von Tirpitz and force this issue at once, even to the point of an Imperial conference. But he did not dare to wait until this final confrontation or even until he had some word from Bernstorff before attempting to assuage American opinion. The Washington government had asked for information about the sinking of the *Arabic*;[68] any delay in replying might prove fatal. Thus on August 24 the Chancellor had a warning sent to the Fleet, reminding U-boat commanders of the limitations formerly imposed by the Emperor,[69] and the following telegram dispatched to Bernstorff for delivery to the State Department and publication in the American press:

> So far no official information about the sinking of the *Arabic* is available. The Imperial Government trusts that the Government of the United States will not take a definite stand after only hearing the reports coming from one side, which, according to the opinion of my Government, can not possibly correspond with the facts, but will give the Imperial Government a chance to be heard equally. . . . In case Americans should actually have lost their life this would naturally be contrary to the intention of the German Government, who would deeply regret this fact and

[67] T. von Bethmann Hollweg to K. G. von Treutler, August 25, 1915, *ibid.*

[68] The Secretary of State to Ambassador Gerard, August 23, 1915, *Foreign Relations, 1915, Supplement*, p. 518.

[69] The Admiralty to the Fleet, August 24, 1915, Tirpitz, *Politische Dokumente*, II, 402.

has instructed me to extend its sincerest sympathy to the Government of the United States.[70]

On the same day, August 24, moreover, Foreign Secretary von Jagow informed Ambassador Gerard privately that the submarine commander had acted contrary to instructions if he had sunk the *Arabic* without warning.[71] And when a news dispatch from Washington, saying that the American government would insist upon a plain disavowal as the price of maintaining diplomatic relations, arrived in Berlin a few hours after this interview, von Jagow called Gerard to his office again. There, on August 25, the Foreign Secretary went all the way, as he had not done the day before, in what was by now becoming this massive German effort to avert a rupture. "We had some conversation," Gerard reported; "he finally said I could cable you and say, if *Arabic* torpedoed as reported in English papers, that the act would be disavowed and reparation made; that torpedoing, if as reported, was contrary to instructions. I asked again what those instructions were: he said not to torpedo passenger ships without notice and giving crew and passengers an opportunity to leave the ship. I asked if these instructions referred to passenger ships only or included merchant vessels also; he said he could not answer that but knew they did refer to passenger ships."[72] Doubting, perhaps, that Gerard would convey this message, von Jagow immediately sent a version of his own to Washington,[73] while the Imperial Chancellor, on the same day, gave a new statement to the American newspapers declaring that the Imperial Government would give "complete satisfaction" to the United States if investigation proved that a German had wantonly attacked and sunk the *Arabic*.[74]

Having thus done everything humanly possible to avert the possibility of an immediate rupture, Bethmann now left Berlin on August 25 for Supreme Headquarters at Pless Castle. At this gloomy Teu-

[70] The German Ambassador to the Secretary of State, August 24, 1915, *Foreign Relations, 1915, Supplement*, p. 524; published in slightly different form in the *New York Times* and other American newspapers by permission of the Secretary of State on August 25, 1915.

[71] Ambassador Gerard to the Secretary of State, August 24, 1915, *Foreign Relations, 1915, Supplement*, pp. 525-526.

[72] Ambassador Gerard to the Secretary of State, August 25, 1915, *ibid.*, p. 526. G. von Jagow to T. von Bethmann Hollweg, August 25, 1915, German F. O. Archives, repeats the gist of Gerard's account of this conversation.

[73] The Foreign Office to Ambassador von Bernstorff, August 25, 1915, *ibid.*

[74] *New York Times*, August 26, 1915.

tonic fortress in Silesia, where the Emperor's own eagles flew, occurred one of the turning points in the history of the war.

Bethmann struck boldly at the outset. Accompanied by von Treutler, he sought out von Tirpitz and Admiral Bachmann, chief of the Admiralty, on the morning of August 26 in an effort to win their cooperation and avoid a direct appeal to the Supreme War Lord. The crisis over the *Arabic* was really very grave, the Chancellor explained. Germany had to avoid a break with America. More than that, Bethmann went on, he had to have the navy's support for his policies, for he "could not walk on a volcano forever," not knowing where he stood in dealing with the United States. He would have to give America definite assurances that submarines would obey the rules of cruiser warfare while attacking all passenger ships; moreover, he would suggest arbitration of the American claims for damages, and he would ask the Washington authorities to take steps to compel England to observe the Declaration of London.

The admirals replied hotly with old arguments. Such a declaration as the Chancellor proposed to give to the United States, Bachmann said, was tantamount to an open confession that the submarine campaign was illegal. Conducting operations according to the rules of cruiser warfare would be suicidal for U-boats, and it would not be much help to Germany if England should consent to observe the Declaration of London in waging maritime warfare. Agreeing, von Tirpitz observed that the Americans were already enemies of Germany, and that such concessions as Bethmann had in mind would not win them to the German side.[75]

Bethmann tried to conciliate his antagonists at the end of this interview but failed, and so the Imperial conference proceeded on schedule soon afterward on the same day, August 26. Arrayed before the Emperor were Bethmann, von Tirpitz, Bachmann, General von Falkenhayn, Admiral von Müller, von Treutler, and Colonel General von Plessen, Chief of the Military Cabinet. The Imperial Chancellor led off, repeating what he had just told Tirpitz and Bachmann. The two admirals replied in the same vein as before, except that Bachmann reported that he had just received word from Berlin that the situation in the United States was much improved, and von Tirpitz added that he did not think that friendly overtures to America could succeed in

[75] "Conference with the Imperial Chancellor and a Joint Meeting in the Presence of His Majesty on August 26, 1915. I. Conference," Tirpitz, *Politische Dokumente*, II, 404-406.

any event. The Emperor then turned to General von Falkenhayn, who said that he must hold to the position that he had taken before, namely, that it was necessary to do anything, even to end the submarine war altogether, to avert hostilities with the United States. The past six months, he added somewhat acidly, had shown clearly enough that the submarines could not really harm England, and it was foolish to think that it would be otherwise in the future.[76]

At this point Bethmann's advantage was considerable. So eager was he, however, to avoid being maneuvered into appearing to oppose the submarine campaign *per se* that he now committed the blunder that nearly cost him the victory. He declared that he did not want to stop the submarine war anywhere, or even to change its method. "He wanted only to be able to give the definite declaration to the United States that we would act in good faith toward passenger ships, so that later, if an infringement should by some chance occur, then the commander involved could be disavowed and the German Government could not be blamed."

This declaration heartened Bethmann's foes and thoroughly con-

[76] Falkenhayn amplified these views a short time later in a letter to Admiral Bachmann. It so well reveals the thinking of the German military leaders about Germany's strategic situation at this time and about the necessity for preserving the neutrality of the United States that it is printed here in full, as follows:

"From my viewpoint, the question shapes up as follows: There can be no more doubt that our enemies, after realizing that they cannot defeat Germany with weapons, will now try to reach their goal by a war of exhaustion. It will be up to us to prevent this with military measures. It is doubtful if we can succeed, but I most firmly hope that we can. At any rate, our situation is so serious that it would be irresponsible to make it worse. An open allying of the United States on the side of our enemies would mean just such a worsening, and a very serious worsening, indeed. Aside from all the immediate effects on public opinion in Germany and on our economic life during the war and afterward, it would bring a chilling of our relations with all the states that have so far been neutral—Holland, Sweden, Denmark, Switzerland, Bulgaria, Greece, and Rumania. In order to break this war of exhaustion, we need the help of the neutrals.

"The open partisanship of the United States against us at this time must be prevented at all costs, if it is possible to prevent it. If the limitation of the submarine war is necessary to avoid such a break, then it has to be done. If a stopping of the submarine war is necessary, then this also cannot be avoided. Whether the submarine war harms England more or less is not important, for the past six months have proved that we do not have the power, either now or in the future, to bring England to her knees.

"If, therefore, the responsible leader of German policy makes demands regarding the conduct of the submarine war in order to maintain peace with the United States, then according to my conviction there is no other choice but to oblige him, unless one could prove that the assumption that the United States would go to war was wrong. However, Your Excellency has not yet proved this." General von Falkenhayn to Admiral Bachmann, September 2, 1915, German F. O. Archives.

fused his friends. Why not wait, Bachmann suggested quickly, to see whether the U-boat commander had blundered in sinking the *Arabic*? If an explanation *were* necessary, then let the Chancellor say that effective measures would hereafter be taken to spare passengers on *large* liners. He would not have to explain what these measures were. This, von Treutler and then von Müller agreed, seemed to offer the best way out; let Bethmann and the naval leaders get together and draft a note along these lines. The Emperor, who had sat in wooden silence, hastened to concur. The Imperial Chancellor, he commanded, should prepare the note in accord with the navy and should present it to him.[77]

Bethmann bowed gravely, but he left the conference in a furious rage. He had, he told Bachmann soon afterward, been surrounded, like the Russians, on all sides. The men upon whom he had depended had left him in the lurch. But, unlike the Russians, he would not surrender. He would not leave Pless until the Emperor had decided in his favor. The American government had to have definite assurances regarding passenger ships; moreover, it had to know that the Imperial political leaders and the navy were in accord. Besides, the matter of a note to America was a political question; he had invited the naval leaders to the conference only to hear their opinions.[78]

Bethmann must have thought long and hard about what he could say to change the Emperor's mind. Then, fortuitously, help arrived during the evening of August 26. It was a telegram from Bernstorff, which the Ambassador had written on August 20, when the situation seemed menacingly critical, and which for some reason had been delayed in transmission. "I fear," it read, "that it will not be possible to prevent rupture this time if our answer about the Arabic is not conciliatory. I advise sending instructions to me immediately to negotiate the entire question. Perhaps it will thus be possible to save the situation."[79]

Armed with this telegram, the Chancellor confronted the Emperor on the following morning, August 27, with the draft of a note of instructions to Bernstorff. Whether the audience was a stormy one; whether Bethmann, for example, threatened to resign if William did

[77] "Conference with the Imperial Chancellor and a Joint Meeting in the Presence of His Majesty on August 26, 1915. II. Conference with His Majesty," Tirpitz, *Politische Dokumente*, II, 406; Spindler, *La Guerre Sous-Marine*, II, 352-355.

[78] Tirpitz, *Politische Dokumente*, II, 406-407.

[79] Ambassador von Bernstorff to the Foreign Office, August 26 [*sic*], 1915, German F. O. Archives. Bernstorff (*My Three Years in America*, p. 146) gives the date of this telegram as August 20, 1915.

not approve the proposed instructions, we do not know. We know only that the Emperor concurred, and that, consequently, the Chancellor at last had a free hand to proceed to what he must have thought would be the concluding phase of the *Arabic* negotiations.[80]

In the meantime, events on the other side of the Atlantic had been moving at a more leisurely pace amid an atmosphere of lessening tension. Wilson's and Lansing's fears of a violent outcome of the crisis had vanished almost altogether after Bethmann's and von Jagow's barrage of reassuring messages arrived in Washington between August 24 and 26. These and Gerard's reports, which, for once, seemed to make sense,[81] made it abundantly clear that the American leaders could obtain almost any reasonable concessions from the German government. Even so, as Wilson and Lansing knew, the task ahead would not be easy. There was, first of all, the necessity of forcing the issue to a conclusion[82] without, however, driving the Germans into desperate resistance and thereby tipping the scales against the Chancellor and the Foreign Office in the struggle for control of German foreign policy.[83] There was, secondly, the fact that the President and Secretary of State, now that they were reasonably certain that a proper disavowal for the destruction of the *Arabic* would come from Berlin in due time, had decided to settle once and for all the question of the inviolability of passenger ships in the war zone.[84]

[80] The Emperor soon afterward made it clear that he understood the basic issues, when he penned the following comment on a letter of resignation from von Tirpitz: "America must be prevented from participating in the war against us as an active enemy. It could offer unlimited financial resources to our enemies who are now in severe financial straits. Our financial situation is not capable of bearing this. It could thereby create a tremendous advantage against us. As supreme commander, I absolutely had to prevent this from happening. That was a wise policy. For that reason I *had* to order limitations with a heavy heart in order to reach the desired goal. The success of a peaceful understanding with the United States can already be seen everywhere in the military and political spheres. . . . First of all, the *war* must be *won*, and for this it is necessary to prevent the entrance of any new enemies into the struggle. It does not matter how that happens, whether with more or less sacrifice, and it is *my affair*. How I use my navy in accomplishing this is, anyway, my affair only." Tirpitz, *Politische Dokumente*, II, 428.

[81] "Gerard is here a little more cogent than usual," Wilson wrote on copies (now in the Wilson Papers) of two dispatches from the Ambassador dated August 25, 1915. They are printed in *Foreign Relations, 1915, Supplement*, pp. 526-527.

[82] As the President said, in W.W. to E. M. House, August 25, 1915, Baker Collection.

[83] As Gerard pointed out in the dispatches cited above.

[84] As the Washington correspondents reported on August 25 and 26. See, e.g., the *New York Times*, August 26 and 27, 1915.

Working confidently for this larger goal, the American leaders took up officially the negotiations that Chandler P. Anderson had begun informally with Ambassador von Bernstorff on August 23, 1915. The Ambassador assumed the initiative on the following day by sending the draft of a proposed message to Berlin to Lansing for the Secretary's comment. "With regard to the confidential negotiations which I hope soon to be able to take up with the American Government," it read, "it seems that the last paragraph of the American *Frye* note of 10th inst, contains a suggestion which may prove useful in the general negotiations concerning *Lusitania* and *Arabic*. I understand the suggestion [to be] . . . that we should refrain from attacking passenger ships without warning pending negotiations, which would put the burden on England to refrain from unlawful blockade pending negotiations. It does, however, not mean that we should give up the whole submarine warfare."[85]

Lansing replied by calling Bernstorff to his office on August 26. Adopting his most official manner, the Secretary of State made it clear that Bernstorff's draft would not do. Bernstorff, he said, had linked the *Arabic* case to the general negotiations that were already in progress over the issue of the safety of Americans traveling on the high seas. The *Arabic* case, he went on, stood alone and would have to be dealt with on its own merits. Meanwhile, the American government would have to know precisely where the German government stood on the question of passenger ships. Bernstorff quickly agreed that this was reasonable enough and promised to rewrite his dispatch.

At this point Lansing began to turn the vise. Feigning a deep gloom, he hinted that he expected a break in relations and warned that the American government could not wait very long for some report on the *Arabic* affair. "The Ambassador," the Secretary of State reported at once to the President, "seemed to be worried over the situation and was, for him, in a very serious mood. He is, however, optimistic that the affair can be amicably settled. I did not indicate to him that I shared his optimism but rather tried to give him the impression that I considered the situation most critical and that Germany would have to act quickly to avoid the consequences of the torpedoing of the *Arabic*, even if it were possible to do so."[86]

Wilson was delighted by this good beginning. "Don't you think

[85] The German Ambassador to the Secretary of State, August 24, 1915, *Foreign Relations, 1915, Supplement*, p. 525.
[86] R. Lansing to W.W., August 26, 1915, *The Lansing Papers*, I, 471-473.

Lansing does these things well," the President jotted on the Secretary's report of the interview as he sent it on for Mrs. Galt to read. He was, moreover, as eager as the Secretary of State to make the most of the present opportunity by driving for a full and unequivocal German pledge of safety for passenger vessels. "It does not seem to me," Wilson replied to Lansing, "that the Ambassador states our position fully enough here, and I should very much dread seeing his Government misled. Our point is, not merely that no passenger ships should be attacked without warning, but that care should be taken to make adequate provision for safe-guarding the lives of non-combatants. Mere warning on a stormy sea, mere putting of passengers and crew into open boats, might be as brutal as giving them no warning at all. 'Without warning and provision for the safety of the lives of non-combatants,' if he would accept the phraseology, would cover my point."[87]

Lansing informed Bernstorff of the President's views on August 27, and the Ambassador straightway revised his message as the two Americans had suggested. Approved by the President and Secretary of State, and dispatched to Berlin over the State Department's wire on August 28, it read as follows:

"It appears that the concluding paragraph of the American Frye note of August 10 contains a suggestion which may prove valuable. I understand the suggestion to be that pending negotiations we should refrain from attacking passenger vessels without warning and providing for the safety of noncombatants, which would put the burden on England to refrain from illegal blockade pending negotiations. It does not, however, mean that we should give up the entire submarine war. General negotiations, however, will be impossible, I am informed, if the Arabic incident is not settled satisfactorily."[88]

On the same day Bernstorff sent two additional messages. The first warned the Foreign Office that the American government, "owing to the state of public opinion," could not wait long for an explanation of the *Arabic* incident; the second relayed Lansing's request for a statement of the instructions that had been given to submarine commanders.[89]

---

[87] W.W. to R. Lansing, August 27, 1915, *ibid.*, p. 473.

[88] Ambassador von Bernstorff to the Foreign Office, August 28, 1915, German F. O. Archives.

[89] Ambassador von Bernstorff to the Foreign Office, two telegrams, August 28, 1915, *ibid.*

The crucial discussions between the Imperial Chancellor and the Foreign Secretary over the drafting of instructions to the Ambassador in Washington had already begun even before these telegrams were written. It seems likely that Bethmann called von Jagow by telephone from Pless after his audience with the Emperor on August 27 and read to him the draft that he, Bethmann, had already prepared and the Emperor had approved. It included everything to make the German surrender complete—a pledge of safety for all passenger ships; a secret provision to the effect that Bernstorff might say that submarines would hereafter observe the rules of cruiser warfare in attacking *all* merchantmen, if this concession were absolutely necessary to avoid a break with America; and a promise to give up the submarine campaign entirely if the Washington government succeeded in forcing the British to observe the Declaration of London.[90] Whether Bethmann would thus go all the way now depended upon what Bernstorff said was the American price of peace.

The word from Washington arrived at the Foreign Office on August 28. Reading between the lines of Bernstorff's dispatches of the same date, Bethmann, who had since returned to the capital, at once perceived that the Ambassador was conveying a message from the President and Secretary of State. Reading on, he saw clearly enough what he would have to do and, more important, what he did not have to do. The American leaders had neither broadened the dispute to include all merchant shipping nor demanded the abandonment of the submarine campaign. Freedom of the seas still meant, in Washington's eyes, freedom for American ships to sail unmolested and for American citizens to travel in safety on any passenger vessel. That, the Chancellor must have told himself, would be a small price to pay for American action to loosen the British hold. Thus he drafted new instructions and sent them off at once to Bernstorff over the American diplomatic wire. They follow:

"I empower you to negotiate confidentially with Wilson or Lansing on the following basis:

"1. American demands for an indemnity for Lusitania and perhaps also Arabic incident will be decided by Hague arbitration. Exclusively for personal information: In the arbitration agreement it will later have to be made clear that the judgment shall not include allowance or disallowance of the German submarine campaign.

[90] Draft of instructions to Ambassador von Bernstorff, dated August 27, 1915, *ibid.*

"2. Passenger liners will be sunk only after warning and the saving of human life, provided they do not flee or offer resistance; upon rejection of the term 'liner,' you will limit yourself to using, at the most, the expression 'passenger ship.' Should England, because of knowledge of this concession, abuse it, we reserve the right to have further talks with America. If you are asked to explain the word 'abuse,' then you could say that we would consider it an abuse if England tried to protect her freighters with single American passengers. Exclusively for your personal information: Assurances about enemy freighters cannot be given.

"3. We expect efforts from the American side to re-establish the freedom of the seas, perhaps on the basis of the Declaration of London, and will be gladly willing to cooperate. If success ensues, we will conduct the submarine war only in accord with the Declaration of London. Otherwise, we reserve the right of decision.

"After agreement on the above basis, I will answer the last Lusitania note, using your proposals. Wire notice of receipt."[91]

The important work was done, and for Bethmann there now remained only the task of seeing that the navy followed through by issuing new instructions to U-boat commanders that would prevent further incidents or protect the Imperial government if they occurred. This was no easy task, for even at this late date, even after they had been informed about the directive to the Embassy in Washington, the admirals took up the fight again more fiercely than before. Tirpitz, trying a bit of obvious blackmail, threatened to resign; Bachmann sent an urgent appeal directly to the Emperor.[92] But William and his personal advisers, particularly Admiral von Müller, held firm; and from Supreme Headquarters the following Imperial command went to the Admiralty: "I order that until further notice the orders for the sparing of *large* passenger ships be changed immediately to read that *all* passenger ships can be sunk only after warning and the saving of passengers and crews."[93] Nor was this all. Determined to have an end to the internecine struggle, the Emperor dismissed Bachmann from his post at the Admiralty and humbled the Grand Admiral (by deny-

[91] Secretary von Jagow to Ambassador von Bernstorff, August 28, 1915, *ibid.*

[92] "My Request for Release from the Position of Secretary of State of the Imperial Naval Office," dated August 27, 1915; Admiral Bachmann to the Emperor, August 30, 1915, Tirpitz, *Politische Dokumente*, II, 409-410, 412-413; Spindler, *La Guerre Sous-Marine*, II, 355-360.

[93] K. G. von Treutler to the Imperial Chancellor, August 30, 1915, German F. O. Archives, transmitting the Imperial order of the same date.

ing him the right of direct access to the throne, which he had enjoyed since the beginning of the war) at the same time that he refused to accept his resignation.[94]

While the Imperial Chancellor was thus finally winning the essential victory, the leaders in Washington were waiting with mounting impatience for some official word from Berlin. Bernstorff received his instructions probably on the day that they were sent, that is, August 28; but he could not use them immediately because they were aimed at a settlement of the general issues, and the Secretary of State had made it clear that he wanted to dispose of the *Arabic* case before moving to the larger questions. The German Ambassador did what he could to encourage the belief that a friendly settlement was imminent,[95] but privately he was far from confident. As he wired somewhat urgently to the Foreign Office on August 31:

"The American Government very impatient because of the domestic situation. If we want to avoid rupture . . . , it is necessary to reply immediately [about the *Arabic*] and at least to make known confidentially the instructions that our submarine commanders have received. American Government satisfied with our declaration but is on guard, believing we wish to evade by dilatory tactics and does not want to discuss other matters until the Arabic incident has been settled. It suffices if we say that the instructions to our commanders were and will be maintained throughout the duration of the negotiations."[96]

The Berlin authorities had no intention of permitting a rupture to occur simply because they did not seem to care. They had already taken steps to inform Bernstorff, "exclusively for [his] personal information," of the recent change in the instructions to submarine commanders by the time that the Ambassador wrote the above dispatch.[97] But the transmission of the Foreign Office's message was delayed because Ambassador Gerard, in a fit of personal pique, refused to send it.[98] The Foreign Office discovered this fact on the following day, Sep-

[94] Spindler, *La Guerre Sous-Marine*, II, 360-362; William II, Cabinet Order dated August 30, 1915, Tirpitz, *Politische Dokumente*, II, 415.

[95] See, e.g., the reports in the *New York Times*, August 29 and 30, 1915, which Bernstorff must have inspired.

[96] Ambassador von Bernstorff to the Foreign Office, August 31, 1915, German F. O. Archives.

[97] The Foreign Office to Ambassador von Bernstorff, No. 478, August 31, 1915, *ibid*.

[98] "The American Ambassador has declined to transmit telegram No. 478 to Washington, since to his regret he is no longer able to do anything for German interests

tember 1. By this time, Bernstorff's urgent warning had arrived in Berlin. Bethmann and von Jagow, consequently, sent the delayed telegram by Stockholm; then they penned an additional message in direct response to Bernstorff's telegram. The submarines that might have torpedoed the *Arabic*, von Jagow wrote, had not yet returned from the war zone; it was, therefore, simply not possible to give any kind of report to the American government at this time. However, the message continued, "You may confidentially inform the American Government that for several months submarine commanders have had orders not to attack large liners without warning and the rescue of passengers and crews. If the Arabic was attacked without warning, this would have been contrary to instructions. The order has now been modified to include all liners (passenger ships). The instructions will be in force for the duration of the negotiations."[99]

This, then, was where things stood between Washington and Berlin by September 1, 1915, when Bernstorff decided to take the initiative aggressively to end the tension and prepare the way for a general settlement. He would do this by giving the American government, as his instructions permitted him to do, the now pivotal pledge of safety for passenger ships. It was not, Bernstorff knew, what Lansing wanted most, namely, an explicit apology or disavowal for the sinking of the *Arabic*; but it would guarantee the peace until the now seemingly inevitable disavowal could be made.

Thus during the morning of September 1, as early as was appropriate, the Ambassador called the Secretary of State by telephone to ask for an appointment right away. He must have divulged his reasons for wanting the conference, for Lansing rushed at once to the White House to talk to the President. He returned to his office a short time later and received the Ambassador. Bernstorff radiated good cheer. He had come, he said, with splendid news; his government had issued

---

so long as we deny to him permanently an audience at Supreme Headquarters, while people like [A. J.] Beveridge and recently Niebuhr, who represents only an obscure newspaper in a provincial town in Illinois, have been received at Supreme Headquarters. . . . It is impossible for him, as an Ambassador, to be treated worse than American newspaper correspondents." Count Montgelas, memorandum dated September 1, 1915, *ibid*. Von Jagow added the following comment: "I spoke today with Gerard, and he seemed to be in a friendly mood. He is still peeved. He wants to be received officially and not privately." Then Bethmann wrote additionally: "Mr. Gerard has written to me and to Secretary von Jagow explicitly that he was withdrawing his request for an audience with His Majesty."

[99] The Foreign Secretary to Ambassador von Bernstorff, September 1, 1915, *ibid*.

new orders to submarine commanders and was now prepared to yield, confidentially, the promise of safety for Americans traveling in the war zone that the President had demanded during the *Lusitania* negotiations. He regretted exceedingly, he went on to say, that his superiors had still received no report about the sinking of the *Arabic*. They would give an explanation when they could; there was no reason, however, why Lansing should not know now how much the Imperial authorities had already done to preserve friendly relations. Lansing was immensely pleased if not surprised. The Ambassador's declaration, he replied, was welcome, to be sure, but it would be of little help in the present situation so long as it remained confidential. Something at all cost had to be done to reassure public opinion. Would the Ambassador, Lansing asked, be willing to put his oral declaration into a statement that could be published in the newspapers?[100]

Without hesitation, even though he knew that he was agreeing to violate his instructions, Bernstorff replied that he would gladly do as Lansing asked. "The attitude here at the end of August," he later explained to his superiors, "was such that something had to calm the waters. Otherwise a break would have been unavoidable."[101] "I could not but admit," he added afterward in his memoirs, "that the view of the Secretary of State was correct. . . . The factor of public opinion obviously appeared of less importance in Berlin than in Washington; besides, I knew from experience that no secret could be kept in Washington for long, and that in a few days this, our first sign of yielding, would be common knowledge. I thought it best, therefore, to get the full diplomatic advantage from the new situation, and took it upon myself . . . to publish my instructions."[102] Having made this decision, Bernstorff left the State Department, beaming at reporters as he went, and returned an hour later with the following letter:

Washington, D.C., Sept. 1

My dear Mr. Secretary:

With reference to our conversation of this morning, I beg to inform you that my instructions concerning our answer to your last Lusitania note contains the following passage:

[100] The above paragraph is based upon a news report in the New York *World*, September 2, 1915; J. von Bernstorff, *My Three Years in America*, pp. 149-150; and R. Lansing, *War Memoirs*, pp. 47-48.

[101] Ambassador von Bernstorff to T. von Bethmann Hollweg, October 2, 1915, German F. O. Archives.

[102] *My Three Years in America*, pp. 149-150.

"Liners will not be sunk by our submarines without warning and without safety of the lives of noncombatants, provided that the liners do not try to escape or offer resistance."

Although I know that you do not wish to discuss the Lusitania question till the Arabic incident has been definitely and satisfactorily settled, I desire to inform you of the above because this policy of my Government was decided on before the Arabic incident occurred.

I have no objection to your making any use you may please of the above information.

I remain, my dear Mr. Lansing,

Very sincerely yours,

J. Bernstorff[103]

To Wilson and Lansing, Bernstorff's giving of what was at once called the *Arabic* pledge brought immeasurable relief and joy. Their long and agonizing struggle to maintain American rights on the seas without resort to war was apparently over. The German government had yielded the concession that had been the most difficult for it to make; the disavowal for the sinking of the *Arabic* would now surely follow quickly, and, after that, negotiations that might lead to complete understanding. "In view of the clearness of the . . . statement," Lansing told reporters as he handed them a copy of Bernstorff's letter, "it seems needless to make any comment in regard to it, other than to say that it appears to be a recognition of the fundamental principle for which we have contended." The President would make no statement for publication, but the White House correspondents who saw him after he had received the Ambassador's letter reported that he was immensely pleased and looked happier than he had appeared in many months.[104]

Everywhere throughout the country the reaction was the same—of pride in the achievement of American diplomacy in vindicating the sacred principles of humanity against the pretensions of German militarism, of relief that the threat of a rupture in relations had passed, and of certain expectation that all phases of the submarine dispute would soon be settled. No sooner had the text of Bernstorff's letter appeared in the late afternoon papers than a flood of congratulatory messages began to pour into the White House. And editors in all sections raised a paean to the man who had led the people out of the dark valley to the plain of light. It was, altogether, the greatest tribute to the Pres-

---

[103] As printed in the *New York Times*, September 2, 1915.

[104] *New York Times*, September 2, 1915; New York *World*, September 2, 1915.

ident that had yet been rendered; it was the virtual apotheosis of the Man of Peace.

"The Observer," declared a North Carolina editor in a typical comment, "is not given to irreverence, but . . . it is [now] strengthened in the conviction that has possessed it for some time past that Wilson was a divinely appointed leader of the people."[105] "Woodrow Wilson," another spokesman concurred, "may well forgive in condescending pity the men who have ridiculed and stabbed him: his patience and self-control and calmness and reason and conscience have now put him far above their criticism and envy. He stands laurelled with victory."[106] But the most moving tribute, and the one that best expressed the national feeling, was written by an editor who was not in the habit of using hyperbole. He said:

"Were the public and our city officials truly alive to the significance of the tremendous moral victory won by the President of the United States yesterday, flags would be flying from every building and bells would be pealing from every church tower in this city today. Because it is a victory of peace, and for peace, and not one purchased at the cost of thousands of human lives on a bloody battlefield, these external signs of thankfulness and of glorification are lacking. Within the hearts of all Americans who have understood the meaning of what has been going on and the gravity of the crisis through which the Republic has passed, there is, however, a devout thankfulness and a profound gratitude to President Wilson which needs no outward expression to render it complete. They know that it has been given to the President to achieve a moral victory for his country and for all humanity, which forever insures him a foremost place in the pages of American history, and has mightily enhanced the power and prestige of the United States. Without mobilizing a regiment or assembling a fleet, by sheer dogged, unswerving persistence in advocating the right, he has compelled the surrender of the proudest, the most arrogant, the best armed of nations, and he has done it in completest self-abnegation, but in fullest, most patriotic devotion to American ideals."[107]

[105] *Charlotte Observer*, September 2, 1915.

[106] *The Presbyterian Banner*, cii (September 9, 1915), 8.

[107] New York *Evening Post*, September 2, 1915. For other significant expressions of editorial opinion, see the surveys in the *New York Times*, September 2, 1915, and "Germany Yields to Wilson," *Literary Digest*, li (September 11, 1915), 509-511; *New York Times*, September 2, 1915; New York *World*, September 2, 1915; *The Public*, xviii (September 3, 1915), 849; *The Congregationalist and Christian World*, c (September 9, 1915), 334; Nashville *Christian Advocate*, lxxvi (September 10, 1915), 1188-

No one was happier on that bright September morning than the man who had performed the rite of yielding. Scanning the editorial pages of a pile of American newspapers, Count von Bernstorff was filled with understandable pride and pleasure. Then he sent a telegraphic report on events of the past days to the Foreign Office and addressed a supplementary letter to his friend, the Imperial Chancellor. It might not be easy to come to a definite conclusion on the *Arabic* case, he wrote, if, as the newspapers had just reported, the German submarine involved had actually been sunk by a British warship. "I can, however, say this much," the Ambassador went on, "that the danger of war or a rupture of diplomatic relations has been definitely eliminated. From now on only details have to be worked out. This will perhaps require work and effort, but it will create no serious friction. President Wilson is very glad about the way things stand at the present and now sees the road open to advance against England. Also, public opinion has changed overnight. After all that has happened, one can hardly believe one's eyes if he reads the editorials of the American press today. And we have done nothing but [reveal the instructions] that have been followed in the submarine war since the Lusitania incident. . . . Pulling everything together, it can be said that the situation here has never been more favorable for us since the beginning of the war than it is today."[108]

It was true, or nearly so, at any rate. Not since the inauguration of the submarine campaign had a complete understanding between Berlin and Washington seemed so near at hand. The next six weeks would show whether from such auspicious beginnings a happy culmination would ensue.

1189; *The Standard*, LXIII (September 11, 1915), 36; *The Independent*, LXXXIII (September 13, 1915), 347.

[108] J. von Bernstorff to T. von Bethmann Hollweg, September 2, 1915, German F. O. Archives. The Ambassador, incidentally, received only a mild reprimand from the Foreign Office for exceeding his instructions by permitting the publication of the new orders to submarine commanders. For the reprimand and Bernstorff's apology, see the Foreign Office to Ambassador von Bernstorff, September 8, 1915, and Ambassador von Bernstorff to T. von Bethmann Hollweg, October 2, 1915, both in *ibid.*

CHAPTER XVII

Alarms and Aftermaths

ALTHOUGH the submarine controversy was their overriding concern during the spring and summer of 1915, the American people and their leaders were confronted with and at times convulsed by other events and issues that must now claim our attention. There was the challenge raised by a large group who were demanding huge increases in the nation's armed forces. There was the old dispute with England, which for various reasons was now more irritating than before. There was the necessity of finding a new policy for a changed situation in Mexico. These were all matters less dramatic than the great dispute with Germany, but they were intimately related and scarcely less important, and they often engrossed the attention of the leaders in Washington in the midst of their deepest involvement in the submarine question.

This chapter and the next tell how President Wilson and his advisers grappled with these issues. This much should be said by way of reminder before we proceed: The one central reality of American national life between the sinking of the *Lusitania* and the final settlement of the *Arabic* controversy in October 1915 was the ever-present possibility of war with Germany. Every decision that the President and his colleagues made during this period was affected if not controlled by this fact. It is not too much to say that the events that we are about to describe, and the decisions that the President made in response to them, were in large measure all aftermaths of the *Lusitania* and *Arabic* crises and the turmoil that they raised.

The earliest of these was the sudden and spectacular burgeoning of the movement for military preparedness. This campaign had begun, the reader will recall, in a feeble way during the late autumn of 1914, when a handful of editors and leaders in Congress had first raised the cry that the nation was totally unready to face the unknown perils of the future. It had immediately foundered upon the rocks of public and congressional indifference and Wilson's stern opposition.[1] Nor did the movement make any better progress during the early months of

[1] See above, pp. 137-143.

1915, in spite of intensified agitation by the recently organized National Security League, the older service organizations, and certain editorial champions of the cause, or in spite of the organization of a new preparedness group, the American Legion, in late February 1915.[2] If anything, the public was less concerned in early May than it had been four months before.

This attitude changed in the twinkling of an eye once the news of the sinking of the *Lusitania* reached American shores. Among a host of leaders in numerous walks of life the shock of realization that the nation might soon be at war was compounded by dismay at the knowl-

[2] *New York Times*, March 1, 1915.

News Note—"Mr. Daniels believes that the President
will keep the country out of trouble."
Weed in the New York *Tribune*

edge of how ill-equipped the republic was either to defend its rights or to avert involvement by effective diplomacy. Almost overnight a faltering movement became a crusade. On May 11, 1915, for example, the executive committee of the Navy League called upon the President to summon Congress into special session to authorize a bond issue of $500,000,000 "to provide this country with adequate means of national defense."[3] A month later, at a special luncheon meeting in New York City attended by more than one hundred leading financiers and businessmen, the League raised $25,000 within five minutes for expansion of its propaganda.[4] Editors and publicists took up the preparedness theme with such obsessive vigor that their outpouring swelled into a mighty flood of words by the end of the summer of 1915. Much of it was sheer yellow journalism that, like the lurid motion-picture contribution to the cause, "The Battle Cry of Peace," played upon the new public fear; but a substantial portion of these articles and books reflected the sober concern that was now gripping a large segment of thoughtful Americans.[5] It was not yet possible to judge the impact of this outpouring upon the rank and file in all sections, but one fact was clear enough by the end of the summer: The discussion begun and the challenge raised by the advocates of military expansion could no longer be ignored by the leaders in Washington. Indeed, by this time the President and his advisers were busily at work upon their own plans to augment the national security.

Wilson's reversal of position, that is to say, his espousal of a cause that he had heretofore steadfastly opposed, occurred with a suddenness

---

[3] *ibid.*, May 12, 1915.   [4] New York *World*, June 11, 1915.

[5] For descriptions and analyses of this vast literature of preparedness, see William W. Tinsley, "The American Preparedness Movement, 1913-1916," unpublished Ph.D. thesis, Stanford University; William H. Harbaugh, "Wilson, Roosevelt, and Interventionism, 1914-1917," unpublished Ph.D. thesis, Northwestern University; and Hermann Hagedorn, *The Bugle That Woke America*, a study of Theodore Roosevelt and the preparedness movement. The reader who wishes to examine the literature himself might well begin with the following: "America Unready," *Literary Digest*, L (June 5, 1915), 1314-1316, and the New York *Outlook*, cx (June 30, 1915), 495-499, for a wide selection of newspaper editorials; Julian Street, "Our Next War," *Collier's*, LV (June 19, 1915), 5-7, 28, 30-31; Richard Washburn Child, "Efficiency for Defense," *ibid.*, LVI (September 18, 1915), 7-8, 34-37; and L. M. Garrison, "The War and America. VIII— What We Need," *Harper's Weekly*, LXI (July 24, 1915), 79-81, for samples of the periodical literature; and Hudson Maxim, *Defenseless America*; Major General Francis V. Greene, *The Present Military Situation in the United States*; R. M. Johnston, *Arms and the Race*; Frederick L. Huidekoper, *The Military Unpreparedness of the United States*; Howard D. Wheeler, *Are We Ready?*; and J. Bernard Walker, *America Fallen!*, for some of the leading preparedness books, both of the sensational and of the more sober type, that crowded the bookstalls during the latter half of 1915.

that confused his friends as well as his political foes. As late as May 5, 1915, the garrulous Secretary of the Interior, Franklin K. Lane, could write complaining that the President was unwilling to approve any increases for the army, and that he, Lane, and Secretary of War Lindley M. Garrison stood alone in the Cabinet in support of military expansion.[6] Yet only two weeks later the President issued a statement calling for steady additions to the navy's strength.[7] Not long afterward he gave public blessing to the War Department's ambitious program for training college students as reserve officers at summer camps at Plattsburg, New York, and elsewhere.[8] Then on July 21, in the most important move of all, he asked Secretary Garrison and Secretary of the Navy Josephus Daniels to set their technical advisers to work on plans for an "adequate national defense," so that the administration might recommend a wise program to Congress when it convened in December.[9] During the following weeks, even while he was on vacation at Cornish, Wilson was hard at work guiding the formulation, in its first stages, of what would be the administration's program[10] and trying to prepare the ground for support among Democratic leaders in Congress.[11] Finally, by giving out his letters of July 21 to the defense secretaries for publication in the newspapers on September 3, 1915, the President tacitly confirmed what everyone now knew, that he would soon lead the fight for military and naval expansion. This was easily the most important decision on domestic policy that Wilson made during the year 1915.

There remains the question of motivation, of why Wilson made this decision and what general objectives he had in mind at this particular time. Right understanding will throw much light upon his character as a public leader and further reveal the impact that the great crisis with Germany was having upon his thought and policy.

Critics who were inclined always to ascribe the most malign motives

[6] F. K. Lane to E. M. House, May 5, 1915, House Papers.

[7] New York *World*, May 21, 1915.

[8] *New York Times*, June 29, 1915.

[9] W.W. to L. M. Garrison, July 21, 1915; W.W. to J. Daniels, July 21, 1915, both in the Wilson Papers.

[10] *New York Times*, July 24 and 25, August 13, 1915; J. Daniels to W.W., August 20, 1915, enclosing Charles J. Badger, Senior Member Present of the General Board of the Navy, to the Secretary of the Navy, July 30, 1915, Wilson Papers; L. M. Garrison to W.W., August 12, 17, and 19, 1915, *ibid.*; W.W. to L. M. Garrison, August 16, 18, and 19, 1915, *ibid.*

[11] W.W. to Representative James Hay, Representative L. P. Padgett, Senator George E. Chamberlain, and Senator B. R. Tillman, letters dated August 2, 1915, *ibid.*

to the President believed that he had espoused preparedness simply because it was politically profitable to do so. Senator Henry Cabot Lodge expressed their sentiments in a frank letter, as follows:

"Wilson evidently has come to the conclusion that there is a rising popular feeling for preparedness and, seeing votes in it, is prepared to take it up. Last winter he did everything he could to stop any improvement in the Army and Navy, sneered at [Representative A. P.] Gardner and held him up as merely trying to make political capital because he was urging then, as he is now, the necessity of doing something, backed by an array of facts which have never been successfully impugned at any point. It is announced with great pomp that he [Wilson] has sent for reports from the War and Navy Departments as to the Army and Navy."[12]

There was at least a grain of truth in the charge that political considerations contributed to President Wilson's decision. He was, assuredly, impressed by the mounting volume of the demand and by the way in which the champions of preparedness *seemed* to speak for the majority in all sections. "The demand for reasonable preparedness is clear enough," he could write on August 19, 1915.[13] Colonel House stated the case even more directly a short time later. "This controversy with Germany," he wrote, "has probably definitely settled one thing, and that is the question of 'preparedness.' Our people are thoroughly aroused to the necessity of this."[14] Since this appeared to be true, there could no longer be any question in Wilson's mind what he had to do. The responsible leader in a democracy had no alternative, he had long taught and firmly believed, but to give voice to the majority demand. Responsible leadership, however, had a higher moral duty than this: to guide the majority to the *right* objectives.

This was particularly true, the President knew, in the present situation. Here was a movement with monstrous potentialities for evil. Demagogues, yellow journalists, and sincere extremists had had an open field and had already convulsed the people with warnings of invasion and subversion. Uncontrolled and unchanneled, the agitation could only culminate in national disaster. There had been agitation enough. It was his task, Wilson thought, to take the initiative from

[12] H. C. Lodge to T. Roosevelt, August 5, 1915, Roosevelt Papers. For a milder statement of the same point of view, see W. H. Taft to Mabel Boardman, November 8, 1915, Taft Papers.

[13] W.W. to L. M. Garrison, August 19, 1915, Wilson Papers.

[14] E. M. House to J. W. Gerard, August 25, 1915, House Papers.

the extremists and to guide public opinion toward a constructive and reasonable solution. "There is no need," he wrote in early September, for example, "to stir the nation up in favor of national defense. It is already soberly and earnestly aware of its possible perils and of its duty, and I should deeply regret seeing any sort of [new] excitement stirred in so grave a matter."[15] "We are not being driven, but are going of our own accord," he told the Secretary of War, who had urged him to follow public opinion in deciding upon the objectives of his program.[16]

Everything, of course, would depend upon the way in which he defined this goal. Ever since the sinking of the *Lusitania*, Wilson had lived under the shadow of a rupture or war with Germany. He knew better than most men what meager armed strength he could immediately muster, and what the implications of this weakness were for his negotiations with Germany. He doubted that there were enough troops available even to cope with an armed uprising of German sympathizers, if one should occur in the event of hostilities.[17] That the military resources of the United States were dangerously weak was certainly one of the lessons that he had learned during the great submarine crisis.

Even so, Wilson had also concluded, the right answer was not to be found in rushing into vast preparations for war, as Theodore Roosevelt and other extreme advocates were now suggesting. It would not be possible to do this in any event, the President believed, because the American people were not ready for such a course, and Congress would scarcely approve it. Nor would such preparations make any difference anyway, for the question of war or peace with Germany would probably be decided long before they could be completed. In these circumstances, there was only one solution, and it was in Wilson's mind the right one. It was a program that promised only to provide a safe defensive capacity both on land and sea.[18] This to him was "reasonable" preparedness, "very self-restrained and judicial"[19]—a program that would do no violence to American institutions and traditions and one to which he could commit his own personal leadership in the months ahead.

[15] W.W. to Thomas Dixon, September 7, 1915, Wilson Papers.
[16] W.W. to L. M. Garrison, August 19, 1915, *ibid.*
[17] See his penciled note on E. M. House to W.W., August 23, 1915, *ibid.*
[18] As he told Colonel House on September 24, 1915, House Diary, September 24, 1915.
[19] W.W. to O. G. Villard, September 7, 1915, Villard Papers.

The threat of war with Germany had another consequence, a negative one, but important all the same. This was the way that the tension with Germany had helped prevent the nagging Anglo-American controversy over neutral trading rights from reaching the crisis toward which it often seemed to be inevitably heading.

The reader will recall how British seizure of American shipments of noncontraband suspected of having a German destination and of American vessels carrying such cargoes had proceeded apace following the issuance of the Order in Council of March 11, 1915, and evoked a mounting wave of bitter feeling in the United States; how President Wilson had been on the verge of taking some kind of diplomatic action and had been deterred by the sinking of the *Lusitania*; and how the President had subsequently attempted to win the adoption of a *modus vivendi* for Anglo-German observance of international law and, when this failed, had applied heavy pressure through Colonel House upon the British leaders for an easing of their blockade.[20]

This, roughly speaking, was the situation in Anglo-American relations by the end of the spring of 1915. It steadily worsened during the following month or six weeks as a consequence not only of the now familiar British deeds but even more of British words. In late June 1915 the London Foreign Office handed Ambassador Page a memorandum on British blockade practices. It was an effort to palliate and assuage, but it revealed in a fairly obvious way the continued British assumption of the right to control all American commerce with Europe.[21] Then on July 23, 1915, the Foreign Office finally delivered its formal reply to the American note of March 30, 1915, concerning the recently announced blockade of the Central Powers. This note was neither rude nor unresponsive, but it made no important concession on the fundamental issues to the American point of view.[22]

Continued reports of British seizures of ships and cargoes, which appeared almost daily in the newspapers, and the publication of the Foreign Office's notes fired strong popular resentment in the United States between late June and early August of 1915. To be sure, most Americans resented the German violations of what the President called the rights of humanity more deeply than they did British violations of the rights of trade; and the British had many more defenders among in-

[20] See above, pp. 395-396.

[21] Ambassador Page to the Secretary of State, June 22, 1915, *Foreign Relations, 1915, Supplement*, pp. 443-446.

[22] Ambassador Page to the Secretary of State, July 24, 1915, *ibid*., pp. 168-171.

fluential newspapers and spokesmen than Germany. Even so, the Anglo-American dispute had reached the point of actual danger by this time because to an increasing number of Americans the controversy no longer concerned superficial questions of property but the fundamental issue of national sovereignty.

This, indeed, was the main theme of editors and public leaders who voiced the resentment in all sections of the country. "When the United States under international law has rights clearly established," cried the editor of the most powerful Democratic newspaper in the country, "what can be more intolerable than to have a professed friend say that those rights will be invaded only with the minimum of inconvenience?

"You shouldn't mind a little thing like that, Sam."
Rehse in the New York *World*

What can be more insolent than to be assured by such a friend that on interrupting our lawful trade with neutrals it will graciously refrain from violence or confiscation? Is there any outrage that one nation can inflict upon another at peace more humiliating than to subject its legitimate commerce to a piratical censorship? . . . We went to war with Great Britain a century ago for a cause no more grievous."[23] In Montana Senator Thomas J. Walsh echoed this outburst when he inveighed against "the outrageous aggressions to which our legitimate foreign commerce is daily subjected under the British orders in council, more flagrant than those which brought on the war of 1812."[24] And while the volume of protests mounted, so also did demands for the sending of a stern protest to London and the adoption of even sterner retaliatory measures if the verbal protest failed to produce respect for American rights at sea. Coming as they did from a host of usually pro-Allied newspapers and, even more important, from some of the most powerful Democrats in the United States Senate, these appeals sounded very much like the authentic voice of the nation.[25]

There were many evidences that Wilson and his advisers shared the public's concern in a substantial if varying degree. The President's initial response to the blockade system inaugurated by the Order in Council of March 11, 1915, had been the essentially pragmatic one of acquiescing in the new method of blockade and of assuming, in spite of the plain words of the Order, that the British would not interfere with "innocent," that is, noncontraband, American commerce with the northern European neutrals, even when such commerce had an ultimate German destination. The development in practice of the new British measures had demonstrated the inaccuracy of this assumption at least by the time the *Lusitania* went to the bottom. The President

[23] New York *World*, June 25, 1915.

[24] T. J. Walsh to the Editor of the New York *American*, July 16, 1915, Walsh Papers. For many editorial expressions in the same vein, see "Our Grievance Against England," *Literary Digest*, LI (July 10, 1915), 45-47, and "England's 'Right' to Blockade Neutrals," *ibid.*, August 14, 1915, pp. 285-287; the widely read commentary on the British blockade measures and their destructive impact on the American economy, which was published at this time, Edwin J. Clapp, *Economic Aspects of the War*; the important article by Edward S. Corwin, "Is the British Embargo Lawful?" *New Republic*, IV (August 14, 1915), 37-38; and editorials in *ibid.*, August 7, 1915, pp. 4-5, and the New York *Nation*, CI (August 12, 1915), 191.

[25] e.g., New York *World*, July 15, 1915; Louisville *Courier-Journal*, July 12, 1915; Senator Hoke Smith to A. S. Burleson, for transmission to the President, June 7, 1915, Burleson Papers; Senator F. M. Simmons to W.W., July 3, 1915, Wilson Papers; Senator T. J. Walsh to the Editor of the New York *American*, July 16, 1915, Walsh Papers; J. P. Tumulty to W.W., July 14, 1915, Wilson Papers.

could no longer misunderstand British intentions or doubt that a controversy, one involving what he thought were fundamental principles of national right and international morality, impended.

This feeling was if anything more intense at the State Department than at the White House. Secretary Lansing told Oswald Garrison Villard on July 13, 1915, for example, that British violations of international law were "indefensible and beyond belief," and that Anglo-American relations were nearing a really serious crisis.[26] The illegal restraints imposed by Great Britain on neutral trade have become intolerable," Chandler Anderson wrote in agreement two days later. "In the packing industry alone on the facts presented by these interests, Great Britain has stopped their entire European trade, except their trade with Great Britain."[27]

Assuredly, then, Wilson and Lansing were moved when demands for redress came pouring into the White House and State Department during June and July of 1915. If there had been no submarine controversy at the same time, they almost certainly would have sent the note to London that they had long been contemplating and forced the issue of American trading rights in some decisive way. This, it will be remembered, was precisely what Wilson (in his conversation with Bernstorff on June 2 and in his third *Lusitania* note) had promised the Germans that he would do if they would only meet him halfway in the submarine controversy.

At the same time, the President and Secretary of State knew that their hands were tied for the time being, because they could not risk a serious crisis with Great Britain while there was a chance of war with Germany. Wilson said this frankly and simply to a senator who had urged him to send a vigorous note to London. "I think I feel to the full the force of what you say," he wrote on July 6, "but I feel, also, that it would be nothing less than folly to press our neutral claims both against Germany and against Great Britain at one and the same time and so make our situation more nearly impossible."[28]

The President's two chief advisers on foreign policy understood the strategic necessity of preserving good relations with Great Britain even more strongly than Wilson did. "I feel," Colonel House wrote to Lansing on July 29, "that Germany's good will is lost irrevocably and we must determine how far we can go counter to the Allies' interests with-

[26] O. G. Villard to Rollo Ogden, July 13, 1915, Villard Papers.
[27] Anderson Diary, July 15, 1915.
[28] W.W. to F. M. Simmons, July 6, 1915, Wilson Papers.

out alienating their friendship as well."[29] "In no event," Lansing replied in emphatic agreement, "should we take a course that would seriously endanger our friendly relations with Great Britain, France or Russia, for . . . our friendship with Germany is a matter of the past."[30]

The American leaders, therefore, did only what they thought they could do safely. Lansing and his assistants at the Department, the American Consul General in London, Robert P. Skinner, and even Ambassador Page maintained a steady pressure upon the British Foreign Office and Admiralty for the release of ships and cargoes or the speedy determination of cases by the Prize Court. As Wilson wrote, "We are . . . constantly in communication with the British Government, pressing upon them our rights and the correction of their wrongs."[31] Such overtures and efforts only palliated and did not go to the root of the differences between the two governments. Whether the controversy would remain mute as before or would burst into a sharp diplomatic interchange would depend in part upon further developments in negotiations between Washington and Berlin and upon the future behavior of submarine commanders. It would depend as well upon decisions that leaders in London made.

The authorities at Whitehall had known that they might have to face the possibility of a reckoning with America over the continuation of the blockade ever since late May and early June, when Colonel House had conveyed the President's blunt warning that he would move hard against them if the Germans yielded to American demands during the *Lusitania* negotiations.[32] However, the British government were so confident of an early German-American rupture and a speedy end to all their own difficulties with the United States that the threat of serious trouble with the Washington administration seemed very remote, indeed. Colonel House had fired British hopes mightily before he returned home in early June. He had predicted that his country would soon be at war with Germany; discussed the ways in which the United States might be of most help to the Allies pending the time when, if necessary, the President put an army into the field;[33] and said

[29] E. M. House to R. Lansing, July 29, 1915, House Papers.
[30] R. Lansing to E. M. House, July 30, 1915, *ibid*.
[31] W.W. to F. M. Simmons, July 6, 1915, Wilson Papers.
[32] House Diary, June 3, 1915; E. M. House to W.W., June 4, 1915, Wilson Papers.
[33] Sir Horace Plunkett to E. M. House, June 8, 1915, Plunkett Papers, recalling a recent conversation among House, Plunkett, and Arthur Balfour, the new head of the Admiralty, and enclosing "Note on the position of the United States in regard to possible intervention."

that in any event the United States could not "take any risk of England being beaten."[34] Consequently, Sir Edward Grey could leave the Foreign Office on about June 1 for a long and much-needed rest at his home in Northumberland, confident that no danger of any serious Anglo-American tension lay immediately ahead.

Grey returned to London on about July 13 to discover in full detail how much the situation had changed during his absence. To begin with, it was now fairly clear that the United States would not only *not* go to war with Germany over the destruction of the *Lusitania*, but also might come to agreement with Germany on freedom of the seas, and that this in turn might lead to American action against Great Britain. There were, besides, all the accumulated evidences of the recent sharp increase in anti-British sentiment in America and piles of protests from the State Department and of warnings from Ambassador Spring Rice in Washington. Most appalling to Grey were the signs that a special crisis was at hand over the one issue, British suppression of American cotton exports to Central Europe, that could do the gravest injury to Anglo-American relations.

This issue had come to a head in such a way, actually, as to involve the entire legality of the British blockade. Between early March and May 19, 1915, the British navy had detained twenty-eight neutral ships, six of which were of American registry, and seized more than 200,000 bales of American cotton consigned mainly to Rotterdam. This was seizure exclusively on grounds of violation of the alleged blockade, for the British government had not dared to affront American opinion by putting cotton on the contraband list, thus establishing a basis in law for suppression of the cotton trade to Germany. The London authorities had released the ships and, whenever possible, had purchased the seized cargoes in order to avoid a legal test.[35] But in certain instances this had not been possible; consequently, a number of cases were now, in early July, pending in the Prize Court, and a decision could not long be postponed. It would, obviously, test the Order in Council of

[34] As House told Sir Horace Plunkett on June 4, 1915, Plunkett Diary for the same date. Plunkett at once conveyed House's statement to the British Cabinet. "In my final talk with House," Sir Horace reported to Arthur Balfour on June 12, 1915 (Plunkett Papers), "we agreed absolutely that, apart from all disputes upon issues raised with Germany, the United States cannot take any risk of either a defeat of the Allies, or an inconclusive or disastrously protracted end to the conflict."

[35] Consul General Skinner to the Secretary of State, July 28 and August 20, 1915, *Foreign Relations, 1915, Supplement*, pp. 502-503, 516.

March 11, 1915, in a precise way. No one doubted how the Prize Court would rule, for it was bound to support what was called municipal law over international law. The only question was whether the American government would choose this opportunity to raise a direct challenge.[36]

Secretary Lansing gave the answer in an unmistakable warning to the Foreign Office on July 14, 1915. "In order to avoid any misunderstanding as to the attitude of Government of United States in regard to prize court proceedings in cases involving American interests," he wrote in a telegram of instruction to Ambassador Page, "inform British Government that in view of differences which are understood to exist between the two Governments as to the principles of law applicable in these cases, the Government of the United States desires to make clear to the British Government that in so far as the interests of American citizens are concerned, it will insist upon their rights under the hitherto established principles and rules of international law governing neutral trade in time of war, without modification or limitation by orders in council or other municipal legislation by Great Britain, and it will not recognize the validity of proceedings taken in prize court under restraints imposed by British municipal law in derogation of their rights."[37]

Grey could not misunderstand; nor could he fail to read the clear signs that an open assertion by his government of the right to suppress the cotton trade to Central Europe, whether by authority of the Order in Council or by making cotton absolute contraband, would provoke Congress to adopt retaliatory legislation. This danger was already abundantly evident by the time that Lansing's warning arrived at the Foreign Office in mid-July. A wave of panic and anti-British anger had already swept through the South in anticipation of the decision of the Prize Court. On June 28, for example, the legislature of Georgia had adopted resolutions calling upon the President to use all means within his power, "diplomatic if possible, retaliatory if necessary," to reopen the Central European market to American cotton.[38] From every corner of the cotton states—from political spokesmen, boards of trade, agricul-

---

[36] The above paragraph is based in part upon the unsigned memorandum on the cotton problem prepared probably by Lord Robert Cecil of the Foreign Office. It is dated July 3, 1915, and printed in the Cabinet paper entitled *Cotton as Contraband. Printed for the use of the Cabinet. July 1915*, Asquith Papers.

[37] The Secretary of State to Ambassador Page, July 14, 1915, *Foreign Relations, 1915, Supplement*, p. 472.

[38] *New York Times*, June 29, 1915.

tural leaders, and editors—came public echoes of these demands.[39] We may be sure that the British Embassy took pains to make certain that the Foreign Office also heard them.

The Foreign Secretary's fears were compounded by demands at home, both in the press and from all sections of the government, that he take the action which would give a more secure basis for suppression of the cotton trade. This was to put cotton on the list of absolute contraband, on the grounds that the raw material was an essential ingredient of gunpowder and that recent action by the Imperial German government establishing a governmental monopoly of raw cotton made it impossible to distinguish between cotton going to Germany for military production and for civilian uses.[40]

The proposal was vigorously made on July 14, 1915, at the first Cabinet meeting that Grey attended after his return to London. The Foreign Secretary fought off the demand on this occasion with the help of the visiting Canadian Prime Minister, Sir Robert Borden, who warned that putting cotton on the list of absolute contraband might well induce the President and Congress to prohibit the export of munitions.[41] The government's spokesman in the House of Lords, Lord Crewe, tried to quiet the public demand by warning that placing cotton on the list of absolute contraband would stir enormous resentment in the South,[42] but the clamor grew apace during the following days.[43] In addition, a group of jingoists in the government were suggesting

[39] e.g., Senator J. S. Williams to W.W., June 29, 1915, Wilson Papers; "Preamble and Resolution Adopted by the Board of Directors of the New Orleans Cotton Exchange," dated June 30, 1915, copy in the Burleson Papers; resolution of the State Council of the Farmers' Union of North Carolina, sent to W.W. on July 3, 1915, Wilson Papers; resolutions of the Savannah Cotton Exchange, dated July 8, 1915, copy in *ibid.*; Representative A. F. Lever, E. J. Watson, Commissioner of Agriculture of South Carolina, and Wade Stackhouse, president of the South Carolina Cotton Congress, to W.W., July 12, 1915, *ibid.*; Augusta, Georgia, Cotton Exchange and Board of Trade to the Secretary of State, June 25, 1915, *Foreign Relations, 1915, Supplement*, pp. 191-192; Galveston Commercial Association to the Secretary of State, July 2, 1915, *ibid.*, p. 192.

[40] A group of British experts estimated that the Central Powers needed 110,000 tons of cotton annually for military purposes. See R. W. Matthew of the Board of Trade to M. Bonham Carter (for the Prime Minister), March 31, 1915, Asquith Papers.

[41] The Prime Minister to the King, July 15, 1915, *ibid.*

[42] *New York Times*, July 16, 1915.

[43] e.g., Ambassador Page to the Secretary of State, July 15, 1915, *Foreign Relations, 1915, Supplement*, pp. 192-193; Clifford Carver (Ambassador Page's secretary) to E. M. House, July 20 and 23, 1915, House Papers; Lord Charnwood to W. H. Page, July 20, 1915, Page Papers; London *Times*, July 20 and 23, 1915; W. H. Page to E. M. House, July 21, 1915, House Papers; W. H. Page to W.W., July 23, 1915, Wilson Papers.

that the time had come for the Foreign Office to stand up to the Americans and tell them that the British meant to cut off all trade with Germany by one means or another and would not be frightened by the threat of an American arms embargo. This, the Committee of Imperial Defence suggested to the Prime Minister on July 20, should be done at once. "It might be pointed out," the Committee added, "that if the Americans refuse to supply us with munitions they will not only continue to lose their trade with Germany but they will also lose the advantage they gain from supplying the Allies with munitions. They will also prolong the war to their own disadvantage . . . [and] inevitably cause much bad feeling between the two countries which it will take years to get over."[44]

"Grey," Page reported on July 21, "is very despondent about the American situation." There was little wonder why. A general American challenge to the Order in Council of March 11, 1915, and to the entire blockade seemingly impended in the near future. A crisis over cotton was immediately at hand. How could he avert the one and solve the other without provoking a rebellion in his own government and a revulsion of sentiment among his own people strong enough to imperil the recently formed Coalition Cabinet?

Pondering a course for the future, Grey could not avoid sharing the feelings of irritation and disappointment over current American policies that were now surging through the thoughtful British public.[45] It was a poor time, he must have told himself, for the Americans to

[44] Committee of Imperial Defence, M. P. A. Hankey, secretary, to Prime Minister Herbert Asquith, July 20, 1915, Asquith Papers.

[45] The following extracts give some indication of this development in British opinion:

"Your friends certainly mis-reported to you what I had said to our Government about Wilson. Public opinion over here [in 1915] had been enraged by some of his phrases (especially 'too proud to fight') and by his apparent agreement with Germany over the use of sea-power. In our music-halls, cinema shows, and even in 'Punch' Wilson was being treated in a way which angered Americans who felt that the disrespect was not to the man only but to his office." H. Plunkett to T. Roosevelt, July 25, 1916, Plunkett Papers.

"I enclose a pamphlet in ridicule of the President. I don't know who wrote it, for my inquiries so far have bro't no real information. . . . This thing alone is, of course, of no consequence. But it is symptomatic [of current British sentiment]. There is much feeling about the slowness with wh. he acts. 120 people (Americans) were drowned on the *Lusitania* and we are still writing notes about it—to the damndest pirates that ever blew up a ship. . . . There is a fast growing feeling here, therefore, that the American Gov't is pusillanimous—dalies [*sic*] with 'em, is affected by the German propaganda, etc. etc." W. H. Page to E. M. House, July 21, 1915, House Papers.

The Word-Lord

Kaiser (to Uncle Sam)—"Everything can be explained:
I can put the whole thing in a nutshell, if you'll only listen to me
for three years, or the duration of the war."

Partridge in *Punch* (London)

be pressing so hard on the issue of neutral rights of trade; indeed, the United States would be at war with Germany now if the President had only done his duty when the *Lusitania* was sunk. Serene in mind and purpose as he usually was, Grey could be petulant and self-righteous at times. But never once during these trying times did he permit momentary irritations to blind him to the main necessity of preserving friendly relations between Great Britain and the United States. That necessity, he assuredly concluded, was more urgent now than during the early months of the war. The British simply could not maintain an effective war effort without American munitions and raw materials; worse still, the day was at hand when the Western Allied war effort would also depend upon an uninhibited and generous flow of credit from the United States.

This was the necessity that overshadowed other considerations in Grey's mind as he set down the alternatives for the purview of his colleagues in the Cabinet. The British government, he wrote, could of course simply adhere to its Order in Council of March 11 and its blockade of Germany. "It seems almost certain," he added, "that this course will lead to a deadlock; protests from the United States about particular cases . . . will accumulate; and the attitude of the United States towards us will become increasingly disagreeable." Then there was a second choice—to abandon the Order in Council rather than have any differences with the United States, and to rely upon the rules of international law regarding contraband and continuous voyage in controlling trade with Germany. "As regards imports into Germany," the Foreign Secretary explained, "I think that we should lose very little by adopting this policy, and we should undoubtedly gain by the diminution of friction with neutral countries. But, on the other hand, we should abandon at a stroke all restriction upon the export trade of Germany to neutral ports." If the Cabinet decided upon this course, Grey went on, then the Foreign Office would have to come to a firm understanding beforehand with the American government about the rights of British sea power under international law.[46] A few days later the Foreign Secretary circulated to the Cabinet "the rough draft of a Note explaining a possible line to be taken with the United States" that he had just completed. It informed the Washington government that the Cabinet had decided to withdraw the Order in Council of March 11, 1915, to conduct its maritime warfare hereafter according

[46] E. Grey, memorandum dated July 22, 1915, printed in *Memorandum. Printed for the use of the Cabinet. July 1915,* Asquith Papers.

to the rules laid down by international law, and to put cotton on the list of absolute contraband.[47]

Grey's own conclusions were not only clearly implied in these two documents; they were also further clarified by certain other things that he said and did at this time. He was obviously prepared to insist that the Cabinet repeal the Order in Council and compel the Admiralty to abandon its long-range blockade, if this were necessary to avert an open showdown with the United States. The dispute with the Washington government must at all costs be maintained on the legal level; nothing but disaster could ensue if he permitted considerations of national right and sovereignty to become directly involved. Repeal of the Order in Council would, he knew, be humiliating and dangerous politically, and he would certainly not demand it unless there were no escape. But it might have to be done if the American government pressed the *legal* argument, for on the sheer *legal* issues of the so-called blockade the American government was clearly right and the British government was wrong.[48]

It was the expectation that the Foreign Office would soon have to beat a general diplomatic retreat that caused Sir Edward to come to a firm decision quickly on the more immediate and specific issue of cotton. Control of this staple had by this time become the test of the effectiveness of the British maritime system in the eyes of the British people; no government that opened passage for American cotton to Germany could have survived for many days in London. Cotton had to be put on the list of absolute contraband as quickly as possible, and for obvious reasons *before* the Order in Council of March 11, 1915, was repealed. It was, Grey knew, a course not without its own perils. Rumors that cotton might be condemned had intensified the panic of the South and spurred new demands for retaliation against Great Britain.[49] There was, furthermore, the danger that the American government would accuse the Foreign Office of bad faith for having reneged on its earlier promise not to make cotton contraband. But Grey had concluded at least by July 19, if not before, that the decision was inevitable and could no longer be postponed.

[47] E. Grey, memorandum dated July 26, 1915, printed in *Memorandum. Printed for the use of the Cabinet. July 1915, ibid.*

[48] Grey may have intimated this line of thought to Ambassador Page. See W. H. Page to E. M. House, July 21, 1915, House Papers; W. H. Page to W.W., July 23, 1915, Wilson Papers.

[49] See especially the long article in the New York *World*, July 22, 1915, and the editorial in the *New Republic*, III (July 24, 1915), 292-293, pointing to the inevitability of congressional retaliation if the British put cotton on the list of absolute contraband.

There now remained the problem of finding a way to prevent the open and "legal" suppression of the cotton traffic to the Central Powers from further convulsing the South, precipitating a general crisis, and provoking the President and Congress to measures of retaliation. For advice Grey turned first, we may surmise, to Ambassador Spring Rice and the staff of the British Embassy in Washington. Then on July 19, 1915, he brought the matter before the Cabinet and apparently after some warm discussion obtained the appointment of a special committee, which included Lords Crewe and Lansdowne, Reginald McKenna, Chancellor of the Exchequer, and Lord Kitchener, the war minister, as well as himself, to "consider at once the best mode of dealing with the latest phase of the cotton controversy."[50]

Whether the committee in London was able to devise a solution we do not know; but within a few days, probably by July 22, Grey had in hand a comprehensive plan that promised to solve the vexing problem forever, and to improve Anglo-American relations in the process. Devised by Sir Richard Crawford, the Trade Adviser to the British Embassy in Washington, after consultation with Theodore Price, a cotton broker of New York, and Benjamin R. Strong, Governor of the Federal Reserve Bank of New York, the plan was nearly breathtaking in its boldness.

The problem, Crawford advised the Foreign Office, was actually quite a simple one. Southerners were in panic because they feared a second collapse of the cotton market more disastrous than the one that had occurred the year before if the British government continued to suppress their exports to Central Europe either by blockade or by putting cotton on the list of absolute contraband. It seemed virtually inevitable that the southern bloc would join with other anti-British elements in the next session of Congress to adopt an embargo on the export of arms to the Allies if a second cotton crisis and bankrupting of the southern economy ensued. The answer, Crawford went on to suggest, was simply to guarantee that this would not happen. This could be done by having the British Treasury instruct its agents to go into the cotton exchanges at Liverpool, New York, and New Orleans and buy enough cotton to maintain the price at from 8 to 10 cents a pound. The cost might run to £20,000,000, especially if the British government had to purchase all the cotton that would ordinarily have gone to Central Europe. But it would pacify opinion in the South and avert the threat of an arms embargo; and it would be a small price

[50] The Prime Minister to the King, July 19, 1915, Asquith Papers.

to pay if the American government agreed to accept the definition of cotton as absolute contraband.[51]

The scanty documents available on the British side do not reveal how Crawford's proposal was initially received in London. Grey and his special Cabinet committee must have been appalled by the potential cost; perhaps they wondered whether such an expenditure was necessary since they could, after all, make an almost unanswerable legal argument for condemning cotton; and they surely wanted some kind of assurances from the American government that it would at least informally approve the Crawford plan. Apparently they hesitated to give endorsement, for we find Sir Richard Crawford telling Chandler Anderson as late as July 30 that he had submitted his plan and implying that the Foreign Office had not yet accepted it.[52] If this is true, then the arrival in London of two messages from Colonel House may have played some decisive role. The first was a cable message dated July 19, which reached London on the following day, warning that British action against cotton would probably provoke Congress to retaliation. The second, a letter dated July 21, which arrived in London on August 3, was more important, for in it Colonel House advised his British friends that he had sent the cablegram of July 19 at the direct request of the President.[53] If Grey and his colleagues had had any doubts about the utter necessity of proceeding as Crawford had suggested, the arrival of House's second message certainly ended their hesitation. It is possible that Grey wired a tentative approval to Washington on the same day, for Ambassador Spring Rice did open certain high-level negotiations at this time.[54]

Discussions had meanwhile been proceeding at least on an informal basis in Washington and New York since about July 22, 1915. On that

[51] This is the plan as Crawford described it to Chandler Anderson on July 30, 1915. Anderson Diary, July 30, 1915. See *ibid.*, July 22, 1915, for a briefer description of obviously the same plan by Ambassador Spring Rice.

[52] This, apparently, was also Lansing's understanding. See R. Lansing to E. M. House, July 30, 1915, House Papers.

[53] E. M. House to H. Plunkett, July 19, 1915, House Papers; H. Plunkett to E. M. House, July 20, 1915, *ibid.*; E. M. House to H. Plunkett, July 21, 1915, *ibid.*; H. Plunkett to Masterton Smith (for transmission to Arthur Balfour), August 3, 1915, repeating House's letter of July 21, 1915, Asquith Papers. Wilson's telegram to House is W.W. to E. M. House, July 19, 1915, Baker Collection.

[54] The reader will recognize the tentative character of the foregoing statement. It is about all that can be said concerning the reaction of the leaders in London to the Crawford plan until the archives of the British Foreign Office are opened to scholarly view.

day Ambassador Spring Rice saw Chandler P. Anderson, whom Lansing had deputized to confer with the British officials about some solution of the cotton problem, and told him that he and Sir Richard Crawford had been hard at work on a plan for British support of the cotton market.[55] Then on July 30 Crawford visited Anderson's office for a longer conference. After explaining his project in careful detail, the Trade Adviser came to what he frankly admitted was the crux of the matter from the British point of view. It was whether the American government would acquiesce in British action putting cotton on the list of absolute contraband if the London government took the steps that he had suggested for support of the American cotton market. Anderson replied cautiously but in terms that left no doubt that the Crawford plan would receive a friendly hearing. The difficulty, he said, was that this was all a matter in which the Washington government could not participate and about which it should not even be consulted. However, he added in the same breath, he would communicate Crawford's views informally to the Secretary of State. Then Anderson went on (in the guise of restating Crawford's position) to say that even if the American government did not admit that cotton was absolute contraband, it would surely recognize that this was entirely a legal question to be adjudicated in a normal way, and that no charge of illegality would be made.[56]

After this encouraging beginning it remained only for Crawford and Spring Rice to obtain some informal confirmation of Anderson's reply from the President and Secretary of State and perhaps the final approval of the Foreign Office. Lansing was in an embarrassing position, but he could in all honesty and without any violation of neutrality say to Anderson on July 30, when Anderson reported his conversation with Crawford to the Secretary of State, that the British project was extraordinarily wise, and that Anderson had characterized the American attitude about cotton as absolute contraband fairly enough.[57] And such a statement, which Anderson surely conveyed at once to the British Embassy, was all the Foreign Office wanted to hear from the Secretary of State.

This was the point at which Spring Rice, who was now at Pride's

[55] Anderson Diary, July 22, 1915.

[56] *ibid.*, July 30, 1915.

[57] We have no *direct* evidence that this is what Lansing said to Anderson, but we do know from R. Lansing to E. M. House, July 30, 1915, House Papers, that Anderson reported his conversation with Crawford at once to the Secretary of State; and it seems fair to infer from this same letter that this was the gist of what Lansing said in reply.

Crossing, Massachusetts, took charge in order to bring the President into the discussions in an unobtrusive way, or rather to gain some intimation that the Crawford plan would be acceptable to him. The Ambassador, consequently, sought out his old friend Colonel House, who was nearby at his summer home at Manchester, Massachusetts, on August 2 and there informed him of the conversations that had taken place.[58] House was enthusiastic and apparently volunteered to help by discussing the arrangements for the British purchase of cotton with Benjamin R. Strong, Governor of the Federal Reserve Bank of New York. "Spring Rice has just left," the Colonel wrote to Wilson on the same day. "We went over the cotton question from beginning to end. He confirmed my opinion as to the length Great Britain would go in the event you brought sufficient pressure."[59] Then House talked with Strong and again with Spring Rice on August 6. As he reported at once to the President:

"I have gone into the cotton situation very fully today. First with Governor Strong of the New York Federal Reserve Bank. He had many useful ideas in connection with it. I later took it up with Sir Cecil.

"Sir Richard Crawford has this matter in hand and I have arranged to bring him and Strong together.

"Strong's idea is that if the British Government will put sufficient money back of a plan to take three million bales off the market, there will be no cotton problem to solve. S. R. says American bankers have expressed a willingness to handle the transaction and to hold the cotton for two years if necessary, in this country, so it will not come in competition with foreign shipments or with present consumption. The British Government are to take what loss, if any, and the bankers have the privilege of selling the cotton above ten cents f.o.b. and make whatever profit they can. The British Government do not want to be in a position of making a profit out of it.

"Strong's idea is that this plan should be carried out quietly. If anything is said about it, the reply should be that it is a matter between the British Government and the American planter and the German, or any other Government, can make a similar arrangement if they desire."[60]

House's letter of August 2 apparently brought to the President, now at Cornish, the first direct information that the British were taking

[58] House Diary, August 2, 1915.
[59] E. M. House to W.W., August 2, 1915, Wilson Papers.
[60] E. M. House to W.W., August 6, 1915, *ibid.*

steps to support the cotton market. However, he had certainly learned something about British intentions before this date, and he had obviously already concluded that something like the Crawford plan offered the best way out of his most vexing domestic problem. Ever since the recent intensification of the trade disputes with Great Britain he had been plagued with doubts as to how far he could wisely go. He wanted, as he wrote to Colonel House, to press for the utmost; and yet he also wanted to be "sensible and practical."[61] He knew that the direst consequences would ensue if the cotton crisis were permitted to run its natural course; at the same time, he was appalled by the thought of serious trouble with the British, and particularly at this time of crisis in German-American relations. As he explained once hyperbolically to a complaining Texas senator, "It does not seem as if we ought to go to the length of involving the country in war and so cut off the market for cotton altogether."[62]

To Wilson another ray of hope came on August 4, 1915, when he received a letter from Page in London saying that there was a good chance that the Cabinet might soon repeal the Order in Council and take steps to avert a crisis in the South. "With my knowledge of the situation (whatever that may be worth)," Page had written, "the programme to (1) make cotton contraband (which they will do anyhow), (2) to buy as much as they will at as high a price as they will, and (3) at the same time rescind the Order in Council—that's as good as we can hope for; and that wd remove our legal difficulties. . . . I confess I have more or less hope: I do not know just how much to have."[63]

Here, indeed, Wilson thought, was a solution of the cotton problem. "Does it not seem to you," he wrote at once, relaying Page's letter, to Colonel House, "that that is a good tip for Spring Rice, and that if they would clear away the so-called blockade and buy an unusual amount of our cotton our public would see that we were getting the best we could out of a bad situation?"[64]

House received this letter on August 6, probably just after he had sent his report of his recent conversations with Strong and Spring Rice off to the President. He went immediately to the Ambassador to convey the message from "Harlarkenden."[65] We may be sure that Spring

[61] W.W. to E. M. House, July 20, 1915, Baker Collection.
[62] W.W. to M. Sheppard, July 28, 1915, Wilson Papers.
[63] W. H. Page to W.W., July 23, 1915, *ibid.*
[64] W.W. to E. M. House, August 5, 1915, Baker Collection.
[65] House Diary, August 6, 1915.

Rice lost no time in telling Sir Edward Grey that the President would be satisfied if the British government rescinded the Order in Council of March 11, 1915, put cotton on the list of absolute contraband, and then took steps to support the cotton market in the United States. We may also be sure that Grey and his special Cabinet committee responded by giving final approval to the Crawford plan, if, indeed, they had not already done so a few days before.

Great activity now ensued on both sides of the Atlantic in preparation for the execution of the plan. In Washington Sir Richard Crawford was busy completing the necessary financial arrangements and making provision for storing the cotton that his agents bought until it could be sold without depressing the market. In taking these steps, he worked closely with William P. G. Harding, a member of the Federal Reserve Board from Alabama and a specialist in the financing of cotton, and with Governor Strong of the New York Federal Reserve Bank. Spring Rice, House reported to the President on August 14, "tells me that Sir Richard Crawford is pleased with his conference with Benjamin Strong and Harding and said the suggestions they made in working out the situation have been invaluable."[66] At the same time, Harding and Secretary of the Treasury McAdoo informed the members of the Federal Reserve Board of the arrangements that were being made[67] and set to work on elaborate plans of their own to avert immediate panic in the South once the British government announced that it had condemned cotton. The President was of course not involved in these proceedings, or even officially informed; but he kept in close touch through Colonel House and approved.

This fact came out clearly enough when the German Ambassador attempted to intervene. Bernstorff somehow learned the precise details of the Crawford plan during the first days of August. He wrote to Lansing on August 6, saying that rumors were afloat in New York that the British government had offered to buy 2,500,000 bales of American cotton at 10 cents a pound, in order to pave the way for making cotton absolute contraband. He assumed that the United States government would not, for reasons of principle, accept the offer. If there was "any chance of this offer being accepted," he went on, he would

[66] E. M. House to W.W., August 13, 1915, Wilson Papers.

[67] This they did at a meeting of the Board on August 10, 1915. See P. M. Warburg to W. P. G. Harding, c. August 11, 1915, quoted in W. P. G. Harding to W. G. McAdoo, August 13, 1915, copy in *ibid.*

like to submit a confidential bid of his own, that the Imperial German government was ready at any moment to buy 3,000,000 bales "at the normal price regulated by supply and demand," provided this cotton could be "transported to Germany through neutral countries according to the rules of international law," that is, provided the United States could guarantee safe delivery at Rotterdam.[68]

Lansing was apparently tempted. The German offer, he wrote the President as he sent Bernstorff's letter to Cornish, might be of great value in clearing up the trouble of the cotton states.[69] Wilson was shocked. What a difference there was between British and German methods, he thought. "Bernstorff's letter to you about the purchase of cotton is, indeed, amazing," he replied to the Secretary of State. "What crude blunderers they are! The idea of offering us a palpable bribe, — or rather, offering it to the Southern planters. How little they understand us!"[70]

In London Grey had been pressing ahead with the final preparations on his side. On August 11 he reported to the Cabinet and received that body's final approval for the Crawford plan and for putting cotton on the list of absolute contraband.[71] Immediately afterward Grey met Théophile Delcassé, French Foreign Secretary, and other representatives of the French government in London to prepare the ground for the adoption of common policies toward the United States. Grey informed the French leaders of the steps that his government had taken to avert the collapse of the cotton market, and the conferees agreed that both governments should put cotton on the list of absolute contraband as soon as the London Foreign Office gave the word. The discussions ranged further, over the whole field of the Anglo-American

---

[68] J. von Bernstorff to R. Lansing, August 6, 1915, *ibid.* Bernstorff repeated this offer on August 22, intimating that the Germans would pay 30 cents a pound for cotton. See the German Ambassador to the Secretary of State, August 22, 1915, *Foreign Relations, 1915, Supplement,* pp. 194-195.

[69] R. Lansing to W.W., August 7, 1915, Wilson Papers.

[70] W.W. to R. Lansing, August 9, 1915, Baker Collection. Colonel House, it might be added, was only too happy to use the German offer to make certain that the authorities in London gave final approval to the arrangements that Crawford was now making. House told Spring Rice about Bernstorff's offer on August 11. "I was glad to see that this excited his interest," the Colonel noted in his Diary on the same date, "for my purpose was to stir his own Government to as liberal terms as it was possible to get. They have in mind to make large purchases of cotton and I wanted to clinch it."

[71] Ambassador Page to the Secretary of State, August 13, 1915, copy in the Wilson Papers. See also the statement by Lord Robert Cecil, Undersecretary of State for Foreign Affairs, on August 13, which virtually announced the decision to condemn cotton. *New York Times,* August 14, 1915.

trade controversy. And on this subject the conferees agreed that nothing could be gained by a continuation of "the polemic on principles"; that the important thing was that neutrals should have means of obtaining "legitimate reparations"; and that some concessions might have to be made to the United States on the question of the import and export of goods to and from Germany when arrangements for these had been made before the announcement of the British blockade measures.[72] This part of the Anglo-French understanding was vague, perhaps deliberately vague. It left Sir Edward Grey free to concede almost anything to the Washington government except the outright repeal of the Order in Council of March 11. He had apparently concluded that this would not have to be done, at any rate not in the near future.

Events on both sides of the water moved swiftly to a culmination after the adjournment of the Anglo-French conference on August 14. The London Foreign Office had asked Spring Rice to choose the psychological moment for the announcement that cotton had been condemned. That moment arrived much sooner than the Ambassador could have hoped, on August 19, 1915, when news came to Washington of the sinking of the *Arabic*. Calling reporters to the British Embassy on the same day, Spring Rice informed them that the Allied governments had agreed in principle that cotton was contraband of war; that proclamations announcing this fact officially would soon be issued; and that the Allied governments were prepared to stand behind the cotton market to prevent the ruin of the southern states.[73]

The Foreign Office in London and the British Embassy in Washington now proceeded in close coordination to put the Crawford plan into operation. The Foreign Office issued the royal proclamation dated August 20, putting cotton, cotton linters, cotton waste, and cotton yarn on the list of absolute contraband, in a special supplement of *The London Gazette* on Saturday afternoon, August 21, at a time when the cotton exchanges were closed. Accompanying this proclamation was an official assurance that "His Majesty's Government contemplate initiation of measures to relieve as far as possible any abnormal depression which might temporarily disturb market conditions."

When the Liverpool Cotton Exchange opened on Monday morning, August 23, agents of the British Treasury bought all cotton offered at

---

[72] E. Grey to C. Spring Rice, August 14, 1915; T. Delcassé to J. Jusserand, August 14, 1915, transmitting the text of the Anglo-French report, both printed in a Cabinet paper entitled *Printed for the Use of the Cabinet, August 1915*, Asquith Papers.

[73] *New York Times*, August 20, 1915.

the closing price on the preceding Saturday morning. When the New York and New Orleans exchanges opened a few hours later, moreover, Sir Richard Crawford's representatives went to work in the same manner. The immediate result was to sustain the price of cotton at its pre-contraband price of 8 cents a pound. Then, much to the surprise of the British economic experts, the price began to rise slowly as the cotton crop of 1915 came to market; by mid-October the price stood at 12 cents a pound. According to one account that has all the appearance of being authentic, the cause of this turn in the tide was not the pressure of British buying, which actually totaled only 275,000 bales during the late summer and early autumn. It was the fact that *Geheimrat* Doctor Heinrich Albert, still the head of the German Purchasing Commission, went into the market and bought 1,000,000 bales on his own account.[74]

Administration leaders in Washington had also been hard at work to avert the outbreak of panic in the wake of the British decree of August 20. From his summer home at North Haven, Maine, Secretary McAdoo issued a statement on August 23 declaring that the Federal Reserve banks in the South had ample resources to enable farmers to hold their cotton; that he was prepared to lend $30,000,000 from the federal Treasury direct to southern national banks if additional funds were needed; and that there was absolutely no reason for concern about the future of the cotton market.[75] Two days later, on August 25, William P. G. Harding of the Federal Reserve Board repeated McAdoo's assurances before a gathering of some 2,000 members of the Alabama Merchants' Association in Birmingham. He also read a letter that the President had prepared for the occasion; it promised an abundance of cheap credit to the South and warned southern bankers not to raise their interest rates.[76]

[74] *New York Tribune*, November 20, 1915. This article is a long account of the Anglo-American discussions about the cotton crisis and the way these discussions culminated in the British decision to adopt the Crawford plan. Astonishingly complete and accurate in detail, this article was a triumph for its unknown author.

[75] *New York Times*, August 24, 1915; W. G. McAdoo to W.W., August 23, 1915, Wilson Papers; W. G. McAdoo to W. P. G. Harding, August 24, 1915, copy in *ibid*. For sharp criticism of McAdoo's action, see the *New York Times*, August 26 and 30, 1915; New York *Sun*, September 5, 1915; New York *Journal of Commerce*, September 8 and 15, 1915.

[76] There is a copy of Harding's speech in the Wilson Papers. For Wilson's letter and its immediate impact, see W.W. to W. P. G. Harding, August 23, 1915; W. P. G. Harding to W.W., August 30, 1915; Governor J. E. Ferguson of Texas to W.W., August 26, 1915; and J. L. McLaurin to W.W., September 1, 1915, all in *ibid*.

The immediate consequence of these somewhat frantic preparations was the absence of any serious crisis. To be sure, there was an outbreak of cries for retaliation from southern Democratic leaders immediately following the issuance of the British decree of August 20.[77] But these demands quickly subsided altogether as the price of cotton began its slow but steady rise. As the discontent lessened in the South so also did the danger to the British of the movement for the adoption of an arms embargo. As we will see in the next volume of this biography, the German Americans and their allies failed in their next great campaign for this measure in early 1916 precisely because no second cotton crisis had occurred, because, in short, the Crawford plan had worked so well.

We cannot bring this long episode to a close without a word about another consequence of the happy outcome of the cotton controversy, namely, the way in which it strengthened Anglo-American relations at a critical time. To the American leaders the extraordinary efforts to which the British were willing to go to avert disaster to the southern states furnished new proof of the sincerity of Sir Edward Grey's oft-repeated assurances that his government meant to avoid as far as possible any substantial injury to American economic interests while prosecuting its maritime war. Needless to say, it made a great deal of difference whether President Wilson believed in Sir Edward's good faith in this matter. In the second place, by putting cotton on the list of absolute contraband, and by hereafter controlling the cotton traffic in a way that was entirely valid under international law,[78] the British removed the main cause of American resentment over and the chief ground of American protest against the so-called blockade. The Anglo-American controversy over neutral trading rights was by no means at

---

[77] e.g., Senator Hoke Smith, statement in the *New York Times*, August 25, 1915; Representative E. Y. Webb to Representative C. Kitchin, September 2, 1915, the Papers of Claude Kitchin, University of North Carolina Library; Representative S. J. Tribble to W.W., September 7, 1915, Wilson Papers; Representative A. F. Lever to W.W., September 22, 1915, *ibid.*

[78] The State Department never openly challenged the definition of cotton as absolute contraband, so patent was the case for such action. As Secretary Lansing pointed out in a letter to Senator Hoke Smith on August 28, 1915, Lansing Papers, the Declaration of London, which forbade belligerents to put cotton on the list of absolute contraband, afforded no ground for protest since it had never been incorporated into the body of international law. Within a few months, moreover, the State Department was virtually admitting that the British decree of August 20, 1915, was legal. See, e.g., Counselor F. L. Polk to H. N. Pope, January 15, 1916, the Papers of Frank L. Polk, Yale University Library.

an end, but it would be vastly less dangerous to the good relations of the two countries in the future because cotton was no longer involved.

Anglo-American relations were further bolstered during the late summer of 1915, when leaders on both sides of the Atlantic found a solution to another crisis of an entirely different kind. This was the disruption of American foreign trade that seemed to impend because of the rapid diminution of Britain's dollar resources since the outbreak of the war. As events turned out, the decision whether to avert the crisis or permit it to run its natural course rested ultimately with the President of the United States and two or three of his intimate advisers. As we will see, the choice that they made was in certain measure a consequence of the overshadowing and ever-present threat of rupture with Germany.

As early as May 1915 it had become evident that the Allied governments, and particularly the British, which had assumed primary responsibility for financing the foreign purchases of its allies, were moving rapidly toward a precipice in their economic relations with the United States. By this date, the English trade deficit in the United States was already running between $50,000,000 and $75,000,000 a month; and the situation was bound to grow worse during the coming months on account of a sharp increase in Allied purchases in America.[79]

For a brief time during the late spring and early summer, authorities in the British Treasury and their New York agents, the firm of J. P. Morgan & Company, thought that the extension of a $100,000,000 "credit" by American banks, of a kind that the State Department had earlier approved, might perhaps suffice.[80] The total inadequacy of this remedy had, however, become apparent by early August, even before negotiations for this loan were completed. By this date, the problem had became clarified in all its appalling dimensions: The deficit in British trade balances with the United States, which had totaled nearly one billion dollars between December 1, 1914, and June 30, 1915, would likely exceed $2,500,000,000 for the calendar year 1915. The British could meet part of this balance by drawing further on their dwindling supply of British-owned American securities and by further payments in gold. But they could not pay the full balance for 1915 this way without imperiling their own national solvency and without so ex-

---

[79] Anderson Diary, May 25, 1915, relating a conversation with a Mr. Kent of the Bankers Trust Company of New York and Sir Richard Crawford.

[80] *New York Times*, July 2, 1915.

hausting their resources for foreign trade as to leave them utterly helpless after the beginning of 1916. At this point, obviously, British and
Allied purchases in the United States would virtually have to cease.

This was the gloomy prospect for the future unless some solution
could be found. In mid-August 1915, however, the immediate necessity was the maintenance of the pound sterling at or near its official
exchange price of $4.86 until the larger problem could be solved. The
British Treasury, acting through the Morgan firm, had been able to
hold the pound nearly at par on the New York money exchanges until
about August 1, 1915. Selling of British pounds was so constant and
heavy during early August, however, that dollars could not be found
fast enough to prevent a gradual decline. It accelerated rapidly between
August 13 and 18, when the pound dropped in price from about $4.73
to $4.65. Something had to be done at once lest further decline threaten
the very existence of the Atlantic trade. The situation was so acute
by mid-August that prominent bankers in New York were openly
saying that the only answer was an enormous American loan to the
British and French governments, one totaling perhaps $500,000,000.[81]

Leaders in the British government were no less alarmed than their
friends across the water, but they were reluctant to take so drastic a
step. For one thing, Ambassador Spring Rice, although he agreed that
a "paralysis of trade" threatened unless the exchange problem were
solved, was warning the Foreign Office that there was a grave risk of
the failure of a large American loan at this time. It was obvious, he
added, that "to attempt to float a loan and to fail would be an immense
disaster." Most American bankers, he reported, were jealous of the
Morgan firm and might refuse to cooperate in floating the loan; moreover, there were strong German sympathizers in almost every bank
who would do all they could to prevent its success. The problem could
be better solved for the moment, and more safely, he advised, by making arrangements for the advancement of short-term credits directly
by American banks, and by the hypothecation, if need be, of the two
and a half to three billion dollars' worth of American securities still
held by British subjects.[82] Then there was the matter of British pride.
It was not easy for people who had been the world's bankers for a cen-

[81] *ibid.*, August 14, 1915.

[82] Ambassador Spring Rice to the Foreign Office, August 17, 1915, copy in the Asquith Papers; C. Spring Rice, "Notes by Sir C. Spring-Rice on the Situation in the
United States," memorandum dated August 19, 1915, printed in a Cabinet paper entitled *Printed for the use of the Cabinet. September 1915, ibid.*

tury to confess their financial impotence by turning to America for a huge loan.

The Chancellor of the Exchequer, Reginald McKenna, laid the situation before the Cabinet on August 18, 1915. He would try, he promised, to stabilize the exchange rate without recourse immediately to a loan, by raising £100,000,000 in gold for export to the United States from British banks and from France and Russia, if they could contribute anything.[83] During the following week or ten days McKenna obviously did the best he could. He was able to raise £40,000,000 in gold at home and an equal sum from the French Treasury for immediate shipment to New York. That, certainly, would save the situation momentarily. But he and the French Finance Minister, with whom he talked at Boulogne, also agreed that vast new sums would be required during the autumn, and that their governments could not escape the necessity of an American loan. The Cabinet gave at least a tentative approval on August 25 and 27,[84] and McKenna must have proceeded to sound out the Morgan firm and other American bankers on the possibilities.

For at least two weeks now certain leaders of the American financial community had been eager to get plans for such a loan under way. They would not begin, however, until the Wilson administration had clarified its anomalous position on the whole question of lending. It will be recalled that in October 1914 Bryan and Wilson had reversed Bryan's earlier ban on loans to the extent of permitting the extension of short-term credits to belligerent governments. But this was not enough to satisfy the bankers in the circumstances of the midsummer of 1915. They now faced the prospect of being asked to float a public issue for one or more belligerents while the Washington authorities were still publicly committed in the clearest possible way against war loans in principle and against raising such loans by the sale of bonds directly to the American public in particular.[85] Moreover, the Federal Reserve Board was still following the rule that it had adopted on April 2, 1915, of forbidding Federal Reserve Banks to rediscount a large part of the bills and drafts, known as bankers' acceptances, arising out of the sale of munitions to belligerents. In their dilemma, not knowing where they stood or how far they could go, the bankers turned to Secretary McAdoo.

[83] The Prime Minister to the King, August 19, 1915, *ibid*.
[84] The Prime Minister to the King, August 27, 1915, *ibid*., reporting on Cabinet meetings of August 25 and 27, 1915.   [85] See above, pp. 135-136.

It was, of course, a decision that only the President could make, and McAdoo, who was still on vacation in Maine, laid the issues squarely before him and made his own recommendations strongly in a long letter to the Chief Executive on August 21, 1915. The growing American prosperity, McAdoo began, depended entirely upon the maintenance of the war trade with the Allies. That trade was now threatened with paralysis if the administration refused to permit private bankers to extend normal credit to the country's best customers. "We have repeatedly declared," he went on, "that it is lawful for our citizens to manufacture and sell to belligerents munitions of war. It is lawful commerce and being lawful is entitled to the same treatment at the hands of our bankers, in financing it, as any other part of our lawful commerce."

One of the chief obstacles to financing the war trade in an ordinary way, McAdoo continued, was the Federal Reserve Board's rule of April 2, 1915, known as Regulation J, against the rediscounting by Federal Reserve Banks of bankers' acceptances based on munitions exports. This rule, McAdoo said, had been adopted at a time when he was ill and was the work of the two "strong pro-German" members of the Board, Paul M. Warburg and Adolph C. Miller. He had, McAdoo went on, persuaded the Federal Reserve Board, at a meeting on August 10, to say that it was legal for member banks of the Federal Reserve System to deal in bankers' acceptances based on munitions exports; but up to this point he had not been able to persuade the Board to repeal Regulation J.[86]

[86] This struggle had been even more intense than McAdoo intimated in this letter. The Secretary was no man to brook opposition, and the frustration of being unable to dominate the Board was beginning to tell on his nerves. "To get rid of Miller is imperative," he wrote, for example, to Colonel House at about this time. "It simply must be done & a man of our kind put in his place or I shall have to quit. My nerves simply will not stand the strain. This Board is my real problem. If I can eliminate this small mischief-maker, all will go right." W. G. McAdoo to E. M. House, August 13, 1915, House Papers.

The crucial question before the Board at this time was whether the Federal Reserve Banks and national banks that were members of the Federal Reserve System were in fact institutions of the United States government. If they were, then their participation in the financing of the war trade would be a clear violation of American neutrality. If they were not, then the Federal Reserve Board would have no ground in *law* for imposing unusual restrictions upon such activity.

Before the summer of 1915 the Board had worked consistently on the assumption that the Federal Reserve Banks, at any rate, *were* public institutions. Warburg had been the chief advocate of this point of view, and his motives were certainly not above suspicion. A German by birth and rearing, with strong family and financial connec-

Meanwhile, the Secretary of the Treasury continued, there was the larger problem of some kind of loan to Great Britain. "It is," he wrote, "imperative for England to establish a large credit in this country. She will need at least $500,000,000. She can't get this in any way, at the moment, that seems feasible, except by sale of short time Government notes. Here she encounters the obstacle presented by Mr. Bryan's letter of Jany 20, 1915 to Senator Stone in which it is stated that 'War loans in this country were disapproved because inconsistent with the spirit of neutrality' etc. and 'this Government has not been advised that any

tions in the Fatherland, he was in every way a loyal partisan of the German cause. It is only fair to say that the other members of the Board (except McAdoo, who was not present) had willingly concurred with Warburg's view at the meeting when Regulation J was adopted. Indeed, there is good reason to believe that it was Charles S. Hamlin, Governor of the Federal Reserve Board, who was mainly responsible for the adoption of Regulation J.

Events following the adoption of this rule had forced Warburg and his ally, Adolph C. Miller, to come out more openly, at least within the privacy of the Board, as pro-Germans. What happened can be briefly told, as follows:

In response to repeated inquiries from bankers and to their own growing doubts, the members of the Board decided to ask their counsel to rule on the legal questions involved in the whole matter of bankers' acceptances. Counsel replied on July 20 and again four days later, saying that Federal Reserve Banks were not institutions of the United States government, and that the Federal Reserve Board could not lawfully forbid the Federal Reserve Banks to discount acceptances based upon any legitimate commercial transactions.

From this point on, Warburg made his fight against permitting the rediscounting of bankers' acceptances based upon munitions on the ground, not of law, but of policy. The first major test occurred at the meeting of the Board in New York City on August 10 to which McAdoo referred in his letter to the President. Governor Benjamin Strong of the New York Reserve Bank had asked the Board to review its position on bankers' acceptances. Warburg and Miller now admitted that the Federal Reserve Banks were not, strictly speaking, governmental institutions, but they contended that they were so heavily clothed with public responsibility that they could not rediscount bankers' acceptances based on munitions exports with violating American neutrality. They also strongly opposed the plans now on foot for the cooperation of the Federal Reserve Banks with British authorities for support of the cotton market. At this meeting on August 10 the Board voted to send a letter to Governor Strong authorizing member banks to buy and renew the controverted bankers' acceptances, but it did not repeal Regulation J which, it will be remembered, forbade Federal Reserve Banks to rediscount them. This, then, was the situation when McAdoo drafted his letter to President Wilson.

The above is based on Paul M. Warburg, "History of the Development of the Acceptance Regulation," MS. dated October 5, 1915, in the Scrapbooks of Charles S. Hamlin, Library of Congress; hereinafter cited as the Hamlin Scrapbooks; C. S. Hamlin to P. M. Warburg, December 30, 1915, *ibid.*; C. S. Hamlin to W. G. McAdoo, August 12, 1915, *ibid.*; copy of the minutes of the meeting of the Federal Reserve Board on August 10, 1915, *ibid.*; W. P. G. Harding to W. G. McAdoo, August 13, 1915, Wilson Papers.

general loans have been made by Foreign Governments in *this country since the President expressed his wish that loans of this character should not be made.*' The underscored part [in italics here] is the hardest hurdle of the entire letter. Large banking houses here which have the ability to finance a large loan, will not do so or even attempt to do so, in the face of this declaration. We have tied our hands so that we cannot help ourselves or help our best customers. France and Russia are in the same boat. Each, especially France, needs a large credit here."

"The declaration," McAdoo continued, "seems to me most illogical and inconsistent. We approve and encourage sales of supplies to England and others but we disapprove the creation by them of credit balances here to finance their lawful and welcome purchases. We must find some way to give them needed credits but there is no way, I fear, unless this declaration can be modified. Maybe the Arabic incident may clarify the situation! I should hate to have it modified that way. . . .

"The problem is so huge that she [England] must go 'whole hog' & she cant do that unless our attitude can be modified. Perhaps it could be done, if you decided that it should be done at all, by some hint to bankers, although I dont think that would do. In fact England & her allies will have great difficulty in getting the amount of credit they need here even if our government is openly friendly. I wish you would think about this so we may discuss it when I see you. To maintain our prosperity, we must finance it. Otherwise it may stop and that would be disastrous."[87]

The question, as it happened, had to be answered even before McAdoo returned to Washington. On August 17, 1915, James B. Forgan, president of the First National Bank of Chicago—acting discreetly, no doubt, for the Morgan partners—addressed a pointed inquiry to his friend, Frederick A. Delano, Vice Governor of the Federal Reserve Board. "To put it bluntly," he wrote, "I would like to know what the attitude of the government administration in Washington would be towards the flotation of a large British loan in this country. . . . You might send me one of the following telegrams to indicate which of the positions you think the government would take . . . and I will understand your meaning:

"1. Parties would be favorable to and would encourage such a transaction.

[87] W. G. McAdoo to W.W., August 21, 1915, *ibid.*

"2. Parties would take no action either for or against such a transaction.

"3. Parties would discourage such a transaction but would not offer any active interference with it.

"4. Parties attitude would be such as to make such a transaction practically impossible."[88]

Delano gave this letter to Charles S. Hamlin, Governor of the Federal Reserve Board, and he in turn passed it on to the Secretary of State. Lansing could no more make the decision on his own than McAdoo could; thus he sent a copy of Forgan's letter to the White House on August 25 with the request that the President tell him how to reply. "I think," he added in a somewhat cryptic recommendation, "we must recognize the fact that conditions have materially changed since last autumn when we endeavored to discourage the flotation of any general loan by a belligerent in this country. The question of exchange and the large debts which result from purchases by belligerent governments require some method of funding these debts in this country."[89]

It was a momentous matter, but we can only speculate about the thoughts that ran through the President's mind. He had McAdoo's letter of August 21 before him now as well as Lansing's, and he must have been impressed by his son-in-law's honest appeal for approval of a British loan on account of the economic benefits that it would bring to the American people. He could not be unmindful of this consideration. He knew also that Lansing's comment on the change in the exchange situation was true. But in making his decision he assuredly was influenced more by the other argument that McAdoo had implied, that the American government would not be truly neutral if it prevented a belligerent from borrowing money from private parties, any more than if it prevented the same belligerent from purchasing munitions or other supplies of war in the United States. Secretary Lansing had been saying the same thing in an indirect way all along, and Sir Edward Grey had earlier protested against the unneutrality of the ban on loans.[90]

We must assume, in addition, that the President was also influenced by recent developments in German-American relations. The first *Arabic* crisis was at its height at the very time that he was reviewing the ques-

[88] J. B. Forgan to F. A. Delano, August 17, 1915, *The Lansing Papers*, I, 142-143.

[89] R. Lansing to W.W., August 25, 1915, *ibid.*, p. 143.

[90] See above, p. 183.

tion of war loans. This is not to say that the knowledge that the United States might soon be at war with Germany was the decisive factor, or that it led Wilson knowingly to give a large advantage to Great Britain. It probably simply confirmed the wisdom of the decision that Wilson would otherwise have made.

Thus the President's choice was virtually foreordained by all the circumstances. "My opinion in this matter, compendiously stated," he wrote to Lansing, giving answer to Forgan's letter, "is that we should say that 'Parties would take no action either for or against such a transaction,' but that this should be orally conveyed, so far as we are concerned, and not put in writing."[91] In other words, the administration would revert to a position of strict neutrality on war loans. It would neither prohibit them, nor encourage them, as McAdoo wanted to do, nor take any official notice of them, as the bankers obviously desired.

Lansing sent a copy of the President's letter to McAdoo and undoubtedly conveyed its purport orally to Hamlin, who in turn must have passed it on to Wall Street. We cannot be altogether certain what took place during the next few days, but it is possible that the bankers came back to Lansing with the plea that the administration's mere acquiescence was not enough; that they needed some sign of public blessing from Washington—not an outright approval, which they knew they could not get, but at least a statement announcing the reversal of the Bryan ban. Selling a British loan of $500,000,000 to the American people, the bankers might have argued, would be a difficult task at best; it might be impossible if the public believed that the administration still adhered to its earlier opposition to public war loans. In any event, we know that this was McAdoo's belief, and that he returned to Washington on about September 1 and put great pressure on Lansing to reopen the question with the President.

Whatever the reason, Lansing took this step in what was for him an extraordinarily strong letter to the President on September 6. After reviewing the Anglo-American exchange situation in great detail, the Secretary of State forecast a gloomy future for the United States if some solution were not found: "restriction of outputs, industrial depression, idle capital and idle labor, numerous failures, financial demoralization, and general unrest and suffering among the laboring classes." Secretary McAdoo was convinced and he agreed, Lansing went on, that "there is only one means of avoiding this situation . . . , and that is the flotation of large bond issues by the belligerent govern-

[91] W.W. to R. Lansing, August 26, 1915, *ibid.*, p. 144.

ments." The difficulty—and it was what McAdoo had come to see him about—was that the administration still stood publicly committed to "the policy of discouraging general loans to belligerent governments." He went on:

"Now . . . we are face to face with what appears to be a critical economic situation, which can only be relieved apparently by the investment of American capital in foreign loans to be used in liquidating the enormous balance of trade in favor of the United States.

"Can we afford to let a declaration as to our conception of 'the true spirit of neutrality' made in the first days of the war stand in the way of our national interests which seem to be seriously threatened?

"If we cannot afford to do this, how are we to explain away the declaration and maintain a semblance of consistency?

"My opinion is that we ought to allow the loans to be made for our own good, and I have been seeking some means of harmonizing our policy, so unconditionally announced, with the flotation of general loans. As yet I have found no solution to the problem.

"Secretary McAdoo considers that the situation is becoming acute and that something should be done at once to avoid the disastrous results which will follow a continuance of the present policy."[92]

It was a fairly obvious trap that Lansing set—this statement of the dire details and need, confession of inability to find the answer, and appeal to the superior intellect for a solution—and Wilson, no doubt, understood. He called the Secretary of State to the White House on September 6, as soon as he had read his letter, and gave him an oral reply. We do not have a record of this conversation, but it is not difficult to deduce what the President said. He must have made it plain that he understood Lansing's and McAdoo's maneuver and had no intention of issuing any public statement repealing the Bryan ban. He may also have added that he would be grateful if his two subordinates did not mention the subject to him again. (In any event, the administration issued no statement; and Lansing and McAdoo said not another word about the matter, insofar as we know.) However, Wilson may have indicated, he was willing to permit Lansing, when the question arose in concrete form, to intimate to the Washington correspondents that the administration did not object to a British loan and in fact viewed it sympathetically on the sole ground that it was essential to the maintenance of America's foreign trade. At any rate, this is what a "highly placed administration official" told reporters on September 14,

[92] R. Lansing to W.W., September 6, 1915, *ibid.*, pp. 144-147.

after negotiations for what soon became an Anglo-French loan were in full swing.[93] "I have no doubt," Wilson wrote to Lansing on the day following this conference, "that our oral discussion of this matter suffices. If it does not, will you let me know that you would like a written reply?"[94] The President apparently had made his views sufficiently clear.

By now preparations for launching the great loan, which the French government had agreed to share, were entering their final stages in England and America. Still fearing that the loan might fail, British Treasury officials had decided to send an impressive commission headed by Lord Reading, the Lord Chief Justice, and composed of other distinguished British and French leaders. They would go to America not merely to negotiate the terms but also to give a proper tone and publicity to the undertaking. For their part, the Morgan partners were busy rallying the leading bankers and making arrangements for the underwriting and distribution of the loan on a nation-wide scale.

The Anglo-French commission arrived at New York aboard the liner *Lapland* on September 10, 1915, at the same time that the presidents of most of the large banks and insurance companies in the United States were gathering in the city at Morgan's invitation. Long and grueling sessions, at which the midwestern bankers took the lead on the American side, ensued during the next two and one-half weeks at the Morgan offices, at Lord Reading's suite on the eighteenth floor of the Hotel Biltmore, and on the yacht *Corsair* owned by J. P. Morgan, Junior. After sharp disagreement over the amount of the loan, whether it should be secured by collateral, and whether any of the proceeds should be used for the purchase of munitions, the conferees finally came to an agreement on September 28, 1915. It provided for a five-year unsecured loan of $500,000,000 to the British and French governments at an interest rate that totaled nearly 6 per cent with commissions and discounts, to be underwritten by a nation-wide banking syndicate headed by the Morgan firm, and the proceeds of which would be used exclusively to pay British and French trade balances in the United States.[95] It was only half what the British had by this time hoped to get, and the interest rate was almost exorbitant; but

[93] *New York Times*, September 15, 1915.
[94] W.W. to R. Lansing, September 8, 1915, *The Lansing Papers*, I, 147.
[95] *New York Times*, September 11, 13, 14, 16, 17, 18, 19, 20, 21, 24, and 29, 1915; New York *World*, September 16, 18, and 29, 1915.

the London Cabinet "with some reluctance sanctioned this plan, as the best available in the circumstances," on September 28 and October 1, and Lord Reading signed the loan papers on behalf of the commission on October 15.[96]

Events soon revealed that it was easier for the bankers to drive a hard bargain with the British government than to sell the Anglo-French bonds to the American people. The project was launched as a patriotic enterprise for the underwriting of American prosperity with much fanfare and with the support of a group of distinguished leaders and most editorial spokesmen. Only a few of them were indiscreet enough to imply that pro-Allied sentiment was involved in any way.[97] Most supporters of the loan said, and many of them indeed believed, that it was, as one prominent New England editor put it, "a business question that should be considered from a purely American point of view."[98]

Such arguments, though widely expressed and sincerely meant, failed either to assuage the consciences of many Americans who were disturbed by what they thought was the moral unneutrality of the loan, or to mollify the pro-German and anti-British elements, or, in the final analysis, to make much impression on the rank and file. "I think it is getting the people of this country to gamble on the war. The Bible says, in effect, 'Where your treasure is, there your heart is also,'" William J. Bryan declared.[99] "I am resolutely opposed to anything, no matter what the excuse," Senator William J. Stone, chairman of the foreign relations committee of the Senate, agreed in a public statement,

[96] The Prime Minister to the King, October 2, 1915, Asquith Papers; *New York Times*, October 16, 1915.

[97] e.g., Robert Bacon, in the *New York Times*, October 3, 1915; "The Big Loan," *Harper's Weekly*, LXI (October 9, 1915), 337; and George Harvey, "Patriotism and Profits," *North American Review*, CCII (November 1915), 648-649, 654-657.

[98] *Springfield* (Massachusetts) *Republican*, September 16, 1915. In this same vein, see the address of J. P. Morgan, Jr., to some 650 bond salesmen at the Waldorf-Astoria Hotel in New York City on October 8, 1915, printed in the New York *Journal of Commerce*, October 9, 1915; the statement of a group of prominent Americans that included Joseph H. Choate, C. W. Eliot, Seth Low, and James J. Hill, printed in the *New York Times*, October 18, 1915; "The Question of a Loan to Europe," New York *Nation*, CI (September 16, 1915), 349-350; New York *Evening Post*, September 16, 1915; New York *Journal of Commerce*, September 16, 1915; *New York Times*, September 17, 1915; *The Independent*, LXXXIII (September 27, 1915), 412-413; *Congregationalist and Christian World*, C (October 7, 1915), 466-467; *Saturday Evening Post*, CLXXXVIII (October 23, 1915), 24; *Bankers Magazine*, XCI (November 1915), 585-586.

[99] *New York Times*, September 21, 1915; see also Bryan's statement of September 11, printed in *The Commoner*, XV (September 1915), 4.

"calculated to convert any part of our people from our national attitude of honest neutrality into an attitude of partisanship in the European struggle."[100] And all the while the Hearst press, Irish-American groups like the American Truth Society, and the German-American organizations, egged on by Ambassador von Bernstorff, raised an enormous hue and cry.[101] At least in the Middle West, where their influence was strongest, they succeeded virtually in paralyzing efforts to distribute the Anglo-French bonds. Every single bank in Milwaukee, for example, announced that it would have no part in the loan.[102]

It might have made some difference in the outcome if the Washington administration had played an active role. As has been noted, the President did perhaps permit Lansing or McAdoo to tell reporters that the administration approved the loan insofar as it was an ordinary commercial transaction for the benefit of American foreign trade. On another occasion he asked the Secretary of the Treasury to explain the administration's point of view—that the "real significance of the loan . . . [was] the maintenance of international exchanges whose breakdown would be absolutely disastrous to the United States"—to a protesting senator. In making this request, however, he was careful to add, "I wonder if you could not get the information conveyed to him without its seeming like an administration announcement in this matter with which we really have nothing to do?"[103] From this point on he said not another word, direct or indirect, about the loan, and other members of the government kept silence accordingly.

For all these reasons, and for others more subtle—like the unfamiliarity of American investors with foreign bonds and the lurking suspicion that they were not safe—the sponsors of the Anglo-French loan failed to make any substantial headway in their campaign. The syndi-

[100] *New York Times*, October 3, 1915.

[101] See the New York *World*, September 17, 1915, and American Truth Society, *A Statement issued by the American Truth Society in defense of its President against an unjust attack made upon him by the President of the United States*, for the role that this organization played; statement of C. J. Hexamer, president of the National German-American Alliance, in the New York *World*, September 16, 1915; various accounts in *ibid.*, September 14, 1915, and the *New York Times*, September 15, 21, and 25, 1915; E. C. Stahl, president of the Deutsch-Amerikanischer National-Bund of New Jersey, to R. Lansing, September 16, 1915, Lansing Papers; and Ambassador von Bernstorff to the Foreign Office, September 21 (No. 408) and 24 (No. 414), 1915, German F. O. Archives.

[102] New York *World*, September 18, 1915.

[103] W.W. to W. G. McAdoo, September 17, 1915, Wilson Papers; for McAdoo's letter, see W. G. McAdoo to G. E. Chamberlain, September 22, 1915, *ibid*.

cate organized by J. P. Morgan & Company to market the bonds came to an end by limitation on December 14, 1915. On this date about $187,000,000 of the half-billion dollar issue were still unsold and had to be taken by the underwriting banks. (The results would have been positively disastrous if six companies with large contracts from the British government had not bought $100,000,000 of the bonds.)[104] More important was the fact that the syndicate had sold only 33,000,000 dollars' worth of the bonds to ordinary noninstitutional investors.[105]

It was, altogether, a spectacular failure with momentous implications for the future. For one thing, it convinced the American bankers and British financial leaders that it would be futile to try to raise any important sums directly from the American people; never again during the period of American neutrality did the British attempt to float a public loan in the United States. This meant that the American people would not give such hostages to an Allied victory as they might have given had the Anglo-French loan and other loans like it succeeded. Hereafter (for the proceeds of the Anglo-French loan enabled the British to solve the exchange problem only for a short period during the closing months of 1915) the British could pay their monstrously growing trade deficits only by short-term loans from American banks, which of course were no solution at all,[106] and by long-term loans secured by such first-class American collateral as the banks were required by law to demand. This in turn meant that the British would become totally dependent upon the good will of the American financial community and, ultimately, of the Washington government itself. It meant, also, that the British had still achieved no permanent solution of the exchange problem; they still faced the prospect of the paralysis of the flow of life-giving supplies from the United States once they had mortgaged all their American securities.

In the long run, therefore, the chief consequence of the failure of the Anglo-French loan of 1915 was an enormous strengthening of the President's hand in dealing with the Allies in the future.

[104] The three largest of these were the DuPont interests, Bethlehem Steel, and Westinghouse, which together bought 70,000,000 dollars' worth of bonds. New York *World*, October 6, 1915.

[105] *ibid.*, December 15, 1915.

[106] The Federal Reserve Board greatly facilitated the extension of such short-term credits by repealing Regulation J on September 7, 1915, and by adopting a new Regulation R specifically authorizing Federal Reserve Banks to rediscount member-bank bankers' acceptances "up to an amount not to exceed the capital stock and surplus of the bank for which the rediscounts are made." Federal Reserve *Bulletin*, 1 (October 1915), 310-311.

CHAPTER XVIII

The Triumph of Carranza

DURING the late summer and early autumn of 1915 the Mexican problem came to the forefront in Washington again, and in such a way
as to compel President Wilson and his advisers finally to adopt the
clear-cut policy which, up to this time, they had thought it wise to
evade. Events in Mexico itself during this period might in any event
have forced them to this course. But they also stood committed to a
decisive confrontation by virtue of the actions of the Pan-American
conference that they had convened at the State Department during
the first days of August. On August 11, 1915, it will be recalled, the
conferees had framed a solemn appeal to the warring Mexican factions
to end their strife and unite in a common government, and they had
accompanied this call with an offer of mediation. Lansing and the
Latin American diplomats had then agreed to meet again as soon as
the Mexican leaders had replied, in order to consider what common
policy they should recommend to their respective governments.[1]

To General Villa, who was now maintaining a precarious front at
Torreón in north central Mexico, the suggestion that the warring chieftains meet under international auspices to form an all-Mexican government came as the first ray of hope since his debacle at Celaya.[2] He
accepted the Pan-American offer on August 16, the day after he had
received it. "All military chiefs and civilian officials affiliated with
the Convention Government," he added assuringly, "desire only to witness the reestablishment of a government in Mexico that will bind itself to hold popular elections by which the people may, with absolute
freedom, designate their representatives in office regardless of any preference which such chiefs and officials may entertain in favor of any
candidate or candidates."[3] Following this lead, all prominent *Villistas*

[1] Above, pp. 492-493.
[2] As he virtually said in a message to his so-called government at Chihuahua City
on August 15. New York *World*, August 16, 1915.
[3] F. Villa, telegram dated August 16, 1915, *Foreign Relations, 1915*, pp. 737-738.

replied with one accord during the following days; and from the South came echoes of approval from Zapata and his chieftains.[4]

This clutching at straws was pathetic in a way but also wholly irrelevant, for everything depended upon how the First Chief would respond. Or it might be more accurate to say that everything depended upon whether Carranza's generals would compel him to accept the Pan-American offer. Herein, Lansing knew, lay the only hope of success, for Carranza had already made it abundantly clear before the Pan-American appeal arrived at his headquarters that he would no more brook outside interference by fellow Latin Americans than by *Yanquis*.[5] The hope that the First Chief's generals might force him to the peace table vanished altogether between August 15 and 23, when all of them said that they had referred the appeal to "the First Chief of the Constitutionalist Army in charge of the executive power," and that he alone was competent to give an answer.[6]

Lansing, actually, was not surprised. A settlement in Mexico, he thought, would not come by appeals and replies in the newspapers but by diplomatic pressure applied strongly enough in the right place at the right time. What should the American government insist upon, and how? The Secretary of State must have gone to the White House on about August 14 and put this question squarely to the President. Only a few days before, it will be remembered, Wilson had insisted that Lansing take no action, as he had then been about to do, to commit the United States to the elimination of Carranza and the support of some other Mexican leader.[7] Now what? Let the First Chief be told frankly and confidentially, Wilson must have instructed the Secretary of State, that the Pan-American conferees did not contemplate armed intervention in Mexico, and that they had no preconceived prejudice against Carranza and indeed might even recommend his recognition to their respective governments. At the same time, the President apparently continued, Carranza must be made to understand that the United States government, at any rate, would extend recognition only to the Mexican leader chosen at a peace conference representing all the contending elements, and that Carranza's present program *could*

[4] C. B. Parker to the Secretary of State, August 29, 1915, with enclosures, *ibid.*, pp. 739-742.

[5] E. Arredondo to the Secretary of State, August 10, 1915, *ibid.*, pp. 734-735; New York *World*, August 16, 1915.

[6] Their replies are listed in *Foreign Relations, 1915*, p. 753; see also the *New York Times*, August 19, 22, and 24, 1915.

[7] Above, pp. 490-491.

not lead to recognition because it aimed at triumph by force of arms.[8]

Probably at Wilson's suggestion, Lansing asked the Washington correspondent, David Lawrence, to convey this message to Eliseo Arredondo, the head of the Constitutionalist mission in Washington. Lawrence found Arredondo at Asbury Park, New Jersey, on August 15, 1915. He not only relayed the President's message but also persuaded the Mexican envoy to urge his superior to accept the American peace plan in principle.[9] Lansing was at least slightly encouraged. "Confidentially," he wrote to Paul Fuller, Senior, on the day after receiving news of Arredondo's report to the First Chief, "I might inform you that I am working through other instrumentalities to bring about the acceptance by General Carranza of the principle which is advanced in our communication to the Mexican factions."[10]

Perhaps it was because they were encouraged that the President and Secretary of State took their next step, which was to send Lawrence at once to Veracruz, there to press their views personally upon the First Chief.[11] Arriving at the temporary Mexican capital on August 28, Lawrence explained what the American President had in mind to the First Chief during a two-hour interview on the same day. He had come, Lawrence said, voluntarily and with no official character; but he was "thoroughly conversant" with the Washington government's point of view. The President and Secretary of State, he went on, feared the dangers of preferring one armed faction to another, "because of resentments which might thereby result," and they believed that "harmonizing elements meant surer domestic peace as well as minimizing chances of foreign intervention." "I outlined," Lawrence reported to the State Department, "what seemed to me [the] method by which he could obtain recognition, suggesting that his note be written so as not to offend any signatories [of the Pan-American appeal] and that some kind of conference be called and if no agreement could be reached [the] more powerful faction probably would be chosen, pro-

[8] At any rate, Wilson's emissary, David Lawrence, on August 15, 1915, told Carranza's Confidential Agent, Eliseo Arredondo, that these were the President's views and policy. D. Lawrence to R. Lansing, August 15, 1915, State Department Papers.

[9] *ibid.*; D. Lawrence to R. Lansing, August 16, 1915, *ibid.*

[10] R. Lansing to P. Fuller, Sr., August 17, 1915, Lansing Papers.

[11] Both Lawrence's leaving and his subsequent negotiations were shrouded in great secrecy, presumably because Lansing did not want his Pan-American colleagues to know that he was conducting such important negotiations as it were behind their backs. In reporting from Veracruz, for example, Lawrence used the code name "Laguirre," which Wilson must have invented, while Wilson and Lansing never used his name even in their private correspondence.

vided it gave promise of satisfying international obligation." Carranza was cordial throughout but made it plain that his government still had no intention whatever of accepting or permitting outside help or interference. On the other hand, he added, he would be glad to discuss international questions officially with Lawrence if the American government would accredit him.[12]

"It does not seem to me," Wilson replied in comment when Lansing sent him this first report, "that our friend has got anywhere in particular in his representations to the stiff-necked First Chief or made any impression on him that is likely, if confirmed, to lead to cooperation on his part with the United States; and therefore it does not seem to me wise that we should do more than this: send word to Silliman that our friend does come fresh from conversations with you and is in a position to know what the real sentiments and purposes of the Government of the United States are.[13] Any sort of official recognition of him [Lawrence] would be a mistake, and quite out of keeping with the understanding upon which he went down there."[14]

It was all very discouraging; and not long after the President wrote the above letter a second and, to Wilson, an even more irritating dispatch from Lawrence arrived in Washington. It described a near crisis in Mexican-American relations on account of the absence of any strong or acceptable American representative at Carranza's headquarters. There was nothing for the President to do, the message continued, but, first, to accept the facts of Mexican life and recognize Carranza, even if he should reject the Pan-American overture, and, second, to send a new envoy who could present the American point of view forthrightly and insist that the Constitutionalists live up to their international obligations.[15]

"As to the course advised," Lansing wrote as he sent this telegram to the President on August 31, "I am much in doubt as I feel that the Pan-American Conferees would be strongly opposed to following it."[16] "I do not think any part of this advice is good," Wilson replied somewhat more testily. "The usual thing has happened: a man is sent down to explain our exact position and purpose and within a day or two

[12] W. W. Canada to the Secretary of State, for "Laguirre," August 29, 1915, State Department Papers.

[13] Lansing sent a message in this vein at once to Silliman. The Secretary of State to Special Agent J. R. Silliman, August 31, 1915, *ibid.*

[14] W.W. to R. Lansing, August 31, 1915, *ibid.*

[15] W. W. Canada to the Secretary of State, for "Laguirre," August 30, 1915, *ibid.*

[16] R. Lansing to W.W., August 31, 1915, *ibid.*

sends us a comprehensive plan of his own entirely inconsistent with what he was sent to say. I think it is best to make no reply at all to this, and simply to let it go at what we replied to the first communication. It is a great pity, but it is clear that nothing can be done either with or through Carranza. I have no doubt that your conversation with General [Hugh L.] Scott[17] strengthened this impression in your mind, as it did in mine."[18]

Whether it was a great pity depended entirely upon the point of view, but there could certainly never be any further doubt that the determined man in the White House had failed in his campaign, now more than two years old, to impose his own will upon the equally stubborn leader of the Mexican Revolution. As if to make certain that the American President understood, Carranza gave an interview to reporters at Veracruz on August 31, 1915. "Under no consideration," he warned, "would I permit interference in the internal affairs of Mexico, as no nation has the right to interfere in the internal affairs of any country. . . . Any doing so must expect to meet resistance, which naturally could not be overcome except by overwhelming force."[19]

Carranza had been maturing a plan of his own, which he frankly divulged to Lawrence on September 1, just before the American agent returned to Washington. It was to render the project of Pan-American mediation obsolete by a smashing campaign that would destroy the last vestiges of *Villista* power in northern Mexico. He would then be able to present the would-be mediators with the *fait accompli* of his own undoubted supremacy when he made formal reply to their appeal.[20]

The First Chief's offensive began in the opening days of September

---

[17] A leader of the anti-Carranza, pro-Villa faction in the administration, whose extraordinary activities at this time are revealed in part in the following letter: "I am very much afraid that the ABC are going to recommend the recognition of Carranza. . . . I told Bonilla and Llorente [Villa's agents in Washington] to get busy now to combat this Carranza propaganda here and regain the standing for Villa that has been lost on account of the Carranza propaganda. I told [Felix] Sommerfeld [another of Villa's agents in the United States] the same thing and urged him to do it. . . . I do not know what we can do further as I have done everything I can think of." H. L. Scott to J. R. Garfield, September 10, 1915, Scott Papers.

[18] W.W. to R. Lansing, August 31, 1915, State Department Papers.

[19] *New York Times*, September 1, 1915.

[20] W. W. Canada to the Secretary of State, for "Laguirre," September 1, 1915, State Department Papers.

and gained momentum with almost incredible speed. On September 4[21] General Obregón, now Constitutionalist commander in chief in the North, hit Villa and his ragged Division of the North at Saltillo, capital of Carranza's native State of Coahuila, and captured the city after a sharp engagement. Villa then fled northward toward Paredon; unable to stem Obregón's onrush there, Pancho retreated eastward to Torreón, an important railroad center and his principal base of operations in north central Mexico. Having lost most of his artillery and many men in flight, Villa dared no longer to stand and fight. He retired to Guanacevi, in the Sierra Madres, while Obregón entered Torreón on September 9 without firing a shot. At about the same time other Constitutionalist forces occupied Piedra Negras on the Mexican-American border opposite Eagle Pass, Texas, and Durango, capital of the state by the same name, southwest of Torreón.[22]

These blows shattered Villa's military power and humbled his political pretensions. He still held the State of Chihuahua and the important port city of Juárez opposite El Paso; but he was by now nothing more than a bandit leader who could hit, run, and elude capture in an uncanny way, but never again offer organized resistance.

All this was obvious when Carranza, speaking through his Foreign Secretary, Jesús Acuña, finally returned his formal reply to the Pan-American mediators on September 10, 1915, the day after the fall of Torreón. It was restrained and friendly but utterly unyielding. Carranza, Acuña said, could not "consent to a discussion of the domestic affairs of the Republic by mediation or on the initiative of any foreign government whatever." Acceptance of the Pan-American offer would gravely prejudice Mexican independence and set a precedent for foreign intervention in the settlement of internal questions. The First Chief, Acuña went on, was not only the guardian of Mexican sovereignty but also the leader of a "genuine revolution, which aims at doing away with the last vestiges of colonial times . . . and satisfying the noble yearning of the Mexican people for well-being and improvement." He could not sit down at the peace table with the men who had attempted to corrupt and destroy the Revolution or permit these enemies of the Mexican people to take direct part in the government, any more than

---

[21] This and the following dates are approximate.

[22] Consul Garrett to the Secretary of State, September 4, 1915, State Department Papers; Consul Williams to the Secretary of State, September 7, 1915, *ibid.*; G. C. Carothers to the Secretary of State, September 8 and 10, 1915, *ibid.; New York Times,* September 9 and 10, 1915.

he could permit outsiders, however friendly, to guide the destinies of the fatherland.

The truth was, the Foreign Secretary continued, that the Constitutional revolution begun by Carranza after Huerta's treason was at the point of culmination. "The strife is now nearing its end and the reactionary faction, annihilated, is seeking refuge on the northern border, controlling only the State of Chihuahua, a small part of the State of Sonora, and, in the center, the State of Morelos [where the *Zapatistas* were entrenched], which the Constitutionalist forces will soon occupy. The First Chief with an army of 150,000 men now dominates the greater part of the national territory. . . . I have no doubt that your excellencies will draw from the foregoing statement the conviction that by entering into agreements with the vanquished faction the First Chief would not only relinquish the victory won at the cost of so many sacrifices but also the First Chieftainship of the Constitutional Army and the Executive Power of the nation and thereby foil the faith and confidence reposed in him by the Mexican army and people."

Although Carranza had to refuse the courteous Pan-American invitation, Acuña concluded, he would none the less be glad to meet the would-be mediators at one of the border towns held by his forces. Such discussions as took place, however, must have the sole object of determining whether the mediators should conclude that Carranza and his government were entitled to *de facto* recognition.[23] "This," the note ended, "would afford a further occasion for drawing closer the relations of friendship between the people and Governments of your excellencies and the Mexican people and Government."[24]

President Wilson and Secretary Lansing were neither surprised by Carranza's formal rejoinder nor much inclined to quarrel with his claim to mastery of Mexico. They had followed the dispatches too closely during the First Chief's last offensive to have any further doubts on this score. And now, at the very time that they were studying the note from Veracruz, further light on the Mexican situation came to Washington from the reports of two of the State Department's most

[23] Carranza was here adopting a suggestion that David Lawrence had made to him in Veracruz, that he at least offer to meet with the mediators if he could not accept their invitation to a peace conference.

[24] "Reply of General Carranza to the Pan American Note," September 10, 1915, *Foreign Relations, 1915*, pp. 746-748.

trusted agents, George C. Carothers and Zach L. Cobb.[25] They made it clear that Villa's power had deteriorated even more than earlier dispatches had indicated, and they told of loss of confidence and widespread suffering in Pancho's territory and of a mass exodus of turncoats and refugees to the United States and Carranza's domain.[26]

There was another reason for coming to terms with Carranza and for indirectly helping him to consolidate his power. German agents, as Wilson and Lansing now knew, had been busy all summer encouraging strife in Mexico in an obvious effort to involve the United States. Writing in his diary in early October 1915, Lansing described these activities and said that discovery of them had forced him to the conclusion that the United States must recognize Carranza in order to avoid intervention which, he said, would mean playing Germany's game.[27] This statement has to be taken with several large grains of salt,[28] but it does make clear that the German-American tension had its impact even on American policy toward Mexico.

In these circumstances how, indeed, could the President and Secretary of State avoid accepting the situation and preparing the way for Carranza's recognition, either in company with the Pan-American mediators or alone if this could not be arranged? This is what Lawrence had earlier advised and what Carothers and Cobb were now strongly urging.

A reading of the First Chief's reply of September 10 nearly confirmed the Secretary of State's hitherto tentative judgment about the necessity of granting an early recognition to the victor in Mexico. "The Carranzistas," he explained to the President on September 12 as he sent him a copy of the note from Veracruz, "are undoubtedly stronger and more cohesive than they have ever been. In fact I have almost reached the conclusion that they are so dominant that they are entitled to recognition. . . . The situation has changed materially since the [Pan-American] communication was sent to the Mexican chiefs. Villa's

---

[25] Carothers, it will be remembered, was the Department's Special Agent assigned to Villa's headquarters. Cobb was Collector of the Port of El Paso and an officer of the Treasury Department, but he served in an unofficial capacity for the State Department.

[26] G. C. Carothers to the Secretary of State, September 10, 1915, State Department Papers; Z. L. Cobb to the Secretary of State, September 11, 1915, *ibid*.

[27] Lansing Diary, October 10, 1915.

[28] Because in this passage Lansing gives the impression that it was the discovery of German intrigues in Mexico that was solely responsible for his decision to recognize Carranza, and that *he* alone made the decision.

power has rapidly waned, his forces have disintegrated, and many of his ablest lieutenants have abandoned him or are quarreling with him. As long as the Villista faction was capable of offering stubborn resistance to the Constitutionalists the desirable thing was to stay the strife by harmonizing the factional differences. That was the purpose of the proposed conference of leaders. Now, it seems to me, the problem is whether or not peace in Mexico will not be more quickly restored by giving moral support to the triumphing faction of Carranza."

The trouble was, Lansing went on, that the Pan-American mediators had invited the Mexican leaders to a conference and the losers had accepted. "Can we consistently or honorably refuse to call such a conference? If we do call it, what will be the practical value of its deliberations? With the utter demoralization of the enemies of Carranza it would be absurd to assert that any government, which they could set up, represented the sovereignty of the Mexican people." It might be possible to hold a conference at which the *Villistas* could meet and draw up a statement of grievances to be presented to Carranza. "As this involves the whole general Mexican policy," he concluded, "I think that I should be advised as to your wishes in the matter."[29]

Calling the Secretary of State to the White House as soon as he had read this letter, the President gave his decision clearly and quickly. We have a record of what he said, written succinctly as usual in Wilson's own words, as follows:

"We have already gone over this matter orally; but perhaps it is best for me to put down what I understand our course of action is to be:

"We are to call our Latin American colleagues together and suggest to them a conference with representatives of Carranza at Washington,[30] on substantially the basis he proposes, to discuss the advisability of recognizing him as the *de facto* head of the Republic; having it clearly understood that we think the acceptance of the Revolution absolutely necessary.

"We are also to keep faith with the leaders of the other factions, who have accepted our proposal for a conference on Mexican affairs,

[29] R. Lansing to W.W., September 12, 1915, *The Lansing Papers*, II, 550-552.

[30] This was Lansing's suggestion, made in his letter of September 12, 1915, as follows: "Of course his [Carranza's] invitation to meet in conference on the border to discuss Mexican affairs from the international standpoint . . . cannot be accepted. The place of a meeting for such purpose could not in any event be Mexican territory. If Carranza had named Washington it might be at least worthy of consideration. . . . Such a conference would in fact review the entire domestic state of Mexico including the power of the factions and their complaints against one another."

and are to call such a conference of their representatives to be convened and held in Mexico; with the understanding that we wish from them any proposals they may wish to make, but with the intimation conveyed to them in some proper way that the best and most helpful thing for them to do is to let us know confidentially the terms upon which they will submit to Carranza in view of the probable necessity we shall be under, because of the utter alteration of conditions since our suggestion of a conference was conveyed to them, of recognizing him as the head of the Republic."[31]

In accomplishing the first task ahead—persuading the Latin American envoys to fall in with President Wilson's plan—Lansing ran into unexpected difficulties largely of his own making. The Pan-American conference reassembled at the Secretary's invitation at the Hotel Biltmore in New York City on September 18, 1915. But the atmosphere was somewhat tense, for Lansing three days before had told reporters that the Pan-American conference would accept Carranza's counterinvitation; he had, moreover, revealed that he had recently warned all Americans in Villa's territory to leave at once and had instructed consular officials in the same area to withdraw quietly.[32] The Latin Americans, particularly the correct and sensitive Brazilian Ambassador, da Gama, obviously deeply resented what they must have regarded as Lansing's attempt to prejudice their decision.

The discussions that ensued at the Hotel Biltmore were not, consequently, always cordial in tone. With great skill Lansing presented the President's plan for two separate Mexican conferences. He argued patiently that the facts of the Mexican situation demanded recognition of Carranza and pleaded for a joint recommendation to this effect to the governments represented. Time and again he was on the verge of success only to be frustrated by Ambassador da Gama, who refused to countenance any suggestion of *joint action* of any kind, either for discussions with the Mexican chieftains or for recognition of the First Chief. At the end of the grueling three-hour session the best Lansing could obtain was approval of a resolution declaring that the conferees should soon make some recommendation to their governments on the question of recognition, and agreement that the Secretary of State

[31] W.W. to R. Lansing, September 13, 1915, *ibid.*, p. 552.

[32] *New York Times*, September 16, 1915. For Lansing's warning to American citizens and consular officials in Villa's territory, see the Secretary of State to certain American Consuls, September 11, 1915, *Foreign Relations, 1915*, p. 837.

should confer with the representatives of Villa and Carranza in Washington and report his own recommendations to the Pan-American envoys on October 9.[33] "I am disappointed, naturally," Lansing wrote at the end of a long report of the meeting to the President, "that the plan that we had agreed upon was not carried through, but as it has failed, to an extent, I think we should follow out some such scheme as the one above proposed."[34]

There was really not much else that the President and Secretary of State could do. Having committed themselves so strongly to collective action, they could not now recognize Carranza on their own. Thus Lansing did no more for the time being than to issue a statement to the newspapers summarizing the conference's decisions of September 18.[35] Then, just before the conference was scheduled to reconvene, he requested and received the statements that he had promised to obtain from the *Carrancista* and *Villista* agents in Washington.[36] With these documents in hand, he met the six Latin American diplomats in his office on October 9, 1915, for what was to be the crucial session. It was another three-hour meeting and presumably a contentious one; but somehow (for we have no full record of the discussion) the Secretary of State carried the day. Smiling as he greeted reporters a short time later, he made the following simple announcement: "The conference, after careful consideration of the facts, have found that the Carranza party is the only party possessing the essentials for recognition as the de facto government of Mexico, and they have so reported to their respective Governments."[37] President Wilson voiced his approval to the newspapermen on the following day.[38]

In Veracruz Carranza received the announcement with unfeigned pleasure. "This news," he told reporters, "puts an end to all efforts of our enemies to bring about foreign intervention. They continue their intrigues and their attacks in the newspapers, but recognition of the Constitutionalist Government naturally will rob them of the fruit

[33] "Conference on Mexican Affairs, September 18, 1915," *ibid.*, pp. 754-762; "Text of Agreement by the Conference of Diplomatic Representatives," *The Lansing Papers*, II, 554.

[34] R. Lansing to W.W., September 18, 1915, *ibid.*

[35] *New York Times*, September 19, 1915.

[36] E. Arredondo to the Secretary of State, October 7, 1915, *Foreign Relations, 1915*, pp. 763-765; E. C. Llorente to the Secretary of State, October 8, 1915, *ibid.*, pp. 765-766; also the statement by General Villa, printed in the *New York Times*, October 9, 1915.

[37] *ibid.*, October 10, 1915.

[38] *ibid.*, October 12, 1915.

of their efforts. When peace is absolutely restored and tranquility really established throughout the republic amnesty will be granted to all these persons, but not now. To permit them to return at this time would be to endure their machinations within the republic."[39]

While Wilson and Lansing were congratulating themselves on their achievement, a storm of almost unprecedented magnitude broke over their heads. It was a violent, last-ditch campaign by the Roman Catholic hierarchy and spokesmen to thwart the final act of recognition of the Constitutionalist regime.

The outbreak was not entirely unexpected, even though no one in Washington had read all the warning signals. They came in a clear way following the Pan-American conference of September 18, after the publication of intimations in the press that the American government had abandoned plans for intervention and was now contemplating the recognition of Carranza. All over the country Roman Catholics reacted bitterly. Carranza, cried the editor of the Church's pre-eminent American weekly, is "a modern Nero, enemy of God and man, a very scourge generated and supported by a power of ill, to revile Heaven and morality and to spread desolation over a fair land that no longer knows human hope, but must trust in God alone, for that the powers of darkness within and without its borders are working unto its destruction."[40] The First Chief, the Bishop of Mobile agreed, "is the lowest of the low, the vilest of the vile."[41] And protests began to appear in the press and to pour into the White House and State Department even before any formal announcement concerning the matter of recognition was made.[42]

[39] *ibid.*, October 11, 1915. For the reaction of Villa and his partisans, see Villa's statement in *ibid.*; the statement of M. Díaz Lombardo and E. C. Llorente printed in *ibid.*; H. L. Scott to J. R. Garfield, October 11 and 14, 1915, Scott Papers; H. L. Scott to C. E. Husk, November 17, 1915, *ibid.*; and J. R. Garfield to H. L. Scott, October 12, 1915, *ibid.*

[40] *America*, XIII (October 2, 1915), 614.

[41] The Most Reverend E. P. Aller to W.W., October 4, 1915, State Department Papers.

[42] e.g., the Reverend John Wynne, editor of the *Catholic Encyclopaedia*, quoted in the New York *World*, October 10, 1915; the Most Reverend J. H. Conroy, Auxiliary Bishop of Ogdensburg, New York, to the Secretary of State, October 5, 1915; E. B. Ledvina, secretary, Catholic Church Extension Society, to W.W., Ocotber 5, 1915; Western Catholic Union to W.W., October 6, 1915; Missouri Federation of Catholic Societies to W.W., October 6, 1915; Slavonic Catholic Union to W.W., October 7, 1915; American Federation of Catholic Societies of Kansas City to W.W., October 7, 1915; E. F. Cooke, president, New York State Federation of Catholic Societies, to W.W.,

This was all merely a prelude to the violent denunciation that followed the adjournment of the Pan-American conference on October 9, 1915. From almost every Roman Catholic bishop and organization, as if in response to orders, came protests and appeals to the President and Secretary of State not to commit the awful act.[43] The Church's newspapers continued their reproaches and added a new warning of political retaliation. As the spokesman of the Archdiocese of New Orleans and the Diocese of Savannah put it in a particularly savage editorial:

"Mr. Wilson's recognition of Carranza, the avowed enemy of the Catholic Church, is an insult to the Catholics of this country. It is a direct challenge to them, and we hope that not only Catholics but every true lover of religious freedom . . . will give him such an open answer at the polls as will prove to him that no President of the United States can so flagrantly ignore the lawful and respectful request of 16,000,000 fellow citizens without paying the penalty. . . . Mr. Wilson stands at the bar of this country and he must answer for his actions."[44]

In spite of the earlier warnings, Wilson and Lansing were obviously surprised and upset by the intensity of the main Roman Catholic attack. Lansing had taken careful pains to give to the press the memorandum that Carranza's Washington agent had submitted to him on October 8; the Secretary had also made a point of saying that this memorandum and other recent statements by the Constitutionalist govern-

---

October 7, 1915; Louisiana Federation of Catholic Societies to W.W., October 9, 1915; and J. W. Gregg, president, Catholic Federation of Santa Clara County, California, to W.W., October 9, 1915, all in the State Department Papers.

[43] See the following appeals addressed directly to the President (all in *ibid.*) from the Bishop of Seattle, October 11, 1915; the Bishop of Sioux City, Iowa, October 19, 1915; the Bishop of Leavenworth, October 18-19, 1915; the Bishop of Ogdensburg, October 18-19, 1915; the Bishop of Wheeling, October 18-19, 1915; the Bishop of Superior, Wisconsin, October 18-19, 1915; the Bishop of Grand Rapids, October 20-21, 1915; the Archbishop of Philadelphia, October 18, 1915; the Bishop of Newark, October 18, 1915; the Bishop of Bismarck, North Dakota, October 20-21, 1915; the Bishop of Rochester, New York, October 18, 1915; the Bishop of Trenton, October 18, 1915; Milwaukee County Federation of Catholic Societies, October 12-13, 1915; Brooklyn Diocesan Union of the Holy Name Society, October 18, 1915; the Grand Knight of the Knights of Columbus, October 18-19, 1915; Federation of Catholic Societies of New Jersey, October 19, 1915; Ancient Order of Hibernians, October 11, 1915; Brooklyn Diocesan Branch of the American Federation of Catholic Societies, October 11, 1915.

[44] *The Morning Star* of New Orleans, October 16, 1915, as quoted in the New York *World*, October 17, 1915. See also *America*, xiv (October 16, 1915), 14; the *Brooklyn Tablet*, October 16, 1915; and J. P. Chew in the St. Louis *Church Progress*, October 18, 1915.

ment included broad guarantees of religious freedom for Mexico.[45] The President and Secretary of State believed that these guarantees were all that any reasonable man could demand. They had no quarrel with Carranza's determination to punish clergymen who had taken an active part in the civil war. Finally, they also knew that the recognition of the Veracruz regime would draw substantial support from important elements in American public opinion, particularly among organized labor and the Protestant churches.[46] Thus the effect of the Catholic campaign at home was, if anything, to harden their determination to proceed to the final stages of the policy they had already announced. One of the two men made this clear on October 17 by telling reporters that the administration was satisfied with Carranza's promises of religious freedom and by adding, somewhat defiantly, that Mexican priests who entered politics must expect to be treated like politicians, and that clergymen, presumably American as well as Mexican, would do better to tend their flock than to "dabble in politics."[47]

The Secretary of State, therefore, proceeded undeterred to play out the drama that had begun so differently more than a year before. The governments whose envoys had participated in the Pan-American conference had given official notice to the State Department by October 16 that they were prepared to implement the recommendation of October 9. Lansing called his Latin American colleagues to his office on October 18 for a final meeting. They quickly agreed that their governments should extend recognition *de facto* on the following day.[48] This is the way it was done, with the governments that had been represented in the conference—the United States, Brazil, Argentina, Chile, Bolivia, Uruguay, and Guatemala—being joined by the governments of Colombia and Nicaragua in a display of hemispheric unity.

[45] *New York Times,* October 10 and 12, 1915; New York *World,* October 10, 1915.

[46] e.g., S. Gompers to W.W., June 14, 1915, Wilson Papers; S. Gompers to W.W., August 9, 1915, enclosing E. E. Martinez to S. Gompers, August 5, 1915, *ibid.*; S. Gompers to W.W., September 22, 1915, enclosing a resolution by the Executive Council of the American Federation of Labor urging the recognition of Carranza, *ibid.; Lutheran Church Work,* III (January 7, 1915), 4-5; Grapho, "Roman Catholic Complaint Concerning Mexico," *The Congregationalist and Christian World,* c (January 21, 1915), 78; *The Churchman,* CXI (February 27, 1915), 261-262; "What the Mexican Revolution Has Done for Protestantism," New York *Christian Advocate,* XC (July 22, 1915), 974; G. B. Winton, D.D., " 'Poor Mexico!' " *ibid.,* December 9, 1915, pp. 1668-1669; G. B. Winton, "Shall the American People 'Recognize' Carranza?" Nashville *Christian Advocate,* LXXVI (December 10, 1915), 1619-1620.

[47] New York *World,* October 18, 1915.

[48] See Lansing's statement announcing the agreement of the conferees, in the *New York Times,* October 19, 1915.

Secretary Lansing granted recognition for the United States in a letter to Carranza's agent in Washington, Eliseo Arredondo:

It is my pleasure to inform you that the President of the United States takes this opportunity of extending recognition to the de facto Government of Mexico, of which General Venustiano Carranza is the Chief Executive.[49]

The Government of the United States will be pleased to receive formally in Washington a diplomatic representative of the de facto Government as soon as it shall please General Carranza to designate and appoint such representative; and, reciprocally, the Government of the United States will accredit to the de facto Government a diplomatic representative as soon as the President has had an opportunity to designate such representative.

I should appreciate it if you could find it possible to communicate this information to General Carranza at your earliest convenience.[50]

The Secretary of State next informed the diplomatic corps at Washington of his action, wired the news to American embassies and legations throughout the world, and sent instructions to the American agent at Carranza's headquarters to convey the tidings to the First Chief in a formal ceremony. Finally, before the day was finished, he issued a proclamation, which the President had already signed, forbidding the export of munitions to Mexico,[51] together with a supplementary order from the White House exempting the *de facto* government from the operation of the embargo.[52]

The news, meanwhile, had spread rapidly through Mexico almost as soon as Lansing sent his letter to Arredondo. Carranza was at his field headquarters in the Hotel Salvador in Torréon. He received official notification from the American Special Agent, John W. Belt, in a simple ceremony that began at about six p.m. on October 19.[53] In Mexico City bells in the cathedral, screaming whistles, and fireworks signaled the receipt of the news, while the newspapers appeared in American colors on the following morning, October 20. The most moving ceremony of all took place in Veracruz at six o'clock in

[49] Carranza had sent word to Washington that he preferred not to be called "President," as he was in fact not President of Mexico but "in charge of the Executive power of the Republic." Special Agent J. W. Belt to the Secretary of State, October 19, 1915, *Foreign Relations, 1915*, p. 770.

[50] The Secretary of State to E. Arredondo, October 19, 1915, *ibid.*, p. 771.

[51] Printed in *ibid.*, pp. 772-773.

[52] It was W.W. to W. G. McAdoo, October 19, 1915, Wilson Papers.

[53] Special Agent Belt to the Secretary of State, October 19, 1915, *Foreign Relations, 1915*, p. 773.

the evening on the same day. The American battleships outside the harbor raised the Mexican flag and fired a salute of twenty-one guns. They were answered immediately by the gunboat *Zaragoza*, which ran up the American flag and returned the salute as enthusiastically if not as loudly.[54] At the same place only seventeen months before had occurred the American attack on Mexican territory which had caused the rupture of diplomatic relations between the two countries.

Did it mean the beginning of a new era of cordial relations between the two republics of North America? This much, certainly, was clear by mid-October of 1915: The recognition of Carranza signified that the leaders in Washington had finally admitted the futility of their own hopes and plans to lead the Mexican people into the paths of peace and self-government. President Wilson must have looked back over events in Mexico since the beginning of the civil war in August 1914 with mixed feelings. Of personal frustration and even bitterness, because his own well-meant offers of assistance had always been rejected. Of pessimism, because even now he had no confidence in Carranza and in his ability to reconstruct Mexico. But perhaps also of relief and even of vindication, because he had (at least since Veracruz) somehow managed to avoid military involvement and consequent disaster, and because he had almost singlehandedly kept the door open for the adoption of policies that bore some relation to reality.

[54] *New York Times*, October 20 and 21, 1915.

CHAPTER XIX

The Brink of War: The Second *Arabic* Crisis

EVENTS in the German-American dispute took an unexpected turn while Carranza was pushing his last great offensive against Villa in northern Mexico. The first week in September 1915 found the American people basking in the afterglow of the *Arabic* pledge, confident that a resolution of the submarine controversy was near at hand. The afterglow dimmed suddenly and turned chill; and by mid-September the nation was once again on the brink of war with Germany, with not much hope of a peaceful solution in sight. "An evil star seems to hang over German-American negotiations on the submarine war," Ambassador von Bernstorff ruefully reported to Berlin on September 8, 1915. "Every time one seems to have reached the goal a new incident occurs to prevent further progress."[1] He was referring to two events that had revived the tension since his giving of the *Arabic* pledge exactly one week before.

The first was an incident that again stirred the American public's alarm and the administration's anger over Teutonic propaganda and meddling in domestic affairs, which had just begun to abate after the Albert affair and the exposure to official view of the Rintelen mission. It happened in the following way:

On August 19, 1915, von Bernstorff, Doctor Konstantin Theodor Dumba, the Austro-Hungarian Ambassador to the United States, and James F. J. Archibald, an American correspondent in the pay of the German Embassy,[2] sat at dinner in a New York hotel. Archibald was

[1] Ambassador von Bernstorff to T. von Bethmann Hollweg, September 8, 1915, German F. O. Archives.

[2] We find Bernstorff complaining as late as October 1916 that he was still having to carry Archibald on his payroll. Archibald, the Ambassador wrote to the Foreign Office in Berlin, was one of the "many more or less honourable persons employed by us in the course of this long war." "'The spirits that one summons from the deep cannot again be got rid of,'" he continued. "These people make themselves useful at first, and in the end for the most part then become mere beggars." Ambassador von Bernstorff to the Foreign Office, October 7, 1916, among the intercepted wireless messages in the Page Papers.

sailing for Europe the following day on the *Rotterdam* and had come to collect a package of bulky documents which he was taking to Berlin and Vienna for various Teutonic agents. While the three men were eating, apparently, a long memorandum arrived for Dumba from one Martin Diennes, alias William Warm, New York correspondent for the Cleveland *Szabadság* (*Freedom*), a Hungarian-American newspaper. It outlined an elaborate plan to stimulate strikes and walkouts among munitions and steel factories from Bethlehem, Pennsylvania, to Chicago. The best strategy, Diennes suggested, would be to use the foreign-language press, paid agitators, and as many union officials as could be bribed to stir the workers' discontent against low wages and bad working conditions.[3]

Dumba read this memorandum with growing enthusiasm. His government had recently instructed him to warn all Austro-Hungarian subjects in the United States that it was an act of treason, punishable by imprisonment or death by hanging, for them to work in any factory that manufactured war matériel for the enemies of the Fatherland. Diennes' plan, Dumba thought, could be carried out cheaply and safely; and it offered a means of at least beginning an attack on the munitions factories. The Ambassador therefore decided to add the Diennes memorandum to the other documents that Archibald was carrying. Then the following morning, August 20, Dumba hastily penned a covering letter to Count Stephan Burián von Rajecz and gave it to the American correspondent before he sailed. "I would like," he wrote to the Foreign Minister in Vienna, "to use this rare, safe opportunity to recommend the [Diennes] proposals most warmly to Your Excellency's favorable consideration. I am under the impression that we could, if not entirely prevent the production of war materials in Bethlehem and the Middle West, at any rate strongly disorganize it and hold it up for months, which, according to the statement of the German Military Attaché, is of great importance, and which amply outweighs the relatively small sacrifice of money. . . . I beg Your Excellency kindly to inform me through wireless reply with respect to this letter, whether you approve of same."[4]

After an uneventful crossing the *Rotterdam* called at Falmouth on August 30. There British naval authorities searched Archibald's cabin, seized the documents in his possession, and arrested him on the flimsy

[3] This memorandum is printed in *Foreign Relations, 1915, Supplement*, pp. 936-938.
[4] K. Dumba to Count Burián, August 20, 1915, translation printed in the *New York Times*, September 10, 1915.

charge of performing an unneutral act. The correspondent was only briefly detained, but the documents went straight to London, where authorities lost no time in giving copies of most of them to Ambassador Page and a copy of Dumba's letter to Burián to the press.[5]

News of the affair broke in the United States on September 6, when the newspapers published the substance of Dumba's letter and the Ambassador's own rather bland admission that he had indeed written it. "There are thousands of workingmen in the big steel industries, natives of Bohemia, Moravia, Carniola, Galicia, Dalmatia, Croatia, Slavonia, and other peoples of the races from Austria-Hungary, who are uneducated and who do not understand that they are engaged in a work against their own country," Dumba told reporters at his summer residence at Lenox, Massachusetts, on September 5. "In order to bring this before them, I have subsidized many newspapers published in the languages and dialects of the divisions mentioned. . . . But this has been difficult. In some of the great steel plants of Pennsylvania these uneducated men of my country are nothing more or less than slaves. . . . It is difficult to get at these workers except en masse, and a peaceful walkout of these workingmen would be of the greatest advantage to my Government."[6]

To most Americans it was all enormously shocking. The Albert documents had revealed a network of German propaganda within their midst. Now here was further evidence that the Austrians and the Germans, too, for the German Military Attaché, Captain von Papen, was heavily implicated in the plot, would not hesitate to disrupt the country's economic life and disturb its domestic peace if they could serve their interests by so doing. The American government, editors throughout the country agreed, should give Dumba his passports at once. "In the whole history of our relations with foreign countries," the *New York Times* declared, for example, "there has never been another diplomatic representative at our national capital who has in such an open and unabashed way taken measures to make himself

[5] Ambassador Page to the Secretary of State, September 1, 1915, transmitting a translation of Dumba's letter, *Foreign Relations, 1915, Supplement*, pp. 932-933; Ambassador Page to the Secretary of State, September 3, 1915, transmitting translations of other documents, *ibid.*, pp. 936-941; *New York Times*, September 10, 1915, printing the full text of Dumba's letter to Count Burián; and *ibid.*, September 22, 1915, printing the text of most of the dispatches that had been seized from Archibald as they had appeared in a parliamentary paper published on September 21, 1915.
[6] *New York Times*, September 6, 1915.

altogether unacceptable."[7] Nor did the furor altogether end when
Dumba was dismissed, for the *New York Times* and particularly the
New York *World* shortly afterward printed further evidence of widespread intrigues and activities by Austro-Hungarian editors and Consuls throughout the Middle West.[8]

Wilson and Lansing had reacted with an acerbity that revealed their
own sensitivity. Their feeling toward Dumba was none too charitable
to begin with, for the Foreign Office in Vienna had recently submitted a fervent public protest against the export of American munitions to the Allies—an obvious attempt, like Bernstorff's earlier effort,
to support the movement in the United States for an arms embargo—
and Lansing had returned a stinging reply aimed at bringing this discussion to an end.[9] Although Dumba was not directly involved, the
Washington leaders must have suspected that he was responsible for
the blast from Vienna. Moreover, Lansing had by now developed a
considerable personal dislike of the Austrian diplomat. He was, the
Secretary of State wrote not long afterward, the most wily and untrustworthy member of the diplomatic corps in Washington: "A natural-
born intriguer he doubtless found congenial occupation in conspiring
and plotting, and to these nefarious enterprises . . . he appears to have
assiduously devoted his peculiar talents."[10]

Lansing sent a copy of Page's dispatch transmitting the text of
Dumba's letter to the White House as soon as it arrived in his office
on September 2. "It seems to me," the Secretary wrote in an accompanying comment, "that the conduct of the Ambassador is of a very
serious nature and that we should consider at once what steps should
be taken in regard to it."[11] There was no doubt about the seriousness
of Dumba's offense, Wilson replied, any more than there was about
Bernstorff's implication in all such plots against American neutrality.
The only question was when and how to take action against *both*

---

[7] *ibid.*, September 7, 1915. See also the New York *World*, September 7, 1915; *New
Republic*, IV (September 11, 1915), 136; and the review of press opinion in the *Literary Digest*, LI (September 18, 1915), 573-574.

[8] *New York Times*, September 11, 1915; New York *World*, September 15 and 17,
1915.

[9] Ambassador Penfield to the Secretary of State, July 2, 1915; the Secretary of State
to Ambassador Penfield, August 12, 1915, *Foreign Relations, 1915, Supplement*, pp. 790-
798; *New York Times*, July 16, August 16, 1915. R. Lansing, *War Memoirs*, pp. 55-62,
gives a detailed account of the drafting of the reply to the Foreign Office in Vienna.

[10] "Constantin Theodor Dumba," in notes dated May 1916, in the Lansing Papers.

[11] R. Lansing to W.W., September 2, 1915, *The Lansing Papers*, I, 79.

culprits. It would, he went on, probably be better to wait until the German government had made full settlement in the *Arabic* dispute. "As for the How, what do you think would be the best course, a private intimation to each of them which would allow them to ask to be relieved, without public rebuke, or a direct request on our part to their Governments? I do not know the practice in these matters."[12]

The answer became clear enough once the story of Dumba's indiscretion appeared in the American newspapers on September 6. American opinion, the President and Secretary of State apparently agreed on the following day, would be satisfied with nothing less than a demand for Dumba's immediate recall, and one unceremoniously made. To dismiss Bernstorff at this point, which Wilson was still eager to do, would, however, be a more difficult matter. As Lansing must have pointed out, the American government really had no evidence upon which to base any serious charges against the German Ambassador; and, as Wilson himself admitted, it would be hard to ask for Bernstorff's recall without giving the impression of a diplomatic breach.[13] There was no alternative, therefore, but to let Bernstorff and other German officials like von Papen escape for the time being, and to make as much capital as possible out of the Dumba affair.

Lansing moved as quickly as he could and ruthlessly, but he had promised Dumba a hearing, and he could not act before going through this formality. The Austrian Ambassador came down from Lenox for a long conference at the State Department in the afternoon of September 7 and did his best to make amends.[14] But Lansing was not moved to charity. "He is evidently very much distressed because of what has occurred," the Secretary reported to the President after Dumba had left, "but I do not think he really repents of his action; he only deplores the fact that he was found out."[15] "I see no alternative," Wilson replied in agreement the next morning, September 8," but to follow the course we decided on yesterday."[16] And so Lansing at once prepared the note asking the Foreign Office to recall its envoy "on account of his im-

[12] W.W. to R. Lansing, September 3, 1915, *ibid.*, p. 80.

[13] W.W. to E. M. House, September 7, 1915, Baker Collection.

[14] Not merely orally but also by bringing a memorandum attempting to explain. See "Memorandum by the Austro-Hungarian Ambassador," *The Lansing Papers*, I, 81-82.

[15] R. Lansing to W.W., September 7, 1915, *ibid.*, p. 81; also R. Lansing, *War Memoirs*, pp. 64-66. For detailed press accounts of this interview, see the *New York Times*, September 8, 1915, and New York *World*, September 8, 1915.

[16] W.W. to R. Lansing, September 8, 1915, *The Lansing Papers*, I, 82.

proper conduct"; Wilson walked over to the State Department in the late morning, read Lansing's draft, and added a final phrase assuring the Imperial and Royal government that the Washington authorities sincerely desired to maintain "cordial and friendly" relations; and Lansing dispatched the note to Vienna at four o'clock in the afternoon and gave it to the press on the following day, September 9.[17] Dumba left for home as soon as the State Department had made arrangements for his safe passage, still in a huff over the treatment he had received[18] and still unrepentant. "As to the unfortunate incident which is the cause of my departure I was certainly wrong," he wrote to Colonel House, "because I made the mistake of being found out."[19]

Dismissing Dumba purged some of Wilson's and Lansing's ill humor over Teutonic intrigues and espionage.[20] But only briefly could their thoughts run undisturbed by reports of alien subversion. Not more than a few days after the dismissal of Dumba the New York *World* published the first account of the attempts by Rintelen and other German agents to gain control of the Longshoremen's Union and provoke dock strikes in various port cities.[21] At about the same time additional new evidence of German intrigues with Huerta and other counterrevolutionary Mexican leaders came to the Secretary of State from London, in papers taken from Rintelen at the time of his arrest and sent on by Ambassador Page.[22] "I have just heard full details," the New

---

[17] The Secretary of State to Ambassador Penfield, September 8, 1915, *Foreign Relations, 1915, Supplement,* pp. 933-934; *New York Times,* September 9 and 10, 1915; New York *World,* September 10, 1915.

[18] In his haste to finish the business, Lansing apparently neglected to inform Dumba that the State Department was requesting his recall. The Austrian struck back in a public letter to the Secretary of State on September 17, 1915. He did not question the American government's right to dismiss him, Dumba said. "When, however," he continued, "your Government sees fit to resort to the extraordinary and to me humiliating course of preferring charges against me to my Government, without advising me of the intended action or even intimating that such action is contemplated and to request my recall upon those charges as confessed, while at the same time refusing me permission even to communicate privately with my Government, I respectfully protest against such action as unjust to me and contrary to diplomatic usage." K. T. Dumba to R. Lansing, September 17, 1915, *New York Times,* September 19, 1915.

[19] K. T. Dumba to E. M. House, September 23, 1915, House Papers.

[20] e.g., see W.W. to R. Lansing, September 15, 1915, *The Lansing Papers,* I, 83.

[21] New York *World,* September 13, 1915. This was the first time that the newspapers had published anything about Rintelen's *activities.* However, the author of this article knew nothing about Rintelen and did not connect him with the events about which he was writing. Wilson and Lansing of course knew.

[22] Charles Warren, Assistant Attorney General, to R. Lansing, September 15, 1915, Lansing Papers, summarizing "the papers sent to this [the Justice] Department yes-

York publisher and sometime correspondent, Oswald Garrison Villard, wrote after talking confidentially to Lansing on September 15. "It is really alarming. The Germans were behind the Huerta uprising & some have actually been collecting & storing arms."[23] Then ten days later there was new confidential revelation of the propaganda work of the German Embassy in Washington and a further hint of the Embassy's intrigues in Latin America.[24]

By such blundering and continuing intrigue did the Austrian and German envoys and agents help to perpetuate the German-American tension at the very time that the dispute over the *Arabic* was being renewed.

The second event to which Bernstorff referred in his letter to Bethmann on September 8, 1915, seemed to be even more menacing to the

---

terday with reference to the arrest of Rintelen in England [Ambassador Page's No 2081 with enclosures]." The latter brackets are in the original text.

[23] O. G. Villard to J. P. Gavit, September 15, 1915, Villard Papers.

[24] This came from Page on September 25, 1915. Ambassador Gerard, a few days before, had inadvertently (he said) opened a large package in the diplomatic pouch from Washington addressed by Ambassador von Bernstorff to the Foreign Office. "In accordance with his custom in opening correspondence, [Gerard] did not tear envelopes or break seals of this parcel but detached bottom flap of envelope without it." Examination quickly revealed the highly important character of the contents, and Gerard sent Alexander Kirk, Third Secretary of the American Embassy in Berlin, to London so that he could safely ask the State Department what to do. Kirk described the contents of the package as follows:

"Package found to contain statements in duplicate of accounts of German Embassy in Washington together with supporting vouchers in the original or certified copy. Vouchers show that $5,000 was paid to Archibald for propaganda, $4,500 to Marcus Braun, editor of *Fairplay*, $3,000 to Miss Ray Beveridge for a lecture tour and $1,000 to Edwin Emerson for traveling expenses. In addition statements from the Western Union Telegraph Cable Company contain names of persons in the United States and elsewhere to whom messages were sent by the German Embassy as well as purpose of message, whether propaganda or official business. These statements show also the bill for cables to Bogotá from April 1 to the 10th amounted to over $4,000 and to Guatemala $3,000 and to Shanghai $2,000. Large sums spent in cables to Mexico City, Manila, Honolulu, Haiti and Buenos Aires in that paper appear to furnish authentic list of all kinds German agents in the United States and elsewhere and also indicate extent and direction of German propaganda." Telegram by A. Kirk, transmitted in Ambassador Page to the Secretary of State, September 25, 1915, *Foreign Relations, 1915, Supplement*, pp. 942-943; decoded personally by the Secretary of State. See R. Lansing to W.W., September 27, 1915, Wilson Papers.

At Lansing's instruction Kirk brought the documents to Washington, where they were presumably photographed. He then took the package back to Berlin, where Gerard was able to deliver it, all properly sealed, to the Foreign Office without arousing any suspicion. See R. Lansing to W.W., October 21, 1915, *ibid*.

German-American peace than the Dumba affair and the further revelations of German intrigue. It was another wanton submarine attack
on a passenger liner only three days after the giving of the *Arabic*
pledge. The Allan liner *Hesperian*, 10,920 tons, bound from Liverpool
to Montreal with some 650 persons aboard and armed with a six-inch
gun on the stern, was heavily damaged by an explosion on the starboard side at 8:30 in the evening of September 4 about eighty-eight miles
southwest of Fastnet. The ship stayed afloat for thirty-four hours, but
eight persons were apparently killed by the detonation. Only one American citizen, a member of the crew, was aboard; he was unhurt. It was
nearly dark, and no one saw any sign of a submarine or even of a torpedo
track in the water. However, the ship's officers swore that the steel
fragments that rained upon the deck when the explosion occurred
were definitely from a torpedo and not a mine.[25]

For a moment it seemed that a really dangerous crisis impended.
The first report from the American Consul on the scene told of a torpedoing by a German submarine,[26] and American newspapers, while
printing this dispatch on September 6, carried headlines announcing
an underwater attack at night without warning.[27] In Washington the
President and Secretary of State tried to reserve judgment until all the
facts were in, but they were shocked and disappointed that a new incident should take place just when it seemed that the *Arabic* case was
about to be happily settled.[28] "My thought just now is full, of course,
of this *Hesperian* business," Wilson wrote in despair to Colonel House
on September 7. "It looks, I fear, as if it were going to be extremely
difficult to get at any real facts in the case; and yet the facts are essential to any intelligent handling of the case. Shall we ever get out of
the labyrinth made for us all by this German 'frightfulness'?"[29]

The crisis, if such it can be called, ended before it could seriously
imperil the final *Arabic* negotiations that were in progress between
Washington and Berlin. Lansing sent an urgent inquiry to the German

---

[25] Consul Wesley Frost at Cork to the Secretary of State, received September 7, 1915,
transmitting affidavit of the officers of the *Hesperian* dated September 6, 1915, *Foreign
Relations, 1915, Supplement*, pp. 534-535.

[26] Consul Frost to the Secretary of State, September 5, 1915, *ibid.*, pp. 533-534.

[27] e.g., *New York Times*, September 6, 1915.

[28] As one of them seems to have told reporters on September 6, *ibid.*, September 7,
1915.

[29] W.W. to E. M. House, September 7, 1915, Baker Collection. See also W.W. to F. K.
Lane, September 7, 1915, and W.W. to L. C. Woods, September 7, 1915, Wilson Papers.

Foreign Office on September 7.[30] Before this message arrived, however, the leaders in the German capital had already sent public and official assurances to America, saying that as far as the Admiralty knew no German submarine was operating off Fastnet on September 4, and that it seemed highly improbable that the *Hesperian* had been torpedoed and altogether likely that it had struck a mine.[31] The Foreign Office repeated this same message a week later; then on September 23 it reported that it was now possible to say with certainty that no German submarine could have attacked the *Hesperian*.[32] Officials in Washington apparently still (and rightly) thought otherwise, but the State Department did not have enough evidence to challenge the German denial.[33] As we will soon see, the *Hesperian* incident did not come and go without having some impact on the development of the larger German-American dispute over submarine warfare.

The big question following the giving of the *Arabic* pledge on September 1 was how long the President and Secretary of State would wait for the Imperial government's formal disavowal of Commander Schneider's deed. Lansing feared that the German authorities might add delay to delay, giving as an excuse the fact, which by this time seemed to be fairly well established, that the *U24* had herself been sunk by a British ship, and that consequently they could obtain no reliable information about the regrettable affair. A letter from Bernstorff to Lansing on September 3, saying that the only submarine which could have sunk the *Arabic* had not yet returned to its home base,[34] tended to confirm the suspicion.

[30] The Secretary of State to Ambassador Gerard, September 7, 1915, *Foreign Relations, 1915, Supplement*, p. 537.

[31] K. II. von Wiegand, dispatch from Berlin dated September 7, in New York *World*, September 8, 1915; the Foreign Office to Ambassador von Bernstorff, September 7, 1915, German F. O. Archives, transmitted in the German Ambassador to the Secretary of State, September 8, 1915, *The Lansing Papers*, I, 476.

[32] Ambassador Gerard to the Secretary of State, September 14 and 24, 1915, *Foreign Relations, 1915, Supplement*, pp. 548-549, 556.

[33] See the Secretary of State to Ambassador Page, November 1, 1915, *ibid.*, p. 607. The truth was later revealed by Admiral Spindler, the German naval historian. The *Hesperian* had indeed been attacked without warning by none other than Commander Walter Schwieger of the *U20*. He fired his torpedo on what seemed to him to be the well-grounded assumption that the *Hesperian* was an auxiliary cruiser. Spindler, *La Guerre Sous-Marine*, II, 336-337.

[34] The German Ambassador to the Secretary of State, September 3, 1915, *Foreign Relations, 1915, Supplement*, p. 533.

Lansing was fast losing patience. "I do not feel that we should wait very long for an explanation in regard to the *Arabic*," he wrote to the President as he sent Bernstorff's letter on for his perusal, "and I am inclined to answer the Ambassador to that effect."[35] When two days passed without bringing any further word from Bernstorff or from the President, Lansing's thoughts began to turn to a somewhat desperate plan of action. It was, apparently, the news of the torpedoing of the *Hesperian* on September 6 that convinced him that he must implement his plan forthwith. As he explained in a memorandum for his Diary on that day:

"I am sure that only strong words will force the German Government to admit liability [in the *Arabic* case] and give guarantees for the future. If at this time we employ mild language, it will be credited to weakness or at least to doubt of popular support. . . . I have, in view of the circumstances, come to the conclusion that it is necessary to 'take the bull by the horns' and put the matter up to the German Ambassador so firmly and emphatically that he will be convinced that, unless his Government repudiates the brutal act of its submarine commander in attacking the *Arabic* and promises not to repeat the offense, it will probably mean war.

"I shall not seek the President's authorization to take this radical course because, if it fails, it may be desirable for him to repudiate my words and to declare that I was not empowered to go so far as to threaten war. I am satisfied, however, that only a blunt statement to Bernstorff will bring results. Believing this my duty seems plain. I must take the personal risk of being humilated in case this course fails, since it appears to be the only way to avoid national humiliation for Germany will certainly continue her submarine war unless she fears that we will resist with force."[36]

Such a maneuver might conceivably have brought Lansing's tenure to an abrupt end. It was fortunate for him, therefore, that events developed as they did during the next few days. To begin with, the President, although he agreed that the American government could not permit the Germans to "wait too long to state their attitude and the course they intend to pursue with regard to the sinking of the

[35] R. Lansing to W.W., September 4, 1915, *The Lansing Papers*, I, 475.

[36] "Embarrassment of Action in the Arabic Case," Lansing Diary, September 5, 1915. In his *War Memoirs*, pp. 45-46, Lansing falsified the date of this memorandum—it was written, he said, on August 25—in order to give the impression that he took this firm stand during the early stage of the *Arabic* crisis.

Arabic," insisted that Lansing take no action until all the facts about the "sinking" of the *Hesperian* were clear.[37] Then, while the leaders in Washington waited for news of that incident, a message from Berlin about the *Arabic* arrived on September 9, 1915. It renewed the submarine crisis in a startling way, and Secretary Lansing was subsequently able to take the United States to the brink of war with the President's full knowledge and approval, and without having to run the risks of a private *démarche*. What occurred to bring the crisis to this final head can be briefly told.

Commander Schneider returned to his base at Wilhelmshaven on August 26 and sent a detailed report on his destruction of the *Arabic* to the Admiralty on September 2. Perhaps he was appalled when he learned what havoc he had caused; perhaps his fellow-officers and superiors made him understand that much—indeed, everything—depended upon his report. Whatever the reason, the U-boat captain now told a story somewhat different from the one that he had recorded in his log on the morning of August 19, 1915. Then he had written a simple recital of simple facts—how he had sunk the British steamer *Dunsley* by cannon fire, had sighted a large vessel and submerged for the attack, had seen the large steamer head toward the straits where the *Dunsley* was sinking, and had fired his torpedo and sunk the still unidentified ship.[38] Writing on September 2, Schneider added some important new details—that the large steamer, while approaching the *Dunsley*, had turned sharply toward the *U24*, and that he, Schneider, had fired his torpedo in the belief that the steamer was attempting to ram him.[39]

With Schneider's report in hand, the Imperial Chancellor and Foreign Secretary set to work to draft what they thought would be their definitive declaration about the *Arabic* affair to the American government. Their task was not an easy one. The Washington authorities had demanded that they disavow and punish Commander Schneider. But upon the basis of his own testimony the commander did not deserve punishment; moreover, there simply were no grounds for an official public apology to the United States. Bethmann and von Jagow could not have contemplated making such apology even had they doubted Schneider's veracity. The risks of provoking a battle over the honor of the navy, which they would inevitably lose; of embarrassing

---

[37] W.W. to R. Lansing, September 7, 1915, *The Lansing Papers*, I, 475.

[38] Spindler, *La Guerre Sous-Marine*, II, 335.

[39] *ibid.*, pp. 346-347, prints Schneider's report of September 2, 1915, in full.

the conciliatory new Chief of the Admiralty, Admiral Henning von Holtzendorff; and of completely alienating an already inflamed public opinion[40] were too great. But these considerations were largely irrelevant anyway, for Bethmann and von Jagow accepted Schneider's report as of course an honest one. They would go to great lengths to conciliate the United States, they must have told themselves, but not to the length of dishonoring themselves, the Imperial navy, and the German nation by craven surrender.

Thus the note that von Jagow handed to Gerard on September 7, although phrased in friendly language, repudiated all the American contentions and demands. The submarine commander, it said, had believed that the *Arabic* was about to attack him. "In order to anticipate this attack he gave orders to have the submarine submerge and fired a torpedo at the steamer." "The German government," the note concluded, "most deeply regrets that lives were lost through the action of the commander. It particularly expresses this regret to the Government of the United States on account of the death of American citizens. The German Government is unable, however, to acknowledge any obligation to grant indemnity in the matter, even if the commander should have been mistaken as to the aggressive intentions of the *Arabic*. If it should prove to be the case that it is impossible for the German and American Government to reach a harmonious opinion on this point, the German Government would be prepared to submit the difference of opinion as being a question of international law to the Hague tribunals. . . . In so doing it assumes that as a matter of course the arbitral decision shall not be admitted to have the importance of a general decision on the permissibility or the converse under international law of German submarine warfare."[41]

Published in the American press on September 9 and 10, the Foreign Office's refusal to make any amends set off a storm of denunciations and demands for the immediate severance of diplomatic relations with the German Empire by editors already distraught by news of German and Austrian intrigues within the United States. "Suspend diplomatic

[40] The publication of Bernstorff's letter to Secretary Lansing of September 1, 1915, in the German press on September 2 and 3 had set off a wave of angry editorial criticism of the Imperial Chancellor and his subordinates. See, e.g., the Berlin *Kreuz-Zeitung*, September 3, 1915; Berlin *Vossische Zeitung*, morning edn., September 6, 1915; Berlin *Taegliche Rundschau*, morning edn., September 6, 1915.

[41] Ambassador Gerard to the Secretary of State, September 7, 1915, *Foreign Relations, 1915, Supplement*, pp. 539-540.

relations!" the New York *World* declared roundly. "A Government that violates international law in general, that violates its treaties with the United States, . . . that systematically violates American neutrality and conspires against the domestic welfare of the American people, may safely be expected to violate all further engagements into which it enters. German faith is quicksand which engulfs everything that trusts in its treachery."[42] "The Arabic memorandum," Ambassador von Bernstorff reported to Berlin on September 13, "has caused a tremendous storm."[43]

The German note arrived at the State Department on September 9, at a particularly unpropitious moment. Administration leaders were already upset by the *Hesperian* incident and the Dumba affair. Washington was in the midst of an almost unendurable heat wave, and there were signs that Wilson, if not Lansing, was in poor condition for another crisis. The President, one keen reporter wrote a few days later, "has felt the heat terribly, and his nerves are frayed, for the first time, so that [Doctor Cary T.] Grayson is making desperate efforts to get him away. . . . The truth is they are all tired out with the thing."[44] We have further revelation of Wilson's mood at this time, among other things, in the comments that he penciled on copies of reports from Gerard as he sent them on for Mrs. Galt to read:

"Is not Gerard extraordinary? He repeats nothing but gossip—and *seems* to intimate that we are being taken in." (About September 2)

"Ordinarily our Ambassador ought to be backed up as of course, but—this ass? It is hard to take it seriously." (September 10)

"Who can fathom this? I wish they would hand this idiot his passports!" (September 11)

Wilson's and Lansing's suspicions of German duplicity were confirmed by a startling dispatch from Gerard that arrived at the State Department early in the afternoon of September 10, 1915. Summarizing the opinions of the American Naval Attaché in Berlin, Walter R. Gherardi, Gerard reported: "The remarkable change in the German attitude between Bernstorff's statement and the last German note regarding the *Arabic* arises from a decision having been reached to follow naval policy rather than the policy of the Foreign Office and to

[42] New York *World*, September 14, 1915.

[43] Ambassador von Bernstorff to T. von Bethmann Hollweg, September 13, 1915; also Ambassador von Bernstorff to the Foreign Office, September 14, 1915, German F. O. Archives.

[44] O. G. Villard to J. P. Gavit, September 15, 1915, Villard Papers.

give no guarantees that the submarine warfare will in any way be modified." Submarine losses as a result of attacks by English warships and armed merchantmen, Gerard went on, had recently been so heavy that the German naval leaders had told "the general Government that to follow the policy laid down for submarine warfare would mean total failure of that method of warfare, involving the destruction of the German submarine fleet." These facts, Gerard concluded, "were used by the Navy to influence the Government and . . . were successful in reversing the policy as laid down by Bernstorff in his conversation and note."[45] It mattered not that this report was wholly inaccurate; it mattered only that the President and Secretary of State believed that it was true, and that they read it in conjunction with the German note.

In a long letter to the President on September 11, Lansing set down his reactions and conclusions as to what the American government should do. He had, he wrote, been through the German note and the affidavits that the State Department had recently received from the survivors of the *Arabic* and the *Dunsley*. The evidence indicated clearly that the submarine commander could not have believed that the *Arabic* was trying to ram him and that he had wantonly attacked the ship without warning. The German authorities should have been able to determine this fact from the newspaper reports alone. "The whole tenor of the note," the Secretary continued, "is a cold and uncompromising declaration that the commanders of submarines have practically a free hand though bound, technically, by some general form of instructions, and that if they make mistakes, however unwarranted, their Government will support them. It seems to me that we must reach a conclusion that the Bernstorff statement of principle is valueless and cannot be relied upon as a protective measure." If this were true, Lansing concluded, then the American government must either peremptorily and publicly demand that the German authorities disavow and punish the submarine commander, or else sever diplomatic relations at once. Any further discussion would be contrary to the dignity of the United States.[46]

Wilson, obviously, agreed with Lansing that the German reply made a mockery of the *Arabic* pledge. "This," he wrote on a draft of the note after he had finished reading it on September 10, "seems to me so obviously disingenuous that I am still further impressed with the

[45] Ambassador Gerard to the Secretary of State, September 9, 1915, *Foreign Relations, 1915, Supplement*, p. 543.
[46] R. Lansing to W.W., September 11, 1915, *The Lansing Papers*, I, 478-480.

feeling that Bernstorff has been misleading us. What is there for the Hague under the terms of this note?[47] The President also agreed that the American government would have to demand an open disavowal and could tolerate no undue delay in Berlin. As he put it in a letter to Colonel House on September 20:

"Bernstorff is evidently anxious to get his government off from any explicit or formal disavowal of the Arabic offence; but I do not see how we can with self-respect do that. The country would consider us 'too easy' for words, and any general avowal of a better purpose on their part utterly untrustworthy. Do you not think so?

"They are moving with intentional, and most exasperating slowness in the whole matter. I fear that when they have gained the time they need, for example in the Balkans, they will resume their reckless operations at sea, and we shall be back of where we started."[48]

He would, therefore, press for this disavowal as a test of German good faith even to the point of threatening a break in diplomatic relations and possible war. "Much to my surprise," Colonel House recorded in his Diary after talking with Wilson on September 22, 1915, "he said he had never been sure that we ought not to take part in the conflict and if it seemed evident that Germany and her militaristic ideas were to win, the obligation upon us was greater than ever."[49]

Resolved though he was to go all the way with the Germans and to accept even the risk of hostilities, the President was not quite ready to follow Lansing's lead in making a formal public demand for disavowal or in severing diplomatic relations immediately. Either step, Wilson must have realized, would mean abandoning diplomacy and inviting war. And this he could not bring himself to do. The country trusted him to keep the peace too much for him to betray that trust; besides, in spite of momentary irritations, he was himself determined to avoid a violent recourse if that were possible. "The country is undoubtedly back of me in the whole matter," he wrote to Colonel House on September 20, in the letter just cited, "and I feel myself under bonds to it to show patience to the utmost. My chief puzzle is to determine where patience ceases to be a virtue."

Wilson replied to Lansing's letter of September 11 orally, perhaps by telephone on that day or the next. We have no record of their con-

---

[47] Penciled comment on copy of Ambassador Gerard to the Secretary of State, No. 2855, September 7, 1915, Wilson Papers.

[48] W.W. to E. M. House, September 20, 1915, Baker Collection.

[49] House Diary, September 22, 1915.

versation, but events immediately ensuing make clear enough what the President instructed Lansing to do. It was to stand firm and insist upon a disavowal and a definitive restatement of the *Arabic* pledge, so as to secure German compliance with American demands for the protection of passenger ships, but to do this with all becoming patience and inoffensiveness, in order to give the German government one last chance. It was one of the most important decisions that the President made during the entire period of American neutrality, for it meant that peace between Germany and the United States was at least still possible.

Consequently, when Ambassador von Bernstorff, startled by newspaper reports of the administration's anger over the German note,[50] requested an early conference with the Secretary of State,[51] Lansing agreed readily enough. Bernstorff hastened from his summer house at Cedarhurst, Long Island, on September 12 and went to the State Department on the following day. The Secretary was suave and seemingly sympathetic and made it clear that the American government was prepared to endure another round of negotiations in order to find a peaceful solution. He would be glad, Lansing said, to send a summary of the evidence that he had on hand relating to the sinking of the *Arabic* to the Foreign Office in Berlin. Negotiations were better conducted privately than in the newspapers, he went on; therefore, he was willing to permit the Ambassador and the German Foreign Secretary to communicate with each other in their own code over the State Department's wire. At the same time, Lansing made it clear, the American government viewed the German note of September 7 as a virtual repudiation of the *Arabic* pledge, demanded a full clarification of German assurances to the United States[52] and a disavowal of the submarine commander, and would sever diplomatic relations if

[50] e.g., *New York Times*, September 11, 1915; New York *World*, September 11, 1915.

[51] "The press reports about the Arabic case are so alarming," Bernstorff wrote to Colonel House on September 11, "that I will have to go to Washington again, although Mr. Lansing has not yet expressed the wish to see me. If there is any truth to the newspaper reports, the situation looks very serious and I will as 'ultima ratio' have to try to see the President again." J. von Bernstorff to E. M. House, September 11, 1915, House Papers.

[52] At this point Lansing *suggested* that it might be well for the German government to consider broadening the *Arabic* pledge to include all merchantmen, since submarines had often warned merchantmen before attacking them and some of the freighters might have Americans aboard.

these demands were not satisfied.[53] As Bernstorff reported to the Foreign Office:

"The Government over here . . . [believes] that a further exchange, which would be published immediately and misinterpreted in both countries, would lead to a rupture. It believes that the only way to gain an agreement is by the way of confidential discussions with me. This would be the only possible way out. The Arabic memorandum has in part been misunderstood here and in part has been viewed as an example of German bad faith. They believe here that we were willing to yield in principle but that we make nothing but evasions in practice. . . . In order to reach a *total* understanding, it would first be necessary to empower me here once more to publish the instructions to the commanders which will totally exclude a repetition of similar occurrences. If, however, we have to hold to the position that the commander in the Arabic incident obeyed his instructions, then I believe that an agreement is out of the question, since confidence in the honesty of our intentions will be lacking. . . . I do not have the slightest doubt that a breach of diplomatic relations will ensue if an agreement cannot be reached.

"Lansing is not going to answer the Arabic memorandum and, as I have already said, the whole diplomatic correspondence about this question will go through me. He considers this way as *ultima ratio* on the basis that Wilson and I are bound to each other by the policy of freedom of the seas."[54]

Throughout the interview Bernstorff left no doubt that he understood the gravity of the situation. "The whole attitude of the Ambassador," Lansing added in his report to the President, "was conciliatory and an evidence of willingness to do anything to avoid a rupture between the two Governments. I think I may say he was extremely 'docile.' There was none of the aggressiveness which he has shown on other occasions. He seemed to be much depressed, and doubtful as to what he could accomplish with his Government."[55]

In order to prepare the American people for what he must have

[53] R. Lansing to W.W., September 13, 1915, *The Lansing Papers*, I, 480-481.

[54] Ambassador von Bernstorff to the Foreign Office, September 15, 1915, German F. O. Archives.

[55] R. Lansing to W.W., September 13, 1915, *The Lansing Papers*, I, 481. Cf., however, Bernstorff's statements to reporters in New York on September 15, *New York Times*, September 16, 1915, and J. von Bernstorff to E. M. House, House Papers.

thought was an inevitable break with Germany, Lansing called reporters to the State Department on September 14, 1915, and told them virtually everything that had taken place at his conference with Bernstorff on the day before. The Secretary was careful to make it plain that he had told the Ambassador that the American government would sever relations and take steps to "protect the nation's honor" if the Berlin authorities did not disavow the attack on the *Arabic* and give proper guarantees for the future.[56] President Wilson confirmed this statement on September 15, in an extraordinary off-the-record interview directed as much to the Berlin government as to his fellow-citizens. The President, White House reporters noted, was determined either to obtain the disavowal and put an end to German submarine operations insofar as they endangered American lives, or else to break diplomatic relations with Germany. He realized, reporters added, that a rupture of relations might mean war, but he would run this risk rather than budge from the position he had taken.[57] Privately, Wilson added that he was not very optimistic about the outcome but was willing to wait, in spite of the almost unbearable strain that he now felt. As he put it in letters to two friends:

"Unfortunately there is no present prospect of a clearing in this complicated German matter. Apparently they do not know how to keep faith with anybody, and we are walking on quicksand.

". . . I am well, and the only weight to business lies just now in its character rather than in its amount: it's the anxiety, not the labour, that gets under one's skin and hurts."[58]

"I must admit that I have at no time recently had any feeling of confidence that the German Government would sufficiently yield to our demands to clear the situation, but you may be sure I have not lost patience and that I shall give the matter abundant time for proof.

"Of course, wear and tear are inevitable and the fatigue of this sort of anxiety is very great, but I am still quite fit, I am happy to say, and do not doubt that I shall have the strength to stick it all out."[59]

The men at the Wilhelmstrasse had never dreamed that the President and Secretary of State would regard the German note of September 7 as a repudiation of the pledges they had given for the con-

---

[56] New York *World*, September 15, 1915; *New York Times*, September 15, 1915.
[57] New York *World*, September 16, 1915.
[58] W.W. to Lucy Smith, September 15, 1915, Baker Collection.
[59] W.W. to O. G. Villard, September 16, 1915, Villard Papers.

duct of submarine operations. They and the new Chief of the Admiralty had no intention at this time, at any rate, of resuming attacks on passenger vessels and driving the United States into the war. News of the violent American reaction to their note fell, therefore, like a bolt out of a clear sky in Berlin. "According to newspaper reports," the Foreign Secretary wired in alarm to Bernstorff, before he had received any official word from Washington, "the American Government considers our note about the Arabic insufficient and prepares new demands. We are without official information. To avoid rupture, we would be ready if absolutely necessary to accept . . . [an] international commission of inquiry according to Title 3 of The Hague Convention of the laws of 1910 [1901]. . . . Would you immediately discuss the Arabic incident personally with Wilson and, as the case may be, suggest to him the proposition mentioned above? It is absolutely necessary that you inform us about the situation by telegram."[60]

After Bernstorff's dispatch reporting his interview with Lansing and saying that the State Department was cabling a summary of its evidence on the sinking of the *Arabic* reached the Foreign Office on September 16, 1915, the Imperial Chancellor and his advisers saw clearly enough what the circumstances demanded. Reading Bernstorff's message soon after it arrived, Bethmann Hollweg concluded, even before he had seen the summary of the evidence from Washington, that the German government would have to admit that Commander Schneider had acted subjectively in good faith but had "misjudged the actual situation and acted wrongly in view of his instructions," and that the sooner this admission were made without asking for an international court of inquiry the better it would be. In addition, the Chancellor further instructed his subordinates, the Foreign Office should tell the Washington government in no uncertain terms that the Imperial government stood faithfully behind the *Arabic* pledge. He was personally willing, he added, to extend that guarantee to all merchantmen, but he did not think it would be possible to obtain the navy's agreement at the present moment.[61]

Soon afterward on the same day, September 16, the summary of the evidence from Washington arrived at the Wilhelmstrasse,[62] along, how-

[60] The Foreign Secretary to Ambassador von Bernstorff, September 13, 1915, German F. O. Archives.

[61] T. von Bethmann Hollweg, memorandum dated September 16, 1915, *ibid.*

[62] It was transmitted in the Secretary of State to Ambassador Gerard, September 14, 1915, *Foreign Relations, 1915, Supplement,* pp. 547-548.

ever, with affidavits from Commander Schneider and the crew of the *U24* testifying that the *Arabic* had indeed attempted to ram their craft, or at least that they had believed this to be the case. Meeting at the Foreign Office late in the evening, undoubtedly after consultation with the Chancellor, Foreign Secretary von Jagow, Undersecretary Arthur Zimmermann, and Count Montgelas, head of the American section, discussed the problem again in the light particularly of the new German evidence. They concluded readily enough to use all possible means of reassuring the American government about the safety of passenger ships. But an outright disavowal of Commander Schneider would not be easy. The most they could do, at least for the moment, the Foreign Office officials agreed, would be to suggest the appointment of an international commission to examine the evidence.[63]

Von Jagow, consequently, prepared new instructions to Bernstorff and sent them to Washington on the following morning, September 17. The important paragraphs follow:

"I empower you to explain the following to Lansing:

"1. Submarine commanders are instructed by order of His Majesty to sink enemy passenger ships only after warning and the saving of human life, provided the ships do not try to escape or offer resistance. The order is formulated in such a way that in cases of doubt the attack is to be halted. Exceeding this order would bring a reprimand in consequence.

"2. Statement in the Arabic memorandum is based on the official report of the commander, whose good faith cannot be doubted. Should we, on the basis of proof which we have just received, conclude that the commander attacked unjustifiably because he thought he was about to be rammed, he would be reprimanded for exceeding his orders. On the other hand, we are prepared to determine the facts by an international commission of inquiry under Title 3 of The Hague Agreement of 1910 [1901], page 25, and if the decision is unfavorable to us, to reprimand the commander. For your exclusive personal information: The reports of the commander and crew under oath state that an attempt to ram had indeed been made, at least that they had the impression that this was true. I ask immediate wireless report of the disposition of the American Government and how they would feel about an international commission of inquiry. Whether such a proposal would lead to an immediate break.

[63] See the detailed account of this conference in the *New York Times*, September 17, 1915.

"3. Question of indemnity for death of American citizens would have to be decided, like the Lusitania case, by The Hague Convention, but judgment could not have any bearing on the admissibility or inadmissibility of the German submarine war.

"To avoid a break, Your Excellency could at the most declare that in the Arabic case, if it is proved that the commander of the submarine exceeded his instructions, we would pay an indemnity out of friendliness on our part; however, without recognition of any international obligation.

"4. Extension of the order to freighters is not possible since English freighters are mainly armed and have been instructed [put under the duty] to attack German submarines. . . . However, warning will be given by us as often as it is possible to do so. . . .

"6. We think it impossible that new incidents will take place in view of the contents of the new order. Should such a thing occur, completely against expectations, it definitely would be contrary to the will of the officials who gave the order and would quickly draw a very sharp reprimand in consequence. . . ."[64]

This was only the first move in what soon developed into an extraordinary campaign to convince the American authorities and people that the Imperial government stood by its promises and would do anything that was honorable to avert a break with the United States.

Von Jagow had already taken steps to clear the docket of the *Hesperian* affair and an earlier incident involving the Cunard liner *Orduna*[65]

[64] The Foreign Secretary to Ambassador von Bernstorff, September 17, 1915, German F. O. Archives.

[65] For the details of the unsuccessful submarine attack on the *Orduna*, see above, p. 445. The State Department had asked the Foreign Office in Berlin for information about the attack in late July 1915, but von Jagow had refused to reply on the ground that the incident involved an enemy ship on which no American lives had been lost. (The Acting Secretary of State to Ambassador Gerard, July 24, 1915, *Foreign Relations, 1915, Supplement*, p. 485; the Foreign Office to Ambassador von Bernstorff, August 2, 1915, German F. O. Archives.) The Imperial Navy Office, however, gave a copy of the submarine commander's report on the *Orduna* incident to the American correspondent, Karl H. von Wiegand, who summarized it in a story in the New York *World*, August 8, 1915. Once the second *Arabic* crisis broke out, von Jagow hastened to hand an official report and explanation to Gerard. (G. von Jagow to Envoy von Treutler, September 9, 1915, German F. O. Archives; Ambassador Gerard to the Secretary of State, September 10, 1915, *Foreign Relations, 1915, Supplement*, pp. 545-546; the Foreign Office to Ambassador von Bernstorff, September 11, 1915, German F. O. Archives.) Von Jagow's report closed the affair. "The Orduna and Hesperian cases are now, after our statement, considered settled. Everything now depends upon the Arabic case." Ambassador von Bernstorff to the Foreign Office, September 21, 1915, *ibid.*

—the only two outstanding cases involving submarine attacks on passenger ships except the *Lusitania* and *Arabic* cases. Now, on September 18, almost as soon as he had finished drafting his instructions to the Ambassador in Washington, the Foreign Secretary called the Berlin correspondent of the Associated Press to his office and gave him a long interview, which was nothing less than a direct appeal to the American people. The German government, he said, hoped and believed that it could settle the *Arabic* case by direct negotiation with the Washington authorities. There could certainly be an honest difference of opinion about the evidence, he went on, and the German government would be glad to examine the materials that the State Department had just submitted. But up to this point, at any rate, the Foreign Office "could not, you will admit, well go behind the report of the commander of our submarine, or question his honest belief . . . that the British Captain was planning to attack his craft." If direct negotiations failed, then the Imperial government hoped that the dispute could be referred to The Hague for adjudication.

"As to the larger question of submarine warfare," von Jagow continued, "the attitude of Germany is perfectly clear. Enemy passenger steamers will not be subjected to attack without warning provided they respect the regular maritime code and will be sunk only when opportunity for safety of passengers and crew is given. Instructions to German submarine commanders on this point are very precise and definite, and go as far as is possible to eliminate the possibility of error or accident. . . . Neutral merchantmen, including Americans, are exempt from interference, as stated long ago, except when carrying contraband and will then be destroyed only under the conditions laid down in the international code concerning maritime war, when provision is made for the safety of those aboard. . . .

"I do not expect . . . [new incidents to occur], and I speak with full confidence. The Government—the whole Government—is agreed upon the instructions to submarine commanders, . . . and our submarine officers have been impressed with the necessity of carrying them out in letter and in spirit. . . . Mischance cannot be eliminated entirely in war time, nor dangers for noncombatants, either in land or sea war, absolutely guarded against, but every precaution has been taken, so far as lies in the power of the Imperial Government, to safeguard the interests of neutrals. Should the present instructions governing the submarine campaign be exceeded in any respect, the Imperial Government, as the Chancellor assured you recently, would not hesitate to give such complete satisfaction to the United States as would conform to the friendly relations between the two Governments."[66]

The Foreign Secretary went the second mile again the next day, September 19, by handing Ambassador Gerard a note aimed at settling the old case of the *William P. Frye*[67] and ending forever all German-American differences over *American* trading rights at sea. In earlier correspondence about the *Frye* case, the Berlin Foreign Office had acknowledged that the German government was financially liable when German warships sank American vessels carrying conditional and absolute contraband according to the rules of cruiser warfare. In the note of September 19, however, the Foreign Office went even further by promising that German naval craft would not sink any American vessel carrying only *conditional* contraband, even though in certain circumstances they had a legal right to do so.[68]

Unknown to the Imperial Chancellor and Foreign Secretary, and of course to the American government and people, the new head of the Admiralty, von Holtzendorff, made his own contribution to the cause of German-American peace by sending the following order to the fleet on September 18:

> Such a general situation exists that, during the course of the following weeks, all possibility of violating the orders which have just been given must be excluded. During this period, therefore, you will cease all submarine activity off the west coast of England and in the Channel, even activity in accordance with prize orders [the rules of cruiser warfare]. In the North Sea you will continue to conduct the submarine war according to these orders. It will be possible to use the submarines which must be disposed of for military missions. The present order must remain top secret; it should be communicated to as small a number of persons as possible.[69]

[66] *New York Times*, September 19, 1915. The Chief of the Admiralty, von Holtzendorff, confirmed von Jagow's statement for the information of the American government in an interview with Gherhardi a few days later. "Admiral," Gerard reported, "said that Naval Department was now in complete accord with general Government and that instructions given to submarines were strict and would be carried out." Ambassador Gerard to the Secretary of State, September 22, 1915, *Foreign Relations, 1915, Supplement*, p. 553.

[67] See above, p. 454.

[68] Ambassador Gerard to the Secretary of State, September 20, 1915, *Foreign Relations, 1915, Supplement*, pp. 551-552.

[69] Spindler, *La Guerre Sous-Marine*, II, 366.

The commanders of the High Seas Fleet and of the Navy Corps ordered an immediate halt to submarine operations against all merchant ships. Thus American pressure had brought, at least momentarily, a complete end to the *Handelskrieg mit U-Booten* announced so confidently on February 4, 1915.

The outcome now depended upon two things—whether the American government would continue uncompromisingly to demand a formal disavowal, and whether it would also press forward in a new campaign to force the German government to expand the *Arabic* pledge to include all merchantmen. It will be recalled that Lansing had suggested to Bernstorff on September 13 that it would be helpful if the Imperial government thus broadened its pledges,[70] and that von Jagow had replied that it was not possible to warn all merchant ships before sinking them because the British were arming merchantmen and ordering them to attack submarines aggressively.

Actually, there was not much likelihood at this point that the Washington authorities would endanger the *Arabic* settlement by demanding that the Germans adhere strictly to the rules of cruiser warfare in *all* their submarine operations. They remembered only too well that the President himself, in the first *Lusitania* note, had narrowed the German-American dispute to the issue of the safety of "unarmed merchantmen."[71] Besides, the President and Secretary of State knew that

[70] "In conclusion, I would like to add that everyone here would be extremely gratified if instructions to submarine commanders could be extended to all merchant ships. They [Lansing and others] argue emphatically that the latter only sail slowly and have thus far always been warned. The advantage of not warning comes into play only with a quick-sailing passenger ship, which we have promised to warn anyway. Therefore, the matter would be of no importance to us, while it would make a fine impression here and would strengthen the position of the United States in its negotiations with England." Ambassador von Bernstorff to the Foreign Office, September 15, 1915, German F. O. Archives.

[71] As the President admitted after Bernstorff, in his first comment on the *Hesperian* affair, had reminded Lansing that this vessel was armed. "This seems exceedingly important," he had added, "as the whole controversy between the United States and Germany turns on the subject of 'unarmed merchant vessels.'" (The German Ambassador to the Secretary of State, September 8, 1915, *Foreign Relations, 1915, Supplement,* p. 539.) "The only present comment necessary on these letters [from Bernstorff], obviously meant to be reassuring," Wilson wrote to Lansing on September 10, "is that my original error in speaking of 'unarmed' vessels when I should have said 'unresisting' is now rising up to embarrass us, for which I am very sorry." (W.W. to R. Lansing, September 10, 1915, *The Lansing Papers,* 1, 477.) For the administration leaders' discussion during the drafting of the first *Lusitania* note, and for Wilson's decision to use the term "unarmed merchantmen," see above, pp. 384-385.

the German claim that the British were arming merchantmen and using them offensively and perhaps illegally was substantially true,[72] and that they would therefore be on extremely weak ground in demanding that submarines expose themselves unduly to destruction. Finally, the reaction of the American press to the torpedoing of the armed liner *Hesperian* had impressively demonstrated that the American people would be reluctant to support their government in any test of strength over armed ships.[73]

Wilson and Lansing might have raised the issue none the less, had they really meant to drive the Germans to the wall. This was far from their intention. And since they agreed with the German point of view about armed ships, they said no more for the time being to the Germans about observing the rules of cruiser warfare in attacking ordinary merchantmen. At the same time, they sent a sharp warning to the British that they might require all British ships calling at American ports to be disarmed unless they stopped using their guns for unprovoked attacks against submarines.[74] And when the First Lord of the

[72] Wilson and Lansing, for example, had been dreadfully shocked by the most famous (or infamous) of these incidents—the so-called *Baralong* affair. On August 19, 1915, one Wegener, commander of the *U27*, stopped the British steamer *Nicosian* preparatory to sinking her some seventy miles off Queenstown in the Irish Sea. While Wegener waited for the crew to evacuate their ship, the British Q-boat *Baralong*, disguised as a tramp steamer and flying the American flag, came upon the scene. About one hundred yards from the *Nicosian* the *Baralong* hoisted the English flag and opened fire on the *U24*, sinking her at once. When the crew of the submarine took to the water, the sailors of the *Baralong* shot as many of them as they could find.

Wilson and Lansing learned about the incident when some American members of the crew of the *Nicosian* reported the details to the American Embassy, and Page telegraphed their affidavits on August 26 and 29. (Ambassador Page to the Secretary of State, August 26 and 29, 1915, *Foreign Relations, 1915, Supplement*, pp. 527-529.)

"To me the conduct of the British naval authorities is shocking," Lansing wrote as he sent a copy of Page's dispatch of August 29 to the President. (R. Lansing to W.W., August 30, 1915, Wilson Papers.) "Isn't this one of the most unspeakable performances? I need add nothing to what Lansing says. It's horrible!" Wilson wrote in comment on the dispatch.

[73] e.g., the Baltimore *Evening Sun*, September 9, 1915, and the *Springfield* (Massachusetts) *Republican*, September 8, 1915.

[74] Early in the war the State Department, following precedent and international law, had adopted the rule that merchant ships that were armed solely for defense might use American ports without being subjected to the rules governing the treatment of auxiliary cruisers and warships. (See the Acting Secretary of State to the Diplomatic Representatives of Belligerent States, September 19, 1914, *Foreign Relations, 1914, Supplement*, pp. 611-612.) The Department reaffirmed this position in March 1915, in response to an inquiry from the Cunard Steamship Company about the entry of two of its defensively armed steamers, the *Orduna* and *Transylvania*, into the Port of New

Admiralty in London, A. J. Balfour, and House's friend, Sir Horace Plunkett, came back with the fervent plea that merchantmen had to

---

York. (The Secretary of State to the Cunard Steamship Company, March 3, 1915, *Foreign Relations, 1915, Supplement*, p. 845.)

The issue did not arise again until May 1915, when the British armed steamer *Asian* entered the Port of New Orleans, and Lansing asked the British Embassy to see to the disarming of the vessel, on the ground that the British government had informed the State Department on September 4, 1914 (the British Ambassador to the Secretary of State, September 4, 1914, *Foreign Relations, 1914, Supplement*, pp. 606-607), that British merchantmen coming to American ports would not carry arms in the future. (Counselor Lansing to the British Ambassador, May 22, 1915, *Foreign Relations, 1915, Supplement*, p. 846.) Actually, the British had never made any such announcement, but the British Ambassador did not challenge Lansing's misinterpretation and apparently ordered that the *Asian* be disarmed.

The issue lay dormant for several months. Then in the late summer an incident occurred that set off the first discussions between the President and Secretary Lansing about the treatment of armed ships. The State Department received word in August that the British steamer *Waimana*, armed with one 4.7-inch gun mounted aft, was about to enter the Port of Newport News to take on a cargo of coal. Lansing at once asked Ambassador Spring Rice to see to it that the gun was removed before the ship left the Virginia port. (The Secretary of State to the British Ambassador, August 25, 1915, *ibid.*, p. 848.) Replying for Sir Edward Grey, Spring Rice refused on the grounds that the *Waimana* was armed defensively within the regulations laid down in the State Department's circular of September 19, 1914, and that disarming her in response to Lansing's official request would create a precedent "for abolishing purely defensive armament on vessels engaged solely in the British mercantile service." (The British Ambassador to the Secretary of State, September 10, 1915, *ibid.*, pp. 848-849.) Lansing replied at once without commenting on Spring Rice's contentions by declaring that the American government knew all about the unprovoked attacks by British merchantmen upon submarines, and by announcing that the Washington government would not grant clearance to the *Waimana* until it had received formal assurances that she would use her gun only for defensive purposes. (The Secretary of State to the British Ambassador, September 11, 1915, *ibid.*, pp. 849-850.)

This was the point at which Lansing referred the question to the President. Spring Rice's argument was sound as far as it went, Lansing wrote on September 12, but the emergence of the submarine had made the old rules obsolete. Armament that might have been purely defensive in the late summer of 1914 was now offensive "against so small and unarmored a craft as a submarine." There could be no doubt that armed British merchantmen, even passenger ships, had been seeking out submarines and attacking them. This made it difficult "to demand that a submarine shall give warning and so expose itself to the heavy guns carried by some of the British passenger vessels." He thought, therefore, Lansing went on, that the American government should amend its rules and announce that it would treat all armed merchantmen, regardless of the number, size, and location of their guns, as warships when they entered American ports. As for the *Waimana*, he concluded, the State Department might well adopt a lenient policy in view of its declaration of September 19, 1914. (R. Lansing to W.W., September 12, 1915, *The Lansing Papers*, I, 330-331.)

Wilson gave his answer orally to the Secretary of State on September 13, 1915. Lan-

act aggressively to protect themselves against underwater attack,[75] Wilson was utterly unmoved. "I read the letters from Plunkett and Balfour with the greatest interest," he wrote to Colonel House, who had forwarded them. "The matter of armed merchantmen is not so simple as Balfour would make it. It is hardly fair to ask Submarine commanders to give warning by summons if, when they approach as near as they must for that purpose they are to be fired upon. It is a question of many sides and is giving Lansing and me some perplexed moments."[76]

As it turned out, Wilson and Lansing did not have to make any decision about armed merchantmen once the *Arabic* affair was settled, simply because the issue had ceased to have any urgency after the German Admiralty called its submarines home from the Irish Sea. The discussions in Washington about this matter were, however, by no means unimportant or irrelevant. For the short run, at any rate, they signified clearly enough that the American leaders would be content to let the *Arabic* negotiations run in the channel already deeply cut by the main course of the German-American discussions up to this time.

Bernstorff, meanwhile, had taken up the negotiations anew in the overriding conviction that nothing could prevent a German-American rupture but a formal disavowal of Commander Schneider.[77] Lansing was now—it was the last week in September—on vacation at his home

---

sing, he said, should let the *Waimana* go "upon a promise by the British Admiralty and a bond by the owners of the vessel that the arms will in no case be used for offense." The Secretary, moreover, should prepare the new rule classifying all armed merchantmen as warships "but not publish it or put it into effect until we see what we are going to be able to work out of this *Arabic* business." (W.W. to R. Lansing, September 13, 1915, *ibid.*, pp. 331-332, summarizing what Wilson had told Lansing earlier in the day.)

As it turned out, neither the British Cabinet nor the owners of the *Waimana* were willing to make a test case at this time. The *Waimana* landed her gun at Newport News on September 21 and sailed the following day. (The Collector of Customs at Norfolk to the Secretary of the Treasury, September 22, 1915, *Foreign Relations, 1915, Supplement*, pp. 850-851.)

[75] A. J. Balfour to E. M. House, September 12, 1915, House Papers, written in response to the Secretary of State to the British Ambassador, September 11, 1915, cited above; H. Plunkett to E. M. House, September 17, 1915, House Papers.

[76] W.W. to E. M. House, October 4, 1915, Baker Collection. House reported the President's views to Balfour in E. M. House to A. J. Balfour, October 6, 1915, House Papers.

[77] As he said in Ambassador von Bernstorff to the Foreign Office, September 22, 1915, German F. O. Archives.

in upstate New York, and the Ambassador, hearing from someone that the President wanted him to hasten the discussion, called upon Colonel House in New York on September 26. For the President's information Bernstorff summarized the instructions that the Foreign Office had sent to him on September 17, saying that he could give additional new assurances to supplement the *Arabic* pledge, and that his government was willing to submit the *Arabic* case to an international inquiry and to accept the principle of financial responsibility for loss of American life. If this were not satisfactory, Bernstorff went on, he would "take the question up with his government as to some form of disavowal based upon American evidence." And if the President decided that a disavowal had to be made, he, Bernstorff, could consult the Foreign Office at once, or he could wait until Lansing had returned to Washington.[78]

Wilson was delighted, almost elated. Actually, it seems highly improbable that he would have pressed his demand for the disavowal to the point where a rupture would have been inevitable if it were not conceded. Certainly he could not have failed to be impressed by the new assurances from Berlin and above all by the German government's offer to submit the facts to an international court of inquiry. On the other hand, after reading House's letter the President must have concluded that Bernstorff was obviously near the point of surrender, and that firmness persevered in would soon bring a reward. "I replied," the President wrote to Lansing as he sent House's letter to him on September 30, "that I was willing to wait until Bernstorff could see you in New York on Saturday [October 2], and that when he did see you I thought it best that he should take it for granted that we would have to insist upon a disavowal of the action of the submarine commander in sinking the *Arabic*. I said that I did not think that public opinion in this country would be in the least satisfied with anything short of that. You will know better than I can as yet just what line to take with the Ambassador when you see him."[79]

It did not work out quite as easily as the President thought it would. On about September 27, before he could again press his advice upon the Foreign Office, the German Ambassador received final instructions from von Jagow in Berlin. Officials there, the Foreign Secretary wrote, had completed their own exhaustive investigation of all the English

[78] E. M. House to W.W., September 26, 1915, *The Lansing Papers*, I, 482.
[79] W.W. to R. Lansing, September 30, 1915, *ibid.*, pp. 482-483.

and German evidence relating to the sinking of the *Arabic* and were sending the German affidavits to Washington by wireless and by mail. "According to this factual report, there is no doubt but that the submarine commander had ample reasons for believing that he was about to be rammed. On the other hand, the German Government does not desire to reject the testimony of the English officers of the *Arabic* given under oath, according to which the *Arabic* did not attempt to ram the submarine. The attack of the submarine has, therefore, to our regret not been in accord with our explicit instructions. The commander has been *informed* in this regard. For the final settlement the German Government is willing out of friendship but without admission of international obligation to pay indemnity for the death of American citizens." Bernstorff, von Jagow went on, might give this communication to the Washington authorities, but additional concessions were impossible. "Should you have to make further proposals or believe that you could push through an international commission of inquiry," the instructions concluded, "I request wire report from you before you go ahead."[80]

Bernstorff read this message with a heavy heart. It was not, he knew, a disavowal; indeed, it was only slightly less unyielding although more friendly in tone than the German note of September 7 had been, and he doubted that it would avert the threatened rupture of relations. In spite of these forebodings he drafted a note reminding the American government of the recent German pledges for the safety of passenger ships and incorporating almost verbatim the Foreign Office's instructions of September 26.[81] This he gave to Lansing at a brief meeting at the Hotel Biltmore in New York City on the morning of October 2, 1915, along with the first draft of a German note on the *Lusitania*[82] and mumbled regrets that his government could not go further toward the disavowal. He then returned to his summer residence at Cedarhurst and in his gloom did not inform the Foreign Office of what he had done.

Lansing took Bernstorff's *Arabic* note with him to Washington and handed it without comment to the President at a conference at the White House during the following evening, October 3. Wilson, one is tempted to assume, replied that there could no longer be any ques-

---

[80] The Foreign Secretary to Ambassador von Bernstorff, September 26, 1915, German F. O. Archives; italics added.

[81] Bernstorff's note, dated October 2, 1915, is printed in *The Lansing Papers*, I, 483.

[82] *ibid.*, pp. 484-485.

tion about the sincerity of the German assurances concerning the conduct of submarine operations in the future. On the other hand, he continued (this we know from the record), the note would not do as a disavowal of the sinking of the *Arabic*. The American government simply "could not accept a note of that sort."[83] Lansing agreed. But how far should they go *now*? Should they reject the German explanation but accept the offer to submit the evidence to an international tribunal for its scrutiny and judgment? Should they demand an immediate disavowal and by so doing run the risk of a diplomatic rupture and of losing everything they had gained? And would the American people support them if they took this last desperate course and found themselves at the point of no return? These were important questions, and we may be certain that Wilson and Lansing pondered them. We have no direct account of what they said, but supporting evidence indicates that their conversation might well have run as follows:

Bernstorff, obviously, has received broad power from the Foreign Office to settle the *Arabic* case. His note of October 2 was an attempt to resolve the controversy in a way that would be least embarrassing to his government. A sharp application of pressure, however, would probably force the Ambassador to an outright disavowal. But what kind of pressure? A threat to break diplomatic relations unless the disavowal is soon forthcoming? It might work; indeed, it probably would work. But it *is* risky. What if the Germans call our bluff? We then might have to break relations. Let us try a safer course—by intimating through the newspapers that we *might* break relations if Bernstorff does not yield. Lansing can determine at his next meeting with the Ambassador what the effect of this announcement has been.

This, at any rate, is how they handled the matter. Following this conference, the Secretary of State (or the President) hinted to reporters that Bernstorff's note of October 2 was unacceptable, and that "final refusal by Germany to meet the American viewpoint on the Arabic case might bring about the threatened rupture in diplomatic relations."[84] Then on the following day, October 4, Lansing sent the Ambassador a telegram asking him to come to Washington at once.

[83] R. Lansing to E. M. House, October 6, 1915, *ibid.*, p. 486, telling about the White House conference of October 3, 1915.

[84] As the correspondent for the *New York Times* put it. *New York Times*, October 4, 1915.

Bernstorff arrived at the Secretary of State's office at 10:30 on the morning of October 5. He was obviously distraught and downcast; and Lansing must have quickly concluded that the newspaper report had hit its mark, and that he should use a low-pressure approach. He congratulated the Ambassador for having influenced his government "to secure an amicable settlement of the controversy." However, he continued *without any hint of a threat*, he had to say that the President and he had agreed that the note of October 2 "was not satisfactory in its present form." When Bernstorff asked what was wrong, Lansing answered gently. But let him tell the story:

"I pointed out to him that in the third (3) paragraph the German Government appeared to support entirely the commander of the submarine in the conviction which he had reached as to the purpose of the *Arabic* to ram the submarine. I told him that in view of the fact that the note stated that the attack of the submarine was against the instructions issued to the commander, this assertion appeared to be contradictory.

"The Ambassador replied that he was willing to omit that from the note.

"I also said that it was very unsatisfactory that the note failed to frankly disavow the act; that there was no question but that the language was open to the interpretation of the disavowal. The Ambassador said that that was his intention and I then asked him why he had not stated it in the note. He said he thought that he possibly could do so.

"In regard to the last paragraph, relating to the payment of indemnity, I said to him that the note offered to pay an indemnity as an act of grace and that this Government could not accept it on that basis, for they considered there was a legal right to an indemnity. I suggested, however, that a controversy on this point could be avoided by a change of language.

"The changes which I proposed I indicated on the note of October 2d, in lead pencil.

"The Ambassador said that he was not sure whether his instructions would permit him to go as far as these changes, but that he would go back to the Embassy and examine the instructions, and if they were broad enough he would make the changes proposed and would send me a new note within an hour."[85]

[85] R. Lansing, "Memorandum by the Secretary of State . . . ," *The Lansing Papers*, I, 485-486.

Bernstorff went through the formality of returning to his office for further thought. But to him the situation was already altogether clear. The question, as he later explained, was now down to its bare essentials—whether it was "worthwhile to break off diplomatic relations with the United States over this incident" and thus incur a hopeless new war.[86] His superiors at the Wilhelmstrasse simply did not understand the danger. Therefore, he would have to make the decision for peace by yielding; he would have to exceed his instructions even though this might bring his own humiliation by repudiation or recall. Following all of Lansing's suggestions, he hastily drafted a new note and had it delivered to Lansing's office at 12:15 p.m. With the new and changed portions printed in square brackets, it follows:

Imperial German Embassy,
Washington, October 5, 1915.

My dear Mr. Secretary:

Prompted by the desire to reach a satisfactory agreement with regard to the *Arabic* incident, my Government has given me the following instructions:

The orders issued by His Majesty the Emperor to the commanders of the German submarines—of which I notified you on a previous occasion—have been made so stringent that the recurrence of incidents similar to the *Arabic* case is considered out of the question.

According to the report of Commander Schneider of the submarine that sank the *Arabic*, and his affidavit as well as those of his men, Commander Schneider was convinced that the *Arabic* intended to ram the submarine. On the other hand, the Imperial Government does not doubt the good faith of the affidavits of the British officers of the *Arabic*, according to which the *Arabic* did not intend to ram the submarine. The attack of the submarine, therefore, was undertaken against the instructions issued to the commander. The Imperial Government regrets [and disavows this act] and has notified Commander Schneider accordingly.

[Under these circumstances my Government is prepared to pay an indemnity for the American lives which, to its deep regret, have been lost on the *Arabic*. I am authorized to negotiate with you about the amount of this indemnity.]

I remain (etc.)

J. v. Bernstorff[87]

---

[86] J. von Bernstorff to T. von Bethmann Hollweg, October 20, 1915, German F. O. Archives.

[87] The German Ambassador to the Secretary of State, October 5, 1915, *Foreign Relations, 1915, Supplement*, p. 560.

Lansing handed the note to the President, and in the privacy of the White House the two men rejoiced together. Then shortly afterward, while giving the text of Bernstorff's letter to reporters, the Secretary announced that the *Arabic* case was settled to the complete satisfaction of the American government and intimated that the long and bitter German-American controversy was "very near at an end." Talking to the correspondents, Wilson agreed, adding that he now felt solid ground under his feet for the first time since the beginning of the submarine dispute.[88]

While editors throughout the country were hailing the *Arabic* note with warm appreciation,[89] Bernstorff was hard at work at the German embassy attempting to prepare his superiors in Berlin to accept the concessions that he had made. In a brief dispatch to be sent over the State Department's wire on October 5 he mentioned only that he had reached "complete agreement with the American Government" and had admitted the responsibility of the Imperial Government "for the loss of human life and for monetary damages."[90] On the following day, however, his courage returned as he read the glowing comments that filled the newspapers, and he penned the following report to the Imperial Chancellor:

"As I have telegraphed Your Excellency, the agreement about the Arabic case has caused joy among general public opinion here. Only a few out-and-out Anglophile newspapers, as, for example, the New York Herald and the New York Tribune, show the cloven hoof in their disappointment that a break in diplomatic relations has been avoided. Since the outbreak of the war we have never had as good a press as today.

"The historian will not have to speculate whether war with the United States has been avoided because of the agreement on the Arabic question. Your Excellency knows that I personally believe that we would have drifted into war without the hope of being saved if the agreement had failed. The avoidance of hostilities, I suggest most respectfully, was reason enough to conclude an agreement. And I had

[88] *New York Times*, October 6, 1915.

[89] *New Republic*, iv (October 9, 1915), 244; New York *Outlook*, cxi (October 13, 1915), 339; New York *Nation*, ci (October 14, 1915), 451; and the review of newspaper editorial opinion in "America's Diplomatic Victory," *Literary Digest*, li (October 16, 1915), 821-824.

[90] Ambassador von Bernstorff to the Foreign Office, October 8, 1915, German F. O. Archives. This dispatch, written on October 5, was delayed in transmission through Secretary Lansing's oversight and hence was postdated.

Dropping Another Pilot

Marcus in the *New York Times*

a further goal in mind—to gain action for us by the Government of the United States in advancing energetically against England in effectively establishing freedom of the seas. . . . One can think about the President as he likes; one may consider him neutral or not. But it cannot be denied that his whole heart is committed to the cause of peace. A Republican President could not have resisted the combined anti-German pressure of Wall Street, the press, and the so-called high society."[91]

As it turned out, Bernstorff was not destined to get much reward on earth for what Colonel House called his "patience, good sense and untiring efforts" for peace.[92] With President Wilson he had apparently earned no credit at all. Having used the Ambassador to win the victory, Wilson, still upset by reports of German intrigues, was now again eager to send Bernstorff packing. "He had in mind to send Bernstorff home, and said he did not see why we should send Dumba and not Bernstorff," House wrote in his Diary after a conference with the President in New York only three days after the settlement of the *Arabic* affair. It was not the first time that Wilson had thought of handing the Ambassador his passports; and the President was apparently deflected from this course only by House's plea that Bernstorff "was about the best of his tribe and had done more to bring about a solution of our differences with Germany than perhaps any one man."[93]

The danger to Bernstorff of humiliation was even greater from Berlin. In that city a near explosion occurred when news of the Ambassador's latest *démarche* arrived there. Bethmann and von Jagow were furious, first of all, because they had to read the text of Bernstorff's letter in English newspapers published on October 5 and received no word at all from their envoy until October 8, 1915.[94] They were alarmed because Bernstorff had failed to make the German pledges concerning the conduct of submarine operations conditional upon American success in winning freedom of the seas from Great Britain, as their gen-

---

[91] J. von Bernstorff to T. von Bethmann Hollweg, October 6, 1915, *ibid*.

[92] E. M. House to J. W. Gerard, October 6, 1915, House Papers.

[93] House Diary, October 8, 1915.

[94] This was true, as we have said, because Lansing failed through an oversight to send Bernstorff's telegram No. 642 of October 5, 1915, until three days later. The German Foreign Office received its first official text of Bernstorff's letter on October 11, when Ambassador Gerard gave a copy to Count Montgelas. Bernstorff sent a copy of the text by wireless on October 19. Ambassador von Bernstorff to the Foreign Office, October 19, 1915, German F. O. Archives.

eral instructions of August 28, 1915, had directed him to do.[95] They were upset most of all by Bernstorff's explicit disavowal and divulging of Commander Schneider's name, for this had set off a wave of indignation in naval circles. As the Chancellor wrote in bitter complaint on October 26 after reading the copy of the *Arabic* note that the Ambassador had just sent by wireless:

"Does this conform to my instructions? It should have been said that Schneider had *reason to assume* that the Arabic meant to ram him. If my assumption is correct, it would be highly regrettable if Bernstorff has chosen a form and has met them halfway in a manner that was not necessary and about which the navy can rightly protest. It will be difficult to repair the damage now that the thing is done. Admiral von Holtzendorff, whom I saw in Charleville today, already was disquieted about the Wolff telegram [in the German press, telling of the *Arabic* settlement], and he asked me if the Arabic case had now been finally settled. And he seemed now—contrary to his former views—in little agreement that we should reform the submarine war totally, if England accepts the Declaration of London and abides by it."[96]

Bethmann and von Jagow could not recall Bernstorff without repudiating him, and they could not repudiate his disavowal outright or add a codicil making the *Arabic* pledge conditional upon American success against the British without, so it seemed, inviting the diplomatic rupture they were still determined to avoid.[97] Yet they had to find some way to mollify naval opinion at home.[98] In the end someone at the Foreign Office found the solution, which was to send a note to the State Department implicitly approving everything that Bernstorff had done but in fact repudiating his disavowal of Commander Schneider

[95] "Have you informed the American Government that we reserve freedom of action for ourselves in the eventuality that its approach to England remains without success?" The Foreign Office to Ambassador von Bernstorff, October 24, 1915, *ibid.*

[96] Bethmann's penciled comments on Ambassador von Bernstorff to the Foreign Office, October 19, 1915, *ibid.*

[97] They were also apparently convinced by Bernstorff's explanation and argument: "*I have always stressed that we would reserve complete freedom of action in case England does not meet us halfway. . . .* This liberty has in fact been curtailed only one way—in that we have agreed not to sink passenger ships without warning, etc. From this assurance we will never be able to withdraw unless we want war with the United States of America. The sinking of a liner with Americans on board once again would—if such a sinking took place without warning, etc., and be justified by the Imperial Government—lead surely and unavoidably to war." J. von Bernstorff to T. von Bethmann Hollweg, November 1, 1915, *ibid.*

[98] e.g., Admiral H. von Holtzendorff to the Foreign Secretary, October 24, 1915, *ibid.*

and qualifying his admission of the German government's legal liability for the loss of American lives aboard the *Arabic*.

Bernstorff, von Jagow wrote to the Secretary of State on October 30, had reported to the Foreign Office about the *Arabic* negotiations and had communicated the text of his letter to Secretary Lansing. "From the Ambassador's report," the Foreign Secretary added mellifluously, "I see with satisfaction that a full understanding has been reached between our two Governments." As Bernstorff had already pointed out, von Jagow went on, the commander of the submarine that sank the *Arabic* was convinced that the liner was about to ram him. He, von Jagow continued, was sure that the American officials would agree that the commander's suspicion had been justified once they had read the German affidavits that he had sent to Washington. But (and from here nearly to the end of his memorandum von Jagow repeated almost verbatim the text of his instructions to Bernstorff of September 26) the German government did not want to reject the testimony of the officers of the *Arabic,* etc. "I may therefore," he went on, "repeat Count Bernstorff's statement that the attack of the submarine, to our regret, was not in accordance with their [the] instructions issued, and that the commander has been *notified* accordingly." As the American government knew, von Jagow concluded (while availing himself again of the opportunity to express his "satisfaction that Count Bernstorff's negotiations with the Secretary of State, Mr. Lansing, have led to a settlement of the incident"), Bernstorff had been instructed to pay an indemnity *"out of friendly consideration* and leaving aside the question of liability resulting from international law."[99]

It was all done so cleverly that no one in Washington realized what had happened—that von Jagow had first approved Bernstorff's disavowal and admission of financial liability and then repudiated them!

Having cleared the record[100] if not the minds of the President and Secretary of State, the Foreign Secretary closed the *Arabic* case by sending a scalding reprimand to Bernstorff.[101]

[99] Ambassador Gerard to the Secretary of State, October 30, 1915, *Foreign Relations, 1915, Supplement*, pp. 603-604; italics added.

[100] For example, von Jagow could later tell the leaders of the Reichstag, as he probably did, that the Foreign Office had in fact not made any formal disavowal of Commander Schneider or admitted any financial liability. See "Memorandum about the Settlement of the Arabic Question, for the Eventual Use of the Foreign Secretary before the Budget Committee, but First to be Presented to the Secretary," by Count Montgelas, dated December 1, 1915, German F. O. Archives.

[101] The Foreign Office to Ambassador von Bernstorff, November 8, 1915, German F. O. Archives.

CHAPTER XX

Neutrality Reaffirmed

THE supreme test of the Wilson administration's good faith in its fight
for the freedom of the seas, most American observers agreed, now lay
immediately ahead during the early days of October 1915. Having persuaded and compelled the German government to afford proper guarantees of safety for American ships and cargoes and American citizens
on all passenger liners, would the leaders in Washington now move,
as they had always said they would, with equal vigor to compel the
British to conduct their maritime warfare more nearly according to
the well-established rules? Upon the answer depended the entire future of American neutrality, whether the Washington government
would remain the authentic champion of neutral rights, or whether
it would drift into a benevolent neutrality that favored the Allies.

All along, actually, it had been a question of *when*, not *if*. Never
at any time during the long summer of 1915 had Wilson and Lansing
ever seriously doubted that the national interest and their own concepts of international morality demanded that they continue to pursue
a course of rigorous impartiality. At fleeting moments they might in-
dulge in private sympathies for the Allies, but such sentiments were
invariably overborne by the responsibility that they always felt as the
spokesmen of a great people dedicated to peace, and as the last effective
defenders of the international order that they ardently wanted to preserve. They had no alternative, they knew, but to defend that order
as much against British assaults as against German.

The important American confrontation of the British maritime system was postponed all during the late spring and summer of 1915[1]
only because the President was not willing to risk a serious controversy

---

[1] I use the qualifying adjective "important" here because, as the reader will recall,
Lansing did give clear notice in his note to London of July 14, 1915, that the United
States government did not recognize the legality of the British blockade established
by the Order in Council of March 11, 1915, and because the President and the State
Department maintained a steady private pressure upon the London Foreign Office on
behalf of American trading rights all during the period of the submarine dispute with
Germany.

with Great Britain while the more serious submarine dispute hung fire. At the first sign that that dispute was nearing settlement, soon after Bernstorff's giving of the *Arabic* pledge on September 1, 1915, Lansing asked his special assistant in the State Department, Chandler P. Anderson, to set to work upon a note to Great Britain. Anderson completed his draft on October 2 and laid it upon the Secretary's desk two days later.[2] Lansing wrestled with the draft during the following days, generally increasing the severity of the language, and sent the revised version to the President on October 9.[3] Wilson made a "few verbal changes" that did "not alter the substance at all" and returned the draft to Lansing on October 21.[4] It was taken to London three days later by Alexander C. Kirk, Third Secretary of the American Embassy at Berlin, who was going back to his post by way of London at this time.[5]

Presented to Sir Edward Grey by Ambassador Page on November 5, the note was, as Lansing said, "unavoidably long"—a massive document some 7,000 words in length, not counting extensive appendices. It began by recalling the British government's previous assurances that it would exercise its belligerent rights with all due regard for the interests of legitimate neutral trade, and by asserting that such promises had, unhappily, not been honored. "On the contrary," it went on, "interferences with American ships and cargoes destined in good faith to neutral ports and lawfully entitled to proceed have become increasingly vexatious, causing American shipowners and American merchants to complain to this Government of the failure to take steps to prevent an exercise of belligerent power in contravention of their just rights."

Here followed a detailed indictment of the method that the British had been using in the exercise of their admitted right to control traffic in contraband—the detention of ships and cargoes for long periods in British ports while the search for contraband was being made, and often without any proof that the vessels and cargoes thus held were liable to seizure. After a long review of American practice during the

---

[2] New York *World*, October 3, 1915; *New York Times*, October 6, 1915.

[3] R. Lansing to W.W., October 9, 1915, *The Lansing Papers*, I, 303.

[4] W.W. to R. Lansing, October 21, 1915, *ibid.*, p. 304. "I had very little hand indeed in the preparation of the note. I merely touched up its phraseology here and there. Lansing wrote it, and it seems to me an unanswerable paper." W.W. to Lucy Smith, November 17, 1915, Baker Collection.

[5] *New York Times*, October 28, 1915.

Civil War and of the clearly established rules of international law on this subject, the note went on rather gently to appeal to the British government to instruct its officers "to refrain from these vexatious and illegal practices."

At this point the paper turned sharply to the "so-called 'blockade' measures imposed by the order in council of March 11." The American government, it explained, at first had been inclined to view these measures leniently because of British assurances that they would be carried out with a minimum inconvenience to neutral trade. It had not worked out this way, and the Washington authorities could "no longer permit the validity of the alleged blockade to remain unchallenged." Lansing then reviewed the accepted principles of international law governing the establishment and maintenance of a blockade—that it must be effectively maintained, must apply impartially to the ships of all nations, and must not operate against neutral ports. On every point, the note asserted, the alleged British blockade failed to meet the test of legality. "It is incumbent upon the United States Government, therefore, to give the British Government notice that the blockade, which they claim to have instituted under the order in council of March 11, can not be recognized as a legal blockade by the United States." In ordinary circumstances, the American government would advise its citizens to seek redress in the British Prize Court, which had the duty of upholding international law. But the British Prize Court, the note went on, had clearly shown itself bound by the illegal Order in Council of March 11 and by oppressive decrees issued by the Admiralty. American citizens, therefore, had only one means of redress— to appeal to their own government for protection. Then followed a summary statement of grievances and a moving declaration of intention:

"I believe that it has been conclusively shown that the methods sought to be employed by Great Britain to obtain and use evidence of enemy destination of cargoes bound for neutral ports, and to impose a contraband character upon such cargoes, are without justification; that the blockade, upon which such methods are partly founded, is ineffective, illegal, and indefensible; that the judicial procedures offered as a means of reparation for an international injury is inherently defective for the purpose; and that in many cases jurisdiction is asserted in violation of the law of nations. The United States, therefore, can not submit to the curtailment of its neutral rights by these measures, which are admittedly retaliatory, and therefore illegal, in conception and in nature, and intended to punish the enemies of Great Britain for alleged illegalities on their part. . . .

"The Government of the United States desires, therefore, to impress most earnestly upon His Majesty's Government that it must insist that the relations between it and His Majesty's Government be governed, not by a policy of expediency, but by those established rules of inter-national conduct upon which Great Britain in the past has held the United States to account when the latter nation was a belligerent en-gaged in a struggle for national existence.[6] It is of the highest impor-tance to neutrals, not only of the present day, but of the future, that the principles of international right be maintained unimpaired.

". . . This task of championing the integrity of neutral rights, which have received the sanction of the civilized world, against the lawless conduct of belligerents arising out of the bitterness of the great conflict which is now wasting the countries of Europe, the United States un-hesitatingly assumes, and to the accomplishment of that task it will devote its energies, exercising always that impartiality which from the outbreak of the war it has sought to exercise in its relations with the warring nations."[7]

So there it finally was for the entire world to read, a clear and ring-

[6] For evidence indicating that Lansing may have overstated this point, see Julius W. Pratt, "The British Blockade and American Precedent," *United States Naval Institute Proceedings*, XLVI (November 1920), 1789-1802; and the following by James P. Baxter, 3rd: "The British Government and Neutral Rights, 1861-1865," *American Historical Review*, XXXIV (October 1928), 9-29; "Papers Relating to Belligerent and Neutral Rights, 1861-1865," *ibid.*, pp. 77-91; and "Some British Opinions as to Neutral Rights, 1861 to 1865," *American Journal of International Law*, XXIII (July 1929), 517-537.

These articles, a distinguished diplomatic historian has written, "show how United States belligerent practice 1861-1865 expanded British practice on continuous voyage, applying it to enforcement of blockade *via* neutral islands and to absolute contraband *via* territorially adjacent neutral countries (Mexico). Far from 'holding the belligerent United States to account' in 1861-1865, as Lansing asserted, the British Government *did not do so*. It deliberately acquiesced in United States belligerent practice *re* contraband and blockade in order to establish a precedent useful to Great Britain as a belligerent in a future maritime war. As Baxter shows from British documents, Great Britain availed herself of this precedent conveniently in 1914-1917. To be sure she exceeded American belligerent practice of 1861-1865 by extending continuous voyage to the in-terception of conditional contraband *via* neutral countries (whether adjacent by land or by sea to Germany); but so had United States belligerent practice 1861-1865 ex-tended British belligerent maritime practice of 1801-1812. A good case can be made that neutral maritime rights were *moot* in Anglo-American relations in 1914-1917." Samuel Flagg Bemis to the author, September 17, 1959.

[7] The Secretary of State to Ambassador Page, October 21, 1915, *Foreign Relations, 1915, Supplement*, pp. 578-589.

The Court—"There is no evidence against you; so we find you guilty."

Kirby in the New York *World*

ing reaffirmation of American neutrality. It was no denial of the legitimate prerogatives of British sea power. It made no threats of immediate retaliation or of a break in diplomatic relations if the British did not yield. It was, none the less, a powerful protest with a profoundly important immediate significance and menacing possibilities for the future.

To begin with, it denied out of hand the British claim to exceptional international virtue by branding the London government as a gross violator of international law. For the American people, confused by the claims of rival propagandists and still wanting to be fair in judgment, this indictment of the British by their own government came as proof that they, or at least a large part of them, had been right all along in their belief that Britain and Germany were both lawbreakers fighting in the wrong way if not for the wrong ends.

Secondly, the note of October 21 defined the issues in dispute between the two governments in the way that Sir Edward Grey had thus far been able to prevent their being defined, that is, in terms of national *right* and *sovereignty*. The fact that the note did not contain any outwardly threatening language was not as important as might appear at first glance. The important fact was that the Washington authorities had taken a position they could not compromise and from which they could not retreat: they had set themselves in direct opposition to an important part of the British maritime system, and relations between the two governments could never be really cordial until the cause of the conflict had been removed. Indeed, all kinds of dangers impended unless the British gave in—unending, nagging disputes that might lead cumulatively to serious tension, retaliation by the United States in ways that would seem unimportant to American officials but have catastrophic consequences for the British, and the like.

In the final analysis, however, the note to Great Britain was most important for its unmistakable assertion that the United States government would continue to pursue a course of neutrality as rigorously as circumstances permitted. It was fair warning from one friend to another to expect no benevolent neutrality, no special help or favors. It reaffirmed the warning that Ambassador Spring Rice had earlier given a friend at home: "I hope the British people will understand that they must help themselves and not depend on American or foreign sympathy. In another sense—

> "Trust not for freedom to the Franks
> "They have a King who buys and sells.
> "In native swords and native ranks
> "Tis there alone that freedom dwells."[8]

Published in American and English newspapers on November 8, 1915, and in the German press on November 9 and 10, the American protest stirred a reaction that revealed that contemporary observers understood at least some of its meaning.

American editors approved the note to London in the same overwhelming way that they had endorsed the President's notes to Berlin

[8] C. A. Spring Rice to Lord Bryce, January 5, 1914 [1915], Bryce Papers.

during the *Lusitania* correspondence. Extreme Anglophiles, like the editor of the New York *Tribune*, denounced it furiously, to be sure, and a larger group, including the editors of the *New Republic* and the *Outlook*, who were committed both to the Allied cause and neutrality for the United States, gave approval only grudgingly.[9] The spokesmen of the German-American communities admitted that the protest was strong and convincing but complained that it came too late and included no hint of an ultimatum.[10] But the great majority of commentators agreed with Frank Cobb, who wrote in the New York *World* on November 8, 1915, as follows:

"On such a showing of outrage as is here made, the terms of the American protest, which are lawyer-like throughout, must be regarded as exceedingly temperate. To gain a military advantage more or less important, Great Britain has become a grievous offender against law, against its own cherished principles, against several of the small nations of Europe which it has assumed to champion and against the best and most powerful friend that it has among the neutrals of the earth. It has not killed Americans; it has killed American rights. It has done more than seize American property; it has . . . [denied] American sovereignty."[11]

The German Ambassador was so impressed by the outpouring of American sentiment that he sent a large number of editorial extracts to the Foreign Office, something he did not ordinarily do.[12]

Leaders and publicists in Germany pored over the note with an astonishment and delight that increased the more they read. Officials on the Wilhelmstrasse did not "entertain exaggerated expectations" of an American "advance against English pirating at sea," mainly because they well knew that it would help them relatively little if the British did conduct their maritime warfare fully according to the rules of international law. None the less, they warmly welcomed the American protest, especially for its help in the ideological struggle; and they agreed that they must give the Washington government "a reasonable

[9] *New Republic*, v (November 13, 1915), 27-28; New York *Outlook*, cxi (November 17, 1915), 650-651.

[10] e.g., *New-Yorker Staats-Zeitung*, Cincinnati *Freie Presse*, Cincinnati *Volksblatt*, and St. Louis *Westliche Post*, all dated November 8, 1915.

[11] For excellent surveys of general American press reaction, see the *New York Times*, November 8, 1915, and "Our Case Against Great Britain," *Literary Digest*, li (November 20, 1915), 1141-1142.

[12] Ambassador von Bernstorff to the Foreign Office, November 10, 1915, German F. O. Archives.

amount of time in which to push its demands against England."[13]

For once the German press was glowing in its praise of the American President. "In one sense," declared the authoritative *Cologne Gazette*, for example, "the note is a historical document of the first importance. It announces to all the world, through the mouth of the mightiest neutral, . . . whose feet have trampled international law, who has destroyed the freedom of the seas. . . . This note has set on Great Britain's forehead a brand which she will never be able to wash away."[14] The most perceptive German analysis, however, came from the pen of Doctor Bernhard Dernburg, the former propagandist in America, whose comment filled the entire front page of the *Berliner Tageblatt* on November 12, 1915. After pointing out that President Wilson had struggled with equal sincerity to bring both Germany and Great Britain back to respect for international law, Dernburg continued:

"The submarine question had to be settled first, because this was not a question, like Great Britain's commercial war against Germany, of replaceable wares or financial losses, but of the lives of American citizens. The differences with Great Britain, therefore, were postponed until the road had been cleared by Germany's wise concessions in the 'Arabic' case. . . .

"The German press has raised the question whether the United States would endeavor to enforce compliance with her demands. According to the diplomatic history of the United States—and the 'Lusitania' case is a page in this history—there is every reason to believe that this will be done at all costs . . . , however little the President desires difficulties with Great Britain (or Germany, either). . . . While only minor measures of compulsion were available against Germany, because of the complete suppression of [her] trade, far more powerful weapons are at hand against Great Britain and her allies, for example, the refusal of credit, prohibiting National banks to discount the notes of the Allies, an embargo on individual trade items useful to the Allies, and finally the prohibition of the export of munitions."[15]

To Britons who were now pouring out their blood and treasure in

[13] Count Max Montgelas, "Memorandum about the Settlement of the Arabic Question, for the Eventual Use of the Foreign Secretary before the Budget Committee . . . ," dated December 1, 1915, *ibid*.

[14] *Kölnische Zeitung*, 1st morning edn., November 10, 1915.

[15] *Berliner Tageblatt*, morning edn., November 12, 1915. For other significant German editorial comments, see the Berlin *Morgenpost*, November 9, 1915; *Frankfurter Zeitung*, evening edns., November 9 and 11, 1915; *Kölnische Volkszeitung*, morning and noon edns., November 12, 1915.

what they thought was America's fight almost as much as their own, who were disheartened by the Allied failures of the past spring and summer and by the prospect of an endless war, and who were coming increasingly to regard the American government with pity, contempt, or loathing for being "too proud to fight" to defend its rights[16]—to such men the Secretary of State's note of protest was final proof of the moral collapse of the American government. "They are," the British Ambassador in Paris wrote in his Diary, "a rotten lot of psalm-singing, profit-mongering humbugs."[17] Sir Edward Grey apparently did not voice his disappointment to his friend Walter Page; or perhaps he did and Page thought it wiser not to convey his remarks to Washington. Most of the newspapers commented in a relatively restrained way, observing, for example, merely that the language of the note was "bald almost to the point of incivility" and "pettifogging,"[18] or that the American arguments were "utterly inapplicable in the world of things as they are."[19] One irrepressible spokesman, however, said what most of his thoughtful fellow-countrymen really believed:

"It is a document unworthy of the best traditions of American statesmanship. . . . When history comes to be written, the Americans of future generations will feel anything but pride when they remember the official action of America during the Great War. They will note how, first, it consisted in maintaining a rigid neutrality on a moral issue—*i.e.*, the brutalizing, as Colonel Roosevelt called it, of Belgium. Further, the Washington Government bore the outrages committed on American subjects in such incidents as the sinking of the 'Lusitania' . . . until the efficiency of the British Navy had abated the under-water menace. Again, when in the supreme moment of England's agony they found, or thought they had found, certain technical infringements of their rights, they vehemently pushed their paper case, and declared that we must only save our lives and our honour and free the world from the inhuman tyranny of Germany if we could manage to do so

[16] As Ambassador Page had already pointed out in a series of letters and messages conveying the growing British disenchantment with the American President and his policies. See Ambassador Page to the Secretary of State, September 8, 1915, *Foreign Relations, 1915, Supplement*, pp. 537-538; W. H. Page to E. M. House, September 8 (two letters) and 21, 1915, B. J. Hendrick, *The Life and Letters of Walter H. Page*, II, 30-40; W. H. Page to W.W., September 9, 1915, Wilson Papers; W. H. Page to W.W., October 5, 1915, B. J. Hendrick, *The Life and Letters of Walter H. Page*, II, 41-43.

[17] Lady Algernon G. Lennox (ed.), *The Diary of Lord Bertie of Thame, 1914-1918*, I, 267.

[18] London *New Statesman*, November 13, 1915.

[19] London *Pall Mall Gazette*, November 8, 1915.

without treading on America's grass-plot or scraping a little paint off her garden fence. . . .

"The American note causes us little concern. . . . Its harsh and unsympathetic tone will not make us relax in the slightest degree the grip on the throat of Germany which sea power gives us. We shall answer the note politely, and, we trust, in a much more human spirit than that which inspires its words, but we shall answer it firmly. That we must do in any case, whatever the consequences. But there will be no consequences of a serious character."[20]

Surveying British reaction some days after the publication of the note in London, Ambassador Page had to report to the President that the British and American peoples were now further apart in spirit than at any time since the American Civil War.[21]

With the dispatch of the note of October 21, 1915, to London, the construction of the edifice of American neutrality was finally completed. Now, more firmly than ever before, the Washington authorities stood committed to defense of historic principles, tempered, however, by an expedient acquiescence in both the British and German maritime systems so long as they did not outrageously infringe American neutral rights.

When, as he probably did, President Wilson looked back over events of the past fourteen months, he surely remembered the clamorous days and sleepless nights and the mistakes that he had made. At the same time, he must have recognized that his record was not altogether one of failure.

In the face of the most sweeping pretensions, he, in company with Secretaries Bryan and Lansing, had won guarantees from the German government for the protection of American ships and cargoes and for the safety of American citizens even on belligerent passenger ships against the peril of unseen attack, and a promise from the Germans to conduct submarine operations against ordinary merchantmen insofar as possible within the rules of visit and search. All this in a sense had been the President's personal achievement—the result of his decision to narrow the submarine dispute at its most critical juncture to an issue of manageable proportions, of his almost endless patience in nego-

[20] *The* (London) *Spectator*, cxv (November 13, 1915), 650. I have transposed the last paragraph.
[21] W. H. Page to W.W., November 19, 1915, Wilson Papers. For extended comment on this theme, see A. S. Link, *President Wilson and His English Critics*, pp. 3-12.

tiation, and of his uncanny ability to press the German leaders in precisely the right way at the right time so as to tip the weight in the struggle for control of submarine policy to the side of the civilian branch of the Imperial government.

He, along with Bryan and Lansing, had accepted the legitimate exercise of British sea power in the suppression of American trade with the Central Powers. At the same time, by public statements and diplomatic correspondence, he had led the American people to understand why their government could pursue no other course within the framework of neutrality. It would have been easy enough, considering the enormity of the interests adversely affected by the British measures and the anti-British undertones of American politics and thought, to stir the people to new heights of chauvinism, and to profit politically from the ensuing agitation.

Against British pretensions to an indiscriminate sea dominion he had fought patiently but almost ceaselessly, even during the long period of the submarine controversy with Germany. And from the London Foreign Office and Admiralty he had won signal concessions to American economic interests. After seeming to acquiesce in the blockade announced in the British Order in Council of March 11, 1915, he had denounced that blockade as illegal and indefensible and declared the American government's determination to stand foursquare for what rights of trade were left to Americans under international law.

After trial and error and some fumbling, he and Bryan and Lansing had worked out policies for the enforcement of neutrality at home. Most important, on the two decisive questions affecting America's economic relations overseas—the export of contraband, and private loans and credits to belligerent governments—they had taken a solidly neutral position that gave no undue advantage to either side.

By the end of the first fourteen months of the war no partisan of either alliance could fairly say that the policies of the United States were unneutral. No belligerent government could fairly complain that the hand of the Washington administration was raised against it.

Finally, at home the President had won the confidence of a large majority of the people, established himself as an authentic national spokesman, and restored a large measure of unity to a hitherto divided and confused nation. And this was true because he had conducted the only kind of foreign policies upon which the preponderant majority could agree.

To say that these were all substantial achievements is not to imply that they were necessarily wise or right. It is to say only that Wilson and his advisers on the whole accomplished what they set out to do, and that they served the national will by doing so. Whether they were also promoting the national interest and serving the peace of the world, only time would tell.

Bibliography of Sources and Works Cited[1]

THE author wishes to acknowledge his indebtedness to the following publisher:

To Constable & Company, Ltd., for permission to quote from *The Letters and Friendships of Sir Cecil Spring Rice*, edited by Stephen Gwynn.

And to the following persons and libraries, for permission to quote from letters and diaries:

Dr. Charles Seymour and the Yale University Library, the Diary of Edward M. House, letters of E. M. House, and letters in the Papers of E. M. House; Mrs. Woodrow Wilson, letters of Woodrow Wilson.

MANUSCRIPTS

The Diary and Papers of Chandler P. Anderson, Library of Congress.
The Papers of Herbert Asquith, Bodleian Library, Oxford.
The Ray Stannard Baker Collection of Wilsonia, Library of Congress.
The Papers of William Jennings Bryan, Library of Congress.
The Papers of William Jennings Bryan, National Archives.
The Papers of James, Viscount Bryce, Bodleian Library, Oxford.
The Papers of Albert Sidney Burleson, Library of Congress.
The Diary and Papers of Josephus Daniels, Library of Congress.
The Papers of the Department of State, National Archives.
The Archives of the German Foreign Office, on microfilm in the National
  Archives.
The Papers of Carter Glass, University of Virginia Library.
The Papers of Thomas Watt Gregory, Library of Congress.
The Scrapbooks of Charles S. Hamlin, Library of Congress.
The Diary and Papers of Edward M. House, Yale University Library.
The Papers of David F. Houston, Harvard University Library.
The Papers of the Japanese Foreign Office, the Foreign Office, Tokyo.
The Papers of William Kent, Yale University Library.
The Papers of Claude Kitchin, University of North Carolina Library.
The Diary and Papers of Robert Lansing, Library of Congress.
The Lodge-Morse Correspondence, Massachusetts Historical Society.
The Diary and Papers of Walter H. Page, Harvard University Library.
The Papers of Frank L. Polk, Yale University Library.
The Papers of Sir Horace Plunkett, the Horace Plunkett Foundation, London.

[1] This bibliography includes *only* those works and sources cited in the footnotes in this volume. For a survey of the literature and sources dealing with the period 1914-1915, see Arthur S. Link, *Woodrow Wilson and the Progressive Era* (New York: Harper & Brothers, 1954), pp. 283-313.

The Papers of Theodore Roosevelt, Library of Congress.
The Papers of Elihu Root, Library of Congress.
The Papers of Hugh L. Scott, Library of Congress.
The Papers of Charles L. Swem, Princeton University Library.
The Papers of William Howard Taft, Library of Congress.
The Papers of Daniel A. Tompkins, University of North Carolina Library.
The Papers of Oswald Garrison Villard, Harvard University Library.
The Papers of Thomas J. Walsh, Library of Congress.
The Papers of Henry Watterson, Library of Congress.
The Papers of Woodrow Wilson, Library of Congress.
The Wilson-Hulbert Correspondence, Princeton University Library.

PUBLIC DOCUMENTS

PUBLICATIONS OF THE UNITED STATES GOVERNMENT

Congressional Record, 63d Cong., 2d through the 3d sess. Washington, 1913-1915.

Department of State. *Papers Relating to the Foreign Relations of the United States, 1909.* Washington, 1914.

Department of State. *Papers Relating to the Foreign Relations of the United States, 1913.* Washington, 1920.

Department of State. *Papers Relating to the Foreign Relations of the United States, 1914.* Washington, 1922.

Department of State. *Papers Relating to the Foreign Relations of the United States, 1914, Supplement, The World War.* Washington, 1928.

Department of State. *Papers Relating to the Foreign Relations of the United States, 1915.* Washington, 1924.

Department of State. *Papers Relating to the Foreign Relations of the United States, 1915, Supplement, The World War.* Washington, 1928.

Department of State. *Papers Relating to the Foreign Relations of the United States, 1916.* Washington, 1925.

Department of State. *Papers Relating to the Foreign Relations of the United States, The Lansing Papers, 1914-1920.* 2 v., Washington, 1939-1940.

Federal Reserve Board. *Federal Reserve Bulletin*, I. Washington, 1915.

[Secretary of the Treasury] *Annual Report of the Secretary of the Treasury on the State of the Finances for the Fiscal Year Ended June 30, 1914.* Washington, 1915.

[Secretary of the Treasury and Secretary of Commerce] *Increased Ocean Transportation Rates, Letter from the Secretary of the Treasury and the Secretary of Commerce.* 63d Cong., 3d sess., Senate Document 673. 2 parts, Washington, 1914-1915.

[United States Senate] *Inquiry into Occupation and Administration of Haiti and the Dominican Republic.* 67th Cong., 2d sess., Senate Report 794. Washington, 1922.

[United States Senate] *Lobby to Influence Legislation on Ship-Purchase Bill.* 64th Cong., 1st sess., Senate Report 25. 2 parts, Washington, 1916.

[United States Senate] *Munitions Industry. Supplemental Report . . . of the Special Committee on Investigation of the Munitions Industry.* 74th Cong., 2d sess., Senate Report 944. Washington, 1936.

PUBLICATIONS OF FOREIGN GOVERNMENTS

Republic of France, Ministry of Foreign Affairs. *Les Violations des lois de la guerre par l'Allemagne.* Paris: Berger-Levrault, 1915.

[United Kingdom] Committee on Alleged German Outrages. *Report of the Committee on Alleged German Outrages.* London: H.M. Stationery Office, 1915.

CORRESPONDENCE AND COLLECTED WORKS

Baker, Ray Stannard. *Woodrow Wilson, Life and Letters.* 8 v., Garden City: Doubleday, Page, and Doubleday, Doran, 1927-1939.

Baker, Ray Stannard, and William E. Dodd (eds.). *The Public Papers of Woodrow Wilson.* 6 v., New York: Harper & Brothers, 1925-1927.

Cambon, Henri (ed.). *Paul Cambon, Correspondance, 1870-1924.* 3 v., Paris: Editions Bernard Grasset, 1940-1946.

Gwynn, Stephen (ed.). *The Letters and Friendships of Sir Cecil Spring Rice.* 2 v., London: Constable, 1929.

Hendrick, Burton J. *The Life and Letters of Walter H. Page.* 3 v., Garden City: Doubleday, Page, 1924-1926.

Morison, Elting E., *et al.* (eds.). *The Letters of Theodore Roosevelt.* 8 v., Cambridge, Mass.: Harvard University Press, 1951-1954.

Seymour, Charles (ed.). *The Intimate Papers of Colonel House.* 4 v., Boston: Houghton Mifflin, 1926-1928.

AUTOBIOGRAPHIES AND MEMOIRS

Bernstorff, Johann H. von. *My Three Years in America.* London: Skeffington & Son, n.d. but 1920.

Bethmann Hollweg, Theobald von. *Considérations sur la Guerre Mondiale.* 2 v., Paris: Charles-Lavauzelle & Cie., 1924.

Bryan, William J. and Mary B. *The Memoirs of William Jennings Bryan.* Philadelphia and Chicago: John C. Winston Co., 1925.

Grey, Edward (Viscount Grey of Fallodon). *Twenty-Five Years, 1892-1916.* 2 v., New York: Frederick A. Stokes, 1925.

House, Edward M. "The Memoirs of Colonel House." Unpublished MS. deposited in the Papers of George Sylvester Viereck, Yale University Library.

Houston, David F. *Eight Years with Wilson's Cabinet, 1913 to 1920.* 2 v., Garden City: Doubleday, Page, 1926.

Lansing, Robert. *War Memoirs of Robert Lansing*. Indianapolis: Bobbs-Merrill, 1935.

Lennox, Lady Algernon Gordon (ed.). *The Diary of Lord Bertie of Thame, 1914-1918*. 2 v., London: Hodder & Stoughton, 1924.

Lloyd George, David. *The War Memoirs of David Lloyd George*. 6 v., London: Ivor Nicholson and Watson, 1933-1936.

McAdoo, William G. *Crowded Years, The Reminiscences of William G. McAdoo*. Boston: Houghton Mifflin, 1931.

Poincaré, Raymond. *Au Service de la France, Neuf Années de Souvenirs*. 10 v., Paris: Plon-Nourrit et Cie., 1926-1933.

Reinsch, Paul S. *An American Diplomat in China*. Garden City: Doubleday, Page, 1922.

Rintelen, Captain von (Franz Rintelen von Kleist). *The Dark Invader, Wartime Reminiscences of a German Naval Intelligence Officer*. London: L. Dickson Ltd., 1933.

Straus, Oscar S. *Under Four Administrations, From Cleveland to Taft*. Boston: Houghton Mifflin, 1922.

Tirpitz, Alfred von. *Politische Dokumente von A. von Tirpitz*. 2 v., Stuttgart and Berlin: Cotta, 1924-1926.

Westarp, Count Kuno F. V. von. *Konservative Politik im Letzten Jahrzehnt des Kaiserreiches*. 2 v., Berlin: Deutsche Verlagsgesellschaft, 1935.

MISCELLANEOUS CONTEMPORARY WORKS

Asquith, Herbert. *The War: Its Causes and Its Message*. London: Methuen, 1915.

Asquith, Herbert. *Why We Are at War*. London: Methuen, 1914.

Beck, James M. *The Evidence in the Case*. New York: G. P. Putnam's Sons, 1914.

Beck, James M. *The War and Humanity*. New York: G. P. Putnam's Sons, 1917.

Bédier, Joseph. *Les Crimes Allemands d'après Témoignages Allemands*. Paris: Colin, 1916.

Bernhardi, Friedrich von. *Germany and the Next War*, translated by Allen H. Powles. New York: Longmans, Green, 1914.

Beveridge, Albert J. *What Is Back of the War*. Indianapolis: Bobbs-Merrill, 1915.

Burgess, John W. *The European War of 1914, Its Causes, Purposes, and Probable Results*. Chicago: A. C. McClurg, 1915.

Chapman, John Jay. *Deutschland Über Alles, or Germany Speaks*. New York: G. P. Putnam's Sons, 1914.

Church, Samuel Harden. *The American Verdict on the War*. Baltimore: Norman, Remington, 1915.

Clapp, Edwin J. *Economic Aspects of the War*. New Haven: Yale University Press, 1915.

Collman, Charles A. *The War Plotters of Wall Street*. New York: Fatherland Corporation, 1915.

Cramb, J. A. *Germany and England*. New York: Dutton, 1914.

Dernburg, Bernhard. *The Case of Belgium*. New York: International Monthly, 1914.

Eltzbacher, Paul (ed.). *Die deutsche Volksernährung und der englische Aushungerungsplan*. Braunschweig: F. Vieweg & Sohn, 1915.

Francke, Kuno. *A German-American's Confession of Faith*. New York: Huebsch, 1915.

Fuehr, Alexander. *The Neutrality of Belgium*. New York: Funk & Wagnalls, 1915.

Fullerton, George S. *Germany of To-Day*. Indianapolis: Bobbs-Merrill, 1915.

Greene, Francis V. *The Present Military Situation in the United States*. New York: Scribner's, 1915.

S.R.H. and J.F.M. *Sixty American Opinions on the War*. London: T. Fisher Unwin, 1915.

Headlam, J. W. *England, Germany, and Europe*. London: Macmillan, 1914.

Hugins, Roland. *Germany Misjudged*. Chicago: Open Court, 1916.

Huidekoper, Frederick L. *The Military Unpreparedness of the United States*. New York: Macmillan, 1915.

Johnston, Robert M. *Arms and the Race, The Foundations of Army Reform*. New York: Century, 1915.

Lauriat, Charles E., Jr. *The Lusitania's Last Voyage*. Boston: Houghton Mifflin, 1915.

Ludwig, Ernest. *Austria-Hungary and the War*. New York: J. S. Ogilvie, 1915.

Mach, Edmund von. *What Germany Wants*. Boston: Little, Brown, 1914.

Maxim, Hudson, *Defenseless America*. New York: Hearst's International Library, 1915.

McGuire, Daniel K. *The King, the Kaiser, and Irish Freedom*. New York: Devin-Adair, 1915.

McGuire, Daniel K. *What Could Germany Do for Ireland?* New York: Wolfe Tone Co., 1916.

Meurer, Christian. *Der Lusitania-Fall. Eine Völkerrechtliche Studie*. Tübingen: J. C. B. Mohr, 1915.

Münsterberg, Hugo. *The Peace and America*. New York: Appleton, 1915.

Münsterberg, Hugo. *The War and America*. New York: Appleton, 1914.

Muir, Ramsay. *Britain's Case Against Germany*. Manchester: University of Manchester Press, 1914.

Murray, Gilbert. *The Foreign Policy of Sir Edward Grey, 1906-1915*. Oxford: Clarendon Press, 1915.

Reed, John. *Insurgent Mexico*. New York: Appleton, 1914.

Sladen, Douglas. *The Real "Truth About Germany," Facts About the War*. New York: G. P. Putnam's Sons, 1915.

Stephen, S. Ivor. *Neutrality? The Crucifixion of Public Opinion*. Chicago: Neutrality Press, 1916.

Thayer, William R. *Germany vs. Civilization*. Boston: Houghton Mifflin, 1916.

Villard, Oswald Garrison. *Germany Embattled*. New York: Scribner's, 1915.

Walker, J. Bernard. *America Fallen!* New York: Dodd, Mead, 1915.

Wheeler, Howard D. *Are We Ready?* Boston: Houghton Mifflin, 1915.

Whitridge, Frederick W. *One American's Opinion of the European War, An Answer to Germany's Appeals*. New York: Dutton, 1914.

Wilson, Woodrow. *Leaders of Men* (T. H. Vail Motter, ed.). Princeton: Princeton University Press, 1952.

Various authors. *Der Lusitania-Fall im Urteile von deutschen Gelehrten*. Breslau: J. U. Kern, 1915.

How the Franco-German Conflict Could Have Been Avoided, reprinted in the *New York Times*, September 11, 1914.

Truth About Germany, Facts About the War. New York: Trow Press, 1914.

A Way to Stop the War. New York: American Truth Society, 1915.

NEWSPAPERS CITED

AMERICAN

Athens (Georgia) *Banner*, 1915.

Atlanta *Constitution*, 1915.

Baltimore *Evening Sun*, 1915.

Birmingham News, 1915.

Boston *American*, 1915.

Boston Evening Transcript, 1914.

Brooklyn Tablet, 1915.

Charlotte Observer, 1915.

Chicago *Abendpost*, 1915.

Chicagoer Presse, 1915.

Chicago Evening Post, 1914.

Chicago News, 1914.

Chicago *Staats-Zeitung*, 1915.

Chicago *Tribune*, 1914-1915.

Cincinnati *Freie Presse*, 1915.

Cincinnati *Volksblatt*, 1915.

Detroit *Abendpost*, 1915.

Fort Worth *Star-Telegram*, 1914.

Johnstown (Pennsylvania) *Democrat*, 1915.

Louisville *Courier-Journal*, 1914-1915.
Milwaukee *Germania Herold*, 1915.
Newport (Rhode Island) *Daily News*, 1914.
New York *American*, 1915.
New Yorker Herold, 1915.
New Yorker Staats-Zeitung, 1915.
New York Evening Post, 1915.
New York *Evening Sun*, 1915.
New York *Journal of Commerce*, 1914-1915.
New York *Sun*, 1914-1915.
New York Times, 1914-1916.
New York *Tribune*, 1914-1915.
New York *World*, 1914-1915.
Providence Journal, 1915.
St. Louis *Church Progress*, 1915.
St. Louis *Republic*, 1915.
St. Louis *Star*, 1914.
St. Louis *Westliche Post*, 1915.
Springfield (Massachusetts) *Republican*, 1915.
Washington Post, 1915.

FOREIGN

Berlin *Boersen Zeitung*, 1915.
Berlin *Deutsche Tageszeitung*, 1915.
Berliner Lokal-Anzeiger, 1915.
Berlin *Kreuz-Zeitung*, 1915.
Berlin *Morgenpost*, 1915.
Berlin *Nord-deutschen Allgemeinen Zeitung*, 1915.
Berlin *Post*, 1915.
Berlin *Taegliche Rundschau*, 1915.
Berlin *Tageblatt*, 1915.
Berlin *Vorwärts*, 1915.
Berlin *Vossische Zeitung*, 1915.
Frankfurter Zeitung, 1915.
Hamburger Nachrichten, 1915.
Kölnische Volkszeitung, 1915.
Kölnische Zeitung, 1915.
London *Pall Mall Gazette*, 1915.
London *Standard*, 1915.
London *Times*, 1915.
London *Westminster Gazette*, 1915.
Montreal Gazette, 1915.
Paris *Action Française*, 1915.

Paris *L'Homme Enchainé*, 1915.
Paris *Liberté*, 1915.
Paris *Le Matin*, 1915.
Tokyo *Yomiuri*, 1915.

PERIODICALS CITED FOR EDITORIAL OPINION

America, 1914-1915.
Bankers Magazine, 1915.
Baptist Standard (Dallas), 1915.
The Christian Advocate (Nashville), 1915.
The Christian Advocate (New York), 1915.
The Churchman, 1915.
Collier's, 1914-1915.
The Commoner (Lincoln, Nebraska), 1914-1915.
The Congregationalist and Christian World, 1915.
The Economist (London), 1914.
Financial Age, 1914.
Financial World, 1914.
Harper's Weekly, 1914-1915.
The Independent, 1914-1915.
Literary Digest, 1914-1915.
The Living Church, 1915.
Lutheran Church Work, 1915.
Lutheran Youth, 1914.
The Nation (London), 1915.
The Nation (New York), 1914-1915.
The New Republic, 1914-1915.
The New Statesman (London), 1915.
The Outlook (New York), 1914-1915.
The Presbyterian, 1914.
Presbyterian Banner, 1914-1915.
The Public (Chicago), 1914-1915.
Saturday Evening Post, 1914-1915.
The Saturday Review (London), 1915.
The Spectator (London), 1915.
The Standard, A Baptist Newspaper (Chicago), 1914-1915.
The Survey, 1915.
World's Work, 1915.

SIGNED CONTEMPORARY ARTICLES

Aked, Charles F., and Walter Rauschenbusch, "Private Profit and the Nation's Honor: A Protest and a Plea," *The Standard*, LXII (July 31, 1915), 1486-1487.

Bernstorff, J. H. von, "Germany and the Great War," *The Independent*, LXXIX (September 7, 1914), 333-334.

Bethmann Hollweg, Theobald von, "Germany's Appeal to America, Chancellor von Bethmann-Hollweg Invites Impartiality," *La Follette's Weekly*, VI (August 29, 1914), 9.

Bethmann Hollweg, T. von, statement in *World's Work*, XXIX (January 1915), 249-252.

Brooks, Sydney, "The United States and the War: A British View," *North American Review*, CCI (February 1915), 231-240.

Bryan, William J., "Neutrality Toward Both," *The Commoner*, XV (August 1915), 1, 3.

Bryan, William J., "No Loans to Belligerents," *The Commoner*, XIV (September 1914), 2.

Bryan, William J., "WRITE AND WRITE *NOW*," *The Commoner*, XV (August 1915), 1, 3.

Bryce, Lord James, "Message to the American People," *The Independent*, LXXXI (March 29, 1915), 464.

Burgess, John W., "England Twists Decisions of Civil War to Prop Weak Case," *New York Evening Mail*, August 14, 1914.

Burgess, J. W., "John W. Burgess on the Present Crisis," *Boston Evening Transcript*, August 19, 1914.

Burgess, J. W., letter to the *Springfield* (Massachusetts) *Republican*, reprinted in *The Open Court*, XXVIII (October 1914), 587-595.

Child, Richard Washburn, "Efficiency for Defense," *Collier's*, LVI (September 18, 1915), 7-8, 34-37.

Cobb, Irwin S., "Being a Guest of the German Kaiser," *Saturday Evening Post*, CLXXXVII (October 24, 1914), 14-15, 48-50.

Cobb, I. S., "Johann Schmidt, Private," *Saturday Evening Post*, CLXXXVII (January 30, 1915), 13-15, 29-30.

Cobb, I. S., "Punitives versus Primitives," *Saturday Evening Post*, CLXXXVII (November 14, 1914), 14-15, 37-38.

Corwin, Edward S., "Is the British Embargo Lawful?" *New Republic*, IV (August 14, 1915), 37-38.

Delbrück, Hans, interview printed in the New York *American*, October 24, 1915.

Dernburg, Bernhard, "Germany and the Powers," *North American Review*, CC (December 1914), 833-846.

Dernburg, B., "The Ties That Bind America and Germany," *World's Work*, XXIX (December 1914), 186-189.

Dernburg, B., "When Germany Wins," *The Independent*, LXXX (December 7, 1914), 361-362.

Dippel, Christian, "A German View of the War," *The Standard*, LXII (October 3, 1914), 102-103.

Dosch, Arno, "Louvain the Lost," *World's Work*, xxviii (October 1914), A-H.

Dumba, K. T., "The Austro-Servian Conflict," *Outlook*, cvii (August 29, 1914), 1028-1030.

Dumba, K. T., "Why Austria Is at War with Russia," *North American Review*, cc (September 1914), 346-352.

Fullerton, George S., "Why the German Nation Has Gone to War," *Lutheran Church Work*, iii (February 4, 1915), 10-13.

Garrison, Lindley M., "The War and America. VIII—What We Need," *Harper's Weekly*, lxi (July 24, 1915), 79-81.

Grant, Robert, "The Superman," New York *Nation*, xcix (October 29, 1914), 521.

Grapho, "Roman Catholic Complaint Concerning Mexico," *The Congregationalist and Christian World*, c (January 21, 1915), 78.

Haeckel, Ernst, and Rudolf Bucken, "An Appeal to the Universities of America," *The Open Court*, xxviii (November 1914), 659-661.

Hapgood, Norman, "Bernhardi and the United States," *Harper's Weekly*, lix (October 17, 1914), 367-368.

Hapgood, N., "Pan-Germanism and the United States," *Harper's Weekly*, lix (October 24, 1914), 391-393.

Hapgood, N., "The Prussian Menace," *Harper's Weekly*, lix (September 19, 1914), 273-274.

Hapgood, N., "Who Made Germany Crazy? I. Bismarck and Von Treitske [*sic*]," *Harper's Weekly*, lix (October 3, 1914), 316-317.

Hapgood, N., "Who Made Germany Crazy? II. The Kaiser and Von Buelow," *Harper's Weekly*, lix (October 10, 1914), 343-345.

Harvey, George, " 'America First!' " *North American Review*, ccii (August 1915), 161-170.

Harvey, G., "The Duty of America," *North American Review*, cci (June 1915), 801-807.

Harvey, G., "Europe at Armageddon," *North American Review*, cc (September 1914), 321-332.

Harvey, G., "Patriotism and Profits," *North American Review*, ccii (November 1915), 641-657.

Hildebrandt, A. W., "About the War," *Lutheran Church Work*, iii (October 15, 1914), 8.

Hopper, James, "Pancho Villa," *Collier's*, lvii (April 29, 1916), 8-10, 43 ff.

Howells, William Dean, "Why?" *North American Review*, cci (May 1915), 676-682.

Keip, B., "The German Social Democracy and the War," New York *Christian Advocate*, xc (June 3, 1915), 743-744.

Lehmann, J. G., "A Message from German Baptists," *The Standard*, LXII (October 3, 1914), 104.

Lodge, Oliver, "The War: A British View," *North American Review*, CCI (January 1915), 45-51.

Mach, Edmund von, "The German Viewpoint," *Boston Evening Transcript*, December 2, 1914.

Marvin, George, "Villa," *World's Work*, XXVIII (July 1914), 269-284.

Mason, Gregory, "The Mexican Man of the Hour," New York *Outlook*, CVII (June 6, 1914), 292, 301-306.

Mason, Gregory, "With Villa in Chihuahua," New York *Outlook*, CVII (May 9, 1914), 75.

Massingham, H. W., "British Policy and the War," *Atlantic Monthly*, CXV (January 1915), 116-123.

Massingham, H. W., "Open Letter to the American People," *Atlantic Monthly*, CXV (May 1915), 701-706.

Mathews, Shailer, *et al.*, "Appeal to the President," Nashville *Christian Advocate*, LXXV (September 4, 1914), 1149.

More, Paul Elmer, "The Lust of Empire," New York *Nation*, XCIX (October 22, 1914), 493-495.

Münsterberg, Hugo, "Fair Play!" Boston *Herald*, August 5, 1914.

Neve, J. L., "Who Is Responsible for This War?" *Lutheran Church Work*, III (September 3, 1914), 8-9.

Parker, Gilbert, "The United States and the War," *Harper's Magazine*, CXXXVI (March 1918), 522.

Patullo, George, "The Enchanted Captain," *Saturday Evening Post*, CLXXXIX (January 20, 1917), 6-7, 73-74, 77.

Perry, Stuart H., "After the War," *North American Review*, CC (November 1914), 732-741.

Rauschenbusch, Walter, "Be Fair to Germany," *The Congregationalist and Christian World*, reprinted in *Lutheran Church Work*, III (November 19, 1914), 8-10.

Reventlow, Ernst von, "German Propaganda for Deliveries of Weapons to Germany's Enemies," Berlin *Deutsche Tageszeitung*, morning edn., June 16, 1915.

Roosevelt, Theodore, "The International Posse Comitatus," *New York Times Magazine Section*, November 8, 1914.

Roosevelt, T., "Our Responsibility in Mexico," *New York Times*, December 6, 1914.

Roosevelt, T., "The World War: Its Tragedies and Its Lessons," New York *Outlook*, CVIII (September 23, 1914), 169-178.

Steel, Henry Wickham, "The German Bluff," *Harper's Weekly*, LIX (September 26, 1914), 295-296.

Street, Julian, "Our Next War," *Collier's*, LV (June 19, 1915), 5-7, 28, 30-31.

Sweetser, Arthur, "A Diary from the Front," *World's Work*, xxix (January 1915), 350-356.

Sweetser, A., "With the German Army in Its Dash Toward Paris," New York *Outlook*, cix (January 27, 1915), 186-190.

Taylor, Joseph R., "'Pancho' Villa at First Hand," *World's Work*, xxviii (July 1914), 265-269.

Whitaker, Herman, "Villa—Bandit Patriot," *The Independent*, lxxviii (June 8, 1914), 450-452.

Willert, Arthur, "Anglo-American Relations—and the War," *World's Work*, xxix (December 1914), 181-185.

Winton, G. B., "'Poor Mexico!'" New York *Christian Advocate*, xc (December 9, 1915), 1668-1669.

Winton, G. B., "Shall the American People 'Recognize' Carranza?" Nashville *Christian Advocate*, lxxvi (December 10, 1915), 1619-1620.

UNSIGNED CONTEMPORARY ARTICLES

"American Feeling About the German Note," New York *Nation*, ci (July 15, 1915), 83.

"The American Protest to Great Britain," New York *Outlook*, cix (January 6, 1915), 10.

"American Sympathies in the War," *Literary Digest*, xlix (November 14, 1914), 939-941, 974-978.

"America's Diplomatic Victory," *Literary Digest*, li (October 16, 1915), 821-824.

"America Unready," *Literary Digest*, l (June 5, 1915), 1314-1316.

"Another Message from the German Protestants," *Lutheran Church Work*, iii (January 28, 1915), 22-23.

"An Appeal from Breklum," *Lutheran Church Work*, iii (October 8, 1914), 8-9.

"Are We Neutral?" *Collier's*, liii (September 12, 1914), 16.

"The Attack on the Arabic," *Literary Digest*, li (August 28, 1915), 387-388.

"Blaming Germany for the War," *Literary Digest*, xlix (August 22, 1914), 292-295.

"British 'Lies' and American Sentiment," New York *Nation*, xcix (November 26, 1914), 621-622.

"Darkest Side of the Great War," *Literary Digest*, xlix (September 12, 1914), 441-443.

"England's 'Right' to Blockade Neutrals," *Literary Digest*, li (August 14, 1915), 285-287.

"The English Point of View," New York *Outlook*, cviii (September 2, 1914), 42-44.

"European and American Neutrality," *The Economist*, lxxix (August 22, 1914), 340-341.

"German Appeals to America," New York *Nation*, xcix (October 15, 1914), 455-456.

"The German Exposures," New York *Nation*, ci (August 19, 1915), 219.

"German Respect for the Monroe Doctrine," *Literary Digest*, xlix (November 7, 1914), 871-873.

"Germany and the Monroe Doctrine," New York *Outlook*, cviii (November 4, 1914), 521-524.

"Germany Yields to Wilson," *Literary Digest*, li (September 11, 1915), 509-511.

"The Growth of American Pacifism," London *Nation*, xviii (October 2, 1915), 9-10.

"Lessons of the War: The German-Americans," *The Open Court*, xxviii (December 1914), 747-751.

"A Letter from a German Theologian," *Lutheran Church Work*, iii (October 1, 1914), 9-11.

"Light on German Propaganda," *Literary Digest*, li (August 28, 1915), 388.

"A Message from German Churchmen," *Lutheran Church Work*, iii (October 8, 1914), 4.

"Nation-Wide Press Poll on Army and Navy Increase," *Literary Digest*, l (January 23, 1915), 137-138, 162, 164-169.

"An Open Letter from the Methodist Ministers in Germany," New York *Christian Advocate*, xc (May 20, 1915), 686.

"Our Case Against Great Britain," *Literary Digest*, li (November 20, 1915), 1141-1142.

"Our Evacuation of Vera Cruz," *Literary Digest*, xlix (December 5, 1914), 1104-1105.

"Our Government's Attitude Toward National Defense," *Literary Digest*, xlix (December 19, 1914), 1205-1207.

"Our Grievance Against England," *Literary Digest*, li (July 10, 1915), 45-47.

"Our Warning to Great Britain," *Literary Digest*, l (January 9, 1915), 37-39.

"The President's Plan for a Commercial Navy," *Literary Digest*, l (January 16, 1915), 81-83.

"Press Poll on Prohibiting the Export of Arms," *Literary Digest*, l (February 6, 1915), 225-226, 274-283.

"The Question of a Loan to Europe," New York *Nation*, ci (September 16, 1915), 349-350.

"The Real Crime Against Germany," New York *Nation*, xcix (August 13, 1914), 181-182.

"The Rise of Villa's Star," *Literary Digest*, xlviii (April 18, 1914), 859.

"Shall We Join Hands with Villa?" *Literary Digest*, xlviii (May 23, 1914), 1235-1238.

"Should We Prepare for Attack?" *Literary Digest*, xlix (December 12, 1914), 1159-1161.

"True Neutrality," *The Presbyterian*, LXXXIV (December 2, 1914), 3.

"Trying to Solve the Deadlock with Germany," *Literary Digest*, LI (July 24, 1915), 141-143.

"Unhappy Mexico: America's Responsibility," New York *Outlook*, CVIII (December 2, 1914), 752-753.

"Voice of the Clergy on the 'Lusitania' Case," *Literary Digest*, L (May 22, 1915), 1218-1219.

"What the German-Americans Are Organizing for," *Literary Digest*, L (February 13, 1915), 299-301.

"What the Mexican Revolution Has Done for Protestantism," New York *Christian Advocate*, XC (July 22, 1915), 974.

"Why the World Is Against Germany," *World's Work*, XXX (June 1915), 135A-135P.

SECONDARY WORKS AND ARTICLES

Baxter, James P., 3d, "The British Government and Neutral Rights, 1861-1865," *American Historical Review*, XXXIV (October 1928), 9-29.

Baxter, J. P., 3d, "Papers Relating to Belligerent and Neutral Rights, 1861-1865," *American Historical Review*, XXXIV (October 1928), 77-91.

Baxter, J. P., 3d, "Some British Opinions as to Neutral Rights, 1861-1865," *American Journal of International Law*, XXIII (July 1929), 517-537.

Beard, Charles A., "New Light on Bryan and War Policies," *The New Republic*, LXXXVII (June 17, 1936), 177-178.

Beers, Burton F., "Robert Lansing's Proposed Bargain with Japan," *Pacific Historical Review*, XXVI (November 1957), 391-400.

Bellegarde, Dantès. *La Nation Haitienne*. Paris: J. de Gigord, 1938.

Bellegarde, D. *La Résistance Haitienne (L'Occupation américaine d'Haiti)*. Montreal: Editions Beauchemin, 1937.

Blum, John M. *Joe Tumulty and the Wilson Era*. Boston: Houghton Mifflin, 1951.

Bond, F. Fraser. *Mr. Miller of "The Times."* New York: Scribner's, 1931.

Buell, Raymond L., "The American Occupation of Haiti," *Foreign Policy Association Information Service*, V (November 27-December 12, 1929), 334-335.

Child, Clifton J. *The German-Americans in Politics, 1914-1917*. Madison: University of Wisconsin Press, 1939.

Churchill, Winston S. *The World Crisis*. 6 v., London: Thornton Butterworth, 1923.

Costrell, Edwin. *How Maine Viewed the War, 1914-1917*. Orono: University of Maine Press, 1940.

Crighton, John C. *Missouri and the World War, 1914-1917*. Columbia: University of Missouri Press, 1947.

Cummins, Cedric C. *Indiana Public Opinion and the World War, 1914-1917.* Indianapolis: Indiana Historical Bureau, 1945.

Digby, Margaret. *Horace Plunkett, An Anglo-American Irishman.* Oxford: Blackwell, 1949.

Fisher, H. A. L. *James Bryce.* 2 v., London: Macmillan, 1927.

Garraty, John A. *Henry Cabot Lodge, A Biography.* New York: Knopf, 1953.

Gibson, R. H., and M. Prendergast. *The German Submarine War, 1914-1918.* New York: R. R. Smith, 1931.

Griswold, A. Whitney. *The Far Eastern Policy of the United States.* New York: Harcourt, Brace, 1938.

Hackett, Roger F. "Biography of Prince Yamagata." MS. in possession of the author.

Hagedorn, Hermann. *The Bugle That Woke America.* New York: John Day, 1940.

Harbaugh, William H. "Wilson, Roosevelt, and Interventionism, 1914-1917." Unpublished Ph.D. dissertation, 1954, Northwestern University Library.

Hoehling, A. A. and Mary. *The Last Voyage of the Lusitania.* New York: Holt, 1956.

Idditti, Smimasa. *The Life of Marquis Shigenobu Okuma, A Maker of New Japan.* Tokyo: Hokuseido Press, 1940.

Jansen, Marius B. *The Japanese and Sun Yat-sen.* Cambridge, Mass.: Harvard University Press, 1954.

La Fargue, Thomas E. *China and the World War.* Stanford: Stanford University Press, 1937.

Lasswell, Harold D. *Propaganda Technique in the World War.* New York: Knopf, 1927.

Lawrence, David. *The True Story of Woodrow Wilson.* New York: Doran, 1924.

Link, Arthur S., "The Cotton Crisis, the South, and Anglo-American Diplomacy, 1914-1915," in J. C. Sitterson (ed.), *Studies in Southern History in Memory of Albert Ray Newsome.* Chapel Hill: University of North Carolina Press, 1957.

Link, A. S. *President Wilson and His English Critics.* Oxford: Clarendon Press, 1959.

Link, A. S. *Wilson the Diplomatist, A Look at His Major Foreign Policies.* Baltimore: Johns Hopkins Press, 1957.

Link, A. S. *Wilson: The New Freedom.* Princeton: Princeton University Press, 1956.

May, Ernest R., "American Policy and Japan's Entrance into World War I," *Mississippi Valley Historical Review,* XL (September 1953), 279-290.

May, Ernest R. *The World War and American Isolation, 1914-1917.* Cambridge, Mass.: Harvard University Press, 1959.

McCroklin, James H. *Garde d'Haiti, Twenty Years of Organization and Training by the United States Marine Corps.* Annapolis: United States Naval Institute, 1956.

Millspaugh, Arthur C. *Haiti Under American Control, 1915-1930.* Boston: World Peace Foundation, 1931.

Montague, Ludwell L. *Haiti and the United States, 1714-1938.* Durham: Duke University Press, 1940.

Mott, T. Bentley. *Myron T. Herrick, Friend of France.* Garden City: Doubleday, Doran, 1929.

Noyes, Alexander D. *The War Period of American Finance, 1908-1925.* New York: G. P. Putnam's Sons, 1926.

Osgood, Robert E. *Ideals and Self-Interest in America's Foreign Relations.* Chicago: University of Chicago Press, 1953.

Peterson, H. C. *Propaganda for War.* Norman: University of Oklahoma Press, 1939.

Ponsonby, Arthur. *Falsehood in War-Time.* London: Allen and Unwin, 1928.

Pratt, Julius W., "The British Blockade and American Precedent," *United States Naval Institute Proceedings*, XLVI (November 1920), 1789-1802.

Puleston, William D. *Mahan, The Life and Work of Captain Alfred Thayer Mahan, U.S.N.* New Haven: Yale University Press, 1939.

Quirk, Robert E. "The Revolutionary Convention of Aguascalientes." MS. in possession of the author.

Rappaport, Armin. *The British Press and Wilsonian Neutrality.* Stanford: Stanford University Press, 1951.

Rappaport, Joseph. "Jewish Immigrants and World War I: A Study of American Yiddish Press Reactions." Unpublished Ph.D. dissertation, 1951, Columbia University Library.

Read, James M. *Atrocity Propaganda, 1914-1919.* New Haven: Yale University Press, 1941.

Shannon, David A. *The Socialist Party of America, A History.* New York: Macmillan, 1955.

Siney, Marion C. *The Allied Blockade of Germany, 1914-1916.* Ann Arbor: University of Michigan Press, 1957.

Smith, Daniel M. *Robert Lansing and American Neutrality, 1914-1917.* Berkeley: University of California Press, 1958.

Smith, D. M., "Robert Lansing and the Formulation of American Neutrality Policies, 1914-1915," *Mississippi Valley Historical Review*, XLIII (June 1956), 59-81.

Spindler, Arno. *La Guerre Sous-Marine*, translated by René Jouan. 3 v., Paris: Payot, 1933-1935.

Squires, James D. *British Propaganda at Home and in the United States from 1914 to 1917.* Cambridge, Mass.: Harvard University Press, 1935.

Stephenson, George M., "The Attitude of Swedish Americans Toward the World War," *Mississippi Valley Historical Association Proceedings*, x (1918-1919), Part I, 79-94.

Strachey, Amy. *St. Loe Strachey, His Life and Paper*. London: Gollancz, 1930.

Syrett, Harold C., "The Business Press and American Neutrality, 1914-1917," *Mississippi Valley Historical Review*, xxxii (September 1945), 215-230.

Tansill, C. C. *America and the Fight for Irish Freedom, 1866-1922*. New York: Devin-Adair, 1957.

Tansill, C. C. *America Goes to War*. Boston: Little, Brown, 1938 and 1942.

Tinsley, William W. "The American Preparedness Movement, 1913-1916." Unpublished Ph.D. dissertation, 1940, Stanford University Library.

Tokutomi, Iichiro. *Koshaku Matsukata Masayoshi Den* [*Biography of Prince Masayoshi Matsukata*]. 2 v., Tokyo: Committee for Publishing the Biography of Prince Matsukata, 1935.

Tokutomi, I. *Koshaku Yamagata Aritomo Den* [*Biography of Prince Aritomo Yamagata*]. 3 v., Tokyo: Committee for Publishing the Biography of Prince Yamagata, 1933.

Trevelyan, George Macaulay. *Grey of Fallodon*. Boston: Houghton Mifflin, 1937.

Viereck, George Sylvester. *Spreading Germs of Hate*. New York: Liveright, 1930.

Wanderscheck, Hermann. *Bibliographie zur englischen Propaganda im Weltkrieg*. Stuttgart: Weltskriegsbücherei, 1935.

Welles, Sumner. *Naboth's Vineyard, The Dominican Republic, 1844-1924*. New York: Payson & Clarke, 1928.

Wittke, Carl. *German-Americans and the World War*. Columbus: Ohio State Archaeological and Historical Society, 1936.

Index

Textual material in footnotes is indexed by reference to the page or pages on which the footnote occurs, but without indication that the item appears in a note. Titles, manuscript collections, authors of letters, etc., in footnotes are not indexed when they have been cited as references.

434; on necessity of concessions to America, 436
Miller, Adolph C., 619-620
Milwaukee Free Press, 397
Milwaukee *Sentinel*, 24
Môle St. Nicholas, 517-518, 520, 525, 530, 531, 532, 535
Montgelas, Max, 450-451, 571, 664, 679
Moore, John Bassett, 45
Morehead, John H., 376
Morgan, J. P., Jr., pro-Allied, 12; and Wall Street crisis, 76; relays British warning on ship transfers, 85
Morgan, J. P., & Company, and French loan, 62; and exchange crisis, 80; and war "credits," 136; plans for large "credit" to British, 616; attempts to maintain pound sterling, 617; American bankers jealous of, 617; and negotiation of Anglo-French loan, 625-626; failure to sell Anglo-French bonds, 628
Müller, Georg von, adviser to Emperor, 313; at Imperial conference on reply to "strict accountability" note, 328-329; at Imperial conference on Bryan's *modus vivendi*, 334; on "monstrosity" of *Lusitania* sinking, 398; at Imperial conference at Pless Castle, May 31, 1915, 406-407; and preparation of reply to second *Lusitania* note, 434-435, 436-438; on necessity of agreement with America, 552-553; at Imperial conference at Pless Castle, Aug. 26, 1915, 574-576; supports Bethmann's demand for safety for passengers on all liners, 581
Münsterberg, Hugo, and German propaganda in United States, 31, 32; summarizes German-American reactions to administration policies, 161-162
Murray, W. H., 96

Naón, Romulo S., 487
Natera, Panfilo, 256
National Bank of Haiti, American ownership in, 517; makes advances to President Zamor, 521; cuts off allowances to government, 526; marines transfer funds from, 527; Bryan warns Haitian government against molesting, 527; French interests seize control of, 530
National City Bank of New York, 133, 135
National Farmers' Union, 95
National German-American Alliance, 20, 21, 195, 440
National German-American League, 163
National Security League, 137-138
Navy League, 137, 590
Nebraskan, attacked by submarine, 405

neutralism, American, *see* public opinion, *American*
neutrality, American, official proclamations of, 57; machinery for enforcement of, 57-58; early problems of, 58-64, 68-70; President's appeals for, 65-67; President's desire to maintain, 54-56, 162, 413; effect of arms embargo on, 166; British charges against, 183-184; Wilson's exposition and defense of, 184-186
Newlands, Francis G., 155
New Republic, condemns arms embargo, 166-167; on first *Lusitania* note, 396-397; on note to England of Oct. 21, 1915, 688
New York, 369
New York *American*, 341
New York Evening Mail, 32
New York Evening Post, ardently pro-Allied, 19; on Wilson's victory in *Arabic* pledge, 586
New York *Evening Sun*, 556
New York *Herald*, 677
New York *Nation*, ardently pro-Allied, 12, 19; on *Lusitania* incident, 373
New York *Outlook*, ardently pro-Allied, 12; urges Belgian protest, 16; and preparedness campaign, 137; on note to Britain of Dec. 26, 1914, 176; article on Villa, 240; on note to England of Oct. 21, 1915, 688
New York Peace Society, 66
New Yorker Staats-Zeitung, 20-21
New York Stock Exchange, 76-77
New York Times ardently pro-Allied, 12; on Dumba affair, 647-648; prints evidence of Austro-Hungarian intrigues, 648
New York Tribune, pro-Allied spokesman, 12, 677; denounces note to England of Oct. 21, 1915, 688
New York *World*, on Ship Registry Act, 83; accuses shipping interests of lobby, 146; on Wilson's "victory" in Mexico, 232; on "strict accountability" note, 324; on Bryan's resignation, 426; on second *Lusitania* note, 430; exposes intrigue about appointment of Minister to Dominican Republic, 499; exposes Minister Sullivan's corruption, 511-512; publishes documents from Albert's briefcase, 554-556; anger at British blockade practices, 595-596; prints evidence of Austro-Hungarian intrigues, 648; publishes first account of Rintelen's activities, 650; demands severance of relations with Germany, 656-657; on note to England of Oct. 21, 1915, 688
Nicolson, Arthur, 303
Norris, George W., thinking about World War,